THE MARSHALS OF ALEXANDER'S EMPIRE

THE MARSHALS OF ALEXANDER'S EMPIRE

Waldemar Heckel

Routledge
Taylor & Francis Group
LONDON AND NEW YORK

First published 1992
by Routledge
2 Park Square, Milton Park, Abingdon, Oxon, OX14 4RN

Simultaneously published in the USA and Canada
by Routledge
711 Third Avenue, New York, NY 10017

Reprinted 2000

Transferred to Digital Printing 2005

© 1992 Waldemar Heckel

*Routledge is an imprint of the
Taylor & Francis Group*

First issued in paperback 2012

All rights reserved. No part of this book may be reprinted or reproduced or utilized in any form or by any electronic, mechanical, or other means, now known or hereafter invented, including photocopying and recording, or in any information storage or retrieval system, without permission in writing from the publishers.

British Library Cataloguing in Publication Data

A CIP catalogue record for this book is available from the British Library

Library of Congress Cataloging in Publication Data
Heckel, Waldemar
  The marshals of Alexander's empire / Waldemar Heckel.
    p.   cm.
Includes bibliographical references and index.
  1. Alexander, the Great, 356-323 B.C.–Friends and associates.
  2. Generals–Macedonia–Biography. I. Title
DF234.2.H38   1992
938'.07–dc20   91–43616

ISBN 978-0-415-05053-1 (hardback)

ISBN 978-0-415-64273-6 (paperback)

For Lois

TABLE OF CONTENTS

List of Abbreviations   xiii
List of Maps   xx
Preface   xxi

Part I

Chapter i: The 'Old Guard'   3
Introduction   3
1.   The House of Attalos   4
1.1.   Attalos: Philip's In-Law   4
1.2.   Hegelochos son of Hippostratos: Conspirator   6
2.   The House of Parmenion   13
2.1.   Parmenion: Philip's General   13
2.2.   Philotas: Parmenion's Son   23
3.   Black Kleitos   34
4.   Antipatros: An 'Old Rope'   38
5.   Antigonos son of Philippos: Monophthalmos   50

Chapter ii: The 'New Men'   57
Introduction   57
1.   Koinos: Changing One's Spots   58
2.   Hephaistion: *omnium amicorum carissimus*   65
3.   Leonnatos: The Makedonian *Cursus Honorum*   91
4.   Krateros: φιλοβασιλεύς   107
5.   Perdikkas: Successor and Failure   134

Chapter iii: Casualties of the Succession   164
Introduction   164
1.   Meleagros son of Neoptolemos   165
2.   Alketas son of Orontes   171
3.   The House of Andromenes   176
3.1.   Amyntas   176
3.2.   Simmias   179
3.3.   Attalos   180
3.4.   Polemon   183
4.   White Kleitos   185
5.   Polyperchon son of Simmias   188

Chapter iv: The So-called 'Boyhood Friends' of Alexander   205
    Introduction   205
    1.   The sons of Larichos   209
    1.1.   Erigyios   209
    1.2.   Laomedon   211
    2.   Harpalos son of Machatas   213
    3.   Ptolemy son of Lagos   222
    4.   Nearchos son of Androtimos   228

Part II

Chapter v: The Somatophylakes   237

A. *Career Progress*   237
    1.   Σωματοφυλακία   237
    2.   *The Education of Aristocratic Youths*   237
      i.   Background   238
      ii.   Recruitment   238
      iii.   Terminology   241
    3. *The Royal Hypaspists*   244
      i.   The ἄγημα   245
      ii.   Royal and Regular Hypaspists   247
      iii.   The ἄγημα and the ἑταῖροι   249
    4. *From Royal Page to Royal Hypaspist*   250
    5. *The Commanders of the Royal Hypaspists*   253
    5.1.   Admetos   253
    5.2.   Seleukos son of Antiochos   253
    6. *Background and Organisation of the Seven*   257

B. *The Careers of the Somatophylakes*   259
    1. *Somatophylakes Appointed in 336 or Before*   259
    1.1.   Ptolemaios ὁ σωματοφύλαξ ὁ βασιλικός   259
    1.2.   Balakros son of Nikanor   260
    1.3.   Arybbas   261
    1.4.   Demetrios   261
    2. *Somatophylakes Appointed by Alexander III*   262
    2.1.   Menes son of Dionysios   262
    2.2.   Peukestas son of Alexandros   263

3. *Problematic Appointments*		267
3. 1. Lysimachos son of Agathokles		267
3. 2. Aristonous son of Peisaios		275
3. 3. Peithon son of Krateuas		276
4. *The Somatophylakes of Philip III*		279
4. 1. Autodikos son of Agathokles		282
4. 2. Amyntas son of Alexandros		282
4. 3. Alexandros son of Polyperchon		283
4. 4. Ptolemaios son of Ptolemaios		283
5. *Somatophylakes of Alexander IV?*		284
5. 1. Philippos son of ?		284
5. 2. Iolaos		285
6. *The case of Ptolemaios son of Seleukos*		286
7. *Conclusion*		286
C. *Pages and Royal Hypaspists*		289
1. *Pages*		289
1. 1.	Antikles	289
1. 2.	Antipatros	289
1. 3.	Aphthonetos	289
1. 4.	Aphthonios (Elaptonius)	289
1. 5.	Archedamos	290
1. 6.	Aretis	290
1. 7.	Charikles	290
1. 8.	Epimenes	291
1. 9.	Eurylochos	291
1. 10.	Excipinus (?)	291
1. 11.	Gorgatas	292
1. 12.	Gorgias	292
1. 13.	Hekataios	292
1. 14.	Hermolaos	292
1. 15.	Iolaos	293
1. 16.	Metron	293
1. 17.	Philippos	294
1. 18.	Philotas	295
1. 19.	Sostratos	295
2. *Some Royal Hypaspists*		295
2. 1.	Alexandros	295
2. 2.	Charos	296
2. 3.	Hegesimachos (Simachos)	296
2. 4.	Limnaios	296
2. 5.	Nikanor	297

2.6.	Pausanias	297
2.7.	Pausanias of Orestis	297
2.8.	Philippos	298

Chapter vi: Commanders of Regular Hypaspists — 299
  1. The ἀρχιυπασπιστής — 299
  1.1. Nikanor son of Parmenion — 299
  1.2. Neoptolemos — 300
  2. *Chiliarchs and Pentakosiarchs* — 303
  2.1. Addaios — 303
  2.2. Timandros — 303
  2.3. Antiochos — 303
  2.4. Atarrhias son of Deinomenes — 304
  2.5. Philotas — 304
  2.6. Amyntas — 305
  2.7. Antigonos — 305
  2.8. Amyntas Lynkestes — 305
  2.9. Theodotos — 305
  2.10. Hellanikos — 306

Chapter vii: Commanders of the Argyraspids — 307
  1. Antigenes — 308
  2. Teutamos — 316

Chapter viii: Commanders of Infantry — 320
  1. *Some Commanders of Pezhetairoi* — 320
  i. Terminology: πεζέταιροι and ἀσθέταιροι — 320
  ii. The Command Structure (Pezhetairoi) — 321
  1.1. Peithon son of Agenor — 323
  1.2. Gorgias — 326
  1.3. Philippos son of Amyntas — 327
  1.4. Philippos son of Balakros — 327
  2. *Commanders of Light Infantry* — 328
  2.1. Philotas — 328
  2.2. Philippos son of Machatas — 331
  2.3. Balakros — 332
  3. *Commanders of Thrakian Infantry* — 332
  3.1. Attalos — 332
  3.2. Ptolemaios — 333
  3.3. Eudamos — 333
  3.4. Sitalkes — 334

4.	*Commanders of Other Allied Troops*	335
4. 1.	Balakros son of Amyntas	335
4. 2.	Karanos (Kalanos)	335
5.	*Commanders of the Archers*	335
5. 1.	Eurybotas	336
5. 2-3.	Klearchos and Kleandros	336
5. 4.	Antiochos	337
5. 5-6.	Brison or Ombrion?	337
5. 7.	Tauron son of Machatas	338
6.	*Commanders of Greek Mercenaries*	339
6. 1.	Menandros	339
6. 2.	Kleandros son of Polemokrates	340
6. 3.	Herakon	341
6. 4.	Andronikos son of Agerros	341
6. 5.	Menedemos	343

Chapter ix: Commanders of Cavalry — 344

1.	*Hipparchs of the Companion Cavalry*	344
1. 1.	Demetrios son of Althaimenes	345
1. 2.	Eumenes son of Hieronymos	346
2.	*Ilarchs of the Companion Cavalry*	348
2. 1.	Ariston	348
2. 2.	Glaukias	348
2. 3.	Herakleides son of Antiochos	348
2. 4.	Meleagros	349
2. 5.	Pantordanos son of Kleandros	349
2. 6.	Peroidas son of Menestheus	350
2. 7.	Sokrates son of Sathon	350
2. 8.	Sopolis son of Hermodoros	351
3.	*The πρόδρομοι ἱππεῖς and the Paionians*	351
3. 1.	Amyntas son of Arrhabaios	352
3. 2.	Protomachos	353
3. 3.	Aretes	354
3. 4.	Ariston: Commander of the Paionians	354
4.	*Commanders of the Thessalian Cavalry*	355
4. 1.	Kalas son of Harpalos	355
4. 2.	Alexandros son of Aëropos	357
4. 3.	Philippos son of Menelaos	358
4. 4.	Polydamas	359

	5. *Commanders of Other Allied Horse*		361
	5. 1.	Agathon son of Tyrimmas	361
	5. 2.	Anaxippos	361
	5. 3.	Koiranos (Karanos)	362
	6. *The Mercenary Cavalry (μισθοφόροι ἱππεῖς)*		362
	6. 1.	Menidas	362
	6. 2.	Andromachos son of Hieron	364
	6. 3.	Epokillos son of Polyeides	364

Appendices 366
  I. Hephaistion's Chiliarchy 366
  II. The Father of Leonnatos 371
  III. The Battle of Amorgos 373
  IV. Artakoana 379
  V. The Marriage of Attalos and Atalante 381
  VI. Asandros son of Philotas 385

General Bibliography 387
Concordance 413

LIST OF ABBREVIATIONS

Anspach i-iii	Anspach, A. E., *De Alexandri Magni expeditione Indica* (Leipzig, 1903).
Atkinson, *Curtius* i	J. E. Atkinson, *A Commentary on Q. Curtius Rufus' Historiae Alexandri Magni, Books 3 and 4* (Amsterdam, 1980).
Badian, *Studies*	E. Badian, *Studies in Greek and Roman History* (Oxford, 1964).
Baumbach	A. Baumbach, *Kleinasien unter Alexander dem Grossen* (Diss. Jena, publ. Weida i. Th., 1911).
Beloch iii-iv^2	K. J. Beloch, *Griechische Geschichte*, 2nd ed., vols. 3-4 (Berlin-Leipzig, 1927).
Bengtson, *Strategie*	H. Bengtson, *Die Strategie in der hellenistischen Zeit* (Munich, 1937-1952).
Bengtson, *Philipp und Alexander*	H. Bengtson, *Philipp und Alexander der Grosse* (Munich, 1985).
Bengtson, *Diadochen*	H. Bengtson, *Die Diadochen. Die Nachfolger Alexanders des Grossen* (Munich, 1987).
Berve i-ii	H. Berve, *Das Alexanderreich auf prosopographischer Grundlage*, 2 vols (Munich, 1925-1926).
Billows, *Antigonos*	R. A. Billows, *Antigonos the One-Eyed and the Creation of the Hellenistic State* (Berkeley and Los Angeles, 1990).
Boerma	R. N. H. Boerma, *Justinus' Boeken over de Diadochen, een historisch Commentaar, Boek 13-15, cap. 2* (Amsterdam, 1979).
Borza	E. N. Borza, *In the Shadow of Olympus. The Emergence of Macedon* (Princeton, 1990).
Bosworth, *Arrian* i	A. B. Bosworth, *A Historical Commentary on Arrian's History of Alexander*, vol. 1 (Oxford, 1980).
Bosworth, *Conquest and Empire*	A. B. Bosworth, *Conquest and Empire. The Reign of Alexander the Great* (Cambridge, 1988).
Breloer, *Kampf*	B. Breloer, *Alexanders Kampf gegen Poros* (Stuttgart, 1933).

Breloer, *Bund*	B. Breloer, *Alexanders Bund mit Poros: Indien von Dareios zu Sandrokottos*, Sammlung orientalistischen Arbeiten 9 (Leipzig, 1941).
Briant	P. Briant, *Antigone le Borgne* (Paris, 1973).
Brunt, *Arrian* i-ii	P. A. Brunt, *Arrian*, Loeb Classical Library, vol. 1 (Cambridge, Mass., 1976), vol. 2 (Cambridge, Mass., 1983).
Carney, Macedonian Aristocracy	E. D. Carney, 'Alexander the Great and the Macedonian Aristocracy' (Diss. Duke University, 1975).
Cary	M. Cary, *A History of the Greek World from 323 to 146 B.C.*, 2nd ed. (London, 1951).
Cauer	F. Cauer, 'Philotas, Kleitos, Kallisthenes: Beiträge zur Alexandergeschichte', *Neue Jahrbücher für classische Philologie*, Supplbd 20 (1894).
Cawkwell, *Philip*	G. L. Cawkwell, *Philip of Macedon* (London, 1978).
Cloché, *La Dislocation*	P. Cloché, *La Dislocation d'un Empire* (Paris, 1959).
Cook, *PE*	J. M. Cook, *The Persian Empire* (New York, 1983).
Davies, *APF*	J. K. Davies, *Athenian Propertied Families 600-300 B.C.* (Oxford, 1971).
Develin, *Athenian Officials*	R. Develin, *Athenian Officials 684-321 B.C.* (Cambridge, 1989).
Dittenberger, *Syll.*^{3}	W. Dittenberger, *Sylloge Inscriptionum Graecarum*, 3rd ed., vol. 1 (Leipzig, 1915).
Dittenberger, *OGIS*	W. Dittenberger, *Orientis Graeci Inscriptiones Selectae* 2 vols (Leipzig, 1903-1905).
Droysen	J. G. Droysen, *Geschichte des Hellenismus*, 3rd ed. (Tübingen, 1952-1953; repr. Darmstadt, 1980).
Eggermont, 'Gandhara'	Eggermont, P. H. L., 'Alexander's Campaign in Gandhara and Ptolemy's List of Indo-Scythian Towns', *Orientalia Lovaniensia Periodica* 1 (1970), 63-123.
Eggermont	Eggermont, P. H. L., *Alexander's Campaigns in Sind and Baluchistan and the Siege of the Brahmin Town of Harmatelia* (Leuven, 1975).

LIST OF ABBREVIATIONS

Ellis, *Philip II*	J. R. Ellis, *Philip II and Macedonian Imperialism* (London, 1976; repr. Princeton, 1986).
Engel, *Machtaufstieg*	R. Engel, *Untersuchungen zum Machtaufstieg des Antigonos I. Monophthalmos* (Kallmünz, 1976).
Engels, *Logistics*	D. W. Engels, *Alexander the Great and the Logistics of the Macedonian Army* (Berkeley and Los Angeles, 1978).
Errington, *Hist. Mac.*	R. M. Errington, *A History of Macedonia*, trans. by C. Errington (Berkeley and Los Angeles, 1990).
FGrHist	F. Jacoby, *Die Fragmente der griechischen Historiker* (Berlin and Leiden, 1923—).
FHG	C. Müller, *Fragmenta Historicorum Graecorum*, 5 vols (Paris, 1841-1870).
Fontana, *Le Lotte*	M. J. Fontana, *Le Lotte per la successione di Alessandro Magno dal 323 al 315* (Palermo, 1960).
Fox	Robin Lane Fox, *Alexander the Great* (London, 1973).
Fuller	Maj.-Gen. J. F. C. Fuller, *The Generalship of Alexander the Great* (London, 1958).
Goukowsky i-ii	P. Goukowsky, *Essai sur les origines du Mythe d'Alexandre*, 2 vols (Nancy, 1978, 1981).
Grainger	J. Grainger, *Seleukos Nikator. Constructing a Hellenistic Kingdom* (London, 1990).
Granier	F. Granier, *Die makedonische Heeresversammlung. Ein Beitrag zum antiken Staatsrecht* (Munich, 1931).
Green	P. Green, *Alexander of Macedon* (London, 1974).
Griffith, *Mercenaries*	G. T. Griffith, *The Mercenaries of the Hellenistic World* (Cambridge, 1935).
Grote	G. Grote, *History of Greece*, 12 vols (London, 1846-1856).
Habicht, *Gottmenschentum*[2]	Chr. Habicht, *Gottmenschentum und griechische Städte*, Zetemata, Heft 14, 2nd ed. (Munich, 1970).
Hamilton, *PA*	J. R. Hamilton, *Plutarch, Alexander: A Commentary* (Oxford, 1969).
Hamilton, *Alexander the Great*	J. R. Hamilton, *Alexander the Great* (London, 1973).

Hammond, *Alexander*	N. G. L. Hammond, *Alexander the Great. King, Commander and Statesman* (London, 1981).
Hammond, *THA*	N. G. L. Hammond, *Three Historians of Alexander the Great* (Cambridge, 1983).
Hammond, *Macedonian State*	N. G. L. Hammond, *The Macedonian State. The Origins, Institutions and History* (Oxford, 1989).
Hauben, *Vlootbevelhebbershap*	*Het Vlootbevelhebberschap in de vroege Diadochen tijd (323-301 v. C.): Een prosopographisch en institutioneel onderzoek* (Brussels, 1975).
Heckel, *LDT*	W. Heckel, *The Last Days and Testament of Alexander the Great: A Prosopographic Study*, Historia Einzelschriften, Heft 56 (Stuttgart, 1988).
HMac ii	N. G. L. Hammond and G. T. Griffith, *A History of Macedonia*, vol. 2 (Oxford, 1979).
HMac iii	N. G. L. Hammond and F. W. Walbank, *A History of Macedonia*, vol. 3 (Oxford, 1988).
Hoffmann	O. Hoffmann, *Die Makedonen: ihre Sprache und ihr Volkstum* (Göttingen, 1906).
Hofstetter	J. Hofstetter, *Die Griechen in Persien: Prosopographie der Griechen im persischen Reich vor Alexander*, Archaeologische Mitteilungen aus Iran, Ergänzungsband 5 (Berlin, 1978).
Holt, *Alexander and Bactria*	F. L. Holt, *Alexander the Great and Bactria*, Mnemosyne Supplements, no. 104 (Leiden, 1988).
Hornblower, *Hieronymus*	J. Hornblower, *Hieronymus of Cardia* (Oxford, 1981).
Jaschinski	S. Jaschinski, *Alexander und Griechenland unter dem Eindruck der Flucht des Harpalos* (Bonn, 1981).
Judeich	W. Judeich, *Kleinasiatische Studien. Untersuchungen zur griechisch-persischen Geschichte des IV. Jahrhunderts v. Chr.* (Marburg, 1892).
Julien	P. Julien, *Zur Verwaltung der Satrapien unter Alexander dem Grossen* (Diss. Leipzig, publ. Weida i. Th., 1914).
Justi	F. Justi, *Iranisches Namenbuch* (Marburg, 1895; repr. Hildesheim, 1963).

LIST OF ABBREVIATIONS

Kaerst i^2-ii^2	J. Kaerst, *Geschichte des Hellenismus*, 2nd ed. (Leipzig and Berlin, 1926-1927).
Kirchner, *PA*	J. Kirchner, *Prosopographia Attica* ((Berlin, 1901-1903).
Kornemann	E. Kornemann, *Die Alexandergeschichte des Königs Ptolemaios I. von Aegypten* (Leipzig, 1935).
Lehmann-Haupt, 'Satrap'	C. F. Lehmann-Haupt, 'Satrap', *RE* iiA (1923), 82-188.
McCrindle	J. W. McCrindle, *The Invasion of India by Alexander the Great* (London, 1896; repr. 1969).
Macurdy, *HQ*	G. H. Macurdy, *Hellenistic Queens: A Study of Woman-Power in Macedonia, Seleucid Syria and Ptolemaic Egypt*, Johns Hopkins University Studies in Archaeology, no. 14 (Baltimore, 1932).
Marsden, *Gaugamela*	E. W. Marsden, *The Campaign of Gaugamela* (Liverpool, 1964).
Mehl	A. Mehl, *Seleukos Nikator und sein Reich. Teil 1. Seleukos' Leben und die Entwicklung seiner Machtposition* = Studia Hellenistica 28 (Leuven, 1986).
Niese	B. Niese, *Geschichte der griechischen und makedonischen Staaten seit der Schlacht bei Chaeronea* (Gotha, 1893).
Olmstead, *HPE*	A. T. Olmstead, *History of the Persian Empire* (Chicago, 1948).
Osborne, *Naturalization*	M. J. Osborne, *Naturalization in Athens* i-iii (Brussels, 1981-1983).
Papastavru	J. Papastavru, *Amphipolis. Geschichte und Prosopographie*, Klio Beiheft 37 (Leipzig, 1936).
Pearson, *LHA*	L. Pearson, *The Lost Histories of Alexander the Great* (New York, 1960).
Pollitt	J. J. Pollitt, *The Art of Ancient Greece: Sources and Documents* (Cambridge, 1990).
Sandberger	F. Sandberger, *Prosopographie zur Geschichte des Pyrrhos* (Stuttgart, 1970).
Schachermeyr	F. Schachermeyr, *Alexander der Grosse: Das Problem seiner Persönlichkeit und seines Wirkens* (Vienna, 1973).
Schachermeyr, *Babylon*	F. Schachermeyr, *Alexander in Babylon und die Reichsordnung nach seinem Tode* (Vienna, 1970).

Schaefer, *Demosthenes* iii[3]	A. Schaefer, *Demosthenes und seine Zeit*, vol. 3, 3rd ed. (Leipzig, 1887).
Schober	L. Schober, *Untersuchungen zur Geschichte Babyloniens und der Oberen Satrapien von 323-303 v. Chr.* (Frankfurt a. M., 1981).
Schubert, *Quellen*	R. Schubert, *Die Quellen zur Geschichte der Diadochenzeit* (Leipzig, 1914).
Seibert, *Ptolemaios*	J. Seibert, *Untersuchungen zur Geschichte Ptolemaios' I.*, Münchener Beiträge zur Papyrusforschung und antiken Rechtsgeschichte (Munich, 1969).
Seibert, *Verbindungen*	J. Seibert, *Historische Beiträge zu den dynastischen Verbindungen in hellenistischer Zeit*, Historia Einzelschriften, Heft 10 (Wiesbaden, 1967).
Seibert, *Eroberung*	J. Seibert, *Die Eroberung des Perserreiches durch Alexander des Großen auf kartographischer Grundlage*, TAVO Beiheft, Reihe B, no. 68 (Wiesbaden, 1985).
Shrimpton, *Theopompus*	G. S. Shrimpton, *Theopompus the Historian* (Montreal-Kingston, 1991).
Smith, *EHI*	V. Smith, *The Early History of India. From 600 B.C. to the Muhammadan Conquest, including the Invasion of Alexander the Great*, 4th ed., revised by S. M. Edwardes (Oxford, 1924).
Stein, *Alexander's Track to the Indus*	Sir Aurel Stein, *On Alexander's Track to the Indus* (London, 1929).
Strasburger	H. Strasburger, *Ptolemaios und Alexander* (Leipzig, 1934).
Tarn i-ii	W. W. Tarn, *Alexander the Great*, 2 vols (Cambridge, 1948).
Tarn, *GBI*	W. W. Tarn, *The Greeks in Bactria and India*, 3rd ed. (Cambridge, 1951).
Tataki, *PB*	A. B. Tataki, *Ancient Beroea. Prosopography and Society* (Athens, 1988).
Vezin	A. Vezin, *Eumenes von Kardia* (Tübingen, 1907).
Welles, *Diodorus*	C. B. Welles, *Diodorus of Sicily*, Loeb Classical Library, vol. 8 (Cambridge, Mass., 1963).
Welles, *AHW*	C. B. Welles, *Alexander and the Hellenistic World* (Toronto, 1970).

LIST OF ABBREVIATIONS

Wilcken U. Wilcken, *Alexander the Great*, translated by G. C. Richards, with notes and introduction by E. N. Borza (New York, 1967).

LIST OF MAPS

Map I:	The Campaigns of Alexander the Great	xxv
Map II:	The Voyage of Nearchos	234
Map III:	The Naval Battles of the Lamian War (322 B.C.)	378

Preface

This book has a rather long and complicated history. It began in the late 1970s as a doctoral dissertation ('Marshals of the *Alexanderreich*', Diss. University of British Columbia, 1978), directed by Phillip E. Harding and the late Malcolm F. McGregor, and concerned itself primarily with the 'New Men', who remain the figures of central interest even in this version. Since 1975, I have devoted myself to matters of prosopography, with the aim of revising, up-dating and continuing the second volume of Helmut Berve's *Das Alexanderreich auf prosopographischer Grundlage* (Munich, 1926). This undertaking has proved long and arduous, often interrupted by other projects. The present book is thus a compromise — much more than the original dissertation, far less than the envisioned prosopography.

I had intended that *The Marshals* should be a collection of biographies illuminating the careers of the most prominent of Alexander's officers, a work aimed not primarily at specialists in the field but useful to them. But as the scope of the book widened, with a concomitant proliferation of pages and footnotes — to say nothing of the escalating price — it became clear that the casual reader might be intimidated by the format of the volume. I have, nevertheless, tried to make the lives contained in the first three or four chapters comprehensible even to those who are not professional students of Alexander; Part II contains career-studies that are supplementary to those of Part I. Whether I have succeeded, the reader will decide. The critic will, of course, find much to criticise. I am acutely aware that, by increasing the number of individuals discussed in the book, I have exposed myself to the criticism that I have not included them all, or that the method of organisation is confusing rather than helpful. A detailed 'Table of Contents', as well as an index and concordance should compensate for certain peculiarities of composition, but there will, no doubt, always be those who prefer an exhaustive treatment and alphabetical arrangement.

Predictably, the work is idiosyncratic, the selection of individuals and topics uneven and arbitrary. In part this is due to the subject-matter and the nature of recent scholarly publications. The famous Diadochoi ('Successors'), Antigonos the One-Eyed, Lysimachos,

Ptolemy Soter, and Seleukos Nikator, are given only partial treatment. Full vitae for these men are virtually impossible to provide in a work of this scope and redundant in the light of the recent books of Richard A. Billows and John Grainger, and the imminent appearance of Helen S. Lund's monograph on Lysimachos. Eumenes of Kardia receives only a brief discussion and will have to await Edward Anson's full-scale study. Furthermore, what I do say about these historical individuals, and indeed many others whose careers intertwined with theirs, owes much to the work of these scholars. To Professor Anson I am particularly grateful for not only reading substantial portions of my work but also allowing me to read the entire typescript of his book on Eumenes. Professor Billows sent me a stimulating (unpublished) discussion of the Philippoi of Alexander's reign, from which I have derived virtually as much profit as from the admirable prosopography that rounds out his *Antigonos the One-Eyed and the Creation of a Hellenistic State* (Berkeley, 1990). Nevertheless, it should be emphasised that the careers of the Diadochoi are, in fact, only peripheral to this study, which concerns itself with men who did not live to become Successors, or died in the attempt.

Except for brief and general introductory comments at the beginnings of most chapters, I have let the careers of Alexander's marshals speak for themselves. Some apparent inconsistencies are, in fact, intentional: each chapter and section attempts to interpret events as they pertained to the individuals in question, and, just as the motives and experiences of each man will have been different, so too the perspectives of each situation will change, if only slightly, in many cases. Furthermore, since the book should serve also as a valuable reference tool, there is the unavoidable — and, indeed, desirable — repetition of historical detail and references. Here the attempt to view the context through the individual, rather than the individual within the context, provides the necessary variation that separates this collection of biographies from the prosopographic catalogue towards which it inclines. *The Marshals* is thus an arabesque of intertwining biography, an interpretative prosopography or, as one scholar has suggested to me, 'prosobiography'.

This book is also, in many ways, a synthesis — though some may call it a collage — of work done since 1975. I am happy to record my thanks to various academic presses, scholarly journals and editors for permission to reuse, in a somewhat modified form, material published previously. I am grateful to: the Johns Hopkins University Press for permission to reuse 'Leonnatos, Polyperchon and the Introduction of *Proskynesis*', *AJP* 99 (1978), 459-461, and a portion of 'Asandros', *AJP* 98

(1977), 410-412; the University of Chicago Press for 'The Flight of Harpalos and Tauriskos', *CP* (1977), 133-135; the University of Toronto Press for 'The Conspiracy *against* Philotas', *Phoenix* 31 (1977), 9-21, and 'Somatophylakia. A Macedonian *cursus honorum*', *Phoenix* 40 (1986), 279-294; E. J. Brill for 'Peithon, son of Agenor', *Mnemosyne* 43 (1990), 456-459; J. D. Sauerländer's Verlag for 'Who was Hegelochos?' *RhM* 125 (1982), 78-87; Oxford University Press for 'On Attalos and Atalante', *CQ* 28 (1978), 377-382; and the Akademie Verlag GmbH for 'The Early Career of Lysimachos', *Klio* 64 (1982), 373-381. The editors of their respective journals have granted permission for the reprinting, almost verbatim, of two articles in their entirety ('The "Boyhood Friends" of Alexander the Great', *Emerita* 53 [1985], 285-289, and 'The Career of Antigenes', *Symbolae Osloenses* 57 [1982], 57-67) and portions of 'Some Speculations on the Prosopography of the *Alexanderreich*', *LCM* 6 (1981), 63-70.

Three maps are included with the text, the first (Map I) illustrating the scope of Alexander's campaigns. The scale, however, prevents the inclusion of all place names mentioned in the text. Modern river systems have been shown with the exception of the lower Euphrates, which has been changed to flow directly into the Persian Gulf, as it did in Alexander's time. Adjustments have also been made to the coastlines of Asia Minor, the upper Persian Gulf and the Indus delta to reflect ancient coastal configurations. Map II, which accompanies the section on Nearchos, is meant to guide the reader. I have not dealt with all the problems of Nearchos' voyage in the text, or on the map. My purpose is to write a brief biography of Nearchos; full discussion of geographical questions goes well beyond the scope of the book. Map III supplements the narrative of Appendix III.

Internal references, to sections within a chapter, are given in the following form: '1. 1 below' or '4. 3 above'. Cross-references to other chapters and sections are made in bold face (**ix 1. 2; ii 3**). Full citations of books and articles are rarely provided in the footnotes (except in the Appendices), for the sake of economy. Many sections (and sub-sections) include short bibliographies; a list of works cited in abbreviated form may be found at the beginning of the work; a full bibliography (387 ff.) gives full citation of all works in the text with the exception of book reviews. The abbreviation of the names of scholarly journals follows the practices common in other works of Classics and Ancient History.

Many individuals have helped with the writing and editing of this book at different stages. I am greatly indebted to Phillip Harding, who directed the original dissertation, and Truesdell S. Brown, who acted as external examiner and continued to provide me with advice and encouragement until his death at the beginning of this year. Professor Erich Gruen read and criticised the section on Krateros and made several suggestions about scope and content that have vastly improved this book. Professors Edward M. Anson, Elizabeth Carney and John Vanderspoel read and commented on the penultimate version of the typescript at a time when they were all burdened with monographs of their own. Professor Brian Bosworth kindly allowed me to see his chapter on 'History and Artifice in Plutarch's *Eumenes*' in advance of publication. My colleague, Dr Michael Walbank, kept me abreast of recent epigraphic publications and gave expert advice on many problems. I am grateful also to John Yardley for putting our joint projects on hold while I completed *The Marshals*; to three student assistants, Mr Ralph Siferd, Mr Thomas Goud, and Miss Vanessa Nugent, for help with the collection of materials; and to Mrs Lillian Kogawa, who typed large portions of the text. The University of Calgary has supported my research, since my appointment to the faculty in 1977, in the form of fellowships, release time, and research and travel grants. It is a pleasure to record my gratitude to Richard Stoneman, who kindly took my proposal to Routledge in the first place, and to Virginia Myers, who saw the book through to publication.

Most of all, I must thank Mr Bill Mills, who not only drew the maps for the book, but read every page of the typescript on two different occasions, saved me from numerous errors, and caused me to rethink many of my arguments. Finally, the dedication of this book to my wife, Lois, represents but a small down-payment on a very large debt.

Calgary, 21 March, 1992

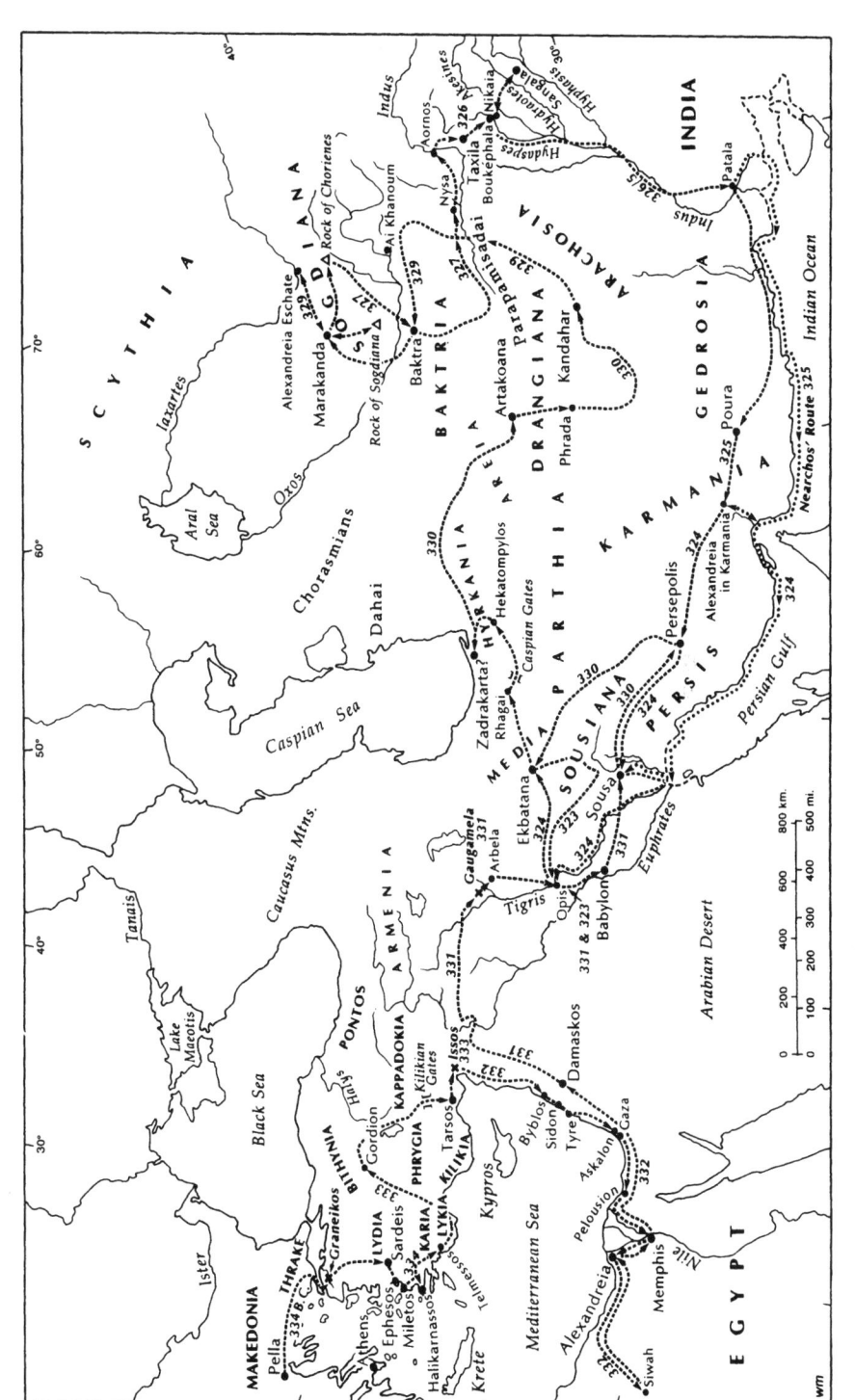

Map I The Campaigns of Alexander the Great

Part I

i. The 'Old Guard'

Introduction

The army that crossed the Hellespont in 334 B.C. was still very much that of Philip II, its leaders chosen from the firmly entrenched aristocratic families of Makedon. Two years earlier, Alexander had had good reason to fear many of them: challenging his right of succession, a powerful faction might, if it chose, reassert the claims of Amyntas son of Perdikkas who, in the face of a national crisis, had been swept aside in favour of Philip. For Alexander, Philip's assassination could scarcely have occurred at a better time, with both Parmenion and Attalos absent in Asia Minor. Antipatros, for reasons that must have been clear to Alexander, engineered the Crown Prince's accession, despite the fact that Alexandros Lynkestes, a brother of the convicted regicides, was his son-in-law. Arrhabaios and Heromenes were promptly arrested and executed, as confidants of the assassin Pausanias; Amyntas Perdikka would be eliminated soon afterwards. But a purge, whether in the name of justice or filial piety, could extend only so far. Alexander would have to make his peace with the 'Old Guard'.

Some could, of course, be left behind to manage the affairs of the homeland, kept in check by Antipatros, if indeed he could be trusted. But the new King lacked the authority to reform but slightly the command structure of the expeditionary force. Morale and efficiency would doubtless suffer. More immediate was the threat of mutiny and assassination that accompanied any attempt to deprive the troops of officers drawn from their regional aristocracies. Philip had begun to strengthen the central authority by educating the sons of the Makedonian nobility at the Court, but these young men were for the most part contemporaries of Alexander. Too young and inexperienced, they and their new King would have to await opportunities for promotion and gradual integration into the power-elite. For the moment, a realignment of the 'Old Guard' would have to suffice. Their impact on the early stages of the campaign was significant, though soon the 'Old Guard' gave way to the 'New Men'. Ultimately, with but a few exceptions, the conquerors of Asia were not destined to rule it.

THE MARSHALS OF ALEXANDER'S EMPIRE

1. The House of Attalos

1. 1. Attalos: Philip's In-Law

Literature. Berve ii 94, no. 182; Judeich 302, 304-305; Kaerst, *RE* ii (1896), 2158, no. 4; A. B. Bosworth, 'Philip II and Upper Macedonia', *CQ* 21 (1971), 102 ff.; Schachermeyr 97.

Born c. 390 B.C.,[1] Attalos was a younger contemporary of Antipatros and Parmenion (born c. 400 and 398 respectively). He was the uncle of Hippostratos (Satyros *ap.* Athen. 13. 557d), and thus apparently the brother of Amyntas (Didymos *ap.* Marsyas of Pella, *FGrHist* 135/6 F17); both had died by the late summer or autumn of 337, when Philip II married Attalos' niece and ward, Kleopatra. Attalos' prayer at the wedding-feast, that Kleopatra might produce legitimate heirs to the Makedonian throne,[2] was both tactless and fatal: Alexander never forgave him and considered him a threat to his life (Curt. 8. 8. 7; cf. 6. 9. 17). But Hamilton's suggestion (*PA* 24) that 'Philip was acting at the behest of an influential group of nobles, headed by Attalus and his father-in-law Parmenio', when he married Kleopatra is not convincing: of Attalos' career before 337 we know nothing, and it is clear that his power at the Court increased only as a result of the marriage (cf. Schachermeyr 97).[3]

According to the popular account, Attalos was a friend of the younger Pausanias, who had confided to him the details of the insults uttered by Pausanias of Orestis and his own plans for a glorious death (Diod. 16. 93. 5). The latter occurred in a battle with the Illyrians of King Pleurias, probably in early 336. Soon thereafter Attalos avenged his friend's death by plying Pausanias of Orestis with wine at a dinner-party and handing him over to his muleteers to be sexually abused.[4] By this time, Attalos had been designated general of the

---

[1] Berve ii 94, 'gegen 380 geboren', is unnecessarily low.

[2] Satyros, frg. 5; Plut. *Alex.* 9. 7 ff.; cf. Justin 9. 7. 3. Ps.-Kall. (L) 1. 20. 1 calls him Lysias; but Ps.-Kall. (A) 1. 21. 1 and Jul. Valer. 1. 13-14 distinguish between Attalos and Lysias. See Berve ii 424, no. 47.

[3] Diod. 16. 93. 7: εἷς ὢν τῶν ἐξ αὐλῆς καὶ πολὺ δυναμένων παρὰ τῷ βασιλεῖ. But this refers only to the time after Philip's marriage to Kleopatra; cf. Heckel, *Ancient Macedonia* iv 297 f.

[4] Diod. 16. 93. 7; Justin 9. 6. 5-6, alleging that he was abused by Attalos himself. For this episode and the sources see Fears, *Athenaeum* 53 (1975), 111-135. There is no need to identify Pleurias with Pleuratos (Marsyas of Pella, *FGrHist* 135/6 F17) or to date the campaign to 344/3. For the date of Pausanias' death see W. Heckel, 'Philip and Olympias (337/6 B.C.)', in

advance force that was to cross into Asia (Diod. 16. 93. 8-9); for this reason, and because of their relationship (cf. 16. 93. 8), Philip was unwilling to reprimand Attalos for his crime against Pausanias, who in turn vented his rage on the King.[5]

Attalos had crossed the Hellespont at the beginning of spring 336 (Justin 9. 5. 8; cf. Diod. 16. 91. 2), sharing the command with Parmenion,[6] whose daughter he had married.[7] Their force of 10,000 advanced as far as Magnesia-on-the-Maiandros, where they were defeated by Memnon the Rhodian, and thus forced to seek refuge in the city (Polyainos 5. 44. 4). On the news of Philip's death, Attalos plotted rebellion,[8] trusting in his popularity with the troops and communicating with the anti-Makedonian party in Athens.[9] Whether he was in fact guilty is a moot point, since Alexander may have used these charges to justify his murder.[10] Judeich's suggestion (304 f.), that the Makedonian retreat from Magnesia to the Hellespont can be explained by Attalos' rebellion against Alexander, is unlikely. Hekataios (perhaps the Kardian[11]) was sent to secure his execution (Diod. 17. 2. 5-6), which he could not have brought about without Parmenion's complicity.[12] Justin's claim that Alexander, before his departure for Asia, killed all Kleopatra's relatives is a rhetorical exaggeration: only Attalos is meant (see below).[13]

Classical Contributions. Studies in Honour of Malcolm Francis McGregor, edited by G. S. Shrimpton and D. J. McCargar (Locust Valley, N. Y., 1981), 56.

[5]That he was the *somatophylax* Attalos of Diod. 16. 94. 4 and one of the Seven (Hammond, *GRBS* 19 [1978], 346, n.37) is impossible, since the *somatophylakes* here are hypaspists and Attalos was, at any rate, in Asia at the time of Philip's death.

[6]Diod. 17. 2. 4; cf. Justin 9. 5. 8-9, adding Amyntas (most likely the son of Arrhabaios) as a third general.

[7]Curt. 6. 9. 17; she was presumably the same woman who married Koinos son of Polemokrates in 334; cf. Curt. 6. 9. 30.

[8]Diod. 17. 5. 1; at 17. 2. 3 he is called a rival for the throne, though he scarcely had any legal claims to it.

[9]Diod. 17. 2. 4, 5. 1; cf. 17. 3. 2, naming Demosthenes; cf. Judeich 304.

[10]Cf. Badian, *Phoenix* 17 (1963), 249-250. Diod. 17. 5. 1 says that although he had been in contact with Demosthenes, Attalos sent Demosthenes' letter to Alexander in order to prove that he was not planning to rebel against him.

[11]Thus Judeich 304 and Beloch iii^2 1. 613; but Berve ii 148, no. 292 rejects the identification (cf. ii 149, no. 294).

[12]Diod. 17. 5. 2; Curt. 7. 1. 3; for his death, see also Curt. 8. 1. 42; cf. 8. 1. 52; and 8. 7. 4; Justin 12. 6. 14.

[13]Justin 11. 5. 1: *omnes novercae suae cognatos, quos Philippus in excelsiorem dignitatis locum provehens imperiis praefecerat, interfecit.*

1. 2. Hegelochos son of Hippostratos: Conspirator

Literature. Berve ii 164-165, no. 341; Hoffmann 183, with n.91; Sundwall, *RE* vii.2 (1912), 2594, no. 1; Baumbach 49 ff.; H. Hauben, 'The Command Structure in Alexander's Mediterranean Fleets', *Anc. Soc.* 3 (1972), 55-65, esp. 56-58; id., 'The Expansion of Macedonian Sea-Power under Alexander the Great', *Anc. Soc.* 7 (1976) 82-87; W. Heckel, 'Who was Hegelochos?' *RhM* 125 (1982), 78-87.

Hegelochos son of Hippostratos, both cavalry commander and, temporarily, admiral of Alexander's fleet,[14] was the great-nephew of Attalos, a relationship which illuminates his career. But modern scholarship resists the identification,[15] which links him with Philip II's last wife, Kleopatra-Eurydike.[16] About her origins very little is known. She was the niece of Attalos, a Makedonian noble;[17] Satyros adds that she was the sister of a certain Hippostratos. No other explicit statement about her family exists, but much can be deduced from evidence hitherto disregarded.

Curtius (6. 11. 22-29) relates that Philotas, under torture, divulged that Hegelochos had conspired with Parmenion in Egypt, but that Parmenion considered it unwise to take action against Alexander while Dareios III lived. The incident has been dismissed as fictitious: 'Curtius ... has a story of a plot between Parmenio and Hegelochus (then dead), which Philotas is said to have divulged under torture. Since no charge was in fact brought against Parmenio, it is almost certain that none could be: the plot with Hegelochus must be an effort of later

---

[14]Cavalry commands: Arr. 1. 13. 1; 3. 11. 8; cf. Curt. 6. 11. 22. On his command of the fleet see Hauben, *Anc. Soc.* 3 (1972), 56-58; Baumbach 49 ff.

[15]See Heckel, *RhM* 125 (1982), 78-87. Doubts expressed most recently by S. Hornblower, *The Greek World 479-323 B.C.* (London, 1983), 285.

[16]Arr. 3. 6. 5 alone calls her 'Eurydike'. On the question of her true name, and possible 'dynastic' implications see Heckel, *Phoenix* 32 (1978), 155-158; Bosworth, *Arrian* i 282 f.; Prestianni-Giallombardo, *ASNP* S. III, 11 (1981), 295-306; E. Badian, 'Eurydice', in *Philip II, Alexander the Great and the Macedonian Heritage*, edited by W. L. Adams and E. N. Borza (Washington, D. C., 1982), 99-110.

[17]Plut. *Alex.* 9. 7; Satyros *ap.* Athen. 13. 557d; Paus. 8. 7. 7; the relationship is confused by Diodoros (17. 2. 3) and Justin (9. 5. 8-9), who make Attalos Kleopatra's brother, though Diod. 16. 93. 9 says he was her nephew. Jul. Valer. 1. 13 has Kleopatra as Attalos' daughter, while Ps.-Kall. 1. 20-21 names Lysias (clearly Attalos is meant) as Kleopatra's brother. Green's stemma (587) attempts to reconcile the variants by postulating a brother, as well as an uncle, of Kleopatra named Attalos; but the sources clearly refer to the same man. See also Hoffmann 157.

apologia.'[18] Now the purpose of Philotas' torture had been to extort a confession of Parmenion's involvement in some crime that could be used to justify his execution. Of Dimnos' crime Philotas, at first, denied all knowledge (*quod ad Dymnum pertinet nihil scio*, 6. 11. 30), but he confessed that Hegelochos, incensed by Alexander's claims to be Ammon's son (*cum primum Iovis filium se salutari iussit rex*, 6. 11. 23), conspired with Parmenion to murder the King. Parmenion, however, approved the measure only if Dareios were dead (6. 11. 29), and the actual conspiracy came to naught.

Whether Philotas did, in fact, confess to the Hegelochos affair or whether it was merely so reported by Alexander's agents, the charge was made: it had equal value for Alexander whether it was exacted under duress or merely invented. And, admittedly, the charge could have been invented — very easily, since Hegelochos had died at Gaugamela in the preceding year. But there must have been something about Hegelochos that would make such a fabrication seem plausible, something that was well known to the Makedonian army. Badian (*TAPA* 91 [1960], 332) alleges that 'no charge was in fact brought against Parmenio'. But is this really so? In Curtius' version, the charges brought against Parmenion undoubtedly included his alleged dealings with Hegelochos. And charges *were* clearly brought against him. To Polydamas, the bearer of Parmenion's writ of execution, Alexander says: 'we are, everyone of us, victims of Parmenion's crime' (Curt. 7. 2. 13). More explicitly, we are told that charges of some sort were used to justify Parmenion's murder by Kleandros and his associates: 'Cleander ordered their leaders [i.e., the commanders of Parmenion's troops] to be admitted and read out to the soldiers the letter written by the King, in which Parmenion's plot against the King ... was contained' (Curt. 7. 2. 30). It follows that the charges extorted from Philotas were used in the condemnation of Parmenion.

But was Hegelochos' plot a fabrication? We are reminded of Philotas' 'conspiracy', related by Arrian (3. 26. 1) and Plutarch (*Alex.* 48. 1 - 49. 2; *de fort. Al.* 2. 7 = *Mor.* 339e-f), which also took place in Egypt and was the result of the same grievances. It is clear that Alexander's journey to the oasis of Siwah and his rejection of Philip as his father exacerbated an already uneasy feeling in the Makedonian

---

[18] Thus Badian, *TAPA* 91 (1960), 332; cf. Fears, *Athenaeum* 53 (1975), 133, n.77. Hegelochos' conspiracy is ignored by Green, Schachermeyr and Hamilton; Fox (289) mentions Hegelochos, inaccurately and without a judgment on the historicity of the incident. Berve treats the matter with caution (ii 165).

army.[19] But a hostile faction existed in Makedonia long before Ammon's fateful utterance, and (as is certainly true in Philotas' case) we ought to look for the seeds of Hegelochos' discontent in some earlier event. The man's identity provides a clue.

Arrian (3. 11. 8) calls Hegelochos' father Hippostratos, a name which occurs only twice in accounts of the period before 336: Marsyas (*FGrHist* 135/6 F17) names a certain Hippostratos son of Amyntas who died in Philip's Illyrian campaign of 344/3 B.C.; Satyros (*ap.* Athen. 13. 557d = Müller, *FGH* iii, frg. 5) adds that the brother of Kleopatra was called Hippostratos. All three references may refer to the same man, the father of Hegelochos. In which case, Hegelochos must have been Kleopatra's nephew.

K. J. Beloch argued that Kleopatra's brother could not have had a son old enough to command a squadron of Companions at Gaugamela: 'Ein Ἡγέλοχος Ἱπποστράτου befehligte bei Arbela eine Ile der Hetaerenreiterei (Arr. *Anab.* III 11, 8); aber Kleopatras Bruder kann nicht wohl einen Sohn gehabt haben, der in 331 alt genug gewesen wäre, ein solches Kommando zu führen...' (iii² 2. 70). But is this actually the case? Plutarch does say that Philip fell in love with Attalos' niece in spite of her age (*Alex.* 9. 6: [Κλεοπάτρα], ἣν ὁ Φίλιππος ἠγάγετο παρθένον, ἐρασθεὶς παρ' ἡλικίαν τῆς κόρης).[20] Berve's estimate that she was born c. 353 appears to suit Plutarch's description; she may, however, have been considered young in comparison with Olympias, then in her late thirties. Hence 355-353 B.C. provides a good, conservative, date for Kleopatra's birth.[21] For the year of Attalos' birth, Berve (ii 94; cf. 1. 1 above) settles on c. 380, making him a contemporary of Philip II. He could have been considerably older. On the assumption that Hippostratos son of Amyntas was the father of Hegelochos, and that Berve's birthdate for Attalos is unnecessarily low, I propose the following stemma:

---

[19]Berve ii 165 concludes from Hegelochos' conspiracy with Parmenion that he was 'ein Träger der philippischen Tradition'. The matter is brought to a head by the affair of Kleitos; cf. Berve ii 206-208, no. 427, s.v. Κλεῖτος; also Cauer 38-58; Schubert, *RhM* 53 (1898), 98-120; the conflict between old and new is clear from the primary sources: Plut. *Alex.* 50. 1 - 52. 2; Arr. 4. 8. 1 - 9. 4; Curt. 8. 1. 19-52. See also **i 3**.

[20]I. Scott-Kilvert translates 'although she was far too young for him' (261).

[21]This age would be supported by the physical evidence, if Kleopatra is indeed the woman in the antechamber of the so-called 'Tomb of Philip II'. But the identities of the occupants are far from certain (cf. Borza 260 ff.).

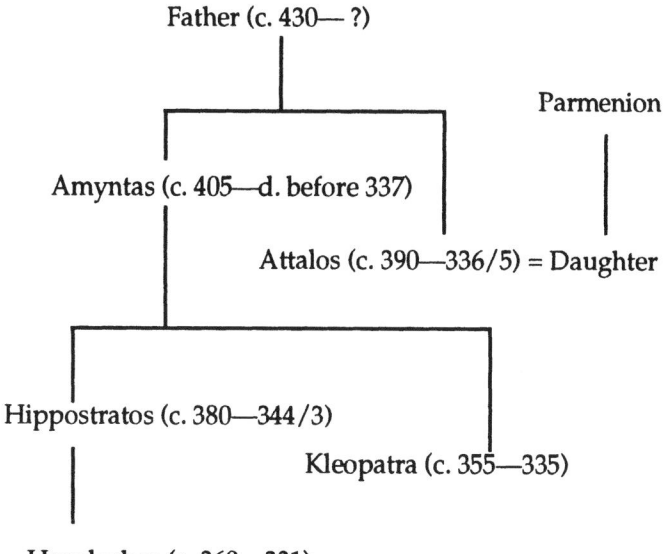

```
                    Father (c. 430— ?)
                           |
          ┌────────────────┤                    Parmenion
          |                |                        |
Amyntas (c. 405—d. before 337)                      |
                           |                        |
                  Attalos (c. 390—336/5) = Daughter
                           |
       ┌───────────────────┴────────┐
       |                            |
Hippostratos (c. 380—344/3)         |
       |                    Kleopatra (c. 355—335)
       |
Hegelochos (c. 360—331)
```

Felix Stähelin, speaking of that Hippostratos who died in the Illyrian campaign, argues: 'man könnte ebensogut an Hippostratos, den Bruder Philipps zweiter Gemahlin Kleopatra denken, den Satyros ... in einer Weise erwähnt, die uns vermuten lässt, das der Mann sich irgendwie besonders hervorgetan haben muss.'[22] Yet, he concludes: 'In keinem Falle ist Hippostratos, der Vater des Hegelochos, mit Hippostratos, dem Bruder der Kleopatra, identisch, denn wir wissen, dass Alexander bei seinem Übergange nach Asien die sämtlichen Verwandten seiner Stiefmutter umbringen liess (Justin 11, 5, 11).'[23] This view, however, places too much faith in the reliability of Justin (or Trogus, for that matter), who was notoriously fond of generalisations and rhetorical plurals.[24]

---

[22]Stähelin, *Klio* 5 (1905), 151.
[23]*Ibid.*
[24]Justin 11. 5. 11: *proficiscens ad Persicum bellum omnes novercae suae cognatos, quos Philippus in excelsiorem dignitatis locum provehens imperiis praefecerat, interfecit.* Justin's Alexander was one who *non in hostem, sed in suos saeviebat* (9. 8. 15). And where Justin knows of only one incident or one victim of Alexander's cruelty, he speaks of many. *hic* [sc. *Alexander*] *amicorum interfector convivio frequenter excessit* (9. 8. 16) refers only to Kleitos' murder (cf. Curt. 3. 12. 19). He speaks of many sons of Philip II, though he can name only one (to except, momentarily, the fictitious Karanos): *genuit ex Larissaea saltatrice filium Arridaeum, qui post Alexandrum regnavit. habuit et multos alios filios ex variis matrimoniis regio more susceptos, qui partim fato, partim ferro periere* (9. 8. 2-3). Likewise, although he names only one brother (the

According to all the sources that record her death (and these include Justin), Kleopatra and her daughter were the victims not of Alexander but of Olympias.[25] On Attalos, however, Alexander did take vengeance, through the agency of a certain Hekataios, and with the acquiescence of Parmenion.[26] There is no mention of any other male relatives of Kleopatra. Her father and her brother were already dead before she married Philip in 337 and this will explain why Kleopatra is consistently identified not as the daughter of Amyntas but as the niece of Attalos. Berve's objection (ii 185) that Satyros speaks of Hippostratos as if he were still alive in 337 is not convincing. Satyros gives no indication about the brother of Kleopatra, whether he was still alive or had already died, nor can any inference be drawn. But the evidence of Satyros may well tell us something about Kleopatra's family history. Amyntas may have died before his son, Hippostratos, and Kleopatra (and possibly her mother) would therefore have passed into the custody of her brother until his death in 344/3. At that time

fictitious Karanos, whose existence is contradicted by Justin himself at 9. 7. 12), whom Alexander put to death, he speaks of *fratres interfecti* (12. 6. 14; cf. Fox 504). *nec suis, qui apti regno videbantur, pepercit, ne qua materia seditionis procul se agente in Macedonia remaneret* (11. 5. 2) refers only to Amyntas Perdikka (*tunc Amyntas consobrinus ... interfect[us]*, 12. 6. 14). And, there is only one relative of Alexander's *noverca* (= Kleopatra) who might be described as [*quem*] *Philippus in excelsiorem dignitatis locum provehens imperiis praefecerat* (11. 5. 1): Attalos (cf. again 12. 6. 14). *omnes novercae suae cognatos ... interfecti* must be another generalisation. Cf. 10. 1. 1, 4 ff.; 11. 6. 11.

[25] Plut. *Alex*. 10. 7, it was done against Alexander's wishes; Justin 9. 7. 12 says that she was forced by Olympias to hang herself; Paus. 8. 7. 7 says that both mother and *son* (unless the adjective νηπιός is two-termination, hence feminine in this case) were forced onto an oven. Karanos, as son of Philip and a wife other than Olympias, has again been resurrected. Tarn rightly did away with him (ii 260-262, Appendix 9: 'Caranus'); he was followed by Burn, *JHS* 67 (1947), 143. But Karanos has been accepted as the son of Kleopatra (denying, therefore, the existence of Europe) by Grote 12. 8; Droysen i^3 70; Welles, *AHW* 15; and as Kleopatra's second child by Fox 503 f. and Green 108 ff., 523-524. That he was the son of another wife, most likely Phila the Elimeiot, is proposed by Willrich, *Hermes* 34 (1899), 177; Stähelin, *RE* xi (1922), 734-735, s.v. 'Kleopatra (12)'; Berve ii 199-200, no. 411, s.v. Κάρανος, and ii 213-214; Wilcken 62; Macurdy, *HQ* 54; Niese i 52; Schachermeyr 102, with n.84, 104. Most recently, Ellis, *Philip II* 306, n.54, correctly supports Tarn. The child is clearly meant to be Kleopatra's (the *noverca* of Justin 11. 2. 3 must be Kleopatra, as Tarn has proved conclusively). The child mentioned by Pausanias is the one referred to as *filia* by Justin 9. 7. 12, and this is Europe, so Satyros *ap*. Athen. 13. 557e. See Heckel, *RFIC* 107 (1979), 385-393; but see Unz, *JHS* 105 (1985), 171-174.

[26] Diod. 17. 2. 5-6; 17. 5. 2; Curt. 7. 1. 3; see Berve ii 148, no. 292, s.v. Ἑκαταῖος. Berve *TAPA* 91 (1960), 327; Green 119 f.

Kleopatra, now between nine and eleven years of age, became the ward of her uncle, Attalos. Thus her only two known male relatives still living in 337 were the prominent Attalos and Kleopatra's nephew Hegelochos, who had only begun his career in the army.

We first encounter Hegelochos as a commander of sarissophoroi (= prodromoi) and 500 light infantry near the Graneikos river (Arr. 1. 13. 1). But, unless Hegelochos exercised an exceptional command, his appearance in this context may be the result of Arrian's clumsy use of his primary sources (cf. Bosworth, *Arrian* i 114: 1. 13. 1 may be a doublet of 1. 12. 7, the mission of Amyntas son of Arrhabaios). When Alexander left Gordion in spring 333, he sent Hegelochos to the coast with orders to build a new fleet at the Hellespont (Arr. 2. 3. 3).[27] After a successful campaign with the fleet, he appears to have handed over naval affairs to Amphoteros, the brother of Krateros, and rejoined Alexander in Egypt in the winter of 332/1 (Arr. 3. 2. 3). He reappears, for the last time, at Gaugamela (Arr. 3. 11. 8: an ilarch in Philotas' Companion Cavalry), where, it seems, he met his end: Arrian says nothing further about him, but Curtius makes Philotas refer to him as *illum ... Hegelochum qui in acie cecidit* (6. 11. 22).

Only a literal interpretation of Justin prevents us from identifying Hegelochos with the nephew of Kleopatra. And this testimony has been discredited. The career of Hegelochos is thus instructive. When Alexander set out for Asia, he left many enemies, potentially dangerous, alive, both in Makedonia and within the army: witness the series of intrigues and conspiracies that followed the death of Philip II. Alexander could, and did, eliminate his most dangerous political rivals, but he was forced to adopt a policy of conciliation; for the very bases of his power were the Makedonian nobles, who had supported Philip and who had now realigned themselves in accordance with the needs of the new regime. There were some casualties, but Alexander will have been anxious to limit the slaughter. Parmenion could buy peace, and indeed strengthen his position in the army, but the price was Attalos' head. Nevertheless, numerous members of the 'opposition' remained alive and in positions of power. Alexandros of Lynkestis came to no harm at this time, though he was later arrested for his

---

[27]Curt. 3. 1. 19: *Amphoterum classi ad oram Hellesponti, copiis autem praefecit Hegelochum, Lesbium et Chium Coumque praesidiis hostium liberaturos*. The apparent contradiction of Arr. 3. 2. 6 (seen by Berve i 161 and ii 32, no. 68, s.v. Ἀμφοτερός) is perhaps explained by Hauben, *Anc. Soc.* 3 (1972), 57, who regards this as 'a diarchic fleet command', in which 'the head of the marines also functioned as the supreme commander of the whole formation.' Thus Amphoteros controlled the purely naval matters, but under Hegelochos' direction.

intrigues. Yet Alexander could have been expected to fear him on account of the execution of Heromenes and Arrhabaios (Berve ii 80, 169, nos. 144, 355). Amyntas, the nephew of Lynkestian Alexandros and the son of the executed Arrhabaios,[28] also retained his rank until the arrest of his uncle led, apparently, to his own fall (cf. Berve ii 30). And so it comes as no surprise that Hegelochos was also left unharmed. Hippostratos had been Kleopatra's brother, but he was long dead and forgotten by the time that the purge took place. Hegelochos presented no challenge to Alexander's sovereignty and the King could ill afford to extend his feud with Attalos to include even Kleopatra's nephew.[29] The Makedonian nobility were too numerous, too influential and too much interrelated to make such an action feasible. We are reminded of Badian's salutary observation that 'Alexander could not afford (and had hardly intended) to engage in wholesale slaughter of the Macedonian nobility' (*TAPA* 91 [1960], 335).

Opposition to Alexander, resulting from the problems of the succession of 336, continued until the death of Alexandros Lynkestes, the *dénouement* of the Philotas affair. Friction existed throughout Alexander's reign between the supporters of Alexander and those whom Schachermeyr (363) terms 'altmakedonisch gesinnt'. In the course of this struggle there were many casualties and, while Hegelochos appears to have died in battle, there is no reason to suspect that he was not hostile to Alexander and capable of plotting against him. If he was in fact the nephew of Kleopatra, the murder of his aunt will have been fresh in his mind in 332/1. Curtius (or his source) did not invent the incident. Now that we have some clue concerning the family of Hegelochos, a more plausible motive for his hitherto disregarded conspiracy emerges.

---

[28]Also the brother of the defector Neoptolemos (Arr. 1. 20. 10; Diod. 17. 25. 5 puts him on the Makedonian side, a view accepted by Welles, *Diodorus* 188 f., n.1; cf. Bosworth, *Arrian* i 145).

[29]In fact, Burstein (*EMC* n.s. 1 [1982], 141-163) sees Alexander's burial of Kleopatra in Philip's tomb as a conciliatory gesture. Burstein rightly speaks of 'the cautious policy Alexander had adopted in dealing with them [i.e., the Attalos faction]' (161).

2. The House of Parmenion

2. 1. Parmenion: Philip's General

Literature. Berve ii 298-306, no. 606; id., *RE* xviii. 4 (1949), 1559-1565, no. 1; Beloch iv² 2. 290-306, Abschn. XV: 'Alexander und Parmenion'.

Ἀθηναίους μὲν οὖν μακαρίζειν ἔλεγεν [sc. Φίλιππος], εἰ καθ' ἕκαστον ἐνιαυτὸν αἱρέσθαι δέκα στρατηγοὺς εὑρίσκουσιν· αὐτὸς δὲ ἐν πολλοῖς ἔτεσιν ἕνα μόνον στρατηγὸν εὑρηκέναι, Παρμενίωνα.
(Plut. *Apophth. Phil.* 2 = *Mor.* 177c)

From the era of Philip II, Parmenion son of Philotas (Arr. 3. 11. 10) emerged as Makedon's foremost general (Curt. 4. 13. 4; Justin 12. 5. 3; cf. Plut. *Alex.* 49. 13; *Mor.* 177c), powerful within the army — where his family and its adherents held major commands — and no less influential at the Court (Plut. *Apophth. Phil.* 28 = *Mor.* 179b).[30] Born c. 400 B.C. (Curt. 6. 11. 32; cf. 7. 2. 33.), he was already a dominant force in Pella in the first years of Philip's reign. On that king's orders, he put to death Euphraios, who had had great influence with Perdikkas III, arresting and executing the former at Oreos (Karystios *ap.* Athen. 11. 508e). News of his victory over the Illyrian Grabos reached Philip at Potidaia, as we are told (Plut. *Alex.* 3. 8), on the same day in 356 as the report of Alexander's birth. Indeed, Philip valued Parmenion's generalship: he was alleged to have remarked that whereas the Athenians elected ten generals every year, he had found only one general in many years — Parmenion (Plut. *Apophth. Phil.* 2 = *Mor.* 177c, quoted above).

About the father Philotas, most likely an important figure at the court of Amyntas III, nothing is recorded but the name. Parmenion himself had only three sons: Philotas (born in the late 360s), Nikanor, Hektor; at least one daughter, whose name has not survived, is indirectly attested.[31] Nothing is known of his connections with the aristocratic factions and families of Makedon before Philip's marriage to Kleopatra-Eurydike, but it appears that his eldest son, Philotas, was brought up at the Court with Philip's nephew, Amyntas Perdikka; for

---

[30] Parmenion, Antipatros and Eurylochos headed the Makedonian embassy which negotiated the Peace of 346 (Demosth. 19. 69; Aesch. 3. 72; Deinarchos 1. 28; cf. Theopompos *FGrHist* 115 F165).

[31] Berve's assumption (ii 298) that Parmenion had at least two daughters (one the wife of Attalos, the other of Koinos) is perhaps unnecessary: Koinos appears to have married Attalos' widow.

the two appear to have been very close in age.³² Nor can we say what were Parmenion's connections with Alexander, Olympias and their supporters. One source calls Philotas a friend of Alexander, yet his actions in 336 will scarcely have endeared him to the Crown Prince.³³ Undoubtedly, Parmenion, who could not himself aspire to the kingship, supported Philip politically with the same enthusiasm as he did militarily. Thus, when Philip married Kleopatra-Eurydike, Parmenion brought himself into closer alignment with the King by marrying his daughter to Attalos,³⁴ with whom he was sent, in spring 336, to prepare a bridgehead in Asia.³⁵ But the assumption — and it is no more than an assumption — that Attalos was of Lower Makedonian origin need not imply the same about Parmenion. The evidence suggests rather that he had strong connections with the highlands: Philotas commanded in the Triballian campaign the cavalry from Upper Makedonia (τοὺς ἐκ τῆς ἄνωθεν Μακεδονίας ἱππέας) and his friends included the sons of Andromenes from Tymphaia;³⁶ Parmenion himself normally commanded the infantry, on the left, at least half of which was recruited from Upper Makedonia;³⁷ he was also associated with Polyperchon (Tymphaia) and the sons of Polemokrates (Elimeia), one of whom, Koinos, became his son-in-law.³⁸

Sent ahead with Attalos and Amyntas to prepare for Philip's invasion (Diod. 16. 91. 2; 17. 2. 4; Justin 9. 5. 8; cf. Trogus, *Prol.* 9),

---

³²See Berve ii 393-397, no. 802, s.v. Φιλώτας. Berve (ii 393) assumes that Philotas was Parmenion's eldest son, since he commanded the Companions, and that he was born 'nicht lange vor 360, da er anscheinend zu den Jugendfreunden Al.s gehörte'. His younger brother, Nikanor, commanded the hypaspists, and it seems that Philotas' birthdate fell between 365 and 360, which would make him roughly contemporary with Amyntas Perdikka. Probably they were *syntrophoi* at the Court, where they became close friends (cf. Curt. 6. 9. 17; 6. 10. 24). See Berve ii 30-31, no. 61, s.v. Ἀμύντας.

³³Plut. *Alex.* 10. 3: the Pixodaros affair. Whether Philotas was brought in to shame Alexander or whether he was Philip's informant (so Hamilton, *G&R* 12 [1965], 121, with n.4, translating παραλαβών as 'taking as witness'), he must have earned Alexander's ill-will.

³⁴Curt. 6. 9. 18; this union probably dates to autumn 337, that is, shortly after Philip's own wedding.

³⁵Diod. 16. 91. 2; 17. 2. 4; Justin 9. 5. 8-9, adding Amyntas (perhaps the son of Arrhabaios?).

³⁶The Triballian campaign (Arr. 1. 2. 5). Connections with sons of Andromenes (Curt. 7. 1. 11).

³⁷Certainly at least four of the six taxiarchs in 334 were of Upper Makedonian origin.

³⁸Polyperchon (Curt. 4. 13. 7 ff.); the sons of Polemokrates: Kleandros and Koinos. Ellis, *Philip II* 253, n.70, cites an unpublished paper by C. D. Edson, arguing that Parmenion was from Pelagonia.

Parmenion enjoyed mixed success in Asia Minor: Polyainos (5. 44. 4) provides a vague account of a defeat at Magnesia-on-the-Maiandros inflicted by Memnon the Rhodian.[39] In 336/5 Alexander sent to him Hekataios, who murdered Attalos, almost certainly with Parmenion's approval.[40] This was Parmenion's token of loyalty, and there is no reason to doubt that Alexander was satisfied.[41] Some time later, Parmenion captured Gryneion and sold its inhabitants into slavery; Memnon, however, forced him to abandon the siege of Pitane (Diod. 17. 7. 9) and drove his accomplice, Kalas son of Harpalos, back to Rhoiteion (Diod. 17. 7. 10). The campaign had not been an overwhelming success: perhaps the Makedonians had underestimated the Persian forces in the region and the skill of their Rhodian general; more likely, Alexander found himself preoccupied with the political turmoil in Europe, leaving Parmenion with limited resources to fend for himself. Parmenion had, however, secured the beach-head and, over the winter of 335/4,[42] rejoined Alexander in Europe. In 334 he transported most of the infantry and cavalry from Sestos to Abydos. Diodoros adds that, in Asia Minor, Parmenion commanded the infantry — 12,000 Makedonians, 7,000 allies and 5,000 mercenaries (Arr. 1. 11. 6; Diod. 17. 17. 3). In fact, his sons also held major commands in the Makedonian army: Philotas led the Companions, Nikanor the hypaspists; only Hektor held no attested office.[43] Asandros son of Philotas, who was promptly installed as satrap of Lydia, was probably not Parmenion's brother.[44] Nevertheless, Parmenion and his sons, the taxiarchs Koinos, Polyperchon,[45] and Amyntas son of

---

[39]The account, and Polyainos' figure of 10,000 Makedonian troops (accepted by McCoy, *AJP* 110 [1989], 424), must be treated with caution (cf. Niese i 59, n.2).

[40]Diod. 17. 2. 4-6, 5. 2. Attalos' widow (apparently) was then given by her father to Koinos son of Polemokrates (Curt. 6. 9. 30; cf. Arr. 1. 24. 1; 1. 29. 4). The product of this union was a son named Perdikkas; see Dittenberger, *Syll.*³ 332; Berve ii 312-313, no. 626.

[41]Diod. 17. 2. 5-6; 17. 5. 2; Curt. 7. 1. 3. Cf. Edmunds, *GRBS* 12 (1971), 367.

[42]Berve ii 299 places Parmenion's advice, that Alexander produce an heir before departing for Asia, in this context (Diod. 17. 16. 2).

[43]For Hektor see Berve ii 149, no. 295; id., *RE* Supplbd iv (1924), 716, no. 10a. Nothing is known about his life except that he drowned in the Nile in 332/1 (Curt. 4. 8. 7-9; cf. 6. 9. 27; Julian, *Epist.* 82 [446a], removes the event to the Euphrates) and that Alexander buried him with suitable honours. Nikanor: Arr. 1. 14. 2; 3. 11. 9; Diod. 17. 57. 1-2; Curt. 6. 9. 27; Berve ii 275, no. 554; see also **vi 1. 1**.

[44]See Appendix VI.

[45]For Polyperchon and Parmenion see Curt. 4. 13. 7 ff. See further **iii 5**.

Andromenes, along with Polydamas (perhaps commander of the Pharsalian horse), formed a powerful faction in Alexander's army.

At the river Graneikos, he is alleged to have advised Alexander not to attack so late in the day, but this counsel was rejected by the King (Arr. 1. 13. 2 ff.; Plut. *Alex.* 16. 3), who argued that he would be ashamed to be held up by a mere trickle like the Graneikos after he had crossed the Hellespont.[46] In the actual battle Parmenion commanded the left, including the Thessalian cavalry (Arr. 1. 14. 1), who acquitted themselves well in the engagement (Diod. 17. 19. 6); soon afterwards, he was sent ahead to Daskyleion, which he captured and garrisoned (Arr. 1. 17. 2). Now since Daskyleion was the residence of the satrap of Hellespontine Phrygia, it appears that Parmenion's task was to ensure that Kalas son of Harpalos, Alexander's newly appointed satrap of the region, was securely established there.[47] Upon his return, Alexander sent Parmenion to Magnesia and Tralles (which had surrendered) with 2,500 infantry, an equal number of Makedonians and 200 of the Companions (Arr. 1. 18. 1). He rejoined the King at Miletos, where he advised against disbanding the fleet,[48] and continued with

---

[46] Diod. 17. 19. 3, says that Alexander attacked at dawn, thus giving the impression that he was following Parmenion's advice. Diodoros may, however, be basing his account on a corrective (pro-Parmenion) version — he does not mention Parmenion's advice, or Alexander's rejection of it — or he may simply have mistakenly translated Parmenion's proposal into action. Beloch iv^2 2. 296-297 accepts Diodoros' version as correct; cf. also Bosworth, *Arrian* i 114-116, with full discussion of the source problem, with earlier literature on the battle at the Graneikos.

[47] Both Parmenion and Kalas were familiar with the region, having campaigned there in 336 and 335 (Diod. 17. 7. 10). It appears that Parmenion took with him to Daskyleion the Thessalian horse, which he left there for the time to help Kalas recover the Troad (Arr. 1. 17. 8). Arrian curiously separates the appointment of Kalas and Parmenion's mission (1. 17. 1-2) from the instructions given to Kalas and Alexandros son of Aeropos concerning 'Memnon's territory' (1. 17. 8; did they set out from Sardeis?). It would be odd if Alexander made the appointment and then took Kalas to Sardeis, only to send him back into his satrapy from Ionia. Kalas replaced Arsites (Arr. 1. 12. 8; 1. 17. 1); for previous rulers of the satrapy see P. Krumbholz, *De Asiae Minoris Satrapis Persicis* (Leipzig, 1883), 93. See also ix 4. 1.

[48] Parmenion drew attention to an omen, an eagle perched on the shore behind Alexander's ships. If the Makedonians won a naval engagement at the beginning of the campaign it would be beneficial to their cause, but a setback would not harm them, since the Persians were already dominant at sea (Arr. 1. 18. 6). But Alexander responded that he would not fight against a force superior in numbers — 400 Persians (Arr. 1. 18. 5) to 160 Makedonians under Nikanor (1. 18. 4) — and in training, and risk good lives to an uncertain element; that a loss would harm Makedonian prestige at a crucial point in the

him into Karia. With winter approaching, Parmenion moved to Sardeis, taking a hipparchy of Companions, the Thessalian horse, the allies and the wagons; his orders were to march ahead into Phrygia and there to await the King (Arr. 1. 24. 3; cf. 1. 29. 3). It was at Gordion that Parmenion apprehended Dareios' agent, Sisines, who had been sent to induce Alexandros Lynkestes to murder the Makedonian King. Sisines was sent in chains to Alexander (now at Phaselis) who, upon interrogating the Persian, sent Amphoteros back to Gordion instructing Parmenion to arrest the Lynkestian.[49] In spring 333, Alexander himself reached Gordion, as did Koinos and Meleagros, leading the newly-weds and fresh reinforcements (Arr. 1. 29. 3-4).

When the expedition moved out of Kappadokia to Kilikia, Parmenion remained at the so-called 'Camp of Kyros' with the heavy infantry while Alexander took the hypaspists, archers and Agrianes in order to occupy the Kilikian Gates (Arr. 2. 4. 3). These had been abandoned by Arsames' guards, who were frightened by the King's approach and alarmed by Arsames' 'scorched earth' policy; and Alexander, fearing lest the satrap should destroy Tarsos, sent Parmenion ahead to capture the city. This, at least, is Curtius' version; Arrian says nothing about Parmenion's contribution (Curt. 3. 4. 14-15; Arr. 2. 4. 5-6). Whether this is the result of abbreviation or a deliberate omission by Arrian's source(s), we cannot be sure. The mission invites comparison with Parmenion's capture of Damaskos soon after the battle of Issos (below). But Parmenion had up to this point been placed in charge of the less-mobile troops, and one suspects that Curtius' source may have written '[Philotas son of] Parmenion'. It was near Tarsos that Alexander fell ill, and Justin's claim that Parmenion wrote to Alexander from Kappadokia, warning the King to beware of Philippos, the Akarnanian physician, may reflect his (or rather Trogus') belief that Parmenion had remained in Kappadokia while Alexander rushed ahead to Tarsos.[50] Now it is precisely in this context

campaign; and that the omen showed that the Makedonians should fight on land, for that was where the eagle was situated, not at sea (Arr. 1. 18. 7-9).

[49]Arr. 1. 25. 4-10; a different version in Diod. 17. 32. 1-2; cf. Curt. 7. 1. 6, and 3. 7. 11-15 (for the arrest and death of Sisines).

[50]Bosworth (*Arrian* i 190) points out that from the Gates to Tarsos it is only about '55 km, a manageable day's stint for the advance column'. And it appears more likely that Alexander himself (or possibly Philotas) advanced with the more mobile troops and that Parmenion remained at the Gates, awaiting further instructions from the King. Parmenion had in fact passed through the Gates (τῇ δὲ ὑστεραίᾳ ἅμα τῇ ἕῳ ξὺν τῇ δυνάμει πάσῃ ὑπερβαλὼν τὰς πύλας κατέβαινεν ἐς τὴν Κιλικίαν, Arr. 2. 4. 4; cf. Atkinson, *Curtius* i 155), but this does not rule out the possibility that he stayed behind or followed at a slower pace. A letter from him might be thought to have come

that the Vulgate discusses the arrest of Alexandros Lynkestes, who, like the doctor Philippos, had allegedly been bribed by the Persian King. On this occasion, as on others, Parmenion's advice was disregarded and proved to be wrong.

From Tarsos, Parmenion advanced to the 'other' or Syrian Gates (Arr. 2. 5. 1; Diod. 17. 32. 2), which he secured before rejoining the King at Kastabalon (Curt. 3. 7. 5; cf. Arr. 2. 6. 1-2, with Bosworth, *Arrian* i 199); thereafter he took Issos and advised Alexander to fight Dareios in the narrows where the numerical supremacy of the Persians could be negated. The advice was accepted (Curt. 3. 7. 6-10)![51] In this first encounter with the Great King, Parmenion acted as commander-in-chief of the forces on the left, and was told to extend his line to the sea (Curt. 3. 9. 8-10; Arr. 2. 8. 4; 2. 8. 9-10). To his contingent Alexander added the Thessalian cavalry (Arr. 2. 8. 9; Curt. 3. 11. 3), who again fought with distinction.

After the battle, Parmenion was sent to capture the treasures at Damaskos,[52] a mission accomplished without difficulty (Arr. 2. 15. 1; Curt. 3. 13. 1 ff., heavily dramatised; cf. Polyainos 4. 5. 1). Athenaios (13. 607f-608a) quotes from what is purportedly a letter of Parmenion to Alexander itemizing the captured spoils, among them 329 of the Great King's concubines. This letter (if genuine) appears to have reached Alexander at Marathos. The King now instructed Parmenion, who was on his way back to Alexander's camp, to send him only the captive Greek envoys and to take the remaining spoils back to Damaskos and guard them there (Arr. 2. 15. 1-2). The captives included Barsine, the widow of both Mentor and Memnon the Rhodians and allegedly the first woman with whom Alexander was intimate. Parmenion, it is said,

---

from the direction of Kappadokia. Diod. 17. 31. 4-6 knows nothing about any warning concerning Philippos and follows his account of Alexander's illness with the arrest of Alexandros Lynkestes (17. 32. 1-2). This was perhaps the original version given by Kleitarchos; Curtius' account is contaminated by Trogus and/or Ptolemy; I cannot agree with Hammond, *THA* 121, who thinks that Trogus and Curtius used a common source (Kleitarchos) for this episode.

[51]Parmenion's activities occupied him for the better part of a month, in which he took precautions against Dareios' advance. Nevertheless, the Persian King took Parmenion and Alexander by surprise, entering Kilikia from the north (via the Bahche Pass). For a full discussion see Bosworth, *Arrian* i 192 f.; cf. also F. Stark, *Alexander's Path from Caria to Cilicia* (New York, 1958), 4, 7; Engels, *Logistics* 42-53, esp. 44, n.97, for a comment on Alexander's alleged ignorance of the Persian position.

[52]Curt. 3. 12. 27; Arr. 2. 11. 10; Plut. *Alex.* 24. 1. Dareios had sent most of his baggage and the Persian women (except those of his immediate family) to Damaskos before he reached Issos (Arr. 2. 11. 9; Diod. 17. 32. 3; Curt. 3. 8. 12).

urged him to take up this relationship.⁵³ She too may have been brought to the King at Marathos.

Parmenion now became military overseer of Koile Syria,⁵⁴ a temporary command: the satrapy was soon assigned to Andromachos, whom the Samaritans later put to death (Curt. 4. 5. 9; cf. 4. 8. 9-11). Curtius places the appointment of Andromachos and Parmenion's reunion with Alexander after the fall of Tyre, when the army prepared to move south towards Gaza, the logical time for such an administrative change. Polyainos gives Parmenion charge of the army at Tyre, while Alexander conducted his Arabian campaign; but Curtius claims that the siege had been entrusted to Krateros and Perdikkas.⁵⁵ The story that Parmenion, hard-pressed by the Tyrians, had to summon Alexander from Arabia sounds like another attempt to discredit the old general. From Gaza, Parmenion accompanied the King to Egypt. There he used his influence to pacify Hegelochos (Curt. 6. 11. 27-29), and his mere presence in the camp sufficed to save Philotas from charges of treason (Arr. 3. 26. 1). Still his sojourn in Egypt was not free of tragedy: his youngest son Hektor drowned in the Nile.⁵⁶

The last two years of Parmenion's life are more difficult to reconstruct. His murder in Ekbatana demanded justification, and both imperial propaganda and *apologia* cast a long shadow over the history of these years. Hence, when Dareios offers Alexander all the territory west of the Euphrates, a large amount of silver and the hand of his daughter in marriage, Parmenion adds that he would accept the offer. To which, Alexander replies arrogantly that he would too, *if he were Parmenion*.⁵⁷ Similarly, the old general's advice that they attack the

---

⁵³Aristoboulos, *FGrHist* 139 F11 = Plut. *Alex.* 21. 9; Parmenion had earlier advised Alexander to produce an heir before leaving for Asia (Diod. 17. 16. 2). For Alexander's intimate relations with Barsine see Justin 11. 10. 2-3: *tunc et Barsinen captivam diligere propter formae pulchritudinem coepit, a qua postea susceptum puerum Herculem vocavit*.

⁵⁴Curt. 4. 1. 4 (cf. Bosworth, *CQ* 24 [1974], 47 f.). It is tempting to see Parmenion as a corruption of Menon (son of Kerdimmas), on whom see Arr. 2. 13. 7. But Justin 11. 10. 4 f., seems to corroborate some kind of independent command for Parmenion, though *Parmeniona ad occupandam Persicam classem* is clearly corrupt, unless it implies that Parmenion was to secure the coast of Koile-Syria. See also Bosworth, *Arrian* i 225.

⁵⁵Parmenion at Tyre: Polyainos 4. 3. 4. Krateros and Perdikkas: Curt. 4. 3. 1; cf. Polyainos 4. 13 (Krateros).

⁵⁶Curt. 4. 8. 7 ff.; 6. 9. 27; cf. Plut. *Alex.* 49. 13.

⁵⁷Plut. *Alex.* 29. 7-9 (10,000 talents; cf. Arr. 2. 25. 1, in a different chronological context); Diod. 17. 54; Curt. 4. 11. 1-14 and Justin 11. 12. 1-10 (30,000 talents).

Persians by night at Gaugamela is rejected as a plan to 'steal victory' (Curt. 4. 13. 4, 8-9; Arr. 3. 10. 1-2; Plut. *Alex*. 31. 11-12). On the morning of the battle, Parmenion frets because the troops are ready for battle but Alexander is still asleep; the King, when he awakes is remarkably calm and confident in face of danger (Diod. 17. 56. 2; Curt. 4. 13. 17 ff., Plut. *Alex*. 32. 1-4). And, in the battle itself, Parmenion is depicted as slack and incompetent, tarnishing the King's total victory over Dareios.

ὅλως γὰρ αἰτιῶνται Παρμενίωνα κατ' ἐκείνην τὴν μάχην νωθρὸν γενέσθαι καὶ δύσεργον, εἴτε τοῦ γήρως ἤδη τι παραλύοντος τῆς τόλμης, εἴτε τὴν ἐξουσίαν καὶ ὄγκον, ὡς Καλλισθένης φησί, τῆς Ἀλεξάνδρου δυνάμεως βαρυνόμενον καὶ προσφθονοῦντα.
(Plut. *Alex*. 33. 10 = *FGrHist* 124 F37)

For there is general complaint that in that battle Parmenio was sluggish and inefficient, either because old age was now impairing somewhat his courage, or because he was made envious and resentful by the arrogance and pomp, to use the words of Callisthenes, of Alexander's power.
(B. Perrin, tr.)

In truth, Parmenion's appeal for help, if it was actually sent, did not reach Alexander, and the old man extricated himself from the difficulties presented by Mazaios and the Persian cavalry. But a few strokes of the pen could now blacken Parmenion's reputation while exculpating the King of any error in leadership. How much of the entire hostile portrait of Parmenion can, in fact, be traced to Kallisthenes? Probably very little. To begin with, it is not at all certain that Kallisthenes himself was responsible for the charge that Parmenion was νωθρὸς καὶ δύσεργος, only that he had at some point in his history described τὴν ἐξουσίαν καὶ τὸν ὄγκον τῆς Ἀλεξάνδρου δυνάμεως. But if Kallisthenes is responsible for this negative view of Parmenion, we must assume that he revised the earlier books of his history, introducing fictitious discussions of policy between the general and the King.

It is difficult to imagine that these episodes could have been written in Parmenion's lifetime, or even in the King's. Just as Lysimachos reacted to Onesikritos' story of the Amazon queen, surely at least one of the King's Companions, a member of the King's *consilium*, might be expected to ask: 'And where was I when all this happened?' Kleitos indeed was outraged when a Greek (Pierion or Pranichos) mocked the failure of certain Makedonian commanders, but no contemporary ever charged Alexander or Kallisthenes with blackening Parmenion's memory by alleging that he gave foolish advice or failed to perform his duties in battle. On the other hand, Kallisthenes may simply have written what the King wanted to read, even if he did alienate members of the Makedonian aristocracy.[58] Or else — and this can be no more than speculation — whoever edited the work for publication after Kallisthenes' death in 327 inserted the passages concerning Alexander and Parmenion.[59] One thing is certain, however: the hostile portrait of Parmenion originated with one of the first Alexander historians, for it found its way into Kleitarchos as well as Ptolemy and was the invention of neither.

There soon developed a corrective view, most easily detected in the Vulgate, notably in Curtius. The latter's obituary notice says of Parmenion: *multa sine rege prospere, rex sine illo nihil magnae rei gesserat* (7. 2. 33). And Beloch (iv^2 2. 295 f.) thinks that Philotas was essentially speaking the truth to his mistress when 'he declared that the greatest deeds were those accomplished by himself and by his father, and he called Alexander a stripling who reaped on their account the fame of empire.'[60] Passages favourable to Parmenion thus appear to be later inventions: his advice that the army fight in the narrows at Issos (Curt. 3. 7. 8-10) and that Alexander not read to his soldiers letters from Dareios urging them to murder their leader (Curt. 4. 10. 16-17) is accepted in each case. Curtius himself regards the criticism of Parmenion excessive and directs against Polyperchon Alexander's rejection of the night-attack at Gaugamela (4. 13. 4, 7-10).[61]

Parmenion commanded the Makedonian left at Gaugamela (Arr. 3. 11. 10; cf. 3. 15) and soon found himself hard-pressed by the Persian cavalry under Mazaios (Diod. 17. 60. 5-7); Skythian horsemen had, furthermore, broken through Makedonian lines and begun to plunder the camp (Curt. 4. 15. 2 ff.). A detachment sent to recall Alexander failed to make contact with the King and returned with its mission unfulfilled (Diod. 17. 60. 7); though Arrian (3. 15. 1) claims that Alexander responded and came to the rescue.[62] Parmenion's skilful handling of the Thessalians, combined with the flight of Dareios from the other part of the battlefield, forced Mazaios to withdraw (Diod. 17. 60. 8). It had

---

[58]Cf. Pearson, *LHA* 48: 'his flights of rhetoric were taken too seriously by some Macedonians.'

[59]As Pearson, *LHA* 23 points out, there is no evidence that Kallisthenes' history was published in instalments; nor do we have any idea who the editor of the work could have been.

[60]ἑαυτοῦ τὰ μέγιστα τῶν ἔργων ἀπέφαινε καὶ τοῦ πατρός, Ἀλέξανδρον δὲ μειράκιον ἀπεκάλει δι' αὐτοὺς τὸ τῆς ἀρχῆς ὄνομα καρπούμενον (Plut. *Alex.* 48. 5).

[61]Cf. also Curt. 4. 12. 21.

[62]Fuller 178 accepts the story; it is rejected by Bosworth, *Conquest and Empire* 82 f.; cf. *Arrian* i 310; cf. Devine, *Phoenix* 29 (1975), 381.

been Parmenion's role to hold the enemy in check on the left while Alexander turned the tide of battle on the right. The victory was won on both sides of the Makedonian line, and Parmenion's contribution cannot be diminished. The horsemen under Aretes' command had, meanwhile, repulsed those who burst into the camp (Curt. 4. 15. 18 ff.). Once the Persians were routed, and Alexander had established his camp beyond the Lykos river, Parmenion occupied the Persian camp, capturing the baggage, the camels and the elephants (Arr. 3. 15. 4).

On the march from Sousa to Persepolis, Parmenion led the slower troops and the baggage train along the wagon road into Persis (Arr. 3. 18. 1), while Alexander took an unencumbered force through the Persian Gates. At Persepolis he advised Alexander not to destroy the palace; for it was unwise to destroy one's own property (Arr. 3. 18. 11). In this instance, we can make little out of Alexander's rejection of the advice, since he was constrained by his own claims to be the 'avenger of Greece' to make a symbolic gesture at Persepolis. Nor, on the other hand, does Parmenion's suggestion that Alexander spare the palace imply any sympathy for Alexander's new role as Great King of Asia or sensitivity to the conquered peoples. From Persepolis the King sent Parmenion to Ekbatana with the accumulated treasure (Justin 12. 1. 3; Arr. 3. 19. 7), details of which are again provided in a letter from Parmenion to Alexander (Athen. 11. 781f - 782a).

Ekbatana was a milestone in Alexander's campaign, and for Parmenion's career: the last of four Persian capitals had been taken, the Panhellenic phase of the war concluded — at least in the opinion of the Greek allies, many of whom were sent home. When Alexander continued in pursuit of Dareios, he left Parmenion in Ekbatana, presumably as *strategos* of Media and possibly as a temporary measure; his instructions to invade the land of the Kadousians and Hyrkania (Arr. 3. 19. 7) were apparently cancelled.[63] But the end was near for the old soldier. The news of Nikanor's death (Curt. 6. 6. 18; Arr. 3. 25. 4) can have reached Parmenion only a few days before he learned of Philotas' execution. To the latter, there was no chance to react militarily. Alexander had removed that option. The decision to condemn and execute Philotas had been made carefully, for it demanded the father's murder. Once made, however, there could be no turning back.

Polydamas, an old friend, delivered the order, travelling on swift dromedaries and accompanied by local guides; kinsmen remained with Alexander as hostages until the mission was fulfilled. In Media, Kleandros, Agathon, Sitalkes and Menidas — the old man's successors

---

[63]See Bosworth, *Arrian* i 337; Seibert, *Eroberung* 110 f.; cf. Brunt, *Arrian* i 529, Appendix xiii 5.

— carried out the sentence, as Parmenion learned of this conviction and of the charges against him.[64] For the troops there was temporary disbelief, then resignation: they had witnessed a cabinet-shuffle, Makedonian style. Opposition to the King and his methods continued, especially amongst the aristocracy. But few outlived any public expression of it.[65]

2. 2. Philotas: Parmenion's Son

Literature. Berve ii 393-397, no. 802; Cauer 8-38; E. Badian, 'The Death of Parmenio', *TAPA* 91 (1960), 324-338; W. Heckel, 'The Conspiracy against Philotas', Phoenix 31 (1977) 9-21; Z. Rubinsohn, 'The "Philotas Affair" — A Reconsideration', *Ancient Macedonia* ii (Thessaloniki, 1977), 409-420; Goukowsky i 38 ff.; ii 118-134; Hamilton, *PA* 132-138; Bosworth, *Arrian* i 359-363.

Philotas was the son of Parmenion, and thus also brother of Nikanor, Hektor and at least one unnamed sister, the wife of Attalos (Curt. 6. 9. 17).[66] Born probably in the late 360s, Philotas appears to have been a *syntrophos* of Amyntas Perdikka; the sons of Andromenes (Curt. 7. 1. 10-11; cf. Arr. 1. 27. 1) and, perhaps, also Amyntas son of Antiochos (cf. Ellis, *JHS* 91 [1971], 15 ff.) were personal friends. Whether he held any military office before Alexander's accession is unknown: he is first attested as a commander of cavalry (from Upper Makedonia) in the Triballian campaign (Arr. 1. 2. 5). It is tempting to see his promotion to hipparch of the Companions as a reward for Parmenion's complicity in the execution of Attalos.

---

[64]For Parmenion's death see Arr. 3. 26. 3-4; Curt. 7. 2. 11-32, with a eulogy at 7. 2. 33-34; Plut. *Alex*. 49. 13; Diod. 17. 80. 3; Justin 12. 5. 3. For Polydamas: Arr. 3. 26. 3; Curt. 7. 2. 11 ff. (7. 2. 12, for the hostages: *fratres* may be an error for *filii*). Parmenion's murderers: Kleandros, Menidas and Sitalkes (Arr. 3. 26. 3); Kleandros (Curt. 7. 2. 19 ff.); Kleandros, Agathon, Sitalkes and Herakon (Curt. 10. 1. 1). The charges against Parmenion were either fabricated (Curt. 6. 9. 13-14) or extracted from Philotas under torture (Curt. 6. 11. 21 ff.). See also **viii 3. 4, 6. 2-3** (Sitalkes, Kleandros and Herakon).

[65]Meleagros (Curt. 8. 12. 18) is a notable exception. Koinos died soon after his opposition to Alexander at the Hyphasis (Curt. 9. 3. 20; Arr. 6. 2. 1), but Alexander cannot be blamed for his death.

[66]Son of Parmenion: Arr. 1. 14. 1; 3. 11. 8; 3. 26. 1, 3-4 (cf. 4. 14. 2); Diod. 17. 17. 4; 17. 57. 1; 17. 80. 1, 3; Curt. 6. 7. 18; 6. 8. 7, 11; 6. 9. 13; 6. 10. 30 ff.; 7. 1. 2 ff.; Justin 12. 5. 3; cf. Diod. 17. 118. 1; Curt. 6. 6. 19. Nikanor: Curt. 6. 6. 19; cf. 6. 9. 13; Diod. 17. 57. 2; Arr. 2. 8. 3; 3. 25. 4. Hektor: Curt. 4. 8. 7-9; cf. 6. 9. 27. The sister who married Koinos (Curt. 6. 9. 30; Dittenberger, *Syll*.³ 332, 10) was probably Attalos' widow; for Koinos was *neogamos* in 334 B.C. (Arr. 1. 24. 1, 29. 4; cf. Heckel, *Historia* 36 [1987], 117 f.: A33, cf. A34).

Before the crossing to Asia, it appears that Philotas commanded only a portion of the Makedonian cavalry (cf. Berve ii 393). Upon surrounding the Illyrians of Kleitos in the town of Pellion, Alexander sent Philotas with sufficient horsemen to protect a foraging party. These, however, were surrounded by Glaukias and the Taulantians, who had come to Kleitos' aid, and had to be rescued by the King (Arr. 1. 5. 9-11).[67] And we hear nothing further about him until the beginning of the Asiatic expedition, when he commands the entire Companion Cavalry (Diod. 17. 17. 4).[68]

At the Graneikos, Philotas' cavalry were drawn up on the right, alongside the archers and the Agrianes (Arr. 1. 14. 1; though we need not follow Berve ii 393 in assuming that these other units were under Philotas' command, especially when Alexander himself took up a position on the right). Of his participation in the critical cavalry engagement nothing is recorded, though he must certainly have been in the forefront of the battle. But the King's confidence in his abilities is clearly shown by the fact that Philotas was sent with the cavalry and three brigades of infantry to Mykale to prevent the Persian fleet, which was being barred from the harbour of Miletos by the Makedonian admiral Nikanor, from disembarking and obtaining water and supplies (Arr. 1. 19. 7-8). Under Alexander's direct command, Philotas took part in the abortive attempt on Myndos (Arr. 1. 20. 5-7). Where he spent the winter of 334/3 — with Alexander in Pamphylia and Lykia, or with his father (so Berve ii 393), who took the army from Sardeis to Gordion — depends on our interpretation of Arrian (1. 24. 3), who gives Parmenion a 'hipparchy' of Companions. At best, Arrian can be referring to only a few *ilai*, though possibly the term 'hipparchy' is wrongly and anachronistically used as a substitute for *ile* (cf. Bosworth *Arrian* i 155).[69] In either case, it would seem that Philotas and the bulk of the Companions remained with Alexander in southwestern Asia Minor.

On the journey from Gordion to Tarsos, the Companion Cavalry accompanied Alexander. In fact, they were probably instrumental in capturing Tarsos before it could be put to the torch by the satrap Arsames; Curtius' claim that this was the work of Parmenion may well be a corruption of an original account which gave credit to [Philotas son of] Parmenion. During the King's lengthy illness, which followed his 'bath' in the Kydnos river, Philotas remained in the camp and, upon

---

[67] Alexander led a force of hypaspists, Agrianes, archers and 400 cavalry (Arr. 1. 5. 10).

[68] Curt. 6. 9. 21 does not fix the time of Philotas' appointment.

[69] Cf. also Brunt, *JHS* 83 (1963), 29; id., *Arrian* i p. lxxv §60; Griffith, *JHS* 83 (1963), 70.

Alexander's recovery, accompanied him to Soloi and via Anchiale to the Aleian plain. Here Alexander turned south to the coastal town of Magarsos, sending Philotas across the plain to Mallos, where the army was later reunited.[70] Of his specific role in the battle of Issos, nothing is recorded.

Dionysios of Halikarnassos (*de comp. verb.* 18 p. 123-126R = Hegesias, *FGrHist* 142 F5) quotes Hegesias' description of the capture of Gaza, in which Philotas and Leonnatos brought the eunuch (Arr. 2. 25. 4; *Itiner. Al.* 45) Batis, whom Dareios had entrusted with the defence of the city, to Alexander as a captive. Hegesias' account is similar, in its main outline, to that given by Curtius (4. 6. 7-29); both may derive from a common source, most likely Kleitarchos.[71] Despite the dramatic touches, which emphasise Alexander's emulation of Achilles,[72] it appears that Batis was in fact executed, and the details about Philotas' involvement in his arrest need not have been fabricated.

The winter of 332/1 in Egypt, and Alexander's adoption by Ammon-Re, marked a turning-point in the relationship between Philotas and Alexander. The 'friendship', of which some writers (ancient and modern) speak, may never have been warm. In 336, Philip had brought Philotas with him 'as a witness' (so Hamilton, *PA* 26) when he reproached his son for his dealings with Pixodaros (Plut. *Alex.* 10. 3). Whether this means that Philotas had informed against the Crown Prince or, what seems more likely, Philip was using Philotas as a paradigm of good behaviour, the incident must have strained the relationship between Parmenion's son and Alexander. In fact, Philotas was not one of Alexander's boyhood friends, but rather a friend and *syntrophos* of Amyntas Perdikka (a rival of the Crown Prince) and the brother-in-law of his bitter enemy Attalos (Curt. 6. 9. 17). When Philotas spoke out against Alexander in Egypt, rebuking him for his divine pretensions and claiming for himself and his father the credit for the Makedonian victories, it was clearly not for the first time. But, on this occasion, it was unfortunate for Philotas that his talk reached the King's ears.

---

[70]For these activities see Arr. 2. 5. 5-9.

[71]Thus Hammond, *THA* 127 f.; Pearson, *LHA* 248, is more cautious: 'Perhaps he (sc. Curtius) knew the work of Hegesias and altered it to suit his own tastes, unless we are to believe that some earlier writer than Hegesias first put the story in circulation.' For the Batis episode see also Tarn ii 265-270: Appendix 11; Berve ii 104-105, no. 209; Atkinson, *Curtius* i 341-344; Bosworth, *Arrian* i 257 ff.

[72]Compare Curt. 4. 6. 29 with Verg., *Aen.* 2. 273; so Pearson, *LHA* 248, n.28; Atkinson, *Curtius* i 342.

Amongst the captives taken by Parmenion at Damaskos at the end of 333 was a Makedonian girl named Antigona (Berve ii 42, no. 86). A Pydnaian or Pellaian by birth,[73] she had been captured, after sailing to Samothrake to celebrate the mysteries, by the Persian admiral Autophradates (Plut. *Mor.* 339d-f).[74] She soon became Philotas' mistress and the sounding-board for his complaints about the King. Alexander's victories in Asia, these had been the work of Parmenion; nor did Philotas make light of his own achievements. And now the King was encouraging reports that he had been sired by the god Ammon. Philotas' comments were related by Antigona, innocently we may assume, to her friends, and eventually the gossip reached Krateros' ears. Others may have dismissed the comments as the grumblings of a chronic malcontent, but Krateros saw political advantage in blackening Philotas' name. He therefore suborned Antigona to report directly to him whatever Philotas said, and he took this, as evidence of treason, to the King himself. These disloyal rumblings constituted Philotas' so-called 'Egyptian conspiracy' (Arr. 3. 26. 1; cf. Plut. *Alex.* 48. 4 - 49. 2), and Alexander rightly took no action against him.

The nature of Philotas' participation in the battle of Gaugamela, where he commanded the Companions (Arr. 3. 11. 8; Curt. 4. 13. 26; Diod. 17. 57. 1), is not recorded. Presumably, he fought in the immediate vicinity of the King and followed him in his pursuit of the fleeing Persians, which, rumour held, was cut short by Parmenion's request for help. At Sousa, he is said to have witnessed Alexander sitting on the throne of the Great King and to have treated with disdain the laments of those Persians who saw Alexander resting his feet on the table from which Dareios used to eat (Curt. 5. 2. 13-15; Diod. 17. 66. 3-7). Anecdotal and perhaps even fictitious, the story nevertheless reflects Philotas' attitude to the conquered peoples. Similarly, Parmenion's advice at Persepolis that Alexander should not destroy what was now his (Arr. 3. 18. 11) was pragmatic rather than sensitive to the political situation.

At the Persian Gates, Philotas was sent with the infantry brigades of Koinos, Amyntas and Polyperchon (Curtius 5. 4. 20, 30; Arr. 3. 18. 6) to circumvent the forces of Ariobarzanes and perhaps begin the bridging of

---

[73]From Pydna (Plut. *Alex.* 48. 4). Hamilton, *PA* 133, rightly rejects Burn's suggestion that she was sold into slavery after Philip's capture of Pydna in 356. From Pella (Plut. *de fort. Al.* 2. 7 = *Mor.* 339e). The use of the word γύναιον in both passages implies that she was of low birth.

[74]Hamilton's suggestion (*PA* 133) that she was captured earlier in 333 leaves little time for her to have found her way to Damaskos. Hamilton rejects Berve's (ii 42) observation that she was captured at sea, on the basis of Plut. *Mor.* 339e (ἡλώκει δ' ὑπ' Αὐτοφραδάτου πρότερον εἰς Σαμοθρᾴκην διαπλεύσασα).

the Araxes river;[75] Polyainos (4. 3. 27) wrongly assigns command of the main camp to Philotas and Hephaistion (cf. Heckel, *Athenaeum* 58 [1980], 169-171). Nothing else is recorded about Philotas until the death of his brother Nikanor in the autumn of 330. He remained behind in Areia for several days to see to his brother's funeral.

Philotas rejoined the army in Phrada (modern Farah?[76]), the capital of Drangiana (Diod. 17. 78. 4), soon to be renamed Prophthasia ('Anticipation'; cf. Steph. Byz. s.v. Φράδα) for the events which would unfold. There Dimnos, an obscure Makedonian from Chalaistra, organised a conspiracy against Alexander, about which virtually nothing is known: motive and mode of execution are completely absent, the conspirators, with the exception of Demetrios the Somatophylax, notable for their obscurity. Curtius alone names them (6. 7. 15): Peukolaos, Aphobetos, Theoxenos, Archepolis, Nikanor, Iolaos, Amyntas, Demetrios.[77] The instigator, his lover (Nikomachos) and his lover's brother (Kebalinos) are equally undistinguished.

Though the details of the story are easily told, there is little of value that can be said with certainty and much room for speculation. About the perpetrators, the motives and the proposed execution of the plot, the sources tell us virtually nothing. Dimnos planned the deed,[78] but he was betrayed by his lover Nikomachos, who revealed the conspiracy to his own brother Kebalinos. Kebalinos, for his part, informed Philotas, believing that he would bring the matter to the King's attention. But Philotas failed to act on the information and, even on the next day, Alexander remained ignorant of the plot, although it was to be carried out on the day that followed (cf. Curt. 6. 7. 6). Kebalinos now approached Metron, one of the Royal Pages, and

---

[75]Thus Arr. 3. 18. 6; but Curt. 5. 4. 30 has Philotas and the taxiarchs participating in the attack on Ariobarzanes, with the bridging of the Araxes taking place later under Alexander's direction (5. 5. 3-4).

[76]See R. Lane Fox, *The Search for Alexander* (Boston-Toronto, 1980), 274 f., with photograph.

[77]Alphabetically, Berve nos. 64, 161, 190, 260, 387, 558, 637; these are Arrian's (3. 26. 3) ὅσοι ἄλλοι μετέσχον αὐτῷ τῆς ἐπιβουλῆς. Amyntas may be the son of Andromenes; but this is not proof of his guilt. See Heckel, *GRBS* 16 (1975), 393-398.

[78]Thus Plut. *Alex.* 49. 3. Curt. 6. 7. 6 does not say that Dimnos himself planned it: cf. 6. 11. 37, where a certain 'Calis' (unnamed by Curt. 6. 7. 15) confesses that he and Demetrios planned the crime. Given Demetrios' importance, it is surprising that so little is said about his involvement or his punishment.

through him the news of the conspiracy reached the King.[79] Philotas would excuse himself by claiming that he had not taken the matter seriously. But, in such a context, negligence implied complicity, and his inaction, at least in the eyes of Alexander's younger companions, was treasonable.

Philotas' arrest was preceded by the apprehending of the chief conspirator. But Dimnos could not be taken alive and the old maxim that 'dead men tell no tales' lends credence to the view that Alexander did not want him to testify. Many scholars have found the view of E. Badian, amplified by P. Goukowsky, that Dimnos' conspiracy was a fabrication designed to 'frame' Philotas, difficult to resist.[80] Alexander is portrayed as bent on the destruction of the house of Parmenion, using Philotas, who was 'plus vulnérable que son père' (Goukowsky i 39), as a pretext for eliminating the old man. While Philotas attended to the funeral rites of his brother, the plot was hatched: Dimnos' imaginary conspiracy would be divulged to Philotas, who, 'comme prévu' (Goukowsky *ibid*.), would then incriminate himself by not bringing the matter to the King's attention. Such a conspiracy *against* Philotas, like the elaborate crimes of Agatha Christie's characters, looks impressive — in retrospect. Because Philotas did not

---

[79]For the minor characters of the drama see Berve ii 142 f., no. 269, s.v. Δίμνος; cf. Hoffmann 206, who rejects Curtius' form, *Dymnus* (6. 7. 2 ff.), on linguistic grounds; Berve ii 143 believes Plutarch's (*Alex.* 49) Λίμνος is a scribal error, Λ written for Δ, but Ziegler's Teubner text retains Limnos; that form is also preferred by Schachermeyr 328 ff.; cf. Kirchner, *RE* v.1 (1903), 648; Hamilton, *PA* 135. See also Berve ii 279-280, no. 569, s.v. Νικόμαχος; Kroll, *RE* xvii.1 (1936), 459, no. 6; Berve ii 203, no. 418, s.v. Κεβαλῖνος; Hoffmann 209; in Plut. *Alex.* 49. 4 the MSS. read Βαλίνῳ or Βαλείνῳ; Kroll, *RE* x (1919), 101; Berve ii 260-261, no. 520; cf. *RE* xv.2 (1932), 1485, s.v. 'Metron (2)'.

[80]Badian, *TAPA* 91 (1960), 324-338; Goukowsky i 38-41, ii 118-134. Although I agree with Badian that Alexander's 'new men' played an important role in the elimination of Philotas, I cannot agree that (i) Alexander had taken an active role in 'extricating himself from the stranglehold of Parmenio's family and adherents' (329); that (ii) Alexander had been steadily undermining Parmenion's reputation; that (iii) Dimnos' conspiracy was fabricated with the destruction of Philotas and, ultimately, of Parmenion in mind. On the first point, it must be noted that Hektor and Nikanor died of natural causes (drowning and illness) and that there is no evidence of foul play; the appointment of Asandros as satrap of Lydia means nothing if, as is likely, Asandros was *not* Parmenion's brother. Point (ii) must be rejected in its entirety: the negative portrait of Parmenion in the Alexander sources can have had no impact on the Makedonian soldiery in Parmenion's own lifetime. As for (iii), Alexander had already removed Parmenion from the army and could now act without his interference. His murder was made necessary only by the execution of Philotas.

reveal Dimnos' plot to Alexander, it is assumed that he would not have done so under any circumstances. J. R. Hamilton rightly asks: 'how could Alexander *know* that Philotas would fail to pass on the information?'[81] Indeed, it would have been embarrassing to the King, had Philotas revealed the conspiracy, if he were then forced to admit to fabricating it in order to test him.

That Philotas was innocent of participating in Dimnos' plot is undeniable. Kebalinos would scarcely have approached Philotas had he known of his involvement, and Philotas could be expected to have taken measures to prevent the conspiracy from coming to light. In fact, nothing could be asserted with confidence, by the prosecution or the King's historians, except that Philotas had been negligent. But this negligence may well indicate Philotas' hopes that the plot should succeed. With Alexander dead, the army would almost certainly turn back, and Parmenion in Ekbatana would be the logical man to assume control of affairs until a new king could be selected. Parmenion's position should not be underestimated: the old general controlled Alexander's lifeline to Makedonia.

The death of Nikanor and Parmenion's consignment to Ekbatana had, however, left Philotas isolated. As a young man he was raised at Philip's court, a *syntrophos* of Amyntas Perdikka. The close friends of the latter, the son of Philip's brother and predecessor, were doubtless sympathetic to his claims to the kingship.[82] Alexander's accession must therefore have been a disappointment, the execution of Amyntas a cause for anxiety. Amyntas son of Antiochos had made no secret of his opposition to Alexander and fled (Arr. 1. 17. 9; cf. Curt. 4. 1. 27). Others weathered the political storm and retained offices only recently acquired. For the new king, conciliation was essential, even if it meant keeping potentially dangerous individuals in positions of power: Hegelochos, Alexandros Lynkestes, and his nephew Amyntas. The elimination of Attalos, Heromenes and Arrhabaios, and Amyntas Perdikka gave Alexander some degree of security, but this could not have been accomplished without the support of Philip's two most powerful generals: Antipatros and Parmenion. Philotas undoubtedly owed much to his father's influence.[83] But he was arrogant and

---

[81]Hamilton, *PA* 134 f. But Goukowsky i 39, nevertheless, remarks: 'Comme prévu, Philotas négligea de révéler au roi la prétendue conspiration qu'un comparse lui avait dénoncée'.

[82]On the vexed question of Amyntas' claim to the throne see J. R. Ellis, *JHS* 91 (1971), 15 ff.; id., *Philip II* 47; Griffith, *HMac* ii 208 f.; cf. Hatzopoulos, *Ancient Macedonia* iv 288 f.

[83]So Fox 287. One wonders if the death of Attalos and the promotion of Philotas were in any way related.

outspoken,[84] and his prestigious command was coveted by the younger commanders, who through their connections with Alexander hoped for greater power.[85] Their envy was fuelled by Philotas' unyielding nature (Themistios, *Or.* 19. 229c-d, remarks on his αὐθάδεια): he had foolishly disregarded Parmenion's advice to 'make less of himself',[86] and his arrogance and general unpopularity made his ultimate deposition only a matter of time. Philotas' enemies were not about to let the opportunity pass. Deep-rooted animosities manifested themselves in the form of vigorous prosecution and, in the face of adversity, Parmenion, through whose influence Philotas had escaped an earlier charge of treason, was not there to help him.

For Alexander's inner circle of friends, Philotas' error in judgment afforded the perfect opportunity for securing his elimination (Curt. 6. 8. 4). Krateros renewed his prosecution of an old enemy. He became the spokesman of this hostile faction, and his words will represent the thinking of his associates. Alexander ought to have consulted them on this matter, he argued. Philotas would continue to plot against him, and Alexander could not keep on excusing him forever. Nor would Philotas be mellowed by his kindness. Alexander must guard himself against the enemy within (Curt. 6. 8. 4). All Philotas' enemies were convinced that he was involved in Dimnos' conspiracy — or, at least, so they said — and now they advocated the use of torture (Curt. 6. 8. 15). When Alexander allowed himself to be persuaded that Philotas must be removed he was not acting entirely against his will. Schachermeyr (334 f.) is quite right to point out that the drastic steps that were taken after Philotas' arrest need not have been taken. But, had Alexander not been strongly influenced by his group of companions, he might well have been content to take less stringent measures and allow the house of Parmenion to lapse into the state of obscurity for which it was destined.[87] It was not the decision about Philotas that had made the King hesitate, rather the question of Parmenion. For the son's execution

---

[84]Plut. *Alex.* 48. 1-3.

[85]The rivalry between the friends of Amyntas Perdikka and those of Alexander calls to mind the remarks of the younger Kyros who (in Xenophon, *Anab.* 1. 7. 6-7) remarks that his brother's friends administer the satrapies of the empire, but, if he (Kyros) should be victorious, he would make his own friends masters over these. See further Heckel, *Ancient Macedonia* iv 293 ff., esp. 302-304.

[86]Plut. *Alex.* 48. 3: ὑποψίαν ⟨εἶχε⟩ καὶ φθόνον, ὥστε καὶ Παρμενίωνά ποτ' εἰπεῖν πρὸς αὐτόν, ὦ παῖ, χείρων μοι γίνου.

[87]One cannot over-emphasise the state of decline of the house of Parmenion already *before* the Philotas affair.

required the murder of the father, and Alexander had to consider the consequences of the second action.[88]

Philotas, at any rate, understood the politics of the moment, pronouncing that the bitterness of his enemies had overcome Alexander's goodwill (*vicit... bonitatem tuam, rex, inimicorum meorum acerbitas:* Curt. 6. 8. 22). And Curtius makes it clear who these *inimici* were: *secunda deinde vigilia, luminibus extinctis, cum paucis in regiam coeunt Hephaestio et Craterus et Coenus et Erigyius, hi ex amicis, ex armigeris autem Perdiccas et Leonnatus* (6. 8. 17). These gained most from Philotas' execution, especially Krateros and Hephaistion, the former being most vigorous in arousing Alexander's hostility toward Philotas, the latter the most vehement of his tormentors.[89] They had all hated Philotas for a long time (Plut. *Alex.* 49. 8 calls them τοὺς πάλαι μισοῦντας αὐτόν). But, since Hephaistion and Krateros had the most influence with Alexander, and emerged as the chief beneficiaries of the affair, we may justly assign to them the leading roles. What parts Perdikkas, Leonnatos and Erigyios played in destroying Philotas, we cannot say; nor are the benefits to them as immediately obvious.

Krateros' opposition to Philotas can be easily understood; he was loyal and ambitious, and in both respects he proved a natural enemy of Philotas. From the time of the *epiboule* in Egypt, he appears to have actively opposed Philotas. Hephaistion, on the other hand, made use of a more subtle power, his personal influence with Alexander. Two other individuals exemplify the opportunism of Makedonian politics, Koinos and Amyntas. Both stood to lose more than they could gain and turned a potentially disastrous situation to their advantage. In Koinos' case, we cannot be sure if he was reacting to an emergency, or if he had

---

[88]Goukowsky ii 133 comments: 'si l'on adopte les vues de Heckel, il faut aussi accorder à Alexandre une surprenante dose d'inconscience'. But Alexander had in the past been reluctant to take measures that would alienate the 'Old Guard': he had assigned the command of the Thessalian cavalry to Alexandros Lynkestes, a brother of the regicides Heromenes and Arrhabaios, and had delayed his trial and execution for over three years; the appointments of personal friends as Somatophylakes (Leonnatos and Perdikkas) were separated by the appointment of Menes; and the promotion of Hephaistion would be tempered by naming Kleitos as his colleague. The thought of punishing Philotas had, indeed, occurred to the King, but the evidence suggests that, had he not been encouraged by Philotas' enemies, he might not have taken such extreme measures. Dimnos too, on the theory expounded by Badian and Goukowsky, emerges as a man of remarkable devotion to his king (to say nothing about the good-natured 'false conspirators' who allowed themselves to be executed for the sake of realism), willing to give his life in order to 'frame' Philotas!

[89]Cf. Carney, 'Macedonian Aristocracy', 124, 127.

merely shifted his loyalties. Koinos was Philotas' brother-in-law, but he did not support him. It appears that he too plotted against Philotas. When Philotas came to trial before the Makedonian army, Koinos was his most outspoken prosecutor (*Coenus, quamquam Philotae sororem matrimonio secum coniunxerat, tamen acrius quam quisquam in Philotan invectus est:* Curt. 6. 9. 30). Koinos would gain from Philotas' ruin, but he also knew that his family connections with him could prove disastrous. Similarly, Amyntas son of Andromenes, averted danger by repudiating his friendship with Philotas.[90]

When Alexander personally called for the death-penalty before the Makedonian army, the enemies of Philotas won the day.[91] Their efforts secured for them commands of major importance, positions that were to bring them into conflict with one another shortly afterwards; for the success of their conspiracy against Philotas only helped to encourage further rivalry. For the King, the primary concern had all along been Parmenion, who was quickly despatched. Alexandros Lynkestes too was executed, though his crimes had no bearing on the Philotas case. Demetrios the Somatophylax was removed from office soon afterwards, in the land of the Ariaspians, and replaced by Ptolemy, son of Lagos:[92] though he was probably guilty of little more than having been Philotas' friend, it was later alleged that he had conspired with Dimnos. The 'Old Guard' were no longer strongly represented in the higher ranks, where Alexander's friends, or at least men of his temperament, were now found in greater numbers. The conservative element had not been totally eradicated,[93] but opposition

---

[90]Curt. 7. 1. 18 ff.; see F. Helmreich, *Die Reden bei Curtius*, Rhetorische Studien 14 (Paderborn, 1927), 168-183; Granier 42-46; Heckel, *GRBS* 16 (1975), 393-398: the *regius praetor* of Curtius (Berve no. 65) is the son of Andromenes.

[91]Philotas' death: Arr. 3. 26. 3 (killed by the javelins of the Makedonians); Diod. 17. 80. 2 (in the customary Makedonian way, which according to Curt. 6. 11. 10 was stoning; cf. 6. 11. 38); Curtius does not actually describe Philotas' execution (but cf. 7. 1. 1); cf. also Plut. *Alex.* 49. 13 and Justin 12. 5. 3. Later references to his death: Arr. 4. 14. 2; Curt. 8. 1. 33, 38, 52; 8. 7. 4-5; 8. 8. 5; Justin 12. 6. 14.

[92]Arr. 3. 27. 5. The case against Demetrios the Somatophylax is suspicious: Arrian reports his removal from office in a different context (in the land of the Ariaspians or 'Euergetai'). In Curtius' version, although he is by far the most important of those named by Dimnos (6. 7. 15), no mention is made of Demetrios' arrest, nor is he given an opportunity to defend himself. It may be that Demetrios was, like Parmenion and Alexandros Lynkestes, a victim of the purge that followed the Philotas affair. Linked in a more general way with Philotas, he was later wrongly named as a party to Dimnos' conspiracy.

[93]Parmenion's murder gave Antipatros greater reason to fear Alexander (Diod 17. 118. 1). Cf. also Plut. *Apophth. Antip.* 1 = Mor. 183f: Ἀντίπατρος

could be suppressed by the formation of a disciplinary unit after the Philotas affair,[94] by means of the psychological effects of the Kleitos affair. Yet mutinies at the Hyphasis and at Opis reminded Alexander that friction between the old and the new was very real.[95]

ἀκούσας τὴν Παρμενίωνος ὑπὸ Ἀλεξάνδρου τελευτήν, εἰ μὲν ἐπεβούλευσεν Ἀλεξάνδρῳ Παρμενίων, εἶπε, τίνι πιστευτέον; εἰ δὲ μή, τί πρακτέον;

[94] The *ataktoi* (Diod. 17. 80. 4; Justin 12. 5. 4-8; Curtius 7. 2. 35 says that Leonidas was their leader, cf. Berve ii 236, no. 470). They did not, however, as Goukowsky i 40 suggests, form a seventh brigade of pezhetairoi.

[95] See Carney, 'Macedonian Aristocracy', *passim*.

3. Black Kleitos

Literature. Berve ii 206-208, no. 427; Cauer 38-58; R. Schubert, 'Der Tod des Kleitos', *RhM* 53 (1898), 99 ff.; Hoffmann 183; Kroll, *RE* xi (1922), 666, no. 9; E. D. Carney, 'The Death of Clitus', *GRBS* 22 (1981), 149-160.

Kleitos son of Dropides (Arr. 1. 15. 8; 3. 11. 8; 3. 27. 4; 4. 8. 1; cf. 4. 9. 3), was surnamed Melas ('the Black') in order to distinguish him from his namesake, the taxiarch and later hipparch, White Kleitos (Berve, no. 428).[96] Although we are reasonably well informed about his family, nothing is recorded about his place of birth or residence. Lanike, his sister, was Alexander's nurse (Arr. 4. 9. 3; Curt. 8. 1. 21 [Hellanice]; cf. 8. 2. 8-9, and Justin 12. 6. 10): born c. 375, she was apparently still alive in 328 and had at least three sons who served Alexander during the Asiatic expedition. Two *anonymi* perished at Miletos in 334 B.C.,[97] while a third son, Proteas — *syntrophos* and drinking companion of Alexander (Aelian, *VH* 12. 26; cf. Athen. 4. 129a and 10. 434a) — was very likely the admiral who defeated Datames at Siphnos, hence the son of Andronikos (Berve ii 328 f., no. 664 = no. 665; thus Carney, *GRBS* 22 [1981], 152 f., an identification which Berve ii 328 considers 'nicht ausgeschlossen'). If the identification is correct, Andronikos — almost certainly the son of Agerros[98] — would have been Lanike's husband and Kleitos' brother-in-law. Theodoros (Berve ii 176, no. 362), identified merely as a 'brother of Proteas' but on intimate terms with Alexander (Plut. *Mor.* 760c), may also have been Lanike's son (cf. Carney 152, with n.10). He appears to have remained in Makedonia,[99] or to have been left behind (in an administrative capacity?), perhaps in Asia Minor; for Alexander wrote to him concerning the purchase of an hetaira. The implications of these relationships are illustrated in the following stemma:

---

[96]Black Kleitos: Diod. 17. 20. 7; 17. 57. 1; Plut. *Alex.* 16. 11; White Kleitos (his father's name is unknown): Athen. 12. 539c; see also **iii 4**.

[97]Curt. 8. 2. 8; cf. Arr. 4. 9. 4; see also Heckel, *L'Antiquité Classique* 56 (1987), 136, nos. 40-41.

[98]So Carney, *GRBS* 22 (1981), 153. Berve ii 39, n.3, leaves open the possibility that Proteas son of Andronikos (no. 664) may be the grandson of Agerros; but Proteas son of Lanike may nevertheless be a different individual (no. 665), and thus Andronikos need not be Lanike's husband. I am, however, inclined to accept Carney's stemma.

[99]Perhaps Philip II's hieromnemon in 339 B.C. (Dittenberger, *Syll.*³ 249B, 32, as suggested by Berve ii 176); but only one letter of the name is visible: [Θε]ο[δώρου].

THE 'OLD GUARD'

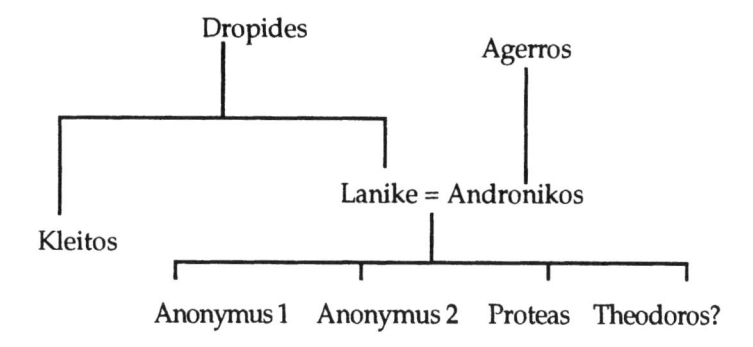

```
         Dropides                Agerros
            |                       |
   ┌────────┴────────┐               |
   |                 |               |
 Kleitos        Lanike  =  Andronikos
                         |
         ┌───────────┬───┴────┬──────────┐
    Anonymus 1   Anonymus 2  Proteas  Theodoros?
```

Of Kleitos' actual career very little is known. His heroic defence of Alexander in the battle of the Graneikos is undoubtedly true and derives from Kallisthenes; but it retained its importance in all subsequent Alexander historians because of the circumstances of Kleitos' death — at the hands of the one he saved. Yet, even this episode is not without its problems. Arrian and Plutarch relate that Kleitos severed Spithridates' arm just as he was about to strike the King; Diodoros, however, records that the man was Rhoisakes, Spithridates' brother.[100] In the final analysis, it makes little difference, since both perished in the battle, the victims of Alexander and Kleitos; but the confusion is inexplicable (cf. Bosworth, *Arrian* i 123; Hamilton, *PA* 40).

Kleitos commanded the Royal Squadron (ἴλη βασιλική) since at least the beginning of the expedition; in what capacity he had served Philip II (Curt. 8. 1. 20), we do not know. At Gaugamela he continued to command the *ile basilike*, as he must have done at Issos, though he is not named in any account of the battle (Arr. 3. 11. 8; Diod. 17. 57. 1; Curt. 4. 13. 26, the cavalry *agema*). An unspecified illness detained Kleitos in Sousa at the end of 331. In the following spring, he proceeded to Ekbatana, whence he set out to rejoin the King in Parthyaia, bringing with him those Makedonians who had guarded the treasures conveyed from Persepolis to Ekbatana (Arr. 3. 19. 8).

In that same year, Philotas was condemned and executed for his alleged role in the conspiracy of Dimnos. His position as hipparch of the Companion Cavalry was now shared by Hephaistion and Kleitos. Arrian (3. 27. 4) says that Alexander no longer thought it wise to entrust so important a command to a single individual, no matter how dear he

---

[100] Arr. 1. 15. 8; Plut. *Alex*. 16. 11; Diod. 17. 20. 7; cf. Curt. 8. 1. 20. The episode may have been the inspiration for the Apelles' portrait of Kleitos on horseback (Pliny, *NH* 35. 93; Pollitt, p. 162; cf. Berve ii 206), but White Kleitos had also been a hipparch and the identity of Apelles' *Kleitos* is not certain.

might be. But the King was clearly concerned to offset the appointment of his personal friend Hephaistion — a blatant case of nepotism — with one that might appease the 'Old Guard'.[101] The brother of his nurse and a man who had once saved his life, Kleitos seemed both trustworthy and acceptable to the more conservative element.[102] Furthermore, given Hephaistion's lack of experience, it would have been difficult to promote him over the head of the ilarch of the Royal Squadron. Curiously, Kleitos plays no attested role in the campaigns of 330-328, and Carney (*GRBS* 22 [1981], 151) suggests that Alexander 'granted Clitus the honor of his position, ... then ... prevented him from acquiring much glory through it'. This is unduly suspicious. Both Arrian (Arr. 4. 8. 1-9. 9) and Plutarch (*Alex.* 50. 1-52. 4) record Kleitos' death out of chronological context, which may explain their failure to mention him again. Diodoros' account of this period is lost, Justin's highly compressed and abbreviated. Hence only Curtius' silence could be regarded as significant, and even from his account Kleitos' absence may be coincidental.

Curtius (8. 1. 19) does, however, tell us that, shortly before the fateful drinking-party in Marakanda (autumn 328), Kleitos had been designated satrap of Baktria and Sogdiana, assuming the office which Artabazos had resigned on account of age. Schachermeyr suggests that the appointment may be linked with the restructuring of the cavalry commands. Krateros, Koinos, Perdikkas and others had all joined Hephaistion as hipparchs, and they now may have contributed to Kleitos' demise. For Kleitos the appointment as satrap was *honor exilii*.[103] The example of Parmenion must have been fresh in his mind and, though he had far less to fear from the King, the prospect of lengthy service in Turkestan, remote and uncivilised, cannot have been appealing. It could be argued that the region had not been subdued, that Alexander perhaps hoped to leave the area in the hands of a competent cavalry commander while he himself moved eastward. But Alexander had made a habit of depositing Philip's officers in the provinces: Kalas, Asandros, Antigonos, Balakros, Parmenion — now Kleitos.

Hence it is significant that the quarrel which precipitated the murder involved the clash of generations and ideologies: Philip

---

[101]Carney, *GRBS* 22 (1981), 150, with n.5, accepts tentatively Badian's suggestion (*TAPA* 91 [1960], 336) that Kleitos' promotion was intended to buy his support for Alexander's policies.

[102]Cf. Schachermeyr 363.

[103]Schachermeyr 364 rightly observes: 'in Wahrheit aber bedeutete es Entfernung aus dem königlichen Kreis, aus der kämpfenden Truppe, ... Isolierung und Kaltstellung'.

against Alexander;[104] the Makedonian kingdom versus the new empire;[105] the methods of each ruler, and the needs of each state. Alexander had slowly but steadily replaced Philip's officers with men of his own generation, men who very often shared his vision of the empire or, even if they did not, were content to say that they did. But the promotion of these men required the demotion, the reassignment, or even the liquidation of the 'Old Guard'. Whether Kleitos' anger was in fact prompted by the verses of Pierion (or Pranichos), mocking a Makedonian defeat,[106] or by fawning courtiers who compared Alexander favourably with Herakles and the Dioskouroi,[107] makes little difference. Nor are stories of Bacchus' wrath (Arr. 4. 8. 1-2; 4. 9. 5)[108] or Kleitos' unyielding belligerence (Arr. 4. 8. 6-9; Curt. 8. 1. 39 ff.; Plut. *Alex.* 51. 8 ff.) intended to do more than exculpate the King. What matters is that Kleitos spoke out, aggressively, against Alexander's personal and political transformation, against the dismantling of the 'Old Guard'. The King, though restrained by his Somatophylakes (Curt. 8. 1. 45 ff.; Plut. *Alex.* 51. 6), seized a spear from a hypaspist on guard in the tent and struck Kleitos (Arr. 4. 8. 8-9; Curt. 8. 1. 49-52; Plut. *Alex.* 51. 9-11; Justin 12. 6. 3) — because he was angry, and drunk (Arr. 4. 9. 1). The words, 'Go now to Philip and Parmenion and Attalos' (Curt. 8. 1. 52), though fictitious, undoubtedly reflect the sentiment that accompanied the fatal blow. The days that followed may in fact have brought genuine remorse (Arr. 4. 9. 2 ff.; Curt. 8. 2. 1 ff.; Plut. *Alex.* 52. 1-2; Justin 12. 6. 7-11). But, in the end, Alexander and his new empire were well rid of Black Kleitos.

---

[104]Arr. 4. 8. 4 ff.; Curt. 8. 1. 23 ff.; Plut. *Alex.* 50. 11; Justin 12. 6. 2-3.

[105]Plut. *Alex.* 51. 2-3, 5.

[106]Plut. *Alex.* 50. 8 ff. For Pierion and Pranichos see Berve ii 320, no. 639 and ii 327, no. 657. The defeat is thought by some to be that suffered by the Makedonian force at the Polytimetos; others, however, suggest it involved Kleitos himself. See Carney, *GRBS* 22 (1981), 155, with n.17 for a survey of views. Holt, *Alexander and Bactria* 78 f., n.118, thinks the poet commemorated the valour of Aristonikos the *kitharoidos*, who was killed by Spitamenes' forces near Baktra.

[107]Arr. 4. 8. 2-3; but Curt. 8. 5. 8 postpones this until his description of the clash between Alexander and Kallisthenes.

[108]Or neglected sacrifices: Plut. *Alex.* 50. 7.

4. Antipatros: An 'Old Rope'

Literature. Berve ii 46-51, no. 94; Kaerst, *RE* i (1894), 2501-2508, no. 12; D. Kanatsulis, *Antipatros. Ein Beitrag zur Geschichte Makedoniens in der Zeit Philipps, Alexanders und der Diadochen* (Diss. Munich 1940; publ. Thessaloniki 1942), superseded by id., 'Antipatros als Feldherr und Staatsmann in der Zeit Philipps und Alexanders des Grossen', *Hellenika* 16 (1958/59), 14-64, and id., 'Antipatros als Feldherr und Staatsmann nach dem Tode Alexanders des Grossen', *Makedonika* 8 (1968), 121-184; W. L. Adams, 'Antipater and Cassander: Generalship on Restricted Resources in the Fourth Century', *AncW* 10 (1985), 79-88.

γράμματα γὰρ ἐξέπεσεν αὐτοῦ, δι' ὧν παρεκάλει Περδίκκαν ἐπιχειρεῖν Μακεδονίᾳ καὶ σώζειν τοὺς Ἕλληνας ὡς ἀπὸ σαπροῦ καὶ παλαιοῦ στήμονος (λέγων τὸν Ἀντίπατρον) ἠρτημένους.
(Plut. *Demosth.* 31. 5)

A letter of his [sc. Demades] ... leaked out, in which he had urged Perdiccas to seize Macedonia and deliver the Greeks, who, he said, were fastened to it only by an old and rotten thread (meaning Antipater).

(B. Perrin, tr.)

Apart from the royal houses, there are few families in Makedonian and Hellenistic history about which we are better informed than that of Iolaos. Nevertheless, what we know about the family's background is disappointing: the attested patriarch appears to have been that Iolaos who appeared at Potidaia with the Makedonian cavalry as the deputy of Perdikkas II in 432 (Thuc. 1. 62. 2). Gomme (*HCT* i 219) speculates that this man, who bears the name of Herakles' nephew, may have been a member of the Makedonian royal family, which claimed descent from Herakles. This is unlikely, if our man is an ancestor of Antipatros; for neither the latter nor his son Kassandros was able to make a claim to the Makedonian throne on the basis of kinship.

Born in 399/8 B.C.,[109] Antipatros son of Iolaos came from Palioura, a place that cannot be identified with certainty.[110] Beloch (iv^2 2. 125)

---

[109] *Suda* s.v. Ἀντίπατρος makes him 79 at the time of his death; cf. Ps.-Lucian, *Macrob.* 11, 'about 80'; he died in the archonship of Apollodoros, according to the Parian Marble, *FGrHist* 239 B12.

[110] Kanatsulis, *Antipatros* (Thessaloniki, 1942), 1, n.2, tentatively suggests Palaeorium, mentioned by Pliny, *NH* 4. 37, on the Athos peninsula; Paliouri at the tip of Pallene also comes to mind; cf. S. Casson, *Macedonia, Thrace and Illyria* (Oxford, 1926), 59.

regards him as coeval with Philip II, pointing to the relative youth of Kassandros, Antipatros' eldest attested son. But Antipatros would scarcely have been described in a letter of Demades as 'an old and rotten rope' (Arr. *Succ.* 1. 14; Plut. *Demosth.* 31. 5; *Phok.* 30. 9)[111] if he had not been well advanced in age in 323/2.

At least ten children are attested: four daughters and six sons, of whom the names of all but one *anonyma* (the wife of Alexandros Lynkestes; cf. Heckel, *Historia* 36 [1987], 118, A37) are known. Phila, Nikaia and Eurydike all played important roles in sealing political alliances in the years before and after Triparadeisos.[112] Philippos, Alexarchos, Iolaos, Pleistarchos and Nikanor are identified as either sons of Antipatros or brothers of Kassandros.[113] About Kassandros' age we cannot be certain, though he was clearly the oldest surviving son: Hegesandros (*ap.* Athen. 1. 18a) shows that Antipatros was still alive when Kassandros was thirty-five, establishing 354 as the *terminus ante quem* for the son's birth.

If the *Suda* is correct both about Antipatros' age and the composition of a historical work on the Illyrian campaigns of Perdikkas III (αἱ Περδίκκου πράξεις Ἰλλυρικαί), he was already militarily active — and possibly influential at the Court — during the reign of Philip II's predecessor. Antipatros will have been almost forty at the time of Philip's accession, and it is doubtful that he rose from obscurity at that age to become perhaps the most powerful of Philip's hetairoi (Plut. *Apophth. Phil.* 27 = *Mor.* 179b; Athen. 10. 435d). He and Parmenion were involved in the peace negotiations in the spring of 346 (Demosth. 19. 69; Aesch. 3. 72; Deinarchos 1. 28);[114] he had earlier campaigned in Thrake, in the war against Kersobleptes.[115] About Antipatros' diplomatic efforts in Athens little is known. It was at this time that he made the acquaintance of Isokrates; his friendship with

---

[111] A letter to Perdikkas; in the *Phokion*, Plutarch wrongly says that it was addressed to Antigonos; cf. also Williams, *AncW* 19 (1989), 27 ff.

[112] References and discussion in Seibert, *Verbindungen* 11-19.

[113] Whether these children were all born to the same wife is unknown, and unlikely. Nor is it probable that Kassandros was the eldest son of Antipatros. We should expect to find the first (or, at least, second) son named for his paternal grandfather. Iolaos, born c. 341 (Berve ii 184, no. 386, suggests c. 350 or possibly after 345; both dates too high), was the youngest of Antipatros' sons, and I suspect that an earlier son of that name had died by the late 340s.

[114] cf. Beloch iii² 1. 504; J. Buckler, *Philip II and the Sacred War* (Leiden, 1989), 132 f. Eurylochos (presumably the man named in Justin 12. 6. 14 as a victim of Alexander) appears as a third ambassador in the *Hypothesis* to Demosth. 19. See also Theopompos, *FGrHist* 115 F165.

[115] Theopompos, *ap.* Steph. Byz., s.v. Ἄπρος = *FGrHist* 115 F160; cf. Kanatsulis, *Hellenika* 16 (1958/59), 19-24.

Phokion (Plut. *Phok.* 26. 4-6; 30. 3) may, however, belong to the period after Chaironeia. Summer 342 saw Antipatros representing Philip II as *theoros* at the Pythian games (Demosth. *Philippic* 3. 32; cf. Libanios 23. 311) and as regent of Makedonia in the King's absence (Isokrates, *Ep.* 4). In 340, when his services were needed in Thrake (Theopompos, *FGrHist* 115 F217), Antipatros turned over the affairs of the state to Alexander, now sixteen (Plut. *Alex.* 9. 1; but see Schachermeyr 93, n.74, against Hamilton, *PA* 22), and campaigned at Perinthos (Diod. 16. 76. 3; cf. Frontinus 1. 4. 13)[116] and, later, against the Tetrachoritai (Theopompos F217). After Chaironeia (338), he was sent to Athens to negotiate a peace and awarded a proxeny and citizenship (Justin 9. 4. 5; Hyper. *Against Demades*, frg. 77 = 19. 2 [Burtt]; cf. *IG* ii² 239).

He played no small part in securing the throne for Alexander after Philip's assassination: it was undoubtedly at his urging that Alexandros Lynkestes was the first to hail his namesake as 'King'.[117] Thereafter, Antipatros appears to have acted as regent whenever the King was absent from Makedonia. Thus we find him sending an embassy — albeit ineffectual — to the Isthmos in an attempt to prevent the Arkadians from aiding Thebes in 335 (Deinarchos 1. 18). Rumour at Thebes held that Antipatros himself was coming to deal with their uprising (Arr. 1. 7. 6), a story encouraged by false reports that Alexander had been defeated in the north (Justin 11. 2. 8). But Polyainos' claim (4. 3. 12) that Antipatros played a significant role in the capture of Thebes is contradicted by the Alexander historians and inherently improbable.[118] When he set out for Asia in 334, Alexander left Antipatros firmly in charge of European affairs,[119] having ignored his advice to produce an heir to the throne before his departure (Diod. 17. 16. 2). For the defence of the fatherland and to maintain the Makedonian hegemony, 12,000 infantry and 1500 cavalry were considered sufficient (Diod. 17. 17. 5).

But his position was soon strained by the recruitment of fresh levies for Asia,[120] the defence of the European mainland against the planned

---

[116]Polyainos 4. 2. 8 is a doublet, assigning the same ruse to a different context.

[117]Arr. 1. 25. 2; Curt. 7. 1. 6-7; cf. Ps.-Kall. 1. 26, version L; Justin 11. 2. 2; Badian, *Phoenix* 17 (1963), 248.

[118]This does not negate Plut. *Alex.* 11. 8. Hamilton, *PA* 30, rightly notes that the demand for Antipatros' surrender was not meant seriously (Berve ii 46 himself, though he rejects its historicity, calls it 'höhnisch'), and it need not imply that Antipatros was present.

[119]Arr. 1. 11. 3; ; Curt. 4. 1. 39; Justin 11. 7. 1; Diod. 18. 12. 1; cf. 17. 118. 1: στρατηγὸς τῆς Εὐρώπης. See also Schol. Lucian, *nav.* 33; *Itiner. Al.* 17.

[120]In 333, Antipatros sent 3000 Makedonian infantrymen, 300 cavalry, as well as 200 Thessalian and 150 Eleian horse to Alexander at Gordion (Arr. 1. 29.

counter-invasion of Memnon the Rhodian, the prosecution of the war against Agis III of Sparta. In response to Memnon's threat, Antipatros commissioned a fleet, under the command of Proteas (apparently a son of Black Kleitos' sister, Lanike: see Berve ii 328 f., nos. 664-665), who defeated the Persian admiral, Datames, at Siphnos (Arr. 2. 2. 4-5). News of the victory, brought by Proteas himself to Alexander in Tyre (Arr. 2. 20. 2), formed part of the on-going communications between the homeland and Alexander.[121]

In 333 Agis gathered forces at Tainaron and on Krete, not only soldiers but a fleet as well (Arr. 2. 13. 4 ff.; Curt. 4. 1. 38 ff.; Diod. 17. 48. 2). Despite the loss of Persian support and Athens' decision to remain aloof (Diod. 17. 62. 7), in 331 Agis rallied the Peloponnesians and easily defeated Antipatros' general, Korrhagos (perhaps a relative of Antigonos' wife Stratonike).[122] The Spartan alliance now included Elis, Achaia (except for Pellene) and all the Arkadians except Megalopolis (Aesch. 3. 165; Deinarchos 1. 34; cf. Curt. 6. 1. 20; cf. also [Demosth.] 17. 7. 10; Paus. 7. 27. 7),[123] which Agis promptly besieged (Aesch. 3. 165) with a force of 20,000 infantry — to which we might add as many as 8,000 mercenaries who had escaped from Issos (Curt. 4. 1. 39; Diod. 17. 48. 1-2; but cf. Brunt, *Arrian* i 481 f.) — and 2000 cavalry (Diod. 17. 62. 7). Antipatros received news of the uprising just as he was dealing with the rebellion in Thrake.[124] Concluding hostilities as best he could under

---

4). In the winter of 332/1, he sent another 400 Greek mercenaries and 500 Thrakian horse to Alexander (Arr. 3. 5. 1), and Amyntas son of Andromenes recruited 6000 infantry and 500 cavalry from Makedonia as well as 50 young men from prominent families to act as Pages, along with 3500 and 600 Thrakian infantry and cavalry respectively, and over 4000 mercenaries (Diod. 17. 65. 1, reading 'Thrakians' for 'Trallians'; Curt. 5. 1. 40-42; cf. 7. 1. 38-40). Thus, by the time of Agis' war, Antipatros' resources had been significantly depleted. See Bosworth, *JHS* 106 (1986), 1-12, for the effects of Alexander's campaigns on the Makedonian state; cf. Adams, *AncW* 10 (1985), 79-82.

[121]Letters from Alexander to Antipatros: Plut. *Alex.* 20. 9; cf. *de fort. Al.* 2. 9 = *Mor.* 341c (about Issos); cf. Plut. *Alex.* 46. 3 (from the Iaxartes); 47. 3 (from Hyrkania); 55. 7 (concerning the Hermolaos conspiracy); 57. 8 (from the Oxos river; cf. Athen. 2. 42f); 71. 8 (from Sousa in 324, concerning the discharged veterans); Diod. 18. 8. 4 (concerning the Exiles' Decree).

[122]Cf. Plut. *Demetr.* 2. 1; see also Kaerst, *RE* i (1894), 2503, for the order of events.

[123]For the background to the uprising in the Peloponnese see McQueen, *Historia* 27 (1978), 40-64.

[124]Diod. 17. 62. 5 ff. Polyainos 4. 4. 1 may refer to this campaign, but appears to belong to 347/6; cf. Steph. Byz. s.v. Τετραχωρῖται. Brunt, *Arrian* i 480, rightly questions whether Memnon himself had rebelled (as Diod. 17. 62. 5 alleges), since he later brought reinforcements to Alexander (Curt. 9. 3. 21), who

the circumstances, he gathered a force of 40,000 (Diod. 17. 63. 1) — greatly augmented by his Greek allies — and invaded the Peloponnese. At Megalopolis he was victorious, and Agis was killed in the engagement,[125] along with 5300 of his men (Diod. 17. 63. 3; Curt. 6. 1. 16: Makedonian casualties are given by these sources as 3500 and 1000 respectively). Order was restored to Greece by referring the matter to the League of Korinth (Curt. 6. 1. 19-20); the Lakedaimonians, for their part, were forced to send ambassadors to Alexander to beg his forgiveness (Aesch. 3. 133; Diod. 17. 73. 5-6; Curt. 6. 1. 20).

There was, however, a rift developing between Alexander and Antipatros. One could point to the King's orientalism, to the fates of Parmenion and Kleitos, and more significantly the execution of Alexandros Lynkestes. Alexander had allegedly disparaged the victory at Megalopolis as a 'battle of mice' (Plut. *Ages.* 15. 6), and there were claims that Antipatros had regal aspirations (Curt. 10. 10. 14), that he had entered into secret negotiations with the Aitolians (Plut. *Alex.* 49. 14-15), and that he had quarrels with Alexander's mother, Olympias (Plut. *Alex.* 39. 13; *Apophth. Al.* 14 = *Mor.* 180d; Diod. 17. 118. 1). Hence Alexander's decision to replace him as regent of Makedon with Krateros (Arr. 7. 12. 4; Justin 12. 12. 9) aroused the suspicions of both ancient and modern writers (Curt. 10. 10. 15). And, not surprisingly, stories that Antipatros and his sons conspired with several of the King's hetairoi to murder him soon began to circulate.[126]

would scarcely have tolerated his disloyalty. Badian's attempt (*Hermes* 95 [1967], 179 f.) to identify him with the man honoured by the Athenians (Tod, *GHI* 199 = *IG* ii² 356) strikes me as implausible. Despite Artabazos' early connections with Philip, and Alexander's later liaison with Barsine, it is doubtful that Alexander would have left as *strategos* of Thrake a close relative of Memnon the Rhodian, who had since 336 led the resistance to Makedon.

[125] Plut. *Agis* 3; Diod. 17. 63. 4; Curt. 6. 1. 1-15; Justin 12. 1. 6-11. The battle took place at about the same time as the trial of Ktesiphon (Aesch. 3. 165; cf. 3. 133; Plut. *Demosth.* 24; Schaefer, *Demosth.* iii² 202, n.1; 211 ff.). Curt. 6. 1. 21 dates it before the campaign of Gaugamela, which is rendered unlikely by Arr. 3. 16. 10, which says that Alexander sent money to Antipatros from Sousa for the prosecution of the war against Agis; if the battle had been fought in September 331, Alexander ought to have heard of it by the time he reached Sousa in early December (cf. Brunt, *Arrian* i 492). For full discussions see esp. Brunt, *Arrian* i 480-485, Appendix VI; Lock, *Antichthon* 6 (1972), 10-27, confirming the view of Badian, *Hermes* 95 (1967), 170-192, esp. 190-192, against Cawkwell, *CQ* 19 (1969), 163-180, esp. 169-173. Most recently, Bosworth, *Conquest and Empire* 198-204, dates the Megalopolis campaign to early spring 330.

[126] See Heckel, *LDT*, with testimonia.

The death of Alexander brought a measure of stability to Antipatros' position in Makedonia: no one save the King himself could remove him from office, and the settlement at Babylon recognised that fact. The compromise proposal that Europe be shared by Krateros and Antipatros (Curt. 10. 7. 9; cf. Arr. *Succ.* 1a. 7, unless the words Κρατερῷ καί are merely an intrusion from a marginal note, so Kanatsulis, *Makedonika* 8 [1968], 124 f.) was soon abandoned and Antipatros recognised as στρατηγὸς αὐτοκράτωρ of Makedonia and Greece (Justin 13. 4. 5; Diod. 18. 3. 2; cf. 18. 12. 1; Arr. *Succ.* 1a. 3) — to which area were added the lands of the Thrakians, Illyrians, Triballians and Agrianes, as well as Epeiros (Arr. *Succ.* 1a. 7; 1b. 3).[127] Lysimachos, the στρατηγός of Thrake, was clearly subject to Antipatros' authority.

To the Athenians, however, news of the King's death was the signal for war (cf. Diod. 18. 8), or rather the resumption of hostilities planned already in 324 in reaction to the Exiles' Decree.[128] Leosthenes gathered mercenaries, ostensibly for some private undertaking, in order that Antipatros might not begin counter-preparations in earnest (Diod. 18. 9. 2-3). But the Athenians soon declared their support for Leosthenes openly and defrayed his expenses with Harpalos' plunder; and they allied themselves with the Aitolians (Diod. 18. 9. 4-5).[129] A fleet of 40 quadriremes and 200 triremes was commissioned (Diod. 18. 10. 2; cf. Justin 13. 5. 8) and eventually much of Greece joined the Hellenic war against Makedon (Diod. 18. 11. 1-2; Paus. 1. 25. 3-4).[130]

Antipatros responded with appeals to Krateros in Kilikia and Leonnatos in Hellespontine Phrygia (Diod. 18. 12. 1 reads 'Philotas'),

---

[127] Kanatsulis, *Makedonika* 8 (1968), 121, argues convincingly that Antipatros was ἄρχων of Thessaly in the absence of the Makedonian king.

[128] Argued persuasively by Ashton, *Antichthon* 17 (1983), 47-63.

[129] See Lepore, *PdP* 10 (1955), 161 ff.; for Leosthenes' career see Berve ii 236-237, no. 471; Geyer, *RE* xii (1925), 2060 ff., no. 2; Kirchner, *PA*, no. 9142 (= 9144); Davies, *APF* 342 ff.; Develin, *Athenian Officials* 408, with references.

[130] The allies of the Athenians are given by Diodoros as: the Messenians, the inhabitants of Akte, Argos, Sikyon, a few Illyrians and Thrakians, Achaia Phthiotis except Thebai, the Melians except for Lamia, the Lokrians and Phokians, Ainianes, Alyzaians, Dolopians, Athamanians, Leukadians, the Oitians except for Herakleia, the Molossians subject to Aryptaios, Thessalians except the Pelinnaioi, and Karystos. Pausanias lists Argos, Epidauros, Sikyon, Troizen, Eleia, Phliasia, Messenia, the Lokrians, Phokians and Thessalians, Karystos, Akarnania and the Aitolian League. For the neutrality of the Arkadians see Paus. 8. 6. 2; 8. 27. 10. Greek contemporaries referred to the war as the 'Hellenic War', which emphasised their bid for freedom from Makedonian oppression. For the epigraphic evidence, and the origins of the term 'Lamian War' (which endured in most literary texts), see Ashton, *JHS* 104 (1984), 152-157.

promising Leonnatos the hand of one of his daughters in marriage. Then he left Sippas in charge of Makedonia and moved into Thessaly with 13,000 Makedonians and 600 cavalry, a small force that attests to the drain of Alexander's campaigns on Makedonian manpower (Diod. 18. 12. 2; Bosworth, *JHS* 106 [1986], 8-9). Antipatros also had a fleet of 110 ships, which had conveyed monies from Asia to Makedonia (Diod. 18. 12. 2). But the desertion of the Thessalians to the Greek cause (18. 12. 3) proved to be a major setback, and Antipatros soon found it necessary to take refuge in Lamia and await reinforcements from Asia.[131]

Leosthenes attempted to invest the city (Diod. 18. 13. 1-3), but when Antipatros made a sortie against some Athenians who were digging the ditch, Leosthenes, coming to the aid of his men, was struck by a stone (perhaps hurled from the city walls);[132] he was carried from the battlefield and died on the third day.[133] Antiphilos, a man of good courage and generalship, replaced him (Diod. 18. 13. 6; Plut. *Phok.* 24. 1; Develin, *Athenian Officials* 411).

Antipatros meanwhile pinned his hopes on Leonnatos, whom he had summoned through the agency of Hekataios (Diod. 18. 14. 4), a Kardian (cf. Plut. *Eum.* 3. 6). Leonnatos crossed into Europe with his satrapal army (spring 322) and enlisted additional troops in Makedonia, finally moving into Thessaly with over 20,000 infantry and 1,500 cavalry (Diod. 18. 14. 5). The Athenians abandoned the siege of Lamia and decided to meet Leonnatos before he could join forces with Antipatros.[134] In numbers of infantry the armies were roughly equal — the Athenians had some 22,000, for the Aitolians had left previously to deal with some local matter (18. 13. 4) and were still absent — but in cavalry the Greeks excelled: 2,000 of their total 3,500 were Thessalians under the command of Menon.[135] Leonnatos himself was cut off in a marshy region and, after suffering many wounds, was carried dead from the battlefield by his own men (Diod. 18. 15. 3); his infantry was forced to retreat to higher ground, where on the following day they were joined by Antipatros (Diod. 18. 15. 4-5). Fortune had been kind to the *strategos* of Europe: one engagement had freed him from Lamia, rid

---

[131] Diod. 18. 12. 4; Plut. *Demosth.* 27. 1; *Phok.* 23. 5; [Plut.] *vit. X or.* 8 = *Mor.* 846d-e; Hyper. 6. 12. Justin 13. 5. 8 has Antipatros shut up in Herakleia.

[132] Cf. Justin 13. 5. 12, who says he was hit by a javelin (*telum*).

[133] Diod. 18. 13. 5; cf. Plut. *Phok.* 24. 1; see also Hypereides 6; cf. [Plut.] *vit. X or.* 9 = *Mor.* 849f.

[134] Diod. 18. 15. 1. The battle appears to have been fought near Pharsalos in Thessaliotis (so Kanatsulis, *Makedonika* 8 [1968], 137; cf. Beloch iv^2 1. 72, n.1).

[135] Diod. 18. 15. 2 for the figures; 18. 15. 4 for Menon's command. Menon's daughter Phthia later married Aiakides; they became the parents of Pyrrhos (Plut. *Pyrrh.* 1. 6-7).

him of a dangerous rival and augmented his forces.[136] Nevertheless, Antipatros chose to avoid giving battle on the plain, owing to his inferior numbers of cavalry; instead he withdrew over more rugged ground towards the Peneus.[137]

In the meantime, Kleitos' naval victories had secured the crossing of the Hellespont for Krateros,[138] who soon entered Thessaly with an additional 10,000 foot, 3,000 slingers and archers and 1,500 cavalry, bringing to about 48,000 the entire Makedonian force,[139] which confronted the Greeks near Krannon on 7 Metageitnion (= 5 August) 322;[140] the Greeks, in comparison, had 25,000 infantry and 3,500 cavalry (Diod. 18. 17. 2). Antipatros, once the Makedonian cavalry had engaged its Greek counterpart, led the phalanx forward and drove the enemy infantry to the high ground. Seeing this, the Greek cavalry disengaged, and the victory went to the Makedonian forces, with more than 500 Greek dead and 130 Makedonians killed.[141] Menon and Antiphilos now sued for peace, but Antipatros refused to deal with the

---

[136] Justin 13. 5. 15. Arr. *Succ.* 1. 9 (Λεόννατος ἐπιβοηθεῖν δοκῶν Ἀντιπάτρῳ) hints at Leonnatos' true designs; cf. Kanatsulis, *Makedonika* 8 (1968), 138, n.1.

[137] Diod. 18. 15. 6-7; cf. 18. 16. 5. Justin 13. 5. 16 (*in Macedoniam concessit*) is inaccurate.

[138] Kleitos' victories at Amorgos and the Echinades (= Lichades islands) had put an end to Athenian naval power in the Aegean (see iii 4 and Appendix III); the naval victory at the Hellespont (cf. *IG* ii² 398a), which secured the crossing for Leonnatos, was fought before Kleitos arrived from the Levant. Ferguson, *HA* 18 writes of White Kleitos landing forces under Mikion at Rhamnous after the battle of Krannon. This cannot be correct: Plut. *Phok.* 25 makes it clear that this expedition took place at about the same time as the Greeks fought the battle in which Leonnatos was killed, hence presumably before the battle of Amorgos. Mikion may have been the commander (or at least one of the commanders) of the fleet that secured the Hellespont and allowed Leonnatos to cross from Hellespontine Phrygia; he was defeated and killed by Phokion's forces. Cf. also Berve ii 264, no. 529.

[139] See Diod. 18. 16. 5 for the figures, but these do not correspond exactly with the breakdown given in 18. 12. 2; 18. 14. 5 and 18. 16. 4, which give a total of 43,000+ infantry; 3600 cavalry; 1,000 archers. Diod. 18. 16. 5 has 40,000+ infantry; 5000 horse; 3,000 slingers and archers. The only really serious problem is presented by numbers of cavalry, since the additional slingers and archers might have been included in the general infantry figures at an earlier point. On the cooperation of Krateros and Antipatros in general see Arr. *Succ.* 1. 12.

[140] Diod. 18. 17; Plut. *Phok.* 26; *Demosth.* 28. 1; *Camill.* 19; Paus. 10. 3. 4; cf. Arr. *Succ.* 1. 12. For the date (7 Metageitnion): Plut. *Camillus* 19. 8; *Demosth.* 28. 1; Beloch iv² 1. 74 (5 August); 2. 237; (30 July); cf. Ferguson, *HA* 18, n.2.

[141] Diod. 18. 17. 4-5; according to Paus. 7. 10. 5, two hundred of the Greek dead were Athenian.

Greeks collectively, demanding instead separate peace terms with each state. The Thessalian towns were taken by siege or storm and offered easy peace terms,[142] leaving the Athenians and Aitolians to face Makedon alone.[143]

In Athens there was great consternation, and a deputation led by Phokion and Demades was sent to Antipatros, who had advanced into Boiotia.[144] Mindful of Leosthenes' hard line at Lamia, Antipatros demanded the unconditional surrender of the city, terms which Athens was forced to accept (Diod. 18. 18. 1-3). Antipatros, however, treated the Athenians with leniency (18. 18. 4), though he insisted on establishing a garrison on Mounychia (Plut. *Phok.* 27. 1 - 28. 1; *Demosth.* 28. 1; cf. Paus. 7. 10. 1) and the punishment of leading anti-Makedonian politicians.[145] About a month and a half after Krannon, on 20 Boedromion (September) 322 (Plut. *Phok.* 28. 2; cf. *Demosth.* 28. 1), Menyllos occupied Mounychia; the anti-Makedonian leaders — Demosthenes, Hypereides, Himeraios (the brother of Demetrios of Phaleron), and Aristonikos — were hunted down by Antipatros' agent Archias and put to death.[146]

Having made peace with Athens, Antipatros and Krateros turned their attention to the Aitolians (Diod. 18. 24-25), only to be forced by the situation in Asia to come to terms with them.[147] Antigonos had arrived during the Aitolian campaign with news of Perdikkas' duplicity (Diod. 18. 23. 4 - 24. 1; 18. 25. 3; Arr. *Succ.* 1. 21, 24); though the full extent of

---

[142]Diod. 18. 17. 7; cf. [Plut.], *vit. X or.* 8 = *Mor.* 846e, for the capture of Pharsalos.

[143]In the Peloponnese, Antipatros installed pro-Makedonian oligarchies, often headed by personal friends and supported by garrisons (Diod. 18. 18. 8; 18. 55. 2; 18. 57. 1; 18. 69. 3). See also *Suda* s.v. Δείναρχος; cf. Beloch iv^2 1. 77, with n.4.

[144]They met him at the Kadmeia in Boiotia (Diod. 18. 18; Plut. *Phok.* 26; Paus. 7. 10. 4; Nepos, *Phoc.* 2). *Suda* s.v. ἀνεβάλλετο shows that some military action had been taken against Attika

[145]But see Polyb. 9. 29. 2-4 (from the speech of Chlaineas the Aitolian), which Kaerst, *RE* i (1894), 2506, properly calls 'einseitig und übertrieben'; cf. Paus. 7. 10.

[146]Arr. *Succ.* 1. 13; Plut. *Phok.* 27 ff.; *Demosth.* 28-29; *vit. X or.*, 9 = *Mor.* 849b-c; Paus. 1. 25. 5; *Suda* s.vv. Ἀντίπατρος, Δημοσθένης; Nepos, *Phoc.* 2. 2. For Demosthenes' famous suicide at Kalauria (by chewing on a poisoned 'pen') see Plut. *Demosth.* 29-30; [Plut.], *vit. X or.* 8 = *Mor.* 846e - 847b.

[147]Diod. 18. 25. 5; cf. Arr. *Succ.* 1. 24. Justin 13. 6. 9 wrongly speaks of peace with the Athenians. The Makedonian army numbered 30,000 infantry and 2500 cavalry, against a force of 10,000 Aitolians. This numerical superiority and the pressures of winter could easily have brought Aitolia to its knees.

the latter's dealings with Kleopatra, now in Sardeis, did not come to Antigonos' attention until his return to Asia (Arr. *Succ.* 1. 26; 25. 1 ff.). News of this hastened on Antipatros, who along with Krateros had advanced to the Thrakian Chersonese; and he sent envoys to secure the defection of White Kleitos and his own safe crossing of the Hellespont (Arr. *Succ.* 1. 26). Friendship with Ptolemy in Egypt had been renewed at the termination of the Aitolian campaign (Diod. 18. 14. 2; 18. 25. 4).

Safely across the Hellespont, Antipatros and Krateros were approached by Neoptolemos, who had recently defected from Eumenes' camp and offered promises of easy victory (Arr. *Succ.* 1. 26; cf. Diod. 18. 29. 4-5). Krateros was left to deal with Eumenes, while Antipatros pressed on in the direction of Kilikia (Diod. 18. 29. 6; Plut. *Eum.* 6. 4). Antigonos in the meantime had taken a fleet from Asia Minor (Karia or the Hellespont?) to Kypros, where the Perdikkan forces under Aristonous were campaigning (Arr. *Succ.* 24. 6; cf. 1. 30). Matters took an unexpected turn when Krateros and Neoptolemos were defeated by Eumenes (Diod. 18. 30-32); the remnants of their army did, however, manage to escape to Antipatros, thus mitigating the effects of the setback (Arr. *Succ.* 1. 28; Diod. 18. 33. 1).

In Egypt, Perdikkas fell victim to the treachery of his own officers and the Nile,[148] to say nothing of Ptolemy's own preparations. But the victory was a mixed blessing for Antipatros, who now found it necessary to deal with what remained of Perdikkas' disgruntled army, which Peithon and Arrhidaios had led to Triparadeisos in Syria. These men were embroiled in a bitter dispute with the queen, Adea-Eurydike, who had usurped the prerogatives of her half-witted husband and was supported by the troops, who demanded their pay (Arr. *Succ.* 1. 31-32; cf. Diod. 18. 39. 1-2). Attalos son of Andromenes now heightened tensions further by journeying inland from Tyre in the hope of winning the army back to the Perdikkan cause (Arr. *Succ.* 1. 33, 39). Hence Antipatros was greeted, on his arrival, by an angry mob, which might have lynched him, had it not been for the efforts of Seleukos and Antigonos (Arr. *Succ.* 1. 33; cf. Polyainos 4. 6. 4; Diod. 18. 39. 3-4).

Once order was restored, and the obstreperous Eurydike frightened into submission (Diod. 18. 39. 4), the satrapies of the empire were assigned anew and the war against the Perdikkans entrusted to Antigonos (Arr. *Succ.* 1. 34-38). But Antipatros took steps to limit Antigonos' power by assigning key satrapies to men whom he regarded

---

[148]For Perdikkas' campaign and his fate see Diod. 18. 33. 1 - 36. 5; Arr. *Succ.* 1. 28; Plut. *Eum.* 8. 2-3; Justin 13. 8. 1-2. For his death see also Nepos, *Eum.* 5. 1; Justin 13. 8. 10; 14. 1. 1; 14. 4. 11; 15. 1. 1; Diod. 18. 36. 5; *Suda* s.v. Περδίκκας; *Heidelberg Epit.* 1; Arr. 7. 18. 5; Paus. 1. 6. 3. See also ii 5.

as loyal to himself,[149] by appointing Somatophylakes for Philip III Arrhidaios (Arr. *Succ.* 1. 38), and by designating his own son Kassandros 'chiliarch of the cavalry' (Arr. *Succ.* 1. 38; Diod. 18. 39. 7), so that Antigonos might not pursue an independent course without Antipatros' knowledge. That he left the Kings in Antigonos' care (Arr. *Succ.* 1. 38: τούτῳ [sc. 'Ἀντιγόνῳ] τοὺς βασιλέας φρουρεῖν τε καὶ θεραπεύειν προστάξας) is surprising only in retrospect. Antipatros had come to regard the Kings as pertinent to the Asiatic empire, and preferred to conduct the affairs of Europe unencumbered by an infant and a half-wit. Their futures were best left to the uncertainties of Asia and the ambitions of Alexander's marshals.

Returning to the west, Antipatros stopped at Sardeis, where he and Kleopatra exchanged recriminations (Arr. *Succ.* 1. 40). Asandros was despatched to engage the forces of Attalos and Alketas, only to be worsted (Arr. *Succ.* 1. 41), and before he could leave Asia Antipatros was met by Kassandros, who had already fallen out with Antigonos. Persuaded that Antigonos harboured designs on a grander scale, he removed the Kings from the latter's custody and took them — reluctantly, we must assume — to Europe (Arr. *Succ.* 1. 42-44). Removing the symbols of authority from Antigonos, Antipatros had nevertheless tacitly recognised him as an equal partner in the empire, as the *strategos* of Asia, and he was content, for the time, to leave him preoccupied with the suppression of the outlawed party.

Antipatros did not long outlive these events. In the autumn of 319 he fell ill and soon died,[150] leaving the conduct of European affairs in the hands of Polyperchon. As Polyperchon's second-in-command (Chiliarch), he appointed his own son Kassandros (Diod. 18. 47. 4; 18. 48. 4-5; cf. Plut. *Phok.* 31. 1). These unprecedented measures were undoubtedly confirmed by a council of hetairoi (cf. Hammond, *HMac* iii 130), though neither Kassandros and — as soon became clear — a substantial number of prominent Makedonians favoured the appointment (Diod. 18. 49. 1-3; Plut. *Phok.* 31. 1; *Heidelberg Epit.* 1. 4 =

---

[149]Kleitos in Lydia (replacing Menandros, a friend and kinsman of Antigonos); Arrhidaios, in place of the dead Leonnatos; Philoxenos instead of Philotas in Kilikia; Amphimachos in Mesopotamia was probably the brother of Arrhidaios the satrap (Arr. *Succ.* 1. 35 wrongly calls him τοῦ βασιλέως ἀδελφός). The Karian satrap Asandros appears to have been loyal to Antipatros.

[150]Diod. 18. 48. The embassy of Demades, who requested that Antipatros remove Menyllos' garrison from Mounychia, helps to date Antipatros' death. The old man was mortally ill when Demades reached him, but the latter did not leave Athens before the end of June 319 (as is clear from *IG* ii^2 383b); cf. Plut. *Phok.* 30. 4-6; *Demosth.* 31. 4-6. Demades was, however, executed (along with his son Demeas) on a charge of having conspired with Perdikkas; for incriminating letters had been found in the royal archives (Diod. 18. 48. 2-3).

FGrHist 155 F1). But Kassandros' pique must have been a small thing compared with the resentment these arrangements elicited from Antigonos the One-Eyed.

5. Antigonos son of Philippos: Monophthalmos

Literature. Berve ii 42-44, no. 87; Kaerst, *RE* i (1894), 2406-2413, no. 3; Billows, *Antigonos*, esp. 1-80; E. M. Anson, 'Antigonus, the Satrap of Phrygia', *Historia* 37 (1988), 471-477; Briant.

> Zu Al[exander]s Zeit ist der gewaltigste der Diadochen für uns nur ein blasser Schatten.
>
> (Berve ii 44)

Born c. 382 B.C.,[151] Antigonos, later known as 'the One-Eyed',[152] was the son of a certain Philippos.[153] The name of his mother is not recorded, but we do know that she was remarried at some time after the birth of Antigonos and his brothers, this time to Periandros (otherwise unknown), to whom she bore a son named Marsyas.[154] Since Marsyas was born c. 356 — he was a *syntrophos* of Alexander the Great (*Suda* s.v. Μαρσύας) — we may assume that the mother was still very young when she bore Antigonos, Demetrios and, apparently, a third son of Philippos, Polemaios (father of Antigonos' nephew of the same name who was active in the early age of the Successors). R. A. Billows' assumption (*Antigonos* 17) that she married 'an important noble from

---

[151] Hieronymos *ap.* Ps.-Lucian, *Macrob.* 11 = *FGrHist* 154 F8; Appian, *Syr.* 55 [279]; cf. Plut. *Demetr.* 19. 4, who says that in 306 he was 'a little short of 80 years old'; Porphyry of Tyre, *FGrHist* 260 F32 says he was 86 at the time of his death!

[152] Cf. Aelian, *VH* 12. 43 (ὁ καὶ ἑτερόφθαλμος καὶ ἐκ τούτου Κύκλωψ προσαγορευθείς); Plut. *Sertorius* 1. 8; Pliny, *NH* 35. 90. Oikonomides, *AncW* 20 (1989), 17-20, suggests that the bust of an old one-eyed man in the Ny Carlsberg Glyptothek (I.N. 212 = G. M. A. Richter, *The Portraits of the Greeks* [London, 1965], fig. 374) may be Antigonos the One-Eyed. Billows follows Charbonneaux, *Rev. des Arts* 2 (1952), 219 ff., in identifying Antigonos with one of the horsemen, shown (significantly?) in profile (cf. Pliny, *NH* 35. 90; Pollitt, p. 161), on the Alexander Sarcophagus (*Antigonos* 8, with n. 19 for earlier literature). Apart from the fact that the sarcophagus could be as early as the mid-320s, it should be noted that the battle-scene depicts, in all likelihood, the battle of Issos, or perhaps Gaugamela; Antigonos participated in neither of these. Antigonos was also painted by Protogenes (Pliny, *NH* 35. 106; Pollitt, p. 173). R. R. R. Smith, *Hellenistic Royal Portraits* (Oxford, 1988), cautiously avoids identifying any surviving portrait as Antigonos I.

[153] Arr. 1. 29. 3; Dittenberger, *Syll.*³ 278, 5; Strabo 12. 4. 7 C565; Justin 13. 4. 14; Aelian, *VH* 12. 43; Plut. *Demetr.* 2. 1; Hieronymos *ap.* Ps.-Lucian, *Macrob.* 11 = *FGrHist* 154 F8.

[154] *Suda* s.v. Μαρσύας. Cf. Berve ii 247 f., no. 489; Heckel, *Hermes* 108 [1980], 444-462; Billows, *Antigonos* 399-400, no. 67; for his career see also Diod. 20. 50. 4; Plut. *Mor.* 182c.

Pella' is unnecessary, perhaps even wrong: the ethnic 'Pellaios', often used of young men raised at the Court, tells us nothing about their fathers' origins (but cf. Berve ii 43: 'vielleicht in Pella ansässig').[155]

Claims that Antigonos himself was of obscure origin, a common labourer (αὐτουργός), are inventions of the propaganda mills of the Diadochic age — the same ones that made Polyperchon a 'brigand', Eumenes a 'funeral musician' (Aelian, *VH* 12. 43), and Marsyas a school-teacher (*Suda* s.v.). On the other hand, the claims of Philip V to be related to Philip II and Alexander (Polyb. 5. 10. 10),[156] although they may have been invented in an age when such things could no longer be put to the test, need not imply (even if they were true) that either Philippos or his wife were Argeads. This is the androcentric view. Stratonike, the daughter of Korrhagos and wife of Antigonos, may well have been related to Philip II; for the name is attested in the Argead house (cf. Thuc. 2. 101. 6).[157] Antigonos himself was an hetairos of Alexander (Aelian, *VH* 14. 47a); Justin describes him as *Philippo regi et Alexandro Magno socius* (16. 1. 12).[158]

At the time of Alexander's crossing into Asia, Antigonos commanded 7000 allied Greek hoplites, though we know virtually

---

[155] For the career of Polemaios (I) and his son see Billows, *Antigonos* 425 ff., nos. 99-100. Billows (17) assumes that Demetrios was the eldest of Philippos' sons. Though not impossible, this strains matters even more, since Demetrios would have been born no later than 383, some 27 years before Marsyas' birth by the same mother.

[156] Some earlier literature in F. W. Walbank, *A Historical Commentary on Polybius*, vol. 1 (Oxford, 1957), 548. Perseus' sons were called (significantly?) Philip and Alexander (Justin 33. 2. 5); whether the Antigonids claimed to have genealogical links with Karanos is not clear from 33. 2. 6.

[157] His marriage to Stratonike, and their children (Plut. *Demetr.* 2). Her possible connections with the Argead house: Edson, *HSCP* 45 (1934), 213-246; cf. Macurdy, *AJP* 48 (1927), 205, comments on the name 'Stratonike' but does not (as Briant 24, n.2, says) regard the woman as an adherent of the Argeadai.

The suggestion of Edson (*op. cit.*) that the Antigonids came originally from Beroia has not found a great deal of favour in recent years (rejected by Lévêque, *Pyrrhos* 156 f., and Billows, *Antigonos* 18), but Tataki's prosopography has brought some new information to light, which appears to strengthen Edson's theory.

[158] His friendship with Eumenes appears to originate in Philip's reign (Plut. *Eum.* 10. 5). Billows' attempt to link Antigonos with 'Antigenes the one-eyed, from Pellene' (27-29) is not convincing: (1) there is uncertainty about whether this is really Antigenes or Atarrhias; (2) Antigonos himself could not have been present in Susa or Opis when the episode with Antigenes (or Atarrhias) occurred; (3) we are dealing in this episode with a relatively low-level commander/soldier, which would suit either of the hypaspist commanders but not Antigonos.

nothing about the nature of this command or the exercise of it.[159] Clearly, he must have participated in the battle at the Graneikos, and at some time before August 334 he was sent to win over Priene to the Makedonian cause. We may assume that Antigonos made the initial arrangements with Priene and that these were confirmed, in terms favourable to the city, by Alexander himself (cf. Tod, *GHI* ii, nos. 184-185). Hence that state, appreciative of Antigonos' efforts,[160] honoured him, bestowing *proxenia*, citizenship, and exemption from taxation (Dittenberger, *Syll.*^{3} 278 = *I.Priene*, no. 2 = Tod, *GHI* ii no. 186). Thus the King had used Antigonos in much the same way as he was employing Parmenion and Alkimachos to secure Makedonian control over the cities of Asia Minor.[161]

It appears that Antigonos remained with Alexander until early spring 333,[162] when he was appointed satrap of Phrygia (capital: Kelainai; Arr. 1. 29. 3; Curt. 4. 1. 35 wrongly says 'Lydia', but see below), which he ruled for the duration of Alexander's life, and beyond. At the time of his appointment, Kelainai had not yet surrendered to the Makedonians, though the inhabitants had promised to do so at the end of the second month, if no help arrived from Dareios III before that time. The garrison of 1000 Karians probably continued to serve Antigonos upon the surrender of the city; the 100 Greek mercenaries may, however, have been handed over to Alexander or shipped to Makedonia for punishment.

As the satrap of Phrygia, which controlled the main lines of communication in Asia Minor, Antigonos became responsible for the

---

[159] For discussions see, however, Briant 27-41; Billows, *Antigonos* 36-41.

[160] Tod, *GHI* ii pp. 245-246.

[161] Arr. 1. 18. 1. The failure to mention Antigonos' mission is almost certainly attributable to Ptolemy's bias.

[162] Berve ii 43 assumes that he remained with Parmenion, but Parmenion did not rejoin Alexander until he reached Gordion, which lay to the northeast of Kelainai. Arrian 1. 29. 3 does not say that Antigonos was appointed satrap *in absentia*, and the provision that Balakros son of Amyntas should replace Antigonos as *strategos* of the allies suggests that that unit was present at Kelainai. Billows' speculation (*Antigonos* 40) that Antigonos may have returned to Makedonia with the 'newly-weds' (Arr. 1. 24. 1, 29. 4) should be rejected. First, it is highly unlikely that someone who was married no later than 338 would belong, in the winter of 334/3, to a group who ἦσαν νεωστὶ πρὸ τῆς στρατιᾶς γεγαμηκότες (Arr. 1. 24. 1). Second, Arrian names only Ptolemaios son of Seleukos, Koinos son of Polemokrates, and Meleagros son of Neoptolemos as commanders of this expedition — though it might be argued that Antigonos was intentionally overlooked by Arrian-Ptolemy. Third, the 'newly-weds' rejoined Alexander at Gordion (Arr. 1. 29. 4), not Kelainai.

suppression of any remnants of Persian resistance in the area.[163] After the battle of Issos (November 333), a substantial force, loyal to the Persian King, escaped from the battlefield and prepared for a counterstrike by enlisting troops in Kappadokia and Paphlagonia (Curt. 4. 1. 35). These forces were, however, crushed in three separate battles in 332: Antigonos himself was victorious in Lykaonia, Kalas in Paphlagonia (an area which had been added to his satrapy of Hellespontine Phrygia, although it had not been adequately subdued[164]), and Balakros expelled the Persians from Miletos (Curt. 4. 5. 13).[165] It appears that, after the departure of Nearchos in 331/0 B.C., Antigonos assumed control of Pamphylia and Lykia (cf. Diod. 18. 3. 1; Curt. 10. 10. 2; cf. Baumbach 57). Stratonike, Antigonos' wife, soon joined him in Kelainai; Philippos, the younger brother of Demetrios Poliorketes, may have been born there (so Berve ii 383, no. 776), though Billows (*Antigonos* 420) suggests plausibly that he was born in Makedonia in 334.

Antigonos now vanishes from the history of Alexander the Great but resurfaces as a major player in the age of the Successors. Confirmed as satrap of Greater Phrygia (Diod. 18. 3. 1, 39. 6; Justin 13. 4. 14; Arr. *Succ.* 1a. 6; 1b. 2), he was nevertheless ordered by Perdikkas to aid Eumenes in the conquest of Kappadokia, and his refusal to obey these

---

[163]For Antigonos' control of the 'lifeline to Europe' see Anson, *Historia* 37 (1988), 471, following Tarn ii 110 f. Anson argues that Antigonos 'did not share power in Phrygia with others as was common in other satrapies' (472). Asandros and Menandros in Lydia did have a garrison commander in Sardeis, but this man (Pausanias) was surely subordinate to the satrap. Alexander's failure to install a *phrourarchos* in Kelainai is explained by the fact that it had not yet surrendered when the King moved on. Antigonos will undoubtedly have appointed his own *phrourarchos*. Anson (474) plausibly ascribes Antigonos' success, despite small numbers of Greek and Makedonian troops, to the use of native levies.

[164]Curt. 3. 1. 22-24. The Paphlagonians had not paid tribute to the Persian kings, and it is doubtful that they were ready to submit completely to Makedonian rule. Billows (*Antigonos* 45, n.85) dates Kalas' death in battle with the Bithynian dynast Bas (Memnon, *FGrHist* 434 F1 §12. 4) to this time; Badian, *JHS* 81 (1961), 18, is probably correct in assigning this disturbance to the end of Alexander's reign.

[165]Curt. 4. 5. 13 merely elucidates the more compressed observation at 4. 1. 35. I do not believe that Antigonos won three successives battles before his victory in Lykaonia. Nor am I inclined to accept the view that 'Lydia' in Curt. 4. 1. 35 is anything more than an error on Curtius' part. That Antigonos assumed 'overall command in Asia Minor', as Billows (*Antigonos* 44, n.80) suggests, can neither be proved nor disproved. In Balakros' absence, Alexander assigned the military responsibilities in Kilikia to Sokrates (apparently the son of Sathon, Curt. 4. 5. 9).

instructions placed him in jeopardy when Perdikkas called him to account (Plut. *Eum.* 3. 4-5; Diod. 18. 23. 3-4; cf. Arr. *Succ.* 1. 20).[166] Rather than risk deposition, and possibly execution, for his insubordination, Antigonos fled to Europe, bringing with him reports of Perdikkas' duplicity and confirmation of what Antipatros and Krateros had suspected: that Perdikkas aimed at complete control of Alexander's Empire.[167] Having persuaded them to terminate the war against the Aitolians and prepare for war with Perdikkas, Antigonos crossed the Aegean with ten Athenian ships and 3,000 troops, landing in Karia, where he was welcomed by the satrap Asandros, who was also a kinsman (Arr. *Succ.* 25. 1: καὶ δέχεται αὐτὸν Ἄσανδρος ὁ Καρίας ξατράπης .... κατὰ γένος ἐπιτήδειος ὤν). It was undoubtedly Antigonos' purpose to gain a foothold in Asia Minor and rally the disaffected satraps until Krateros and Antipatros could cross the Hellespont. Menandros immediately went over to Antigonos, angered by the high-handedness of Perdikkas, who had left him in charge of the satrapal forces but placed him under the authority of Kleopatra (Arr. *Succ.* 25. 2). Furthermore, he gave damning evidence that Perdikkas intended to send Nikaia back to her father and marry Alexander's sister instead (Arr. *Succ.* 1. 26). Reports of this hastened the invasion from the north by Krateros and Antipatros, who persuaded White Kleitos to abandon the Perdikkan cause and allow their entry into Asia (Arr. *Succ.* 1. 26).

Antigonos, in the meantime, had moved inland, intending to catch Eumenes in an ambush. But his troop movements were reported to Kleopatra at Sardeis, and Eumenes managed to escape to Phrygia (Arr. *Succ.* 25. 6-8). It was presumably soon afterwards that Antigonos joined Krateros and Antipatros near the Hellespont where a council of war was held. Krateros, it was decided, would deal with Eumenes, while Antipatros pushed on to Kilikia; Antigonos meanwhile was sent to Kypros to engage the forces under the command of Aristonous (thus Arr. *Succ.* 1. 30; cf. 24. 6).[168] Whether Antigonos won a clear victory there is debatable (*pace* Billows, *Antigonos* 68): nothing is recorded of the campaign except his participation in it. It appears that he came to terms with Aristonous' forces once news of Perdikkas' death became

---

[166] I see no good reason for suspecting, as Billows (*Antigonos* 58 f., with n. 15) does, the truth of the charges against Antigonos. Diod. 18. 23. 4 says they were slanders and false accusations. But this is just the kind of defence one should expect from Hieronymos. Billows (*ibid.*) is right, however, to reject Müller's suggestion (*Antigonos Monophthalmos* 19 f.) that Antigonos was piqued at the loss of Paphlagonia, which, as Billows points out, had belonged to Hellespontine (not Greater) Phrygia.

[167] Diod. 18. 23. 3-4; Arr. *Succ.* 1. 20, 24.

[168] Billows, *Antigonos* 66. Antigonos was perhaps accompanied by Dionysios of Herakleia Pontika (Memnon, *FGrHist* 434 F2 §§3-6).

known. Of the enemy commanders there, at least one, Medeios of Larisa, joined him.[169] From Kypros, Antigonos was summoned to northern Syria, where, at Triparadeisos, he was recognised as a virtual equal partner with Antipatros, whom he had saved from the rampaging mob that had once been Perdikkas' Royal Army (Arr. *Succ.* 1. 32-33; Polyainos 4. 6. 4).

At Triparadeisos, he was appointed *hegemon* of the Royal Army (Diod. 18. 39. 7; Arr. *Succ.* 1. 38) and presumably recognised as *strategos* of Asia Minor (cf. Diod. 18. 50. 1). In theory, he was second only to Antipatros in the hierarchy of Alexander's orphaned empire. Perhaps, Antipatros sensed that his own end was near and regarded Antigonos as the most worthy to exercise the supreme authority. But the decision to leave the Kings with Antigonos and his chiliarch, Kassandros, suggests that Antipatros was content to rule Makedonia and Europe and to leave the problems of Asia and the misfit Kings to another. Antigonos and Kassandros soon fell out, however, and Antipatros, acting on his son's advice, took the Kings back to Europe. He had thus taken back the symbolic authority over the empire as a whole, but in fact left Asia to Antigonos, who lacked neither the ambition nor the resources to gain supremacy.

A towering man, larger than his own son Demetrios (Plut. *Demetr.* 2. 2), who was himself reputedly tall (Diod. 19. 81. 4; 20. 92. 3), Antigonos became exceedingly corpulent late in life — to the extent that this rather than old age hampered his performance on the battlefield (Plut. *Demetr.* 19. 4; cf. *Mor.* 791e). Both jovial (Plut. *Demetr.* 28. 8) and witty (*Demetr.* 14. 3-4; *Mor.* 182d-e; cf. 633c), he could nevertheless be loud and boastful (Plut. *Eum.* 15. 3; *Demetr.* 28. 8). And, though affectionate at home (Plut. *Demetr.* 3) and clearly devoted to his wife Stratonike, he was driven by *philotimia* and *philarchia* to the extent that he alarmed Alexander (Aelian, *VH* 12. 16; 14. 47a) and alienated many others (Diod. 18. 50. 1; 21. 1. 1; Plut. *Demetr.* 28. 8). In some areas of his personal life he was less tolerant of criticism: he allegedly executed Theokritos for a tactless remark about his eyes, though he had himself once joked that the characters of a letter were large enough for a blind man to read (Plut. *Mor.* 633c).[170]

---

[169] Aristonous is later found in Makedonia, supporting Polyperchon and Olympias. He may, however, have returned there with Antipatros. Billows' comment that 'Sosigenes joined Eumenes' (*Antigonos* 68) is misleading: Sosigenes was apparently serving Polyperchon, who was now cooperating with Eumenes (Polyainos 4. 6. 9).

[170] For the fate of Theokritos see Teodorsson, *Hermes* 118 (1990), 380-382, with further references.

In his dealings with political and military foes, he could be ruthless: Alketas' body was denied burial (Diod. 18. 47. 3); and, of the officers taken captive at Kretopolis, only Dokimos managed to save himself (and this was through treachery; Diod. 18. 45. 3; 19. 16; cf. R. H. Simpson, *Historia* 6 [1957], 504 f.); White Kleitos and Arrhidaios were driven from their satrapies (Diod. 18. 52. 3-6); Peukestas was deposed (Diod. 19. 48. 5), Peithon eliminated through treachery (Diod. 19. 46. 1-4), and Antigenes burned alive in a pit (Diod. 19. 44. 1). The claim that Eumenes was murdered by his guards without Antigonos' permission is feeble and transparent *apologia* (Nepos, *Eum.* 12. 4). In one case, his own son Demetrios was forced to betray his father's trust to secure the escape of his friend Mithridates (Plut. *Demetr.* 4. 1 ff.). Despite the propaganda he used in his quest for legitimacy and the goodwill of the Greek cities, Alexander's marshals soon learned to fear his ruthless ambition and calculated brutality.

ii. The 'New Men'

Introduction

The emergence of Alexander's 'New Men' was both the result and the cause of the erosion of the entrenched aristocracy's domination of the highest military commands, which represented nothing less than the chief magistracies of a Makedonian state on the move. The state had quickly formed around Alexander, whose kingship came to be regarded as personal rather than circumscribed by geography. The success of Alexander's conquests likewise relegated the homeland to little more than a side-show on the western fringe of the burgeoning empire, a source of reinforcements and the guarantor of European stability. It was perhaps a logical development of their training as *syntrophoi* of the Crown Prince that the 'New Men' also identified the state with the person of the King.[1] Friendship and trust played no small part in advancing their careers, and — as hetairoi, taxiarchs, hipparchs, and Somatophylakes — they formed and dominated the King's Consilium. Publicly, and in private, they influenced his policy, advanced and jeopardised the careers of others. Inevitably, they came into conflict with one another.

Divided on the matter of Alexander's orientalising policies, they nevertheless exhibited an unshakeable loyalty to the King, whom they served unsparingly. Each shared in his exploits, all died young. So that their lives intertwined with that of Alexander in fate's Gordian knot. But because they laboured in the shadow of the great man, their own careers have received too little attention from historians, ancient and modern. Heroic fame (*kleos*) eludes them, a reward their own service has helped to bestow upon Alexander. The Hellenistic kingdoms too were destined for other, arguably lesser, men. It is idle to speculate what may have been, but the path that led the Makedonian state to Triparadeisos reveals that, although each of the 'New Men' had striven to be second only to Alexander, none could be justly considered a second Alexander.

---

[1] Koinos was, of course, not a *syntrophos* of Alexander. In the other aspects of his career, however, he belongs to the 'New Men' rather than the 'Old Guard', despite his early associations with Parmenion.

THE MARSHALS OF ALEXANDER'S EMPIRE

1. Koinos: Changing One's Spots

Literature. Berve ii 215-218, no. 439; Honigmann, *RE* xi (1921), 1055-1057, no. 1; Tarn ii 192-197; J. R. Hamilton, 'The Cavalry Battle at the Hydaspes', *JHS* 76 (1956), 26-31; A. M. Devine, 'The Battle of the Hydaspes: A Tactical and Source-Critical Study', *AncW* 16 (1987), 91-113, esp. 102-107.

When, at the Hyphasis river, Koinos espoused the cause of the common soldier, thereby calling to a halt Alexander's relentless march eastward, he had come full circle. A son-in-law of Parmenion and, in all likelihood, the husband of Attalos' widow, he betrayed his family connections in 330 and repudiated his friendship with Philotas for the sake of survival and, indeed, political gain. The acceleration of his military career is unmistakable, and Koinos has been regarded, not unjustly, as one of Alexander's 'New Men'. In the end, however, his traditional Makedonian values placed him at odds with his King. Other officers will have shared his sentiments, but few, if any, dared express them publicly. His sudden death, so soon after the Hyphasis mutiny, makes the impact of this challenge to Alexander impossible to assess and easy to misinterpret. Ultimately, he had shown himself to be one of the King's men, though not necessarily one of Alexander's 'Boys'.

Koinos son of Polemokrates (Arr. 1. 14. 2; cf. Dittenberger, *Syll.*³ 332, 7-8) is usually identified as an adherent of the Elimeiot nobility. This assumption is based solely on the ethnic composition of his brigade,[2] but may nevertheless be correct; for Perdikkas of Orestis commanded the Orestian and Lynkestian brigade, Polyperchon that from his native Tymphaia.[3] Polemokrates had been allotted estates in the Chalkidic peninsula, and Koinos too received additional land in Philip's reign, all of which Koinos' son Perdikkas inherited.[4] If this grant of land

---

[2] Diod. 17. 57. 2. Griffith, *HMac* ii 396, for example, does not hesitate to speak of 'Polemocrates of Elimeia (father of Coenus)...'. Berve ii 215 is more cautious: '...vielleicht aus der Landschaft Elimiotis, wie die Tatsache, daß er unter Al. eine aus diesem Bezirk sich rekrutierende τάξις der Pezhetairen führte.'

[3] Diod. 17. 57. 2; Curt. 4. 13. 28 correctly identifies Perdikkas' troops but does not understand the composition of Polyperchon's brigade. We are not told the origins of the troops under Krateros, Meleagros and Amyntas.

[4] Dittenberger, *Syll.*³ 332: ἐφ' ἱερέως Κυδία· βασιλεὺς Μακεδόνων Κάσσανδρος δίδωσι Περδίκκαι | Κοίνου τὸν ἀγρὸν τὸν | ἐν τῆι Σιναίαι καὶ τὸν ἐπὶ Τραπεζοῦντι οὓς ἐκληρούχησεν Πολεμοκράτης ὁ πάππος αὐτοῦ | καὶ ὃν ὁ πατὴρ ἐπὶ Φιλίππου, καθάπερ καὶ Φίλιππος ἔδωκεν ἐμ πατρικοῖς καὶ αὑτοῖς καὶ ἐκγόνοις, κυρίοις οὖσι κεκτῆσθαι καὶ | ἀλλάσσεσθαι καὶ ἀ[π]οδόσθαι κτλ.

dates, as Dittenberger assumes,[5] to 348/7 or shortly thereafter, Koinos' birth should be dated no later than 367. Indeed, it is doubtful that he would have defended his right to speak out at the Hyphasis with reference to his age, had he not been at least forty in 326 (Arr. 5. 27. 3). Kleandros son of Polemokrates appears to have been his (older?) brother.[6]

Although his brigade is first named in the surprise attack on Glaukias' Taulantians near Pelion in 335 (Arr. 1. 6. 9),[7] Koinos may have commanded the Elimeiot infantry already in the final years of Philip's reign. Arrian relates that, during the first year of the Asiatic campaign he led back to Makedonia the newly-weds (νεόγαμοι), to which number he too belonged, sharing the command with the taxiarch, Meleagros son of Neoptolemos, and Ptolemaios son of Seleukos. Koinos had married Parmenion's daughter — her name has not survived — perhaps in 335.[8] She appears to have been none other than the widow of Attalos, to whom she was married for not much more than a year.[9] No later than the end of 333 B.C. she bore Koinos a son named Perdikkas.

At the Graneikos river, Koinos was stationed on the right, between the brigades of Perdikkas and Amyntas son of Andromenes, that is, in the second position after the hypaspists (Arr. 1. 14. 2). In the subsequent major engagements at Issos and Gaugamela, he occupied the first position, replacing Perdikkas. Griffith argues that Koinos' shift towards the centre indicates that this brigade had, at the Graneikos or at some other time before the battle of Issos, distinguished itself and thus become known as the 'best Companions'.[10] But we do not know why Alexander changed the order of the brigades, and the term ἀσθέταιροι, in all likelihood, was used generally of the brigades from Upper Makedonia.

After the Graneikos victory, we hear nothing of Koinos until he is sent home from Karia with the newly-weds (Arr. 1. 24. 1). This was also a recruiting mission (1. 24. 2): in spring 333, he rejoined Alexander at Gordion with 3000 infantry and 300 cavalry from Makedonia, 200 Thessalian horse and 150 Eleian cavalry under the command of

---

[5]*Syll.*[3] 332, p. 553, n.5, followed by Berve ii 215.
[6]Berve ii 204, no. 422.
[7]Berve ii 215, following Honigmann, *RE* xi (1921), 1055, wrongly calls it the Triballian campaign; see now Hammond, *HMac* iii 46-47.
[8]Curt. 6. 9. 30; cf. Heckel, *Historia* 36 (1987), 117, A33. This marriage, coming soon after Alexander's accession, would appear to argue against the view that Parmenion and his family were out of favour at the Court because of their connections with Attalos.
[9]Their marriage must date to sometime after Philip's union with Kleopatra-Eurydike in autumn (?) 337.
[10]*HMac* ii 712; cf. **viii 1 (i)** for further discussion.

Alkias.[11] We next encounter him at Issos, occupying the first infantry position on the right, next to Nikanor's hypaspists, but nothing else is known of his role in the battle.[12] In the final assault on Tyre, Koinos' brigade (or rather a portion of it) boarded a ship suitable for landing troops (Arr. 2. 23. 2), and once inside the city-walls distinguished itself in a particularly bloody engagement (Arr. 2. 24. 3). At Gaugamela Koinos held the same position as at Issos[13] and was wounded by an arrow in the heavy fighting.[14]

In his haste to reach Persepolis, Alexander followed the shorter route through the mountains, intending to enter Persis via the Persian or Sousian Gates. Here the Makedonian army was held at bay by the satrap Ariobarzanes until an encircling path was revealed to the King by captives. Once it became clear that Alexander would be able to circumvent the enemy's position, Koinos, Amyntas, Polyperchon and Philotas[15] were detached from the encircling force in order to begin the bridging of the Araxes river (Curt. 5. 4. 20, 30; Arr. 3. 18. 6). Following the sack of Persepolis, the removal of the treasures to Ekbatana was entrusted to Parmenion and some of the heavy infantry. Koinos, however, accompanied Alexander as far as the Caspian Gates, where he was detached with a small party to forage for supplies needed in the pursuit of Dareios (Arr. 3. 20. 4).[16] But news of Dareios' arrest by Bessos and his accomplices caused Alexander to push ahead without awaiting Koinos' return (Arr. 3. 21. 2); the latter rejoined Krateros, who followed the King at a more leisurely pace. In the campaigns against the Mardians (Arr. 3. 24. 1) and Satibarzanes near Artakoana (Arr. 3. 25. 6), Koinos and Amyntas son of Andromenes were again directly under the King's command.

The events of Phrada (330 B.C.) placed Koinos in jeopardy, with allegations of Philotas' involvement in the conspiracy of Dimnos. Philotas was his brother-in-law (Curt. 6. 9. 30), but Koinos belonged to

[11] Arr. 1. 29. 4; cf. Curt. 3. 1. 24; for Alkias see Berve ii 23, no. 46. He is otherwise unattested.

[12] Arr. 2. 8. 3; Curt. 3. 9. 7.

[13] Arr. 3. 11. 9; Diod. 17. 57. 2; Curt. 4. 13. 28, who claims, incorrectly, that Koinos' troops stood in reserve (Atkinson, *Curtius* i 422; cf. Berve ii 216, rejecting Honigmann, *RE* xi [1921], 1056).

[14] Curt. 4. 16. 32; Diod. 17. 61. 3; according to Arr. 3. 15. 2, he was wounded in the heavy fighting near Parmenion (cf. Honigmann, *RE* xi [1921], 1056); but see Bosworth, *Arrian* i 311.

[15] Almost certainly the son of Parmenion, as is clear from Curt. 5. 4. 20 (cf. Bosworth, *Arrian* i 327; Heckel, *Athenaeum* 58 [1980], 171).

[16] He accompanied Alexander from Awan-i-Kif, through the Caspian Gates — usually identified with Sar-i-Darreh (Seibert, *Eroberung* 112; cf. Bosworth, *Arrian* i 340, with map opposite) — and gathered provisions in the region of Choarene (mod. Khar).

the King's *consilium*, which was convened to discuss the matter (Curt. 6. 8. 17). His actions are, in fact, quite understandable: the vehemence with which he assailed Philotas — denouncing him as a parricide and a traitor to his country (Curt. 6. 9. 30) — reflects the danger in which he found himself. Few scholars today credit Curtius' statement that it was the law in Makedon to put to death the relatives of those who plotted against the King, yet Koinos, by inveighing against his wife's brother and calling for his torture, was attempting first and foremost to establish his own innocence;[17] certainly, he did not belong to the faction which had long hated Philotas (τοὺς πάλαι μισοῦντας αὐτόν, Plut. *Alex*. 49. 8).

Did his career suffer as a result of Philotas' disgrace? There is brief hiatus in our knowledge of Koinos' activities between 330 and 328, but this may be due to the nature of the sources, which become confused and uneven at this point. To seek political causes for Koinos' brief disappearance from history is perhaps unwise; for we should then be hard pressed to explain the man's prominence in the years 328-326 B.C. In 328, Alexander conducted a sweep-campaign in Sogdiana, dividing the mobile portion of the army into five units, one of them under Koinos' command.[18] He was instructed to take his troops and Artabazos (at that time the satrap of the region) in the direction of Skythia, where, it was reported, Spitamenes had taken refuge (Arr. 4. 16. 3). This brief campaign accomplished little, however, since Spitamenes had crossed the Oxos and attacked Baktra (Zariaspa), only to driven out again by Krateros (Arr. 4. 16. 4 - 17. 2). In late summer or early autumn, Koinos rejoined Alexander at Marakanda where Artabazos relinquished his satrapy on account of old age (Arr. 4. 17. 3; Curt. 8. 1. 19). Hence Koinos undoubtedly attended the drinking-party at which Kleitos, designated to succeed Artabazos, was murdered by the King. As winter approached, Koinos remained in Sogdiana with the new satrap, Amyntas son of Nikolaos, two brigades of pezhetairoi, 400 Companion cavalry and the *hippakontistai* with orders to defend the territory

---

[17]Curt. 6. 9. 30; 6. 11. 10-11. His dilemma and the emotional torment are perhaps brought out in Curt. 6. 9. 31: *saxumque quod forte ante pedes iacebat, corripuit emissurus in eum, ut plerique crediderunt, tormentis subtrahere cupiens.* Schachermeyr 327 emphasises his loyalty to the King ('...Koinos, der biedere Haudegen, wohl dem Bergadel entstammend. Zwar Schwiegersohn des Parmenion, jedoch von betonter Loyalität'). But Koinos did not want to be tarred by the same brush as Philotas and there was political gain in the demise of his in-laws.

[18]Arr. 4. 16. 2-3: Hephaistion, Perdikkas, Ptolemy, Koinos (with Artabazos) and Alexander each led one unit; Curt. 8. 1. 1 says there were only three divisions, led by Alexander, Hephaistion and Koinos. The heavy infantry (at least four brigades) remained with Krateros in Baktria (Arr. 4. 16. 1; 4. 17. 1).

against Spitamenes and the Massagetai.[19] These he defeated with heavy casualties, and after coming to terms with the Massagetai — who soon showed their good faith by sending Spitamenes' head to Alexander — Koinos rejoined the King at Nautaka before winter's end.[20]

Koinos had proved himself in Sogdiana, and it is not surprising to find him in more independent roles during the Swat campaign.[21] Against the Aspasian hyparch, Koinos remained with Alexander (Arr. 4. 24. 1) and also against the Gourians and Assakenians as far as Massaga (Arr. 4. 25. 6); from Massaga he was sent against Bazeira (Bir-Kot),[22] where he inflicted heavy losses on the natives while Alexander took the nearby town of Ora (Ude-gram).[23] The natives of Bazeira fled to Aornos (Pir-Sar), to which the King advanced via Embolima, taking Koinos and some more nimble troops.[24] On his return from Aornos, Alexander learned that Aphrikes (or Airikes?) was preparing to blockade his path, and he left Koinos to bring up the slower troops while he himself advanced to meet the enemy.[25]

---

[19] Arr. 4. 17. 3. Koinos retained his own brigade (perhaps already led by Peithon son of Agenor) and that of Meleagros. The 400 Companions may represent what were to become Koinos' hipparchy (cf. Arr. 5. 16. 3).

[20] For the battle with the Massagetai, who suffered over 800 casualties, see Arr. 4. 17. 5-6. Spitamenes' death: Arr. 4. 17. 7 (a much different story in the vulgate: Curt. 8. 3. 1-15; ME 20-23). Koinos rejoins Alexander: Arr. 4. 18. 1.

[21] For the Swat Campaign in general see Fuller 245 ff.; Seibert, *Eroberung* 150-154.

[22] For the identification of Bazeira (Beira) see Stein, *Alexander's Track to the Indus* 46-48; Eggermont 184.

[23] Arr. 4. 27. 5-8; Curt. 8. 10. 22 (Beira); *Itiner. Al.* 107. Ora (= Ude-gram; Stein, *Alexander's Track to the Indus* 58-60; cf. Seibert, *Eroberung* 152, with n.40, and Karten 25-26): Arr. 4. 27. 5 names Attalos, Alketas and Demetrios the hipparch as the commanders in charge of the siege of Ora; Curt. 8. 11. 1 names Polyperchon and credits him with the capture of the town. Arr. 4. 27. 7, 9 gives Alexander the honour of taking Ora.

[24] Arr. 4. 28. 8: in addition to Koinos' brigade, Alexander took the archers, the Agrianes, select troops from the phalanx, 200 Companion cavalry and 100 mounted archers.

[25] Aphrikes: Diod. 17. 86. 2; perhaps Αἰρίκης, Anspach i 32, n.92; Curt. 8. 12. 1 (Erices); ME 42 (Ariplex). Perhaps a brother of Assakenos, the deceased dynast of the Assakenians, and of Amminais (ME 39); thus also a son of Kleophis, together with whom he is found at Massaga in spring 326 B.C. (ME 42). Aphrikes attempted to block one of the passes of the Buner region (near Embolima) with a force of 20,000 Indians (Curt. 8. 12. 1; Diod. 17. 86. 2, giving him also 15 elephants) and he was killed by his own troops, who sent his head to Alexander in order to win his pardon (Diod. 17. 86. 2; Curt. 8. 12. 3 suggests that the troops may have acted out of hatred). Eggermont 183-184 sees Assakenos as ruler of the western Swat basin, Aphrikes as chief of the eastern Swat (or Udyana); Berve ii 26 identifies the unnamed brother of Assakenos (Arr. 4. 30. 5)

By the time the Makedonians reached the Hydaspes (Jhelum), Koinos had effectively become hipparch. His name continued to be applied to his former brigade, though the commander of that unit was in all probability Peithon son of Agenor (Tarn ii 190 implausibly assigns it to Antigenes). Before the battle with Poros, he was sent back to the Indus to dismantle the ships and transport them overland to the Hydaspes (Arr. 5. 8. 4). In the actual engagement, Koinos' brigade and hipparchy crossed the river upstream along with the King and took part in the initial assault on Poros:[26] he and Demetrios son of Althaimenes attacked the cavalry (about 2000 in number) on the Indian right, pursuing them as they transferred their position to the left, where Poros' horsemen were outnumbered by Alexander's.[27]

At the Akesines (Chenab) Koinos was left behind to oversee the crossing by the bulk of the army and to forage for supplies; a similar task was given also to Krateros.[28] He rejoined Alexander at or near the Hyphasis (Beas) after the bloody Sangala campaign. Here, when the troops were stubborn in their refusal to continue eastward, Koinos rose to put the soldiers' case to the King. The speeches put into his mouth by Arrian and Curtius are undoubtedly rhetorical creations of those same authors, but the essence of the arguments made will reflect accurately the feelings of the Makedonians, and of Koinos himself: in short, he reminded the King of the sufferings and losses of the army, of their desire to see their homeland and loved ones, of the need to find new and younger troops for Alexander's further expeditions.[29] Curtius adds an appeal to the poor state of the soldiers' equipment, a point which may well be true, but which contributes to the general irony of the situation: Koinos, who spoke so passionately in favour of returning to Makedonia,

---

with Amminais and distinguishes him from Aphrikes. But both are found in the city of Massaga (*ME* 39, 42, though only Amminais is described as *frater regis*; Ariplex belongs to the *amici*, that is, to the advisors, of Kleophis) and it seems odd (*pace* Berve ii 97-98) that we should find both opposing Alexander after the fall of Aornos. There are several possibilities: Arrian (4. 30. 5) may be wrong in calling the Indian leader Assakenos' brother; Diod. 17. 86. 2 and Curt. 8. 12. 1 wrongly name Aphrikes (or Erices) in place of Amminais; or, what seems most likely, the vulgate simply failed to note that Aphrikes was a member of the royal family. See further Berve ii 97-98, no. 191; id., *RE* Supplbd. iv (1924), 44; Eggermont 183-184.

[26] Arr. 5. 12. 2; Curt. 8. 14. 15, 17; Plut. *Alex.* 60.

[27] Arr. 5. 16. 3; 5. 17. 1. For a discussion of Koinos' role in the battle see Devine, *AncW* 16 (1987), 102 ff., largely summarising Hamilton, *JHS* 76 (1956), 26-31 (against Tarn ii 192 ff.). Curt. 8. 14. 15 must be emended to make sense of Koinos' activities (Devine, *Phoenix* 39 [1985], 297).

[28] Arr. 5. 21. 1, 4.

[29] Arr. 5. 27. 2-9; Curt. 9. 3. 3-15.

died soon afterwards (Curt. 9. 3. 20),[30] and there arrived shortly after his death 25,000 splendid suits of armour (9. 3. 21). Whatever suspicions his death at the Hydaspes arouses, coming as it did so soon after his opposition to Alexander, there is no good reason to assume that it was not caused by illness.[31]

Berve aptly concludes (ii 218): 'Mit K[oinos] starb einer der echtesten Makedonen des Heeres, keine der glanzvollen Erscheinungen seiner Zeit, aber in anspruchsloser, soldatischer Pflichterfüllung, in zuverlässigen Einsetzen seiner bedeutenden militärischen Gaben und nicht zuletzt in seiner aufrechten Männlichkeit einer der wertvollsten Gehilfen Al[exander]s.'

---

[30] According to Curtius, Alexander could not resist an uncharitable comment: *adiecit tamen propter paucos dies longam orationem eum exorsum, tamquam solus Macedoniam visurus esset.*

[31] Arr. 6. 2. 1. His death occurred at the Hydaspes (cf. Arr. 5. 29. 5; 6. 1. 1), not at the Hyphasis (so Berve ii 218, probably a misprint); Curt. 9. 3. 20 places his death at the Akesines (on the confusion see Hammond, *THA* 152 f.) and mentions it immediately after the speech for dramatic (ironic) effect. Badian (*JHS* 81 [1961], 22), however, comments on 'how Coenus' *rash* championship of the common soldiers at the Hyphasis was at once followed by his *opportune* death' (my italics).

2. Hephaistion: *omnium amicorum carissimus*[32]

Literature. Plaumann, *RE* viii (1913), 291-296, no. 3; Hoffmann 170 f.; Berve ii 169-175, no. 357. Cf. Kornemann 242 f.; Schachermeyr 511-515 and *passim*; cf. id., *Babylon* 31-37; Bengtson, *Philipp und Alexander* 194 f.; W. Heckel, 'Hephaistion "the Athenian"', *ZPE* 87 (1991), 39-41.

ἅπαξ δὲ περὶ τὴν Ἰνδικὴν καὶ εἰς χεῖρας ἦλθον σπασάμενοι τὰ ξίφη, καὶ τῶν φίλων ἑκατέρῳ παραβοηθούντων προσελάσας Ἀλέξανδρος ἐλοιδόρει τὸν Ἡφαιστίωνα φανερῶς, ἔμπληκτον καλῶν καὶ μαινόμενον, εἰ μὴ συνίησιν ὡς, ἐάν τις αὐτοῦ τὸν Ἀλέξανδρον ἀφέληται, μηδέν ἐστιν.

(Plut. *Alex.* 47. 11)

Once, during the Indian campaign, they [Krateros and Hephaistion] actually drew their swords and came to blows, and as the friends of each were rushing to bring aid, Alexander rode up and openly berated Hephaistion, calling him a fool and a madman if he did not know that without Alexander he was nothing.

In October 324 B.C., Hephaistion died at Ekbatana of a fever aggravated by immoderate eating and drinking.[33] He ended his life the dearest of Alexander's friends, the most influential man in the newly-won empire. From Alexander himself, the untimely death evoked an almost boundless display of grief, reminiscent, as he was doubtless aware, of Achilles' sorrow at the fate of Patroklos. Whatever the source of the parallel of Patroklos and Hephaistion, and the claim that Alexander consciously emulated Achilles, who had been his hero ἐκ παιδός (Arr. 7. 14. 4), there is no reason to doubt that the grief was genuine. The accounts of Alexander's reaction to his friend's death were many and varied, as Arrian tells us, and in each case strongly prejudiced by the φθόνος or εὐνοία that each author felt for Hephaistion or for Alexander himself.[34] Alexander's actions were unusual, indeed controversial: these manifestations of grief were not only typical of the oriental despot that he had shown increasing signs of becoming,[35] but were clear indications that the relationship between

---

[32] Curt. 3. 12. 16.

[33] Arr. 7. 14. 1; Plut. *Alex.* 72; Diod. 17. 110. 8; cf. Polyainos 4. 3. 31 (wrongly placing his death in Babylon); Beloch iii² 2. 321-322, for the date of the Kossaian campaign. An account of how Hephaistion 'drank himself to death' was also given by Ephippos of Olynthos in a work entitled Περὶ τῆς Ἀλεξάνδρου καὶ Ἡφαιστίωνος τελευτῆς (or ταφῆς: *FGrHist* 126).

[34] In spite of this statement (Arr. 7. 14. 2), the surviving accounts of Hephaistion's career and character are surprisingly consistent, reflecting no great divergence of opinion.

[35] Cf. Plut. *Pelop.* 34. 3.

Hephaistion and the King was, to use one modern scholar's phrase, 'not purely Platonic'.[36]

Hephaistion son of Amyntor came from Pella[37] and, according to Curtius (3. 12. 16), was educated along with Alexander.[38] Like the sons of other noble Makedones, he was brought up at the Court, a Page (παῖς βασιλικός) of Philip II and a *syntrophos* of his sons. Born c. 356, he entered the ranks of the Pages no later than c. 343 and heard at Mieza the lectures of Aristotle.[39] W. W. Tarn, however, questioned the existence of the famed boyhood friendship and drew attention to the hetairoi of Alexander who were exiled in the aftermath of the Pixodaros-affair, from whose number Hephaistion was conspicuously absent.[40]

Tarn also rejected, on the ground that it was a λόγος, Arrian's (1. 12. 1) remark that Hephaistion crowned the tomb of Patroklos at Ilion, often interpreted as evidence of his long-standing, intimate, friendship with Alexander, which was common knowledge already at the time of the crossing into Asia.[41] As political propaganda, Alexander's visit to

---

[36]Hamilton, *Alexander the Great* 31.

[37]Arr. 6. 28. 4; *Ind.* 18. 3. Amyntor son of Demetrios (*IG* ii² 405) may be Hephaistion's father (see below). *P.Oxy.* 2520, an epic poem on Philip of Makedon, frg. 1, line 15, reads:].ιναμυντορας·αλλ[....]αυτ[. Lobel's commentary reads: 'If ρoc could be read, which I doubt, there would emerge the possibility of a reference to Amyntor, father of Alexander's companion, Hephaestion...', *Oxyrhynchus Papyri* XXX, ed. E. Lobel, Egypt Exploration Society, Graeco-Roman Memoirs, 44 (London, 1964), 46. The adjective Πελλαῖος need not mean, however, that Hephaistion's family was from Pella, only that he was brought up there, at the Court of Philip II (cf. the case of Leonnatos).

[38]*cum ipso* [sc. *Alexandro*] *pariter eductus*. Ps.-Kall. 1. 18. 5 and Jul. Valer. 1. 10 depict Hephaistion and Alexander as boyhood friends, but their information is late and unreliable.

[39]Diog. Laert. 5. 27 mentions letters from Aristotle to Hephaistion. For the date of Aristotle's sojourn in Makedonia (343) and for a realistic view of his reputation at this time, see W. K. C. Guthrie, *A History of Greek Philosophy*, vol. 6 (Cambridge, 1981), 35 f.; against the view that he was Alexander's chief preceptor, A. H. Chroust, *Aristotle*, vol. 1 (South Bend, Indiana, 1973), 125-132, with notes on 358-364.

[40]Tarn ii 57. Named by Plut. *Alex.* 10. 4 (Ptolemy, Harpalos, Nearchos, Erigyios); Arr. 3. 6. 5 adds Erigyios' brother, Laomedon. For a full discussion see iv. Badian, *TAPA* 91 (1960), 327, regards the role of Philotas in the Pixodaros affair as significant: '...he clearly placed good relations with the king above excessive loyalty to a discredited crown prince.'

[41]Cf. Aelian, *VH* 12. 7. Fox (113) serves as an excellent example: 'Already the two were intimate, Patroclus and Achilles even to those around them; the comparison would remain to the end of their days and is proof of their life as lovers....' Cf. Luschey, *Archaeologische Mitteilungen aus Iran* 1 (1968), 121: 'Er

the site of Troy will have had great appeal for the Greek city-states; one thinks of Agesilaos' abortive sacrifice at Aulis.[42] But, if Alexander made use of the incident to promote his Panhellenic crusade, he did so through his Court historian, Kallisthenes, and the latter, it appears, did not cast Hephaistion in the role of Patroklos.[43]

Alexander, it is true, claimed descent from Achilles; for his mother belonged to the Aiakidai of Epeiros, who, from at least the late fifth century, traced their ancestry to a certain Molossos, son of Neoptolemos and Andromache.[44] And Olympias may well have encouraged her son's interest in the family hero. But many of the details that link Achilles and Alexander appear to derive from the work of the poetasters, especially a certain Choirilos of Iasos, who accompanied Alexander on the expedition and recorded his exploits in the form of an epic poem in which the King appeared as Achilles. His tribute was wasted on Alexander, who remarked: 'I would much rather be Homer's Thersites than the Achilles of Choirilos.'[45] Whether the King was consciously imitating Achilles when he grieved for Hephaistion cannot be known. Certainly writers would have been more inclined to make the comparison after 323, when both Alexander and his best friend had died young (cf. Bosworth, *Arrian* i 103 f.).

To reject the existence of the boyhood friendship on the basis of the sources' failure to mention Hephaistion in connection with the

[sc. Alexander] wird den Tod Hephaistions als eine Art Omen betrachtet haben: stirbt Patroklos, so stirbt auch bald Achill.' More credible is the generally overlooked work of B. Perrin ('Genesis and Growth of an Alexander-myth', *TAPA* 26 [1895], 56-68), where it is pointed out that the 'romantic attachment in which the two friends were delighted to pose as Achilles and Patroklos evidently dates from the last years of this period [i.e., after Gaugamela]. But romantic tradition confidently, and in a very telling way, transposes this relation to the earlier periods' (58).

[42]Xen. *Hell.* 3. 4. 3; Plut. *Agesilaos* 6. 6-11. Cf. Cawkwell, *CQ* 26 (1976), 66-67: '...Agesilaus sought, by sacrificing at Aulis as Agamemnon had done..., to give the campaign a grandiose significance, to open as it were a new chapter in the great conflict of East and West.' Cf. also J. Rehork, 'Homer, Herodot und Alexander', *Beiträge zur Alten Geschichte und deren Nachleben, Festschrift für F. Altheim* (Berlin, 1969), 257-258; Dobesch, *GB* 3 (1975), 88, n.34.

[43]Kallisthenes: Jacoby, *FGrHist* 124; Pearson, *LHA* 22-49; on the propaganda value, see Prentice, *TAPA* 54 (1923), 74-85; Brown, *AJP* 70 (1949), 233-234; cf. Golan, *Athenaeum* 66 (1988), 99 ff.

[44]See Heckel, *Chiron* 11 (1981), 79-86, esp. 80-82; cf. Bosworth, *Conquest and Empire* 39.

[45]Constant. Prophyr., *Horat. AP* 357 = *FGrHist* 153 F10a: *Poeta pessimus fuit Choerilus, qui Alexandrum secutus opera eius descripsit...cui Alexander dixisse fertur, multum malle se Thersiten iam Homeri esse quam Choerili Achillen* (cf. Jul. Valer. 1. 47). For Choirilos see Berve ii 408-409, no. 829; Crusius, *RE* iii (1899), 2361-2363, no. 5; Tarn ii 55-62.

Pixodaros affair is, however, unwise. Scholars have mistaken the ἑταῖροι of Alexander for his closest boyhood friends, his σύντροφοι, but the evidence appears to suggest that those 'friends' who were exiled by Philip in the spring of 336 were not contemporaries of the Crown Prince.[46] In fact, Alexander's closest boyhood friends remained with him.

Hephaistion's activities before the battle of Gaugamela are ill attested and derive primarily from the Vulgate,[47] but they are consistent in depicting him as one who was close to the King and whose talents were organisational rather than military. Hence Lucian (*Pro Lapsu* 8), our first reference to Hephaistion after Arrian's λόγος and purportedly based on a letter of Eumenes of Kardia to Antipatros, claims that Hephaistion gave Alexander an auspicious — though embarrassing to himself — greeting on the morning of the battle of Issos.

He next appears, on the day after that battle, in one of the most popular anecdotes about Alexander.[48] Among the captives taken after the Persian disaster were the wife, the mother and the children of Dareios III. Hearing that they mourned Dareios as already dead, Alexander sent to them Leonnatos (or possibly Laomedon[49]), who informed them that Dareios had, in fact, escaped from the battlefield of Issos and that Alexander would see to their own safety. On the following morning, Alexander, accordingly, went to visit the Persian women, accompanied by Hephaistion, who was both taller and more striking in appearance.[50] The Queen Mother, Sisygambis, began to

---

[46]See iv (Introduction).

[47]The evidence of Ps.-Kall. 1. 18. 5 and Jul. Val. 1. 10 can carry little weight, but Diogenes Laertius' evidence for a relationship between Hephaistion and Aristotle (5. 27) is supported by Curt. 3. 12. 16. Diod. 17. 114. 1, 3 mentions Alexander's love for Hephaistion and Olympias' jealousy; cf. Lucian, *Dial. mort.* 12. 4, where Philip is said to have disapproved of Alexander's devotion to Hephaistion; also Athen. 10. 435a, claiming that Alexander's indifference to women prompted Philip to send the Thessalian courtesan Kallixeina to their son. Plut. *Alex.* 28. 5 mentions a gift of little fishes from Alexander to Hephaistion (which Freya Stark, *Alexander's Path* [New York, 1958], 205, compares with the younger Kyros' gifts of food to his closest friends; cf. Xen. *Anab.* 1. 9. 25-26); he read Olympias' letters and shared Alexander's secrets: Plut. *Alex.* 39. 8; *apophth. Al.* 14 = *Mor.* 180d; *de fort. Al.* 1. 11 = *Mor.* 332f-333a, but these may refer to late in the campaign.

[48]Arr. 2. 12. 6-7; Diod. 17. 37. 5-6; 17. 114. 2; Curt. 3. 12. 15 ff.; Val. Max. 4. 7 ext 2; *Itiner. Al.* 37; *Suda* s.v. Ἡφαιστίων.

[49]See Heckel, *SIFC* 53 (1981), 272-274; cf. ii 3.

[50]*Et sicut aetate par erat regi, ita corporis habitu praestabat* (Curt. 3. 12. 16); cf. *et statura et forma praestabat* (Val. Max. 4. 7 ext 2); and ὅτι μείζων ἐφάνη ἐκεῖνος (Arr. 2. 12. 6). The scene is depicted on a painting of Veronese in the National Gallery, London. Similar references to Hephaistion's youthful appearance are made by Curtius (7. 9. 19) and Justin (12. 12. 11). According to

prostrate herself at Hephaistion's feet when one of the eunuchs pointed out the true Alexander. But the King dismissed the incident, adding that 'Hephaistion too is Alexander', and, with this gesture of magnanimity, acknowledged Hephaistion as his *alter ego*.[51]

In December 333 or January 332, Alexander bestowed upon Hephaistion the singular honour of choosing a king for the Sidonians.[52] According to Curtius and Diodoros, two 'hosts' of Hephaistion recommended for the kingship a certain Abdalonymos, a man of exceptional character and habits, whom poverty had constrained to labour as a gardener; and, indeed, he was found at his work, unperturbed by the commotions of war.[53] In spite of dramatic and cynic touches, the Vulgate gives some insight into the factional strife at Sidon, which was bound to follow the Persian defeat and the arrival of foreign troops. Abdalonymos was favoured by the popular party (Diod. 17. 47. 6), which may indeed have played a role in deposing Straton (cf. Curt. 4. 1. 16); but opposition to the appointment came from the wealthy, who sought to influence Alexander's decision by lobbying his Companions (Curt. 4. 1. 19, 24). Hephaistion's role suggests that Alexander had recognised early his best friend's administrative and organisational skills.[54]

From the accounts of the Tyrian campaign, Hephaistion is conspicuously absent. But, in late summer 332, he conveyed the fleet, and the siege-equipment, from Tyre to Gaza, a relatively minor task

---

Pliny (*NH* 34. 64; Pollitt, p. 98), Lysippos (or, as some said, Polykleitos [the younger]) produced a statue of Hephaistion; see H. Rackham's note in *Pliny: Natural History*, Loeb Classsical Library, vol. 9 (Cambridge, Mass., 1968), 174, n.b; cf. Franklin P. Johnson, *Lysippos* (Durham, N.C., 1927), 25, 230; Gebauer, *MDAI (A)* 63-64 (1938-39), 67-69, believes he can identify this. He was also identified in Aëtion's painting of the marriage of Alexander and Rhoxane, as the best man (νυμφαγωγός), standing to the right of Alexander and holding a torch; the description given by Lucian (*Aëtion* 5; Pollitt, pp. 175-176) is followed in the painting on the north wall of the Farnesina in Rome by 'Il Sodoma'. M. Bieber, *Alexander the Great in Greek and Roman Art* (Chicago, 1964), 51, identifies Hephaistion as the central figure in the battle scene of the so-called Alexander Sarcophagus from Sidon.

[51]καὶ γὰρ καὶ οὗτος Ἀλέξανδρός ἐστιν (Diod. 17. 37. 6; cf. Val. Max. 4. 7 ext 2; Arr. 2. 12. 7; *Suda* s.v. Ἡφαιστίων; Curt. 3. 12. 17). Schachermeyr 512, takes this one step further and sees Alexander as continually striving to bestow honours upon Hephaistion: 'Alexander, der in seiner Neigung für Hephaistion niemals genug zu tun glaubte....'

[52]Curt. 4. 1. 15-26; Plut. *de fort. Al.* 2. 8 = *Mor.* 340c-d (at Paphos); Diod. 17. 46. 6 ff. (at Tyre) . See Berve ii 3, no. 1, s.v. Ἀβδαλώνυμος.

[53]Justin 11. 10. 9; Diod. 17. 47. 1-6; Curt. 4. 1. 17-26; for the motif, cf. Cincinnatus in Livy 3. 26, but the story is clearly of Greek origin.

[54]Cf. Plaumann, *RE* viii (1913), 291: 'Alexander übertrug ihm die Regelung der Verwaltung in Sidon.'

now that Alexander controlled the seas.⁵⁵ After this, he is not heard of again until 331, when Alexander moved out of Egypt. Marsyas of Pella, a half-brother of Antigonos the One-Eyed and a σύντροφος of the King, records that Demosthenes tried to bring about a reconciliation with Alexander by sending to Hephaistion a young Samian (or Plataian, so Diyllos, FGrHist 73 F2) named Aristion.⁵⁶ His presence at Alexander's court is dated by an Athenian embassy, which found him there in 331; Aeschines appears to corroborate Marsyas' testimony, but it is possible that he was in fact one of the latter's sources.⁵⁷ But the information about Hephaistion comes directly from Marsyas, who was well placed to assess that man's position at Court.⁵⁸

A possible explanation of Hephaistion's role may be found in IG ii² 405, a decree of Demades granting Athenian citizenship to Amyntor son of Demetrios (Kirchner, PA 750) and his descendants in 334 B.C.⁵⁹ It is tempting to see Amyntor son of Demetrios as the father of Hephaistion. Amyntor may have used his influence (perhaps even through Hephaistion) to persuade Alexander to treat the Athenians with leniency in 335, or to back down on his demand for the expulsion of the prominent Athenian orators. At any rate, Hephaistion himself was thus, by extension, awarded Athenian citizenship and became the contact for Demosthenes at Alexander's court.⁶⁰

At Gaugamela he was wounded while 'commanding the *somatophylakes*' (τῶν σωματοφυλάκων ἡγούμενος, Diod. 17. 61. 3), which must mean that he commanded the *agema* of the hypaspists (that is, the ὑπασπισταὶ βασιλικοί). The context of his appointment to the Somatophylakes (the Seven) is not recorded, but it appears that he

---

⁵⁵Curt. 4. 5. 10. Curtius must be speaking of the Phoinikian and Kypriot fleet, which defected to Alexander after the battle of Issos. The Greek contingents were still in the Aegean with Hegelochos and Amphoteros. See Hauben, *Anc. Soc.* 7 (1976), 82 ff.

⁵⁶FGrHist 135/6 F2 = Harpokration, s.v. Ἀριστίων. For Marsyas and his history see Heckel, *Hermes* 108 (1980), 444-462. For Aristion see Berve ii 63, no. 120; Kirchner, RE ii (1896), 900, no. 12.

⁵⁷Note the close similarity between Aeschines, *In Ctesiphontem* 160, 162 and the Marsyas fragment.

⁵⁸J. A. Goldstein, *The Letters of Demosthenes* (New York, 1968), 42 f., n.33, is almost certainly correct in rejecting Badian's suggestion that Hephaistion was Demosthenes' 'powerful protector at the Court' (*JHS* 81 [1961], 34).

⁵⁹Δημάδης ‖[Δημέου Πα]ι[α]νιεὺς εἶπε‖[ν· ἐπαινέσαι] Ἀμύντορα, [ἐ‖πειδὴ εὔνοι]αν ἐνδείκν‖[υται περὶ Ἀθ]ηναίους, εἴ‖[ναι δ' Ἀμύντορ]α Δ[ημ]ητρίο‖[υ Ἀθηναῖον α]ὐτὸν καὶ ἐκ‖[γόνους αὐτο]ῦ.... See Heckel, *ZPE* 87 (1991), 39-41.

⁶⁰See C. Schwenk, *Athens in the Age of Alexander* (Chicago, 1985), 132-134, no. 24, though I see no good reason for doubting Amyntor's Makedonian connections.

THE 'NEW MEN'

replaced the obscure, but not unimportant, Ptolemaios (Berve, no. 672),[61] who died at Halikarnassos in the first year of the Asiatic campaign. If this is so, then he will have been the first of Alexander's σύντροφοι, the first of the 'New Men', to have been promoted. Ptolemaios (672), at the time of his death, had commanded hypaspists as well,[62] but it does not appear that Hephaistion replaced him both as a member of the Seven and as leader of the *agema*. In 332, we find a certain Admetos distinguishing himself in the final attack on Tyre. Tarn (ii 151) argues plausibly that he was the commander of the *agema*. In that event, Hephaistion is more likely to have been Admetos' successor.

A review of Hephaistion's career after the battle of Gaugamela illuminates his debt to his relationship with Alexander.[63] The Philotas affair and the events that followed show that he was not only the chief beneficiary of Alexander's friendship but also a skilful manipulator of the King's power of command. Hephaistion's was, in fact, an unusual career: until the death of Philotas, he held no major (independent) military command;[64] the majority of his commands thereafter were of a predominantly non-military nature, and those that did involve military skill were often conducted in concert with a more experienced commander; and he owed his promotion more to nepotism than to his own ability.[65] It is the last of these points that

[61]Perhaps the father of Ptolemaios the Somatophylax of Philip III Arrhidaios in 320 B.C. (Arr. *Succ.* 1. 38). See, however, Billows, *Antigonos* 426 ff., no. 100 ('Polemaios II, son of Polemaios I, Macedonian'), who thinks that the Somatophylax of Philip III is actually Polemaios, the nephew of Antigonos Monophthalmos. On the *agema* see vA 3.
[62]Arr. 1. 22. 4: Πτολεμαῖος ὁ σωματοφύλαξ ὁ βασιλικός, τήν τε 'Αδαίου καὶ Τιμάνδρου ἅμα οἷ τάξιν ἄγων.
[63]He was wounded in the arm at Gaugamela: Arr. 3. 15. 2; Diod. 17. 61. 3; Curt. 4. 16. 32.
[64]Polyainos 4. 3. 27 records that Hephaistion and Philotas (apparently the son of Parmenion) commanded the forces directly opposed to Phrasaortes (Polyainos' mistake for Ariobarzanes; cf. Berve ii 60-61, no. 115; ii 400, no. 813), while Alexander led the encircling forces at the Persian Gates. But both Arrian (3. 18. 4, 7-8) and Curtius (5. 4. 14-15, 29) relate that Krateros commanded the main force; Diod. 17. 68 does not understand the strategy (cf. Heckel, *Athenaeum* 58 [1980], 168-174). No other source names Hephaistion in this context. Philotas son of Parmenion appears not to have remained with the main force. Arr. 3. 18. 6 may refer to him (so Bosworth, *Arrian* i 327) and not to the taxiarch (Berve, no. 803); Curt. 5. 4. 20, 30 is clearly thinking of the hipparch. But see Milns, *GRBS* 7 (1966), 159-160; rejected by Bosworth, *CQ* 23 (1973), 252 f. As commander of the *agema* at Gaugamela (Diod. 17. 61. 3), Hephaistion was supervised directly by Alexander.
[65]So Welles, *AHW* 47; against Hamilton, *PA* 130; Kornemann 242; Berve ii 171. But see Bengtson, *Philipp und Alexander* 194: 'Hephaistion war ein tapferer Offizier, zunächst als Führer der Leibhypaspisten. Später war er der

merits first consideration; for nowhere is Hephaistion's influence more evident than in the Philotas affair.

The intricacies of the affair have already been discussed: Dimnos' plot was the catalyst that allowed Alexander's younger commanders to work for the elimination of Philotas. It would be naïve to suppose that his ruin and the sudden, unprecedented, rise of Hephaistion were in no way related. In part, Philotas had himself to blame: he was arrogant, and he disparaged the achievements of Alexander, claiming for Parmenion the credit for Makedon's victories. No less a Makedonian than Kleitos, he did not make light of his own contribution. But his overbearing and impulsive nature was inclined to arouse the hostility not so much of Alexander as of his younger Companions. These were men of the aristocracy, from whom the Makedonians drew their generals and governors. Young and eager for promotion, they were consequently jealous of another's success. Thus, while success came easily to the son of Philip's general, it was not without odium. Plutarch (*Alex.* 49. 8) says that Alexander's friends had long hated Philotas — long before his outspokenness in Egypt,[66] or even his role in the Pixodaros affair.[67] At the time of the Egyptian *epiboule*, Parmenion's influence was sufficient to deflect charges of treason. But Parmenion's power was waning, his retirement made imminent by each of Krateros' successes. At the time of Dimnos' plot, Philotas was at the mercy of his political enemies: his father in Ekbatana, his brothers dead, he was isolated within the Makedonian army.[68] The command of the Companion Cavalry was undoubtedly a coveted post, and it is not surprising that Hephaistion, who was the first amongst Alexander's friends, should cherish the hope of becoming his foremost commander — and no unit was used more effectively after Gaugamela than the Makedonian cavalry. The record of Hephaistion's dealings with individuals shows that he was of a particularly quarrelsome nature[69] and not above

Kommandeur der ersten Hipparchie der Hetairenreiterei. ...er erscheint ... als der bedeutendste Helfer des Königs neben Krateros. ... Als militärischer Führer zeigte er eine hohe Begabung....'

[66]Plut. *Alex.* 48. 4 - 49. 2; *de fort. Al.* 2. 7 = *Mor.* 339d-f; Arr. 3. 26. 1.

[67]Plut. *Alex.* 10. 3. Philip II used Philotas as an example of good conduct in a manner intended to shame Alexander. Hamilton, *PA* 26 (repeating the views expressed in *G&R* 12 [1965], 121, n.4), may be correct, however, to take παραλαβών to mean 'taking as witness' and to assume that Philotas reported Alexander's intrigues with Pixodaros to Philip. In either case, Philotas' role will not have endeared him to Alexander.

[68]Parmenion sent to Ekbatana: Arr. 3. 19. 7; Hektor's drowning: Curt. 4. 8. 7-9; Nikanor's death from illness: Arr. 3. 25. 4; Curt. 6. 6. 18-19. See also i 2. 1-2.

[69]Plut. *Alex.* 47. 11-12; *de fort Al.* 2. 4 = *Mor.* 337a; *Eum.* 2. 1-3; Arr. 7. 13. 1; 7. 14. 9. Berve ii 173 aptly describes his behaviour as 'das Benehmen eines verzogenen Kindes'. Cf. Badian, *CQ* 8 (1958), 150: 'Even the character and intrigues of the sinister Hephaestion are not illuminated by Arrian-Ptolemy.'

maligning others to Alexander, even when this afforded no obvious personal gain.[70] Philotas would be Hephaistion's first victim.

But neither Hephaistion's hatred of Philotas nor his influence with Alexander was sufficient in itself to dislodge Philotas from his command. He was a high-ranking officer, descended from a noble Makedonian family; nor had Parmenion failed to win a large following in the army. Yet Philotas' foolish handling of the news of Dimnos' conspiracy gave his adversaries the perfect opportunity to secure his elimination. Philotas' guilt cannot be proved: that he was negligent in not passing on Kebalinos' information is certain, and he may secretly have hoped that Dimnos' plot would succeed. Alexander, it appears, was still reluctant to take action against him, and he might well have shown clemency a second time had not Philotas' enemies intervened.[71]

As before in Egypt, Krateros was his most vigorous opponent, and his benefit from the destruction of Philotas and Parmenion is clear; but Krateros had already superseded Parmenion, and his success as a commander was based on his ability. What then of Hephaistion's role, which cannot be passed over lightly? Exactly how he influenced Alexander's thinking in private we cannot know; undoubtedly Alexander discussed the matter with him, and we may suppose that Hephaistion was not loathe to speak ill of Philotas.[72] Certainly Hephaistion was part of the *consilium*, which Alexander called after his initial meeting with Philotas, when he may still have been inclined towards leniency. Curtius portrays Krateros as the chief spokesman on this occasion, but Hephaistion was among those who voiced the opinion that Philotas must have been guilty of participating in Dimnos' conspiracy[73] and that he should be forced to

---

[70]Plut. *Alex*. 55. 1: Hephaistion claimed that Kallisthenes had promised to do *proskynesis* but went back on his word. Some scholars believe that Hephaistion lied 'to save his own skin' (so Brown, *AJP* 70 [1949], 244); cf. Schachermeyr 384; Hamilton, *PA* 153.

[71]Curt. 6. 7. 32 suggests that Alexander was willing to forgive him, if only he could deny complicity. Philotas could not absolve himself entirely and did admit to negligence. Alexander was, to some extent, satisfied (or, at least, he was temporarily reconciled with Philotas), though Curt. 6. 7. 35 expresses doubts about Alexander's true feelings. Nevertheless, it is clear from 6. 7. 1 ff. that a lengthy denunciation of Philotas by the other generals played no small part in influencing Alexander's decision. The case of Alexandros Lynkestes provides a good parallel: καὶ ἐδόκει τοῖς ἑταίροις μήτε πάλαι εὖ βεβουλεῦσθαι τὸ κράτιστον τοῦ ἱππικοῦ ἀνδρὶ οὐ πιστῷ ἐπιτρέψας, νῦν τε χρῆναι αὐτὸν κατὰ τάχος ἐκποδὼν ποιεῖσθαι... (Arr. 1. 25. 5).

[72]It is hard to believe Plutarch (*de fort. Al.* 2. 7 = *Mor*. 339f) that Alexander did not discuss the matter of Philotas with Hephaistion.

[73]Curt. 6. 8. 10: *nec ceteri dubitabant, quin coniurationis indicium suppressurus non fuisset nisi auctor aut particeps.*

reveal the names of his fellow-conspirators under torture.[74] Once it is decided to take action against Philotas, then Hephaistion comes to the fore. His name heads the list of those who came to Alexander's tent during the second watch on the night of Philotas' arrest.[75]

In the actual trial before the army, Hephaistion is not mentioned; Koinos and Amyntas were outspoken, both eager to repudiate their ties with Philotas.[76] By now Alexander himself had been won over by Philotas' enemies. Hephaistion's influence was on a personal level, with Alexander; his popularity with the army cannot have been great. True to his nature, he reappears as the foremost of Philotas' tormentors. The Makedonians demanded that Philotas be executed by stoning, but Hephaistion and his associates persuaded that he be tortured first: *Hephaestio autem et Craterus et Coenos tormentis veritatem exprimendam esse dixerunt* (Curt. 6. 11. 10). From Curtius' account (6. 11. 10-18) we gain a picture of the deep-rooted enmity between Philotas and Krateros — one which goes back to Philotas' disaffection in Egypt — but we also see Hephaistion's darker side; Plutarch (*Alex.* 49. 12) explicitly refers to Philotas' tormentors as οἱ περὶ τὸν Ἡφαιστίωνα. In view of Hephaistion's later dealings with rivals, and his obvious gain from Philotas' downfall, we must regard him as a most formidable opponent and no less responsible for Philotas' demise than Krateros.

One of the blackest chapters in the history of Alexander closed with the execution of Philotas and, in fearful haste, the murder of his father. The King had known all along that Parmenion's death must follow that of his son, and it is for this reason that he had resisted prosecuting the latter. For Hephaistion a new chapter opened with his appointment as hipparch of one-half of the Companion Cavalry, a direct consequence of his role in the Philotas affair.

After Philotas' execution, the command of the Companion Cavalry was divided between Hephaistion and Black Kleitos, the son of Dropides,[77]

---

[74]Curt. 6. 8. 15: *omnes igitur quaestionem de eo, ut participes sceleris indicare cogeretur, habendam esse decernunt.*

[75]Curt. 6. 8. 17: *cum paucis in regiam coeunt Hephaestion et Craterus et Coenus et Erigyius, hi ex amicis, ex armigeris autem Perdiccas et Leonnatus.*

[76]Koinos was Philotas' brother-in-law (Curt. 6. 9. 30), having married his sister only shortly before the Asiatic campaign (cf. Arr. 1. 24. 1; 1. 29. 4; cf. Dittenberger, *Syll.*³ 332). Amyntas and his brothers had been friends of Philotas (Curt. 7. 1. 11); both were perhaps σύντροφοι of Amyntas Perdikka (cf. Heckel, *Ancient Macedonia* iv 304). Amyntas himself had been named by Dimnos as a conspirator (Curt. 6. 7. 15; see Badian, *TAPA* 91 [1960], 334, n.30; Heckel, *GRBS* 16 [1975], 393-398), though his name may have been added later because of his connections with Philotas; Polemon fled from the camp after Philotas' arrest (Arr. 3. 27. 1-3; Curt. 7. 1. 10 ff.). See also Granier 42-46; Lock, *CP* 72 (1977), 101 f.

[77]See Berve ii 206-208, no. 427; Kroll, *RE* xi (1921), no. 9; cf. i 3.

since Alexander no longer thought it wise to entrust this important post to any one person, even to his closest friend (Arr. 3. 27. 4). Fear of conspiracy will not, in itself, explain this dual appointment: there were political and military factors. Politically, it was necessary to temper the elevation of the untried and abrasive Hephaistion with the appointment of Kleitos. As ilarch of the Royal Squadron (ἴλη βασιλική), Kleitos had undoubtedly been second only to Philotas in the hierarchy of the Companions, but his promotion was clearly a move to conciliate the more conservative Makedonians, who did not look with favour upon the treatment of Parmenion and his son[78] and could be expected to regard Hephaistion's promotion as blatant nepotism.[79] Furthermore, Alexander recognised that Hephaistion, whose loyalty could scarcely be called into question, was not equal to the task of commanding the entire unit.

How this division of the cavalry worked in practice is unknown, owing to the lamentably vague nature of the evidence. Of Kleitos' activities as hipparch, from his appointment to the time of his death, we know nothing.[80] At the time of his death, Kleitos had been offered the satrapy of Baktria, but it is unlikely that Alexander appointed him originally with the intention of replacing him by means of a further revision of the cavalry.[81] The sources are misleading. Two years of warfare separate Kleitos' promotion from his death, yet there is no mention of his participation in the campaigns from 330 to 328 B.C. Some scholars attribute his absence to a wound sustained in battle or to illness, though there is no hint of this in the sources.[82] Possibly an explanation is to be found in the structure of the extant histories of Alexander: the Kleitos episode is related out of its historical context

---

[78] The disapproval of the common soldier could be silenced. Alexander is alleged to have formed a 'Disciplinary Unit', the ἄτακτοι (Diod. 17. 80. 4; Justin 12. 5. 4 ff.; Curt. 7. 2. 35 ff., who says that their leader was named Leonidas). But the opposition of the aristocracy is seen in the attitudes of Kleitos (Curt. 8. 1. 52) and Hermolaos (Arr. 4. 14. 2; Curt. 8. 7. 4). Carney, *GRBS* 22 (1981), 151, goes too far in suggesting: 'It is just as likely that Clitus' new command was the result of the king's determination to play his leading officers off against one another, thus preventing them from uniting against him.'

[79] Cf. Schachermeyr 363; Fox 311.

[80] The poem of Pranichos (Berve ii 327, no. 657), if it refers to a historical incident (so Hamilton, *PA* 141), such as the defeat at the Polytimetos River (Arr. 4. 3. 7; 4. 5. 2-6. 2; Curt. 7. 6. 24; 7. 7. 30 ff.), cannot mean that Kleitos took part in the affairs at Marakanda or at the Polytimetos, as is suggested by J. Benoist-Méchin, *Alexander the Great: The Meeting of East and West*, Mary Ilford tr. (New York, 1966), 81-82. For a different interpretation of Pranichos' poem see Holt, *Alexander and Bactria* 78 f., n.118.

[81] See especially Brunt, *JHS* 83 (1963), 27-46; Griffith, *JHS* 83 (1963), 68-74; Berve i 104-112; Tarn ii 154-167; cf. also Beloch iii² 2. 322-352.

[82] Thus Fox 311. Cf. Arr. 3. 19. 8 for a previous illness.

by Plutarch and Arrian in order that the three great catastrophes (Philotas, Kleitos, Kallisthenes) may be recorded in a sequence.[83] Perhaps this format can be traced to the primary sources and, if so, these sources will have begun to conceive of Kleitos as dead, hence omitting him from their accounts of events in which he must certainly have taken part.

Hephaistion's own role also requires an explanation. Never do we hear of his commanding the half of the Companions that had been assigned to him; in fact, in the year 329, when the cavalry was Alexander's main striking force in Sogdiana, Arrian makes no mention of Hephaistion (cf. Berve ii 171), while Curtius records only that he was one of the counsellors who came to Alexander's tent before the battle with the Skythians at the Iaxartes River (Curt. 7. 7. 9). During this year it appears that the cavalry was either directly under Alexander's command or, as in the case of the attempted relief of Marakanda and the battle at the Polytimetos River,[84] divided into small detachments under minor commanders.

What we learn of Hephaistion's later career as a cavalry-officer confirms our suspicions that his promotion to hipparch was owed to his friendship with Alexander rather than to military genius. In the spring of 328, Alexander moved out of his winter-quarters in Baktria, re-crossed the Oxos River and conducted a sweep-campaign against the rebellious Sogdiani. The forces were divided into five parts, with Hephaistion commanding one contingent.[85] But the project appears to have accomplished little more than to win back several small fortresses to which the rebellious natives had fled; the most important action was fought, in that season, by Krateros against the Massagetai.[86]

---

[83]Kornemann 138, assumes that 'die Verkoppelung der beiden Katastrophen [i.e., Kleitos and Kallisthenes] in der Umgebung Alexanders erst von der Vulgata und ihr folgend von Arrian vollzogen worden ist.'

[84]Arr. 4. 5. 2 - 6. 2; Curt. 7. 7. 31 ff., for a different version. This should not lead us to Welles' conclusion (*AHW* 40) that Alexander, fearing powerful rivals, sent 'incompetents' against Spitamenes.

[85]Arr. 4. 16. 2. The other contingents were commanded by Perdikkas, Ptolemy and Alexander, while Koinos and Artabazos held a joint command; Curt. 8. 1. 1 speaks of three divisions under Alexander, Hephaistion and Koinos; Curt. 8. 1. 10 says Artabazos accompanied Hephaistion. Arrian speaks of *stratia*, implying that the entire force was divided into five parts, but a large portion of the army (the infantry-brigades of Polyperchon, Attalos, Gorgias, Meleagros and Krateros, who commanded them, Arr. 4. 16. 1, 17. 1; Curt. 8. 1. 6) was in Baktria. The main striking force in Sogdiana was the cavalry.

[86]See, however, Holt, *Alexander and Bactria* 62 f.: 'It was probably during Hephaestion's mission to colonize the eastern Oxus and its tributaries that Ai Khanoum (Alexandria-Oxiana?) was founded at the strategic juncture of the

THE 'NEW MEN'

When the columns reunited at Marakanda in the summer of 328, Hephaistion's functions began to be adapted to suit his talents. There is no reason to suppose that he had any extraordinary abilities as a general; his previous military record precludes this, and his later role as a 'utility-man' leads to the same conclusion. His first mission in Sogdiana was to synoecise the local settlements (Arr. 4. 16. 3), an assignment that was to guarantee the loyalty of the native population by means of the establishment of garrisons, while it provided Alexander with a network of communications in the region. Alexander now used Hephaistion regularly for non-military operations — perhaps these were activities that Hephaistion himself enjoyed. In fact, it is the founding of cities, the building of bridges, and the securing of communications that constitute his major contribution to Alexander's expedition.[87]

Apart from the synoecisms in Sogdiana, little else is known of his activities before the army moved into India. Curtius (8. 2. 13) tells us that, ten days after Kleitos' murder, Hephaistion was responsible for acquiring provisions for the winter of 328/7. The remainder of the campaign, which saw the death of Spitamenes and the capture of the Rock of Chorienes, does not include another reference to him.[88]

When the expedition set out for India at the end of spring 327, Hephaistion and Perdikkas were sent ahead with a substantial force to act as an advance guard, to subdue the area around Peukelaotis, and to build a boat-bridge on the Indus.[89] Berve poses the question, who had the *imperium maius* in this venture?[90] Nominally, it appears that

---

Oxus and Kochba Rivers.' Krateros against the Massagetai: Arr. 4. 17. 1; Curt. 8. 1. 6-7.

[87]Milns 112 credits Hephaistion with bridging the Euphrates river (in two places) at Thapsakos, which is interesting in view of his later activities (e.g., bridging the Indus) but his role is not documented, as far as I can tell, by the ancient sources (cf. Arr. 3. 7. 1; Curt. 4. 9. 12).

[88]There is no mention in the historical sources of Hephaistion's role in the marriage of Alexander and Rhoxane, painted by Aëtion and described by Lucian, *Aëtion* 5.

[89]Arr. 4. 22. 7-8; 4. 23. 1; 4. 30. 9; 5. 3. 5; Curt. 8. 10. 2-3; 8. 12. 4; *ME* 48. See Smith, *EHI* 53 and 63, who follows the suggestion of M. Foucher, *Sur la Frontière Indo-Afghane* (Paris, 1901), 46, that the crossing took place at Ohind or Und, sixteen miles north of Attock (Atak), which was formerly thought to be the location of Hephaistion's bridge; see also Eggermont, 'Gandhara', 102-110.

[90]Berve ii 171; cf. ii 314, where Berve suggests 'dass P. die Fußtruppen, Hephaistion die Reiter kommandierte'. This is not convincing: Perdikkas no longer commanded infantry; his brigade had been given to his brother Alketas (Berve ii 22, no. 45). Perdikkas was himself a hipparch and, if one hipparchy was inferior to another (as was the case in the last years of Alexander's reign; cf. Arr. 7. 14. 10; Diod. 18. 3. 4; App. *Syr.* 57; Plut. *Eum.* 1. 5), then Perdikkas was possibly inferior to Hephaistion in this venture.

Hephaistion had it, for Curtius' account of the dealings with Omphis, son of Taxiles, makes no mention of Perdikkas, who must certainly have been present; no details are given by Arrian.[91] It appears, however, Perdikkas' presence in this, Hephaistion's first major independent command, can be attributed to the need for a competent military man,[92] and to their apparent compatibility. In the late stages of the campaigns, both Hephaistion and Perdikkas had developed strong personal ties with Alexander, and it is not surprising that Perdikkas replaced the dead Hephaistion as Alexander's most trusted general and friend; for the two seem to have been sympathetic towards Alexander's orientalising policies.[93]

Together with Perdikkas, Hephaistion advanced to the Indus along the Kabul River valley, subduing some natives who resisted but winning the majority over by negotiation and show of force. At Peukelaotis (Pushkalavati = modern Charsada), however, they found that the local ruler, Astis, had rebelled.[94] He had perhaps been among the Indian hyparchs who had submitted to Alexander along with Omphis (Taxiles),[95] and his rebellion may have been caused not by anti-Makedonian sentiment but by the fear of his rival Sangaios, who had now allied himself with Omphis. Only after thirty days of siege did Hephaistion and Perdikkas take the city, handing it over to Sangaios, who later made an official surrender to Alexander; Astis himself was killed in the defence of his city. By the time that Alexander reached the Indus, Hephaistion had built the boat-bridge

---

[91]Curtius, who last mentions Perdikkas at 8. 10. 2, leaves him in limbo, failing to mention him in connection with Omphis (Curt. 8. 12. 6; cf. ME 48: *magnumque commeatum ab Hephaestione compara[tum in] venit* [sc. *Alexander*]; Curt. 8. 12. 15). For Omphis (*ME* 49 has Mophis) see Berve ii 369-371, no. 739, s.v. Ταξίλης. Berve's book is not properly cross-indexed, thus neither Omphis or Mophis appears in the alphabetical listing. He is in fact the Indian Ambhi (McCrindle 412 f.); cf. Smith, *EHI* 63 ff.

[92]Bengtson, *Philipp und Alexander* 194, gives a much more positive assessment of Hephaistion: 'Als militärischer Führer zeigte er eine hohe Begabung, und dies vor allem auf dem Indienzug. Hier hat er ganz im Sinn Alexanders gewirkt, und zwar nicht nur auf dem Schlachtfeld, sondern auch in der Organisation des Landes.'

[93]For his character see Miltner, *Klio* 26 (1933), 52; Schachermeyr, *Babylon* 16; also ii 5.

[94]Arr. 4. 22. 8; cf. Berve ii 89-90, no. 174, s.v. "Αστης. The MSS. of Arrian have "Αστις. Rapson, *CHI* i 318 suggests that the name 'is short for Ashtakaraja, king of the Ashtakas.' Cf. Breloer, *Bund* 108-110. The Kabul valley leads straight to Peukelaotis; the old view that Hephaistion and Perdikkas reached Peshawar via the Khyber Pass is convincingly rejected by Eggermont, 'Gandhara', 69-70; cf. Engels, *Logistics* 108. Cf. also Badian, *CQ* 37 (1987), 117-128.

[95]Arr. 4. 22. 6. So Anspach i 13; cf. Berve ii 90.

and acquired provisions, chiefly from Omphis, for the bulk of the army.[96]

In the battle with Poros at the Hydaspes (Jhelum), Hephaistion and Perdikkas both commanded cavalry and were directly under Alexander's control on the left wing;[97] more precise information is lacking. In concert with the hipparch Demetrios son of Althaimenes,[98] Hephaistion led a smaller force into the kingdom of the so-called 'cowardly' Poros (Πῶρος ὁ κακός), a cousin of the recently defeated king.[99] This man, alarmed at the friendly treatment of his namesake, left his kingdom and fled eastward to the Gandaridai.[100] Alexander pursued him as far as the Hydraotes (Ravi) river, whence he sent Hephaistion — with his own hipparchy and that of Demetrios son of Althaimenes, two brigades of infantry and half the archers — into the defector's kingdom in order to hand it over to the friendly Poros.[101] Whether 'cowardly' Poros' defection was in any way connected with the uprising among the Assakenians cannot be determined.[102] Perhaps Alexander had already intended to give the (now) friendly Poros authority over the kingdom of his namesake, who fled for this very reason. At any rate, Hephaistion's mission was primarily organisational — to oversee the transfer of the kingdom and establish a Makedonian outpost on the Akesines (cf. Arr. 5. 29. 3) — and hardly a war of conquest: Diodoros' claim (17. 93. 1) that he returned to Alexander, 'having conquered a large part of India' (πολλὴν τῆς Ἰνδικῆς καταπεπολεμηκώς), does him more than justice. He rejoined the King after the Sangala campaign — a particularly bloody undertaking[103] — and before the expedition reached the Hyphasis (Beas).[104]

Thus, in India as in Baktria-Sogdiana, Hephaistion's duties continued to be primarily non-military. With Perdikkas he had

---

[96]Arr. 5. 3. 5; Curt. 8. 10. 2-3; 12. 4, 6, 15; *ME* 48; Fuller 126-127; Breloer, *Kampf* 22.

[97]Arr. 5. 12. 2; Curt. 8. 14. 15. For the battle in general see Schubert, *RhM* 56 (1901), 543-562; Veith, *Klio* 8 (1908), 131-153; Tarn ii 190-198; Hamilton, *JHS* 76 (1956), 26-31; Devine, *AncW* 16 (1987), 91-113. See also Breloer, *Kampf* 51; Fuller 180-199; esp. 186-187.

[98]See **ix 1. 1** and Berve ii 134, no. 256.

[99]Berve ii 345, no. 684; Breloer, *Bund* 125, n.2.

[100]Diod. 17. 91. 1-2; cf. Arr. 5. 21. 3-4. The Gandaridai or Gangaridae (Curt.) were thought to live beyond the Ganges (Curt. 9. 2. 3; Diod. 17. 93. 2).

[101]Arr. 5. 21. 5; Diod. 17. 91. 2 does not give the exact composition of Hephaistion's troops (μετὰ δυνάμεως). Demetrios son of Althaimenes may have been Hephaistion's cousin (see above).

[102]Arr. 5. 20. 7; the (unnamed) hyparch there was murdered; Alexander sent Philippos son of Machatas to restore order.

[103]Just under 100 dead and over 1200 wounded, among them the Somatophylax Lysimachos (Arr. 5. 24. 5).

[104]Diod. 17. 93. 1; Curt. 9. 1. 35.

founded the city of Orobatis *en route* to the Indus[105] (which he bridged), and gathered provisions from Omphis. After transferring the territories of 'cowardly' Poros to his namesake, he established a fortified site near the Akesines (Chenab);[106] later he founded settlements at Patala and in the land of the Oreitai (Arr. 6. 21. 5). The latter, named Alexandreia, may in fact have been the synoecism of Rhambakia, which Leonnatos completed.[107]

Nevertheless, in 326 Hephaistion emerged as the most powerful of Alexander's marshals. The army had mutinied at the Hyphasis, no longer willing to proceed ever-eastward. Alexander may have felt that Koinos, the spokesman for the war-weary troops, had betrayed him.[108] Koinos soon died of illness, but Alexander, retracing his steps only grudgingly, came to rely more and more on Hephaistion.[109] On his return to the Hydaspes, Alexander appointed trierarchs for the fleet that would descend the Indus river system. Following the Athenian practice, the King assigned to his wealthiest and most prominent officers, among them Hephaistion,[110] the responsibility for meeting the expenses of the fleet. For the expedition towards the Indus delta, Alexander divided the bulk of his land forces into two parts: Hephaistion took the larger portion, including two hundred elephants, down the eastern bank, while Krateros with the smaller force descended on the west.[111] It was Alexander's custom to divide his forces whenever possible, to expedite the subjugation of enemy territory, but at this time the separation of Hephaistion and Krateros had become a virtual necessity. Friction between Alexander's dearest friends, which had existed for some time, erupted during the Indian campaign into open hand-to-hand combat, with the troops ready to come to the aid of their respective leaders.[112] Now it seemed that the only way to ease the tension was to keep the two commanders apart as much as possible.

---

[105] Arr. 4. 28. 5.

[106] Arr. 5. 29. 3. The transfer of inhabitants from neighbouring villages and the imposing of a garrison was done by Alexander himself on his return from the Hyphasis.

[107] See Hamilton, *Historia* 21 (1972), 603-608.

[108] For Koinos' speech: Arr. 5. 27. 2-9; Curt. 9. 3. 5-15; Alexander's reaction, Arr. 5. 28. 1; cf. **ii 1**.

[109] Koinos' death: Arr. 6. 2. 1; Curt. 9. 3. 20. Badian is suspicious of his sudden death: *JHS* 81 (1961), 22. Carney, 'Macedonian Aristocracy', believes that Alexander now came to regard Krateros as 'potentially dangerous' (216) and that 'he did not fear [Hephaistion] as he did Krateros' (220); but see my discussion of their relationship below. Hephaistion had rejoined Alexander before the Hyphasis mutiny (Diod. 17. 93. 1; Curt. 9. 1. 35).

[110] Nearchos, *FGrHist* 133 F1 = Arr. *Ind.* 18. 3.

[111] Arr. 6. 2. 2; Arr. *Ind.* 19. 1-3; Diod. 17. 96. 1.

[112] Plut. *Alex.* 47. 11-12; cf. Diod. 17. 114. 1-2.

The Indus proved useful. The rivals were given instructions to proceed downstream, each on his side of the river, and to await the fleet, which would join them three days' sail from the point of departure.[113] Two days after Alexander's arrival at the predestined location, Hephaistion continued south toward the junction of the Hydaspes and Akesines, toward the territory of the peoples allied to the Mallians, who had prepared to resist the invader (Arr. 6. 4. 1). By the time Hephaistion arrived, he found that Alexander (who had sailed ahead) had subdued the tribes of that region and was preparing to march directly against the Mallians; these lived between the Hydraotes and Akesines Rivers.

For this campaign, Alexander devised the following strategy. First the slower troops, Polyperchon's brigade and the elephants, were transferred to the western bank and placed under Krateros' command, as were the *hippotoxotai* and the force with which Philippos (the brother of Harpalos, the Treasurer) had followed the course of the Akesines River.[114] Hephaistion and the troops that remained with him were to march five days in advance toward the confluence of the Akesines and Hydraotes. Nearchos was to sail down the Akesines with the fleet, and Ptolemy was to follow Hephaistion's route after a delay of three days. Alexander meanwhile crossed the desert region between the rivers with the intention of taking the Mallians off guard. He hoped that those of the Mallians who escaped southward would be driven into the arms of Hephaistion, while Ptolemy would lie in wait for those who attempted to escape to the west (Arr. 6. 5. 6). The elaborate strategy proved unnecessary, for Alexander took the Mallians completely by surprise. They had not expected that the enemy would arrive from the west, through the waterless region. Those who retreated to their chief city, where Alexander was critically wounded, were slaughtered, while those of another town, if they did not find refuge in the marshes, were butchered by the forces of Perdikkas (Arr. 6. 6. 6).

The army continued southward, both Hephaistion and Krateros now occupying the eastern bank, since the terrain on the western side proved too difficult for Krateros' troops (Arr. 6. 15. 4). But before the army reached Patala news came of unrest in the west. Thus Krateros was despatched with the elephants, such Makedonians as were unfit for service (ἀπόμαχοι) and the brigades of Attalos, Meleagros and Antigenes, with instructions to police the regions of Arachosia, Drangiana and finally Karmania, where he was to rejoin Alexander.[115] For Hephaistion it must have been welcome news that Krateros, his

---

[113] Arr. *Ind.* 19. 3; Arr. 6. 4. 1; cf. Milns 227.

[114] Arr. 6. 5. 5. See Breloer, *Bund* 29-56 (despite the objections of Brunt, *Arrian* ii 443); Fuller 259-263; Smith, *EHI* 94 ff.

[115] Arr. 6. 17. 3; on the error at 6. 15. 5 see Bosworth, *CQ* 26 (1976), 127 ff.

most powerful rival, had been sent to the west; for he now became, undisputedly, Alexander's second-in-command.

At Patala, Alexander made good use of Hephaistion's organisational skills, instructing him to fortify the place while he himself sailed to the mouth of the Indus via the west arm of the river (Arr. 6. 18. 1). On his return, he found the task completed and he assigned to Hephaistion the work of fortifying the harbour and building the dockyards at the city, while he himself sailed to the Ocean along the eastern arm of the Indus (Arr. 6. 20. 1). Hephaistion appears to have completed this work by the time of Alexander's return, although it is possible that Patala harbour, which became the base for Nearchos' Ocean-fleet, was set in final order by Nearchos himself (Arr. 6. 21. 3).

Hephaistion, however, accompanied Alexander to the west. At the Arabios River, Alexander left him behind with the main force, while he, Leonnatos and Ptolemy ravaged the land of the Oreitai in three columns (Arr. 6. 21. 3; Curt. 9. 10. 6). Hephaistion, it appears, had been instructed to lead his forces to the borders of the Oreitai, where all the contingents reunited (Arr. 6. 21. 5). In the land of the Oreitai, Hephaistion made preparations for the synoecism of Rhambakia, while Alexander attended to military matters on the frontiers of Gedrosia. But Hephaistion was soon replaced by Leonnatos and sent to join Alexander, who now prepared to take the army through the Gedrosian desert (Arr. 6. 21. 5, 22. 3). Leonnatos remained behind, for a time, with the satrap Apollophanes, in order to settle affairs among the Oreitai, complete the synoecism of Rhambakia, and prepare for the needs of Nearchos, who would be stopping there *en route* to the Persian Gulf.[116]

Of Hephaistion's part in the Gedrosian expedition we know nothing, except that he accompanied Alexander. After the ordeal and a rest in Karmania, Hephaistion led the slower troops and the baggage-train into Persia along the coastal route (παρὰ θάλασσαν). Alexander took the lighter troops through the mountains to Persepolis and through the Persian Gates; Hephaistion must have followed, for the last portion of his march, the wagon-road (ἁμαξιτός) that by-passed the Gates, which Parmenion had used in the winter of 331/0, when he led a similar force.[117] On the road to Sousa, the forces were reunited. And it was at Sousa that Hephaistion reached the pinnacle of his career.

---

[116] Arr. 6. 22. 3: *Ind.* 23. 5-8; Curt. 9. 10. 7; Diod. 17. 104. 5-6; 105. 8; Pliny, *NH* 6. 97; cf. Hamilton, *Historia* 21 (1972), 603-608.

[117] Arr. 6. 28. 7. Parmenion's route around the Persian Gates: Arr. 3. 18. 1; Curt. 5. 3. 16.

From his role in the Philotas affair, we gain a picture of Hephaistion as an unpleasant, jealous individual.[118] Perhaps encouraged by his success against the rival Philotas, Hephaistion continued to be at odds with leading figures in Alexander's entourage; Kallisthenes, Eumenes, Krateros. Towards the end of his career, as we have seen, there was open conflict between Hephaistion and Krateros, who was equally ambitious but more capable. Yet Krateros' hitherto meteoric rise reached a plateau in India, when Hephaistion became a powerful and dangerous rival. There had been friction, and Alexander appears to have kept them apart deliberately. But, while the King professed to love them both dearly,[119] some of the blame for Krateros' less-than-spectacular career after 326 must be attached to Hephaistion's influence and to Alexander's willingness to promote the latter's interests.[120]

Hephaistion's dealings with individuals reveal that he was quarrelsome, deliberately incompatible. We do not know the exact nature of his quarrel with Kallisthenes, or why he maligned him. Perhaps Kallisthenes' way of life did not appeal to Hephaistion,[121] who showed an enthusiastic preference for Alexander's orientalisms and was himself given to the same excesses that at times afflicted the King.[122] Plutarch tells us that Hephaistion was sympathetic to Alexander's oriental policies — which Alexander, no doubt, explained to him and won his support for — and that he was used by Alexander in his dealings with the Persians (Plut. *Alex.* 47. 9). Perhaps this attitude toward the orientals earned him the disfavour of both Makedonians and Greeks, though his rise to power through Alexander's

---

[118]Carney, 'Macedonian Aristocracy', 221: 'One forms a picture of Alexander's closest friend which is not attractive. Yet it is easy to see why such a man would be both useful and attractive to Alexander: he was attractive to no one else, and therefore to Alexander alone.'

[119]For Alexander's devotion to Hephaistion: Curt. 3. 12. 16; Plut. *Alex.* 47. 9-10; Diod. 17. 114. 1-3; cf. Arr. 1. 12. 1; Aelian, *VH* 12. 7 (cf. Bosworth, *Arrian* i 103 f.); Lucian, *dial. mort.* 12. 4 (397). Krateros: *erat Craterus regi carus in paucis,* Curt. 6. 8. 2; ὅντινα ἴσον τῇ ἑαυτοῦ κεφαλῇ ἄγει, Arr. 7. 12. 3; cf. Plut. *Alex.* 47. 9-10; *Apophth. Al.* 29 = *Mor.* 181d; Diod. 17. 114. 1-2.

[120]Carney ('Macedonian Aristocracy') suspects Alexander's motives: '...Alexander was careful to balance the duties and honours of Krateros with those of other top men, especially with Hephaistion' (214). 'Alexander carefully monitored his activities and consciously played him off against others. Krateros was potentially dangerous ... and had to be watched closely' (216). For full discussion see **ii 4**.

[121]Arr. 4. 10; Plut. *Alex.* 53. Hephaistion shared many of the sentiments of Alexander's flatterers, who contributed to Kallisthenes' ruin.

[122]Cf. Ephippos of Olynthos and his work περὶ τῆς Ἀλεξάνδρου καὶ Ἡφαιστίωνος τελευτῆς (or ταφῆς), *FGrHist* 126, which doubtless exaggerated their vices.

favouritism was a major cause of hostility; there will have been a number of his contemporaries who encouraged rumours that Hephaistion was Alexander's minion.[123] Perhaps he organised the unpopular *proskynesis* affair, as modern scholarship likes to assume,[124] though Chares of Mytilene, whom Schachermeyr regards as Alexander's 'Chef der Kanzlei', would be a more suitable candidate for such work.[125] At any rate, Kallisthenes had promised Hephaistion that he would perform *proskynesis* — or so, at least, the latter claimed — but went back on his word. Hephaistion wasted no time in maligning Kallisthenes, once the sycophant, Demetrios son of Pythonax, had brought Kallisthenes' defiance to Alexander's attention.[126] We cannot say to what extent he carried his hostility, but he will scarcely have done anything to enhance Kallisthenes' already-declining popularity. Kallisthenes, however, made little or no effort to redeem himself.

The accounts of Hephaistion's quarrels with Eumenes are lost from the manuscripts of Arrian and Curtius.[127] Plutarch speaks of two separate occasions on which they disagreed. The first instance involved the allotment of living-quarters: Hephaistion gave the quarters previously assigned to Eumenes to the flute-player Euios.[128] This was clearly an arrogant gesture on Hephaistion's part and an affront to the Greek Eumenes, a man of no mean station. This incident is presumably one that is lost from Arrian's manuscript, for it took place at Ekbatana, precisely the historical context in which the *lacuna* occurs. The second quarrel, again the result of a relatively minor issue, involved a gift or a prize (περὶ δωρεᾶς τινος); Plutarch does not give the details.[129] The quarrels evoked Alexander's anger, first against Hephaistion (who appears to have instigated them) and later against Eumenes, and it appears that ever since the first incident the two were

---

[123] Aelian, *VH* 12. 7; Justin 12. 12. 11; Lucian, *dial. mort.* 12. 4 (397); Diod. 17. 114. 3; cf. Tarn ii 319-326, Appendix 18: 'Alexander's Attitude to Sex', esp. 321.

[124] Droysen i³ 312; Berve ii 171; Schachermeyr 383; Hamilton, *Alexander the Great* 105; *PA* 153; Wilcken 169; Welles, *AHW* 41; Green 375 f.

[125] Schachermeyr, *Babylon* 17-18; 34.

[126] Plut. *Alex.* 55. 1. For Demetrios son of Pythonax, see Arr. 4. 12. 5; see also Berve ii 134-135, no. 258; Hamilton, *PA* 153.

[127] Arr. 7. 12. 7 breaks off with the quarrels of Antipatros and Olympias, and resumes with the reconciliation of Hephaistion and Eumenes (τούτῳ τῷ λόγῳ ὑποπτήξαντα Ἡφαιστίωνα συναλλαγῆναι Εὐμενεῖ, οὐχ ἑκόντα ἑκόντι); the actual quarrel itself is lost. Curt. 10. 4. 3 breaks off at Opis and resumes with the account of Alexander's death, 10. 5. 1 ff.

[128] Plut. *Eum.* 2. 2; cf. Berve ii 155-156, no. 315, s.v. Εὔιος. Euios was himself a source of trouble, for he quarrelled with Kassandros over the boy Python (Berve ii 339, no. 678, s.v. Πύθων), so Plut. *Apophth. Al.* 20 = *Mor.* 180f.

[129] Plut. *Eum.* 2. 8. Cf. Vezin 16-17; Berve ii 156-158, no. 317; Kaerst, *RE* vi (1909), 1083 f.; for his later career see H. D. Westlake, 'Eumenes of Cardia', *Essays on the Greek Historians and Greek History* (New York, 1969), 313-330.

at odds with one another; for the cause of the enmity must be sought in the struggle for power within the army, and in the unpleasant nature of Hephaistion. Fortunately for Eumenes, the animosity and Hephaistion were short-lived; nevertheless, Eumenes was careful to avert any suspicion that he rejoiced at Hephaistion's death by proposing that honours be granted to him posthumously (Arr. 7. 14. 9; Diod. 17. 115. 1).

Most revealing, however, are the accounts of Hephaistion's stormy relations with Krateros. The two had worked together against Philotas, a common enemy; now ambition for power and Alexander's favour led inevitably to jealous rivalry. In the early stages of the campaign there had been less conflict: Krateros had been steadily proving himself the most likely man to replace Parmenion, Hephaistion was busily ingratiating himself with Alexander. Both were dear to the King, and he used them according to their abilities: Krateros for important military assignments and for dealings with Greeks and Makedonians (for he was very 'traditional' in his thinking), Hephaistion for organisational work, both in conquered territory and at the Court. But, as Hephaistion's aspirations extended to higher commands in the army, jealousy erupted into open hand-to-hand fighting, with the supporters of each ready to join in the fray (Plut. *Alex.* 47. 11). Undoubtedly this accounts for the fact that Hephaistion and Krateros were seldom in the same camp together (for any length of time) after 326.

The incident in India, where Hephaistion and Krateros came to blows, is instructive. We are told (Plut. *Alex.* 47. 11) that Alexander rode up and openly reproached Hephaistion, calling him a madman if he did not know that 'without Alexander he would be nothing' ('Αλέξανδρος ἐλοιδόρει τὸν Ἡφαιστίωνα φανερῶς, ἔμπληκτον καλῶν καὶ μαινόμενον, εἰ μὴ συνίησιν ὡς, ἐάν τις αὐτοῦ τὸν Ἀλέξανδρον ἀφέληται, μηδέν ἐστιν). This was not the case with Krateros, whom Alexander chided in private; for Krateros was not one to be dishonoured before his own troops, and before the hetairoi. Alexander recognised the value of Krateros to the King and to the army, and, undoubtedly, he was pained by the friction between Krateros and Hephaistion. His relationship with the latter, on the other hand, was a much more personal one; ruffled feathers could later be smoothed over in private. And probably he understood that Hephaistion's nature was largely to blame. No two individuals are more aptly characterised than are Hephaistion and Krateros by the epithets φιλαλέξανδρος and φιλοβασιλεύς.[130]

In view of Hephaistion's rivalry with Krateros and the previous downfalls of Philotas and Kallisthenes, the somewhat unspectacular last years of Krateros under Alexander suggest that Hephaistion's influence with Alexander had again been at work. We cannot say what would have happened had Krateros actually become Regent of

---

[130]Plut. *Alex.* 47. 10; *Apophth. Al.* 29 = *Mor.* 181d; Diod. 17. 114. 2.

Makedonia in Antipatros' place. But, for Hephaistion in Asia, the base of Alexander's integrated empire, Krateros' departure for Europe left him without a serious rival as Alexander's dearest friend and foremost general.[131]

Sousa in the spring of 324 saw not only the clearest manifestation of Alexander's orientalism in the mass-marriages between the Iranian and Makedonian nobilities, but also the culmination of Hephaistion's unusual career. Already he had become the army's most important officer, for he commanded the first hipparchy (= chiliarchy) of the Companions (Arr. 7. 14. 10). Very soon he would be crowned for his exploits on the campaign, along with the other members of the Somatophylakes (Arr. 7. 5. 6). But now he received, at the mass-mariages, what must be regarded as the greatest honour of his career, no less than a symbolic share in the empire.

For Alexander the marriage to Rhoxane, in spite of the strong romantic tradition that it had been a love-match, had been the first experiment in political marriage; Philip II had exploited political marriages to their fullest, and now Alexander secured the goodwill of the stubborn Sogdiani by marrying one of their race.[132] In 324, firmly established on the throne of the Great King, Alexander sought to legitimize his own position by marrying the Achaimenid Stateira,

---

[131]For Krateros' departure see Arr. 7. 12. 3-4. The ambitious and somewhat unscrupulous Perdikkas, however, lurked in the shadows.

[132]Alexander had given his first thoughts to political marriage in 337, at the time of the ill-advised communications with Pixodaros (Plut. *Alex.* 10. 1-4). At the Iaxartes River, some two years before his marriage to Rhoxane, he rejected a union with the daughter of the Skythian king (Arr. 4. 15. 1-5). For the marriage to Rhoxane see Arr. 4. 19. 4 - 20. 4; Plut. *Alex.* 47. 7; *de fort. Al.* 1. 11 = *Mor.* 332e; *de fort. Al.* 2. 6 = *Mor.* 338d; Curt. 8. 4. 21-30; ME 28-29; Zon. 4. 12, p. 296, 6; Strabo 11. 517. For the political motives Plut. *Alex.* 47. 8; cf. Curt. 8. 4. 25. See Hamilton, *PA* 129-130; on the marriage Renard and Servais, *L' Antiquité Classique* 24 (1955), 29-50; Tarn ii 326; but see Schachermeyr, *Babylon* 22: 'man gewinnt den Eindruck, als ob sich Roxane im Liebesleben Alexanders gegenüber den neuen, aus Staatsräson geschlossenen Ehen recht wohl zu behaupten wusste.' See Berve ii 346-347, no. 688, s.v. Ῥωξάνη. Alexander held both her father and brother in great honour, see Berve ii 292-293, no. 587, s.v. Ὀξυάρτης; ii 186, no. 392, s.v. Ἰτάνης. Rhoxane was, one might add, with the exception of Alexander's mistress Barsine (whose son Herakles is now accepted by Brunt, *RFIC* 103 [1975], 22-34, against Tarn, *JHS* 41 [1921], 18-28, and ii 330-337; cf. Berve ii 102-104, no. 206, s.v. Βαρσίνη, ii 168, no. 353, s.v. Ἡρακλῆς, who accepts his existence), the only woman to bear children by Alexander; that is to omit his fictitious children by the Indian queen Kleophis (Berve, no. 435) and Thalestris the Amazon.

daughter of Dareios III.[133] To Krateros he gave Amastris, daughter of Dareios' brother, Oxyathres, a bride worthy of the King's most capable commander.[134] But to Hephaistion he wedded Drypetis, the sister of his own bride Stateira, for, according to Arrian, 'he wished his children to be the first-cousins of Hephaistion's children'.[135] By marrying Stateira, Alexander had strengthened his claim to the rule over Asia — and clearly the marriage must have had great popular appeal for the Persians, who hoped to see the grandsons of Dareios on the throne[136] —, but he also conferred upon Hephaistion, who married his new sister-in-law, more than just the honour of relationship by marriage: this was a legitimate, though lesser, claim to a share in the empire.

Whatever the exact nature of Alexander's plans for Hephaistion — including his role as Chiliarch in the Persian sense of *hazarapatis*[137] — they were never fully realised. From Sousa, he led the bulk of the infantry to the Persian Gulf, while Alexander sailed down the Eulaios River to the coast (Arr. 7. 7. 1), and from here he followed the Tigris upstream where the army and fleet reunited (Arr. 7. 7. 6). Together they proceeded to Opis, and from Opis to Ekbatana. It was now autumn 324 B.C.

At Ekbatana Alexander offered sacrifice and celebrated athletic and literary contests.[138] There were bouts of heavy drinking, and

---

[133] Plut. *Alex.* 70. 3; *de fort. Al.* 1. 7 = *Mor.* 329e-f; Diod. 17. 107. 6; Justin 12. 10. 9-10; Arr. 7. 4. 4 (from Aristoboulos) mistakenly calls her Barsine. Berve ii 363-364, no. 722, s.v. Στάτειρα. Tarn ii 334, n. 4, followed by Hamilton, *PA* 195, thinks Barsine was her official and correct name (against Berve); Schachermeyr, *Babylon* 22, regards Barsine as her 'Mädchenname'.

[134] See Arr. 7. 4. 5; Memnon, *FGrHist* 434 F4. Berve ii 24, no. 50; Wilcken, *RE* i (1894), 1750, s.v. 'Amastris (7)'. Berve ii 291-292, no. 586, s.v. Ὀξυάθρης. See also Macurdy, *HQ* 60, 107.

[135] Arr. 7. 4. 5. For Drypetis see also Diod. 17. 107. 6; cf. Curt. 10. 5. 20. Berve ii 148, no. 290. For her death (along with her sister) at the hands of Rhoxane and Perdikkas Plut. *Alex.* 77. 6.

[136] Alexander strengthened this claim by marrying also Parysatis, daughter of Artaxerxes III Ochos, who had ruled Persia before Dareios III (Arr. 7. 4. 4). See Berve ii 306, no. 607. For the family-connections see Neuhaus, *RhM* 57 (1902), 610-623; but Bosworth, *Arrian* i 218, treats Neuhaus' theory with caution.

[137] See Junge, *Klio* 33 (1940), 13-38; E. Benveniste, *Titres et noms propres en iranien ancien* (Paris, 1966), 51-71. Cf. Schachermeyr, *Babylon* 31-37: 'Der Unterschied zum Reichsvezierat des persischen hazarapatis lag also darin, daß der Chiliarch Alexanders überhaupt keine dauernden und fixen Befugnisse zu eigen hatte, daß er nichts war, solange ihm der Herrscher keinen Auftrag gab, daß er aber als vollwertiger alter ego des Herrschers auftreten konnte, sobald ihn dieser mit einem diesbezüglichen Auftrag und einer diesbezüglichen Vertretung betraute' (36).

[138] Plut. *Alex.* 72. 1 says that some 3000 artists had arrived from Greece; cf. Arr. 7. 14. 1; Diod. 17. 110. 7-8 (dramatic contests only).

shortly thereafter Hephaistion fell ill with a fever.[139] We do not know the precise nature of his ailment; even Plutarch, who gives the most detail, is vague (*Alex.* 72. 2). Invariably, Hephaistion's death is linked with heavy drinking: Arrian implies that the drinking-bouts were the cause of Hephaistion's illness, Diodoros is more explicit, but Plutarch does not specify the cause of Hephaistion's fever, only that immoderate eating and drinking were the proximate cause of his death.[140] Ephippos of Olynthos, in his scandalous pamphlet 'On the Death of Alexander and of Hephaistion', will have attributed it solely to barbaric drinking-habits.[141] At any rate, it was on the seventh day of his illness that Hephaistion died (so Arr. 7. 14. 1). The only other details are supplied by Plutarch, according to whom, Hephaistion disregarded the strict diet imposed by his doctor Glaukos (Glaukias in Arr. 7. 14. 4), who had gone off to the theatre.[142] Eating a boiled fowl and drinking a great quantity of wine, Hephaistion heightened his fever and died (Plut. *Alex.* 72. 2); news of his deteriorating condition reached Alexander at the stadium, where he was watching the boys' races, but he returned too late and found Hephaistion already dead (Arr. 7. 14. 1).

From the accounts of what followed it is virtually impossible to separate fact from fiction. Arrian provides a catalogue of λεγόμενα, but his criteria for discerning what is reliable and what is not — when indeed he does make such an attempt — amount to little more than accepting what is honourable in a king's behaviour and rejecting what is not; in this respect he recalls the rather naïve basis for his trust in Ptolemy's *History*, which he related in the prooemium.[143] Alexander's

---

[139]The heavy drinking was exaggerated by Ephippos of Olynthos, *FGrHist* 126, and played down by Aristoboulos, 139 F62 = Arr. 7. 29. 4.

[140]For the accounts of his death: Arr. 7. 14. 1 ff.; Diod. 17. 110. 8; Polyainos 4. 3. 31 (incorrectly, it happened at Babylon!); Justin 12. 12. 11; Arr. 7. 18. 2-3; Epiktetos 2. 22. 17; Plut. *Alex.* 72; *Pelopidas* 34. 2; Nepos, *Eumenes* 2. 2; Appian, *BC* 2. 152.

[141]For Ephippos of Olynthos see Jacoby, *FGrHist* no. 126, and iiD 437-439.

[142]Plut. *Alex.* 72. 2 (Glaukos). See Berve ii 112, no. 228, s.v. Γλαυκίας.

[143]Arr. 7. 14. 2-10. In the prooemium Arrian says that he based his history on the works of Aristoboulos and Ptolemy, whom he judged to be the most reliable of the historians of Alexander 'because Aristoboulos had accompanied Alexander on the expedition, and Ptolemy, in addition to campaigning with him, was a King himself, and it would have been more despicable for him to lie than for anyone else' (*prooem.* 2). Arrian did not ignore Alexander's faults, it is true, but he coupled his criticisms of his hero with whole-hearted (often excessive) praise not only of his virtues but of his readiness to repent of his crimes (e.g. 4. 9. 1; 4. 19. 6). On the whole there is a reluctance to accept stories that cast Alexander in a bad light, and the attitude prevails that, if we are to judge Alexander's character, we must base this on all the evidence, not on a portion of it: ὅστις δὲ κακίζει Ἀλέξανδρον, μὴ μόνον ὅσα ἄξια κακίζεσθαί

grief was excessive; on this point all the sources concur, but there were some who thought it noble that he should display his sorrow, others who found it unfitting for Alexander or for any other king. Those who saw in Alexander's grief an emulation of Achilles reported that he shaved the manes of his horses and his mules, tore down city-walls, and lay upon the corpse of his Patroklos, refusing food and water; the last point is at least typical of Alexander.[144] Magnificent, indeed ostentatious, were the funeral arrangements, some of which were later cancelled at the instigation of Perdikkas, who conveyed Hephaistion's body to Babylon.[145] In his role as Great King, Alexander ordered that the sacred fire of Persia be extinguished until such time as Hephaistion's last rites had been taken care of.[146] Such were the honours accorded the dead Hephaistion. But there were stories of Alexander's anger. Blame was cast on Glaukias the physician and on the healing-god Asklepios: Glaukias was cruelly executed, and the temple of Asklepios at Ekbatana razed.[147] On the Kossaians too, a

ἐστι προφερόμενος κακιζέτω, ξύμπαντα τὰ ᾿Αλεξάνδρου εἰς ἓν χωρίον ξυναγαγών ... (7. 30. 1). For a useful discussion of Arrian's attitude to his subject see J. R. Hamilton's 'Introduction' in Aubrey de Sélincourt's Penguin translation, *Arrian: The Campaigns of Alexander* (Harmondsworth, 1971), 17-34, though Hamilton's comment (*Alexander the Great* 20) that Arrian, 'a Stoic himself, ...avoided the doctrinaire condemnation of Alexander popular in Stoic circles', falls short of expressing Arrian's willingness to make excuses for Alexander (or, at least, to overlook what is unpleasant).

[144]For Alexander's excessive grief and the agreement of the sources see Arr. 7. 14. 2; for different attitudes towards the display of emotion, Arr. 7. 14. 3. The emulation of Achilles: Arr. 7. 14. 4 (he also cut his own hair); Aelian, *VH* 7. 8; Plut. *Pelop.* 34. 2 (horses' manes, demolished walls), cf. *Alex.* 72. 3. For his refusal of food and drink, Arr. 7. 14. 8. Cf. Alexander's behaviour after Kleitos' death, Arr. 4. 9. 1 ff.; Plut. *Alex.* 51. 10 - 52. 1; Curt. 8. 2. 1 ff.

[145]For the funeral pyre: Justin 12. 12. 12; Diod. 17. 115. 5 (both put the cost at 12,000 talents); Arr. 7. 14. 8 (10,000); cf. Hamilton, *Prudentia* 16 (1984), 14. Diod. 17. 115. 6 speaks of the slaughter of 10,000 sacrificial victims; for the cancellation of Hephaistion's monument see Diod. 18. 4. 2 (who wrongly calls it the pyre, which had already been completed; see *Diodorus of Sicily*, vol. 9, Loeb Classical Library [Cambridge, Mass., 1947], R. M. Geer, tr., 21, n. 1); cf. Badian, *HSCP* 72 (1967), 200-201. According to Plut. *Alex.* 72. 5 the work was to be undertaken by Stasikrates (Deinokrates? see Berve, nos. 249, 720), who had offered to shape Mt. Athos into a giant likeness of Alexander. See Hamilton, *PA* 202. For Perdikkas' instructions to take the body to Babylon, Diod. 17. 110. 8; it is not mentioned by Arrian.

[146]For the sacred fire see Diod. 17. 114. 4. Schachermeyr, *Babylon*, 'Das persische Königsfeuer am Hof Alexanders', 38-48, esp. 47.

[147]For Glaukias' fate see Arr. 7. 14. 4; Plut. *Alex.* 72. 3 Arrian claims that Glaukias was executed for giving bad medicine, which may be the 'official version', so Berve ii 112 and Hamilton, *PA* 200. That Alexander did in fact execute Glaukias does not seem unlikely, for he was known to interfere in the

barbaric people to the west of Ekbatana, Alexander vented his anger.[148] And, not surprisingly, history was quick to discover prophecies of Hephaistion's death.[149] The 'Son of Ammon' sent envoys of Siwah to inquire if Hephaistion should be worshipped as a god; the prudent father replied that he should be revered as a hero.[150]

business of physicians (cf. his advice to Pausanias the doctor of Krateros on how to treat his patient with hellebore [Plut. *Alex.* 41. 7], or his letter to Peukestas' doctor, Alexippos, congratulating him on his healing talents [Plut. *Alex.* 41. 6]; and it is not surprising that we know the names of several other doctors in Alexander's entourage, see Berve i 79-80). For the temple of Asklepios see Epiktetos 2. 22. 17; but cf. Arr. 7. 14. 6: οὐκ ἐπιεικῶς κέχρηταί μοι ὁ Ἀσκληπιός, οὐ σώσας μοι τὸν ἑταῖρον ὅντινα ἴσον τῇ ἐμαυτοῦ κεφαλῇ ἦγον.

[148]Arr. 7. 15. 1 ff.; Diod. 17. 111. 4 ff.; Polyainos 4. 3. 31.

[149]Arr. 7. 18. 2 = Aristoboulos, *FGrHist* 139 F54. The seer Peithagoras foretold the deaths of both Alexander and Hephaistion (cf. Appian, *BC* 2. 152). The prophecy was given to Apollodoros, his brother, who feared both Hephaistion and Alexander. Had he also found Hephaistion difficult to deal with?

[150]Arr. 7. 14. 7: envoys are sent to Ammon. Arr. 7. 23. 6: the response comes that he should be revered as a hero; cf. Plut. *Alex.* 72. 3, but incorrectly that he should be deified Diod. 17. 115. 6; Justin 12. 12. 12: *eumque post mortem coli ut deum iussit*; Lucian, *Cal.* 17. The hero-cult of Hephaistion is alluded to by Hypereides 6. 21: καὶ [τ]οὺς τούτων οἰκέτας ὥσπερ ἥρωας τιμᾶν. Cf. Treves, *CR* 53 (1939), 56-57 (the cult was in place already in April/May 323); Bickerman, *Athenaeum* 41 (1963), 70-85; Habicht, *Gottmenschentum* 28-36. But P. M. Fraser, in his review of Habicht, *CR* 8 (1958), 153 f., does not think the allusion to Hephaistion is so obvious. See Hamilton's comments (*PA* 200-201), where these views are summarised; the notion that Alexander sought to introduce his own deification by means of Hephaistion's hero-cult antedates Habicht, see Kornemann, *Klio* 1 (1901), 65, who makes a good case for this. Arr. 7. 23. 6-8 relates that Alexander was willing to forgive Kleomenes (Berve, no. 431) his crimes in Egypt if he saw to a hero's shrine there.

For the small likenesses of Hephaistion made by the hetairoi see Diod. 17. 115. 1. The lion of Hamadan — 3. 56 m. long and of brown sandstone (remarkably similar in size and style to the lions of Chaironeia and Amphipolis) — may be the one surviving monument of Hephaistion. For this statue, and its history, see Luschey, *Archaeologische Mitteilungen aus Iran* 1 (1968), 115-122, esp. 121 f. Cf. Fox (435): '...centuries later, when Hephaistion had long been forgotten, the ladies of Hamadan would smear the nose of their lion with jam, hoping for children and easy childbirth. Hephaistion ended his fame as a symbol of fertility.'

3. Leonnatos: The Makedonian *Cursus Honorum*

Literature. Berve ii 232-235, no. 466; Hoffmann 168-170; Geyer, *RE* xii.2 (1925), 2035-2038, no. 1.

Leonnatos, according to the evidence of the *Suda*, was a relative of Eurydike, the mother of Philip II, hence an adherent of the Lynkestian royal house; he was a *syntrophos* of Alexander and it is presumably because he was brought up at the Court that he was referred to as Pellaian.[151] Four different patronymika are attested, but there is good reason to favour Ἀντέου (cf. Arr. *Succ.* 1a. 2, Ἄνθους).[152] About the life of Anteas nothing is known, though he was most likely an hetairos of Philip II. Leonnatos himself best illustrates the career of the gifted and well-born Makedonian.

Leonnatos appears in our sources for the first time on the day of Philip II's assassination: he is named, along with Perdikkas and Attalos (son of Andromenes?[153]), among the *somatophylakes* who pursued the assassin Pausanias (Diod. 16. 94. 4). Berve (ii 233, n.1) is certainly correct in assuming that these men were hypaspists, for neither Leonnatos nor Perdikkas was a member of the Seven in 336, nor did that unit ever include anyone named Attalos — certainly not the son of Andromenes.[154] That Perdikkas, Leonnatos and Attalos were at this time members of the Pages (παῖδες βασιλικοί) is virtually impossible:[155] Perdikkas was certainly too old, as was Leonnatos himself, to belong to the Pages; and it is doubtful that any one of them was the commander of that unit.

Whether the son of Anteas is identical with that Leonnatos named in a recently published inscription concerning Philippoi, cannot be determined.[156] The coincidental appearance on the stone of the names Leonnatos and Philotas (without patronymika) has led editors to identify the latter as Parmenion's son, and to date their mission to

---

[151] *Suda* s.v. Λεόννατος = Arr. *Succ.* 12; cf. Curt. 10. 7. 8: *stirpe regia genit[us]*. For Eurydike's connections with the Lynkestian royal house see Macurdy, *HQ* 17; Bosworth, *CQ* 21 (1971), 99-101; Geyer, *RE* xii.2 (1925), 2035; cf. also Oikonomides, *AncW* 7 (1983), 62-64. Πελλαῖος: Arr. *Anab.* 6. 28. 4; *Ind.* 18. 3.

[152] See Appendix II.

[153] So Welles, *Diodorus* 101, n.2. Hammond, *GRBS* 19 (1978), 346, n.37, implausibly identifies him with the uncle of Kleopatra-Eurydike; against this view, Heckel, *LCM* 4 (1979), 215-216. See iii 3. 3.

[154] See iii 3.

[155] Suggested by Droysen i^3 70; rejected by Geyer, *RE* xii.2 (1925), 2035.

[156] Vatin, in *Proceedings of the 8th Epigraphic Conference* i (Athens, 1984), 259-270; Missitzis, *AncW* 12 (1985), 3-14; Hammond, *CQ* 38 (1988), 382-391.

Philippoi to 'either before the Triballian campaign in 335 or before the Persian expedition in 334, when Philotas was available.'[157] We know of a certain Leonnatos son of Antipatros of Aigai, a man of some importance (Arr. *Ind.* 18. 3), who could have acted as Alexander's ambassador on this occasion; the name Philotas is far too common to allow a positive identification. The son of Anteas would have been about twenty-one or twenty-two years of age at this time, and if he is indeed the Leonnatos in question, this could perhaps be his first diplomatic mission.[158]

At Issos in late 333 B.C., the women of Dareios III (his mother, wife and daughters[159]) were captured by the Makedonians. Misled by false rumours, they believed that Dareios had fallen in battle and began to mourn him. Hence Alexander planned to free them from unnecessary sorrow by sending to them Mithrenes, the former satrap of Sardeis, who spoke Persian.[160] According to Curtius (3. 12. 7-12), however, Alexander thought that the sight of a traitor might only heighten the anguish of the captive women and sent instead Leonnatos, one of his hetairoi (*ex purpuratis* = τῶν ἑταίρων). But it may be that Leonnatos played no part in this famous episode. That the situation required someone of linguistic skill is unlikely to be mere embellishment on Curtius' part. Why, then, would Alexander substitute for Mithrenes a man who did not know the barbarian tongue? Arrian tells us that Peukestas was the only Makedonian to acquire a speaking knowledge of the Persian language,[161] but from the same source we learn that, after the battle of Issos, the King placed Laomedon — a Greek from Mytilene who had been settled in Amphipolis — in charge of the Persian captives precisely because he was bilingual.[162] And it seems odd that Alexander

---

[157] Missitzis, *AncW* 12 (1985), 9.

[158] Hammond, *CQ* 38 (1988), 383, n.2, points out that 'the lack of patronymics, especially with a name as common as that of Philotas, is striking.' This may argue in favour of identifying the Leonnatos of the inscription with the son of Anteas, but I would draw no firm conclusions.

[159] Also his young son, Ochos. For the captive women: Arr. 2. 12. 4-5; Curt. 3. 12. 4 ff.; Diod. 17. 37. 3; Plut. *Alex.* 21. 1-2. See Berve ii 356-357, no. 711, s.v. Σισύγαμβις (Dareios' mother; Diod. 17. 37 has Σισύγγαμβρις); ii 362-363, no. 721, s.v. Στάτειρα (sister and wife of the King). The daughters were named Stateira and Drypetis. For Sisygambis' family see Neuhaus, *RhM* 57 (1902), 610-623; but cf. Bosworth, *Arrian* i 218.

[160] Curt. 3. 12. 6-7; see Berve ii 262-263, no. 524. Cf. also Baumbach 39-40; Julien 27-28, for his later career as satrap of Armenia.

[161] Arr. 6. 30. 3: ...μόνος τῶν ἄλλων Μακεδόνων μεταβαλὼν τὴν Μηδικὴν καὶ φωνὴν τὴν Περσικὴν ἐκμαθὼν καὶ τἆλλα ξύμπαντα ἐς τρόπον τὸν Περσικὸν κατασκευασάμενος.

[162] Arr. 3. 6. 6: Λαομέδοντα..., ὅτι δίγλωσσος ἦν ἐς τὰ βαρβαρικὰ γράμματα, ἐπὶ τοῖς αἰχμαλώτοις βαρβάροις [κατέστησε]. But Bosworth, *Arrian* i 283 suggests that the words ἐς τὰ βαρβαρικὰ γράμματα may mean

should have a man of such ability in his inner circle of friends and not make use of him. If the story derives ultimately from Ptolemy — and this would require that Ptolemy wrote before Kleitarchos and Aristoboulos[163] — then it is possible that he deliberately substituted the name of Leonnatos for Laomedon; for Ptolemy was to fall out with his former friend, driving him out of Syria in 319.[164]

Hegesias (*ap.* Dion. Hal. *de Comp. Verb.* 18 p. 123-126R = *FGrHist* 142 F5) claims that Leonnatos and Philotas son of Parmenion brought Batis, the eunuch to whom Dareios had entrusted the garrison at Gaza, in chains to Alexander.[165] The story of how Alexander, in imitation of Achilles, dragged the captive commander behind his chariot has been rejected as fiction by W. W. Tarn and B. Perrin.[166] But Batis himself is historical, as is his surrender to Alexander. And there is no good reason for denying Leonnatos' role in bringing the eunuch to the King.

In 332/1 Leonnatos joined the Seven (the Somatophylakes), filling the position left vacant when Arybbas died of illness in Egypt.[167] This is the earliest recorded promotion to the office, but it is possible that Alexander's first appointee was Hephaistion, the successor of Ptolemaios (Berve, no. 672) who fell at Halikarnassos in the first year of the campaign (see vA 6). Up to this point, Leonnatos had accompanied the King as one of his hetairoi, though he fought as a member of the *agema* of the hypaspists. The Seven, we may suppose, fought in the immediate vicinity of the King — this, at least, is

---

'that Laomedon's bilingual capacities extended only to documents not to actual speech.' Even if this is so, Alexander clearly placed him in charge of the captive barbarians because he knew something of their language, and, for the same reason, Laomedon was the obvious person to attempt to communicate with the Persian queens.

[163]For this theory see especially Errington, *CQ* 19 (1969), 241 f. Arr. 2. 12. 5 comes from Ptolemy and Aristoboulos (so 2. 12. 6), and thus ultimately from Ptolemy; 2. 12. 6-7, by contrast, is a λόγος. Hammond, *THA* 128, traces Curtius' account of Leonnatos' visit to Kleitarchos. Kleitarchos may have taken the information from Ptolemy.

[164]Laomedon was defeated and captured by Ptolemy's general, Nikanor (Diod. 18. 43. 2; App. *Syr.* 52 says he fled to Alketas). We do not know what became of him. See also Heckel, *SIFC* 53 (1981), 272-274, and **iv 1. 2**.

[165]Arr. 2. 25. 4 (cf. *Itiner. Al.* 45) adds the information that Batis was a eunuch; cf. also Bosworth, *Arrian* i 257 f.

[166]Perrin, *TAPA* 26 (1895), 59-68; Tarn ii 265-270, Appendix 11: 'The Death of Batis.' Compare also Curt. 4. 6. 29 with Verg. *Aen.* 2. 273, as noted by Pearson, *LHA* 248, n.28; cf. Atkinson, *Curtius* i 342. For the full story in Curtius see 4. 6. 7-29.

[167]Arr. 3. 5. 5 gives the form Ἀρρύβας. The form Ἀρύββας is supported by inscriptional evidence; see Berve ii 85, no. 156; Hoffmann 176-177. The name was popular with the Aiakidai of Epeiros, and Arybbas may have been an adherent of that family, hence a relative of Alexander.

implied by their name and origin — unless they were given special commands in another sector. Hence Leonnatos, who held no independent command before the campaign in Sogdiana, is not mentioned by the sources except in non-military contexts.

According to Curtius (6. 8. 17), Leonnatos accompanied Perdikkas, Krateros, Hephaistion, Koinos and Erigyios (and some others, unnamed) to Alexander's tent shortly before Philotas' arrest in 330; for the Companions also formed the King's council.[168] It is likely that he joined his colleagues in condemning Philotas, but we have no explicit information concerning his views or his possible involvement in Philotas' torture. Certainly he was not one of the obvious beneficiaries of the affair.

He is not heard of again until the Kleitos episode (328 B.C.), again in the account given by Curtius, which poses some difficulties. According to this source, when Alexander assailed Kleitos at the banquet in Marakanda, Perdikkas and Ptolemy attempted to restrain him, while Lysimachos and Leonnatos took away his spear (Curt. 8. 1. 46); all appear to have been acting in their capacities as Somatophylakes. But Curtius' version appears to be vitiated by the testimony of Plutarch (*Alex.* 51, apparently from Chares of Mytilene[169]), which is preferred by most modern scholars.[170] Plutarch claims that a certain Aristophanes, a σωματοφύλαξ, disarmed Alexander and that the weapon was not a spear but a dagger ('Αλέξανδρος ... τὸ ἐγχειρίδιον ἐζήτει. τῶν δὲ σωματοφυλάκων ἑνὸς 'Αριστοφάνους φθάσαντος ὑφελέσθαι, Plut. *Alex.* 51. 5-6). Now the identity of this σωματοφύλαξ is a matter of some dispute, for there was no known member of the Seven named Aristophanes. Palmerius suggested 'Aristonous' (cf. Arr. 6. 28. 4), a simple and sensible emendation. Berve's rejection of it as 'nicht nur reine Willkür, sondern auch sachlich falsch'[171] in favour of an actual Aristophanes, who was a member of the hypaspists (also called *somatophylakes* on occasions[172]), has been shown by K. Ziegler to be incorrect.[173] In the very sentence in

---

[168]Cf. Arr. 1. 25. 4: ξυναγαγὼν δὲ τοὺς φίλους βουλὴν προὐτίθει, ὅ τι χρὴ ὑπὲρ 'Αλεξάνδρου γνῶναι (the case of Alexandros Lynkestes in 333 B.C.).

[169]So Schachermeyr 364. Athen. 7. 277a = *FGrHist* 125 F9 informs us that, according to Chares, Alexander was fond of apples. The throwing of apples in Plutarch's version argues for an eye-witness source. Chares gave information of this sort — from daily life at the Court — and the detail about the apples (though hardly a firm basis for evaluation) may point to Chares as the source.

[170]Brown, *AJP* 70 (1949), 237; Hamilton, *PA* 139; Schachermeyr 362 ff.; Berve ii 207-208; Kornemann 248-251. But Schubert, *RhM* 53 (1898), 99, recognises 'eine Verschmelzung von zwei verschiedenen Originalberichten.'

[171]Berve ii 69, n.2; cf. ii 74, no. 136.

[172]Berve i 28, n.1; Tarn ii 135-142; see v.

[173]'Plutarchstudien', *RhM* 84 (1935), 379-380.

which Aristophanes appears, Plutarch makes a clear distinction between the σωματοφύλαξ, who removed the dagger, and the ὑπασπισταί, whom Alexander summoned; it is doubtful that Plutarch used two different terms to apply to the same office within the same sentence. According to the 'corrected' version of Plutarch, therefore, it was Aristonous the Bodyguard, and not Lysimachos and Leonnatos, who disarmed the King. But is this actually the case?

To determine who did what in such a chaotic instance is not possible. But it also is not true that Curtius' account is vitiated by that of Plutarch. Plutarch's version involves the removal of Alexander's own dagger, which was the first weapon that he might be expected to reach for, if he carried it on his person. The wording of the Greek in this instance makes it unlikely that this was a case of Aristonous taking the dagger from Alexander; indeed, it would have been a rather comic scene. Plutarch says that Alexander searched for his dagger, but Aristonous had anticipated the events and removed it. Now, unless we are to imagine Alexander groping in vain at his waist for the weapon, which Aristonous, like some light-fingered thief, had dexterously snatched away, we must assume that the dagger lay nearby and that Aristonous, with forethought, had taken it out of harm's way. Quite different, and in no way contradictory, is the account given by Curtius, in which Alexander, in need of a weapon, snatches a spear from one of the bodyguards (*Alexander rapta lancea ex manibus armigeri*: 8. 1. 45). This then is the weapon that Leonnatos and Lysimachos wrested from Alexander, who was now incensed by the insolence of Kleitos. Certainly all the Somatophylakes were present at the banquet, as Plutarch (*Alex.* 51. 11) implies, and as we should expect. Very likely each one attempted, in his own way, to avert the disaster, but we are not in a position to say who did what.

Leonnatos, according to Arrian (4. 12. 2), ridiculed the attempt to introduce *proskynesis* at the Makedonian Court. Arrian writes:

ἀλλὰ σιγῆς γὰρ γενομένης ἐπὶ τοῖς λόγοις ἀναστάντας Περσῶν τοὺς πρεσβυτάτους ἐφεξῆς προσκυνεῖν. Λεοννάτον δέ, ἕνα τῶν ἑταίρων, ἐπειδή τις ἐδόκει τῶν Περσῶν αὐτῷ οὐκ ἐν κόσμῳ προσκυνῆσαι, τὸν δὲ ἐπιγελάσαι τῷ σχήματι τοῦ Περσοῦ ὡς ταπεινῷ· καὶ τούτῳ χαλεπήναντα τότε Ἀλέξανδρον ξυναλλαγῆναι αὖθις.

When, however, a silence fell after these words, the senior Persians arose and did obeisance one by one. Leonnatos, one of the Companions [hetairoi], thinking that one of the Persians made his obeisance ungracefully, mocked his posture as abject; Alexander was angry with him at the time, though reconciled later.

(P. A. Brunt, tr.)

Berve believes that the man in question is not Leonnatos the Somatophylax (though Arr. 2. 12. 5 calls him ἕνα τῶν ἑταίρων), since Arrian refers to him in all other instances (where he is specifically identified) as ὁ σωματοφύλαξ (4. 21. 4; 4. 24. 10; 6. 9. 3; 6. 22. 3), once he has related that Leonnatos became one of the Seven (3. 5. 5). Therefore, Berve concludes, this Leonnatos is the son of Antipatros of Aigai, the same Leonnatos whom Nearchos named as one of the trierarchs at the Hydaspes River.[174]

Berve's argument is too dogmatic and over-simplifies Arrian's use of terminology.[175] There can be no talk of consistent or inconsistent usages in Arrian: he does not apply the epithet ὁ σωματοφύλαξ to Leonnatos until 4. 21. 4 (that is, after he has related the *proskynesis* episode), nor does this epithet derive from the same source as the phrase ἕνα τῶν ἑταίρων. Both passages in which Leonnatos is described as a member of the hetairoi derive from writers other than Ptolemy, who is clearly responsible for the designation of him as Somatophylax.[176] Thus it is perfectly reasonable to find Leonnatos referred to as a member of the hetairoi at 4. 12. 2, even though he became Somatophylax at 3. 5. 5 (one does not exclude the other).[177] Furthermore, if we are to confine the argument to what is, and what is not, explicitly stated in the sources, we cannot say with certainty that Antipatros' son, Leonnatos, was a member of the hetairoi; Berve's guess (i 31) that he was may be correct, but that is implicit.

More important is the historical situation. The man who laughed at the spectacle of Persians grovelling before Alexander was a man of rank, to whom the act of prostration was abhorrent and who must certainly have regarded the Makedonian king as *primus inter pares* and Persians as inferiors.[178] This will have been true of Leonnatos the Bodyguard, who was of the highest nobility. Alexander's anger was short-lived, as we are told; he might have dealt more severely with a lesser individual. Leonnatos son of Antipatros must be regarded as the

---

[174] Berve ii 235, no. 467. Cf. Arr. *Ind.* 18. 6 = Nearchos, *FGrHist* 133 F1. He is not the son of Antipatros the Regent, who was from Paliura.

[175] 'Dass es sich nicht um den gleichnamigen Somatophylax ... handelt ..., zeigt *deutlich* [my italics] der erklärende Zusatz Arrians...ἕνα τῶν ἑταίρων' (ii 235).

[176] For Arr. 4. 12. 2 see Kornemann 142, who thinks chapters 10-12 comprise 'Einlagen...aus anderen Quellen'; cf. Strasburger 40, who categorises chapters 10-12 as λεγόμενα.

[177] The Somatophylakes were all hetairoi, though only seven hetairoi were Somatophylakes.

[178] The fact that Leonnatos himself was addicted to oriental extravagance and emulous of Alexander's ostentatious behaviour (*Suda* s.v. Λεόννατος = Arr. *Succ.* 12) does not rule out his ridiculing of Persian practices. He was, at once, attracted to the luxury of Persian royalty and contemptuous of (what he regarded as) the obsequiousness of barbarian courtiers.

less likely candidate. Arrian's use of the phrase ἕνα τῶν ἑταίρων, which does not rule out Leonnatos the Somatophylax, will more likely refer to him than to the obscure and once-attested son of Antipatros.[179] The latter's temporary disfavour with Alexander would scarcely be significant.

The same story is told by Curtius (Kleitarchos?) about Polyperchon, though in a more sensational form (8. 5. 22), while Plutarch substitutes the name of Kassandros, the eldest son of Antipatros the Regent.[180] Curtius is certainly wrong: on his own testimony, Polyperchon was not present when the *proskynesis* scene took place. Arrian tells us that Polyperchon, Attalos and Alketas were left behind with Krateros in Sogdiana to complete the subjugation of Paraitakene, while Alexander moved south into Baktria; it was in Baktria that the conspiracy of the Pages was uncovered (Arr. 4. 22. 1-2). Since Attalos, Alketas and Krateros, with whom Polyperchon had left Alexander's camp, were informed of the Pages' conspiracy by letter (Plut. *Alex*. 55. 6) and since their departure from the main camp is dated by Curtius (8. 5. 2) to before the *proskynesis* episode, it appears that Polyperchon was not present when Alexander attempted to introduce *proskynesis* and could not have ridiculed it.[181] Plutarch's failure to mention Polyperchon among those who were informed by letter is perhaps explained by Polyperchon's separate mission to Bubacene, of which only Curtius (8. 5. 2) speaks. Polyperchon, therefore, should not be connected with this incident; Curtius has confused him with Leonnatos, who certainly was present. As for Kassandros, son of Antipatros, his participation in the affair must be the product of later writers, influenced by the antipathy of Kassandros and Polyperchon, and by the tradition that Alexander was hostile to Antipatros and his sons.[182]

Leonnatos thus incurred Alexander's displeasure, though only briefly, as Arrian implies and as we may deduce from his career.[183] Badian (followed by Hamilton, *PA* 54) speaks of this incident as 'retard[ing] his advancement' and believes that Leonnatos 'rehabilitated himself by outstanding courage', whereby Badian must

---

[179]Arrian mentions no other Leonnatos in the *Anabasis*. The name is only twice attested in this period, but it is known in later times; cf. Hoffmann 168-169, n.75. See also Badian, *TAPA* 91 (1960), 337, n.34, who rejects Berve's identification with Leonnatos no. 467.

[180]Plut. *Alex*. 74. 2-5; cf. Hamilton, *PA* 206. See Berve ii 201-202, no. 414, s.v. Κάσσανδρος.

[181]Berve ii 326 believes that 'die Tatsache [i.e., Polyperchon ridiculing the Persians] selbst ist nicht zu bezweifeln, zumal sie zu dem starr makedonischen Charakter des P. stimmt....' See further Heckel, *AJP* 99 (1978), 459-461, and iii 5.

[182]Plut. *Alex*. 74. 2: Μάλιστα δ' Ἀντίπατρον ἐφοβεῖτο καὶ τοὺς παῖδας, ὧν Ἰόλας μὲν ἀρχιοινοχόος ἦν, ὁ δὲ Κάσανδρος ἀφῖκτο μὲν νεωστί....

[183]In the case of Polyperchon, Curt. 8. 6. 1 says that his disfavour lasted some time: *Polyperconti quidem postea castigato diu ignovit*.

refer to the heroism against the Mallians.[184] But Alexander's anger must have been very short-lived, for Leonnatos' military career, which had only begun in the spring of 327 (i.e., just before the experiment with *proskynesis*), suffered nothing adverse when the army set out for India at the end of spring of that same year.[185]

If we are to single out any event that may have won back the King's favour for Leonnatos, we might consider his role in saving Alexander from Hermolaos' conspiracy. According to Curtius, Eurylochos, the brother of Charikles, brought the news of the Pages' conspiracy to Alexander through the agency of Ptolemy, son of Lagos, and Leonnatos.[186] Arrian does not mention Leonnatos, only Ptolemy, who was doubtless eager to win for himself sole credit for the disclosure.[187] We know nothing further of his activities in this connection.

Leonnatos' first military command dates to the spring of 327 and, therefore, chronologically before the conspiracy of the Pages. This involved the leadership of the forces that besieged the 'Rock of Chorienes' by night, a task that Leonnatos fulfilled in rotation with his fellow Somatophylakes, Perdikkas and Ptolemy.[188] We know nothing else about this command, but it marks (as far as we can tell) Leonnatos' entry into the military sphere. When the army left Baktria for India, with Hephaistion and Perdikkas sent to the Indus,[189] Leonnatos and Ptolemy emerged as prominent commanders of that segment of the army under Alexander's personal leadership. Both were wounded in the territory around the Choes River (Arr. 4. 23. 3),[190] though not seriously, for each commanded one-third of Alexander's

---

[184]Badian, *TAPA* 91 (1960), 337: '...Leonnatus seems to have incurred the king's displeasure by contributing to the ridicule that killed the attempt to introduce *proskynesis* among the Macedonians. This must have retarded his advancement. When he rehabilitated himself by outstanding courage and loyalty, his rise was rapid, culminating in the great honor he received at Susa.'

[185]The affair of the Pages, and the arrest of Kallisthenes, occurred in Baktria in 327 (Arr. 4. 22. 2); the *proskynesis* episode must have been shortly before this, and after the marriage of Alexander and Rhoxane. Cf. Berve ii 346-347, no. 688 (Rhoxane); id., *Klio* 31 (1938), 152 f.; Brown, *AJP* 70 (1949), 249; Fox 320 ff.

[186]Curt. 8. 6. 22. See Berve ii 159, no. 322 (Eurylochos); ii 407, no. 824 (Charikles); cf. Brown, *AJP* 70 (1949), 240 ff.; Seibert, *Ptolemaios* 18 f.

[187]Arr. 4. 13. 7. Cf. Berve ii 152-153, no. 305 (Hermolaos); ii 191-199, no. 408 (Kallisthenes). See Seibert, *Ptolemaios* 18 f.; Strasburger 40; Kornemann 143.

[188]Arr. 4. 21. 4. Cf. F. von Schwarz, *Alexanders des Grossen Feldzüge in Turkestan* (Munich, 1893), 21-23, 83 ff.; Fuller 244 f. For the identification of Chorienes and Sisimithres (as recognised by Berve ii 354 f., no. 708) see Heckel, *Athenaeum* 64 (1986), 223-226, against Bosworth, *JHS* 101 (1981), 29 ff.

[189]Arr. 4. 22. 7; 4. 30. 9; 5. 3. 5; Curt. 8. 10. 2-3; ME 48; Smith, *EHI* 53, 63.

[190]The Choes is probably the Kunar (thus Brunt, *Arrian* i 508); Engels, *Logistics* 108, identifies it with the Choaspes, which must be the Swat.

THE 'NEW MEN'

forces in the campaign that drove the Aspasians into the hills; Leonnatos' forces included the brigades of pezhetairoi under the command of Attalos son of Andromenes and Balakros.[191] While Ptolemy relates the activities of his own division in some detail, we know little about Leonnatos' forces other than that they were equally successful in driving the Aspasians from their positions in the hills and bringing about their defeat (Arr. 4. 25. 3). Leonnatos had, at least, proved himself a competent commander.

At the Hydaspes (Jhelum) River, Alexander faced Poros with his entire force and, since he had more experienced military men at his disposal, he used Leonnatos in a lesser capacity. Curtius names Leonnatos as an infantry commander, together with Antigenes and Tauron,[192] and says that he crossed the Hydaspes some distance upstream from the main camp that faced Poros' army. But Berve has correctly maintained that a comparison of the texts of Arrian and Curtius reveals that Curtius has mistaken Leonnatos for Seleukos, and that the infantry in question are, in fact, the hypaspists (Arr. 5. 12. 1 ff. Berve ii 233). Other than this, there is no mention of Leonnatos in the battle against Poros.

Presumably his activities were similar to those of Ptolemy, with whom he shared the rank of Somatophylax and whose earlier military career was somewhat similar.[193] But this is of little help, for we know only that the Somatophylakes, Perdikkas, Ptolemy and Lysimachos, crossed the Hydaspes in the same triakonter as Alexander;[194] of the other Somatophylakes Arrian says nothing, though Hephaistion, as hipparch, certainly crossed the river at the same time. Curtius, on the other hand, is of little use, for he greatly exaggerates the role and importance of Ptolemy in this battle (Curt. 8. 13. 17-27). We must assume that, as Somatophylax, Leonnatos accompanied Alexander when he crossed the Hydaspes and that he fought among the troops that were directly under Alexander's control, namely, the cavalry-units of Hephaistion and Perdikkas and the *ile basilike* (Arr. 5. 16; Curt. 8. 14. 15).

On the march to the Hyphasis (Beas) and back Leonnatos did not distinguish himself in any way. His name reappears in the list of some thirty trierarchs at the Hydaspes River in late 326, and some three or

---

[191] Arr. 4. 24. 10. Cf. Berve ii 101, no. 201 (Balakros); Kaerst, *RE* ii.2 (1896), 2816, no. 4.

[192] Curt. 8. 14. 15. Cf. Berve ii 41, no. 83 (Antigenes); ii 371-372, no. 741 (Tauron).

[193] Berve ii 329-335, no. 668. Seibert, *Ptolemaios*, omits this part of Ptolemy's career entirely. Leonnatos and Ptolemy appear together in a number of instances during these years: Curt. 8. 1. 45-46; Arr. 4. 21. 4; Curt. 8. 6. 22; Arr. 4. 23. 3; 4. 24. 10; 4. 25. 2-4; Curt. 8. 14. 15; Plut. *Mor.* 344d; Arr. 6. 28. 4.

[194] Arr. 5. 13. 1. But cf. Berve ii 172, n.1.

four months after the battle with Poros.[195] These thirty were given trierarchies of the Attic type, that is, they were responsible for meeting the expenses of fitting out a trireme.[196] But he did not command a ship; this is clear from the roles of some of the other trierarchs and from Leonnatos' activities near Patala.[197] Since he was among the forces that habitually accompanied the King, he very likely sailed down-river with him as far as the confluence of the Hydaspes and the Akesines (Chenab) and later accompanied him by land in the campaign against the Mallians, who lived between the Akesines and Hydraotes (Ravi) Rivers (Arr. 6. 2. 3 ff.; Curt. 9. 3. 24).

It was in this campaign against the Mallians that Leonnatos played one of his most noteworthy — though again disputed — roles. Alexander had taken the Mallians by surprise, crossing the desert that lay between the rivers, rather than marching north, as the Indians themselves anticipated, from the junction of the rivers.[198] When the Mallians withdrew to their main city, Alexander sought to inspire his war-weary Makedonians by being the first to scale the city-walls. This nearly ended in disaster; for very few of the Makedonians managed to join Alexander at the top before the ladders gave way under the weight of the troops. Alexander, seeing that he was cut off, leapt from the walls inside the city, where he was wounded by an enemy missile.[199] Several of his followers rushed to his aid, though the sources disagree on exactly who these were. One is certain: Peukestas, who was later appointed an eighth Somatophylax for his part in saving the King's life.[200] The rest are problematic. Aristonous and Ptolemy are named, the former only by Curtius; Ptolemy himself

---

[195] Arr. *Ind.* 18. 3-10 = Nearchos, *FGrHist* 133 F1. For a discussion of the chronology of Alexander's expedition see Beloch iii² 2. 304-322, 'Die Chronologie der Feldzüge Alexanders', esp. 320. The departure of the fleet and the land-forces is dated by Strabo 15. 1. 17 C691 (= Aristoboulos, *FGrHist* 139 F35) to 'a few days before the setting of the Pleiades' (πρὸ δύσεως Πληιάδος οὐ πολλαῖς ἡμέραις).

[196] See most recently Hauben, *Anc. Soc.* 7 (1976), 91; Wilcken 188 suggested that this had a further consideration: 'to give a personal interest in the enterprise to his immediate followers'. See also Berve i 165 f.

[197] E.g., Hephaistion and Krateros, who commanded the land-forces in the descent of the Indus. For Leonnatos' activities see below.

[198] Arr. 6. 4, esp. 6. 4. 3; Curt. 9. 4. 15 ff. is ignorant of Alexander's strategy. See Fuller 259-263; Wilcken 190; Hamilton, *PA* 176; Smith, *EHI* 98 ff.; Breloer, *Bund* 29 ff.

[199] Arr. 6. 8. 4 - 13. 5 for a full account of Alexander's activities; cf. Curt. 9. 4. 26 - 5. 30; Diod. 17. 98. 1 - 100. 1; Plut. *Alex.* 63; *Mor.* 327b; 341c; 343d; 344c-d; Strabo 15. 1. 33 C701; Justin 12. 9. 3-13; Oros. 3. 19. 6-10; *Itiner. Al.* 115-116; *ME* 76-77; cf. Ps.-Kall. 3. 4. 12-15; Zon. 4. 13; p. 299, 16; cf. also Hamilton, *PA* 176 ff.; Kornemann 82-85.

[200] Berve ii 318-319, no. 634; Hoffmann 177-178; Arr. 6. 28. 3-4.

(in conflict with the testimony of Kleitarchos) said that he was not present at the battle.[201] Three others are mentioned by various sources: Habreas and Limnaios (= Timaeus), both killed in the skirmish,[202] and Leonnatos, who for his heroism was crowned at Sousa by Alexander.[203]

Both Habreas and Leonnatos are disputed, as Arrian (6. 11. 7) tells us. But this does not mean, as Berve suggests, that '[Limnaios] wird von einem Teil der Überlieferung ... an Stelle des auch nicht sicher bezeugten Leonnatos ... beim kampf um die berühmte Mallerstadt genannt' (Berve ii 237). Plutarch (*Alex.* 63; *Mor.* 327b) does fail to mention Leonnatos, but he does not substitute Limnaios for Leonnatos (in fact, they appear together in *Mor.* 344d). Instead the Limnaios-Timaeus of Plutarch-Curtius replaces Habreas, who is known only to Arrian (Ptolemy and/or Aristoboulos).[204] But, when Arrian says that there was no agreement on the matter of Leonnatos (ὑπὲρ Λεοννάτου δὲ οὐκέτι ξυμφέρονται), he must mean that Leonnatos was not named by every work that he consulted; this is indeed true of the *extant* authors. If the extant records reflect accurately their primary sources, then this means that Arrian's sources were not unanimous on the subject of Leonnatos among the Mallians. If there was a dispute about individuals, it involved Limnaios and Habreas, both of whom were killed in the battle. Certainly, it will have been easier to confuse the names of the obscure dead than of a wounded, but living, hero.

From the city of the Mallians to the junction of the Akesines and Hydraotes, and thence to Patala, Leonnatos accompanied Alexander by ship. In the first instance, this will have been on account of his wounds, in the second, because he belonged to *eos ..., qui comitari eum* [sc. *Alexandrum*] *solebant*, whom Curtius speaks of as accompanying Alexander by ship (Curt. 9. 8. 3). At Patala, Leonnatos, now recovered from his wounds, led a force of one thousand cavalry and eight

---

[201]Curt. 9. 5. 21: *Ptolomaeum, qui postea regnavit, huic pugnae adfuisse auctor est Clitarchus et Timagenes; sed ipse, scilicet gloriae suae non refragatus afuisse se, missum in expeditionem, memoriae tradidit.* Cf. Arr. 6. 11. 8; 6. 5. 6-7; Kornemann 82-85. See also Errington, *CQ* 19 (1969), 235, 239.

[202]Berve ii 5-6, no. 6, s.v. Ἀβρέας; Kirchner, *RE* i.1 (1893), 110; Hoffmann 222; he is named only by Arrian, whom Droysen i³ 368 f., follows; cf. Schachermeyr 455; Kornemann 254. Limnaios (Plut.), Timaeus (Curt.), see Berve ii 237, no. 474, s.v. Λιμναῖος; Hoffmann 147.

[203]Curt. 9. 5. 15, 17 (with Peukestas, Aristonous, Timaeus); Plut. *Mor.* 344d (with Ptolemy, Limnaios); not mentioned by *Mor.* 327b (only Ptolemy and Limnaios); Arr. *Ind.* 19. 8 = Nearchos, *FGrHist* 133 F1 (with Peukestas); Arr. 6. 9. 3; 6. 10. 1-2 (with Peukestas, Habreas); 6. 11. 7 (his role is not attested by all sources). And cf. Arr. *Ind.* 23. 6; Arr. 7. 5. 5, where he is crowned, in part for saving Alexander's life.

[204]For the confusion of Habreas and Limnaios (Timaeus) see my groupings above, where it is clear that there is no confusion of Limnaios for Leonnatos (against Berve ii 237).

thousand hoplites and lightly armed troops along the shore of the island (which formed the delta of the Indus) while Alexander took the fleet to the Ocean via the western arm of the river (Arr. 6. 18. 3). With Alexander returning upstream, Leonnatos now retraced his steps to Patala. From there he accompanied the King, by land, along the eastern arm of the river as far as a great lake, where he remained in charge of his own troops and those ships with their crews that Alexander left behind as he took a smaller detachment to the Ocean (Arr. 6. 20. 3). When Alexander returned, it seems, Leonnatos led the land forces back to Patala.

Having reached the Ocean, Alexander now gave thought to returning to the west. Presumably his native informants had told him that the region to the west lacked water, and so he sent Leonnatos ahead to dig wells along the route that the army was to follow (Curt. 9. 10. 2). When he had completed this task, Leonnatos awaited Alexander on the borders of the land of the Oreitai; this was late in the summer of 325 (Beloch iii^2 2. 320). Reaching the Arabios River, Alexander left the bulk of the army under the command of Hephaistion and, dividing the rest of the army into three parts (as he had done against the Aspasians two years earlier), under the command of Ptolemy, Leonnatos and himself, he moved south of the Arabios into the territory of the Oreitai, who had not submitted to him. By means of a vigorous sweep-programme, like the one he had employed in Sogdiana in 329, Alexander ravaged the land and subdued the Oreitai.[205] The columns of Ptolemy and Leonnatos reunited first with Alexander and then with Hephaistion's troops. In one body they proceeded to Rhambakia, where Hephaistion was left to settle the city, while Alexander took a force to the Gedrosian border, where the Oreitai and the Gedrosians were preparing to resist (Arr. 6. 21. 5 - 22. 2). When these had been overcome without much difficulty, Alexander sent Leonnatos, together with Apollophanes, whom he had appointed satrap of the area, to Rhambakia, presumably with instructions to send Hephaistion ahead to Gedrosia. But Leonnatos, with the Agrianes, some archers and cavalry, and a force of mercenary cavalry and infantry, was ordered to remain in the land of the Oreitai (ἐν Ὤροις), with instructions 'to await the fleet until it sailed past this region, to synoecise the city and to settle affairs among the Oreitai' (Arr. 6. 22. 3).[206] J. R. Hamilton[207] has argued convincingly that not only does ἐν Ὤροις mean 'among the Oreitai' but the use of the definite article in τὴν πόλιν ξυνοικίζειν refers to the city mentioned previously (i.e.,

---

[205]Curt. 9. 10. 6-7; Diod. 17. 104. 5-6; cf. the similar strategy in Sogdiana, Arr. 4. 16. 1-3; Curt. 8. 1. 1 ff.

[206]τό τε ναυτικὸν ὑπομένειν ἔστ' ἂν περιπλεύσῃ τὴν χώραν καὶ τὴν πόλιν ξυνοικίζειν καὶ τὰ κατὰ τοὺς Ὠρείτας κοσμεῖν.

[207]*Historia* 21 (1972), 605 f.

Rhambakia, which Hephaistion had begun to synoecise),[208] and not another city, as was formerly thought.[209]

Sometime between Alexander's departure and the arrival of Nearchos with the fleet, Leonnatos won an impressive victory over the Oreitai, who had risen against him. According to the partisan account of Nearchos, he inflicted upon the enemy heavy casualties: 'he killed six thousand of them, and all their leaders'.[210] And of his own forces Leonnatos lost only fifteen cavalrymen and a handful of infantry; though Apollophanes the satrap fell in the battle.[211] When Nearchos arrived at the shore near Rhambakia (Arr. 6. 22. 3; cf. *Ind*. 23 = 133 F1), Leonnatos had prepared provisions for his Ocean voyage. He also exchanged troops with Nearchos, taking with him those men who, on account of their laziness, had caused or might cause disciplinary problems in the fleet (Arr. *Ind*. 23. 8). After Nearchos' departure, Leonnatos put everything in order among the Oreitai (as he had been instructed) and set out for Gedrosia by land. The news of his exploits had already reached Alexander by letter (Curt. 9. 10. 19), but it is uncertain where Leonnatos himself rejoined Alexander; perhaps it was in Karmania, though possibly only at Sousa.

Sousa marked the high-point in Leonnatos' career under Alexander. He was awarded a golden crown in honour of his courage in India and his victory over the Oreitai.[212] Presumably he took a Persian bride in the marriage-ceremony at Sousa, though we have no record of this; nor is there any mention of his bride. Whoever she was, she was doubtless repudiated by Leonnatos shortly afterwards and, unlike Amastris, the Persian bride of Krateros, has no known history under the Diadochoi.[213]

When Alexander died suddenly in Babylon, Leonnatos emerged as one of the leading men of the succession crisis: together with Perdikkas and Ptolemy, he belonged to οἱ μέγιστοι τῶν ἱππέων καὶ τῶν ἡγεμόνων, as opposed to those lesser lights, [οἱ] μετ' ἐκείνους (Arr. *Succ*. 1a. 2). In the debate that followed, in which the supporters of Perdikkas proposed that Rhoxane's child (if male) should inherit the kingdom, it was suggested by Peithon, one of the Bodyguard, that Leonnatos share with

---

[208] Arr. 6. 21. 5.

[209] Wilcken 199; see also the literature cited by Hamilton, *Historia* 21 (1972), 603, n.1; Droysen i³ 391, appears to agree with Hamilton that Leonnatos finished Hephaistion's work at Rhambakia: 'die Kolonisation der neuen Stadt zu vollenden.'

[210] Arr. *Ind*. 23. 5 = Nearchos, *FGrHist* 133 F1; cf. Curt. 9. 10. 19.

[211] On the fate of Apollophanes see Badian, *JHS* 81 (1961), 21.

[212] Arr. *Ind*. 23. 6; 42. 9; *Anab*. 7. 5. 5. It is doubtful that he was crowned a second time when 'Hephaistion and the other Somatophylakes' were crowned (7. 5. 6).

[213] Berve ii 24, no. 50, s.v. Ἀμαστρις; cf. Wilcken, *RE* i.2 (1894), 1750, no. 7.

Perdikkas the guardianship of the child, on the ground that both were of royal stock (*stirpe regia genitos*: Curt. 10. 7. 8).[214] But when the common soldiery, incited by Meleagros, declared for the feeble Arrhidaios, whom they hailed as King under the title Philip III, Leonnatos led the cavalry, the backbone of Perdikkas' support, outside the city of Babylon, while Perdikkas himself remained within the city in the hope of winning over the infantry. Perdikkas' stay was brief, owing to the hostility of Meleagros, who induced Arrhidaios to order his assassination, and he soon rejoined Leonnatos and the cavalry (Curt. 10. 7. 20, 8. 4). At this point our knowledge of Leonnatos' activities in the struggle for power at Babylon breaks off, for his cause was essentially that of Perdikkas, the dominant figure in the ancient sources.[215] Whatever Leonnatos' expectations were (and his earlier naming as a guardian together with Perdikkas — whose ambitious designs Leonnatos was intended to keep in check — suggests that he could have hoped for considerable power), he must have been disappointed by the outcome. Perdikkas, once he had overcome Meleagros, became the *de facto* ruler of the Asian empire, for he had both the figure-head, Philip Arrhidaios, and the royal armies firmly under his control; there was no further talk of special authority for Leonnatos once the cavalry and infantry had been reconciled.

In the settlement at Babylon (323), Leonnatos found himself sidelined. A strong supporter of Perdikkas (at least in the struggle with Meleagros), he must have been dissatisfied with the satrapy of Hellespontine Phrygia, despite its strategic location.[216] Did Perdikkas, in fact, think that Leonnatos would act in his interests? If so, he was quickly disappointed, for Leonnatos began immediately to intrigue against Perdikkas and the marshals of the empire. He had been contacted by the sister of Alexander, the widow of Alexandros of Epeiros, Kleopatra, through whom he hoped to gain power; for she had offered her hand in marriage, perhaps at Olympias' instigation, and such a marriage carried with it a serious — possibly 'legitimate' — claim to the throne of Makedon.[217]

---

[214]Cf. Justin 13. 2. 13-14.

[215]That Leonnatos whole-heartedly supported Perdikkas' regency is doubtful, but the high-ranking officers will have been unanimous in their opposition to Meleagros and Philip Arrhidaios.

[216]Arr. *Succ.* 1a. 6; 1b. 2; Curt. 10. 10. 2; Diod. 18. 3. 1, and 18. 12. 1 (where 'Philotas' occurs instead of Leonnatos); Justin 13. 4. 16. Consider Errington's remarks: 'Leonnatus acquired a crucial satrapy in exchange — which Perdiccas could scarcely deny him — but his subsequent career shows his thwarted ambition, and his later disloyalty to Perdiccas may have originated in this rebuff' (*JHS* 90 [1970], 57).

[217]Plut. *Eum.* 3. 9. For Kleopatra see Berve ii 212-213, no. 433; Stähelin, *RE* xi.1 (1921), 735-738, no. 13. See also Macurdy, *HQ* 30 ff., esp. 36-37; Droysen ii³

THE 'NEW MEN'

Leonnatos certainly was not content to play second fiddle to Perdikkas. When he received orders to aid Eumenes in wresting Kappadokia from Ariarathes (Plut. *Eum.* 3. 4-5), he had already formulated his plan to overthrow Perdikkas. Undoubtedly he was encouraged by the insubordination of Antigonos, satrap of Phrygia, who refused Perdikkas' instructions that he also should support Eumenes; nor will he have failed to recognise that Perdikkas did not have the strong backing of the generals. Peithon, Ptolemy, Philotas, Antigonos, all were seditious.[218] And renewed turmoil in Greece offered Leonnatos his pretext for crossing the Hellespont and seeking the throne; for Antipatros, blockaded at Lamia in Thessaly by the allied Greek forces, sent Hekataios of Kardia to summon him to Greece.[219]

At this point, Leonnatos attempted to persuade Eumenes to cross into Europe with him — ostensibly in aid of Antipatros, but in reality to seize the Makedonian throne. He revealed to Eumenes the details of his correspondence with Kleopatra. But in this matter he misjudged Eumenes, who shunned the proposal, either from loyalty to Perdikkas or fear of his archrival Hekataios. While Alexander lived, Eumenes had denounced Hekataios, urging the King to depose him and restore freedom to the Kardians. Now he feared lest Antipatros should kill him in order to please Hekataios.[220] During the night, Eumenes and his forces slipped away from Leonnatos, bringing the news of his designs to Perdikkas.[221]

Disappointed by Eumenes, Leonnatos crossed into Europe. His satrapal army cannot have been very large, and he stopped in

37; Geyer, *RE* xii.2 (1925), 2037; Errington, *JHS* 90 (1970), 60; Carney, *Historia* 37 (1988), 385 ff., esp. 394-403.

[218] For Peithon's designs in the upper satrapies see Diod. 18. 4. 8; 18. 7. 1-9. Ptolemy's opposition to Perdikkas' regency can be seen in the succession debate, Curt. 10. 6. 13-16; Justin 13. 2. 11-12; for his fear of Perdikkas' intentions Diod. 18. 14. 1-2. Philotas was removed from his satrapy (Justin 13. 6. 16) on account of his loyalty to Krateros (Arr. *Succ.* 24. 2). For Antigonos' insubordination see Plut. *Eum.* 3. 4-5.

[219] Plut. *Eum.* 3. 6; Diod. 18. 12. 1; 18. 14. 4-5; Justin 13. 5. 14.

[220] Plut. *Eum.* 3. 8-10. Vezin (27 f.) argues that Eumenes, as a Greek, was not eager to assist in suppressing this most recent Greek uprising, and 'daß Leonnats übereilte Offenheit ihn nicht als den Mann erwies, solch eine Absicht zu verwirklichen' (28). Macurdy, *HQ* 36-37, describes Leonnatos as 'impetuous and easily carried away by enthusiasm', but he did have the support of Olympias and her daughter (the family of Alexander still counted for something), and he was himself related to the royal house; thus his bid for power could not be taken lightly.

[221] Plut. *Eum.* 3. 10; Nepos, *Eum.* 2. 4-5, claims that Leonnatos planned to kill Eumenes when he could not persuade him. Perhaps it was from Eumenes' report that Perdikkas first gave thought to marrying Kleopatra for political advantage.

Makedonia to recruit both infantry and cavalry. With a force of more than 20,000 foot and 1500 cavalry he pushed south towards Lamia. But the Athenian general Antiphilos decided to engage Leonnatos before he could join forces with Antipatros. The exact location of the battlefield is not given, but it could scarcely have been far north of Lamia itself.[222] Although the infantry were evenly matched, Leonnatos had fewer than half the enemy's number of cavalry, and he soon found himself cut off in a marshy region. There, overcome by his wounds, Leonnatos was carried dead from the battlefield by his own men.[223] Antipatros may indeed, as Justin claims, have welcomed the death of Leonnatos:[224] not only had the engagement removed a dangerous rival, but it had lifted the siege of Lamia and augmented Antipatros' forces substantially.[225]

'Kurz, aber glänzend ist die Rolle, welche L[eonnatos] unter Al[exander] spielt, und sie stellt ihn in die Reihe der ersten Heerführer seiner Zeit.' Thus Berve (ii 235) summarizes Leonnatos' career. He was a potential unfulfilled. For the Successors of Alexander the Great his death was a timely one: there were already too many rivals for the empire. In his arrogance, his fondness for Persian luxury[226] — evinced by his dress and the decoration of his arms, even the gilded bridles of his Nisaian horses — and in the style of his hair, Leonnatos was clearly emulous of his kinsman Alexander and jealously eager to exercise at least some of his power. Noblility, beauty and physical strength were his by birth, as was the expectation of military office. In the exercise of the latter, he displayed exemplary courage but also recklessness and ambition. And in the end Fortune abandoned him, just as it had Alexander.

---

[222]Antiphilos will scarcely have considered abandoning Lamia until he heard that Leonnatos had entered Thessaly. Diod. 18. 15. 5 tells us that Antipatros joined Leonnatos' army on the day after the battle (τῇ δ' ὑστεραίᾳ).

[223]Diod. 18. 15. 3; Justin 13. 5. 14; cf. Plut. *Phocion* 25. 5; Strabo 9. 5. 10 C434.

[224]Justin 13. 5. 15; cf. Arr. *Succ.* 1. 9, where Λεόννατος ἐπιβοηθεῖν δοκῶν 'Αντιπάτρῳ expresses Leonnatos' duplicity.

[225]Antipatros had come into Thessaly in autumn 323 with 13,000 infantry and 600 cavalry; he now inherited what remained of Leonnatos' 20,000 foot and 1500 horse.

[226]Arr. *Succ.* 12. He was also passionately fond of wrestling and gymnastics (Plut. *Alex.* 40. 1; Pliny, *NH* 35. 168); or hunting (Athen. 12. 539d = Phylarchos, *FGrHist* 81 F41 and/or Agatharchides of Knidos, 86 F3; Aelian, *VH* 9. 3); cf. also Hamilton, *PA* 106.

4. Krateros: φιλοβασιλεύς

Literature. Berve ii 220-227, no. 446; Geyer, *RE* Supplbd iv (1924), 1038-1048; Kornemann 245-246.

καὶ ὅλως τὸν μὲν ἐφίλει μάλιστα, τὸν δὲ ἐτίμα, νομίζων καὶ λέγων ἀεὶ τὸν μὲν Ἡφαιστίωνα φιλαλέξανδρον εἶναι, τὸν δὲ Κρατερὸν φιλοβασιλέα....

(Plut. *Alex.* 47. 10)

In general, he loved the one best, and honoured the other most; for he considered, and always commented, that Hephaistion was fond of Alexander, but Krateros fond of the King.

Krateros was a soldier and a patriot, loyal to his King, faithful to his Makedonian origins.[227] Throughout Alexander's reign he won the respect and devotion of both the King and the army through an unusual combination of ability and loyalty. Yet he did not attain greatness even when the opportunity presented itself. As a personality he appears to have been somewhat uninspired, and his reluctance to make a bid for supreme power after Alexander's death may well betray a lack of statesmanship.[228] But he gained quickly a reputation as a soldier, and, among Alexander's new commanders, he was arguably the best.

The son of Alexandros, Krateros came from the mountainous canton of Orestis.[229] Of his family background very little is known: the mother was apparently named Aristopatra,[230] Amphoteros (later Alexander's admiral) was his brother.[231] Presumably, the family belonged to the

---

[227]Plut. *Alex.* 47. 9-10.

[228]Cf. P. Green, *Alexander to Actium: The Historical Evolution of the Hellenistic Age* (Berkeley, 1990), 8, who gives the following description of Krateros: 'A genial bear of a man, in his broad-brimmed Macedonian slouch hat, he was popular with the troops; but he lacked that fine edge of ruthlessness necessary for supreme power'.

[229]For his father's name: Arr. *Ind.* 18. 5; Arr. 1. 25. 9; cf. also Perdrizet, *JHS* 19 (1899), 274. For his Orestian background, Arr. *Ind.* 18. 5.

[230]Strabo 15. 1. 35 C702 = *FGrHist* 153 F2 (a letter from Krateros to his mother); the letter itself is spurious, but the mother's name may well be correct.

[231]Berve ii 32-33, no. 68, s.v. Ἀμφοτερός. Cf. Kaerst, *RE* i (1894), 1977, no. 4. During the winter of 334/3 he was sent by Alexander from Phaselis to Parmenion in Gordion with orders that the latter arrest Alexandros Lynkestes on a charge of treason (Arr. 1. 25. 9-10). Amphoteros travelled in native dress, accompanied by guides from Perge, in order to avoid detection (Arr. 1. 25. 9). In

high nobility of Upper Makedonia, for Krateros was one of the most influential of Alexander's hetairoi.[232] But, since we do not know the names of any other relatives, by blood or marriage, further deductions about the family's position within the Makedonian aristocracy are impossible.

Although the year of Krateros' birth is unknown, the argument that Amphoteros was the younger brother (Berve ii 32) is not persuasive. Krateros' achievements outshine those of his brother, but do not impute seniority. The case of Alkimachos, generally considered the eldest of Agathokles' known sons, invites comparison: far more influential at Alexander's court was his younger brother Lysimachos; Philippos died young in 328/7, while Autodikos appears to have reached manhood only shortly before 320 B.C.[233] The fact that Alexander used Amphoteros for some rather delicate missions,[234] and even appointed him navarch of the Aegean fleet, suggests that, like Alkimachos, he was a man of some experience.[235] Krateros himself appears to have been considerably younger than the field-marshals of Philip II: Parmenion, Antipatros, Antigonos, Attalos.[236] His promotion was quick and steady, suggesting that he was younger and able, rather

spring 333, he proceeded to the coast to share the command of the reconstituted Aegean fleet with Hegelochos (Curt. 3. 1. 19; cf. 4. 5. 14 ff.; Arr. 2. 2. 3; 3. 2. 6).

[232]Curt. 6. 8. 2 ff.; 6. 8. 17; 6. 11. 10; 9. 6. 6. Krateros did not become one of the Somatophylakes, however, and this might imply that his family was of lesser importance (cf. Berve's comments i 25-26); certainly three Somatophylakes had connections with the Makedonian royal house (Leonnatos and Perdikkas; cf. Ptolemy's claim to be a bastard son of Philip). If there was a regional basis for recruitment of Somatophylakes, then it might be argued that Orestis was already represented by Perdikkas. But note that in 325 there were two representatives from Eordaia: Ptolemy son of Lagos and Peithon son of Krateuas.

[233]For Alkimachos, see Arr. 1. 18. 1-2; Hyper. 19. 2 (Burrt) = Harpokration s.v. Ἀλκίμαχος; Anaximenes, FGrHist 72 F16. Cf. also Berve ii 23, no. 47. The death of Philippos (Curt. 8. 2. 35-39; Justin 15. 3. 12); Autodikos was Somatophylax of Philip III Arrhidaios (Arr. Succ. 1. 38).

[234]The arrest of Alexandros Lynkestes (Arr. 1. 25. 9-10); his mission to Krete and the Peloponnesos (Arr. 3. 6. 3; Curt. 4. 8. 15; cf. Bosworth, Phoenix 29 [1975], 27-43).

[235]Curt. 3. 1. 19: *Amphoterum classi ad oram Hellesponti, copiis autem praefecit Hegelochum, Lesbium et Chium Coumque praesidiis hostium liberaturos.* Hauben, Anc. Soc. 3 (1972), 57, sees Hegelochos as Amphoteros' superior: this was 'a diarchic fleet command', in which 'the head of the marines also functioned as the supreme commander of the whole formation'; cf. id., Anc. Soc. 7 (1976), 82 f.

[236]Parmenion was born c. 400; Antipatros in 398 and Antigonos in 382. For Antigonos' early career see i 5 and Billows, Antigonos 15 ff. I would put Attalos' birthdate closer to 390: see i 1. 1; cf. Heckel, RhM 125 (1982), 83.

than a middle-aged man whose progress had been retarded for some reason under Philip II. Perhaps he was born after 370 — a conservative estimate, but still a guess. Later cases of illness will be ascribable to the effects of his wounds and hard campaigning rather than to old age.[237]

Krateros' story is predominantly military. We know nothing about him before 334, although he must have taken part in the European campaigns. From the start of the Persian expedition, he commanded his own brigade of pezhetairoi, though apparently not the regional troops of Orestis.[238] In this capacity, we find him at the River Graneikos, stationed on the left side with the brigades of Philippos son of Amyntas and Meleagros.[239] By the following year, he had gained in authority, commanding all the infantry on the left at Issos, though still subordinate to Parmenion, who exercised supreme command over that wing.[240]

Early in 332 B.C., he and Perdikkas were entrusted with the siege of Tyre in Alexander's absence;[241] in that time, a Tyrian sortie was

---

[237] Krateros' wounds: Plut. *Alex.* 41. 5; Arr. 4. 3. 3. Illness: Arr. 7. 12. 4; Plut. *Alex.* 41. 6-7.

[238] Orestians and Lynkestians were commanded by Perdikkas (Diod. 17. 57. 2). Berve i 114-115 recognised that there were three Upper Makedonian taxeis (those of Koinos, Polyperchon and Perdikkas), and that the remainder were, in all likelihood, manned by 'Kernmakedonen' (but see the apparent contradiction at ii 220, where Krateros is described as leading 'eine, vielleicht aus der Landschaft Orestis sich rekrutierende Taxis der Pezhetairen'). Cf. the term ἀσθέταιροι, which Bosworth, *Arrian* i 252, assumes referred only to the three brigades from Upper Makedonia.

[239] Krateros' brigade appears twice in Arrian's description of the battle-order (1. 14. 2, 3). Bosworth, *CQ* 26 (1976), 126, is probably right in supposing that Ptolemy and Aristoboulos gave conflicting versions and that 'Arrian has absorbed both versions without reconciling the contradiction'. Arr. 1. 14. 2 places Krateros' brigade between those of Koinos and Amyntas, on the centre right; 1. 14. 3 places him on the left, where he ought to belong (so Roos' Teubner text [Leipzig 1967], 32, and Brunt, *Arrian* i 59, n.3; cf. Köpke, *Jahrb. f. cl. Philologie* 99 [1869], 263; Droysen, *Hermes* 12 [1877], 242). But Bosworth, *Arrian* i 118, prefers not to remove Krateros from 1. 14. 2, arguing that 'the author of the variant, whether Aristobulus or Ptolemy, assumed wrongly that it occupied the position at the extreme left which it was to have at Issus and Gaugamela...'.

[240] Arr. 2. 8. 4; Curt. 3. 9. 8. Krateros was regularly on the left side, a point which favours Köpke's and Droysen's preference (above) for a position on the left at the Graneikos (Arr. 1. 14. 3). He commands the left of the fleet at Tyre (Arr. 2. 20. 6; Curt. 4. 3. 11), and of the land forces at Gaugamela (Arr. 3. 11. 10; Curt. 4. 13. 29; Diod. 17. 57. 3).

[241] Curt. 4. 3. 1. Arrian's (2. 20. 4) reticence is hardly surprising, since the command was held jointly by Krateros and Perdikkas, the latter a victim of Ptolemy's bias. See Errington, *CQ* 19 (1969), 237, who thinks this may 'conceivably be an omission of Arrian's.'

effectively countered by Krateros' troops.²⁴² But Alexander soon summoned him to Sidon, where the Kypriot kings who had defected from Dareios had gathered with their fleets. In the naval assault on Tyre, Krateros commanded the left with Pnytagoras, the Salaminian king.²⁴³ Of his part in the actual capture of the city, nothing is known.²⁴⁴ In fact, there are no further references to his military activity until the battle of Gaugamela (331 B.C.), where, as at Issos, he led the infantry-brigades on the left wing, again under Parmenion's general command.²⁴⁵

His position on the left — and with the infantry — makes it more difficult for us to monitor his activities;²⁴⁶ for the Alexander historians focussed on the deeds of the King, on the right, and on the sweeping charges of the horsemen. By comparison the grappling phalanx offered little to excite the reader. From the descriptions of Gaugamela, however, we can draw certain inferences about Krateros' generalship, precisely because a second cavalry engagement took place on the left. As Alexander's forces pushed forward on the right, Parmenion found himself hard pressed on the left, and a gap developed in the infantry-line between the brigades of Polyperchon and Simmias, when the latter could not keep up with the surging phalanx. Now this appears to have come about less by accident than by design, for Simmias and his men were informed that the left was in trouble (ὅτι τὸ εὐώνυμον τῶν Μακεδόνων πονεῖσθαι ἠγγέλλετο).²⁴⁷ That the young and inexperienced Simmias — he commanded the brigade in the absence of his brother Amyntas²⁴⁸ — had the presence of mind to hold back his

---

²⁴²Polyainos 4. 13; cf. Berve ii 220.

²⁴³Arr. 2. 20. 6; Curt. 4. 3. 11. Bosworth, *Arrian* i 245, supposes that Parmenion had returned and assumed command of the besieging force.

²⁴⁴I suspect that Krateros was not with the fleet when it anchored in the harbour facing Sidon. In this engagement Pnytagoras' quinquereme was sunk (**Arr. 2. 22. 2**).

²⁴⁵Arr. 3. 11. 10; Diod. 17. 57. 3; but Curt. 4. 13. 29 is corrupt: *in laevo Craterus Peloponnesium equites habebat Achaeorum et Locrensium et Maleion turmis sibi adiunctis*; cf. Berve ii 221, n.1: this is an error for Philoxenos (no. 442).

²⁴⁶Note that Marsden (*Gaugamela*) does not mention him once.

²⁴⁷Arr. 3. 14. 4.

²⁴⁸Arr. 3. 11. 9 says that the brigade of Amyntas 'son of Philippos' was commanded by Simmias (both were sons of Andromenes); Diod. 17. 57. 3 and Curt. 4. 13. 28 assign the command to Philippos son of Balakros (otherwise unknown); cf. Bosworth, *Arrian* i 300-301, and *Entretiens Hardt*, 22 (Geneva, 1976), 9 ff.; Atkinson, *Curtius* i 423 f. Bosworth makes the appealing suggestion that Simmias may have been a subordinate of both Amyntas and Philippos. It is interesting that Arrian (3. 14. 4) writes οἱ δὲ ἀμφὶ Σιμμίαν, a group which might have included Philippos son of Balakros. For Philippos son of Balakros see **viii 1. 4**.

troops seems less likely than that the order came from Krateros, who, when he saw the Indians and Persians burst through to the baggage, also sent the infantry in reserve to fall upon the plunderers.[249] Schooled by Parmenion, Krateros now helped to extricate him from a dangerous situation, one which might have proved disastrous had the infantry on the left tried to keep pace with the right.

After Gaugamela, Krateros' advancement was steady and rapid. On the road from Sousa to Persepolis, in the land of the Ouxians, Krateros was given his first independent command over a portion of the army other than his own brigade. He did not disappoint. When the Ouxians refused to allow Alexander passage through their territory, the King took a picked force along one of the lesser-known roads and fell upon them, as they were unprepared for an attack from that quarter. He had sent Krateros ahead to occupy the heights, to which, he assumed, the Ouxians would flee. The strategy proved sound, and large numbers were butchered by Krateros' men.[250] From this point onward, Alexander regularly divided his forces, leaving the larger — and slower — portion with Krateros.[251] Later, as Hephaistion, Perdikkas, Ptolemy and Leonnatos gained in importance, they also held independent commands; nevertheless, those tasks that involved the greatest risk and responsibility were, for the most part, reserved for Krateros.[252]

---

[249]Simmias and the gap in the phalanx: Arr. 3. 14. 4. Marsden, *Gaugamela* 59: 'In view of the fierce fighting in progress on the left, Simmias made the wise decision.' I suspect, however, that the decision was made for him by Krateros. Bosworth, *Arrian* i 300-301, 309, thinks that Ptolemy wrote maliciously to discredit the family of an enemy (Perdikkas' sister, Atalante, married Attalos son of Andromenes). For the Indian and Persian cavalry: Arr. 3. 14. 5-6. But the problems with this episode are summarised by Bosworth, *Arrian* i 308 f. Cf. Devine, *Phoenix* 29 (1975), 381, n.21: '...it is evident that its object (whether intended or not) was merely the field baggage-park, and not Alexander's fortified four-day camp...'.

[250]See Arr. 3. 17. 4 ff. Diod. 17. 67 and Curt. 5. 3. 1-16 make no mention of Krateros' role. Bosworth (*Arrian* i 321 ff.) assumes that Arrian and the vulgate sources are referring to two different engagements. For the roles of Tauron and Krateros in this campaign see also **viii 5. 7**. Cf. Fuller 226-228; Olmstead, *HPE* 519; Stein, *Geog. Journal* 92 (1938), 313 ff. Also Strabo 11. 13. 6 C524; 15. 3. 6 C729.

[251]Krateros' independent commands: *ME* 35, 59, 60; Polyainos 4. 13; Curt. 4. 3. 1; Arr. 3. 17. 4 ff., 18. 4 ff.; Curt. 5. 4. 14-16, 29, 34; 5. 6. 11; Arr. 3. 21. 2; Curt. 6. 4. 2, 23-24; Arr. 3. 25. 6, 8; Curt. 6. 6. 25, 33; Arr. 4. 2. 2; Curt. 7. 6. 16, 19; 7. 9. 20-22; Arr. 4. 17. 1; Curt. 8. 1. 6; 8. 5. 2; Arr. 4. 18. 1; 4. 22. 1-2; 4. 23. 5; Curt. 8. 10. 4; Arr. 4. 24. 6-7; 4. 28. 7; 5. 12. 1; 5. 18. 1; 5. 21. 4; Diod. 17. 96. 1; Arr. 6. 2. 2; 6. 4. 1; 6. 5. 5, 7; Arr. *Ind.* 19. 1, 3; Curt. 9. 8. 3; 9. 10. 19; Arr. 6. 15. 5, 7; 6. 17. 3; 6. 27. 3; 7. 12. 3-4.

[252]Against the Ouxians: Arr. 3. 17. 4 ff.; against Ariobarzanes: Arr. 3. 18. 4 ff.; Curt. 5. 4. 14 ff.; against the Massagetai in Baktria: Curt. 8. 1. 6; Arr. 4. 17. 1; at

Some five days after defeating the Ouxians, the Makedonian army reached the Persian (or Sousian) Gates, where they found the road barred by the satrap of Persis, Ariobarzanes.[253] The position was virtually impregnable, and the defending force more than adequate;[254] hence a frontal assault was repulsed with heavy losses.[255] Informants and an alternative route were sought. There was, of course, the wagon-road through the plain, by which Parmenion was leading the baggage-train and its heavily-armed escort into Persia, but it was feared that delay would allow the Persians time to remove the treasures from Persepolis, which lay beyond the 'Gates' and the Araxes River.[256] Therefore, since he had learned of a difficult encircling path, Alexander led a select force to Ariobarzanes' rear and left the rest of the troops at the foot of the 'Gates' under the direction of Krateros.[257] Alexander's strategy anticipates that used at the Hydaspes in 326:

the Hydaspes: Arr. 5. 12. 1 (Curtius fails to mention Krateros' important role); policing the satrapies in the west: Arr. 6. 17. 3; cf. Curt. 9. 10. 19.

[253] For the chronology: Diod. 17. 68. 1; cf. Curt. 5. 3. 17, with an apparent textual problem, since Curtius says that Alexander entered Persis on the third day but reached the 'Gates' on the fifth; cf. F. Schmieder, *Quinti Curtii Rufi: De Rebus Gestis Alexandri Magni*, vol. 2 (London, 1825), 1089. Complete accounts of the battle: Arr. 3. 18. 1-9; Curt. 5. 3. 16 - 4. 34; Diod. 17. 68. 1 - 69. 2; Polyainos 4. 3. 27; Plut. *Alex.* 37. 1-2 (the beginning only; cf. Hamilton, *PA* 96-97); also Strabo 15. 3. 6 C729. Modern discussions: Sir Aurel Stein, *Geog. Journal* 92 (1938), 313 ff.; Olmstead, *HPE* 519; Fuller 228-234; Heckel, *Athenaeum* 58 (1980), 168-174. Berve ii 60-61, no. 115, identifies Ariobarzanes with the son of Artabazos; Bosworth, *Arrian* i 325, rightly distinguishes between them. Polyainos mistakenly has Φρασαόρτης (Berve ii 400, no. 813), the later satrap of Persis; cf. Kaerst, *RE* ii (1896), 833, 'Ariobarzanes (4).'

[254] The figures vary: Curt. 5. 3. 17 gives Ariobarzanes 25,000 infantry; Diod. 17. 68. 1, 25,000 infantry and 300 cavalry; Arr. 3. 18. 2 has 40,000 foot, 700 horse.

[255] Curt. 5. 3. 22 is over-dramatic (*tunc haesitabat deprehensa felicitas, nec aliud remedium erat, quam reverti qua venerat*). But there is here a tendency to see this event as the Persian Thermopylai (cf. A. R. Burn, *Alexander the Great and the Middle East* [London, 1973], 121-122).

[256] Arr. 3. 18. 1; Curt. 5. 3. 16. According to Curt. 5. 5. 2 and Diod. 17. 69. 1, Alexander learned of the treasure after he had cleared the 'Gates'. Surely his choice of the shorter mountainous route suggests that he hastened to Persepolis for the very purpose of capturing its treasure (so Schachermeyr 286; Olmstead, *HPE* 519 ff.; cf. Droysen i³ 227, who gives equal emphasis to Alexander's pursuit of Dareios).

[257] Arr. 3. 18. 4 says the information came from prisoners; Plut. *Alex.* 37. 1-2; Diod. 17. 68. 5-6; Polyainos 4. 3. 27; Curt. 5. 4. 10-13 speak of a Lykian *boukolos*, a Persian Ephialtes, part of the Thermopylai-motif. Diod. 17. 68 has misunderstood the strategy completely or so greatly compressed his account as to make Alexander's purpose unintelligible. Polyainos (4. 3. 27) wrongly leaves the camp in the charge of Hephaistion and Philotas; the latter certainly could not have been present.

Krateros was to attack Ariobarzanes if he turned to deal with Alexander's force; if, however, Alexander reached the rear of Ariobarzanes' position undetected, Krateros was to await a trumpet-signal, whereupon both divisions of the army would attack the 'Gates' simultaneously.[258] The latter actually happened, and Ariobarzanes' men, hemmed in by the cliffs, were virtually annihilated.[259] The road to Persepolis lay open for Alexander; Krateros brought up the rest of the troops with forced marches.[260]

Persepolis fell. It was not much later that Alexander conducted a thirty-day campaign into the interior of Persia, leaving the bulk of the army behind with Parmenion and Krateros.[261] Probably it was their task to arrange for the removal of the treasures. It is doubtful, however, that Krateros took part in the actual transporting of the treasures to Ekbatana, a task given to Parmenion.[262] Some units of the pezhetairoi did remain behind to guard the treasure,[263] but Krateros appears to have set out with Alexander from Ekbatana toward the Caspian Gates, and, when Alexander hurried after Dareios and his captors, Krateros led the slower forces eastward from the Gates and awaited the return of Koinos and his party, who had been on a foraging mission.[264] Parmenion's orders to march north into Hyrkania, through the land of the Kadousians, once he had conveyed the treasures to Ekbatana, were apparently rescinded, and the divisions of the army that had served as his escort returned to Alexander under the command of Kleitos, who had recovered from his illness in Sousa.[265]

---

[258] Arr. 3. 18. 4-5; Curt. 5. 4. 14-16.

[259] Arr. 3. 18. 9 says that Ariobarzanes and a few horsemen escaped; Curt. 5. 4. 33-34 says that he was killed before Persepolis. The two accounts can be reconciled, if we assume that Arrian did not record the second engagement and that Ariobarzanes was not the son of Artabazos named at Arr. 3. 23. 7.

[260] The Araxes River (Curt. 5. 5. 3; Strabo 15. 3. 6 C729) was bridged by Koinos, Amyntas and Philotas (the hipparch), while the battle with Ariobarzanes was being fought (so Arr. 3. 18. 6), instead of later by Alexander himself (Curt. 5. 5. 3-4; Diod. 17. 69. 2). Krateros' forced marches to Persepolis: Curt. 5. 4. 34.

[261] Curt. 5. 6. 11.

[262] Arr. 3. 19. 7. Berve ii 221 assumes that Krateros helped Parmenion.

[263] Alexander had gone ahead to Ekbatana, which he left taking with him τὴν φάλαγγα τὴν Μακεδονικὴν ἔξω τῶν ἐπὶ τοῖς χρήμασι ταχθέντων (Arr. 3. 20. 1).

[264] Koinos' foraging-party: Arr. 3. 20. 4; 3. 21. 2. Krateros took the slower troops at a moderate pace: μὴ μακρὰς ὁδοὺς ἄγοντα (Arr. 3. 21. 2).

[265] Parmenion's orders: Arr. 3. 19. 7; cf. Schachermeyr 295; Berve ii 304; Bosworth, *Arrian* i 337; Seibert, *Eroberung* 110 f. There is, at least, no evidence that Parmenion carried out these orders. For Kleitos' instructions: Arr. 3. 19. 8; cf also Berve ii 206, no. 427. He had rejoined Alexander by the time of the Philotas affair (Arr. 3. 27. 4).

The campaign in the north-east saw Krateros emerge as Alexander's foremost general, and for some three years he had no serious rivals. After the death of Dareios, Alexander found it necessary to secure Hyrkania, which Seibert (*Eroberung* 114) aptly describes as 'die einzige Landbrücke nach Osten', a 75 km-wide strip between the Caspian and the desert to the south. For the undertaking, Krateros and Erigyios commanded one-third of the army each. But Erigyios' task was merely to lead the baggage-train along the easiest path to Hyrkania, while Krateros took his own brigade and that of Amyntas son of Andromenes, the archers and some cavalry against the Tapourians.[266] Curtius claims that Krateros was left behind to guard Parthiene against invaders (*ut ab incursione barbarorum Parthienem tueretur*, 6. 4. 2), but this is misleading. His mission was clearly to patrol, round up fugitive mercenaries[267] and set in order Parthiene, since Alexander had no time to deal with the natives. Thus he and Erigyios reunited with Alexander at Zadrakarta (Sari or Gorgan?) in Hyrkania, their arrival coinciding with that of Autophradates, satrap of the Tapourians, whose fate was to be decided by Alexander.[268]

When the news came that Satibarzanes, satrap of Areia, had defected to Bessos, who had now assumed the tiara and the title of Artaxerxes, Alexander hastened to deal with him. But Krateros' role is difficult to ascertain, owing to the diverging accounts of Arrian and Curtius, the only sources for his activities. According to Curtius, Krateros was left behind at the foot of a rocky outcrop (Kalat-i-Nadiri?[269]), on the plateau of which — some thirty-two stades in circumference (Curt. 6. 6. 23; about 3.5 miles) — 13,000 Areians had taken refuge. But Alexander, who had intended to pursue Satibarzanes, soon returned and conducted the siege in person; for he learned that Satibarzanes was too far off. Alexander's reconnaissance may have informed him that Satibarzanes had moved to Artakoana (usually

---

[266] Arr. 3. 23. 2; cf. Curt. 6. 4. 2.

[267] Arr. 3. 23. 6 says that he did not, however, fall in with any of Dareios' mercenaries.

[268] Arr. 3. 23. 6; Curt. 6. 4. 23-24 has 'Phradates'; see Berve ii 221; ii 96-97, no. 189; Kaerst, *RE* ii.2 (1896), 2608, s.v. 'Autophradates (2)'. Arr. 3. 24. 3 says that he surrendered of his own accord; this must have been a direct consequence of Krateros' activities. Alexander, nevertheless, reinstated Autophradates as satrap (Arr. 3. 23. 7). For the identification of Zadrakarta with Sari (instead of Astarabad/Gorgan) see Engels, *Logistics* 84, n.64; but there are good arguments for Gorgan: see Seibert, *Eroberung* 117, with n.66; cf. also W. Vogelsang, 'Some Observations on Achaemenid Hyrcania: A Combination of Sources', in A. Kuhrt and H. Sancisi-Weerdenburg, eds., *Achaemenid History* iii (Leiden, 1988), 121-135.

[269] Curt. 6. 6. 23-25. For the identification and a description of the place see Engels, *Logistics* 87-88.

identified as Herat and equated with Alexandreia in Areia[270]). Perhaps he sent Krateros ahead to Artakoana, which he besieged in the King's absence, but allowed him the honour of taking it.[271] In Arrian's version, Alexander breaks off his march to Baktra, leaving him with the rest of the army, and rushes to Artakoana; no satisfactory account of the town's surrender is given. Some time later, when Alexander had already made administrative changes in the satrapy, Krateros and the remainder of the army joined him.[272] Arrian's version is, in all probability, more reliable, since Artakoana lay a considerable distance east of Zadrakarta, and Alexander's more mobile troops will have reached the city some time before Krateros and the rest of the army arrived.[273]

By the year 330, there had been significant changes in the command structure of the Makedonian army, especially insofar as it involved the house of Parmenion. He himself had been left behind at Ekbatana. Nikanor, who commanded the hypaspists, died of illness in Areia;[274] a second son, Hektor, who might otherwise have been considered as Nikanor's successor, had drowned in the Nile in 331. Thus, a family which had, at the beginning of the campaign, exercised considerable influence, was now in eclipse at the Court. But it was worse than that: Philotas, commander of the Companion Cavalry, had foolishly allowed himself to be implicated in the abortive conspiracy of an obscure Makedonian named Dimnos.[275] To Krateros this was welcome news; for the brother of Dimnos' confederate (and lover) had given damning testimony against Philotas, whom Krateros had hated at least since Egypt.[276] Protecting the King from treason — for this is how he regarded Philotas' crime — had its personal advantages, even for one who was already the King's strong right hand.

In Egypt, Philotas had voiced his opinions carelessly, especially his annoyance at Alexander's recent adoption by Ammon. This evoked resentment from many prominent Makedonians, including Hegelochos, who may in fact have influenced Philotas.[277] Arrian mentions

[270]See Appendix IV.
[271]Curt. 6. 6. 33.
[272]Arr. 3. 25. 6-8.
[273]Berve ii 221-222 prefers Arrian, as does Geyer, RE Supplbd iv (1924), 1039. Cf. Droysen i 262; Niese i 110; Schachermeyr 313; Hamilton, *Alexander the Great* 93.
[274]Arr. 3. 25. 4; Curt. 6. 6. 18-19; Berve ii 275, no. 554.
[275]Dimnos: Berve ii 142-143, no. 269.
[276]Kebalinos the informant (Berve ii 203, no. 418); his brother Nikomachos was Dimnos' lover (ii 279-280, no. 569).
[277]Arr. 3. 26. 1; cf. Plut. *Alex.* 48. 4 - 49. 2. For Hegelochos' conspiracy see Curt. 6. 11. 22-29. There is no good reason to regard Hegelochos' treason as a fabrication (*pace* Badian, *TAPA* 91 [1960], 332; Fears, *Athenaeum* 53 [1975], 133,

Philotas' *epiboule* in Egypt (3. 26. 1), and, while his intrigues with Hegelochos went undetected at the time, they were part of the 'treasonous activity' to which Krateros and those loyal to Alexander objected. Arrian gives no details of the Egyptian conspiracy, but it appears to be identical with the affair described at some length by Plutarch (*Alex.* 48. 4-49. 2; *de fort. Alex.* 2. 7 = *Mor.* 339d-f). Among the spoils taken by Parmenion at Damaskos in 333 was Antigona, a young Makedonian girl.[278] She became the mistress of Philotas, who confided in her, claiming that Alexander's victories had been won through his efforts and those of Parmenion, that the King's pretensions about Ammon were an insult to the Makedonian nobility.[279] But what Philotas told her, by way of bragging or complaint, Antigona entrusted to a friend and, ultimately, the rumour reached Krateros.[280] He wasted no time in bringing the matter, and Antigona, to the King's attention. And, while Alexander forgave Philotas his outspokenness, Krateros remained suspicious of him and kept him under surveillance, using the girl as his informant.[281] How long this 'prolonged espionage'[282] lasted is unknown, though it undoubtedly did not span the years between the disaffection in Egypt and the Dimnos affair; indeed, Antigona's information, which cannot have revealed much that was not already known about Philotas, may well have disappointed Krateros' hopes of building a case against his rival. But, when the opportunity presented itself, Krateros and his associates were quick to press their advantage.

n.77); so Heckel, *RhM* 125 (1982), 78-87. For Philotas' 'conspiracy' in Egypt see also Cauer 8 ff.

[278]Antigona's capture at Damaskos: Plut. *Alex.* 48. 4 (where it is stated that she came originally from Pydna); *Mor.* 339d (from Pella). According to the latter version, she had crossed from Pella to Samothrake (for the worship of the Kabeiroi? Cf. Hamilton, *PA* 2; Kern, *RE* x.2 [1919], 1399 ff., esp. 1423-1437, s.vv. 'Kabeiros und Kabeiroi'), where she was captured by Autophradates (Berve ii 96, no. 188). Antigona: the name occurs among the Makedonian nobility (cf. Hoffmann 216) — it was the name of Pyrrhos' wife, a daughter of Berenike — see Berve ii 42, no. 86 (*Mor.* 339d-f has the more correct Ἀντιγόνα); Wilcken, *RE* i (1894), 2404, s.v. 'Antigone (7)'; Hamilton, *PA* 133; Hofstetter 16-17, no. 19a.

[279]Plut. *Alex.* 48. 5; *Mor.* 339d. But, in support of Philotas' arguments, see Beloch iv² 2. 290-306.

[280]Plut. *Alex.* 48. 6; *Mor.* 339e-f.

[281]Plut. *Alex.* 48. 7 - 49. 1. For this conspiracy *against* Philotas (ὁ μὲν οὖν Φιλώτας ἐπιβουλευόμενος οὕτως ἠγνόει καὶ συνῆν τῇ Ἀντιγόνῃ, 49. 1), in which Badian (*TAPA* 91 [1960], 326) attempts to find support for his arguments concerning Dimnos' conspiracy, see Hamilton, *PA* 135.

[282]Badian's phrase (*TAPA* 91 [1960], 331), but he regards this as part of Alexander's conspiracy against Philotas.

Kebalinos exposed Dimnos. But the latter could not be taken alive and could not be used to indict Philotas.[283] Alexander, it appears, had made no firm decision on how he would deal with this case of negligence — the only offence of which Philotas was clearly guilty.[284] The actual decision on Philotas' fate must have been the one advocated by Alexander's friends when a council was held. Krateros spoke first and most effectively, for he was dear to Alexander and exceedingly hostile to Philotas.[285] Whether or not Krateros was attempting to disguise his ill-will towards Philotas with a show of piety, as Curtius claims, is debatable; for Krateros had already gained in power and importance as a result of Parmenion's relegation to Ekbatana.[286] He was, most likely, sincere in both motives: he earnestly desired to protect Alexander from the insidious, and he sought to ruin Philotas for personal reasons. Perhaps friction had developed between the two when it became clear that Krateros was being groomed as Parmenion's successor, but, by the time of the Philotas affair, Krateros had little to fear from either Philotas or Parmenion. In this respect, his role in the affair is much less complicated and less sinister than that of the unaccomplished Hephaistion.[287]

Krateros' speech was to the point and, from the standpoint of the younger commanders, who owed so much to Alexander's favour, perfectly reasonable. In some respects it was strongly reminiscent of the advice given concerning Alexandros Lynkestes. Alexander could not go on excusing Philotas forever, nor would Philotas cease to plot against the King. Beware the enemy within, warned Krateros. And he had not forgotten the threat of Parmenion: the father would not endure the son's execution.[288] Clearly, Krateros understood what was at stake, what could be gained from Philotas' removal. But his condemnation of Philotas served better the wishes of his accomplices in the conspiracy *against* Philotas. All were hostile and unyielding. By the time that Philotas' enemies met, during the second watch on the night of his arrest, Alexander had been strongly influenced — by Hephaistion in private, openly by Krateros. An unprecedented unanimity prevailed among Alexander's young commanders, united in a common purpose,

---

[283]Cf. Badian, *TAPA* 91 (1960), 331: 'Dimnus conveniently killed himself (or was killed while resisting arrest)...'.

[284]In fact, Philotas himself admitted to the charge: *culpam, silentii tamen, non facti ullius...* (Curt. 6. 7. 34).

[285]His relationship with Alexander: Arr. 7. 12. 3; Plut. *Alex.* 47. 9-10; Diod. 17. 114. 1-2; and in this instance, Curt. 6. 8. 2.

[286]*Erat Craterus regi carus in paucis, et eo Philotae ob aemulationem dignitatis adversus* (Curt. 6. 8. 2). *Non aliam premendi inimici occasionem aptiorem futuram ratus odio suo pietatis praeferens speciem* (Curt. 6. 8. 4).

[287]See ii 2.

[288]Curt. 6. 8. 7.

against a common enemy. To Alexander and to the army they denounced Philotas, until even his relatives and friends saw fit to abandon him. Koinos and Amyntas repudiated their earlier ties: it was as much a personal defence as a prosecution of Philotas. The whole affair is aptly summed up by the bitter pronouncement which Curtius puts into Philotas' mouth: *vicit ... bonitatem tuam, rex, inimicorum meorum acerbitas.*[289]

For the next two years Krateros was unchallenged as the foremost of Alexander's generals: Hephaistion had only begun his rise to power with his promotion to hipparch; Parmenion, who had already ceased to be an obstacle before his death, was eliminated as a consequence of the Philotas affair.[290] In Baktria-Sogdiana, as earlier in Hyrkania and Areia, Krateros had supreme authority over the army while Alexander led detachments on special missions. Thus, while Alexander subdued the rebellious outposts along the Iaxartes River (Syr-Darya), Krateros supervised the siege-work at the largest of these, Kyroupolis (Kurkath),[291] which was then taken under the King's leadership — though both Alexander and Krateros were wounded.[292] We know nothing of his role in the brief skirmish with the Skythians who lived beyond the Iaxartes. Curtius (7. 7. 9-10) says that he, along with Erigyios and Hephaistion, attended the council held in Alexander's tent before the battle, but no source records his participation in the actual fighting.[293] It seems likely that he retained the bulk of the army on the south bank of the river when Alexander crossed with a select force to attack the Skythians.

In the meantime, the contingent sent to relieve Marakanda (Samarcand), where Spitamenes had appeared unexpectedly, was ambushed and massacred at the Polytimetos river (Zeravshan).[294]

---

[289]Curt. 6. 8. 22; cf. Plut. *Alex.* 49. 8.

[290]Hephaistion's promotion: Arr. 3. 27. 4. Parmenion's death: Arr. 3. 26. 4; Curt. 7. 2. 11 ff.; Diod. 17. 80. 1, 3; Plut. *Alex.* 49. 13; Justin 12. 5. 3; Strabo 15. 2. 10 C724; cf. Justin 12. 6. 14; Arr. 4. 14. 2; Curt. 8. 1. 33, 52; 8. 7. 4.

[291]So Engels, *Logistics* 103, following Benveniste, *Journal Asiatique* 234 (1943-45), 163-166.

[292]Kyroupolis: Arr. 4. 2. 2; Curt. 7. 6. 16 (Krateros' siege); Arr. 4. 3. 1; Curt. 7. 6. 20 (founded by Kyros the Great); Arr. 4. 3. 1-4; Curt. 7. 6. 19-21 (captured by Alexander). Krateros was wounded by an arrow (Arr. 4. 3. 3); Alexander's wound was more serious (Arr. 4. 3. 3; Plut. *Mor.* 341b, incorrectly placing it in Hyrkania; Curt. 7. 6. 22, saying it happened at the town of the Memaceni, after the fall of Kyroupolis). For the campaign see Fuller 234-236.

[293]Arr. 4. 4. 1-9; Curt. 7. 8. 6 - 9. 17 is quite different; cf. Fuller 237-241, for an analysis.

[294]Arr. 4. 3. 6-7; 4. 5. 2 - 6. 2; Curt. 7. 7. 30-39; cf. 7. 6. 24. See also **ix 6. 2** (Berve ii 38, no. 75: Andromachos); **viii 4. 2** and **ix 5. 3** (Berve ii 200-201, no. 412:

Alexander, learning of the disaster, hurried south, leaving Krateros to follow with the main body at a more restrained pace.[295] The pattern had been set: it was not a glorious role, but Alexander was not one to grant his commanders many opportunities for glory.[296] Nevertheless, when the occasion presented itself, Krateros proved his worth.

In the spring of 328, Alexander moved out of winter-quarters at Baktra (Balkh) and re-crossed the Oxos River (Amu-Darya), leaving behind the brigades of Polyperchon, Attalos, Gorgias and Meleagros, all under the command of Krateros.[297] Their instructions were to prevent further defection in Baktria and to crush the insurrection (τούτοις μὲν παρήγγειλεν [sc. Ἀλέξανδρος] τήν τε χώραν ἐν φυλακῇ ἔχειν, ὡς μή τι νεωτερίσωσιν οἱ ταύτῃ βάρβαροι, καὶ τοὺς ἔτι ἀφεστηκότας αὐτῶν ἐξαιρεῖν [Arr. 4. 16. 1]). But, while Alexander and the mobile troops conducted a sweep-campaign in Sogdiana, the rebel Spitamenes, supported by horsemen of the Massagetai, attacked the smaller Makedonian garrisons in Baktria.[298] Krateros drove the Massagetai to the edge of the desert, where he defeated them in a bitter struggle — killing 150 of 1000 horsemen — only to be forced by the desert to abandon his pursuit.[299] But, by driving Spitamenes and his supporters out of Baktria, Krateros inadvertently took some of the lustre off his own victory; for Koinos, who had been left in Sogdiana at the beginning of winter 328/7, won a more decisive battle, as a consequence of which the Massagetai delivered Spitamenes' head to

---

Karanos); **viii 6. 1** (Berve ii 256, no. 504: Menedemos); also Berve ii 380-381, no. 768: Pharnouches). See now Hammond, *AncW* 22 (1991), 41-47.

[295]Curt. 7. 9. 20. Alexander's relief of Marakanda: Arr. 4. 5. 3 - 6. 5; Curt. 7. 9. 20-21; *Itiner. Al.* 39; *ME* 13. Krateros' arrival: Curt. 7. 9. 22.

[296]I would, however, stop short of Carney's view that 'Alexander carefully monitored [Krateros'] activities' because K. was 'a potentially dangerous leader of opposition and had to be watched closely' ('Macedonian Aristocracy', 216).

[297]Arr. 4. 16. 1 does not mention Krateros, though his position is clear from Arr. 4. 17. 1 and corroborated by Curt. 8. 1. 6. There is some difficulty with Meleagros' role: if he was, in fact, left with Krateros in Baktria he was soon summoned to Sogdiana, where he was left with Koinos late in 328 (Arr. 4. 17. 3). Possibly, Meleagros' name was added in 4. 16. 1 by mistake.

[298]For the fate of the phrourarch Attinas: Curt. 8. 1. 3-5; cf. Arr. 4. 16. 4-5, who does not mention his name; Berve ii 95 writes of Attinas: 'Sein weiteres Schicksal ist nicht bekannt.' But Curt. 8. 1. 5 says he was killed in the engagement, Arr. 4. 16. 5 that he was taken prisoner; if Arrian is correct, Attinas was probably executed afterwards. For Zariaspa-Baktra, where the sick were left behind, and for Peithon son of Sosikles and the harpist Aristonikos, both of whom met noble deaths (see Arr. 4. 16. 6-7).

[299]Thus Arr. 4. 17. 1-2; Curt. 8. 1. 6 claims that the Massagetai fled but that Krateros slew 1000 Dahai, perhaps confusing this battle with the one fought by Koinos (Arr. 4. 17. 6-7).

Alexander.[300] Both Koinos and Krateros rejoined the main force at Nautaka for the remainder of that winter.[301]

Krateros was not present in Marakanda during the summer or early autumn when Alexander murdered Kleitos. The King may have given his version in a letter (just as in the following year the Hermolaos conspiracy was so reported) or through a messenger, perhaps at the same time as Krateros was instructed to send Meleagros' brigade to join Koinos in Sogdiana. What the official version was, and how Krateros reacted to the news, we cannot say. Koinos and Krateros maintained the traditional values of Makedon — they shared Kleitos' sentiments, to a point — and Koinos later became the spokesman of the Makedonian soldiery at the Hyphasis.[302] Krateros, Plutarch tells us, opposed the King, especially for his orientalism,[303] but his objections appear to have been tactful and restrained; for he retained the love and respect of Alexander.

In early 327 B.C., Krateros remained with Alexander in Sogdiana, witnessing the marriage to Rhoxane, of which he doubtless disapproved in private. This followed the capture of the Rock of Chorienes (Koh-i-nor), in which undertaking Krateros may have directed affairs under Alexander's leadership during the day; Perdikkas, Ptolemy and Leonnatos supervised the operations during the night.[304] But, when Alexander moved south into Baktria, Krateros remained in Sogdiana with the brigades of Polyperchon, Attalos and Alketas (Perdikkas' brother) in order to deal with Haustanes and Katanes, who continued the resistance in Paraitakene. Haustanes was captured, Katanes killed.[305] Polyperchon went on to subdue the region

---

[300]Arr. 4. 17. 3-7. Curt. 8. 3. 1-15 and ME 20-23 give a more sensational, but less plausible, account of Spitamenes' decapitation.

[301]Arr. 4. 18. 1-2; Curt. 8. 4. 1 says that when Alexander moved out of winterquarters in spring 327 (cf. Arr. 4. 18. 4) he had stayed there only a little more than two months: *tertio mense ex hibernis movit exercitum.* Cf. Beloch iii² 2. 319.

[302]Kleitos was 'altmakedonisch gesinnt' (so Schachermeyr 363); cf. Arr. 4. 8. 4 ff.; Curt. 8. 1. 22 ff.; Plut. *Alex.* 50-51. Badian is suspicious of Koinos' death, coming so soon after his opposition to Alexander (*Studies* 200). Similar cases of ill-advised opposition to the King: Arr. 4. 12. 2 (Leonnatos); Curt. 8. 12. 17 (Meleagros). Krateros' traditional attitudes: Plut. *Alex.* 47. 9; cf. Carney, 'Macedonian Aristocracy', 216.

[303]Plut. *Eumenes* 6. 3: καὶ γὰρ ἦν ὄντως ὄνομα τοῦ Κρατεροῦ μέγα, καὶ μετὰ τὴν Ἀλεξάνδρου τελευτὴν τοῦτον ἐπόθησαν οἱ πολλοί, μνημονεύοντες ὅτι καὶ πρὸς Ἀλέξανδρον ὑπὲρ αὐτῶν ἀνεδέξατο πολλάκις ἀπεχθείας πολλάς, ὑποφερομένου πρὸς τὸν Περσικὸν ζῆλον ἀντιλαμβανόμενος καὶ τοῖς πατρίοις ἀμύνων διὰ τρυφὴν καὶ ὄγκον ἤδη περιυβριζομένοις.

[304]Arr. 4. 21. 4.

[305]Arr. 4. 22. 2; Curt. 8. 5. 2.

which Curtius (8. 5. 2) calls Bubacene.[306] It was perhaps no coincidence that Alexander's attempt to introduce the Persian practice of *proskynesis* at his own court was made during Krateros' absence. But, even without him, the resistance to oriental custom was strong amongst the Makedonians; soon, there occurred the conspiracy of the Pages, the details of which were reported to Krateros by letter.[307] And some time later, Krateros and his troops rejoined Alexander in Baktria, whence the army set out for India.

In early summer 327, the Makedonians moved to Alexandreia-of-the-Kaukasos (Kunduz[308]); thence to Nikaia and the Kophen River (Kabul).[309] When Perdikkas and Hephaistion led the advance force to the Indus, Krateros at first remained with Alexander, following the course of the Choes (Kunar). But the heavy infantry and siege-equipment crossed the river with great difficulty and made slow progress through the mountains, and Alexander left them behind to follow at their own speed, presumably under Krateros' command.[310] Probably they did not reunite with Alexander until they reached Andaka, where Krateros was left with instructions to subdue those neighbouring cities that had not submitted voluntarily. We are not told about the composition of his force, but it can have included not more than two brigades of pezhetairoi (Polyperchon, Alketas): Alexander had taken the brigades of Attalos and Koinos, while those of Kleitos, Meleagros and Gorgias (formerly Krateros' own) had accompanied Hephaistion and Perdikkas to the Indus.[311] From Andaka, he led his division to Arigaion, where Alexander again left him behind, this time with instructions to fortify the main wall, to settle in the city those of the neighbouring peoples who so wished, and

---

[306]Otherwise unattested.

[307]Plut. *Alex*. 55. 6. *Proskynesis*: Arr. 4. 12. 2 says that it was Leonnatos who mocked the ceremony (Berve ii 235, no. 467, identifies him as Leonnatos of Aigai, which is almost certainly incorrect); see Geyer, *RE* xii.2 (1925), 2035; Badian, *TAPA* 91 (1960), 337; cf. Hamilton, *PA* 54, 206. Curt. 8. 5. 22 names Polyperchon, who on Curtius' own evidence was not present (8. 5. 2); see Heckel, *AJP* 99 (1978), 459-461.

[308]See Holt, *Alexander and Bactria* 20, n.35, for the identification.

[309]Arr. 4. 22. 3: ἑξήκοντος ἤδη τοῦ ἦρος. Cf. Beloch iii² 2. 319. They reached Alexandreia in ten days (Arr. 4. 22. 4); Nikaia and the Kophen (4. 22. 6).

[310]Alexander's route along the Choes and through the mountains: Arr. 4. 23. 2. For the division of the forces cf. Curt. 8. 10. 4 (*Cratero cum phalange iusso sequi*), which refers to a time before Alexander's arrival at Andaka.

[311]Andaka: Arr. 4. 23. 5; Curt. 8. 10. 5: *Iam supervenerat Craterus. Itaque, ut principio terrorem incuteret genti nondum arma Macedonum expertae, praecipit ne cui parceretur, munimentis urbis quam obsidebat incensis*. The description appears to suit Andaka. Koinos and Attalos: Arr. 4. 24. 1; Kleitos, Meleagros, Gorgias: Arr. 4. 22. 7. For the Swat Campaign see Fuller 245 ff.; Stein, *Alexander's Track to the Indus* 41 ff.

to leave behind such Makedonians as were unfit for service (ἀπόμαχοι).[312] Having done this, Krateros led his troops and the siege-equipment into the land of the Assakenians, where he rejoined the King.[313] From here he appears to have remained with the main army until it reached Embolima, which lay near Aornos (Pir-sar). Krateros was ordered to gather provisions at Embolima, which Alexander intended to use as his base of operations against Aornos.[314]

From Aornos, where Krateros is unattested, the main force advanced to the Indus, which had been bridged by Hephaistion and Perdikkas, and thence to the Hydaspes (Jhelum). Here Poros awaited the Makedonians with a sizeable force. In the ensuing battle — Alexander's last major engagement — Krateros' role was similar to that at the Persian Gates. He was to hold the attention of the enemy while Alexander attempted an encircling manoeuvre: if Poros turned to deal with Alexander, Krateros was to cross the river and attack him from the rear; if he remained in place, Krateros was instructed not to attempt the crossing until Alexander had joined battle.[315] In these simplified terms, Krateros played an unspectacular but vital role.

To see in this battle the beginnings of Krateros' decline is to deny the importance of Krateros' division to the success of Alexander's battle-plan.[316] But Krateros had perhaps advanced militarily as far as Alexander was to allow. After the Hydaspes battle we hear of the fortification of Nikaia and Boukephala,[317] of a foraging expedition conducted with Koinos near the Hydraotes (Ravi).[318] And there was open conflict with Hephaistion.[319] The struggle for power and Alexander's affection had led inevitably to rivalry, and this manifested itself in the form of hand-to-hand combat some time after the battle at the Hydaspes. The King himself was forced to intervene, and soon he found it necessary to keep them on opposite banks of the Indus. But the advantage was beginning to shift to Hephaistion, who commanded, at least temporarily, the larger force.[320] On either side of the river, they descended the Indus in stages, but it was Hephaistion

---

[312] Arr. 4. 24. 6-7.
[313] Arr. 4. 25. 5.
[314] Arr. 4. 28. 7.
[315] Arr. 5. 12. 1, 18. 1. Curtius does not mention Krateros, but his account is highly unsatisfactory. For analysis of Krateros' position see Fuller 189.
[316] Cf. Carney, 'Macedonian Aristocracy', 214: '...we see that Alexander never gave him a prominent role to play in battle once Krateros had distinguished himself...against Spitamenes' rebels...'.
[317] Arr. 5. 20. 2.
[318] Arr. 5. 21. 4.
[319] Plut. *Alex*. 47. 11-12. Cf. also Plut. *Mor.* 337a.
[320] Arr. 6. 2. 2; *Ind*. 19. 1.

who figured in Alexander's elaborate strategy against the Mallians;[321] a year earlier, the task might have been entrusted to Krateros. Only Curtius mentions him in this context at all: when Alexander returned critically wounded to the junction of the Akesines (Chenab) and the Hydraotes rivers, it was Krateros who acted as the spokesman of the hetairoi, begging him not to risk his life unnecessarily.[322] But Krateros never regained his pre-eminence in the army.

From the junction of the Indus and Akesines rivers, he led the greater part of the army and the elephants along the left (i.e., east) bank of the Indus, arriving at Mousikanos' capital (near Rohri and ancient Alor[323]) after Alexander's fleet. It was now the end of spring 325. Mousikanos argued that Alexander had arrived in his kingdom before he was able to send envoys to him, and he was pardoned, but Krateros was ordered to garrison and fortify his capital nonetheless. It was his last major operation — and one that he completed while Alexander himself was present[324] — before he was sent westward through Arachosia and Drangiana with instructions to rejoin Alexander in Karmania.[325] Arrian, however, records Krateros' departure twice (6. 15. 5, 17. 3), first from Mousikanos' kingdom, then from Sind. In the first passage, the words διὰ τῆς Ἀραχωτῶν καὶ Δραγγῶν γῆς are correctly excised by editors as an obtrusive gloss.[326] Krateros had continued south with his troops, not much beyond Pardabathra,[327] where he appears to

---

[321] Descent of the Indus river-system: Arr. 6. 2. 2; 6. 4. 1; 6. 5. 5; 6. 5. 7; *Ind.* 19. 1, 3; Diod. 17. 96. 1. See also Breloer, *Bund* 29-56, for the Mallian campaign; cf. Fuller 259-263.

[322] Curt. 9. 6. 6-14; he continued downstream (9. 8. 3).

[323] Although the Indus river-bed lay further to the east (both above and below Alor) in ancient times, Alor (Rohri) and Attock (near modern Und), where Alexander first crossed the Indus, represent two fixed spots past which the river flowed throughout history (see Eggermont 8). Thus Alor was located in Alexander's time, as it is today, on the east bank of the Indus. Arr. 6. 15. 4 says that Alexander transferred Krateros and his forces to the left side of the river because the route was easier than that on the right side, and because there were tribes living there who were as yet unsubdued. This coincides with the view of Eggermont (16-22) that Sambos ruled the hill-country between Alor and the Bolan Pass and that he had been made satrap of this region by Alexander (cf. Arr. 6. 16. 3); hence the right bank of the river would have been more difficult to traverse but friendly (until Sambos' rebellion).

[324] Arr. 6. 15. 7.

[325] Arr. 6. 15. 5 records Krateros' departure for the west before his activities in Mousikanos' kingdom (6. 15. 7). His departure is then recorded a second time at 6. 17. 3.

[326] For the textual problem see Bosworth, *CQ* 26 (1976), 127-129.

[327] He appears to have taken no part in the campaigns against Oxikanos (Arr. 6. 16. 1-2; I can see no evidence for the form 'Oxykanos', found in much modern scholarship; cf. Berve ii 293, no. 589 s.v. Ὀξυκανός) and Portikanos (Curt. 9. 8. 11-12; Diod. 17. 102. 5; Strabo 15. 1. 33 C701). Eggermont (9-15) is

have remained with the main force while Alexander dealt with Sambos, the defecting satrap of the hill-country to the west of the Indus.[328] Soon it was learned that Mousikanos had rebelled — perhaps massacring the Makedonian garrison. Reprisals were conducted by Alexander, and Peithon son of Agenor (the new satrap of the region) soon brought Mousikanos prisoner to Sind, where he was executed.[329] At this point, Krateros was sent back to Rohri-Alor to restore order there — in the absence of Peithon, who continued south with Alexander — and also in Arachosia and Drangiana.

Thus Krateros, with the brigades of Attalos, Meleagros, Antigenes and Polyperchon,[330] some of the archers, all the elephants and the ἀπόμαχοι, moved westward, policing Arachosia and Drangiana, which were reported to be in a state of unrest.[331] The ringleaders of the

probably right to see them as separate rulers, one of Azeika (Axika), the other of Pardabathra. Lassen ii² 186 identifies them but prefers the name Portikanos; most modern scholars equate them under the name 'Oxykanos'.

[328] Arr. 6. 16. 3-5; Curt. 9. 8. 13 ff.; Diod. 17. 102. 6-7, Sambos himself escaped beyond the Indus with 30 elephants. Eggermont (16-22) plausibly identifies him with the 'Samaxus' of Curt. 8. 13. 4, who delivered the regicide Barsaentes to Alexander near Taxila. He had earlier been reinstated as satrap (cf. Arr. 6. 16. 3: τῶν ὀρείων Ἰνδῶν σατράπην ὑπ' αὐτοῦ κατασταθέντα), and his territory extended along the western bank of the Indus. Since Krateros was transferred to the eastern shore, because the terrain was unsuitable for his forces, it is doubtful that he and his contingent took part in the campaign against Sambos.

[329] Arr. 6. 17. 2; Curt. 9. 8. 16 has him executed before Alexander returned to his camp and the fleet. I would identify the son of Agenor with Peithon the taxiarch (Arr. 6. 6. 1; 6. 7. 2-3), who (significantly?) is not named again as a brigade-commander after Alexander's departure from India. Berve ii 311, no. 620, for no good reason, identifies the taxiarch with the son of Antigenes (Nearchos, FGrHist 133 F1 = Arr. Ind. 15. 10).

[330] Arr. 6. 17. 3 omits Polyperchon, but Justin 12. 10. 1 reads: *Itaque ex magna desperatione tandem saluti redditus Polyperconta cum exercitu Babyloniam mittit, ipse cum lectissima manu navibus conscensis Oceani litora peragrat.* Despite the inaccuracy concerning Babylonia, Justin appears to be speaking of Krateros' mission to Karmania, on which Polyperchon may also have gone. Polyperchon had accompanied Krateros in the past (Arr. 4. 16. 1; 4. 17. 1; cf. Curt. 8. 5. 2) and was to do so again in 324 (Arr. 7. 12. 4; Justin 12. 12. 8-9, cf. Bosworth, CQ 26 [1976], 129, n.65). For Polyperchon with Attalos (his relative, so Berve ii 325 and Hoffmann 156, n.59) see Arr. 4. 16. 1, where Meleagros is also named; with Amyntas, brother of Attalos, Curt. 5. 4. 20, 30; with Antigenes, Justin 12. 12. 8-9. On the other hand, Justin substitutes the name Polyperchon for Krateros on a number of occasions (13. 8. 5; 13. 8. 7; 15. 1. 1).

[331] News of the revolt was probably brought to Alexander by his father-in-law (Arr. 6. 15. 3; cf. Berve ii 292-293, no. 587).

uprising — Arrian names Ordanes, Curtius has Ozines and Zariaspes[332] — were arrested and brought in chains to Alexander, who was by this time in Karmania.[333] Stasanor, satrap of Areia and Drangiana, may very well have been summoned to Karmania by Krateros on the march.[334]

After Karmania there were further honours, but Krateros never fulfilled the promise of his early career. At Sousa he wedded Amastris, daughter of Dareios' brother Oxyathres.[335] She was indeed a worthy bride, but of lesser importance than Drypetis, Alexander's new sister-in-law, who was given to the rival Hephaistion.[336] There is, however, no record of a crown at Sousa.[337]

Then, from Opis, Alexander sent home the veterans, 10,000 in number, under the leadership of Krateros,[338] whom he instructed to assume the regency of Makedon in place of Antipatros; the latter was to report to Alexander in Babylon with reinforcements. This move has vexed historians, who suspect a sinister motive on Alexander's part and

---

[332] Arr. 6. 27. 3; cf. Berve ii 293-294, no. 590. Curt. 9. 10. 19: Berve ii 282, no. 579 does not believe that Ozines and Ordanes are identical; Droysen i³ 377, prefers Arrian's testimony; Badian, JHS 81 (1961), 19, wonders if they were in fact different people. For Zariaspes see Berve ii 162-163, no. 335. Alexander had them executed (Curt. 10. 1. 9).

[333] Arr. 6. 27. 3; cf. Strabo 15. 2. 11 C725, who says that Krateros followed the quickest route to Karmania, where both forces arrived at about the same time.

[334] Arr. 6. 27. 3. Stasanor of Soloi: Berve ii 361-362, no. 719; Badian, JHS 81 (1961), 18, incorrectly maintains that he was detained at Alexander's Court. Arr. 6. 29. 1 says that he was sent home shortly afterward; cf. Bosworth, CQ 21 (1971), 123, n.3.

[335] Arr. 7. 4. 5 has Ἀμαστρίνη (cf. Steph. Byz. s.v. Ἀμαστρίνη); Polyainos 6. 12 has Ἀμηστρις. Her life: Wilcken, RE i.2 (1894), 1750, no. 7; Macurdy, HQ 107 ff.; Berve ii 24, no. 50 ("Ἀμαστρις); cf. also Berve ii 291-292, no. 586 for Oxyathres (Oxathres).

[336] See ii 2.

[337] Golden crowns were given to Peukestas and Leonnatos for their heroism in India, to Nearchos and Onesikritos, and to Hephaistion and the other Somatophylakes. Krateros is not mentioned. This does not coincide well with Geyer's conclusion: 'Der beste Beweis für das unbedingte Vertrauen, das der grosse König zu K. gehabt hat, ist wohl der Befehl, eine bedeutende Truppenmacht mit den Kampfunfähigen und die Elefanten vom Indos...nach Karmanien zu führen, und glänzend hat K. dieses Vertrauen gerechtfertigt' (RE Supplbd iv [1924], 1046).

[338] Cf. Justin 12. 12. 8-9 (he was accompanied by Kleitos, Gorgias, Polydamas and Antigenes; Amadas is almost certainly dittography after Polydamas, though Berve ii 24, no. 49 gives him a separate entry). See Curt. 10. 10. 15: *credebant etiam Craterum cum veterum militum manu ad interficiendum eum missum*, where *eum* refers to Antipatros (wrongly 'Alexander' in J. C. Rolfe's Loeb translation, ii 557). According to Plut. *Phokion* 18. 7, Krateros was to offer Phokion the revenues from one of four Asian towns.

are troubled by the slow-progress of Krateros' march: by the time of Alexander's death, some nine months later, Krateros' forces had not advanced beyond Kilikia. Was he simply disobeying Alexander's orders?[339] Or was he waiting until the new recruits had left Makedonia?[340] Had he made a secret 'deal' with Kassandros, who met him in Kilikia on his way to Babylon?[341] Was he involved in a conspiracy against the King?

We need not look for sensational explanations. A reasonable solution may be found in the conditions that prevailed in Kilikia and in Arrian's own description of Krateros' departure:

Κρατερῷ δὲ τούτους τε ἄγειν ἐκέλευσε καὶ ἀπαγαγόντι Μακεδονίας τε καὶ Θρᾴκης καὶ Θετταλῶν ἐξηγεῖσθαι καὶ τῶν Ἑλλήνων τῆς ἐλευθερίας· Ἀντίπατρον δὲ διαδόχους τοῖς ἀποπεμπομένοις ἄγειν Μακεδόνας τῶν ἀκμαζόντων ἐκέλευσεν. ἔστειλε δὲ καὶ Πολυπέρχοντα ὁμοῦ τῷ Κρατερῷ, δεύτερον δὲ ἀπὸ Κρατεροῦ ἡγεμόνα, ὡς εἴ τι κατὰ πορείαν Κρατερῷ συμπίπτοι, ὅτι καὶ μαλακῶς τὸ σῶμα ἔχοντα ἀπέπεμπεν αὐτόν, μὴ ποθῆσαι στρατηγὸν τοὺς ἰόντας.

(7. 12. 4).

Craterus was not only appointed to be their leader but, after conducting them back, he was to take charge of Macedonia, Thrace, Thessaly and the freedom of the Greeks, while Antipater was to bring drafts of Macedonians of full age to replace the men being sent home. He also despatched Polyperchon with Craterus, as the officer next in seniority to Craterus, so that in case of harm coming to Craterus on the way, since he was an invalid when sent off, they should not want a general on their route.

(P. A. Brunt, tr.)

When Krateros left Opis, his condition was so serious that Alexander could not be sure that he would survive the journey home; for that reason, he had named Polyperchon as Krateros' second-in-command and possible successor. Age and ill health will have taken their toll on many of the veterans as well, and the expedition, which proceeded at a leisurely pace, was further encumbered by baggage and camp-followers. Illness alone will not explain Krateros' delay, nor was

---

[339]Badian, *JHS* 81 (1961), 34 ff., believes that Alexander feared the power of Antipatros and sought to depose him. Krateros lingered in Kilikia because he was unwilling to challenge Antipatros.

[340]Thus Griffith, *PACA* 8 (1965), 12-17, concludes that Krateros had orders not to enter Makedonia until Antipatros had left; for the disgruntled veterans might have an adverse effect on the new recruits.

[341]So Green 460.

Kilikia an ideal place to convalesce.³⁴² Whatever it was that threatened his life, it was not a disease that impaired Krateros for the rest of his life: certainly he was well enough to take an active part in the Lamian War and the first war of the Successors. Thus, we may assume that he regained his health by the time he reached Kilikia, or at least before he left it.

But Harpalos had been there not long before, residing at Tarsos with his harlot-queen, Glykera, and doubtless plundering the treasury before seeking refuge in Athens. The satrap, Balakros son of Nikanor (a son-in-law of Antipatros), had been killed in a skirmish with the Pisidians.³⁴³ Krateros spent the winter and the following spring (323) restoring order to the satrapy, intending to hand it over to the taxiarch Philotas, who was probably appointed by Alexander but had not yet set out for the province in late spring 323.³⁴⁴ When Alexander died suddenly in early June 323, Krateros and his veterans remained in Kilikia virtually in a state of limbo.

To replace Antipatros, whether it was prompted by Alexander's fear of his growing power in Europe or by the man's age, was a delicate matter even while the King lived. With Alexander dead, Krateros was trapped between *Staatsrecht* and *Faustrecht*.³⁴⁵ Antipatros, if anyone, was secure in his position; Krateros knew that. For the moment, there was some hope in Babylon, but this was quickly dispelled.

Modern interpretations of Krateros' προστασία cover the whole spectrum of possibilities, from the view that it was the highest honour

---

³⁴²Kilikia is described as 'the most virulent malarial location in Anatolia': Engels, *CP* 73 (1978), 226.

³⁴³Diod. 18. 22. 1: αὗται [the Pisidians] γὰρ ἔτι ζῶντος Ἀλεξάνδρου Βάλακρον τὸν Νικάνορος ἀπέκτειναν, ἀποδεδειγμένον στρατηγὸν ἅμα καὶ σατράπην. Cf. Arr. 2. 12. 2: Balakros ceased to be a Somatophylax and was appointed satrap of Kilikia. He married Phila, the daughter of Antipatros (Antonius Diogenes *ap*. Phot. *Bibl*. cod. 166, p.111b); Antipatros, son of Balagros (*IG* xi.2 161b, line 85; 287b, line 57), who dedicated a golden laurel-wreath at Delos in the late fourth or early third century, may have been their son (Heckel, *ZPE* 70 [1987], 161-162; cf. Badian, *ZPE* 73 [1988], 116-118). For Krateros in Kilikia, see Higgins, *Athenaeum* 58 (1980), 150; Heckel, *SO* 57 (1982), 61.

³⁴⁴Identification with the infantry commander, first mentioned at Arrian 3. 29. 7 seems likely; the 'Philotas Augaeus' (or 'Aegaeus'?) of Curtius 5. 2. 5, appears to be a different individual. His loyalty to the party of Krateros, which resulted in his being deposed by Perdikkas in 321/0 (Φιλώταν μὲν τὸν ξατράπην τῆς χώρας ἐπιτήδειον τοῖς ἀμφὶ Κρατερὸν γιγνώσκων παρέλυσεν τῆς ἀρχης: Arr. *Succ*. 24. 2; Justin 13. 6. 16), will go back to this time or even much earlier. He reappears as a supporter of Antigonos in 318 (Diod. 18. 62. 4 ff.), when he tries to win the loyalty of the Argyraspids away from Eumenes. For his career see Billows, *Antigonos* 423-424, no. 95.

³⁴⁵Schachermeyr's terms (*Babylon* 149 ff.).

in the empire to utter disbelief in its existence. As an academic exercise, the succession problem holds a certain fascination, and it does not want for innovative solutions.[346] But there has been a tendency to overlook one fundamental point: Krateros' προστασία was never realised, nor did Perdikkas intend it to be.[347] The army in Babylon demanded an immediate resolution of the succession question. They were not prepared to await the birth of Rhoxane's child; indeed, they had no desire to see a continuation of Alexander's oriental policies, which Hephaistion and then Perdikkas embraced. Hence they demanded that the half-witted son of Philip II, Arrhidaios, be proclaimed King, designating also as his guardian a man who shared their sentiments — Krateros. Perdikkas remained in control of Hephaistion's Chiliarchy. The *prostates* of King Philip III was his superior *de iure*. But Krateros' office turned out to be nothing more than a temporary concession to the phalanx.

It would be rash, however, to suggest that the *prostasia* was a fiction, that it was not part of the compromise at Babylon. The evidence points to an office, created to placate the phalanx but never actually held by Krateros himself. Quite naturally the position was associated with Arrhidaios, whom the conservative infantry revered as the last male descendant of Philip II. Nor is it surprising that Perdikkas agreed to the arrangement, at least for the moment: Krateros was absent in Kilikia, Arrhidaios in Perdikkas' control. *Faustrecht* prevailed in Babylon. The Chiliarch was supreme commander of the army, and he used his position to crush the insidious. Arrhidaios proved a convenient pawn in Perdikkas' hands, and there was little talk about Krateros' *prostasia*.

For the time, there was nothing for Krateros to do but wait in Kilikia. He had already recognised the futility of attempting to wrest Makedonia from Antipatros now that Alexander was dead. Perdikkas, meanwhile, had made himself *de facto* ruler of the east, and Krateros' veterans, we may be sure, were in no mood to return to Babylon in order to decide the issue.[348] Even now Perdikkas dealt the crippling blow by

---

[346] For earlier literature see J. Seibert, *Das Zeitalter der Diadochen* (Darmstadt, 1983), 84 ff.

[347] Thus Errington, *JHS* 90 (1970), 55: '...we can readily assume that the Perdiccans did not intend Craterus ever to adopt this newly created post, for in the final settlement after Meleager's death they reverted to their original arrangement of making him share Europe with Antipater: and there is no doubt that the Perdiccans were responsible for that arrangement.'

[348] It is likely that Krateros heard the details of the settlement at Babylon from Philotas, who had been sent out as satrap of Kilikia. His arrival there (perhaps in the company of the other satraps bound for the west) occurred shortly before Antipatros' appeal for help. From Philotas he learned not only of the phalanx's wish that he assume the guardianship of Arrhidaios, but also that Alexander's orders that he should replace Antipatros in Makedonia had been

revoking, with the assent of the army, the orders that Krateros should replace Antipatros in Makedonia.[349]

Krateros might well have remainded an outsider, had not the outbreak of the Lamian war on the Greek mainland forced Antipatros to cast about for aid. Both he and Leonnatos were summoned to Greece.[350] Antipatros' appeal included, in all probability, an offer of marriage to his eldest daughter Phila, a woman now in her early thirties but of exceptional qualities.[351] They will have needed no introduction: Krateros probably found Balakros' widow in Tarsos in 324 and later escorted her to Makedonia. That a marriage alliance was included in Antipatros' appeal is suggested too by the fact that Krateros took pains to find a suitable husband for his Sousan bride, the Persian Amastris. From what we know of Krateros' character, it is not surprising that he should willingly repudiate Amastris, but he did arrange an honourable marriage for her, to Dionysios, tyrant of Herakleia Pontika.[352]

Some scholars have charged that Krateros was deliberately slow in responding to Antipatros' call.[353] It must have taken a considerable

cancelled by the army. Given the situation in Europe and the condition of his troops, it is perhaps unfair to speak of the 'Kleinmut' of Krateros (so Schur, *RhM* 83 [1934], 145).

[349] Demonstrated convincingly by Badian, *HSCP* 72 (1967), 201-204.

[350] Diod. 18. 12. 1, where Philotas is incorrectly named as the satrap of Hellespontine Phrygia (18. 14. 4 says the message is brought by Hekataios of Kardia to Leonnatos; cf. Plut. *Eum.* 3. 6); Diodoros, who was speaking of Kilikia earlier, wrote Philotas by mistake.

[351] A similar offer was made to Leonnatos (Diod. 18. 12. 1; cf. Seibert, *Verbindungen* 12, n.6. See Berve ii 382, no. 772 s.v. Φίλα. Phila will have been born shortly before 350 B.C.; she married Balakros no later than 334 (cf. Heckel, *ZPE* 70 [1987], 161 f., and id., *Classicum* 15 [1989], 32 f.). See further Hoffmann 221; Macurdy, *HQ* 58-69, esp. 60; and also Tarn's eulogy in *Antigonos Gonatas* (Oxford 1913), 17 f. (based on Diod. 19. 59. 3-6); Droysen ii³ 51; Kaerst ii² 19; also Wehrli, *Historia* 13 (1964), 140-146.

[352] Memnon, *FGrHist* 434 F1 §4. 4 = Phot. *Bibl.* 224. For the date of this union see Seibert, *Verbindungen* 12-13; Macurdy, *HQ* 60; S. M. Burstein, *Outpost of Hellenism: The Emergence of Heraclea on the Black Sea* (Los Angeles-Berkeley 1976), 75.

[353] Badian, *HSCP* 72 (1967), 202 ('for a time Craterus refused to come to the aid of the hard-pressed Antipater in Thessaly') and *JHS* 81 (1961), 41 ('Yet Craterus hesitated. For several months, even after the outbreak of the Lamian War and the desperate plight to which it soon reduced Antipater, he did nothing to help him, leaving Leonnatus to go to his death'). Schwahn, *Klio* 24 (1931), 331-332, thinks that it was Perdikkas' campaign in Kappadokia that induced Krateros to leave Kilikia; in this he is followed by Errington, *JHS* 90 (1970), 61. But Diod. 18. 16. 4 synchronised Krateros' arrival in Makedonia with Perdikkas' war on Ariarathes: ὑπὸ δὲ τοὺς αὐτοὺς καιροὺς καὶ Κρατερὸς ἐκ Κιλικίας ἀναζεύξας ἧκεν εἰς Μακεδονίαν.

time for the message to reach Krateros in Kilikia, and winter was approaching. Over the winter he supplemented his forces; for he had decided to leave Antigenes and the three thousand Argyraspids in Kilikia for security, other troops were given to Kleitos, who was preparing a fleet with which he would sail to the Hellespont.[354] Krateros therefore recruited fresh troops, perhaps from the satrapies of Asia Minor. Diodoros' description (18. 16. 4) is instructive: ἦγε δὲ πεζοὺς μὲν τῶν εἰς Ἀσίαν Ἀλεξάνδρῳ συνδιαβεβηκότων ἑξακισχιλίους, τῶν δ' ἐν παρόδῳ προσειλημμένων τετρακισχιλίους.... This has been taken to mean that Krateros' infantrymen were divided into two units: 6,000 who had campaigned with Alexander since 334 (who had crossed the Hellespont with him at that time), and another 4,000 who had joined Alexander's in the course of his campaigns.[355] But this is a curious distinction for the historian to make, and ἐν παρόδῳ probably refers to Krateros' own march. The 1,000 Persian archers and slingers, as well as the 1,500 horse, were part of the original force that left Opis.[356]

Despite these extensive preparations, Krateros will have awaited the outcome of Leonnatos' relief efforts. Plutarch (*Phok.* 26. 1) says that the battle of Krannon was fought a short time afterwards (ὀλίγῳ δὲ ὕστερον χρόνῳ), but, since it is dated to 7 Metageitnion (probably 5 August; cf. Beloch iv[2] 1. 74), Krateros will not have reached the Hellespont until late June or early July 322 (for Kleitos' activities in the Aegean see iii 4, and Appendix III). Upon joining Antipatros, Krateros may have been formally engaged to Phila, as Niese suggests, though there is no evidence for this.[357] The advent of Krateros greatly augmented the Makedonian fighting force, but Krateros willingly yielded the supreme command to Antipatros.[358] Together with the remnants of Leonnatos' army, the Makedonians numbered 40,000 infantry, 5,000 cavalry and 3,000 archers and slingers.[359] With these numbers, Krateros and Antipatros won a decisive victory at Krannon, and thereafter broke the Greek alliance by taking the Thessalian cities

---

[354]Kleitos' activities: Diod. 18. 15. 8-9; Plut. *Demetr.* 11. 4; Droysen ii[3] 39-40; Beloch iv[2] 1. 74; cf. Berve ii 209, no. 428; and see iii 4 and Appendix III (with Map III). Antigenes was with Perdikkas in Egypt, where he murdered him (Arr. *Succ.* 1. 35); the only way to explain his presence in Egypt is to assume that he joined Perdikkas in 321/0 in Kilikia (cf. Heckel, *SO* 57 [1982], 60-62). Schachermeyr 489, estimates that Krateros' veterans included 6,000 heavy infantry and 3,000 hypaspists.

[355]E.g., Brunt, *Arrian* ii 489.

[356]Diod. 18. 16. 4.

[357]Niese i 207.

[358]καὶ τοῦ πρωτείου παραχωρήσας ἑκουσίως Ἀντιπάτρῳ (Diod. 18. 16. 5).

[359]Krateros' forces: Diod. 18. 4. 1 (cf. 17. 109. 1; Arr. 7. 12. 3); Diod. 18. 12. 1; 18. 16. 4; more generally, Plut. *Phokion* 26. 1; Leonnatos' troops: Diod. 18. 14. 4-5 (20,000 infantry, 1500 cavalry); for all the forces combined see Diod. 18. 16. 5.

THE 'NEW MEN'

one by one. This resulted in wide-spread defection from the Hellenic cause; peace treaties were made with individual cities (τὰς κατὰ πόλιν διαλύσεις).[360] The army moved as far south as Boiotia, where negotiations took place between Antipatros and the Athenians. Plutarch (*Phokion* 26. 6) says that Krateros favoured invading Attika on the ground that Makedonian forces were being maintained at the expense of their Boiotian allies, while the territory of the Athenian enemy remained untouched. Antipatros, for Phokion's sake, overruled him. Mounychia was, nevertheless, garrisoned on the twentieth day of Boëdromion (17 September, 322; cf. Beloch iv² 1. 76).[361]

Antipatros and Krateros now returned to Makedonia, where they celebrated the latter's wedding to Phila; the bride's father now heaped honours and gifts upon the groom and prepared for his 'return to Asia' (τὴν εἰς τὴν Ἀσίαν ἐπάνοδον συγκατεσκεύασεν).[362] But this was delayed by the necessity of dealing with the Aitolians, the only participants in the Lamian war who remained unconquered.[363] The campaign against them does not appear to have been a reaction to an unexpected emergency, but rather a deliberate act of policy. Therefore, it is doubtful that Antipatros planned to send Krateros back to Asia shortly after the wedding. For what purpose? He had not yet learned of Perdikkas' intrigues, and he believed that he had secured his goodwill through the marriage-alliance with Nikaia.[364] There was no place for Krateros in Asia that would not be a source of trouble.

From the account given by Diodoros (18. 25), it appears — and it is certainly likely — that Krateros was the chief prosecutor of the war against the Aitolians; undoubtedly, he employed his experience gained in the East with Alexander to his advantage. It was now the height of winter, and Krateros built shelters for his troops, forcing the Aitolians, who had forsaken their cities for the highlands, to hold out against the elements and a shortage of food; for it appears that Krateros

---

[360] Diod. 18. 17. 7; for the victory at Krannon, Arr. *Succ.* 1. 12; Plut. *Demosth.* 28. 2; *Phokion* 26. 1; Diod. 18. 17. Lamian war in general: Droysen ii³ 26-52; Kaerst ii² 14-19; Niese i 200-212; Beloch iv² 1.68-78; Tarn, *CAH* vi 454-460; and , for its background, Ashton, *Antichthon* 17 (1983), 47 ff.

[361] Plut. *Phokion* 28. 2-3; *Demosth.* 28. 1; *Camillus* 19.10. Cf. Schaefer, *Demosthenes* iii³ 391 (16 Sept.); see also Berve ii 259, no. 513, s.v. Μένυλλος. Cf. Diod. 18. 18. 5.

[362] Diod. 18. 18. 7. Antipatros, who was on friendly terms with Perdikkas — he had not yet heard of the latter's plan to marry Kleopatra, the sister of Alexander the Great —, was nevertheless supporting Krateros' claim to the *prostasia* of Arrhidaios' kingdom. The sources seem to connect Arrhidaios and the *prostasia* with Europe, which is clearly not how Antipatros understood it (cf. Arr. *Succ.* 1b. 4; 1a. 7; Curt. 10. 7. 9).

[363] Diod. 18. 24-25. For the Aitolians see also Mendels, *Historia* 33 (1984), 129-180.

[364] Berve ii 274, no. 552.

controlled the lines of communication.³⁶⁵ But events in Asia were to extricate the Aitolians from this grave situation and lead Krateros to his doom.

Antigonos the One-Eyed, satrap of Phrygia, alarmed by the growing power of Perdikkas, contrived the latter's ruin by bringing allegations of political duplicity. For Perdikkas, who had earlier secured Antipatros' friendship by marrying (or at least summoning to Asia for the purpose of marriage) the regent's daughter, Nikaia, now aspired to the throne of Makedon itself. And he hoped to achieve his purpose by marrying Alexander's sister. Antigonos' suspicions were not confirmed until his return to Asia (Arr. *Succ.* 1. 26), but the report given to Krateros and Antipatros in Aitolia was seasoned by a vivid account of the senseless murder of Kynnane by Perdikkas' brother, Alketas.³⁶⁶ Events in Asia took precedence. Peace was made with the Aitolians and attention redirected towards the East.³⁶⁷

Together with Antipatros, Krateros departed from Makedonia for the last time in the spring of 320, leaving behind Phila and an infant son.³⁶⁸ Crossing the Hellespont, they found that Eumenes' army stood between them and the Perdikkan forces, who were making their way to Egypt and Ptolemy. Neoptolemos, hostile to Eumenes, under whose authority Perdikkas had placed him, soon deserted to them, an auspicious beginning.³⁶⁹ But, while Neoptolemos may have judged rightly the mood of Eumenes' troops and their devotion to Krateros, he sadly underestimated the generalship and psychology of the Greek; for Eumenes had no intention of revealing to his forces with whom the issue

---

³⁶⁵Diod. 18. 25. 1.

³⁶⁶Arr. *Succ.* 1. 24: ἀνεδίδαξέ τε καὶ τὸ τῆς Κυνάνης ἐκτραγῳδήσας πάθος. Cf. Arr. *Succ.* 1. 22-23; the incident is not mentioned by Diodoros. For the source-question, see Heckel, *RSA* 13-14 (1983-84), 193-200. The fate of Kynnane will not have saddened Antipatros, who had attempted to bar her crossing of the Strymon sometime earlier (Polyainos 8. 60).

³⁶⁷Peace with the Aitolians: Diod. 18. 25. 5; Justin 13. 6. 9 wrongly speaks of peace with the *Athenians*, adding that Polyperchon was left in charge of Europe; he dealt effectively with the Aitolians, Diod. 18. 38. For the decision to go to war with Perdikkas see Arr. *Succ.* 1. 24; also an alliance was made with Ptolemy (Diod. 18. 25. 4; cf. 18. 14. 2). Cf. Seibert, *Ptolemaios* 96 ff.

³⁶⁸He was also called Krateros. Seibert, *Verbindungen* 13, n.17, thinks he was born after his father's death; but this is based on the assumption that Krateros left for Asia in spring 321. The son's own evidence shows that he was born before his father's death. In the dedication of the younger Krateros to Delphoi (lines 3-4) he describes himself as τὸν ἐμ μεγάροις ἐτεκνώσατο καὶ λίπε παῖδα. See Perdrizet, *JHS* 19 (1899), 273-279.

³⁶⁹Diod. 18. 29. 1 - 30. 3; Arr. *Succ.* 1. 26 says that he was lured away; Plut. *Eum.* 5. Neoptolemos: Berve ii 273, no. 548; he was an adherent of the Epeirot royal house; cf. Hoffmann 202, n.119.

was to be decided.[370] Sooner Krateros gasped out his life on the battlefield, the victim of a nameless Thrakian or of his own horse's hoofs.[371] That the much-glorified Eumenes found him semi-animous defies credulity, and it conjures up the image of Alexander's tender, but utterly fictitious, moments with the dying Persian king.[372] One can see the hand of Douris of Samos at work, and what makes the scene more unlikely is that Eumenes had only shortly before overcome his arch-rival Neoptolemos in a bloody hand-to-hand encounter.[373] That he was remorseful and treated Krateros' body with respect is another matter.[374]

---

[370]Nepos, *Eum.* 3. 5-6; Plut. *Eum.* 6. 7 (Eumenes had told his troops that they would be fighting against Neoptolemos and a certain Pigres, perhaps a local dynast); Arr. *Succ.* 1. 27. See Vezin 43 ff. Schubert, *Quellen* 139 ff., following the account of Diod. 18. 29-32 (from Hieronymos), disbelieves the version that Eumenes was afraid that his troops would desert if they learned that they were fighting Krateros, ascribing it to Douris. Schubert goes to great lengths to disprove the claims of Krateros' popularity. But Krateros could not have failed to develop a reputation, through his own successes and his connections with Alexander. Certainly both Neoptolemos and Alketas were reluctant to aid Eumenes — Alketas not even joining the army of Eumenes, Plut. *Eum.* 5. 3 — and both were, significantly, commanders of Makedonian infantry. For Plutarch's version (*Eum.* 6. 8-11) of Eumenes' dream about the aid of Demeter see Vezin (130), who thinks it is a late element, and Schubert (167-170), who traces it to Hieronymos.

[371]Plut. *Eum.* 7. 5-6 claims that he was wounded in the side by a Thrakian and fell from his horse; Arr. *Succ.* 1. 27 says a Paphlagonian; Nepos, *Eum.* 4. 3-4, does not specify. Diod. 18. 30. 5 alone dissents, saying that he was thrown from his horse and trampled. Nevertheless he perished unrecognised (ἀγνοηθεὶς ὃς ἦν συνεπατήθη καὶ τὸν βίον ἀλόγως κατέστρεψεν); perhaps Hieronymos attempted to make Krateros responsible for his own death, absolving Eumenes of blame. Plutarch (*Eum.* 7. 6) relates that a certain Gorgias, one of Eumenes' generals (Berve ii 114, no. 235) recognised the fallen Krateros.

[372]Recognised by Köhler, *SB Berlin* (1890), 594; Schubert, *Quellen* 142.

[373]Nepos, *Eum.* 4. 2: *ab hoc aliquot plagis Eumenes vulneratur*; cf. Justin 13. 8. 8: *mutuis vulneribus acceptis*; Plut. *Eum.* 7. 7-12; Diod. 18. 31. Justin 13. 8. 5, 7 writes Polyperchon where Krateros is clearly meant (cf. Trogus, *Prol.* 13).

[374]Plut. *Eum.* 7. 13; *Suda* s.v. Κράτερος = Arr. *Succ.* 26; Nepos, *Eum.* 4. 4: *amplo funere extulit ossaque in Macedoniam uxori eius ac liberis remisit*. Thus Macurdy comments: '[Phila] was then hurried...into another marriage so speedily that when the body of Craterus, sent to her by Eumenes for burial, arrived, she was already married to a youth of barely eighteen years' (*HQ* 61). But Diod. 19. 59. 3 states that Eumenes kept the bones of Krateros and only when he himself was on the point of dying gave them to Ariston to convey to Phila (315 B.C.).

5. Perdikkas: Successor and Failure

Literature. Berve ii 313-316, no. 627; Geyer, *RE* xix.1 (1937), 604-614, no. 4; Hoffmann 153, 168; Kornemann 247.

> ...es könnte gewiß mit Recht gesagt werden, daß nur in Alexander die Einheit des Reiches gewesen, daß sie ohne ihn oder einen größeren als ihn unmöglich sei....
> (Droysen ii³ 6)

> In Perdikkas hat Alexander eine Persönlichkeit erkannt, die ihm an Temperament, Begabung und Ehrgeiz, wie überhaupt an Format, irgendwie noch am nächsten zu stehen schien.
> (Schachermeyr, *Babylon* 16)

> Perdikkas, dessen besondere Vertrauensstellung bei Alexander uns Gewähr sein darf, daß er Alexanders Absichten verstand und teilte, hatte zuerst in Babylon versucht, die völlige Reichseinheit ... zu gewährleisten....
> (Miltner, *Klio* 26 [1933], 52)

> Perdiccas, of the princely line of Orestis, was brave and a good soldier; he was probably loyal to Alexander's house, and meant to keep the empire together; but he saw that someone must exercise the actual power, and he meant it to be himself. He was, however, unconciliatory and inordinately proud, and probably difficult to work with.
> (Tarn, *CAH* vi 462)

Perdikkas deserves to be considered the first of the Diadochoi: to him Alexander had given his signet ring and, with it, all the uncompleted projects, all the unresolved and festering problems of an empire too quickly subdued and ruled, primarily, by force. For the King's own reputation, it was a good thing, dying young. Posterity knew only his youthful brilliance, lamenting that time alone had defeated him. But his death was the signal for rebellion — to the Greeks in Europe and the Upper Satrapies, to the conservative Makedones who wished to return to the state of Philip II. While the King lived, they dared not oppose him; but now they rejected his policies when they were carried on by other men. In order to continue Alexander's work Perdikkas would have to be another Alexander, and this he was not. Hesitant in situations that required decisive action, he lost ground to his political foes, who cast him in the role of usurper. Thereafter, he moved too quickly, desired too much, and risked all on a single throw of the dice. Confounded in every undertaking by the jealousy of his colleagues and maligned after his death in the memoirs of an enemy, Perdikkas is remembered as a man of far-reaching ambition, ruined by his own incompetence and abrasive personality.[375]

Perdikkas son of Orontes, like his later rival Krateros, came from Orestis,[376] an adherent of that canton's royal house.[377] Two other members of his immediate family are known: a brother, Alketas, who attained the rank of taxiarch (probably of Perdikkas' former brigade),[378] and a sister, Atalante, who married Attalos son of Andromenes.[379] It was a corner-stone of Philip's Makedonian policy that the sons of his hetairoi — especially the highland aristocracy — should be brought to the Court at Pella to begin their training as Pages of the King and *syntrophoi* of his sons.[380] Perdikkas is first mentioned by the historians as a *somatophylax* on the day of the assassination of Philip II (summer 336): together with Leonnatos and Attalos he pursues and kills Pausanias, Philip's assassin.[381] But, as we have seen in the case of Leonnatos, these *somatophylakes* were most likely hypaspists and not the Seven; Welles' suggestion that they were Alexander's

---

[375]Justin 13. 8. 2: *Sed Perdiccae plus odium adrogantiae quam vires hostium nocebat....* Cf. Diod. 18. 33. 3: καὶ γὰρ φονικὸς ἦν καὶ τῶν ἄλλων ἡγεμόνων περιαιρούμενος τὰς ἐξουσίας καὶ καθόλου πάντων βουλόμενος ἄρχειν βιαίως....

[376]Son of Orontes: Arr. 3. 11. 9; 6. 28. 4; *Ind.* 18. 5. For his Orestian origin: Arr. 6. 28. 4; Diod. 17. 57. 2 (implied by τὴν τῶν Ὀρεστῶν καὶ Λυγκηστῶν τάξιν...., Περδίκκου τὴν στρατηγίαν ἔχοντος); Krateros was also from Orestis (Arr. *Ind.* 18. 5).

[377]Curt. 10. 7. 8: *stirpe regia genit[us]*. See F. Geyer, *Makedonien bis zur Thronbesteigung Philipps II.* (Munich-Berlin, 1930), 82-83; Droysen i³ 62. Meleagros' remark about Perdikkas (Curt. 10. 6. 20) can only be intended as an insult: *Nihil dico de nobilioribus quam hic est.*

[378]Berve ii 22-23, no. 45; Hoffmann 153; Kaerst, *RE* i (1894), 1514 f., s.v. 'Alketas (5)'. For his command of Perdikkas' brigade see Droysen i³ 62 (cf. Berve ii 22); but Berve ii 209, n.2, holds Anspach's view (ii 10, n.141), that White Kleitos commanded Perdikkas' brigade, as 'möglich, aber nicht zu erweisen.'

[379]Berve ii 90, no. 177; Kaerst, *RE* ii (1896), 1894-1895, s.v. 'Atalante (5)'; cf. Kaerst, *RE* ii (1896), 2158, s.v. 'Attalos (5)'.

[380]For a full discussion see v A; cf. also Heckel, *Phoenix* 40 (1986), 279-294; cf. Hammond, *Historia* 39 (1990), 261-290.

[381]Diod. 16. 94. 4. See most recently Fears, *Athenaeum* 53 (1975), 111-135. Cf. Berve ii 308-309, no. 614.

personal Bodyguard, and not Philip's, is unconvincing.[382] The proponents of the theory that Alexander himself instigated his father's assassination have attempted to see Perdikkas, Leonnatos and Atttalos as agents of the Crown Prince, who killed Pausanias in order to ensure his silence; but we do not know the exact nature of their relationships with Alexander,[383] nor is it certain that Pausanias was actually killed while attempting to escape.[384] One is tempted to draw inferences: Perdikkas was a young man, presumably in his early twenties,[385] at the time of Philip's death; he appears in the next year leading the brigade from Orestis and Lynkestis in the Illyrian campaign against Kleitos and Glaukias.[386] A reward for service to Alexander? But rapid promotion need not always be cause for suspicion — only when it appears unwarranted. And Perdikkas evinces a high degree of military competence, a fact obscured, but not concealed, by Ptolemy's *History*.

---

[382]For the view that these *somatophylakes* were hypaspists see Berve ii 92, n.3; ii 233, n.1; ii 308; ii 313; confused by Errington, *CQ* 19 (1969), 236. That they were Alexander's Bodyguard: Welles, *Diodorus* 101, n.2. But cf. Schachermeyr 100, n.81.

[383]Hamilton, *G&R* 12 (1965), 122: Pausanias was killed, 'significantly, by three close friends of Alexander. The prince was taking no chances; Pausanias knew too much.' Cf. Welles, *loc. cit.*; Green 108: 'The three young noblemen who pursued and killed Pausanias...were all close and trusted friends of Alexander.' We cannot be sure of this. Pausanias, Leonnatos, Perdikkas were not *all* from Orestis, as is often repeated (most recently by Green 108); Leonnatos was Lynkestian (so Geyer, *RE* xii.2 [1925], 2035; wrongly called Orestian by Berve ii 232; recognised by Fox 505), a *syntrophos* of Alexander (*Suda*, s.v. Λεοννάτος) and related to Philip II. We do not know when Perdikkas became a close friend (but cf. Plut. *Alex.* 15. 3-4); I do not see why Fox 505 supposes that Perdikkas may have been 'middle-aged'); as for Attalos, it is fairly safe to assume that he was the son of Andromenes, not the uncle of Kleopatra-Eurydike, as is suggested by Hammond, *GRBS* 19 (1978), 346, n.37 (see further, Heckel, *LCM* 4 [1979], 215-216). His marriage to Atalante belongs in all likelihood to 323/2.

[384]*P. Oxy.* 1798 = *FGrHist* 148 appears to say that Pausanias (?) was arrested and executed, so Wilcken, *SB* Berlin (1923), 151-157. Rejected by Welles, *Diodorus* 101, n.2. The idea has been revived by Bosworth, *CQ* 21 (1971), 94: 'The papyrus then is unreliable evidence, but that does not mean that Diodorus' account of Pausanias' death should be taken without question.' Against Bosworth see Green 524, n.65: 'He [Paus.] is not in fact named in this text, and the person referred to could equally well be a brother of Alexander the Lyncestian.'

[385]Cf. Berve ii 313: 'unter Al. erscheint er in seiner frischesten Manneskraft.' K. Kraft, *Der 'rationale' Alexander*, Frankfurter Althistorische Studien, Heft 5 (Frankfurt, 1971), 35.

[386]Arr. 1. 6. 9; for the composition of the brigade, Diod. 17. 57. 2.

Modern scholarship has only recently become sufficiently sceptical of Arrian's faith in Ptolemy's *History*. In the 1930s W. Schwahn and H. Strasburger adumbrated the matter of Ptolemy's bias,[387] but the era of W. W. Tarn and C. A. Robinson Jr. took comfort in the apologetic tone of the 'official' version, and Arrian-Ptolemy was preferred at all costs until R. M. Errington produced a systematic analysis of Ptolemy's tendency to denigrate the achievements of Perdikkas and his followers (notably Aristonous).[388]

To determine the truth about Perdikkas' early career is, therefore, no easy task. But the reader who has guarded himself against Ptolemy's distortions recognises in Perdikkas an active and capable leader. In his account of the capture of Thebes, Arrian (1. 8. 1-3) asserts that Perdikkas' troops acted without orders from the King. Diodoros (17. 12. 3) says otherwise. Nevertheless Perdikkas' role, even as described by Arrian, appears to have been somewhat heroic, and Amyntas son of Andromenes was not reluctant to bring up his Tymphaian brigade in support of the Orestians and their leader, who was critically wounded in the battle.[389] Whatever the truth concerning the action taken by Perdikkas' troops, it is clear that Alexander took no disciplinary measures against him, for Perdikkas continued to command his brigade when the army crossed into Asia. At the Graneikos River he was stationed between the hypaspists of Nikanor and Koinos' brigade,[390] roughly the same position that he occupied at Issos and Gaugamela.[391] After a relatively easy victory at the Graneikos, Alexander encountered stubborn defenders at Halikarnassos. In an abortive attempt on Myndos he took with him the infantry-brigades of Perdikkas, Amyntas and Meleagros; but the place could not be taken in the initial assault and Alexander, having brought no siege engines or

---

[387]Schwahn, *Klio* 23 (1930), 228; Strasburger 47: 'die wohlüberlegte Verschweigung dieser Tatsache [i.e., Perdikkas' assumption of Hephaistion's chiliarchy]...'.

[388]Errington, *CQ* 19 (1969), 233-242. The most obvious bias can be seen in Arrian's failure to mention that Alexander gave Perdikkas his signet-ring, and in the claim that Hephaistion's chiliarchy remained vacant. On the other hand, Arrian-Ptolemy is our only source for some of Perdikkas' activities: 3. 18. 5 against Ariobarzanes; 4. 16. 2, he commanded one of five divisions of the army (Curt. 8. 1. 1 mentions only three units, led by Koinos, Hephaistion and Alexander himself); 4. 21. 4 at the Rock of Chorienes; and, most notably, Perdikkas' independent mission against the Mallians, 6. 6. 4-6. See, however, Roisman, *CQ* 34 (1984), 373-385; cf. also A. B. Bosworth, *From Arrian to Alexander* (Oxford, 1988), for a synthesis of his important views on Arrian.

[389]For Amyntas' support see Arr. 1. 8. 2; Perdikkas' wound (1. 8. 3).

[390]Arr. 1. 14. 2.

[391]Arr. 2. 8. 3; Curt. 3. 9. 7 (Issos); Arr. 3. 11. 9; Curt. 4. 13. 28: *post eum* [sc. *Coenon*] *Orestae Lyncestaeque sunt positi* (Gaugamela). The brigades of Koinos and Perdikkas have changed position.

ladders, was forced to withdraw.[392] Perdikkas is mentioned a second time in connection with Halikarnassos: two of Perdikkas' men, motivated by drunkenness and *philotimia*, led an unauthorised assault on the city-walls. Soon the Makedonian forces became embroiled in the struggle but, unlike Thebes, Halikarnassos did not fall as a consequence. The ancient historians explained the failure in part by the drunkenness of the Orestian-Lynkestian brigade, thus assigning blame to Perdikkas, not Alexander.[393] During the siege of Tyre, Alexander conducted a raid on some neighbouring Arabs, leaving the siege-operations under the joint command of Krateros and Perdikkas. Thus Curtius (4. 3. 1). Krateros' role is corroborated by Polyainos, and Arrian's failure to mention the joint command may again reflect Ptolemy's bias.[394]

Whether acting on Alexander's orders or on his own initiative, Perdikkas had a tendency to come to the fore. It was Perdikkas, according to Plutarch (*Alex.* 15. 4-5; cf. *Mor.* 342d-e), who declined Alexander's gifts, as the army departed for Asia, preferring to share the King's fortune; this he did, in some respects perhaps more than any man. Thus, in success as in adversity, he is conspicuous, in spite of Ptolemy's calculated omissions. At Gaugamela he threw himself whole-heartedly into the fray and was wounded.[395] Then, at the beginning of 330 B.C., his unit alone accompanied Alexander as he circumvented the Persian Gates.[396]

What part Perdikkas played in the controversial Philotas affair must be deduced from Curtius, the only author to mention him. Perdikkas came to Alexander's tent on the night of Philotas' arrest, in the company of Hephaistion, Krateros, Koinos, Erigyios and Leonnatos,

---

[392] Arr. 1. 20. 5; Fuller 202.

[393] Arr. 1. 21. 1-3; but the poor discipline of Perdikkas' troops is corroborated by Diod. 17. 25. 5; Fuller 200-206; cf. Welles, *Diodorus* 189, n.2.

[394] Polyainos, 4. 13. Cf. Errington, *CQ* 19 (1969), 237. See also Fuller 206-216.

[395] Curt. 4. 16. 32 (along with Koinos and Menidas); Diod. 17. 61. 3 (with Hephaistion and Koinos); Arrian 3. 15. 2 mentions Hephaistion, Menidas and Koinos, but does not name Perdikkas. See Errington, *CQ* 19 (1969), 237.

[396] Arr. 3. 18. 5. Ptolemy is certainly the source of this passage, as the emphasis given to his role (3. 18. 9) in capturing the wall (found only in Arrian) indicates. But Seibert, *Ptolemaios* 8-10, debates the issue and argues that there is no good reason to identify the Ptolemy of this passage with the son of Lagos (against Berve ii 330). Ptolemy is not identified by patronymic, but Seibert's conclusion must be regarded as short-sighted, especially in view of the fact that Arrian alone gives a version in which a certain Ptolemy distinguishes himself. That Perdikkas had not yet given up his brigade is clear; cf. Milns, *GRBS* 7 (1966), 159, against Tarn ii 143. Of the other taxiarchs, Krateros and Meleagros had remained at the foot of the 'Gates' (Arr. 3. 18. 4), while Polyperchon (Curt. 5. 4. 20, 30), Amyntas, and Koinos were bridging the Araxes River, along with Philotas son of Parmenion (so Bosworth, *CQ* 23 [1973], 252 f.).

in order to discuss the crisis.³⁹⁷ Very likely, he was part of the *consilium amicorum*, which had met with Alexander earlier that day and urged that Philotas be punished: in short, he was party to the conspiracy *against* Philotas.³⁹⁸ The advantages that Philotas' downfall brought to Hephaistion can be gauged by his sudden rise from obscurity; Krateros' activities and benefits are clearly documented, as is Koinos' hostility toward his brother-in-law.³⁹⁹ But what of Perdikkas? Unlike Ptolemy, he did not become Somatophylax as a result of the affair, for Curtius makes it clear that he was already a member of the Seven at the time of Philotas' arrest.⁴⁰⁰ He did not become hipparch, as did Kleitos and Hephaistion (Arr. 3. 27. 4), but continued as taxiarch for a time;⁴⁰¹ nor did he enjoy the great influence exercised by Krateros for almost three years after the deaths of Philotas and Parmenion. But Perdikkas clearly did benefit from Philotas' demise: on Hephaistion's death, he emerged as the foremost of the marshals, having gained steadily in authority. The stages of his military and political development have been obscured by the pre-eminence of Hephaistion and Krateros, and by Ptolemy's sinister *History*.

Although Perdikkas replaced Menes (who had been appointed hyparch of Kilikia and Phoinikia) as Somatophylax shortly after Gaugamela, he continued, for a time, to command his brigade. Thus he was both taxiarch and Somatophylax from the end of 331 until at least the campaigning season of 329. In Sogdiana, Meleagros and Perdikkas, functioning as taxiarchs, besieged one of seven fortresses that had been established along the Iaxartes River (Syr-Darya) by Kyros the Great; Krateros undertook a similar task at Kyroupolis (Kurkath).⁴⁰² But, in the following season, Perdikkas was promoted to hipparch and led one of five divisions that swept Sogdiana; the pezhetairoi of Orestis and Lynkestis were now entrusted to his younger brother, Alketas.⁴⁰³ As Somatophylax, on the other hand, he occupied a seat near the King at the fateful banquet in Marakanda (late summer 328). Together with

---

³⁹⁷Curt. 6. 8. 17.

³⁹⁸Curt. 6. 8. 1 ff. See also Heckel, *Phoenix* 31 (1977), 9-21.

³⁹⁹See also ii 2. For Krateros see especially the versions of Plutarch and Curtius (for details see ii 4); for Koinos' hostility see Curt. 6. 8. 17; 6. 9. 30-31 (also ii 1).

⁴⁰⁰For Ptolemy's promotion to Somatophylax see Arr. 3. 27. 5; for Perdikkas, who appears to have replaced Menes (Arr. 3. 16. 9), Curt. 6. 8. 17: *ex armigeris autem Perdiccas et Leonnatus*.

⁴⁰¹This appears to be his rank at Curt. 7. 6. 19, 21.

⁴⁰²Curt. 7. 6. 19, 21 (Perdikkas, Meleagros); Arr. 4. 2. 2; Curt. 7. 6. 16 (Krateros.); cf. Holt, *Alexander and Bactria* 54 f.

⁴⁰³Arr. 4. 16. 2 (the other four divisions were commanded by Alexander, Hephaistion, Ptolemy and Koinos-Artabazos); Alketas first appears as taxiarch at Arr. 4. 22. 1.

Ptolemy he attempted to restrain the King, who was incensed by Kleitos' frankness; they were aided, in vain, by Lysimachos and Leonnatos.[404] Three of these Somatophylakes — Ptolemy, Leonnatos, Perdikkas — conducted the night-operations against the Rock of Chorienes (Koh-i-nor) early in the following spring.[405]

As the army set out for India, Perdikkas was overshadowed by Hephaistion, who had rapidly acquired prestige and authority since Philotas' demise. With Hephaistion, Perdikkas led an advance force to the Indus, which they were to bridge.[406] Hephaistion was, as it seems, the nominal commander, Perdikkas the more experienced military man. Alexander's selection of Perdikkas as Hephaistion's successor and the lack of friction between the two suggest that they shared Alexander's attitudes and were generally compatible. For this reason, and because Hephaistion needed the support of a competent commander, Perdikkas accompanied him to the Indus.[407] En route they subdued Peukelaotis, whose ruler Astis offered stubborn resistance.[408] By the time Alexander arrived at the Indus, Perdikkas and Hephaistion had brought the natives under the Makedonian yoke, gathered provisions from Omphis (Taxiles),[409] and bridged the river by means of what clearly was a boat-bridge.[410] On their way they had also fortified a city called Orobatis, in which they left an armed guard (Arr. 4. 28. 5).

From the Indus, Perdikkas appears to have accompanied Alexander and the main force to the Hydaspes (Jhelum), where, when the battle with Poros took place, he crossed the river in the same triakonter as Alexander, Lysimachos, Ptolemy and Seleukos (Arr. 5. 13. 1). In the actual battle he commanded one of the hipparchies directly under Alexander's control, the main striking force against Poros.[411]

---

[404]Curt. 8. 1. 45, 48; for Lysimachos and Leonnatos see 8. 1. 46. For the reliability of Curtius' version see **ii 3**.

[405]Arr. 4. 21. 4; cf. Fuller 243-245. For the identification of Chorienes and Sisimithres see Heckel, *Athenaeum* 64 (1986), 223-226.

[406]They led half the Companion cavalry and the brigades of Gorgias, Meleagros and Kleitos (Arr. 4. 22. 7; cf. Curt. 8. 10. 2 without specifics).

[407]See the discussion in **ii 2**.

[408]Arr. 4. 22. 8. See Berve ii 89-90, no. 174, s.v. Ἄστης (the MSS. of Arrian have Ἄστις).

[409]Curt. 8. 12. 6; 8. 12. 15; *ME* 48. Only Hephaistion is named, but Perdikkas must have been present. For details on Omphis (= Ambhi; Diod. and *ME* call him 'Mophis') see Berve ii 369-71, no. 739, s.v. Ταξίλης; Smith, *EHI* 63 ff.; on Taxila see now Karttunen, *Arctos* 24 (1990), 85 ff.

[410]See Curt. 8. 10. 2 for a description. Arr. 5. 7. 1-2 relates that Aristoboulos and Ptolemy did not explain in what manner the river was bridged, but Arrian supposes that boats were tied together to form a bridge.

[411]Arr. 5. 12. 2 (cf. 5. 13. 1); Curt. 8. 14. 15. See Fuller 180-199, esp. 186-187; Breloer, *Kampf*.

THE 'NEW MEN'

After his victory over Poros, Alexander turned his attention to the Kathaioi at Sangala, entrusting the left wing to Perdikkas, who commanded his own hipparchy and the infantry brigades; but Arrian, who reports Perdikkas' battle-position, tells us only what Alexander did on the right and says nothing further about the left.[412] The Sangala campaign was a particularly bloody one, and the numbers of Alexander's wounded high, among them the Somatophylax Lysimachos (Arr. 5. 24. 5). The morale of the troops, who had found Poros a more formidable enemy than Dareios, was reaching a low ebb. Perdikkas himself escaped being wounded and was despatched to ravage the region around Sangala with a lightly armed force (Curt. 9. 1. 19).

To the hardships of the campaign and the terrors of India were added rumours of an impending expedition to the Ganges. The army refused to advance beyond the Hyphasis (Beas). Shortly thereafter Koinos, who had been the spokesman for the disgruntled soldiery, died of illness at the Hydaspes.[413] By this time, many of the Old Guard were gone, and the careers of more conservative officers began to decline, as Alexander turned to his most trusted friend Hephaistion. No doubt it was through Hephaistion's urging that Alexander gave less authority to Krateros, to whom he joined Polyperchon, Gorgias, White Kleitos and Attalos, the mainstays of the phalanx.[414] New leaders emerged, notably Ptolemy, Leonnatos, and to a lesser extent Lysimachos.[415] But quite clearly Alexander placed greater faith than ever in the steady and loyal Perdikkas.

In the campaign against the Mallians, Perdikkas accompanied Alexander through the waterless region between the Akesines (Chenab) and Hydraotes (Ravi) Rivers and then took a special force against one of the Mallian towns. This town he captured, killing those inhabitants who did not manage to escape into the marshes (Arr. 6. 6. 4, 6). Reunited with Alexander for the assault on the main Mallian stronghold, he commanded a portion of the army, which Arrian (Ptolemy) implies was, through its sluggishness, responsible for

---

[412] Arr. 5. 22. 6. The command of the left had been Parmenion's responsibility in most engagements, then Krateros', but the latter was not present at Sangala (cf. Arr. 5. 21. 4: Krateros was on a foraging expedition with Koinos; both appear to have rejoined Alexander at the Hyphasis). For an analysis of the Sangala campaign see Fuller 255-258; cf. Breloer, *Bund* 75 ff. and 223.

[413] Arr. 6. 2. 1; Curt. 9. 3. 20 says that he died near the Akesines. For his career see Berve ii 215-218, no. 439, and **ii 1**.

[414] This group will also have included Meleagros, later the spokesman of the phalanx in the succession-debate.

[415] For Leonnatos see **ii 3**; for Ptolemy see **iv 3**. For their commands in India see Breloer, *Bund* 220-221. See also Heckel, *Klio* 64 (1982), 379.

Alexander's critical wounding there (Arr. 6. 9. 1-2). The near-fatal wounding of Alexander in the Mallian town can scarcely have been Perdikkas' fault, though it may well reflect the increasing reluctance of Alexander's troops to emulate his daring and recklessness; and, if this is a case of Ptolemy detracting from Perdikkas' reputation, it does not deserve serious consideration, for Ptolemy, by his own admission, was not present at the battle.[416] According to one branch of the tradition — Arrian does not name his sources in this case — it was Perdikkas who cut the arrow from Alexander's body; others attribute the surgery to Kritoboulos, a doctor from Kos.[417] The truth of this matter eludes us. But, after Alexander was taken downstream by ship to the junction of the rivers, Perdikkas completed the subjugation of the region before rejoining the main force.[418]

Curiously, this is where our information for Perdikkas' military career under Alexander breaks off. Although he became, with the departure of Krateros, Polyperchon, Attalos and Meleagros for the West, the second most influential man after Hephaistion, there is no further record of his activities. Smaller operations were entrusted to Ptolemy and Leonnatos, larger ones to Hephaistion. Yet, when Hephaistion died and Alexander soon afterward, there was no one more powerful in Asia than Perdikkas himself.

At Sousa in 324 Perdikkas wedded the daughter of Atropates, satrap of Media, as part of Alexander's mass-marriage between the Makedonian and Iranian nobilities.[419] Here too he was crowned, along with the other Somatophylakes.[420] But his greatest honours came later in the year, when Hephaistion drank himself to death at Ekbatana. Hephaistion indeed was irreplaceable, owing to the personal nature of his relationship with Alexander, but the King found in Perdikkas at least some of those qualities that he valued in Hephaistion:

---

[416]Curt. 9. 5. 21; Arr. 6. 5. 6-7; 6. 11. 8. Cf. Errington, CQ 19 (1969), 239; Kornemann 82-85; and Breloer, Bund 29-56.

[417]Arr. 6. 11. 1, the sources are not named (οἱ μὲν...οἱ δέ). For Kritoboulos see Curt. 9. 5. 25; Arrian has Kritodemos, which is surely an error. Both are said to have come from Kos (which in itself suggests a confusion of names), but Kritodemos is unattested, while Kritoboulos is known from Pliny, NH 7. 124 as the physician who extracted the arrow from Philip's eye at Methone. According to Arrian, Ind. 18. 7, he was a trierarch of the Hydaspes-fleet. See Berve ii 228, nos. 452, 453 though Berve regards Arrian's version as correct. But Arrian must certainly be wrong; Kritodemos did not exist. For a full discussion see Heckel, Mnemosyne 34 (1981), 396-398.

[418]Arr. 6. 15. 1; he subdued the Abastanoi. See Smith, EHI 104; Breloer, Bund 48, 223-224.

[419]Arr. 7. 4. 5. Her name is not given, but see Berve ii 91-92, no. 180, s.v. Ἀτροπάτης. Cf. Justin 13. 4. 13.

[420]Arr. 7. 5. 6.

undoubtedly there was a strong personal bond, but Perdikkas' later striving to maintain the unity of the empire suggests that he also understood Alexander's policies.[421] Thus, it was to Perdikkas that Alexander entrusted Hephaistion's corpse, which he was instructed to convey to Babylon and prepare for burial.[422] It is significant, though hardly surprising, that Arrian, who mentions Hephaistion's pyre, says nothing about Perdikkas.[423] And there was more than just this honour. Perdikkas now assumed Hephaistion's command, the first hipparchy or chiliarchy of the Companion Cavalry — though the unit, out of respect for the dead Hephaistion, retained the name of its original commander.[424] More than a mere hipparchy, it implied a position as Alexander's second-in-command; hence, when the office was later conferred upon Seleukos by Perdikkas, Justin describes it as *summus castrorum tribunatus*.[425]

Then Alexander died. The army in general was not prepared for this disaster; witness the confusion of the subsequent years.[426] Perdikkas himself could scarcely have hoped for a better position: since Hephaistion's death he had become Alexander's closest personal friend; he was by far the most influential of the generals[427] and of the Somatophylakes, who had by this time developed into a powerful *clique*;[428] supreme military power was his by virtue of his chiliarchy. His prestige was further enhanced by the significant gesture of Alexander, who on his death-bed and in the presence of the other generals handed to Perdikkas his signet-ring, a fact that Ptolemy the

---

[421] See Schachermeyr, *Babylon* 16; Miltner, *Klio* 26 (1933), 52. For Hephaistion's attitude toward the Persians see Plut. *Alex*. 47. 9-10.

[422] Diod. 17. 110. 8.

[423] Arr. 7. 14. 8 speaks of the pyre at Babylon. For the suppression of this information see Errington, *CQ* 19 (1969), 239.

[424] Arr. 7. 14. 10. It was called 'Hephaistion's chiliarchy' in order to 'distinguish it from other chiliarchies', so Griffith, *JHS* 83 (1963), 74, n.17.

[425] Justin 13. 4. 17; cf. earlier where Perdikkas as chiliarch and Meleagros as hyparch are described as follows: *castrorum et exercitus et rerum* [MSS.] *cura Meleagro et Perdiccae adsignatur* (13. 4. 5).

[426] Against Bosworth, *CQ* 21 (1971), 112-136, esp. 134-136.

[427] Nepos, *Eumenes* 2. 2, draws attention to the reason for Perdikkas' ascendancy: *aberat enim Crateros et Antipater, qui antecedere hunc videbantur; mortuus erat Hephaestio...*

[428] For the composition and development of the Somatophylakes see Heckel, *Historia* 27 (1978), 224-228; full discussion in vA. Note that the most powerful men among the cavalry after Alexander's death were reported by Arrian (*Succ*. 1a. 2) as Perdikkas, Leonnatos, Ptolemy, Lysimachos, Aristonous, Peithon, Seleukos, Eumenes. Only the last two were not Somatophylakes, though Seleukos had commanded the foot-guard (the royal hypaspists), while Eumenes was the chief secretary.

historian took pains to suppress.[429] According to the *Liber de Morte*, Alexander also entrusted to Perdikkas his wife, Rhoxane, with instructions that he should marry her.[430] Rhoxane's role at the time of Alexander's death is heavily romanticised by the *Liber de Morte*,[431] but the suggestion that she marry Perdikkas is in itself not entirely implausible. It was only when the conservative phalanx violently opposed Rhoxane's child in particular and Alexander's policy of fusion in general that a union with her ceased to be a viable means of gaining power. Still she remained a valuable commodity; though it was the unborn child that mattered, not the woman.[432]

Droysen rightly observed that the empire could be maintained only by an Alexander or by a greater man yet.[433] And perhaps it was Perdikkas' fatal error that he attempted to preserve the integrity of the new Empire under Argead rule. In this respect, Ptolemy was more pragmatic and less an idealist, but he was also less to be admired. But Perdikkas had not taken full account of the conservative Makedonian phalanx and their longing for the state of Philip II. They could not endure a second Alexander, if indeed such a man was to be found, and they showed their determination to return to the traditional ways by demanding as their King a man whom no rational thinker could have considered: Arrhidaios, a mentally deficient son of Philip II by the Thessalian Philine. That his mother was a dancing-girl, or a harlot, from Larissa is, almost certainly, a fabrication; Arrhidaios' mental state was not.[434] Fontana's doubts are ill advised: Arrhidaios was

---

[429]Curt. 10. 5. 4; cf. 10. 6. 4-5; Justin 12. 15. 12; Diod. 17. 117. 3; 18. 2. 4; Nepos, *Eum.* 2. 1; *LM* 112. Ptolemy fails to mention not only the ring, but also the care of Hephaistion's body, which was entrusted to Perdikkas, and Perdikkas' elevation to Hephaistion's chiliarchy, which Ptolemy underhandedly denies, Arr. 7. 14. 10. Cf. Schwahn, *Klio* 23 (1930), 223; Strasburger 47; Errington, *CQ* 19 (1969), 239 f.

[430]*LM* 112, 118.

[431]*LM* 101-102, 110 and especially 112: *at Rhoxane magno cum clamore capillos sibi ipsa scindens conata est ad Perdiccae pedes se advolvere. hanc Holcias excepit et eam ad Alexandrum adduxit. ille dentibus frendens cum se iam in extremo spiritu videret, eam complexus osculari coepit dexteramque eius tenens in dexteram Perdiccae indidit nutuque commendationem fecit. deinde cum morte opprimeretur, oculos eius Rhoxane oppressit animamque eius ore suo excepit.* For Rhoxane's life see Berve ii 346-347, no. 688. For the 'historical' significance of the *Liber de Morte* see Heckel, *LDT*.

[432]For her pregnancy: Curt. 10. 6. 9; Justin 13. 2. 5; cf. 12. 15. 9; Arr. *Succ.* 1a. 1; 1b. 1. *ME* 70 mentions an earlier son of Alexander and Rhoxane, who died at the Akesines (sc. Hydaspes) River.

[433]Droysen ii³ 6.

[434]For Philine (Philinna) see Satyros' account of Philip's wives, *FHG* iii (Müller) 161 = Athen. 13. 557b-d; for her alleged low birth see Justin 9. 8. 2 (*saltatrix*); 13. 2. 11 (*scortum*); Athen. 13. 578a: Plut. *Alex.* 77. 7 (ἐκ γυναικὸς

present in Babylon when his brother died, and the marshals could scarcely have overlooked him had he not been totally unfit to rule.[435]

Things went wrong for Perdikkas from the beginning, though everything appeared to be in his favour. He had the support of at least one Somatophylax, Aristonous;[436] Peithon may also have been an ally in the early going.[437] But Perdikkas faced an unusual problem: he could not be acclaimed King and rule securely as long as Rhoxane carried the potential heir; he could not act as regent for a child as yet unborn;[438] and an *interregnum* was out of the question, owing to the mood of the army.[439] Whatever title Perdikkas was to take as ruler, he was anxious

---

ἀδόξου καὶ κοινῆς Φιλίννης). Beloch iii² 2. 69, followed by Griffith, *CQ* 20 (1970), 70-71 and Ellis, *Philip II* 61, thinks she was clearly of a good family, probably the Aleuadai. See also Ehrhardt, *CQ* 17 (1967), 297; Schwahn, *Klio* 24 (1931), 312; Niese i 191, n.5. For Arrhidaios' ailment see App. *Syr.* 52 (οὐκ ἔμφρονα); Justin 13. 2. 11; 14. 5. 2; Diod. 18. 2. 2 (ψυχικοῖς δὲ πάθεσι συνεχόμενον ἀνιάτοις); Plut. *Alex.* 10. 2; 77. 7-8; *Mor.* 337d = *de fort. Al.* 2. 5; *Heidelberg Epitome* (ἐπιληπτικός); Porphyr. Tyr., *FGrHist* 260 F2. According to Plut. *Alex.* 77. 8, his mental condition was brought on by drugs given to him, while he was still a child, by Olympias. Curt. 10. 7. 4-6; the manner in which Peithon speaks of Arrhidaios suggests that he was a pathetic character. See further Hamilton, *PA* 216 f.; Berve ii 385-386, no. 781, s.v. Φίλιππος Ἀρριδαῖος; Hoffmann 134. But see now Greenwalt, *AncW* 10 (1984), 69-77.

[435]Fontana, *Le Lotte* 128 ff. and 128, n.20; cf. Badian's review in *Studies* 263 f.; Errington, *JHS* 90 (1970), 51, n.23.

[436]Berve ii 69, no. 133. For his support of Perdikkas see Curt. 10. 6. 16-18. Like Perdikkas he was loyal to the house of Alexander and, faithful to the end, he perished in 316/5 (Diod. 19. 50. 3 - 51. 1). Predictably, he too was the victim of Ptolemy's bias: see Errington, *CQ* 19 (1969), 235.

[437]Berve ii 311, no. 621. Although he was soon among those who worked to undermine Perdikkas, he appears to have supported him immediately after Alexander's death, though perhaps only on the condition that his power be limited by attaching Leonnatos to him as his colleague. See Curt. 10. 7. 4-8; cf. Schur, *RhM* 83 (1934), 133, 139 f.

[438]For Perdikkas' dilemma see Errington, *JHS* 90 (1970), 50, who comments on the 'possibility of the child's exploitation by anyone unscrupulous enough among Perdiccas' opponents who was prepared to depict Perdiccas as a usurper.' In fact, according to Curtius 10. 6. 21, Perdikkas was accused by Meleagros of planning to usurp power through the regency of Rhoxane's child.

[439]The army had two main objections to Perdikkas' proposal that the Makedonians should await the birth of Rhoxane's child: their more immediate concern was for pay and discharge from duty (so Schwahn, *Klio* 24 [1931], 308; Errington, *JHS* 90 [1970], 51), but they were, at the same time, opposed not to Perdikkas' personal ambition (Badian, *Studies* 263, rightly refuting Fontana, *Le Lotte* 121: 'Causa principale fu l'opposizione a Perdicca, ritenuto colpevle di aspirare al trono; concause evidenti le gelosie personali e il desiderio di dominio degli altri generali') but to Perdikkas' enthusiasm for Alexander's *Verschmelzungspolitik*. To deny this fact is to make light of the inner

that it should be sanctioned by the army. At the urging of Aristonous, he was offered the kingship. Who could deny that Alexander had marked him out as his successor? But Perdikkas unwisely put the army to the test, hoping that, by feigning reluctance, he would have the crown virtually forced upon him. Thus Curtius, drawing heavily on Roman precedent.[440] Again Perdikkas had miscalculated, for the hesitation encouraged only further dissension. His opponents were quick to point out that Perdikkas sought the crown through Rhoxane's son, that he would follow the example of the great Philip, who usurped the kingdom from the legitimate heir, Amyntas Perdikka, his nephew.[441] An illegitimate son of Alexander, Barsine's child Herakles, was scorned by the army, as was Nearchos, who suggested him;[442] Rhoxane's potential son was unpopular with the army, whether Perdikkas alone or a college of guardians acted in his interests.[443] Then the unexpected happened: the common soldier called out for Arrhidaios, for the family of Philip II.[444] And it was at this juncture that Perdikkas lost control of the situation completely; for Meleagros, a taxiarch since at least the beginning of Alexander's Asiatic

resentment of the troops, who mutinied at the Hyphasis River and at Opis, towards their King's orientalisms and those who supported him in his designs.

[440]Curt. 10. 6. 18: *haerebat inter cupiditatem pudoremque et, quo modestius quod spectabat appeteret, pervicacius oblaturos esse credebat*. For the Roman elements in Curtius' history see Sumner, *AUMLA* 15 (1961), 30-39; Devine, *Phoenix* 33 (1979), 142-159.

[441]Curt. 10. 6. 21. See Berve ii 30-31, no. 61. For Philip's usurpation see Ellis, *Philip II* 45 ff. and 250, n.10; id., *JHS* 91 (1971), 15-24. Against this interpretation: Griffith, *HMac* ii 208 ff.; Borza 200 f.; more cautiously, Errington, *Macedonia* 37, with 271, n.9.

[442]Curt. 10. 6. 10-12;. he is mentioned as a possible candidate by Justin 12. 15. 9. Justin 13. 2. 7 makes Meleagros bring Herakles into the discussion; Nearchos is more likely, for he was a relative, having married the daughter of Barsine and Mentor (Arr. 7. 4. 6). Cf. Badian, *YCS* 24 (1975), 168-169: 'The army, reluctant to wait for the legitimate offspring of Alexander's marriage to an Oriental princess, was by no means willing to consider the succession of a semi-Oriental bastard.' For Barsine see Berve ii 102-103, no. 206; cf. also Berve ii 168, no. 353, s.v. Ἡρακλῆς. In favour of Herakles' existence, see now Brunt, *RFIC* 103 (1975), 22-34, and Badian *YCS* 24 (1975), 167, n.51, against Tarn ii 330-337, and id., *JHS* 41 (1921), 18-28.

[443]The joint guardianship of Rhoxane's child is suggested by Peithon, who realises that the army is now suspicious of Perdikkas' designs and hopes to win the phalanx back to Perdikkas' policy by limiting his power. Thus Leonnatos is proposed as co-guardian, while a similar arrangement is sought for Europe (Antipatros and Krateros); Curt. 10. 7. 8-9; cf. Justin 13. 2. 14, who has Perdikkas, Leonnatos, Krateros and Antipatros all acting as guardians for the unborn child. See the comments of Schur, *RhM* 83 (1934), 133, who sees Leonnatos as 'ein wirksames Gegengewicht'.

[444]Curt. 10. 7. 1: *quidam plerisque Macedonum ignotus ex infima plebe.*

campaign, saw in the advocacy of the inept Arrhidaios a means of acquiring power for himself.[445] Undoubtedly, Perdikkas also saw in Arrhidaios a useful pawn, but the initiative had unexpectedly been taken from him. Encouraged by the phalanx, Meleagros had the support of its leaders, with the exception of Perdikkas' brother, Alketas.[446] A wave of irrationality carried Meleagros to the fore, and he acted decisively, challenging Perdikkas' supremacy with a show of arms. Perdikkas withdrew to the chamber that housed Alexander's body, supported by a mere six hundred men, but Meleagros had incited the mob, who burst through the barricades and forced the Perdikkan party to quit the city.[447] The cavalry thus hastened from Babylon under the leadership of Leonnatos; for Perdikkas remained within the city, hoping to re-assert his authority over the infantry.[448] He had been a taxiarch himself, and his brigade was now led by Alketas; doubtless he had some followers among the upper ranks of the phalanx. But Meleagros instigated his assassination, acting in the name of King Philip Arrhidaios, and Perdikkas, who foiled the attempt, now thought it wise to abandon the city and rejoin Leonnatos.[449]

For the moment it looked as if Meleagros had conducted a successful *coup*. But the army soon came to regard him as an opportunist and a demagogue, and they regretted having risen against the marshals of the empire; doubtless their enthusiasm for Arrhidaios waned as they

---

[445]In Curtius' version, Meleagros seems to be acting on his own when he incites the army, but the accounts of Diod. 18. 2. 2-3 and Justin 13. 3. 1-2 (both drawing on Hieronymos) suggest that Meleagros — Justin includes Attalos — was sent to the phalanx by the cavalry and that he betrayed the latter. This might be an attempt to justify Meleagros' punishment, who, according to Diod. 18. 4. 7, was charged with plotting against Perdikkas: ὡς ἐπιβουλὴν κατ' αὐτοῦ πεποιημένον ἐκόλασε. Cf. Schachermeyr, *Babylon* 113, 125; also Wirth, *Helikon* 7 (1967), 291.

[446]Attalos son of Andromenes; Philotas the taxiarch and later satrap of Kilikia, Berve nos. 181 and 803 (= 804?).

[447]Curt. 10. 7. 14: Meleagros assumes the initiative by becoming self-appointed guardian of Arrhidaios; Curt. 10. 7. 16: Perdikkas withdraws with 600 followers; Curt. 10. 7. 17-20: the cavalry are driven from the city and encamp on the plains under the leadership of Leonnatos. This is followed closely, but in abbreviated form, by Justin 13. 3. 3-6; cf. Diod. 18. 2. 3-4.

[448]Curt. 10. 7. 21; implied by Justin 13. 3. 7-8.

[449]Curt. 10. 8. 1-4. Justin 13. 3. 7-8 mentions the assassination bid, ascribing it to Attalos, but he does not mention Perdikkas' flight from Babylon; instead Perdikkas appears to win the phalanx over with a passionate appeal and a denunciation of civil war (13. 3. 9-10); cf. 13. 4. 1: *haec cum pro singulari facundia sua Perdicca perorasset, adeo movit pedites, ut probato consilio eius dux ab omnibus legeretur*. See Wirth, *Helikon* 7 (1967), 291, without critical comment; but cf. Schachermeyr, *Babylon* 125 f.: 'So haben wir bei Iustin mit gewaltigen Kürzungen zu rechnen.'

recognised in him a front for the ambitions of Meleagros.[450] Furthermore, the cavalry now intended to force the issue, cutting off the food-supply. Curtius' description of the resulting confusion among the townspeople and the deterioration of conditions in Babylon is more appropriate to a protracted siege than to this stand-off of scarcely one week; starvation was simply out of the question.[451] Morale suffered nonetheless. Disillusioned with Meleagros and the pathetic Arrhidaios, the phalanx began to negotiate with the Perdikkans. Eumenes was particularly effective in reconciling the factions,[452] and, as a Greek, he may have acted as a mediator; though it is clear from Arrian's *Events after Alexander* and what happened later that he was far from a disinterested party.[453] The actual liaison between factions was conducted by Pasas the Thessalian, Perilaos, and Damis the Megalopolitan.[454] To them Perdikkas responded that he would accept the demands of the infantry — by which we shall take the recognition of Philip Arrhidaios to be meant — only on the condition that the phalanx surrender the authors of the discord.[455] That Perdikkas sought the sanction of the phalanx for the elimination of Meleagros is clear,[456] but Meleagros was himself actively involved in the negotiations and understandably concerned for his own well-being. By this time, Perdikkas (perhaps through the agency of Eumenes, if we may assume co-operation between the two at this early time)[457] had secured the

---

[450]For their regrets and anger at Meleagros: Curt. 10. 8. 5-8; for the disillusionment with Arrhidaios see Curt. 10. 8. 9: *et ex comparatione regis novi desiderium excitabatur amissi.* Cf. Curt. 10. 7. 5, where the army is said to favour Arrhidaios out of pity. Appian's description (*Syr.* 52) also shows that Arrhidaios' acclamation was an irrational and emotional act.

[451]Curt. 10. 8. 12 exaggerates the conditions in Babylon (*itaque inopia primum, deinde fames esse coepit*), after only one week's siege (cf. 10. 10. 9).

[452]Plut. *Eum.* 3. 1-2; cf. Vezin 20 f.; Cloché, *La Dislocation* 12.

[453]Plut. *Eum.* 3. 1 says that he favoured the cavalry but tried to remain neutral; Arr. *Succ.* 1a. 2 names him among the leading cavalry-officers. See also Droysen ii³ 8; Niese i 94; Vezin, *loc. cit.*

[454]Berve ii 306-307, no. 608; ii 317, no. 630, s.v. Πέριλλος (for the name see Hoffmann 212); Curt. 10. 8. 15 reads *Amissus*, which Hedicke emended to *Damyllus* in his Teubner edition (Leipzig, 1908); he is followed by Rolfe, in the Loeb, ii 542. Amissus is otherwise unknown (though Berve ii 25, no. 53, accepts him as genuine); Damyllus is unattested; but Damis is a more common name, and a known Megalopolitan. See Berve ii 115, no. 240, s.v. Δᾶμις. Perhaps Damis has been corrupted to Amissus here; cf. Niese i 245, n.3; see also Hornblower, *Hieronymus* 172.

[455]Curt. 10. 8. 15.

[456]Niese i 194, n.2: 'die Auslieferung der Empörer, also auch des Meleager...'.

[457]Droysen ii³ 8: 'Er [sc. Eumenes] begann mit dem und jenem von den Führen anzuknüpfen und zum Frieden zu reden', by which he certainly means

THE 'NEW MEN'

goodwill of the taxiarchs, most notably Attalos son of Andromenes.⁴⁵⁸ Their own distrust of Meleagros' ambitions will have played no small part in causing them to re-align themselves with the Perdikkan party. But Meleagros, sensing their opposition, indicated a willingness to relinquish his 'control' over Arrhidaios to the more popular and respected Krateros — if the *prostasia* is not, in fact, an invention of Douris of Samos⁴⁵⁹ — though he demanded to be accepted as *tertius dux*.⁴⁶⁰

For the moment, Perdikkas was willing to concede: there was no difficulty in accepting Arrhidaios, who would easily be manipulated once free of Meleagros' influence. As for Krateros, his absence would give Perdikkas sufficient time to secure his own position. More troublesome was the presence of Meleagros, now Perdikkas' lieutenant (ὕπαρχος).⁴⁶¹ It is no accident that the final settlement at Babylon resembled in no way the conditions of the compromise; for Perdikkas had no intention of acceding to the wishes of the phalanx, beyond the recognition of Arrhidaios. He would indeed be King, but Perdikkas meant to rule through him. The decisive act would be the elimination of Meleagros, and in this matter he must have the support of the taxiarchs. Meleagros had been a bitter enemy in the days that preceded the reconciliation, and he continued to be a threat; it is not unlikely that Perdikkas encouraged rumours that Meleagros was plotting against him.⁴⁶² Careful to attach a show of legality to Meleagros' elimination, he called for a lustration of the army in the name of Philip Arrhidaios and on the pretext of punishing the seditious.⁴⁶³ With the King and the army firmly in his grip, Perdikkas crushed the ringleaders of the uprising; the taxiarchs acquiesced in the liquidation of Meleagros; the army, thunderstruck by the show of power and, to an extent, satisfied with the recognition of Philip Arrhidaios, accepted Meleagros' death as necessary for the welfare of

---

the *taxiarchs*, since the *hipparchs* had abandoned the city. Cf. Cloché, *La Dislocation* 12: he shared Perdikkas' loyalty to the Royal House.

⁴⁵⁸For details see Heckel, *CQ* 28 (1978), 377-382, and Appendix V.

⁴⁵⁹Schubert, *Quellen* 139-149, traces the accounts of Krateros' overwhelming popularity to Douris. Arrian's account of Krateros' death is certainly from Douris (*Succ.* 1. 27; 26 = *Suda* s.v. Κρατερός), and the mention of the *prostasia* (which is echoed by Justin 13. 4. 5: *regiae pecuniae custodia Cratero traditur*) may also derive from Douris; see Schwahn, *Klio* 23 (1930), 229 f.; also 235: 'Auffällig ist bei Justin die vielfache Übereinstimmung mit Arrian.... Sie sind allein durch eine gemeinsame Quelle zu erklären; diese kann nur der vielgelesene und oft zitierte Duris sein, auf den Arrian direkt ... zurückgeht.'

⁴⁶⁰Curt. 10. 8. 22; Justin 13. 4. 5; Arr. *Succ.* 1a. 3.

⁴⁶¹Arr. *Succ.* 1a. 3.

⁴⁶²Curt. 10. 9. 7: *Perdicca unicam spem salutis suae in Meleagri morte reponebat*. For rumours of Meleagros' plotting: Diod. 18. 4. 7; cf. Curt. 10. 9. 8 ff.

⁴⁶³Curt. 10. 9. 11 ff.; Justin 13. 4. 7; cf. Diod. 18. 4. 7.

the state: *nam et insociabile est regnum*.[464] Perdikkas had taken the first step in recouping his losses. Power was now once again securely in his hands.

In the name of the King, though doubtless in consultation with the marshals, Perdikkas allotted the satrapies.[465] The most important regions went, not surprisingly, to the most powerful of Perdikkas' 'supporters'. But there was another consideration: Perdikkas found it desirable to remove from Babylon those officers with the greatest influence. It proved to be a futile exercise; for, while Perdikkas worked to establish a strong central government, the new satraps made use of their regional resources to plot a course of separatism — few more vigorously than Ptolemy in Egypt.[466]

At the Court, Perdikkas retained those men whom he felt he could trust: his brother Alketas, Attalos son of Andromenes, to whom he had betrothed his sister Atalante, Seleukos son of Antiochos, whom he now advanced to the command of Hephaistion's chiliarchy, and Aristonous, the only Somatophylax not awarded a satrapy. Nor had he forgotten Rhoxane, whose child (if male) was to be recognised as *symbasileus* with Arrhidaios.[467] Allegedly in Rhoxane's interests, he arranged the murder of the Achaimenid Stateira and her sister Drypetis (Plut. *Alex.* 77. 6). Plutarch depicts it as an act of jealousy, but Rhoxane was educated in the ways of court intrigue and she meant to secure her own position and that of her unborn child: as long as Perdikkas chose to pursue Alexander's policies of unity and fusion, she could not allow Stateira or her sister to remain as potential rivals.[468] That Perdikkas

---

[464]Curt. 10. 9. 1. For Meleagros' end see Curt. 10. 9. 20-21; Arr. *Succ.* Ia. 4-5; Justin 13. 4. 7-8 does not mention Meleagros' death, but it is clear that his description of Perdikkas' acting *ignaro collega* suggests that Meleagros' elimination was part and parcel of the lustration of the army. Diod. 18. 4. 7 places his death after the allotment of the satrapies and the cancellation of Krateros' orders, surely an error.

[465]Diod. 18. 3. 1-3; Justin 13. 4. 10-23; Curt. 10. 10. 1-4; Arr. *Succ.* 1a. 5-7; 1b. 2-7. See also Schachermeyr, *Babylon* 142, 144.

[466]Ptolemy appears from the outset to have favoured a wide distribution of power, a policy that would lead inevitably to the disintegration of the empire; cf. Curt. 10. 6. 15; Justin 13. 2. 12. Paus. 1. 6. 2 portrays Ptolemy as the instigator of the division of the satrapies, which suits both Ptolemy's character and his policies as satrap; cf. Droysen's appraisal (ii^3 13). See also Wirth, *Helikon* 7 (1967), 316 ff., and the rather sterile conclusion of Seibert, *Ptolemaios* 38, based on a rigid analysis of the sources.

[467]Badian, *Studies* 264, suggests that it was intended that Arrhidaios rule until Alexander IV came of age.

[468]For Drypetis and Stateira see Berve ii 148, no. 290; ii 363-364, no. 722. The time of the incident is fixed by the fact that Rhoxane had not yet given birth; she was seven months pregnant at the time of Alexander's death (see

acted as her accomplice in this affair suggests, however, that he had not considered the Achaimenid women as political tools, probably because he had already pinned his hopes on the effective manipulation of Arrhidaios. Rhoxane's child might prove useful — chiefly because of his paternity — and Perdikkas meant to keep him firmly in his control. But, like Rhoxane, he was content to eliminate any potential rivals, or persons whom contenders for the throne might exploit in the future.

Perdikkas' career is an unfortunate tale of lofty ideals combined with excessive ambition and political myopia. He showed a determination to keep the empire intact, and for this idealism — though it was motivated by a quest for personal glory — he is to be admired. Yet his own ambitions blinded him to political realities and he failed largely through his mismanagement of vital issues. He had recovered his position as the guiding force in Babylon, but only by compromising his ideals; had Alexander's son been acceptable to the Makedonians, he might have ruled as Rhoxane's husband, as the 'King's' adoptive father. He had reasserted his power by wresting from Meleagros control of Arrhidaios, only to incur the suspicion of his colleagues (Arr. *Succ.* 1a. 5). These men he attempted to appease by means of the satrapal allotments, in part a concession, but also a plan to remove any threat from the Court.[469] Here too he undermined his cause, for the division of the satrapies led only to the disintegration of the empire; Alexander had been careful to keep the provinces in the hands of lesser men.[470] For the time, at least, Perdikkas will have been happy to see the departure of the generals from Babylon. He now turned his attention to the consolidation of his own position.

As a last act of the Makedonian assembly before the dispersal to the satrapies, Perdikkas freed himself of the burden of Alexander's plans, as they were set out in the *Hypomnemata*.[471] Therefore, he

---

Hamilton, *PA* 216). According to Plutarch (*Alex.* 77. 6), who attributes the act solely to Rhoxane's jealousy, Stateira and Drypetis were summoned by means of a forged letter (ἐξηπάτησεν αὐτὴν ἐπιστολῇ τινι πεπλασμένῃ παραγενέσθαι), whereafter they were murdered and their bodies thrown into a well and covered over. Cf. Schachermeyr, *Babylon* 22, n.33. There is no mention of the fate of Parysatis, Alexander's other royal bride.

[469] See Seibert, *Ptolemaios* 28.

[470] Badian, *JHS* 81 (1961), 24: 'It is worth noting that, having dealt with his excessively formidable subordinates, the King took care to see that their places were taken by unimportant men.'

[471] For the authenticity of the *Hypomnemata* and the plans contained therein see Badian, *HSCP* 72 (1967), 183 ff., against Tarn ii 378-398, who believes they are a late forgery. See also Schachermeyr, *JÖAI* 41 (1954), 118-140 (with pertinent bibliography, 118-119), who argues that the plans are genuine; against this view Hampl, in *Studies Presented to D. M. Robinson*, vol. 2 (Washington University Publications, 1953), 816-829.

called the army together in order to cancel, with a show of legality, Alexander's instructions. This had a two-fold purpose: firstly, it freed Perdikkas of any possible future charge of having failed to carry out Alexander's final instructions and, secondly (what is more important), it cancelled Krateros' orders to replace Antipatros as regent of Makedonia, orders that, according to Diodoros (18. 4. 1), were recorded in the *Hypomnemata*.[472] Again there is a strong indication that Eumenes had already allied himself with Perdikkas, for it was Eumenes, as Royal Secretary, who had prepared the *Hypomnemata*, and he may well have revealed to Perdikkas the possibility of negating Krateros' instructions by asking the army to reject the 'future plans' as a whole; certainly the army was openly opposed to these extravagances.[473] Thus, in one vote, the army set aside the grandiose plans for further conquest, extravagant buildings and Hephaistion's pyre, and, with these, Krateros' orders to replace Antipatros (Diod. 18. 4. 6). Perdikkas was now ready to seek an alliance with the ruler of Makedonia.

Having robbed Krateros of his legal designation as Antipatros' successor, Perdikkas now gave his attention to securing the goodwill and support of the old Regent. These negotiations are not recorded in their historical context, but Diodoros gives us an insight into the circumstances surrounding Antipatros' betrothal of his daughter Nikaia to Perdikkas. He writes:

ὁ δὲ Περδίκκας πρότερον μὲν ἦν κεκρικὼς κοινοπραγίαν Ἀντιπάτρῳ καὶ διὰ τοῦτο τὴν μνηστείαν ἐπεποίητο μήπω τῶν κατ' αὐτὸν πραγμάτων βεβαίως ἐστερεωμένων· ὡς δὲ παρέλαβε τάς τε βασιλικὰς δυνάμεις καὶ τῶν βασιλέων προστασίαν, μετέπεσε τοῖς λογισμοῖς

(Diod. 18. 23. 2).

Perdiccas had formerly planned to work in harmony with Antipater, and for this reason he had pressed his suit when his position was not yet firmly established; but when he had gained control of the royal armies and the guardianship of the kings, he changed his calculations.
(R. Geer, tr.)

From this passage it is quite clear that Perdikkas entered into negotiations with Antipatros when his own position was not yet secure, before he had taken control of the 'Royal Armies and the guardianship (*prostasia*) of the kings'. Now the reference to the 'Royal Armies' cannot be accurate, for it is certain that Perdikkas, as Chiliarch,

---

[472]So Badian, *HSCP* 72 (1967), 201-204.
[473]For Eumenes' role see also Badian, *ibid*. 204.

THE 'NEW MEN'

commanded them from the start.[474] The assumption of the guardianship of the Kings almost certainly indicates that, upon the birth of Rhoxane's son, Perdikkas assumed a second *prostasia*; for Diodoros clearly uses the plural, 'Kings' (τὴν τῶν βασιλέων προστασίαν). At that time Perdikkas was formidable: he exercised, at least by default, the guardianship of Philip Arrhidaios and had assumed the *prostasia* of Alexander IV; the imperial forces in Asia were under his command. Krateros' office, though legally sanctioned, meant nothing if he could not exercise it.[475] Before the birth of Alexander's son, Perdikkas had isolated Krateros in Kilikia and was himself in a precarious state, having incurred the suspicion of the Makedonians in Babylon through his treacherous elimination of Meleagros (Arr. *Succ.* 1a. 5). But Antipatros too was prepared to deal: there was the matter of the Lamian war, and he wanted Krateros in Europe. Thus he recognised Perdikkas' claim to a share of the supremacy in Asia and bound him to a political alliance by promising his daughter Nikaia in marriage. Perdikkas, in turn, acknowledged Antipatros as *strategos autokrator* of Europe.

Perdikkas' negotiations with Antipatros must belong, therefore, to the period of instability at Babylon. One of those who brought Nikaia to Perdikkas in the following year was Iolaos, the girl's brother, who had been present at Alexander's death.[476] It is quite possible that Perdikkas, after the allotment of the satrapies and the cancellation of Krateros' orders, sent Iolaos to his father to report the developments in Babylon and to convey his wish for a marriage-alliance.

Now there were additional problems in the empire: the upper satrapies, where Alexander had settled the Greek mercenaries, were in a state of revolt, a direct consequence of Alexander's death.[477] Accordingly, Perdikkas sent out Peithon, formerly one of the Somatophylakes, who had been allotted Media and now showed the first signs of seditious intent. His army, augmented by contributions from the other satraps (in accordance with Perdikkas' instructions),

---

[474]Curt. 10. 10. 4; Justin 13. 4. 5; Diod. 18. 3. 1 (παραλαβὼν τὴν τῶν ὅλων ἡγεμονίαν). As chief commander he conducted the lustration of the army: Justin 13. 4. 7 ff.; Arr. *Succ.* 1a. 4; Curt. 10. 9. 11 ff.

[475]See Errington, *JHS* 90 (1970), 61; cf. Schur, *RhM* 83 (1934), 144 ff.

[476]See Berve ii 184, no. 386; Arr. *Succ.* 1. 21 has the form Ἰόλλας, for which see Hoffmann 207 f.

[477]Diod. 18. 4. 8; 18. 7. 1: ζῶντος μὲν τοῦ βασιλέως ὑπέμενον διὰ τὸν φόβον, τελευτήσαντος δὲ ἀπέστησαν. Tarn's attempt (*CAH* vi 455-456) to link the disturbances in the east with the Lamian war can be no more than speculation. The rebels, who numbered 20,000 foot and 3,000 horse, were led by Philon the Ainianian (Diod. 18. 7. 2; cf. Berve ii 392, no. 798). See also Beloch iv² 1. 67; Niese i 199-200; Droysen ii³ 24-26; Kaerst ii² 12-13.

overcame the Greek force partly by deceit.[478] Whether the ensuing slaughter of the Greeks who had surrendered was indeed ordered by Perdikkas at the outset of the campaign is difficult to determine.[479] In view of Perdikkas' growing dependence on Eumenes, the annihilation of the Greek force was scarcely good politics. It is possible, however, that Peithon's troops got out of control and that the blame for the slaughter devolved upon Perdikkas.

In the west, Antigonos and Leonnatos had been instructed to aid Eumenes in conquering his satrapy of Kappadokia, which had been bypassed by Alexander.[480] Antigonos, hostile and suspicious from the start, defected from the Perdikkan cause and refused aid to Eumenes. Leonnatos, on the other hand, bolstered his army over the winter of 323/2 and joined Eumenes in the spring.[481] At that point, however, Hekataios, tyrant of Kardia, arrived with an urgent appeal from Antipatros, asking Leonnatos to come with all haste to Europe; for he was besieged in Lamia by the Hellenic forces under Leosthenes.[482] For Leonnatos it was the perfect opportunity for seeking the throne. He had already had communications with Olympias, the unyielding foe of Antipatros, and had received from her daughter Kleopatra, Alexander's sister, a promise of marriage.[483] So much he confided to Eumenes, with whose support he hoped to gain the throne. But Eumenes, whether wary of Leonnatos' impetuosity or sincerely devoted to the Perdikkan cause, rejected the appeal on the ground that he feared that Antipatros would betray him to his arch-enemy

---

[478]Diod. 18. 7. 3. Perdikkas gave Peithon 3800 troops and sent instructions to the eastern satraps to supply a further 10,000 infantry and 8000 cavalry. Peithon persuaded a certain Letodoros to desert, thereby throwing the Greeks into confusion (Diod. 18. 7. 5-7). See Berve ii 237, no. 473; see also ii 311, no. 621, s.v. Πείθων.

[479]Diod. 18. 7. 5, 8-9. See also Cloché, *La Dislocation* 19-20.

[480]Plut. *Eum.* 3. 4. Ariarathes maintained his independence in Kappadokia during Alexander's lifetime (Diod. 18. 16. 1). See Berve ii 59-60, no. 113; Vezin 26 ff.; Briant 146 ff.

[481]For Antigonos' refusal to give aid see Plut. *Eum.* 3. 5; for Leonnatos' dealings with Eumenes, Plut. *Eum.* 3. 5 ff.

[482]Hekataios' appeal: Diod. 18. 14. 4-5; Plut. *Eum.* 3. 6. See Berve ii 149, no. 294.

[483]Plut. *Eum.* 3. 9; cf. Macurdy, *HQ* 30 ff.; Seibert, *Verbindungen* 20.

Hekataios.[484] Therefore, he slipped away from Leonnatos' camp during the night, leaving Leonnatos to take his chances in Europe.[485]

The episode had great significance for Perdikkas, for it was surely through Eumenes that he first came to regard Kleopatra as a means of gaining supreme power. Eumenes, deserted by Antigonos and Leonnatos, appealed to Perdikkas for help and divulged the details of Leonnatos' intrigues. For the moment, there was nothing to be done about him; but events in Greece brought the matter to a speedy conclusion. Perdikkas moved to join Eumenes for an invasion of Kappadokia; it was late spring or early summer 322.[486]

The Kappadokian campaign would give Perdikkas an opportunity to gain prestige: he would complete the conquest of Alexander's empire and punish Ariarathes for his refusal to submit. As he moved westward, Krateros now also abandoned Kilikia in answer to Antipatros' call; whether the two actions were in fact related cannot be determined.[487] In Kappadokia, Perdikkas made short work of Ariarathes, whom he defeated in two decisive engagements.[488] In a single campaigning season, he had extended the boundaries of Alexander's empire and taken a barbarian king captive. But the victory was tarnished by his cruel treatment of Ariarathes, who was impaled (Arr. *Succ.* 1. 11) along with his relatives (Diod. 18. 16. 3).[489] Thereafter, he instructed Eumenes to settle affairs in Armenia, which had been thrown into confusion by Neoptolemos,[490] while he himself

---

[484] Plut. *Eum.* 3. 8. If this was in fact the reason given by Eumenes to Leonnatos, it is surprising that Leonnatos did not offer him support against Hekataios in order to win his support against Antipatros. The knowledge of Leonnatos' dealings with Kleopatra can only have come down to us through Eumenes himself (via Hieronymos); Diodoros, however, says nothing of this.

[485] Plut. *Eum.* 3. 10; cf. Nepos, *Eum.* 2. 4-5, who claims that Leonnatos planned to kill Eumenes when he failed to win his support.

[486] Not long after Leonnatos' departure for Greece; cf. Anson, *AJP* 107 (1986), 214, who dates the campaign to 'August or September 322'.

[487] Diod. 18. 16. 4. Errington, *JHS* 90 (1970), 61: 'It is therefore difficult to believe that Perdiccas' approach to Cilicia on his way against Ariarathes in Cappadocia was not the final stimulus which drove Craterus into supporting Antipater.' Cf. Schwahn, *Klio* 24 (1931), 331 f.; Badian, *JHS* 81 (1961), 41.

[488] Arr. *Succ.* 1. 11 (δυσὶ νικήσας μάχαις); Diod. 18. 16. 1-3 gives Ariarathes 30,000 infantry and 15,000 cavalry; cf. 18. 22. 1; Appian, *Mithr.* 8 = Hieronymos, *FGrHist* 154 F3; Arr. *Succ.* 1. 11; Justin 13. 6. 1-3, who conflates the Kappadokian and Pisidian campaigns; Diod. 18. 16. 2 says that 4000 of Ariarathes' men were killed, more than 5000 captured. Cf. [Lucian], *Macrob.* 13 = *FGrHist* 154 F4; and Hornblower, *Hieronymus* 239-243.

[489] See Cary 11. Plut. *Eum.* 3. 13 says only that he was captured; Vezin 29. Diod. 31, frag. 19. 3-5, from a different source, says Ariarathes fell in battle.

[490] Plut. *Eum.* 4. 1; see also Berve ii 273, no. 548. Perhaps Perdikkas was already distrustful of Neoptolemos; cf. Droysen ii³ 58.

directed his attention to Pisidia.⁴⁹¹ Here the Isaurians and Larandians had risen against and killed Alexander's satrap Balakros son of Nikanor.⁴⁹² These cities Perdikkas took without great difficulty, and they proved a source of plunder for his men. Victorious in the field and offering lucrative rewards to his soldiers, Perdikkas now enjoyed his greatest success.⁴⁹³

It was at this time that Antipatros' daughter Nikaia was brought to Asia by Iolaos and Archias.⁴⁹⁴ But Perdikkas, who had found a marriage-alliance with Antipatros' family desirable in 323, now had second thoughts. To make matters worse, Kleopatra, Alexander's sister, had arrived in Sardeis, having been sent out (no doubt) at the instigation of Olympias.⁴⁹⁵ Eumenes may have had a hand in the affair: Leonnatos had opened his eyes to Kleopatra's potential, and Eumenes, who urged Perdikkas to marry her in place of Nikaia, may have corresponded with the scheming Olympias, encouraging her to send out her daughter.⁴⁹⁶

Kleopatra would tempt Perdikkas to ruin. Already he had begun to formulate a new policy, one that he hoped would win for him the throne. With the Kings securely in his possession and the army favourably disposed towards him on account of his recent successes in Kappadokia and Pisidia, Perdikkas was prepared to take two final steps to the kingship: union with Kleopatra and the ceremonious return of Alexander's body to Makedonia. What army would oppose the man returning to Makedonia with the son of Philip II, the wife, son and sister — indeed, the very body — of Alexander himself?⁴⁹⁷

---

⁴⁹¹Diod. 18. 22. 1. Droysen ii³ 57 places this campaign in the summer of 322, immediately after the Kappadokian affair, and regards it as a move on Perdikkas' part towards Antigonos, who had been guilty of insubordination. Errington, more plausibly, dates the Pisidian campaign to 321 (*JHS* 90 [1970], 77); but cf. Briant 216 ff.

⁴⁹²Diod. 18. 22. 1. This occurred shortly before Alexander's death; cf. Berve ii 100; Julien 20; Baumbach 45, 65, 69. Berve ii 100-101, no. 200; he had been one of the Somatophylakes of Alexander.

⁴⁹³Laranda was taken without difficulty (Diod. 18. 22. 2), though Isaura held out for three days (18. 22. 4). For the self-immolation of the Isaurians see Diod. 18. 22. 4-5; Justin 13. 6. 2-3. For the booty see Diod. 18. 22. 8, disagreeing with Justin 13. 6. 1: *victor nihil praemii praeter vulnera et pericula rettulit*.

⁴⁹⁴Diod. 18. 23. 1; Arr. *Succ*. 1. 21; Justin 13. 6. 4-6. Iolaos had perhaps been sent to Makedonia for the purpose of bringing Nikaia to Asia. The identity of Archias is uncertain.

⁴⁹⁵Arr. *Succ*. 1. 21: ἀλλά γέ καὶ Ὀλυμπιὰς ἡ Ἀλεξάνδρου μήτηρ ἔπεμπε παρ' αὐτὸν κατεγγυωμένη τὴν θυγατέρα Κλεοπάτραν. Cf. Justin 13. 6. 4.

⁴⁹⁶On the basis of Arr. *Succ*. 1. 21, the initiative is always given to Olympias, acting out of hatred for Antipatros.

⁴⁹⁷At this time Arrhidaios (Berve ii 80, no. 145) was still preparing the funeral wagon with the intention of taking the body to Egypt. See details below.

THE 'NEW MEN'

But it was Perdikkas' fate that things should go drastically wrong at the critical moment: he was not destined to rule. The almost contemporaneous arrivals of Nikaia and Kleopatra were most inopportune. In fact, Nikaia's very presence was an indication of changing events: the Makedonians had been victorious in the Lamian war, Antipatros' power restored. And he meant to achieve stability by wedding Phila to Krateros, Nikaia to Perdikkas.[498] By rejecting Nikaia now, Perdikkas would certainly invite civil war.[499] But there was also the matter of the rebellious Antigonos, satrap of Phrygia and friend of Antipatros.[500] What Perdikkas needed was time enough to settle affairs in Asia to his satisfaction.[501]

Against Antigonos he attempted to use tactics similar to those employed with great success against Meleagros: he hoped to remove him under the guise of legality (Diod. 18. 23. 3-4). But Antigonos, who knew well the designs of Perdikkas, made no attempt to clear himself of the charges brought against him — for clearly he was guilty of insubordination in the Kappadokian affair — and fled from his satrapy.[502] He had, however, seen enough of Perdikkas' dealings with the Makedonian women to know that Perdikkas' marriage to Nikaia was merely a front, intended to keep Antipatros satisfied for the time. Whatever Antigonos suspected about Perdikkas' designs he presented to Antipatros and Krateros as fact, and he spiced the information with a highly dramatised account of the fate of Kynnane, about which he had learned before his departure for Europe.[503]

---

[498]It does not follow, however, as Errington (*JHS* 90 [1970], 61 f.) wishes to conclude, that 'by being brought into a family connection with Antipater (and indirectly with Craterus) Perdiccas might peacefully be made to accept a more equitable arrangement (in Asia) for Craterus.' Cohen, *Historia* 22 (1973), 355, is rightly sceptical of the power of such alliances.

[499]Diod. 18. 23. 3; the sentiment at least is expressed by Justin 13. 6. 5; see also Macurdy, *HQ* 37-38; Vezin 39; cf. Beloch iv² 1. 83.

[500]For Antigonos see i 5 and Berve ii 42-44, no. 87; cf. Kaerst, *RE* i (1894), 2406, no. 3; Briant; Billows, *Antigonos*.

[501]To this time belongs the restoration of the Samian exiles, a matter referred by Antipatros to the Kings and carried out by Perdikkas in the name of Philip Arrhidaios; Diod. 18. 18. 6, 9. Perhaps Perdikkas received news of this from Iolaos and Archias, when they brought out Nikaia. See also Habicht, *MDAI(A)* 72 (1957), 152 ff.; id., *Chiron* 5 (1975), 45-50; Errington, *Chiron* 5 (1975), 51-57; Badian, *ZPE* 23 (1976), 289-294.

[502]Diod. 18. 23. 4; 18. 25. 3; Justin 13. 6. 7-9; Arr. *Succ.* 1. 24.

[503]For Perdikkas' designs see Droysen ii³ 59: 'seine Absicht war, den Satrapen von Phrygien, dem aus dem fernen Aegypten nicht so bald Hilfe kommen konnte, zu überrennen, sich dann durch Vermählung mit Kleopatra offen als Gegner der Antipatros zu erklären...'. See Briant 145 ff., esp. 153 ff. For Antigonos' dramatisation of the Kynnane episode see Arr. *Succ.* 1. 24 (ἐκτραγῳδήσας).

Kynnane indeed represented the unexpected, but Perdikkas lost control of affairs when he failed to act decisively on the matter of Nikaia and Kleopatra. After a brief hesitation, which could not have failed to attract attention, he married Nikaia, hoping to forestall a confrontation with Antipatros.[504] As for Antigonos, it proved difficult to mete out punishment, which he clearly deserved, without earning the suspicion and resentment of the other satraps; on this matter the fate of Meleagros had proved instructive.

The year 322/1 witnessed an exodus of prominent Makedonian ladies from their homeland to the vicinity of Perdikkas and the royal army. Atalante, Perdikkas' sister, we may assume was the first, perhaps joining her brother and her intended husband, Attalos, in Pisidia.[505] Then Nikaia's departure was followed closely by that of Kleopatra.[506] Nor did the plans of Antipatros and Olympias go unnoticed by another Makedonian princess, the daughter of Philip II and the Illyrian Audata-Eurydike, Kynnane, a woman of indomitable spirit.[507] She had been married by her father to the innocuous Amyntas Perdikka, rightful heir to the Makedonian throne; but he had lived like an exile in his own land, deprived of his title and bound to allegiance by Kynnane, who proved more than his match in character and in deed. After Philip's death, Amyntas was executed on charges of conspiracy; perhaps he had been incited by Kynnane, who, though loyal to her father, will have preferred that her husband rule in place of her half-brother Alexander (cf. Arr. *Succ.* 1. 22). Now, over the winter of 322/1, as she saw Antipatros and Olympias intriguing with Perdikkas, Kynnane was determined to exert her influence and secure for herself and for her daughter Adea a share of the power.

---

[504]Justin 13. 6. 6; Diod. 18. 23. 3; Arr. *Succ.* 1. 21 says that Eumenes urged him to marry Kleopatra, Alketas advocated Nikaia; Perdikkas chose Nikaia for the time.

[505]For the marriage of Attalos and Atalante see Heckel, *CQ* 28 (1978), 377-382.

[506]For Nikaia and Kleopatra see Berve ii 274, no. 552 (cf. Beloch iv^2 2. 127) and ii 212-213, no. 433. For Perdikkas' dealings with these women see Macurdy, *HQ* 37-38; Cloché, *La Dislocation* 51-53; Seibert, *Verbindungen* 13-16 and 19ff.; Briant 174-175; Errington, *JHS* 90 (1970), 63 ff., who accepts the date given by the Babylonian Chronicle for Perdikkas' death (320 B.C.) and postpones Nikaia's arrival in Asia in summer 321.

[507]Droysen's description is worth quoting: 'Sie hatte das wilde illyrische Blut ihrer Mutter; sie zog mit in die Kriege; Abenteuer und Kriegsfahrten waren ihre Lust, und mehr als einmal nahm sie am Kampf persönlich teil; in einem Kriege gegen die Illyrer erschlug sie mit eigener Hand deren Königin und trug durch ihr wildes Eindringen in die Feinde nicht wenig zur Entscheidung des Tages' (ii^3 60). See Polyainos 8. 60, s.v. Κύννα. Cf. also Heckel, *RSA* 13-14 (1983-84), 193-200; Carney, *Historia* 37 (1988), 392-394.

THE 'NEW MEN'

Once more Philip Arrhidaios proved to be Perdikkas' undoing. Kynnane saw the futility of vying for a union with Perdikkas: Antipatros could offer political advantages, and Kleopatra had more prestige than her half-sister.[508] Therefore, she resolved to by-pass the negotiating parties and to subvert their plans by wedding her daughter Adea to Arrhidaios. Antipatros was not eager to see Kynnane leave Makedonia — doubtless he was already troubled by the recent departure of Kleopatra — and he left a force to turn her back at the Strymon. But the warrior princess had surrounded herself with a small but efficient mercenary-force with which she broke through Antipatros' guard. When the word of her coming reached Perdikkas, he sent Alketas with orders to dissuade her, by force if necessary. Kynnane was not one to be dissuaded; defiant, she was cut down by Alketas' men in full view of the Makedonian army. Surely this was not how Perdikkas had envisioned Alketas' mission.[509] The army mutinied and demanded that Kynnane's purpose be fulfilled, that Adea be taken to Arrhidaios.[510] What support Perdikkas had gained in the past year was now quickly eroding. His officers grew increasingly suspicious of his aspirations, the common soldier was alienated by his acts of barbarity.[511]

Now things began to deteriorate rapidly. Antigonos sought refuge with Antipatros and Krateros, warning them of Perdikkas' intention to march on Makedonia.[512] Ptolemy, who had long feared Perdikkan intervention in Egypt (Diod. 18. 14. 2; 18. 25. 4), made an alliance with the *strategoi* in Europe, who now abandoned their Aitolian war in midwinter 321/0 and prepared to cross into Asia (Diod. 18. 25. 5; Justin 13. 6. 9).[513] Polyperchon held Europe (Justin 13. 6. 9).

Perdikkas, meanwhile, abandoned Nikaia and openly courted Kleopatra, sending Eumenes with gifts to Sardeis, where she had taken up residence.[514] Antigonos' defection had been followed by that of

---

[508] Like Alexander, Kleopatra was the child of both Philip and Olympias.

[509] It is generally held that Perdikkas instigated Kynnane's murder: so Droysen ii³ 61; Niese i 214; Vezin 36; Cloché, *La Dislocation* 55. Beloch iv² 1. 83 has her murdered by Perdikkas himself; Welles, *AHW* 53, thinks Perdikkas was incited by Kleopatra. I prefer Macurdy's suggestion that 'Perdiccas saw the fatal stupidity of his brother's act...' (*HQ* 50).

[510] Kynnane: Polyainos 8. 60; Arr. *Succ.* 1. 22-24; cf. Heckel, *RSA* 13-14 (1983-84), 193-200.

[511] Meleagros, the Greek mercenaries, Ariarathes, now Kynnane.

[512] Diod. 18. 23. 4; 18. 25. 3-4; Justin 13. 6. 7-9; Arr. *Succ.* 1. 24. Cf. Vezin 37; Kaerst ii² 21, for Perdikkas' intention to march on Makedonia.

[513] Seibert, *Ptolemaios* 64 ff.

[514] Arr. *Succ.* 1. 26; Eumenes' visit to Kleopatra follows Polemon's attempt to retrieve Alexander's body (1. 25), but the phrase ἐν τούτῳ shows the events were contemporaneous. Perdikkas was still hoping to recover the body and to march on Makedonia with both the funeral-car and Kleopatra. See Engel,

Asandros, the Karian satrap, and now Menandros of Lydia also took flight.[515] Perdikkas knew that a confrontation with Antipatros and his allies was inevitable, and he meant to bolster his position by marrying Kleopatra before he took to the field and marched on Makedonia. But at this point the bottom fell out of Perdikkas' carefully conceived scheme: Arrhidaios (not the King) had completed the funeral-car in Babylon and had begun to transport Alexander's body to Egypt.

It would be rash to deny that Alexander had requested burial at the oasis of Ammon; on this point the sources concur.[516] But Arrhidaios, who spent almost two years overseeing the funeral-arrangements, was surely instructed by Perdikkas that there would be a change in plans: Alexander's body would be taken to Makedonia, not Egypt.[517] We can

---

RhM 115 (1972), 215-219. The 'gifts' to Kleopatra appear to have included turning over to her the satrapy of Lydia, for Menandros is described as δι' ὀργῆς ἔχων Περδίκκαν ὅτι τὴν μὲν σατραπείαν ἣν εἶχεν αὐτὸς Κλεοπάτρᾳ ἐπιτετρόφει (Arr. *Succ.* 25. 2). Seibert, *Verbindungen* 21, is too brief to be useful; see, however, Vezin 40-41. Beloch iv^2 1. 86, n.6, thinks the marriage did not take place on account of Kleopatra's unwillingness; cf. Cary 12: '...she was as good a wrecker as her mother, and preferred, like Queen Elizabeth, to have many lovers so that she might disappoint them all.' Droysen, ii^3 62, is probably right in saying that she accepted Perdikkas' proposition ('die Königin gab sofort ihre Zustimmung'); but there was not sufficient time for the marriage to take place. She was favourably disposed toward the Perdikkans (Arr. *Succ.* 25. 6), though she repudiated her *philia* — for this remained the extent of her relationship with Perdikkas — once her intended husband had died in Egypt (Arr. *Succ.* 1. 40).

[515] Arr. *Succ.* 1. 26; 25. 2; cf. Engel, *RhM* 115 (1972), 215-219.

[516] Diod. 18. 3. 5; Justin 12. 15. 7; 13. 4. 6; Curt. 10. 5. 4. Paus. 1. 6. 3 does say that the body was destined for Aigai, but this was in accordance with Perdikkas' change of policy (Μακεδόνων τοὺς ταχθέντας τὸν Ἀλεξάνδρου νεκρὸν ἐς Αἰγὰς κομίζειν); there is no mention of Alexander's wishes here. Cf. Arr. *Succ.* 1. 25, where Arrhidaios acts against Perdikkas' wishes (παρὰ γνώμην ... Περδίκκου); the matter is completely misinterpreted by R. M. Geer, *Diodorus*, Loeb, vol. 9 (Cambridge, Mass., 1947), 19, n.4. Seibert, *Ptolemaios* 110-111, also supposes that there is a contradiction between Pausanias' account and the version given by Diodoros, Justin and Curtius. For Perdikkas' change of policy see Droysen ii^3 67, n.2, placing Pausanias' testimony in the proper light. The most thorough discussion is that of Schubert, *Quellen* 180-189; see also Badian, *HSCP* 72 (1967), 185-189; Errington, *JHS* 90 (1970), 64 f.; Beloch iv^2 1. 86-87. Tarn ii 355 f., predictably, disbelieves Alexander's wish to be buried at Siwah, ascribing these reports to Ptolemy's propaganda; less dogmatic is the account given in *CAH* vi 467.

[517] For Arrhidaios see Berve ii 80, no. 145; Kaerst, *RE* ii (1896), 1249, s.v. 'Arridaios (5)'. He is not, as Justin (13. 4. 6) wrongly states, to be identified with Philip Arrhidaios, but one of the later guardians of the Kings (Arr. *Succ.* 1. 31; Diod. 18. 39. 1-2); for the funeral-car see Diod. 18. 3. 5; 18. 26-28; cf. Arr. *Succ.* 1. 25.

only assume, as Perdikkas himself did, that there had been collusion between Ptolemy and the satrap of Babylonia, Archon; it was symptomatic of widespread disaffection among the officials of the empire.[518] News came to Perdikkas that Arrhidaios had turned southward and was making for Egypt. But a contingent headed by the sons of Andromenes, sent out to retrieve Alexander's body, proved inadequate; for Ptolemy had marched out in full force to meet Arrhidaios' procession and escort it to Egypt.[519] Significantly, none of the satraps between Babylonia and Egypt made an effort to intercede.

Robbed of his most valuable tool, Perdikkas abandoned all thoughts of marching against Antipatros. The haste of Antipatros' preparations had caught Perdikkas off-guard: he had not completed the prerequisites for his march on Europe and neither Kleopatra nor the King's body was in his possession. Thus he had already turned his attention to Egypt, where Ptolemy had been increasing steadily in power; news of the 'body-snatching' only further emphasised his need to secure Asia first.[520]

Some re-alignments were made for the sake of security: Philotas, a known supporter of Krateros, was deposed from the satrapy of Kilikia as Perdikkas entered that territory; there too provisions were made for the fleet, and Dokimos was despatched to Babylon with orders to replace Archon, suspected of collusion with Arrhidaios in the highjacking of Alexander's corpse.[521] Eumenes held the western front: his domain was enlarged to include Lykia, Karia and Phrygia, which had been abandoned by Nearchos,[522] Asandros and Antigonos

---

[518]See Arr. *Succ.* 24. 3. One would like to know where the Chiliarch Seleukos and Peithon, satrap of Media, were at this time and how they reacted to the incident.

[519]Diod. 18. 28. 2 ff.; Arr. *Succ.* 1. 25; Paus. 1. 6. 4; cf. Curt. 10. 10. 20. For the sons of Andromenes see Arr. *Succ.* 1. 25 (Polemon only) and 24. 1 (both Attalos and Polemon). Cf. Badian, *HSCP* 72 (1967), 189, n.34.

[520]Diod. 18. 25. 6; Justin 13. 6. 10-13; Arr. *Succ.* 24. 1. Seibert, *Ptolemaios* 110 ff. Perdikkas had other grievances against Ptolemy: his execution of the hyparch Kleomenes and his expansionist war against Kyrene.

[521]For Philotas see Berve ii 397, nos. 803 and 804, s.v. Φιλώτας; id., *RE* xx.1 (1939), 177-178, no. 2; 179, nos. 7-9; P. Schoch 179-180, no. 10 and 180, no. 11; Arr. *Succ.* 24. 2. Philotas' replacement was Philoxenos (cf. Justin 13. 6. 16). For Dokimos and Archon see Arr. *Succ.* 24. 3-5; cf. Berve ii 86-87, no. 165, s.v. Ἄρχων; Kaerst, *RE* ii (1896), 564, s.v. 'Archon (5)'; Berve ii 147, no. 285, s.v. Δόκιμος; Kaerst, *RE* v (1905), 1274, s.v. 'Dokimos (4)'.

[522]Lykia was joined to Greater Phrygia after 330 and is usually given to Antigonos in the satrapy-lists: Arr. *Succ.* 1a. 6, 1b. 2; Curt. 10. 10. 2; Diod. 18. 3. 1; App. *Syr.* 53; though Justin 13. 4. 15 gives Lykia and Pamphylia to Nearchos, who had ruled it from 333 to 330. See Berve i 276 opp.; Baumbach 57, with n.2, who believes that Justin is wrong concerning the satrapy in 323; Nearchos was later a supporter of Antigonos (Diod. 19. 19; cf. Polyainos 5. 35), and he may have

respectively, and doubtless he kept a watchful eye on Kleopatra in Lydia. Under his command were placed also Neoptolemos and Alketas.[523] To White Kleitos, Perdikkas entrusted the defence of the Hellespont,[524] while another fleet was despatched to Kypros, under the command of Sosigenes the Rhodian and Aristonous, his most faithful supporter throughout the war, in order to deal with Ptolemy's allies there.[525] At the same time, Attalos, who had now married Atalante, was ordered to accompany the army to Egypt with a third fleet; in the present turbulence, Perdikkas thought it best to keep his sister in the camp.[526]

Dokimos secured Babylon without difficulty, defeating in battle Archon, who soon died of his wounds (Arr. *Succ.* 24. 5). Meanwhile, Perdikkas marched to Damaskos, where he probably replaced the satrap of Syria, Laomedon, an old friend of Alexander who had gone over to Ptolemy, and awaited reinforcements (likely headed by Peithon, satrap of Media). From here he made his assault on Egypt.

In the west Perdikkas experienced further difficulties. Neoptolemos, long an enemy of Eumenes (Plut. *Eum.* 1. 6; 7. 7), abandoned the Perdikkan forces and joined Krateros' army; Alketas, perhaps stinging from a reproach over the manner in which he handled the affair of Kynnane, refused to serve under Eumenes, protesting that his Makedonians would not go into battle with the illustrious Krateros.[527] Nevertheless, Eumenes and his troops were victorious, though Perdikkas was never to learn the news.[528]

The Egypt against which Perdikkas led his forces had been carefully prepared for the confrontation by Ptolemy, who realised from the start that war with Perdikkas was a strong possibility; he had

---

controlled Lykia under Antigonos' direction; cf. Droysen, ii³ 16; Schachermeyr, *Babylon* 144, n.91. See also Julien 17; Berve ii 269-272, no. 544, s.v. Νέαρχος, esp. 271; Capelle, *RE* xvi.2 (1935), 2134; Niese i 197, n.2; Badian, *YCS* 24 (1975), 169, n.58; Lehmann-Haupt in Papastavru, *Amphipolis* 137. Eumenes' territory: Justin 13. 6. 14-15; Plut. *Eum.* 5. 1-2; Nepos, *Eum.* 3. 2; cf. Diod. 18. 25. 6; 18. 29. 1.

[523]Justin 13. 6. 15; Diod. 18. 29. 2; Arr. *Succ.* 1. 26; Plut. *Eum.* 5. 2-3.

[524]Justin 13. 6. 16; cf. Arr. *Succ.* 1. 26; corroborated by Keil, *JÖAI* 16 (1913), 235, II*n*.

[525]Arr. *Succ.* 24. 6. Aristonous was to be *strategos*; Sosigenes *nauarchos* (Berve ii 369, no. 737); Medios the Thessalian *xenagos* (Berve ii 261-262, no. 521); and Amyntas *hipparchos* (Berve ii 26, no. 56; cf. Kaerst, *RE* i [1894], 2007, no. 20). The Kyprian allies of Ptolemy were Androkles, Nikokles, Nikokreon and Pasikrates (Berve nos. 73, 567, 568, 610). See Briant 205; Niese i 219.

[526]The women in camp included also Rhoxane and Adea-Eurydike.

[527]Plut. *Eum.* 5. 3; but see Schubert, *Quellen* 139-149.

[528]Diod. 18. 33. 1 says that Perdikkas heard and was encouraged by the news of Eumenes' victory. But this is contradicted by Diod. 18. 37. 1 (cf. Plut. *Eum.* 8. 2-3), who says the news arrived in Egypt two days after Perdikkas' murder.

spent the two years after the settlement at Babylon fortifying his satrapy and winning the loyalty of his followers (Diod. 18. 33. 3-4). Perdikkas, if indeed he did try to win support among his generals through gifts and promises (so Diod. 18. 33. 5), was less successful; as Beloch rightly remarks, 'Perdikkas hatte nie die Gabe besessen, sich bei seinen Untergebenen beliebt zu machen' (iv² 1. 88; cf. Justin 13. 8. 2).

At first he made a daring assault on Kamelon Teichos ('The Fort of the Camels'), but failed to take it by storm. The following night, he broke camp and marched upstream from Kamelon Teichos to an island that lay opposite Memphis. But here Perdikkas made a grave error, for, in attempting to reach the island, his troops were subjected to great hardships and danger owing to the unexpected swiftness and depth of the Nile at that point. Only a small number crossed to the island successfully, and the bulk of the army found it an impossible feat; many were drowned in the attempt. What made matters worse was that Perdikkas, who had reached the opposite bank, had too few men for an assault on Memphis and was forced to re-cross the treacherous river. In all, according to Diodoros (18. 36. 1), some 2000 men were lost, including some prominent officers (ἐν οἷς καὶ τῶν ἐπιφανῶν τινες ἡγεμόνων ὑπῆρχον), though none of these is named. It was as much as the army was willing to endure from Perdikkas, whom they held responsible for their present miseries. He had failed for the last time. The foremost of his generals, including Peithon and Seleukos, conspired against him during the night and murdered him in his tent.[529] With him died the last hope for the empire as Alexander had envisioned it.[530]

---

[529]For Perdikkas' campaign against Ptolemy see Diod. 18. 33-37 (the only extensive account); also Arr. *Succ.* 1. 28; Plut. *Eum.* 8. 2-3; Justin 13. 8. 1-2; see Seibert, *Ptolemaios* 118-128 for an analysis of the accounts. For his death: Arr. 7. 18. 5 (it was prophesied by the seer Peithagoras); Nepos, *Eum.* 5. 1; Justin 13. 8. 10; 14. 1. 1; 14. 4. 11; 15. 1. 1; Diod. 18. 36. 5; Paus. 1. 6. 3; *Suda* s.v. Περδίκκας; *Heidelberg Epit.* 1; cf. G. Bauer, *Die Heidelberger Epitome* (Greifswald, 1914), 34-36.

[530]About Antigonos Monophthalmos, Wirth, *Tyche* 3 (1988), 243 f., rightly observes: 'daß er je im Sinne des Perdikkas eine Art von Reichseinheit anstrebte, ist zu bezweifeln und auch aus den Quellen mit ihrer Argumentation nicht zu beweisen....'

iii. Casualties of the Succession

Introduction

The triumph of the 'New Men' proved both ephemeral and incomplete. At Triparadeisos in northern Syria (320 B.C.), the Makedonian empire redefined itself and submitted to the will of two grisled veterans, Antipatros son of Iolaos and Antigonos Monophthalmos ('the One-Eyed'). The champions of its integrity were outlawed by the assembled veterans of the eastern campaigns, while the guardians of the Kings pursued a relentless course of separatism. Antipatros, who had quietly resisted Alexander's authority, reluctantly escorted the inept living symbols of Argead rule to Europe; clearly, he would have preferred to leave them in Asia. To Antigonos he assigned the extirpation of the Perdikkan party — now dispersed among the forces of Eumenes, Perdikkas' brother Alketas, and Attalos son of Andromenes — thereby supplying both the resources for, and the impediments to, the rise of Asia Minor's oldest satrap.

The casualties of the first Diadochic wars included the most eminent remaining commanders of the pezhetairoi, scions of the ruling houses of Upper Makedonia, and two enigmatic officers — Meleagros and White Kleitos. The former, perhaps a supporter of Krateros, had done little to distinguish himself until he made a brief and fatal bid for power in the days that followed Alexander's death on 10 June 323. The latter achieved spectacular prominence through his naval victories at Amorgos and the Echinades, but soon found himself trapped between Monophthalmos' ambitions and the political and military impotence of Polyperchon. The men whose careers are discussed below were harnessed, by family connections or simply by lack of foresight, to losing causes.[1] Hence, they may justly be called 'casualties of the succession'.

---

[1] Amyntas son of Andromenes died long before these events, as may well be true also of Simmias. I have included them with Attalos and Polemon in order to present a complete picture of the family's political affiliations and fortunes.

1. Meleagros son of Neoptolemos: Alexander's 'Petty' Officer

Literature. Berve ii 249-250, no. 494; Hoffmann 146 f., 187; Geyer, *RE* xv.1 (1932), 478-479, no. 2.

> *Quae liberalitas sicut Barbarum obstrinxerat, ita amicos ipsius vehementer offendit. E quibus Meleager super cenam largiore vino usus gratulari se Alexandro dixit, quod saltem in India repperisset dignum talentis M. Rex haud oblitus, quam aegre tulisset quod Clitum ob linguae temeritatem occidisset, iram quidem tenuit, sed dixit invidos homines nihil aliud quam ipsorum esse tormenta.*
> (Curt. 8. 12. 17-18)

> While it put the barbarian under an obligation to him, this generosity of Alexander's seriously offended his own friends. One such was Meleager who, having drunk too much at dinner, offered Alexander his congratulations on having at least found in India a man worth 1,000 talents. The king did not forget how remorseful he had been over killing Clitus for his hasty tongue and so he repressed his anger, though he did comment that envious men only torment themselves.
> (J. C. Yardley, tr.)

The regional background of Meleagros son of Neoptolemos (Arr. 1. 24. 1; 1. 29. 4) is unknown. One suspects a Lower Makedonian origin. He had no strong connections with the adherents of Upper Makedon's aristocracy, although his brigade was often deployed along with Krateros'. But this is perhaps best explained in terms of the composition of their forces: neither brigade belonged to the ἀσθέταιροι and thus both appear to have been recruited from the peasant stock of Lower Makedonia. Krateros, of course, was Orestian, commanding troops who were not from his own region, but not all taxiarchs will have been Upper Makedonians. Indeed, it would be surprising if there were not commanders from the lowlands. On the other hand, the name Neoptolemos (Meleagros' father) suggests the western highlands, the only attested examples in Alexander's reign coming from Epeiros and Lynkestis.[2] Nor can we say with confidence when Meleagros was born. That he was not dismissed with the veterans in 324 suggests that he may have been one of the younger marshals. Similarly, the fact that he had only recently married in 334 implies (though it does not prove) a birthdate perhaps in the 360s.[3]

---

[2] It was the name of Alexander's Epeirot grandfather (Justin 7. 6. 10; 17. 3. 14), nephew (Plut. *Pyrrh.* 5. 2 ff.), and of the ἀρχιυπασπιστής, whom Plutarch (*Eum.* 1. 6) calls one of the Aiakidai. Neoptolemos son of Arrhabaios was Lynkestian (Arr. 1. 20. 10; Diod. 17. 25. 5). Cf. also Hoffmann 202, n.119.

[3] Cf. Berve ii 249.

Whether he was appointed taxiarch by Philip II or by Alexander himself is also uncertain. In 335 he and Philippos (perhaps the son of Balakros? or Amyntas?) were ordered by Alexander to convey back to the Makedonian base the booty taken from the Getai beyond the Danube (Arr. 1. 4. 5). That he was already taxiarch on this occasion is not explicitly stated; it may be inferred from association with Philippos. Meleagros is not mentioned again in the accounts of Alexander's European campaigns, although three other taxiarchs are — Perdikkas, Koinos, Amyntas. Krateros too is conspicuously absent, and it may be that Alexander employed fewer, or different, brigades in Illyria and Greece.

At the Graneikos river Meleagros was stationed on the left wing between the brigades of Philippos and Krateros (Arr. 1. 14. 3), and at Halikarnassos he joined Perdikkas and Amyntas, as Alexander led three brigades of infantry in an unsuccessful attack on Myndos (Arr. 1. 20. 5). From Karia he was sent by Alexander as one of the leaders of the newly-weds (he too had recently married,[4] though his wife's name and family are unknown), along with Koinos son of Polemokrates and Ptolemaios son of Seleukos, to winter in Makedonia and bring back recruits; he rejoined the King at Gordion in the spring of 333, bringing 3,000 infantry and 300 cavalry from Makedonia, along with 200 Thessalian horse, and 150 Eleians under the command of Alkias.[5] Of his participation in the battles at Issos and Gaugamela, nothing is known beyond his position in the battle-line.[6] At the Persian Gates, at the end of 331 B.C., Meleagros and his brigade remained with Krateros, holding the attention of Ariobarzanes, while Alexander conducted the encircling manoeuvre (Arr. 3. 18. 4; Curt. 5. 4. 14).

We do not encounter Meleagros again until the summer of 329 B.C., when Alexander attacked Kyroupolis (Kurkath) and the fortresses along the Iaxartes river (Syr-Darya) in Sogdiana. But here we have only Curtius' testimony, which is not corroborated by Arrian. Meleagros and Perdikkas were entrusted with the besieging of the Memaceni, a people otherwise unknown but said to have killed some 50

---

[4]Arr. 1. 24. 1.

[5]Return to Makedonia: Arr. 1. 24. 1. Reinforcements: Arr. 1. 29. 4. Alkias: Berve ii 23, no. 46.

[6]Issos: Curt. 3. 9. 7; Arr. 2. 8. 4. Gaugamela: Diod. 17. 57. 2; Arr. 3. 11. 9; but Meleagros has dropped out of the battle order at Curt. 4. 13. 28, perhaps out of confusion with his namesake, the ilarch mentioned at 4. 13. 27. He was stationed between Perdikkas and Ptolemaios at Issos, and in the same position at Gaugamela, except that Polyperchon had replaced Ptolemaios, who fell at Issos.

Makedonian horsemen by treachery.⁷ Their city was, however, captured by Alexander himself, despite the fact that he had sustained a serious wound to the neck in the assault on the walls (Curt. 7. 6. 22-23). Arrian (4. 3. 3), however, claims that Alexander suffered this wound at Kyroupolis, and it cannot be determined if Arrian has conflated the sieges of Kyroupolis and the Memaceni or if Curtius has embellished and garbled a more simplified account of the Kyroupolis campaign. But Curtius gives independent, circumstantial, evidence concerning Meleagros' participation, and his account cannot be dismissed out of hand. In the spring of 328, when the main force returned to Sogdiana, Meleagros was left with Polyperchon, Attalos and Gorgias in Baktria,⁸ but Meleagros soon joined Koinos, with whom he spent the remainder of the campaigning season and the winter of 328/7 in Sogdiana.⁹

In 327, his brigade, along with those of White Kleitos and Gorgias¹⁰ (that is, the non-ἀσθέταιροι), accompanied Perdikkas and Hephaistion to the Indus, subduing the local dynast Astis *en route* (Arr. 4. 22. 7; cf. Curt. 8. 10. 2). On this mission, Meleagros will have met the son of the local dynast of Taxila, Omphis.¹¹ Some time later, when Alexander gave Omphis 1,000 talents at a banquet, Meleagros is said to have remarked to his King that 'at least in India he had found a man worth one thousand talents' (Curt. 8. 12. 17-18, quoted above; cf. Strabo 15. 1. 28 C698; Plut. *Alex.* 59. 5). Whether this reflects Meleagros' personal dislike of Omphis, or his opposition to Alexander's favourable treatment of orientals, or perhaps his own pettiness, we cannot say. Curtius claims that Alexander suppressed his anger, remembering Black Kleitos, but remarked that Meleagros, in his envy, was tormenting only himself (Curt. 8. 12. 18). Some modern scholars have seen in this episode, or perhaps in Meleagros' personality in general, the reason for his failure to be promoted to hipparch.¹² Certainly, he was the only surviving taxiarch of those who held the office in 334 who had not risen above that rank. Furthermore, he

---

⁷For the Memaceni see Curt. 7. 6. 17 ff. The treacherous murder of the Makedonian horsemen: Curt. 7. 6. 17-18. For the roles of Meleagros and Perdikkas see 7. 6. 19 (with textual difficulties) and 7. 6. 21.

⁸Arr. 4. 16. 1; Berve ii 249 thinks that each taxiarch had his own command in a separate part of Baktria, but there is no good evidence for this. The cavalry units were active in Sogdiana, and it seems unlikely that individual brigades would have operated in Baktria without cavalry support.

⁹Arr. 4. 17. 3.

¹⁰Krateros' brigade.

¹¹Ambhi. Diodoros and the *Metz Epitome* call him Mophis. When he succeeded his father, he took the official name Taxiles (see Berve ii 369-371, no. 739, s.v. Ταξίλης). On Taxila see Karttunen, *Arctos* 24 (1990), 85-96.

¹²Thus Green 388: 'if Meleager never reached field rank this was, in a sense, just retribution for plain stupidity'.

appears never to have exercised an independent command. Of his personality, little else is known, except that his conservative attitudes led him to reject the kingship of Alexander IV or of Herakles son of Barsine and to espouse the cause of the incompetent Arrhidaios. His fondness for wrestling is attested by Pliny, who claims that he imported powdery dust from the Nile region for this very purpose.[13] But he was clearly not a man of learning, nor politically astute.[14]

At the Hydaspes, Meleagros, Attalos and Gorgias occupied the camp at the halfway point between Krateros' position (opposite Poros) and Alexander's crossing-point (Arr. 5. 12. 1). These three taxiarchs were placed in command of the mercenary cavalry and infantry, almost certainly in addition to their own brigades.[15] And, in accordance with their instructions, they crossed the Hydaspes, once Alexander's forces had successfully diverted Poros' attention, and helped to secure the Makedonian victory (Arr. 5. 18. 1). In 325 Meleagros returned from India via Arachosia and Drangiana along with Attalos and Antigenes, all under the leadership of Krateros (Arr. 6. 17. 3).

The pamphlet on 'The Last Days and Testament of Alexander the Great' includes Meleagros amongst the guests at Medios' dinner-party, at which it is alleged that the King was given poison sent by Antipatros to his sons in Babylon.[16] According to this story, Meleagros was one of some fourteen guests who were involved in the plot against Alexander, and the forged Testament contained in the pamphlet awards the satrapy of Koile-Syria and Phoinikia to Meleagros (*LM* 117; Jul. Valer. 3. 58; Leo 33; Ps.-Kall. 3. 33. 15). The whole story of the poisoning is almost certainly a fabrication of the age of the first Successors, and it is not even certain if the Meleagros of the pamphlet is the taxiarch, or the ilarch and friend of Peithon son of Krateuas.[17] The satrapy of Koile-Syria was, in fact, awarded to Laomedon.

In the events that followed Alexander's death, Meleagros championed the cause of the conservative phalanx (Arr. *Succ.* 1a. 2) and opposed the kingship of Alexander's sons by barbarian women (Justin 13. 2. 6-8; Curt. 10. 6. 20-21). He quickly became the spokesman for the common soldier and for those veteran commanders who had

---

[13]*NH* 35. 167-168; the story is told also of Krateros and Leonnatos.

[14]Berve ii 250 concludes: 'daß er zu den energischen Vertretern des starren und in politischen Dingen beschränkten Makedonentums gehörte, sicher ein gewissenhafter und dem König unbedingt ergebener Soldat war, aber über die engen Grenzen eines gewissen subalternen Wesens nicht hinaus konnte. Al. scheint ihn in diesem Sinne eingeschätzt und ihm deshalb niemals ein größeres selbständiges Kommando anvertraut zu haben.'

[15]So Berve ii 249 (cf. Anspach ii 7, n. 134). Bosworth, *CQ* 23 (1973), 247, n.2, thinks that Gorgias, Meleagros and Attalos commanded only the mercenaries.

[16]For details see Heckel, *LDT*.

[17]Cf. Berve ii 250, no. 495.

looked with disfavour on Alexander's orientalising policies. In an unexpected move, which set the stage for the bitter struggles of the Diadochoi, Meleagros espoused the hereditary claims of Arrhidaios to the Makedonian kingship.[18] The aristocratic faction, stunned by the unexpected turn of events and cowed by the surging mob, withdrew from the phalanx, eventually leaving Babylon altogether (Curt. 10. 7. 10-21). But Meleagros' victory was temporary and hollow: agents sent to assassinate Perdikkas, who had remained briefly in the city in the hope of retaining some support with the infantry, were unwilling to do so, placing little confidence in the authority of Meleagros or his puppet Arrhidaios; Attalos son of Andromenes was easily detached by the prospect of alliance with Perdikkas, who offered his sister Atalante in marriage.[19] The phalanx in general soon repented and called for Meleagros' head and reconciliation with the cavalry.[20] But the cavalry refused to cease hostilities unless the ring-leaders of the uprising were handed over. The fact that the infantry made an exception of Meleagros, demanding that he should be accepted as a third leader (along with Perdikkas and Krateros), shows that at this time there was still considerable support for him.[21] The agreement, which ended the discord, recognised the kingship of Arrhidaios, but it also saw Krateros replace Meleagros as his guardian. This was, of course, much more to the liking of the common soldier, and, Meleagros, although recognised as *tertius dux*,[22] was now isolated and soon abandoned by the infantry, who saw his death as beneficial, indeed essential to the well-being of the empire.[23] Disguising his intentions, Perdikkas arranged with Meleagros himself a lustration of the

---

[18] Whether he took his cue from an *ignotus*, as Curtius (10. 7. 1-3, 6-7) says, is impossible to determine (but cf. Martin, *AJAH* 8 [1983], 162 ff.). Justin 13. 3. 2 and Diod. 18. 2. 2-3 (probably based on Hieronymos) say that Meleagros was sent by the cavalry to negotiate with the infantry but betrayed the former group. Geyer (*RE* xv.1 [1932], 479) prefers this version to that of Curtius, but Curtius appears to be based on Kleitarchos (who used eye-witnesses; so Schachermeyr, *Babylon* 85), and the story that Meleagros betrayed the cavalry may have been a later invention intended to justify his execution.

[19] Assassins sent by Meleagros and Arrhidaios: Curt. 10. 8. 1-3; but Justin 13. 3. 6-8 names Attalos as the instigator of the assassination attempt. For the marriage alliance between Perdikkas and Attalos see Diod. 18. 37. 2; Heckel, *CQ* 28 (1978), 377-382.

[20] Curt. 10. 8. 5 ff. Meleagros appears to have bought time for himself by alleging that the order to murder Perdikkas had come from Philip Arrhidaios himself.

[21] For these negotiations see Curt. 10. 8. 14-22.

[22] Curt. 10. 8. 22-23; Arr. *Succ.* 1a. 3 makes Meleagros Perdikkas' hyparch; Justin 13. 4. 5 treats them as equals: *castrorum et exercitus et rerum* [MSS.] *cura Meleagro et Perdiccae adsignatur*.

[23] Curt. 10. 9. 1: *nam et insociabile est regnum*.

Makedonian army, officially on the instructions of the new King (Curt. 10. 9. 7-11).[24] But, at the head of the cavalry and the elephants, Perdikkas suddenly called for the surrender of the authors of the discord. Some three hundred were handed over for punishment and trampled beneath the feet of the elephants (Curt. 10. 9. 11-18). Meleagros, their leader, sought refuge in a nearby temple, only to be murdered there.[25]

---

[24]Cf. Justin 13. 4. 7: *ignaro collega* must refer to Meleagros' ignorance of the fact that the plan was directed against him as well; cf. Curt. 10. 9. 20.

[25]Curt. 10. 9. 20-21; cf. Diod. 18. 4. 7; Arr. *Succ.* 1a. 4. Justin 13. 4. 7-8 does not name Meleagros, but it is clear that he was among those who were executed. The number of those punished is given in the MSS. of Curt. 10. 9. 18 as 'CCC', but Rolfe, following Bentley, reasons 'XXX', which may be preferable.

2. Alketas son of Orontes: Perdikkas' Brother

Literature. Berve ii 22-23, no. 45; Kaerst, *RE* i (1894), 1514-1515, no. 5; G. Kleiner, *Diadochen-Gräber* (Wiesbaden, 1963), 70 ff.

Born no later than the mid-350s,[26] Alketas was the younger brother of Perdikkas, his successor as taxiarch and partial heir to his war with Antipatros and Antigonos. Although the sources do not give a patronymikon, his father was undoubtedly Orontes.[27] He was thus from the canton of Orestis and related in some way to the Argead royal house.[28] Alketas succeeded his brother as commander of the brigade of Lynkestians and Orestians, perhaps as early as 331/0,[29] but is not named until 327, when he campaigned with Krateros, Polyperchon and Attalos in Paraitakene.[30] In his absence there occurred both the failed attempt to introduce *proskynesis* and the Hermolaos conspiracy, which was reported in a letter of Alexander (Plut. *Alex.* 55. 6).[31]

During the Swat campaign of 327 B.C., Alketas, Attalos and Demetrios the hipparch attacked the town of Ora (Ude-gram), while Koinos besieged Bazira (Bir-Kot);[32] Arrian speaks of οἱ ἀμφὶ Ἀλκέταν (4. 27. 6), as if to suggest that Alketas was the commander-in-chief on this mission. The actual capture of the city was, in Arrian's account, the work of Alexander himself (4. 27. 9). But Curtius has a different version, in which the taking of Ora is assigned to Polyperchon (8. 11. 1), and it is possible that Polyperchon was in fact the leader of the forces named by Arrian.[33] Alketas appears only once more in the Alexander-

---

[26] Although we have no record of when he joined the expedition, there is nothing to suggest that he did not accompany Alexander, and his brother Perdikkas, from the very beginning.

[27] Justin 13. 6. 15; Diod. 18. 29. 2; Arr. *Succ.* 1. 21 all identify him as Perdikkas' brother. Orontes the father of Perdikkas: Arr. 3. 11. 9; 6. 28. 4; *Ind.* 18. 5.

[28] Cf. Curt. 10. 7. 8, unless the reference is to the royal house of Orestis.

[29] Perdikkas appears to have replaced Menes as Somatophylax (Arr. 3. 16. 9); at the Persian Gates (Arr. 3. 18. 5), Perdikkas' brigade is mentioned, but it is not certain if he commanded it in person or if it was already being led by Alketas. In 330, at the time of the Philotas affair, Perdikkas is referred to as *armiger* (Curt. 6. 8. 17).

[30] Arr. 4. 22. 1; cf. Curt. 8. 5. 2, naming only Krateros and Polyperchon, with a separate mission for the latter.

[31] For the authenticity of the letter see Hamilton, *PA* 155; cf. Heckel, *AJP* 99 (1978), 459-461.

[32] Arr. 4. 27. 5. For the identifications of Bazira and Ora see Stein, *Alexander's Track to the Indus* 46-48, 58-60; cf. Seibert, *Eroberung* 152.

[33] Whether Arrian's failure to name Polyperchon was intentional or not is impossible to determine. At 4. 16. 1, he fails to mention that Krateros had

historians: at the Hydaspes (Jhelum) his brigade and that of Polyperchon were assigned to Krateros and stationed in the main camp directly opposite Poros' army.[34] Thus, Alketas participated in only the second stage of the battle, crossing with Krateros after Alexander had engaged Poros.

Between 323 and 320, Alketas served, as we might expect, as an officer of his brother Perdikkas. Initially, it seems, Alketas remained with his brother in Babylon, along with Attalos, Polemon, Dokimos and Aristonous, Perdikkas' chief supporters. But the failure of both Leonnatos and Antigonos to aid Eumenes in securing Kappadokia and Paphlagonia, forced Perdikkas to take the Royal Army to Asia Minor. Leonnatos already aspired to the throne of Makedon, tempted by letters from Olympias, who urged him to depose Antipatros and marry Alexander's sister Kleopatra. To this end, he had tried to enlist Eumenes as an ally, but in vain.[35] Antigonos' refusal is likewise ascribed to arrogance and personal ambition,[36] but the unwillingness of Makedonian officers to take orders from a Greek was clearly a factor, as the conduct of Neoptolemos and Alketas shows.[37] In 321, while Perdikkas was in Pisidia, Nikaia the daughter of Antipatros was brought by her brother Iolaos and a certain Archias. Since suing for her hand in 323, Perdikkas had, however, entered into negotiations with Kleopatra, whom he planned to marry instead. In this matter he was supported by Eumenes, while Alketas urged him to marry Nikaia and remain on friendly terms with Antipatros.[38] Alketas' advice prevailed — at least, for the moment. For Perdikkas sought to cloak his grand scheme by openly marrying Nikaia while Kleopatra played a waiting-game in Sardeis. These intrigues came to the attention of Antigonos the One-Eyed, whom Perdikkas had summoned from Greater Phrygia to answer charges that he had failed to support Eumenes in Paphlagonia and Kappadokia as he had been ordered.[39] When word

supreme command of the forces in Baktria: he names Gorgias, who commanded Krateros' brigade, as becomes clear from Arr. 4. 17. 1.

[34] Arr. 5. 11. 3. I see nothing significant in his failure to be named as a trierarch of the Hydaspes-fleet (Arr. *Ind.* 18); these trierarchies appear to have been restricted to one member of each family, in this case to Perdikkas (18. 5).

[35] Plut. *Eum.* 3. 9-10; cf. Nepos, *Eum.* 2. 4-5, who adds that Leonnatos planned to kill Eumenes when he could not persuade him to share in his enterprise.

[36] Plut. *Eum.* 3. 5: μετέωρος ὢν ἤδη καὶ περιφρονῶν ἁπάντων.

[37] See also Anson, *AncW* 3 (1980), 55-59.

[38] Arr. *Succ.* 1. 21.

[39] The original orders: Plut. *Eum.* 3. 4. Arr. *Succ.* 1. 20 has Perdikkas call Antigonos to account before the arrival of Nikaia and Kleopatra in Asia Minor; Diod. 18. 23. 3-4 says that Antigonos was aware of Perdikkas' intrigues and that it was for this reason, and because Antigonos was a friend of Antipatros and a capable commander, that Perdikkas brought unjust charges against him. The

reached the Perdikkan camp that Kynnane had forced a crossing of the Hellespont and was bringing her daughter Adea to marry Philip Arrhidaios, Alketas was sent north to prevent her from reaching Pisidia.

Alketas' troops must have included many of his own — formerly Perdikkas' — Orestians and Lynkestians and perhaps also Attalos' brigade, now under Polemon's command; these were supplemented by a substantial force of Pisidians, whose friendship and loyalty he began to cultivate through military honours.[40] It is tempting to speculate that Alketas was to take up a position in Hellespontine Phrygia, which had now become vacant with the departure and death of Leonnatos, but this seems unlikely since Alketas made no effort to draw on the resources of that province and used as his base instead Karia and Pisidia. Alketas' approach may have hastened Antigonos' move from Kelainai to Ephesos, whence he would be able to sail to Makedonia. Alketas took the extreme measure of putting Kynnane to death, whereupon the army, mindful of its heritage, insisted that Adea be taken to Perdikkas and that the mother's death should not be in vain.[41] This news too reached Ephesos before the departure of Antigonos, who now brought a variety of charges against Perdikkas and persuaded Antipatros and Krateros to declare war on him.

Preparations were made for war on two fronts: Alketas was instructed to take orders from Eumenes,[42] now overseer of western Asia Minor and entrusted with its defence against Antipatros and Krateros. Perdikkas directed his attention towards Egypt, and Ptolemy. Alketas, perhaps in a fit of pique because the conduct of the war (which he desired for himself) had been given to Eumenes, refused to cooperate, saying that his Makedonian troops would not fight against Antipatros and were favourably disposed towards Krateros.[43] Thus he held himself and his troops aloof, though we cannot say where.

News of disaster at the Nile came swiftly. Perdikkas and his sister Atalante had been killed near Memphis; later, at Triparadeisos, Alketas and some fifty of his brother's officers were outlawed by the

---

full extent of Perdikkas' duplicity, in the Nikaia affair, did not become known to Antigonos until his return to Asia, where he received up-to-date information from Menandros of Lydia (Arr. *Succ.* 1. 26).

[40] Diod. 18. 46. 2.

[41] Arr. *Succ.* 1. 22-23; Polyainos 8. 60; cf. Diod. 19. 52. 5. See Heckel, *RSA* 13-14 (1983-84), 193-200; Macurdy, *HQ* 48-52; Carney, *Historia* 37 (1988), 385-404, esp. 392-394; cf. ead., *Historia* 36 (1987), 496-502, esp. 497-498.

[42] Diod. 18. 29. 2; Justin 13. 6. 15; Plut. *Eum.* 5. 2. Neoptolemos was also ordered to support Eumenes.

[43] Plut. *Eum.* 5. 3.

173

Makedonian assembly and condemned to death.[44] At this time, Alketas was in contact with Eumenes in Phrygia,[45] but the two would not reconcile their differences and Alketas, supported by Dokimos and Polemon son of Andromenes, moved south to Karia, where he was soon joined by Attalos.[46] There, Alketas and Attalos defeated the local satrap Asandros, whom Antipatros had sent against them,[47] whereafter they withdrew into Pisidia, which had only recently been subdued by Perdikkas.

Late in 319, Antigonos — to whom the task of dealing with the outlaws had been entrusted[48] — hurried south from Kappadokia with an army of 40,000 infantry, 7,000 cavalry and an unspecified number of elephants,[49] covering 2500 stades in seven days.[50] Alketas and his followers knew of Antigonos' approach, for they had taken up a position in the so-called Pisidic Aulon, through which an enemy coming from Kappadokia would have to pass,[51] and were surprised only by the

---

[44]Diod. 18. 37. 2; cf. 18. 39. 7; Justin 13. 8. 10 (with textual problems); Arr. *Succ.* 1. 30, 39.

[45]Plut. *Eum.* 8. 7-8 implies that they were both at Kelainai: [Εὐμένης] ἐξήλασεν εἰς τὴν ἄνω Φρυγίαν καὶ διαχείμαζεν ἐν Κελαιναῖς. ὅπου τῶν μὲν περὶ τὸν Ἀλκέταν καὶ Πολέμωνα καὶ Δόκιμον ὑπὲρ ἡγεμονίας διαφιλοτιμουμένων πρὸς αὐτόν....

[46]For the rift between Alketas and Eumenes see Arr. *Succ.* 1. 41; Plut. *Eum.* 8. 8. Plutarch's failure to mention Attalos suggests that the latter was not with Alketas at this time but that he joined him and his brother Polemon in Karia after his unsuccessful naval battle with the Rhodians (Arr. *Succ.* 1. 39). At this time too Laomedon son of Larichos, the satrap of Koile-Syria who had been deposed by Ptolemy's general Nikanor, escaped his captors and joined Alketas in Karia (App. *Syr.* 52 [265]).

[47]Arr. *Succ.* 1. 41.

[48]Diod. 18. 39. 7; cf. Arr. *Succ.* 1. 43 (naming only Eumenes). Battle of 'Kretopolis' or the Pisidic Aulon: Diod. 18. 41. 7 (Antigonos turns his attention to Alketas); 18. 44-45 (the actual battle); 18. 50. 1; Polyainos 4. 6. 7; cf. Engel, *Historia* 21 (1972), 501-507.

[49]Troop figures: Diod. 18. 45. 1.

[50]Diod. 18. 44. 2. At 582. 5 feet per stade, this would work out to 275 miles, or an average of 39. 4 miles per day (R. M. Geer, *Diodorus*, Loeb, vol. 9, p. 135, n.3, says 'about 287 miles, or 41 miles in each 24 hours').

[51]See Ramsay, *JHS* 43 (1923), 1-10, esp. 2-5. Just how well informed Alketas was about Antigonos' movements is difficult to say. Ramsay stresses that 'Alketas and the associated generals were on their march against Antigonus' (5), quoting Diod. 18. 41. 7: ὥρμησεν ἐπὶ τοὺς ἐπιπορευομένους ἡγεμόνας τῶν πολεμίων. But the MSS. reading here is πορευομένους and Geer (Loeb, vol. 9) reads περιγενομένους (cf. Reiske ὑπολειπομένους). Furthermore, Diod. 18. 44 seems to suggest that Alketas had taken no precautions against Antigonos, for he would surely have occupied the foothills before settling down for the night in the plain, if he had suspected that Antigonos might arrive at any time. But cf. Billows, *Antigonos* 78, n.50.

speed of his march. Antigonos, however, was betrayed by the noise of his elephants, and Alketas rushed to seize the foothills overlooking the Aulon with his cavalry. From here, it would have been possible to attack the enemy's flank, had not Alketas' forces been vastly inferior in numbers — 16,000 infantry and 900 horse. Thus Antigonos, engaging him with his right wing, managed to cut off Alketas' retreat to the phalanx with 6,000 cavalrymen. Meanwhile the centre and left of the Antigonid army made short work of the infantry, still in disarray. Hemmed in by the advancing elephants and the cavalry on all sides, Alketas made a daring escape from the battlefield with his hypaspists and the Pisidians, reaching Termessos in safety.[52] There, despite the loyalty of the younger Pisidians, Alketas fell victim to the treachery of the city's elders. Though he eluded capture by suicide, his body was handed over to Antigonos, who, in a not entirely uncharacteristic display of barbarity, maltreated it for three days and then left it unburied.[53] The younger Pisidians, however, recovered the body and buried it with appropriate honours.[54]

[52]Diod. 18. 45. 2-3. Diod. 18. 45. 5 says that the Pisidians numbered 6,000 but this creates some problems. Arr. *Succ.* 1. 39 says that 10,000 infantry and 800 cavalry fled with Attalos after the death of Perdikkas (cf. Diod. 18. 37. 4, no figures given). These troops, minus those who were lost in the battle with the Rhodians, joined Alketas in Karia. Now 10,000 deserters from Memphis and 6,000 Pisidians would indeed give us a figure of 16,000 infantry, and Attalos' 800 horse are only 100 short of the total cavalry at Kretopolis. But Alketas had an army of his own, which Attalos joined and which could not have been composed of Pisidians alone. Plut. *Eum.* 5. 3 speaks of the Makedonians in Alketas' service, and I take these to have been at the very least Alketas' own brigade and the one formerly led by Amyntas and Attalos, now under the command of their youngest brother Polemon. Hence Alketas' army in 321/0 would have included not fewer than 3,000 Makedonians. We may, of course, assume that the casualties in Attalos' *naumachia* against the Rhodians were significant (Arr. 1. 39 does say ὑπὸ 'Ροδίων καρτερῶς ἀπεκρούσθησαν) and that further losses were incurred in the battle with Asandros.
[53]Diod. 18. 47. 3. Antigonos was perhaps venting his anger against Perdikkas. Compare Antigonos' treatment of Eumenes (though Nepos seeks to exculpate him by saying that Eumenes was killed without Antigonos' knowledge — an absurd suggestion. How could one kill the captive leader of the enemy without the permission of one's own commander-in-chief?). Antigenes was burned alive (Diod. 19. 44. 1); cf. Hornblower, *Hieronymus* 215.
[54] Diod. 18. 47. 3. For what appears to be Alketas' tomb, see G. Kleiner, *Diadochen-Gräber* (Wiesbaden, 1963), 71 ff.; Picard, *Journal des Savants* (1964), 298 ff.; and most recently Hornblower, *Hieronymus* 119-120, 206, with earlier literature on 119, n.51. The tomb depicts a rider in relief, armed in Makedonian fashion, but characteristic of the phalangite rather than the cavalryman. The short sword in his hand appears to be of the Illyrian sort — 'was gerade zu dem Orestier Alketas und der orestischen "Taxis" paßt' (Kleiner 76). A larger shield to the right of the rider (Alketas) exhibits 'erst nachträglich eingeritzte

3. The House of Andromenes: A Family at the Crossroads

Four sons of the Tymphaian Andromenes are known — Amyntas, Simmias, Attalos and Polemon — all of whom appear as commanders in the years 335-320, three of them as taxiarchs. The eldest, Amyntas, commanded his own brigade from at least 335; Simmias replaced him briefly at Gaugamela, but after Amyntas' death in 330 the brigade was entrusted to Attalos and not Simmias. Polemon, hurt by connections with Philotas and his own disgraceful flight in 330, never attained military office in Alexander's lifetime; in 321/0, he shared a command with Attalos.

3. 1. Amyntas

Literature. Berve ii 26-28, no. 57; Kirchner, *RE* i.2 (1894), 2007, no. 17; W. Heckel, 'Amyntas son of Andromenes', *GRBS* 16 (1975), 393-398.

Presumably the eldest son of Andromenes (Arr. 1. 8. 2; 1. 14. 2; Diod. 17. 45. 7) and one of Alexander's hetairoi (Diod. 17. 45. 7), Amyntas was a close friend of Philotas son of Parmenion. He was perhaps born soon after 365 and brought up at the court of Philip II as a *syntrophos* of Amyntas Perdikka (Curt. 7. 1. 11). This accords well with the view that Attalos, his (second) younger brother, appears to have been a contemporary and *syntrophos* of Alexander the Great. Amyntas commanded a brigade of pezhetairoi as early as the Theban campaign of 335, where his unit was teamed with that of Perdikkas, which it followed in the assault on the city (Arr. 1. 8. 2). At the Graneikos he was stationed to the right of centre (Arr. 1. 14. 2); nothing else is known about his role in the battle. He was sent to Sardeis to secure the city, which Mithrenes had surrendered to Alexander, but he remained there only until Pausanias had been placed in charge of the citadel.[55] Whether his was one of the three brigades assigned to Philotas at Miletos (Arr. 1. 19. 8), we cannot say; he reappears in the attack on Myndos, together with the Companion Cavalry and the brigades of Perdikkas and Koinos (Arr. 1. 20. 5-7).

At Issos, Amyntas' brigade is found next to that of Ptolemaios son of Seleukos, the successor of Philippos son of Amyntas (or Balakros?), but again his participation in the battle is not otherwise documented (Arr.

Buchstaben' (these are not reproduced and difficult to read from Kleiner's photograph ['Tafel V']), but a contemporary inscription between the rider and the shield appears to have been erased (Kleiner 78).

[55] Arr. 1. 17. 4. Pausanias' appointment: Arr. 1. 17. 7. See Berve ii 308, no. 613, s.v. Παυσανίας. Nothing else is known about him. For Mithrenes see Justi, p. 214; Berve ii 262 f., no. 524.

2. 8. 4; Curt. 3. 9. 7). That he shared Alexander's determination not to break off the siege of Tyre, as Diodoros (17. 45. 7) maintains, is incapable of proof,[56] unless we regard his recruiting mission in Makedonia as a reward for his support. Soon after the capture of Gaza (late 332 B.C.), Alexander despatched Amyntas to Makedonia with ten triremes for the purpose of enlisting reinforcements (Diod. 17. 49. 1). There he appears to have been over-zealous in his recruitment: Gorgias, Gorgatas and Hekataios, young men who had found favour with Olympias in Pella, were coerced against the queen mother's wishes, to serve in Asia, perhaps amongst the fifty Pages who accompanied Amyntas to Sousiana (Curt. 7. 1. 38). He rejoined the King near Sittakene in late 331, bringing 6000 Makedonian infantry and 500 cavalry, along with 3500 Thrakian foot and 600 horse, 4000 Peloponnesian mercenary foot and 380 cavalry, in addition to the 50 aforementioned Pages.[57]

Upon his return, Amyntas resumed the command of his brigade, which was sent with Koinos and Polyperchon, and some cavalry under Philotas, to bridge the Araxes river while Alexander dealt with Ariobarzanes at the Persian Gates.[58] In the Mardian campaign, his brigade and Koinos' accompanied the King (Arr. 3. 24. 1); the same force was led by Alexander against Satibarzanes at Artakoana (Arr. 3. 25. 6).

But Amyntas and his brothers soon fell into disgrace on account of their friendship with Philotas, a connection which threatened their careers and lives. Arrian (3. 27. 1) says that the sons of Andromenes were charged with joining Philotas in a conspiracy against the King. But no one could prove that Philotas was actually involved in Dimnos' conspiracy, only that he had not passed on to Alexander information concerning the plot. Curtius (6. 7. 15) includes a certain Amyntas in the list of conspirators. The others were obscure, like Dimnos himself, and only Demetrios the Somatophylax stands out as a man of note. Hence Amyntas the conspirator may be an otherwise unknown individual with a common Makedonian name (cf. Bosworth, *Arrian* i 360). On the other hand, it is possible that the charges brought against the son of

---

[56]Cf. Berve's claim (ii 27) that the scene 'einem beliebten Effekt des Kleitarchos ihre Entstehung verdankt.'

[57]Curt. 5. 1. 41-42; Diod. 17. 65. 1 gives the same figures but makes the 3500 Thrakian infantry 'Trallians' and gives the number of Peloponnesian cavalry as 'a little under a thousand'; cf. also Arr. 3. 16. 10.

[58]Arr. 3. 18. 6; Curt. 5. 4. 20, 30 adds Polyperchon. Philotas is clearly Parmenion's son and not the infantry-commander: see Bosworth, *Arrian* i 327, against Berve ii 397, no. 803; Milns, *GRBS* 7 (1966), 160.

Andromenes afterwards caused his name to be included (mistakenly) in Curtius' list.[59]

The case against Amyntas did not amount to much: he had been arrogant in his dealings with Antiphanes, the *scriba equitum* (Curt. 7. 1. 15); during a recruiting mission to Makedonia, he had pressed into service some young men from Olympias' court (7. 1. 37-38), and indeed Olympias had written damaging letters about him and his brothers to her son (7. 1. 12); but, most of all, he had close ties of friendship with Philotas (7. 1. 11; cf. Arr. 3. 27. 1). Amyntas seems to have been coeval with Philotas, thus also a *syntrophos* of Amyntas Perdikka and presumably a friend of Amyntas son of Antiochos: of the last two, one had been executed, the other fled to the Persian king and, after the battle of Issos, to Egypt, where he met his end. The charges against Philotas were more serious: culpable negligence on this occasion, treasonous conduct in Egypt in 331. And even now Philotas had to be prosecuted with the utmost vigour. Convicting Amyntas would be more difficult. Fully one-third of the Makedonian infantry could be expected to stand by him — his own brigade and that of Polyperchon; his brother Attalos had been raised at the Court with the then Crown Prince, Alexander. The Philotas affair stopped short of a full-scale purge. But, before it was over, the casualties included Alexandros Lynkestes, Demetrios, Parmenion, and Philotas himself.[60]

After their acquittal in the trial that followed Philotas' arrest, there is no further mention of the sons of Andromenes in the accounts of the next two years, apart from Arrian's brief notice (3. 27. 3) that Amyntas was killed during the siege of a small town shortly after his exoneration. Suspicions that he was deliberately exposed to danger can neither be disproved nor proved. Amyntas may have exposed himself to unnecessary risk in an attempt to vindicate himself. Of Polemon and Simmias we hear nothing further during Alexander's lifetime, though the former reappears in the history of the Successors (Arr. *Succ.* 1. 25; 24. 1 ff.). Simmias vanishes from our records completely.

---

[59]Cf. Badian, *TAPA* 91 (1960), 334, n.30; Heckel, *GRBS* 16 (1975), 394 f. The name of Demetrios the Somatophylax may have been included for similar reasons.

[60]Alexandros: Curt. 7. 1. 5-10. Demetrios: Arr. 3. 27. 5; Curt. 6. 11. 35 ff. Parmenion: Arr. 3. 26. 3-4; Curt. 7. 2. 11 ff.

3. 2. Simmias

Literature. Berve ii 353-354, no. 704; Bosworth, *Arrian* i 300-301; id., *CQ* 26 (1976), 125; id., 'Arrian and the Alexander Vulgate', in *Entretiens Hardt* 22 (Geneva, 1976), 9-14.

Born c. 360, Simmias appears to have been the second oldest of Andromenes' sons and the logical choice to command Amyntas' brigade in his absence.[61] Since Amyntas did not rejoin the expedition until after Gaugamela, his brigade was commanded on that occasion by Simmias. Thus Arrian (3. 11. 9). But the Vulgate names, in this context, Philippos son of Balakros (Diod. 17. 57. 3; Curt. 4. 13. 28, 'Phaligrus'). Until recently, it has been fashionable to reject the testimony of the Vulgate in favour of Arrian, but Bosworth argues that the former is more likely to be correct, that Arrian (Ptolemy) claimed that Simmias commanded his brother's unit 'so that he could lay at his door, by implication at least, the break of the Macedonian line and the attack upon the base camp.'[62] It may be, therefore, that because of Simmias' inexperience and the importance of the battle, Amyntas' brigade was commanded by Philippos son of Balakros, with Simmias in a subordinate role.[63]

Upon his return in late 331, Amyntas reclaimed the command of his brigade. The absence of Simmias from our records and the appointment of Attalos as Amyntas' successor as taxiarch suggests that Simmias was deliberately passed over in favour of his younger brother because of his earlier associations with Philotas and Amyntas Perdikka. The charge that Simmias was, indirectly, responsible for the attack on the Makedonian camp, may have been used to justify Alexander's decision to give Amyntas' command to Attalos, one of his own *syntrophoi*. On the other hand, Simmias may have left the army in 331/0 or died of illness. It is remotely possible that Sippas, whom Antipatros left in charge of Makedonia, when he moved south into Thessaly in 323 (Diod. 18. 12. 2), was in fact correctly named Simmias.[64] Identification with the son of Andromenes is made less likely by this man's limited military experience.

---

[61] I suspect that Simmias was the name of his maternal grandfather, who was likewise the father of Polyperchon. See my stemma of Polyperchon's family (**iii 5**).

[62] Bosworth, 'Arrian and the Alexander Vulgate', 14.

[63] Bosworth, *ibid*.

[64] Cf. Hoffmann 214, who suggests that Σίρρας is also possible, perhaps even more likely. Sippas is otherwise unattested.

3. 3. Attalos

Literature. Berve ii 92-93, no. 181; Kaerst, *RE* ii (1896), 2158, no. 5; R. Schubert, 'Die Porus-Schlacht', *RhM* 56 (1901), 467 f.; R. H. Simpson, 'A Possible Case of Misrepresentation in Diodorus XIX', *Historia* 6 (1957), 504 f.; Schachermeyr, *Babylon* 125; W. Heckel, 'The *somatophylax* Attalos: Diodoros 16. 94. 4', *LCM* 4 (1979), 215 f.

A *somatophylax* (Royal Hypaspist) of Philip II in 336,[65] Attalos had undoubtedly been one of that king's Pages and a *syntrophos* of the Crown Prince, Alexander. Hence a birthdate c. 356 is consistent with the evidence for Attalos' career before and after Alexander's reign. Nothing is known of his career between 336 and 330 B.C., but two years after the family's brief disgrace at Phrada, Attalos is found at the head of Amyntas' brigade (Arr. 4. 16. 1). The curious fact that Attalos alone attained high office after 330 B.C. is ascribed by some scholars to the influence of Perdikkas. But the argument depends upon whether Attalos and Perdikkas were already brothers-in-law at this time.[66] Perdikkas is certainly not the only individual who could have intervened on behalf of the sons of Andromenes, if, in fact, anyone did. Berve (following Hoffmann)[67] assumed that Polyperchon, son of a certain Simmias, and Andromenes (both of Tymphaian origin) were related; I would suggest that a daughter of Simmias (hence a sister of Polyperchon) married Andromenes. If this is so, then Polyperchon may have supported the latter's sons at the time of the Philotas affair. The younger Simmias may have died, or perhaps left the army, while Polemon's youth and disgraceful flight from Alexander's camp will account for his failure to attain higher office before 323.

As for Attalos, he is first mentioned as leader of an infantry-brigade in Baktria in 328; here he appears with Krateros, Gorgias, Polyperchon and Meleagros (Arr. 4. 16. 1). In the following spring, he campaigned in Sogdiana with Krateros, Polyperchon and Alketas (Arr. 4. 22. 1), where he received by letter the news of the Pages' conspiracy in Baktria (Plut. *Alex.* 55. 6). During the Swat campaign, Attalos and his brigade served with Koinos, against the Aspasians (Arr. 4. 24. 1), and Alketas, in the siege of Ora (Arr. 4. 27. 5).

---

[65]Diod. 16. 94. 4; cf. Heckel, *LCM* 4 (1979), 215 f.

[66]For the view that they were related by marriage already in 336 see Welles, *Diodorus* 101, n.2: 'Pausanias was from Orestis, and so were two of his slayers, while Attalus was Perdiccas's brother-in-law'; cf. Green 108. Badian, *TAPA* 91 (1960), 335, suspects that the relationship between Perdikkas and Attalos may have influenced the trial of the sons of Andromenes, after the Philotas affair; I myself echoed these suspicions in *GRBS* 16 (1975), 393, n.5.

[67]Berve ii 325-326, no. 654, s.v. Πολυπέρχων; cf. Hoffmann 156, n.59; but see iii 5.

Curtius (8. 13. 21), in his account of the Hydaspes campaign, describes a certain Attalos as *aequalem sibi* [sc. *Alexandro*] *et haud disparem habitu oris et corporis*, which appears to suit the son of Andromenes. This man remained in the main camp, opposite Poros' forces, disguised as Alexander, who, in the meantime, took a portion of the army upstream in an effort to cross the river undetected. But the identification must be resisted (*pace* Berve ii 93). Arrian (5. 12. 1) tells us that Attalos, Gorgias and Meleagros were stationed halfway between the main camp and Alexander's crossing-point (cf. Schubert, *RhM* 56 [1901], 467 f.). Furthermore, the description of him in the *Metz Epitome* (58) as *Attalus quidam* suggests that we are not dealing with the well-known taxiarch. In 325 B.C. the son of Andromenes accompanied Krateros, Meleagros, Antigenes, and (possibly) Polyperchon westward to Karmania via Arachosia and Drangiana.[68]

In the eastern satrapies, Attalos had served with Alketas, the brother of Perdikkas, on two attested missions, but more often he is associated with the more conservative leaders of the phalanx: Krateros, Koinos, Polyperchon, Meleagros.[69] Hence it is not surprising to find him closely linked with Meleagros in the days that followed Alexander's death. Koinos had died at the Hydaspes in 326; Krateros and Polyperchon were in Kilikia, bound for Makedonia. That left Attalos and Meleagros as natural allies, and the spokesmen of the infantry (cf. Justin 13. 3. 2, 7-8). But their joint opposition to the *principes* in Babylon came to naught and Attalos was easily induced to abandon his colleague by the prospect of marriage to Perdikkas' sister Atalante (Diod. 18. 37. 2).[70] This new alliance isolated Meleagros, who, despite his appointment as Perdikkas' *hyparchos*, fell victim to the purge that followed the reconciliation of cavalry and infantry. For Attalos, and indeed for the bride, it was a fateful union.

First attested in Perdikkas' service during the winter of 321/0, Attalos attempted, with his brother Polemon, to recover Alexander's funeral-carriage. This had been diverted from its westerly route at Damaskos by Arrhidaios, who was taking it to Egypt against the expressed orders of Perdikkas.[71] Furthermore, Ptolemy had come with an army to escort

---

[68]Arr. 6. 17. 3. For Polyperchon see Justin 12. 10. 1.

[69]Attalos' commands (328-325): with Alketas, Arr. 4. 27. 5; with Koinos, Arr. 4. 24. 1; Meleagros, Arr. 4. 16. 1; 5. 12. 1; 6. 17. 3; Krateros, Arr. 4. 16. 1 (implied by 4. 17. 1); 4. 22. 1; 5. 12. 1; 6. 17. 3; Polyperchon, Arr. 4. 16. 1; 4. 22. 1; implied by Justin 12. 10. 1 (to be taken with Arr. 6. 17. 3; cf. Bosworth, *CQ* 26 [1976], 129, n.65).

[70]For a full discussion see Heckel, *CQ* 28 (1978), 377-382, and Appendix V: 'The Marriage of Attalos and Atalante'.

[71]Arr. *Succ.* 1. 25 (naming Polemon alone); *Succ.* 24. 1 (line 3: [οἱ] ἀμφὶ Ἀτταλόν τε καὶ Πολέμωνα).

the King's body to his own satrapy (Diod. 18. 28. 3); Attalos' efforts were thwarted and he rejoined Perdikkas, who had now invaded Kilikia and deposed Philotas.

Here Perdikkas equipped two fleets. One, led by Aristonous, the former Somatophylax, was to suppress the Ptolemaic faction on the island of Kypros. The other was entrusted to Attalos, who skirted the coast of Phoinikia and secured the Pelousiac mouth of the Nile, where he remained, guarding the entrance to the Delta against the naval forces of Antigonos and Antipatros. Attalos was near Pelousion in May 320 when he received word that Perdikkas had been assassinated and Atalante murdered by the raging army (Diod. 18. 37. 3). From Pelousion, he took the fleet to Tyre, where the Makedonian garrison-commander Archelaos received him into the city and handed back 800 talents, which Perdikkas deposited there for safe-keeping. There too Attalos received those troops who had remained loyal to the Perdikkan cause and had fled from the army near Memphis (Diod. 18. 37. 3-4). There were further defections at Triparadeisos, where Attalos appeared in person (Arr. *Succ.* 1. 33, 39) to incite the army, which now rejected the leadership of Peithon and Arrhidaios.[72] Attalos thus gathered a force of 10,000 infantry and 800 cavalry, with which he set sail for Karia, intending to attack Knidos, Kaunos and Rhodes.[73] But the Rhodians, led by their navarch Demaratos, defeated him, and Attalos soon rejoined that portion of the Perdikkan army under Alketas, which had only recently separated from Eumenes in Phrygia.[74]

Reunited, Alketas and Attalos successfully repulsed an attack from the Karian satrap Asandros, acting on Antipatros' orders (Arr. *Succ.* 1. 41). Nevertheless, they now withdrew into Pisidia, where in the following year, they were defeated near Kretopolis by Antigonos.[75]

---

[72]Cf. Errington, *JHS* 90 (1970), 67, n.131; Briant 278, n. 6; Billows, *Antigonos* 68.

[73]Arr. *Succ.* 1. 39. Arrian's account does not say that Attalos and his fleet actually attacked the Kaunians and Knidians. Either these states joined forces with the Rhodians, with the credit for the victory going to Rhodes and Demaratos, or Attalos' strike against them was pre-empted by the Rhodian victory. R. M. Berthold, *Rhodes in the Hellenistic Age* (Ithaca and London, 1984), 60 treats them as separate battles. Hauben, *Vlootbevelhebbershap* 21, speaks of 'een aanval op Rhodos en de tegenover gelegen steden Knidos en Kaunos', as if referring to a single engagement.

[74]The rupture between Alketas and Eumenes: Plut. *Eum.* 8. 8. Alketas' supporters were Polemon and Dokimos. Plutarch's failure to mention Attalos may be an oversight, but it appears more likely that Attalos did not rejoin Alketas until the latter had moved into Karia.

[75]Diod. 18. 44-45; 18. 50. 1. Diod. 18. 41. 7 says that Antigonos set out against Alketas and Attalos, 'who commanded the entire fleet' (τὸν τοῦ στόλου παντὸς κυριεύοντα). What had become of Attalos' fleet, or what remained of it after its

Attalos was captured, together with his brother Polemon, Dokimos, and two otherwise unattested commanders named Antipatros and Philotas.[76] They were imprisoned in a secure fortress which, although unnamed, appears to have been in Greater Phrygia; for Stratonike, Antigonos' wife, who resided in Kelainai, was said to have been nearby (Diod. 19. 16. 4).[77] In 317, when Antigonos had moved to the East to campaign against Eumenes, the captives overpowered their guards and planned to escape, but Attalos' health was failing and the Antigonid forces from neighbouring garrisons arrived quickly to lay siege to the place. Dokimos, who had planned the whole affair, escaped by a secret route and betrayed his former comrades. The fortress was recaptured after a siege of one year and four months.[78] If Attalos lived to see its capture, he did not outlive it by much.

3. 4. Polemon

Literature. Berve ii 322, no. 644; Hoffmann 157; R. H. Simpson, 'A Possible Case of Misrepresentation in Diodorus XIX', *Historia* 6 (1957), 504 f.; Bosworth, *Arrian* i 363 f.

About Polemon we know very little indeed. Born soon after 350 B.C., he was the youngest of four brothers: he appears to have been in his late teens when Amyntas was implicated in the Philotas affair (Curtius 7. 2. 4 describes him as *iuvenis ... primo aetatis flore pubescens*). Thus he

---

defeat by the Rhodians, we do not know. Hauben thinks Attalos' fleet might have been at anchor in Lykia or Pamphylia (*Vlootbevelhebbershap* 22 f.).

[76]Diod. 18. 45. 3; 19. 16. 1. Dokimos, who is unattested in the Alexander-historians, had been a supporter of Perdikkas, capturing Babylon and deposing Archon, who had colloborated with Arrhidaios in diverting Alexander's corpse to Egypt (Arr. *Succ.* 24. 3-5). After the failure of Perdikkas' expedition he joined Alketas and Eumenes, but was reluctant to serve the latter (Plut. *Eum.* 8. 8). He served with Alketas in Karia (cf. Arr. *Succ.* 1. 41) and at Kretopolis (Diod. 18. 44-45), where he was captured (Diod. 18. 45. 3). Imprisoned in Greater Phrygia (?), he planned to escape, eventually betraying his comrades to Antigonos' forces (Diod. 19. 16; cf. Simpson, *Historia* 6 [1957], 504 f.). Antigonos took him into his service, and in 313 Dokimos and Medios captured Miletos (Diod. 19. 75. 3-4). Shortly before the battle of Ipsos (301), Dokimos went over to Lysimachos and secured for him Pergamon, together with its wealth and the treasurer Philetairos (Paus. 1. 8. 1; cf. Diod. 20. 107. 4-5). For his career see also Billows, *Antigonos* 382 f., no. 35; Berve ii 147, no. 285 (very brief); Kaerst *RE* v (1905), 1274, nos. 4-5. Antipatros cannot be identified; Philotas may have been the chiliarch (or pentakosiarch) of Curt. 5. 2. 5.

[77]Ramsay, *JHS* 40 (1920), 107 identifies it as Afiom-Kara-Hissar (Leontos-Kephalai).

[78]Diod. 19. 16 for the full account. For Attalos' poor health, caused by incarceration, see 19. 16. 3. The length of the siege: 19. 16. 5. Diodoros does not say what became of the prisoners, but it is likely that they were executed.

was probably a Page or a Royal Hypaspist in 330 B.C. His flight from the camp on the occasion of Philotas' arrest heightened suspicions that Amyntas and his brothers had been in some way involved in the affair (Arr. 3. 27. 1-2; Curt. 7. 1. 10). But Polemon was persuaded by Amyntas to return and, in the subsequent trial, acquitted (Arr. 3. 27. 3; cf. Curt. 7. 2. 1-10 for a different version).[79]

Nothing else is known of his career during the King's lifetime. Alexander was undoubtedly distrustful of the youth. But the subsequent marriage of Attalos to Perdikkas' sister Atalante brought the sons of Andromenes into renewed prominence. Perdikkas sent Polemon (Arr. *Succ.* 1. 25), together with Attalos (Arr. *Succ.* 24. 1), to prevent the funeral carriage of Alexander from continuing south to Egypt. But Arrhidaios, supported now by Ptolemy, rebuffed them, despite repeated attempts, and sent them back to Perdikkas empty-handed. Whether Polemon served with the land-army that approached Memphis or remained with his brother and the fleet, we cannot say. Certainly he is found with Attalos and Alketas (cf. Plut. *Eum.* 8. 8) after Perdikkas' death: at Kretopolis (319 B.C.) Polemon, Attalos, Dokimos, Antipatros and Philotas were captured by Antigonos (Diod. 18. 45. 3; 19. 16. 1). Imprisoned in a fortress not far from Kelainai, he and his fellow-captives made a desperate bid for freedom, only to be hemmed in and besieged for one year and four months (Diod. 19. 16). In all likelihood, he was executed upon his surrender.[80]

---

[79] According to Curtius, Polemon was captured by others and brought in after Amyntas had made his defence; his tears contributed in no small way to the acquittal of Amyntas. Bosworth (*Arrian* i 364) argues that Ptolemy misrepresented the facts — because Polemon was later an enemy of his — suggesting that Polemon owed his acquittal to Amyntas. Curtius 7. 2. 1 does not, however, say that Polemon returned of his own volition (thus Bosworth, *ibid.*), and in this respect Arrian's version is perhaps more sympathetic. Now much of Curtius' account is heavily dramatised and the trial of Amyntas is clearly modelled on that of M. Terentius, who had been a friend of Sejanus (Devine, *Phoenix* 33 [1979], 150 ff., building on the work of Sumner, *AUMLA* 15 [1961], 30-39). Curtius 7. 2. 4, plausibly, adds that Polemon was carried away by the panic amongst the cavalrymen who had served Philotas: he was not the only one to flee from the camp.

[80] Cf. Billows, *Antigonos* 383, s.v. 'Dokimos'; Simpson, *Historia* 6 (1957), 504-505.

4. White Kleitos: 'Tin-Pot Poseidon'

Literature. Berve ii 209, no. 428; Schoch, *RE* xi (1922), 666-668, no. 10; J. Keil, 'Ephesische Bürgerrechts- und Proxeniedekrete aus dem vierten und dritten Jahrhundert v. Chr.', *JÖAI* 16 (1913), 235; T. Walek, 'Les Opérations navales pendant la guerre lamiaque', *RPh* 48 (1924), 23-30; R. Engel, 'Polyäns Strategem IV 6, 8 zur "Seeschlacht am Hellespont"', *Klio* 55 (1973), 141-145; N. G. Ashton, 'The *Naumachia* near Amorgos in 322 B.C.', *ABSA* 72 (1977), 1 ff.; J. S. Morrison, 'Athenian Sea-Power in 323/2 B.C.: Dream and Reality', *JHS* 107 (1987), 88-97.

Κλεῖτος ἐν Ἀμοργῷ τρεῖς ἢ τέτταρας Ἑλληνικὰς ἀνατρέψας τριήρεις Ποσειδῶν ἀηγορεύθη καὶ τρίαιναν ἐφόρει.
(Plut. *de fort. Al.* 2. 5 = *Mor.* 338a)

Kleitos, after he had destroyed three or four Greek triremes at Amorgos, had himself proclaimed Poseidon and carried a trident.

A prominent Makedonian, but of unknown family, Kleitos was nicknamed 'the White' (ὁ λευκός, Athen. 12. 539c) to distinguish him from his namesake 'Black' Kleitos, the son of Dropides. He first appears as taxiarch in 327, at the beginning of the Indian campaign: his brigade (the seventh), along with those of Gorgias and Meleagros, accompanied Perdikkas and Hephaistion to the Indus river (Arr. 4. 22. 7). In the Hydaspes battle, Kleitos and Koinos made the river-crossing with the King (Arr. 5. 12. 2), while the other five brigades remained on the western bank. When Kleitos next appears, it is as hipparch in the Sangala campaign (Arr. 5. 22. 6), a position which he held also in the Mallian campaign (Arr. 6. 6. 4). Who assumed control of Kleitos' brigade and what became of it, we do not know. Kleitos himself was dismissed with the veterans at Opis and accompanied Krateros as far as Kilikia (Justin 12. 12. 8; cf. Arr. 7. 12. 4). There Krateros appears to have entrusted him with the task of building a fleet with which to guard the Hellespont.[81]

Kleitos' responsibility was undoubtedly to secure the crossing of the Hellespont by Krateros himself, not by Leonnatos, as some have maintained. The latter's crossing into Europe was clearly facilitated by Antipatros' fleet, some 110 ships sent in 324/3 by Alexander which defeated the Athenians near Abydos at the beginning of spring 322 (*IG* ii² 398; ii² 493, neither of which names Kleitos).[82] Krateros, at any rate, was likely to have taken a 'wait and see' attitude, pending the outcome of Leonnatos' battle with the Greeks in Thessaly. The death of

---

[81]Cf. Schoch, *RE* xi (1922), 666; Beloch iv² 1. 72.

[82]Perhaps under the command of Mikion (cf. Plut. *Phok.* 25. 1-4). On the Hellespontine engagement see also Walbank, *AHB* 1 (1987), 10-12, with earlier literature. See also Appendix III.

Leonnatos and Antipatros' deficiency in cavalry made it necessary for Krateros to leave Kilikia, probably in early June. The Athenian admiral Euetion, having been unable to prevent reinforcements from reaching Antipatros from Hellespontine Phrygia, returned to Peiraieus, whence he set out in June to intercept Kleitos' fleet as it entered the Aegean. Near the island of Amorgos, Kleitos defeated the Athenian fleet in the last major naval engagment of the year of Kephisodoros (323/2 B.C.; *Marm. Par.* = *FGrHist* 239 B9).[83] At this point, Kleitos' fleet could not have numbered much more than 130 ships, a force which the Athenians, defeated at the Hellespont and forced to keep ships in reserve in the Malian Gulf, would nevertheless have had difficulty matching. After his victory near Amorgos, Kleitos added the Hellespontine fleet to his own and sailed to the Malian Gulf, where he caught the rest of the Athenian fleet off the Lichades islands and inflicted heavy casualties.[84]

With some justification, Kleitos could now play the part of Poseidon and carry the trident; Phylarchos and Agatharchides go so far as to claim that he conducted business while walking on purple robes. But where Kleitos' showmanship ended and their malice begins is impossible to say. Justin 13. 6. 16 claims that Kleitos commanded Perdikkas' fleet just before Perdikkas invaded Egypt, and it is tempting to emend the text to read *Attalo cura classis traditur* instead of *Clito cura classis traditur*.[85] But a decree from Ephesos, dating to the period before the death of Krateros and granting citizenship to Kleitos and Alketas, shows that the two were still cooperating in the year 322/1.[86] Arrian (*Succ.* 1. 26) tells us that Antipatros and Krateros won over those who were guarding the Hellespont in early 320 (τοὺς τὸν πόρον φυλάσσοντας διὰ πρεσβείας ὑπαγόμενοι), and this appears to indicate the time of Kleitos' defection.

In the settlement at Triparadeisos (320 B.C.), he received Lydia as his satrapy (Diod. 18. 39. 6; Arr. *Succ.* 1. 37), replacing Antigonos' friend, Menandros, who had governed the region since 331 (Arr. 3. 6. 7). Antipatros had clearly intended to keep Antigonos, whom he had

---

[83]For the date cf. Ashton, *ABSA* 72 (1977), 10 f.; and for Kleitos' late departure from the Levant see also Cary, 383. The battle is alluded to in Plut. *Demetr.* 11. 4, in a discussion of character of Stratokles of Diomeia; Plut. *de fort. Al.* 2. 5 = *Mor.* 338a shows that the commander was Kleitos.

[84]Diod. 18. 15. 8-9. The 'Echinades' must be the Lichades (Walek, *RPh* 48 [1924], 28 f.) or near Cape Echinos (cf. Morrison, *JHS* 107 [1987], 95).

[85]Schoch, *RE* xi (1922), 667: 'K. blieb auch im Jahre 321 treu auf der Seite des Antipatros, als Perdikkas seine Expedition nach Ägypten führte. Wenn Iustin XIII 6, 16 berichtet, K. habe dem Perdikkas auf dieser Expedition als Flottenkommandant gedient, so ist ihm ein Versehen unterlaufen, wie Beloch (III 1, 90, 2) richtig bemerkt.'

[86]Thus Keil, *JÖAI* 16 (1913), 235 (for the text, II*n*) and 241 (commentary).

appointed general of the Royal Army and entrusted with the war against the remnants of Perdikkas' party, in check by giving Hellespontine Phrygia to Arrhidaios, Kilikia to Philoxenos and Lydia to Kleitos. But Antigonos, soon after the death of Antipatros made short work of these satraps. Antigonos' move to suppress the activities of Arrhidaios in Hellespontine Phrygia caused Kleitos to garrison some of the cities in his satrapy and flee to Makedonia in order to bring charges against Antigonos (Diod. 18. 52. 5-8). There he served Polyperchon, first by taking the Athenian prisoners, including Phokion, to Athens for execution (Plut. *Phok.* 34. 2-4; 35. 2), and later as admiral of the Makedonian fleet.

As admiral he at first repeated his successes of 322, this time defeating Nikanor's fleet of one hundred ships in the Propontis (Diod. 18. 72; cf. Polyainos 4. 6. 8, who gives Nikanor 130 ships); but the victory was short-lived, for Antigonos brought lightly armed troops up by land and attacked Kleitos' fleet at anchor. When the Makedonians put out to sea, ill prepared and in a state of panic, the remnants of Nikanor's fleet fell in with them and inflicted a decisive defeat upon this self-styled Poseidon (Diod. 18. 72. 5-8; cf. Engel, *Klio* 55 [1973], 141-145). Kleitos escaped to shore, only to be captured by Lysimachos' troops as he made his way by land to rejoin Polyperchon. He was put to death, doubtless on Lysimachos' orders (Diod. 18. 72. 9).

5. Polyperchon son of Simmias: A Jackal among Lions

Literature. Berve ii 325-326, no. 654; Hoffmann 156; Beloch iv² 1. 97 ff.; Lenschau, *RE* xxi.2 (1952), 1798-1806, no. 1; Bengtson, *Diadochen* 39 ff.; Errington, *Hist. Mac.* 123 ff.; Heckel, *LDT* 48-54.

Polyperchon son of Simmias[87] began as a major player in the wars that followed the death of Antipatros the Regent in late 319, wars fought with equal (or, sometimes, greater) vigour by political pamphleteers and partisan historians. Hence Plutarch, drawing on an unnamed source, ascribes to Pyrrhos praise of the man's generalship (Plut. *Pyrrh.* 8. 7; cf. *Mor.* 184c), yet Douris of Samos (*ap.* Athen. 4. 155c = *FGrHist* 76 F12), in the seventeenth book of his *Histories*, said that Polyperchon, though he was an old man and held in honour by the Makedonians, would dance whenever he was under the influence of wine, and that he would wear a saffron robe and Sikyonian slippers. The latter scene reminds us of Philip II, who was chastised after the victory at Chaironeia for 'playing Thersites when history had cast him in the role of Agamemnon' (Diod. 16. 87. 1-2).[88] Aelian (*VH* 12. 43) adds that Polyperchon once made his living as a brigand (ἐλῄστευε), a slanderous charge which may have its origins in the nature of his campaigns in the last decade or so of his life. Driven from the Makedonian homeland, he saw many reversals of fortune in his struggles to assert his authority. Though tenacious, resilient, and surprisingly durable, he nevertheless ceased to be reckoned among the great Diadochoi. He had become little more than a marauder, a jackal among lions.

Polyperchon was of Tymphaian origin.[89] Hence Berve (ii 440: Stammbaum V: 'Fürstenhaus von Tymphaia') assumes that Andromenes and Polyperchon were brothers, sons of the elder Simmias. But their relationship might be more distant. Possibly Andromenes married a sister of Polyperchon; their (second?) child, Simmias, thus bears the name of the maternal grandfather. That Amyntas son of

---

[87]The form Πολυσπέρχον found in some literary sources (Plut. *Mor.* 184c; Aelian, *VH* 12. 43; Athen. 4. 155c) is etymologically sound ('eilig', Pape-Benseler 1230), but the epigraphic and papyrological evidence supports Polyperchon, as found in the Latin sources (cf. Polypercon): *IG* ii² 387 (an Athenian decree of 319/8), line 8; *OGIS* i 4, line 24 (with n.14); i 5, line 39; cf. *P.Cas.* 30. 5 for the occurrence of the name in Egypt. Son of Simmias: Arr. 2. 12. 2; 3. 11. 9.

[88]Beloch (iv² 1. 97), describing Polyperchon as 'ein jovialer alter Herr, der gern einmal eins über den Durst trank, und es dann nicht unter seiner Würde hielt, einen Tanz zu riskieren', is not sufficiently sceptical of Douris (cf. Bengtson, *Diadochen* 39).

[89]Tzetz. *ad Lyc.* 802; Diod. 17. 57. 2; cf. 20. 28. 1; F. Hackmann, *Die Schlacht bei Gaugamela* (Halle, 1902), 10.

Andromenes was named for his paternal grandfather is consistent with Greek and Makedonian practice, but we know too little about the occurrence of the names of maternal grandfathers to establish any rules. But a connection of Polyperchon and the sons of Andromenes by marriage would make it easier to explain their political differences in the late 320s. I would propose the following stemma:

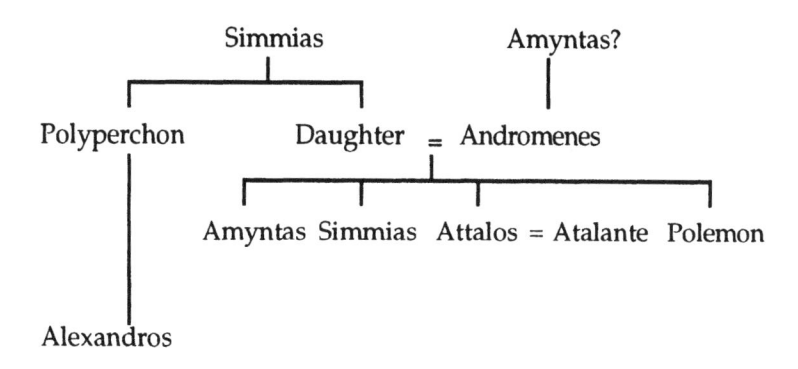

```
            Simmias                    Amyntas?
        ┌──────┴──────┐                    │
   Polyperchon     Daughter    =    Andromenes
        │          ┌────┬────┬────┬────┐
        │       Amyntas Simmias Attalos = Atalante  Polemon
        │
   Alexandros
```

Born between 390 and 380 B.C., Polyperchon was among the prominent veterans sent home in 324 from Opis.[90] His son, Alexandros (cf. Plut. *Demetr.* 9. 5), can scarcely have been born long after the late 340s: he was appointed Somatophylax of Philip III Arrhidaios at Triparadeisos in 320 and was old enough to lead an army in 319/8.[91] Lenschau's (1798) identification of Polyperchon with the mercenary of the same name, who served Kallippos at Rhegion and took part in his murder in 351/0 B.C. (Plut. *Dion* 58. 6), should be rejected as implausible.[92]

Although he was a contemporary of Philip II, nothing is known of Polyperchon's career during that man's reign. It appears that he set out for Asia with Alexander in 334 and, late in the following year, assumed command of the Tymphaian brigade of pezhetairoi, replacing Ptolemaios son of Seleukos, who fell at Issos (Arr. 2. 12. 2); thus he is found at Gaugamela, leading the 'so-called Stymphaians' (Diod. 17. 57. 2), between the brigades of Meleagros and Amyntas.[93] The story that he supported Parmenion's strategy at Gaugamela and was therefore reproached by Alexander is found only in Curtius (4. 13. 7 ff.),

---

[90]Justin 12. 12. 8 names also Antigenes, Gorgias, Kleitos, Polydamas.

[91]Somatophylax of Philip III: Arr. *Succ.* 1. 38. Commander of a force sent to Attika: Diod. 18. 65. 3; Plut. *Phokion* 33. 1. Cf. Berve ii 21, no. 39; Kaerst, *RE* i (1894), 1435, 'Alexandros (13)'.

[92]Possibly the confusion of the two Polyperchons gave rise to Aelian's story (*VH* 12. 43) that the son of Simmias was formerly a brigand.

[93]Arr. 3. 11. 9; cf. Diod. 17. 57. 2-3 and Curt. 4. 13. 28, both with textual problems; Atkinson, *Curtius* i 422-423. For 'Stymphaia' cf. Diod. 20. 28. 1.

who almost certainly inserted it for artistic reasons.[94] But why Polyperchon? In the light of his family connections with sons of Andromenes, whose friendship with Philotas is well attested, the choice is not unusual. Perhaps the story has its origins in the hostile literature of the late fourth century[95] or derives from a pro-Parmenion source.[96] At any rate, it is, like the false claim that Polyperchon was imprisoned for ridiculing *proskynesis*, a fiction.

At the Persian Gates (winter 331/0), Polyperchon, Amyntas and Koinos, along with some cavalry under Philotas' command, were sent ahead to bridge the Araxes river, while Alexander dealt with Ariobarzanes.[97] Polyperchon is not heard of again until 328, when he is left at Baktra with Meleagros, Attalos and Gorgias, during Alexander's cavalry campaigns in Sogdiana. Their instructions were to protect the area against the incursions of rebels like Spitamenes.[98]

According to Curtius, Polyperchon mocked the Persians who did *proskynesis* at Alexander's court in 327. Consequently, he was roughly handled and imprisoned by the King (8. 5. 22 - 6. 1). Arrian (4. 12. 2) gives a less dramatic account, naming Leonnatos, apparently the true culprit. Berve, nevertheless, accepts Curtius' story as historical, and in keeping with Polyperchon's nature: 'die Tatsache selbst ist nicht zu bezweifeln, zumal sie zu dem starr makedonischen Charakter des P. stimmt...' (ii 326; cf. Lenschau, 1799). Although such behaviour may have been consistent with Polyperchon's character (as far as this may be determined), his role in the affair is suspect, on Curtius' own evidence. Arrian tells us that in 327 Polyperchon, Attalos and Alketas were left behind in Sogdiana, under the command of Krateros, to complete the subjugation of Paraitakene, while Alexander returned to Baktria.[99] Curtius (8. 5. 2) records Polyperchon's mission before the introduction of *proskynesis* at Baktra (8. 5. 5 ff.). Furthermore, Krateros and his force were still in Sogdiana when the Hermolaos conspiracy was uncovered; for we are told that Alexander informed them of it by letter.[100] Plutarch says that the letter was addressed to Krateros, Attalos and Alketas. His failure to mention Polyperchon

---

[94]Curtius recognised that Parmenion had been reproached by Alexander too often in a short period and directed the criticism, which other sources level at Parmenion, towards Polyperchon (Curt. 4. 13. 8). Curtius was probably familiar with a tradition hostile to Polyperchon.

[95]Heckel, *AJP* 99 (1978), 459-461.

[96]Atkinson, *Curtius* i 415-416; cf. Rutz, *ANRW* 32.4 (Berlin, 1986), 2350-2351.

[97]Curt. 5. 4. 20, 30; cf. Arr. 3. 18. 6, who does not name Polyperchon.

[98]Arr. 4. 16. 1. The commander-in-chief of the contingent in Baktria must have been Krateros (cf. Arr. 4. 17. 1). Lenschau, 1799, mistakenly asserts that these men were left behind in Baktria, when Alexander advanced into India(!), 'doch wurden seine Truppen später nachgezogen'.

[99]Arr. 4. 22. 1.

[100]Plut. *Alex.* 55. 6; cf. Hamilton, *PA* 155.

indicates merely that he was absent from Krateros' camp: Curtius tells us that Polyperchon conducted a separate mission into the region of Bubacene at that time.[101] Certainly it is unlikely that he completed this mission and returned to Baktra in time to witness the *proskynesis* ceremony.

It remains to explain Polyperchon's presence in Curtius' account. Did Curtius himself introduce him into this episode, or is this the version of Kleitarchos (or of an intermediary source)? Diodoros' version is, unfortunately, lost; the summary of Book 17 gives no evidence as to how the episode might have been handled. Nor do Justin-Trogus and the *Metz Epitome* offer any enlightenment. But Plutarch has a similar story about Kassandros at Babylon.[102] It is, however, a common theme in the history of the Successors that Alexander was at one time or another hostile to them,[103] and the stories that Kassandros and Polyperchon were roughly treated for their opposition to Alexander may have been influenced by their antipathy after the King's death or, in Polyperchon's case, by his general unpopularity.[104]

When the expedition moved towards India, Polyperchon remained with the main army under Alexander's command, while Perdikkas and Hephaistion led the advance-party to the Indus.[105] In the early stages, he accompanied Krateros, whom Alexander left in the vicinity of Andaka to subdue the neighbouring towns.[106] Once this mission had been completed Polyperchon rejoined Alexander briefly at Arigaion, only to be left there again with Krateros to fortify the city, which the Indians had put to the torch and abandoned.[107] Reunited with Alexander a second time, he joined in the attack on the Assakenoi (Arr. 4. 25. 6) and fought at Massaga.[108] Curtius (8. 11. 1) says that it was Polyperchon who was sent to attack Ora (MSS. Nora); Arrian (4. 27. 5) names only Attalos, Alketas and Demetrios the hipparch. Has Curtius

---

[101] Curt. 8. 5. 2. Bubacene cannot be located with certainty: cf. Seibert, *Eroberung* 144; his 'Karte 25' locates it northeast of Paraitakene between the Wakhsh and Amu Darya.

[102] *Alex.* 74. 3: ὁ δ' Ἀλέξανδρος ὠργίσθη, καὶ δραξάμενος αὐτοῦ τῶν τριχῶν σφόδρα ταῖς χερσὶν ἀμφοτέραις, ἔπαισε τὴν κεφαλὴν πρὸς τὸν τοῖχον (cf. Curt. 8. 5. 24: *tum detractum eum* [sc. *Polyperconta*] *lecto rex praecipitat in terram et, cum is pronus corruisset ... inquit...*).

[103] Aelian, *VH* 12. 16; 14. 47a; Justin 15. 3. 3-10.

[104] Cf. Berve ii 326: '...die wenig sympathische Rolle, die er in den Diadochenkämpfen spielte....'

[105] The brigades of *asthetairoi* all remained with Alexander (Arr. 4. 23. 1).

[106] Arr. 4. 23. 5 (Krateros at Andaka). Alexander left Andaka with only the brigades of Koinos and Attalos (Arr. 4. 24. 1). Alketas and Polyperchon clearly remained with Krateros.

[107] Arr. 4. 24. 6-7.

[108] Arr. 4. 26. 1 - 27. 4.

again inserted Polyperchon's name in error?[109] This seems unlikely, since those earlier passages where Polyperchon obtrudes appear to come from a hostile source, and the details concerning Ora are flattering. Arrian may have omitted Polyperchon's name through oversight. But the details are significantly different, and it looks suspiciously as if Arrian (Ptolemy?) denies Polyperchon's capture of Ora and gives it instead to the King himself.

For the remainder of the Indian campaign, Polyperchon is regularly found in that contingent of the army led by Krateros. At the Hydaspes, his brigade, and that of Alketas, remained with Krateros in the main camp, across the river from Poros' position, and thus played only a secondary role in the defeat of Alexander's most formidable Indian adversary (Arr. 5. 11. 3; cf. 5. 15. 3 ff.). In the descent of the Indus river system, Polyperchon served briefly under Hephaistion, but was soon transferred to the west bank, thus rejoining Krateros (Arr. 6. 5. 5). Whether Polyperchon left India with Krateros or continued with Alexander through Gedrosia is uncertain. Justin (12. 10. 1) mentions Polyperchon's departure for Babylonia just before Alexander's Gedrosian march. But Justin regularly substitutes the name of Polyperchon for Krateros (cf. 13. 8. 5, 7; 15. 1. 1). It was shortly before Alexander reached the mouth of the Indus that he sent Krateros to Karmania via Arachosia and Drangiana: according to Arrian (6. 17. 3), Krateros took with him the brigades of Attalos, Meleagros, Antigenes, as well as those hetairoi and other Makedones who were unfit for military service. Polyperchon does resurface in the company of Krateros, at Opis in 324, but, unless Arrian has failed to mention him (deliberately or by accident), there is no good reason for preferring the evidence of Justin, who appears once more to have confused the two marshals.[110]

When Krateros was sent from Opis, with some 10,000 discharged veterans, to replace Antipatros as regent of Makedonia, Polyperchon was designated his second-in-command; for Krateros was in very poor health, and it was not at all certain that he would survive the journey (Arr. 7. 12. 4; cf. Justin 12. 12. 8). Arrian explains the purpose of this appointment: 'so that, if something should happen to Krateros along the way, ... those who were making the journey would not lack a general' (7. 12. 4). And, from this wording, one might conclude that Polyperchon's status pertained only to the march home. But Alexander was eager to replace Antipatros and for the latter to bring reinforcements to him in Asia, and it is doubtful that he would have

---

[109] Thus Berve ii 326, followed by Lenschau, 1799.

[110] On the confusion see Schachermeyr, *Klio* 16 (1920), 332 f.; R. N. H. Boerma, *Justinus' Boeken over de Diadochen, een historisch Commentaar: Boek 13 - 15 cap. 2* (Amsterdam, 1979), 199.

sent Krateros, whose chances of surviving the trip home were questionable, without designating an alternative regent. That man must have been Polyperchon.

At the time of Alexander's death (June 323), Polyperchon, Krateros and the veterans had not advanced beyond Kilikia, where they now remained for a second winter. In 322, they answered Antipatros' call and returned to Makedonia and Thessaly. Augmenting the Makedonian forces, they contributed in no small way to the defeat of Antiphilos at Krannon.[111] What role Polyperchon played, either militarily or politically, during the Lamian War is impossible to determine. But, when Krateros and Antipatros made a truce with the Aitolians in the winter of 321/0, in order to give themselves a free hand to deal with Perdikkas (Diod. 18. 25. 4-5), Polyperchon was entrusted with the defence of Makedonia in their absence (Justin 13. 6. 9). The Aitolians, however, had made a secret pact with Perdikkas to invade Thessaly in order to distract Antipatros. Quickly they attacked Amphissa, defeating and killing the Makedonian general, Polykles, who had been left behind in Lokris, and moved into Thessaly where they incited rebellion and threatened Makedon with a force of 25,000 infantry and 1500 horse.[112] But the danger was lessened by the sudden departure of the Aitolians themselves — in response to an attack by the Akarnanians — and Polyperchon won a decisive victory over the Thessalians and their general, Menon of Pharsalos, the maternal grandfather of Pyrrhos.[113]

Upon Antipatros' death in late 319, Polyperchon assumed the regency and guardianship of the Kings, with Kassandros designated his Chiliarch. In short, Polyperchon had inherited the political and military leadership of Makedonia.[114] But Kassandros, who had

---

[111]Diod. 18. 16. 4 ff.

[112]The Aitolian general Alexandros had brought 12,000 infantry and 400 cavalry, which are surely included in this number (Diod. 18. 38. 1, 3).

[113]Diod. 18. 38. 5-6. This Menon was apparently descended from the commander of the same name who served Kyros the Younger at Kounaxa (see Xen. *Anab.* 2. 6. 21 ff., for an unfavourable character-sketch). That man was alleged to have been intimate with Tharyps the Molossian (Xen. *Anab.* 2. 6. 28), and it was the daughter of the younger Menon, Phthia, who married Aiakides, son of Arrybas and Troas, of the Molossian royal house (Plut. *Pyrrh.* 1. 6); cf. Heckel, *Chiron* 11 (1981), 81, n.11. For his death see also Plut. *Phokion* 25. 5. The Akarnanian invasion of Aitolia is treated by Diodoros as a chance occurrence; it may have been prompted by Makedon.

[114]Diod. 18. 47. 4: ἡ δὲ τῶν ὅλων ἡγεμονία καὶ τῶν βασιλέων ἡ ἐπιμέλεια. Diod. 18. 48. 4: ἐπιμελητὴς τῶν βασιλέων καὶ στρατηγὸς αὐτοκράτωρ. Cf. Plut. *Phokion* 31. 1. The decision was doubtless made in consultation with Antipatros' *consilium* (cf. Hammond, *HMac.* iii 130, with n.3) and not, as Lenschau, 1800, suggests, by the terms of Antipatros' testament. Will, *CAH* vii.1 (1984), 41 (with n.47), thinks that Ptolemy's invasion of Koile-Syria and the

already played second-fiddle to Antigonos in 320, was not inclined to do so again,[115] and Polyperchon sought to strengthen his own position by offering the guardianship of Alexander IV to Olympias and by proclaiming the 'Freedom of the Greeks'.[116]

In Makedonia, and in the Greek states to the south, support was divided between the newly-appointed guardian of the Kings and his rebellious Chiliarch. Loyalty to the latter was, predictably, based on allegiance to Antipatros and an endorsement of his policies. And, whether or not Polyperchon shared these sentiments initially, he was soon forced into a political stance that was diametrically opposite. In retrospect, it is easy to regard this policy as reactive and myopic.[117] But there must have been many in Polyperchon's council who had returned to Europe from Opis and scarcely needed reminding that it had been Alexander's intention to replace Antipatros and to bring a new order to Europe. For Alexander in 324, just as for Polyperchon in 319/8, the reassertion of Argead power in the European part of the Empire required the eradication of the house of Iolaos from power. Hence, not only Antipatros himself needed to be replaced, but the pro-Antipatrid oligarchies which had been established in the south. Polyperchon could now claim to be reviving Alexander's instructions to Krateros, to guard 'the freedom of the Greeks', which must have been closely connected with the so-called Exiles' Decree,[118] proclaimed at Olympia in summer 324. Polyperchon had been Krateros' second-in-command at that time (Arr. 7. 12. 4), but Alexander's death in the following year

---

expulsion of Laomedon were triggered by news of Antipatros' death (cf. p. 42: 'the Syrian venture was a challenge to the order which Polyperchon symbolized and as it could be foreseen that the new regent would find it difficult to keep his position it was important for Ptolemy to be on the side of his opponents'). But Diod. 18. 43 places these events before Antipatros' death, and App. *Syr.* 52, which Will calls 'confused and inaccurate' (41, n.47), shows that Laomedon joined Alketas in Asia Minor. It was after the defeat and death of Alketas that Antigonos learned of Antipatros' death; Ptolemy could scarcely have had the news sooner!

[115]Diod. 18. 49. 1-3; cf. Plut. *Phok.* 31. 1; *Heidelberg Epit.* 1. 4 = *FGrHist* 155 F1. For Kassandros as Antigonos' chiliarch, see Arr. *Succ.* 1. 38; Diod. 18. 39. 7.

[116]Diod. 18. 55. 2 - 57. 1; Plut. *Phok.* 32. 1. I see no evidence for Bengtson's suggestion (*Diadochen* 40) that the revival of the *koine eirene* was Adea-Eurydike's idea.

[117]Thus Errington, *Hist. Mac.* 124 f.

[118]Bosworth, *Conquest and Empire* 224 does not link the Exiles' Decree with Krateros' mission but does comment that Philip III's and Polyperchon's 'famous *diagramma* ... re-enacted the Exiles' Decree...'. Cf. also Mendels, *Historia* 33 (1984), 129 ff., esp. 143-146. Less convincing is Will's view (*CAH* vii.1 [1984], 43) of Polyperchon's actions as 'completely original, without antecedent and without sequel'. Cf. also J. Seibert, *Die politischen Flüchtlinge und Verbannten in der griechischen Geschichte* (Darmstadt, 1979), 167 ff.

put the proposed changes on hold. Krateros reacted to the situation, the danger to Makedon from Leosthenes and the Greeks, and the aspirations of Perdikkas, by throwing in his lot with Antipatros. But the death of the old Regent and his designated successor gave Polyperchon the opportunity to champion the cause of the royal house. Ironically, similar action by the Greek Eumenes elicited praise from ancient and modern writers; the Makedonian Polyperchon is, instead, accused of 'grand-standing', of making transparent gestures in the hope of holding on to power. Nothing can be further from the truth. For Polyperchon harmed his cause by giving away too much power — by offering to share it, with Olympias and with Eumenes, all in the name of the Kings.

In the beginning support for Polyperchon was strong in Makedonia (Diod. 18. 54. 2), and he was soon joined by White Kleitos, driven from Asia by Antigonos (Diod. 18. 52. 6); Olympias was slower to respond to Polyperchon's invitation.[119] Threatened by Kassandros, Polyperchon extended an amnesty to Eumenes and the outlaws, if they supported the cause of the Kings, promising also to come in person to Asia with an army to oppose Antigonos.[120] In addition to Eumenes, Polyperchon wrote also to the Argyraspids, who were guarding the treasures at Kyinda in Kilikia (Diod. 18. 58. 1) and with whose commander Antigenes he was doubtless well acquainted.[121]

Things could hardly have started better. Eumenes and the generals in Kilikia rallied to support the Kings.[122] Athens was quick to dissociate itself from the pro-Antipatrid policies of conservatives like Phokion, and in February 318 made public its enthusiasm for Polyperchon.[123] But the March deadline for the implementation of

---

[119] Diod. 18. 57. 2 does not imply a second invitation. 18. 49. 4 records the original decision of Polyperchon and his Council, 18. 57. 2 the issuing of the invitation to the queen mother. For her reluctance to come immediately see 18. 58. 3-4.

[120] Diod. 18. 57. 3-4.

[121] Engel, *Machtaufstieg* 42, sees Antigonos' preoccupation with affairs in western Asia Minor as the main reason for the 'defection' of the Argyraspids from Antigonos. But Antigonos was surely regarded as an appointee of the Kings, and as such he had now been deposed in favour of Eumenes. The Argyraspids could be expected to remain loyal to Antigonos only as long as he exercised authority on behalf of the royal house.

[122] Letters to Eumenes and the commanders in Kilikia: Diod. 18. 57. 3-4, 58. 1. Eumenes was appointed στρατηγὸς τῆς ὅλης Ἀσίας αὐτοκράτωρ, essentially the same office which Antipatros had conferred upon Antigonos (Diod. 18. 58. 1; cf. 18. 39. 7, 40. 1). The Silver Shields resisted the appeals of Ptolemy (Diod. 18. 62. 1-2) and Antigonos' agent Philotas (Diod. 18. 62. 4 ff.). A fleet was prepared for Polyperchon in Phoinikia (Diod. 18. 63. 6).

[123] See *Syll.*³ 315 = *IG* ii² 387 for Athenian support of Polyperchon in February 318. For the popular support for Polyperchon cf. Nepos, *Phocion* 3. 1.

Philip III's decree passed, with Nikanor still firmly entrenched in Mounychia.[124] A force led by Polyperchon's son Alexandros advanced to Attika, bringing with it many of the exiles and putting pressure on Nikanor, who had seized and fortified Peiraieus and was ignoring orders from Olympias to withdraw his garrison.[125] But Polyperchon's duplicity soon became evident: Alexandros entered into frequent and secret negotiations with Nikanor, perhaps even through the agency of Phokion, who thought to ingratiate himself with the Polyperchan party and to protect himself at home if he could persuade Nikanor to turn over Mounychia and Peiraieus to Alexandros.[126]

Polyperchon, meanwhile, held the bulk of the Makedonian army in reserve in Phokis, that is, inside Thermopylai, where he was met by delegations of the Athenians.[127] One of these was headed by Phokion, whose crimes included collaborating with Nikanor in his seizure of Peiraieus and whose favourable stance towards the house of Iolaos now placed him in jeopardy; nevertheless, his recent negotiations with Alexandros must have caused him to hope for a better reception from Polyperchon.[128] The latter made a great show of ceremony — with Philip III enthroned beneath a golden canopy — but the process quickly degenerated into a shouting-match, and Polyperchon was forced to restrain the enraged King, who nearly transfixed Phokion's comrade, Hegemon, with his spear.[129] In the end, White Kleitos was instructed to take the opponents of the new regime under guard to Athens, where they were denounced and executed (Plut. *Phok.* 34-35).[130]

---

[124] The thirtieth day of Xanthikos (Diod. 18. 56. 5), the 6th Makedonian month. Ferguson, *HA* 30-32, dates Alexandros' arrival in Attika to March 318. For the events of 319-317, I have adopted the changes suggested by Williams, *Hermes* 112 (1984), 300-305, to the chronology of Errington, *Hermes* 105 (1977), 478 ff.

For Nikanor — whom Kassandros had installed in Mounychia as a replacement for Menyllos before the news of Antipatros' death became known (Plut. *Phok.* 31. 1) — see also Berve ii 276-277, no. 557.

[125] Olympias' letter: Diod. 18. 65. 1. Olympias' reluctance to return to Makedonia at this time does not rule out her intervention in Athenian affairs on behalf of Polyperchon and the Kings. Alexandros in Attika: Diod. 18. 65. 3 ff.

[126] So Diod. 18. 65. 3-5; but Plut. *Phok.* 33 (understandably) does not mention Phokion's role. See Gehrke, *Phokion* 115, n.39.

[127] Polyperchon in Phokis: Diod. 18. 68. 2; Plut. *Phokion* 33. 4-12; cf. Nepos, *Phoc.* 3. 3.

[128] Thus Gehrke (*Phokion* 115, n.39) notes that, had Phokion not received some reassurances from Alexandros, his visit to Polyperchon would have been little more than 'glatter Selbstmord'.

[129] Plut. *Phok.* 33. 7-12.

[130] Phokion drank hemlock on 19 Mounychion (= 7 May) 318; cf. Williams, *Hermes* 112 (1984), 304 f. For the final stages of Phokion's career see Gehrke, *Phokion* 108-120; also L. A. Tritle, *Phocion the Good* (London, 1988), 133-140.

Unable to win Athens for himself,[131] Polyperchon left behind a small force under Alexandros, and proceeded against Megalopolis, which had mustered some 15,000 men and prepared to withstand a siege.[132] Elsewhere in the Peloponnese, his envoys called upon the cities to overthrow the oligarchies of Antipatros and even to put the latter's supporters to death, and in this Polyperchon was generally successful.[133] The Megalopolitans, however, led by Damis, a man who had served with Alexander in Asia and had experience of elephants, prevailed militarily and soon turned the swelling political tide in Greece against Polyperchon. Although the Makedonians had been successful in breaching the walls, Damis planted spikes in the path of the elephants, injuring the beasts who, in their frenzy, fell back on their own troops and inflicted numerous casualties.[134] Perseverance was not Polyperchon's strong point, and he soon withdrew to tackle more pressing matters.

Diodoros (18. 72. 1) does not say what these matters were, but it appears that Polyperchon was concerned that Kassandros would soon make an expedition into Makedonia, whither he returned. Satisfied that affairs there were in order, he seems to have moved south to Epeiros — in order to prepare for Olympias' return to Makedonia, which he entrusted to his ally, and Olympias' own nephew, Aiakides[135] — and, from there, perhaps to the Aitolians, whose

[131] Polyperchon did manage to send relief to Salamis, which was being besieged by Kassandros' forces (Diod. 18. 69. 2).

[132] Diod. 18. 70. 1-3.

[133] Diod. 18. 69. 3-4.

[134] For the campaign see Diod. 18. 70-71. Polyainos 4. 14, describing how Polyperchon encouraged his men by assuming the dress of the Arkadians, in order to show them what sort of enemy they were up against, and then appearing in Makedonian armour for the sake of comparison, must refer to the Megalopolitan campaign. Berve's entry on Damis (ii 115, no. 240) contains misleading errors. Damis may be identical with the Amisus of Curt. 10. 8. 15 (Berve's no. 53; Niese i 245, n.3; cf. Heckel, *LCM* 6 [1981], 63); see also Kirchner, *RE* iv (1901), 2056, no. 1. His support for Kassandros was rewarded in 315, when the latter appointed him *epimeletes* of Megalopolis (Diod. 19. 64. 1).

[135] Diod. 19. 11. 1-2. Against the view, prevalent in much modern scholarship (see, most recently, Hammond, *HMac* iii 139), that Alexander IV and Rhoxane were left for some time in Epeiros, see Macurdy, *JHS* 52 (1932), 256-261. Polyperchon could be expected to leave Philip III and Adea-Eurydike in Makedonia, rather than bring them to Epeiros, where their 'enemy' Olympias resided. I see no other good reason for Polyperchon to separate himself from Philip III. Certainly, he is unlikely to have done so *after* Adea-Eurydike announced that she was transferring the 'guardianship' of the 'King' (Hammond, *HMac* iii 140, n.1, may be correct in suggesting that Justin's [14. 5. 3] use of the singular *rex* is significant, 'indicating a rejection of "reges" by Eurydice') to Kassandros.

friendship he cultivated.¹³⁶ In his absence, the Queen, Adea-Eurydike, persuaded her husband, Philip III, to transfer the 'guardianship' of his kingdom to Kassandros (cf. Justin 14. 5. 1-3).

This shrewd move, which may have been instigated by Kassandros himself,¹³⁷ meant an immeasurable loss of prestige for Polyperchon, for whom it now became imperative either to reassert his control over the half-witted King and (what was more difficult) his rebellious wife or to establish the primacy of Alexander IV. It is, most likely, in this historical context that a pamphlet on 'The Last Days and Testament of Alexander the Great' was published. The emphasis placed on the legitimate kingship of Alexander IV and the favourable treatment of Olympias and Rhoxane, in sharp contrast to the accusations of regicide levelled against the family of Kassandros and the supporters of Antigonos, leave little doubt that the original version of this pamphlet — which was soon embellished, contaminated and otherwise distorted in the interests of other parties — originated in the Polyperchan camp.¹³⁸

The failure at Megalopolis had had devastating effects in the south: contemptuous of Polyperchon, some Greek cities went over to Kassandros,¹³⁹ who had pursued his goals with great energy and through the formidable alliances secured by his father in the first years that followed Alexander's death.¹⁴⁰ To counter the most dangerous of these alliances — that with Antigonos, who had supplied Kassandros with thirty-five ships to secure Nikanor's position in Peiraieus — Polyperchon sent out Kleitos with the Makedonian fleet. This man had a score to settle with Antigonos, who had driven him from Lydia soon after Antipatros' death. But his initial success near Byzantion, in which he destroyed or captured about half Nikanor's fleet, was followed by an overwhelming disaster; for Antigonos, with a large contingent of lightly armed troops, fell upon Kleitos' sailors after they had disembarked for the night. Those who managed to board

---

¹³⁶For Polyperchon's relationship with the Aitolians see Mendels, *Historia* 33 (1984), 158 ff.

¹³⁷Perhaps during Kassandros' first return to Makedonia (probably in spring 317; so Hammond, *HMac* iii 137; Diod. 18. 75. 2; cf. 19. 35. 7 and Polyainos 4. 11. 2).

¹³⁸For a full discussion see Heckel, *LDT*.

¹³⁹Diodoros' claim that 'most of the cities defected from the Kings and inclined towards Kassandros' (αἱ πλεῖσται τῶν Ἑλληνίδων πόλεων ἀφιστάμεναι τῶν βασιλέων πρὸς Κάσανδρον ἀπέκλιναν, 18. 74. 1) is grossly exaggerated, as Beloch iv² 2. 440 f. recognised. It is to this period that we should date Polyainos' reference to ἡ πρὸς Πολυσπέρχοντα ὀργή amongst the Makedonians (4. 11. 2).

¹⁴⁰His sisters Eurydike, Nikaia and Phila had married Ptolemy, Lysimachos and Demetrios Poliorketes respectively. See Beloch iv² 2. 125 ff.; Seibert, *Verbindungen* 11 ff., 72, 93; Heckel, *Classicum* 15 (1989), 32 ff.

ship and make for open water fell in with the remnants of Nikanor's fleet and were annihilated. Kleitos himself fled to shore and attempted to reach Makedonia by land, only to fall into the hands of Lysimachos' troops, who put him to death.[141]

In contrast to the lethargy and ineffectiveness of Polyperchon's party, Kassandros had shown himself a force to be reckoned with. Now the return of Nikanor's fleet, sailing into Peiraieus with the beaks of Kleitos' warships, spelled the end of Polyperchon's hopes in Athens.[142] The Athenians, having flirted briefly with democratic revolution, came to terms with Antipatros' son and Greece in general reverted to a pro-Antipatrid stance. Polyperchon could do little but concentrate his efforts on driving Kassandros and his supporters from Makedonia, while hoping that his son Alexandros could keep in check the dissension in the Peloponnese.

In the northwest, Olympias and Aiakides brought their forces to Euia, on the Makedonian-Epeirot border,[143] where they confronted Philip III and Eurydike. Douris' description of the battle as one fought between women, with Olympias in Bacchic attire and Eurydike in Makedonian armour, is surely a later embellishment.[144] At first, the benefits of alliance with Olympias became clear: overawed by the prestige of the queen mother, the troops of Philip and Eurydike deserted, leaving their 'King' to fall into enemy hands and his bride to make a desperate bid at escape (Diod. 19. 11. 1 ff.). She was captured as she made her way to Amphipolis with her advisor, Polykles, perhaps a relative of the general who had been killed by the Aitolians in 321/0.[145] But Polyperchon would have been wise to curtail Olympias' power: her reprisals against personal enemies, and those of her family, soon turned the reverence of the Makedonians into disgust, and this

---

[141]Kleitos' naval campaign: Diod. 18. 72. 2-9; Polyainos 4. 6. 8; cf. Engel, *Klio* 55 (1973), 141-145; Beloch iv^2 1. 103 f.; Billows, *Antigonos* 86-88. See also iii 4. Lysimachos was, as a result of his marriage to Nikaia, an ally of Kassandros. But I see no strong evidence for Engel's characterisation of him as 'Polyperchons persönlicher Feind Lysimachos' (*Machtaufstieg* 98, n.166). Cf. Will, commenting on Polyperchon's appointment as *epimeletes*: 'The illegality of the procedure was not what shocked the new masters of the empire, however, but the fact that the succession to Antipater aroused secret ambitions in some of them. Lysimachus, Macedon's immediate neighbour, would certainly not have disdained the idea of one day restoring for his advantage the union of Macedon and Thrace ...' (*CAH* vii.1 [1984], 41).

[142]Diod. 18. 75. 1.

[143]For the location of Euia see Hammond, *HMac* iii 140, with n.2.

[144]Douris *ap.* Athen. 13. 560f = *FGrHist* 76 F52; cf. Heckel, *Chiron* 11 (1981), 83 f.; Carney, *Historia* 36 (1987), 496 ff., esp. 500.

[145]Diod. 19. 11. 3. For Polykles the general see Diod. 18. 38. 2.

feeling for the woman was extended also to the man who had summoned her.[146]

Polyperchon now took extensive military precautions against Kassandros, who was at the time besieging Tegea in the Peloponnese. He himself occupied Perrhaibia, while his son Alexandros threatened the Peloponnese; the approach from the south was further secured by the Aitolians, who blocked Kassandros' advance at Thermopylai (Diod. 19. 35. 1-2). But Kassandros ferried his men around the pass, landing them in southern Thessaly, and sent one of his officers, Kallas, to hold Polyperchon in check. A second general, Deinias, secured the entrances to Makedonia before Olympias' forces could seize them (Diod. 19. 35. 3).[147] Olympias for her part took refuge in Pydna (Diod. 19. 35. 5-7; Justin 14. 6. 1-4) and entrusted the campaign against Kassandros to Aristonous (Diod. 19. 35. 4).

Besieged at Azoros,[148] Polyperchon now suffered the indignity of watching his troops desert to Kallas (Diod. 19. 36. 6), and he was forced to sit idle as Kassandros starved Olympias and the remnants of the royal family into submission;[149] nor was he able to bring much-needed relief to Monimos in Pella or Aristonous, both of whom remained loyal to the house of Alexander (Diod. 19. 50. 7-8).[150] Indeed, it was only with difficulty that he escaped to Aitolia (Diod. 19. 52. 6). Little remained of his former power, except perhaps those cities of the Peloponnese that retained their allegiance thanks to the presence of

---

[146]Diod. 19. 11. 4-9. Philip III was stabbed by his Thrakian guard and Adea-Eurydike forced to commit suicide. Kassandros' brother, Nikanor, was executed on Olympias' orders and the grave of another brother, Iolaos, overturned. Diodoros (19. 11. 8) further adds that she murdered a hundred prominent supporters of Kassandros. Cf. Diod. 19. 51. 5; Justin 14. 5. 1 ff.
Despite Polyperchon's (and Olympias') blunders at home, the authority of their name could still be used to inspire the troops in Asia (Diod. 19. 23. 2); Polyperchon's crossing into Asia was, however, fabricated by Eumenes himself.

[147]Kassandros also sent Atarrhias (possibly the former hypaspist commander of Alexander) against Aiakides in Epeiros (Diod. 19. 36. 2-3), a move which soon led to the expulsion of the king and his replacement by Kassandros' agent Lykiskos (Diod. 19. 36. 3-5).

[148]Or Azorios (Diod. 19. 52. 6).

[149]With her were Rhoxane and Alexander IV, as well as Deidameia, Aiakides' daughter, to whom Alexander was betrothed (Plut. *Pyrrh.* 4. 3; cf. Sandberger, no. 27), Thessalonike, the daughter of Philip II and Nikesipolis, the daughters of Attalos (and, presumably, of Atalante), and the relatives of some of Olympias' friends (Diod. 19. 35. 5; cf. Justin 14. 6. 2-3). An attempt to help her may have misfired (Polyainos 4. 11. 3).

[150]Monimos appears to have had earlier connections with Olympias (cf. Phylarchos *ap.* Athen. 13. 609c = *FGrHist* 81 F21).

Alexandros[151] — and even he soon found himself hard-pressed by Kassandros. Alexandros had blocked the Isthmus, but Kassandros was able to land his troops in the Argolid[152] and capture Argos. From there he marched across to Messenia and won over all the towns of the region except Ithome. On his return to the north, he left 2,000 troops with Molykkos at the passes between Megara and the Korinthiad.[153]

A rift between Kassandros and his former ally, Antigonos, offered Polyperchon some hope of recouping his losses. In 315, Antigonos sent his agent Aristodemos to secure a pact with Polyperchon and his son, whereby Polyperchon was recognised as *strategos* in the Peloponnese. Oaths were exchanged by Aristodemos and Polyperchon; Alexandros sailed to Asia to complete negotiations with Antigonos.[154] But, despite Lenschau's (1804) belief that this was a contract between equal parties, Polyperchon had clearly accepted a subordinate role in return for Antigonid support in Greece;[155] for Aristodemos brought to his new allies some 8,000 mercenaries recruited in the Peloponnese.[156] Kassandros meanwhile secured Orchomenos in Arkadia but failed to make further gains in Messenia and prepared to return to the north, stopping first to celebrate the Nemean games (Diod. 19. 64. 1). It was presumably during this brief respite that he tried, in vain, to persuade Polyperchon to abandon Monophthalmos. On his return to Makedonia, Kassandros sent Prepelaos to Alexandros, offering him the title of 'general of the Peloponnese' — the very office which the father exercised for Antigonos — and inducing him to defect. Thus Kassandros did even greater harm to Polyperchon's credibility.[157] Or so Diodoros (and presumably his source, Hieronymos) alleges. This may simply be hostile propaganda, intended to discredit Polyperchon, who would thus seem to be unable to command the loyalty of even his own son.

Now Lenschau (1804) has suggested that Alexandros' defection may have been little more than a ploy, to buy time from Kassandros. But, if this was mere deception by Polyperchon and his son, Antigonos too was taken in; for he sent his nephew Telesphoros to liberate the cities in which Alexandros (and Kassandros) had placed garrisons. Soon only

---

[151]Diod. 19. 35. 1, 53. 1.

[152]Beloch iv² 2. 441 assumes that Kassandros' landing-place, Epidauros, had been captured in the campaign of the preceding year.

[153]Diod. 19. 54. 3-4.

[154]Diod. 19. 57. 5; 19. 60. 1; 19. 61. 1; cf. 19. 62. 5.

[155]Polyperchon's *strategia* involved recognition of Antigonid claims to the regency (Diod. 19. 61. 3; cf. Billows, *Antigonos* 114, with n.41), and probably also his territories in Asia, which had been threatened by the coalition of Lysimachos, Kassandros and Ptolemy (Diod. 19. 57. 1).

[156]Diod. 19. 60. 1.

[157]Unsuccessful attempts to enlist Polyperchon: Diod. 19. 63. 3. Alexandros corrupted by Prepelaos: Diod. 19. 64. 3-5.

Sikyon and Korinth held out against Antigonos and these are described by Diodoros in the following terms: ἐν ταύταις γὰρ Πολυπέρχων διέτριβεν δυνάμεις ἁδρὰς ἔχων καὶ πιστεύων ταύταις τε καὶ ταῖς τῶν τόπων ὀχυρότησιν (19. 74. 2). It appears also that the willingness of the Aitolians to join Aristodemos — they had formerly been allies of Polyperchon — was prompted by Polyperchon's alliance with Kassandros. Beloch suggests, plausibly, that Alexandros served as Kassandros' *strategos* because Polyperchon could not bring himself to serve the younger man.[158] Now seventy years old, Polyperchon may have relinquished control of affairs to his son, allowing him to make his best deal, which, in this case involved abandoning Antigonos in favour of his father's bitter enemy. Polyperchon's 'retirement' thus paved the way for *rapprochement*. But Alexandros was quickly swept aside by Aristodemos, and his alliance with Kassandros was perhaps the cause of his assassination and the uprising in Sikyon (314).[159] These events drew Polyperchon out of retirement to pursue an independent policy. Hence, in the Peace of 311, Polyperchon plays no part, and Antigonos' letter to Skepsis (Dittenberger, *OGIS* i 5 = Welles, *RC* 1) shows that Antigonos at least was anxious to deprive him of allies. In lines 37 ff., Antigonos writes:

> οὐ μὴν ἀλλὰ
> διὰ τὸ ὑπολαμβάνειν καὶ τῶν πρὸς τοῦτον
> συντελεσθέ[ν]των τὰ πρὸς Πολυπέρχοντα
> θᾶσσον ἂν διοικηθῆναι, μηθενὸς αὐτῶι συν-
> ορκοῦντος....

> Nevertheless, because we thought that after a settlement had been reached with him [sc. Ptolemy] the matter of Polyperchon might be arranged more quickly as no one would then be in alliance with him....
> (tr. Welles, *RC*, p. 6)

---

[158] 'Es erklärt sich auch sehr einfach, dass nicht Polyperchon, sondern Alexandros die Strategie des Peloponnes von Kassandros erhalten hat. Es war nur eine Frage der Anciennetät; Polyperchon konnte sich dem viel jüngeren Kassandros nicht unterordnen' (iv^2 2. 443).

[159] Diod. 19. 66-67. The assassins were a Sikyonian named Alexion and some others who pretended friendship; these were clearly the anti-Makedonian faction, who took seriously Antigonos' proclamation of Greek autonomy (cf. A. Griffin, *Sikyon* [Oxford, 1982], 77). By allying themselves with Kassandros, Alexandros and Polyperchon went back on their own promises of 319/8 B.C. The uprising in Sikyon was, however, quelled by Alexandros' widow, Kratesipolis (Diod. 19. 67. 1-2), who appears to have held the city for Polyperchon until 308 (Diod. 20. 37. 1). See further Macurdy, *AJP* 50 (1929), 273-278, with some speculation on the woman's family background (esp. 277 f.).

This suggests that Polyperchon would be cut off from all potential allies, if Ptolemy were included in the treaty, and this was surely one of the aims of the Peace.[160]

Polyperchon made one last bid for power, bringing Herakles, the illegitimate son of Alexander and his Persian mistress, Barsine, from Pergamon to Greece.[161] The claims of this child to the throne had been rejected as early as in 323 (Curt. 10. 6. 11-12; cf. Justin 13. 2. 7), but at that time the marshals were already divided on the question of Rhoxane's unborn child. But, in 310, Kassandros laid that problem to rest by ordering the murder of Alexander IV and his mother in Amphipolis.[162] Herakles, a boy of seventeen or eighteen years, could now be exploited for political gain (Diod. 20. 20). Polyperchon brought him to his native Tymphaia in Upper Makedonia, at the head of an army of 20,000 infantry and 1,000 horse, and seriously threatened Kassandros, who remembered with anxiety the enthusiasm which had gripped the Makedonians earlier on Olympias' arrival at Euia. But Kassandros had come to know Polyperchon's nature and the limits of his ambitions. He persuaded the old man to murder the boy in exchange for a share of power, which amounted, in fact, to little more than the theoretical *strategia* of the Peloponnesos (Diod. 20. 28. 2).[163]

With the murder of Alexander's son in Tymphaia in 309,[164] Polyperchon lost all credibility. Satisfied that he had obtained as

---

[160]Lenschau, 1805, takes the phrase διὰ τὴν οἰκειότητα τὴν ὑπάρχουσαν ἡμῖν πρὸς αὐτόν (lines 41-42) as referring to Polyperchon, when in fact they refer to Ptolemy. M. M. Austin (*The Hellenistic World from Alexander to the Roman Conquest* [Cambridge, 1981]) is ambiguous: 'nevertheless, because we understood that a settlement with him too (Ptolemy) would speed up a solution to the question of Polyperchon, and also *because of our relationship with him...*' [my italics]. See, however, Billows (*Antigonos* 132): 'Excluded from direct participation in the peace were Polyperchon and Seleukos; they were implicitly placed under the authority of Kassandros and Antigonos respectively, who were evidently given a free hand to deal with them more or less as they pleased.'

[161]For Barsine and Herakles see Berve ii 102-104, no. 206, s.v. Βαρσίνη, and ii 168, no. 353, s.v. Ἡρακλῆς. Cf. Brunt, RFIC 103 (1975), 22-34; against Tarn, JHS 41 (1921), 18-28.

[162]Diod. 19. 105. 1-2; Paus. 9. 7. 2; Justin 15. 2. 5; cf. also Schachermeyr, *Klio* 16 (1920), 332-337, esp. 334 ff. Hammond, *HMac* iii 165 f., reverses the order of the deaths of Alexander's sons, placing that of Herakles before Alexander IV's, and thus prefers the garbled evidence of Justin (which Hammond has earlier recognised as confused, 165, n.1) and Pausanias to that of Trogus, *Prol.* 15.

[163]Since Polyperchon's support came primarily from the Aitolians, Mendels (*Historia* 33 [1984], 176) reasonably infers that the agreement may have included territorial concessions for the Aitolians as well.

[164]Tarn, *CAH* vi 493, n.2, suggests 308, since Kassandros concealed the death of Alexander IV for some time.

much as he could from the exercise, he attempted to return to the south, only to be forced by a coaliton of Peloponnesians and Boiotians to winter in Lokris (Diod. 20. 28. 4; Trogus, *Prol*. 15).[165] Kratesipolis, holding Korinth and Sikyon in his absence, was forced to turn the cities over to Ptolemy Soter (Diod. 20. 37. 1), who in 308 made his only serious bid for power in Europe and revived the old slogan of 'Greek Liberty'. That the daughter-in-law acted with Polyperchon's approval is doubtful; nor is it likely that she felt a great deal of affection for the most disreputable of Alexander's Successors.

Polyperchon nevertheless continued to wreak havoc in the Peloponnese in the years between Ptolemy's defeat at Salamis and the battle of Ipsos in 301. In 304, Demetrios was still intent on liberating the Greek cities from Kassandros and Polyperchon, and indeed he captured and crucified the latter's garrison commander in Arkadian Orchomenos (Diod. 20. 100. 6, 103. 5-7). What became of Polyperchon himself is unknown. Lenschau (1806) assumes that he died shortly before Ipsos; Beloch iv² 2. 445 thinks that Demetrios' campaign against Messene in 295 (Plut. *Demetr*. 33. 3-4) was directed against him, though he was by now nearly 90 years old!

Throughout the last years of his life, Polyperchon displayed an astonishing durability. His political longevity is difficult to explain; for, although Pyrrhos is said to have praised him for his generalship, he demonstrated considerable ineptitude in military affairs as well as in public relations. His duplicity and ruthlessness towards the Greek states and the Makedonian royal family followed closely the proclamations of his political idealism. Perhaps he owed his survival to the fact that, after 317/6, he ceased to be a major player in the struggles of the Successors. Difficult to dislodge from southern Greece, he was a thorn in the side of, and an embarrassment to, Kassandros and Antigonos alike. In the end, he was little more than the scavenger of the Peloponnese, feasting briefly — now here, now there — on the decaying carcass of Alexander's Empire.

---

[165] Kassandros gave him 4,000 Makedonian infantry and 500 Thessalian horse (Diod. 20. 28. 3).

iv. The so-called 'Boyhood Friends' of Alexander

Introduction[1]

Plutarch, *Alex.* 10. 4, names four ἑταῖροι of Alexander the Great who were banished for their part in the so-called 'Pixodaros affair': Harpalos, Nearchos, Ptolemy son of Lagos, Erigyios; Arrian (3. 6. 5), in a less precise context, adds Laomedon, Erigyios' brother. Modern scholars have had a tendency to refer to them as Alexander's 'boyhood friends', that is, his contemporaries. J. R. Hamilton went so far as to argue that their banishment left Alexander 'isolated' at the Court.[2] And, because there is meagre evidence for the ages of these men, the preconception that they were coeval with Alexander has on occasion led to the rejection of what evidence there is. Hence the statement of Ps.-Lucian (*Macrob.* 12), that Ptolemy died at the age of 84 two years after the accession of his son Philadelphos (i.e., winter 283/2), is discarded because it would force us to place his birthdate in 367/6. Beloch comments: 'Wie weit diese Angabe glaubwürdig ist, mag dahingestellt bleiben; nach Plut. *Alex.* 10 und Arr. *Anab.* III 6, 5 würden wir Ptolemaios eher für etwa gleichen Alters mit Alexander gehalten haben; dafür spricht auch die untergeordnete Stellung, die er am Anfang des asiatischen Feldzuges noch inne hatte' (iii^2 2. 126). But we have here two false assumptions: first, that the ἑταῖροι of Alexander were men of his own age-group; second, that youth alone could account for Ptolemy's low rank in the early years of the campaign.

Curtius' description of Erigyios (7. 4. 34) shows that he was considerably older than the King, and this raises some questions about the ages of the rest. There is no explicit statement about the age of Laomedon. But, if Erigyios was considerably older than Alexander, his brother is less likely to have been the King's near contemporary. Nor do we know which brother was older. Arrian (3. 6. 6) tells us that Laomedon was δίγλωσσος, that he knew the Persian language. A. B. Bosworth

---

[1] For an earlier discussion see Heckel, *Emerita* 53 (1985), 285-289.
[2] Hamilton, *G & R* 12 (1965), 120-121. Equally misleading is Hamilton's statement that 'it is noticeable that among Alexander's close friends were few of the greater Macedonian nobility' (120). The truth of such a statement can only be determined by a study of the origins of the Crown Prince's *syntrophoi*.

(*Arrian* i 283) notes that 'Peucestas is explicitly attested to have been the only Macedonian to speak Persian' (Arr. 6. 30. 3; 7. 6. 3), and concludes that Laomedon could read the language but not speak it. But it seems that Laomedon was placed in charge of the Persian captives after the battle of Issos precisely because he could communicate with them (cf. Heckel, *SIFC* 53 [1981], 272 ff.). Perhaps Arrian's source called Peukestas the only Makedonian to speak Persian because he considered Laomedon a Greek. For Philip II had settled the family of Larichos in Amphipolis, transferring it from Mytilene (Justin 13. 4. 12; Arr. *Succ.* 1. 34; Dexippos, *FGrHist* 100 F8 §2; App. *Syr.* 52 [263]; Diod. 18. 3. 1; Arr. *Indike* 18. 4 lists Laomedon with the Makedones; but Diod. 17. 57. 3 refers to Ἐρίγυιος ὁ Μιτυληναῖος). And it is more likely that Laomedon developed his linguistic skills as a young man on Lesbos rather than in Amphipolis — much less at the Court in Pella; thus Berve (ii 231) rightly speaks of Laomedon's 'Kenntnis der persischen Sprache, die er von seiner Heimat her besaß...'. When he came to the Court, he was considerably older than Alexander.

Nearchos is described as Kretan, once as Amphipolitan — apparently on his own testimony (Arr. *Indike* 18. 4) —, but he appears not to have been raised at the Court. By contrast, the sons of Agathokles, a newly enfranchised ἑταῖρος from Krannon, were raised at Philip's court, and Lysimachos is described as Πελλαῖος, as Μακεδών, as ὁμόφυλος with Demetrios Poliorketes.[3] And, if Nearchos took pains to include himself (and Laomedon) among the Makedones, other writers clearly regarded him as Greek and his influence with the marshals of the empire can be seen from Curtius' description of the succession struggle of 323 to have been negligible. He is last heard of in the year 313/2 as an advisor of Demetrios (Diod. 19. 69. 1), at which time he and his three colleagues are termed πρεσβύτεροι. Perhaps significantly, Alexander's great admiral — at least, in his own estimation (cf. Badian, *YCS* 24 [1975], 147-170) — played no attested role in the great naval victory at Salamis in 306 B.C., although Medios of Larissa and Marsyas of Pella did, the latter a true

---

[3]This is contrary to my own views, expressed in *Klio* 64 (1982), 374 (written in 1976). I now feel that Lysimachos' father was a Thessalian from Krannon, and that it was simply characteristic of Theopompos to represent Greeks who cooperated with Philip II as δοῦλοι or κόλακες and as traitors to the Greek cause. See Theopompos, *FGrHist* 115 F81; cf. F209 on Thrasydaios and Daochos. Lysimachos' early appointment to the Somatophylakes may indicate an attempt by Philip to get regional representation within the group. Aryabbas (Arr. 3. 5. 5) was apparently of Epeirot origin — perhaps even a relative of Olympias — and one of Philip's Somatophylakes. For Lysimachos' acceptance as Makedonian see Arr. *Indike* 18. 3; *Anab.* 6. 28. 4; Plut. *Demetr.* 44. 6; Justin 15. 3. 1; Paus. 1. 9. 5.

contemporary of Alexander (cf. Heckel, *Hermes* 108 [1980], 446-448). Was he too old? Or was he already dead?[4]

Harpalos is the most difficult individual to assess. Berve (ii 75-76) assumed that he was the son of that Machatas whose sister, Phila, married Philip II in 360 or 359 (Satyros *ap.* Athen. 13. 557c). He may have been a *syntrophos* of the Crown Prince, but there is no explicit evidence to this effect. But, he may have been born in the mid-360s, which is what Ps.-Lucian tells us about Ptolemy son of Lagos. The consensus of modern scholarly opinion places Ptolemy's birth just before 360, but this still makes him a 'late bloomer', coming onto the scene as Somatophylax in 330; thirty years constituted almost a full lifetime not just for Alexander but for Leonnatos, Perdikkas, even Hephaistion, men of the King's own age, his *syntrophoi*. They formed the true inner circle of friends, a circle that had developed at the Court already in Alexander's youth and in theirs. Youth will not explain Ptolemy's slow advancement; for younger men than he mirrored Alexander's brilliance and likewise died young. We might speculate that illegitimacy retarded his progress, or that Alexander secretly feared him as a bastard son of Philip, but rumours of Arsinoë's affair with Philip were probably Ptolemy's own creation once he became master of Egypt and Alexander's corpse.[5]

It appears that these ἑταῖροι were older than Alexander and appointed by Philip as his advisors, just as later Antigonos the One-Eyed appointed advisors (including Nearchos) for his young son Demetrios (Diod. 19. 69. 1). It was, after all, one of the functions of the ἑταῖροι to advise (συμβουλεύειν), and it is because they gave bad advice concerning Pixodaros, advice that was against Philip's interests, that they were banished. This short-lived and dangerous office may have saved them from obscurity, for Alexander rewarded their loyalty with a significant, if not dazzling, display of gratitude. But the memoirs of two of their number translated this gratitude into lifelong devotion. Like Arrian, who used them both, we trust the authority of their works because of

---

[4]Polyainos 5. 35 calls a certain Antipatrides a παλαιὸς φίλος of Nearchos, but their friendship need not antedate 334 B.C. On the other hand, Nearchos' Delphic proxeny, which Dittenberger (*Syll.*³ 266) dates to 336, suggests some earlier noteworthy activity (but cf. n.57 below). His history too appears to have been completed before 310, which is regarded as the terminus for Kleitarchos, who used Nearchos' work (Lehmann-Haupt in Papastavru, *Amphipolis* 105; but see Schachermeyr in *Entretiens Hardt* 22, p. 34).

[5]This does not prove that Ptolemy was of humble origin: cf. Justin 13. 4. 10: *ex gregario milite Alexander virtutis causa provexerat*. But for Arsinoë and Philip, cf. H. Bengtson, *Herrschergestalten des Hellenismus* (Munich, 1975), 11: 'Es handelt sich hier sicherlich um eine spätere Konstruktion, wie sie in der Diadochenzeit nicht für sich allein steht.'

their connection with Alexander, and we accept this connection on their authority.[6]

[6]See the *praefatio* to Arrian's *Anabasis*. In Nearchos' case, Badian's introduction to the problem is to the point: 'The reputation of Nearchus, the Cretan from Amphipolis, shines like a good deed in the admittedly naughty world of Alexander historians' (*YCS* 24 [1975], 147).

THE 'BOYHOOD FRIENDS' OF ALEXANDER

1. The Sons of Larichos

Nearchos (*ap.* Arr. *Ind.* 18. 4 = *FGrHist* 133 F1) lists Laomedon son of Larichos amongst the Makedones from Amphipolis; other sources describe him as 'Mytilenaian', the ethnic also applied (once) to his brother Erigyios. Thus it appears that the family left Lesbos — perhaps in the political upheavals of the early 340s — and was settled by Philip II in Amphipolis.[7] Erigyios' position as ἑταῖρος of the Crown Prince, Alexander, indicates that the family belonged to the most highly favoured of Philip's naturalised Makedones.

1. 1. Erigyios

Literature. Berve ii 151-152, no. 302; Lehmann-Haupt in Papastavru, *Amphipolis* 85-86, no. 35; Kirchner, *RE* vi (1909), 452; W.Heckel, 'The "Boyhood Friends" of Alexander the Great', *Emerita* 53 (1985), 285-289.

Erigyios son of Larichos (Arr. 3. 6. 5; 3. 11. 10) was a Mytilenaian by birth (Diod. 17. 57. 3) and presumably, like his brother Laomedon, a naturalised Makedon who had been granted property in Amphipolis. An ἑταῖρος of Alexander, Erigyios was nevertheless not coeval with the Crown Prince: if Curtius' description[8] of him as 'white haired' and *gravis aetate* in 330 is correct, he was more likely to have been born c. 380 and to have acted as an advisor of the young Alexander. Thus he was banished by Philip in the spring of 336 for his role in the Pixodaros affair. On Philip's death in the autumn of that year, Erigyios returned to Makedonia (Arr. 3. 6. 6) and accompanied Alexander on his Asiatic expedition, although we cannot be certain in what capacity. Diodoros (17. 17. 4) claims that he commanded, from the very beginning, 600 Greek allied cavalry; but it becomes clear from Arrian that Erigyios was appointed hipparch only after Alexandros Lynkestes was deposed as the leader of the Thessalians in the winter of 334/3. When Philippos son of Menelaos succeeded Alexandros, the vacant command of the Peloponnesian allies was assumed by Erigyios.[9] Thus he commanded the

---

[7]Papastavru, *Amphipolis* 92, lists only the younger Larichos (no. 51) in his Prosopographia Amphipolitana, perhaps correctly, since we cannot be sure if the elder Larichos was ever settled in Amphipolis.

[8]Curt. 7. 4. 34: *non tulit ferociam barbari dux illius exercitus Erigyius, gravis quidem aetate, sed et animi et corporis robore nulli iuvenum postferendus. is galea dempta canitiem ostentans....*

[9]Arr. 3. 6. 6; Arr. 1. 14. 3: Philippos son of Menelaos commanded the allied cavalry at the Graneikos. At Gaugamela we find him in command of the

allied horse at Issos, where he was stationed on the left wing with Parmenion, and at Gaugamela.[10] Between these two battles, from winter 333/2 until spring 331, Erigyios appears to have remained with Menon son of Kerdimmas, the new satrap of Koile-Syria, protecting the area with the allied cavalry (Arr. 2. 13. 7; cf. Berve ii 151); hence he played no part in the siege of Tyre or the Egyptian campaign.

Soon after the destruction of Persepolis and the transferring of the treasures to Ekbatana, Erigyios accompanied the King in his pursuit of Dareios III, at least as far as the Caspian Gates.[11] He is next attested leading the baggage-train through Parthiene (Curt. 6. 4. 3) and rejoining the King at Arvae (Curt. 6. 4. 23) or Zadrakarta (Arr. 3. 23. 6).[12] At Phrada he is named as a member of the King's consilium, which met to discuss the Philotas conspiracy (Curt. 6. 8. 17); we may expect that he shared the view of the more prominent marshals that Philotas should be eliminated. Not much later, and together with Karanos, Andronikos and Artabazos, he campaigned against the rebel Satibarzanes (Curt. 7. 3. 2; Arr. 3. 28. 2 omitting Andronikos), whom he slew in single combat (Curt. 7. 4. 32-38; Arr. 3. 28. 3). It was perhaps the crowning achievement of his career; for he did not live much longer and little else is recorded about him.

At the Iaxartes (Syr-Darya), Erigyios is mentioned once more as one of the King's advisors: he urged him not to cross the river to campaign against the Skythians (Curt. 7. 7. 21 ff.). But this advice was ignored by Alexander without serious consequence, except that a bout of dysentery forced the King to break off his pursuit of the enemy (Arr. 4. 4. 9). In the winter of 328/7, soon after the capture of the Rock of Sisimithres (= Chorienes), Erigyios died in Sogdiana, apparently from illness. Alexander buried him, and Philippos son of Agathokles (who had died at about the same time), with due honours (Curt. 8. 2. 40). Curtius' claim that he had been one of Alexander's foremost commanders (*inter claros duces*, 8. 2. 40) appears to be true and more than just eulogy.

Thessalians (Arr. 3. 11. 10; Diod. 17. 57. 4; Curt. 4. 13. 29), and we must assume that the shuffling of commands was made during the winter of 334/3 or in the spring of 333 at the latest in Gordion.

[10]Issos: Arr. 2. 8. 9; Curt. 3. 9. 8 (both sources mention only the Peloponnesians without naming their commander). Gaugamela: Arr. 3. 11. 10; Diod. 17. 57. 3; garbled by Curt. 4. 13. 29, who gives the command to Krateros (cf. Atkinson, *Curtius* i 425).

[11]Arr. 3. 20. 1; he appears to have commanded a hipparchy of the ἱππεῖς μισθοφόροι (Berve ii 151, n.3, followed by Lehmann-Haupt in Papastavru, *Amphipolis* 86).

[12]For his route, to Shahrud and through the Elburz range via the Chalchalyan pass to Zadrakarta (Gorgan), see Seibert, *Eroberung* 116; but cf. Bosworth, *Arrian* i 349-351, identifying Zadrakarta with Sari.

1. 2. Laomedon

Literature. Berve ii 231-232, no. 464; W. Judeich, 'Der Grabherr des Alexandersarkophages', *Arch. Jahrb.* 10 (1895), 164 ff.; Stähelin, *RE* xii (1925), 755, no. 6; Bux, *RE* xii (1925), 756, no. 7; Hoffmann 118, n.2; Lehmann-Haupt in Papastavru, *Amphipolis* 88-92, no. 50; W. Heckel, 'The "Boyhood Friends" of Alexander the Great', *Emerita* 53 (1985), 285-289.

Laomedon son of Larichos (Arr. 3. 6. 5; *Ind.* 18. 4) was apparently the younger brother of Erigyios and a Mytilenaian by birth (Arr. *Succ.* 1b. 2; 1. 34; Diod. 18. 3. 1; 18. 39. 6; Justin 13. 4. 12; App. *Syr.* 52 [263]; cf. Diod. 17. 57. 3). Nearchos lists him as Amphipolitan (*FGrHist* 133 F1 §18. 4 = Arr. *Ind.* 18. 4), hence a naturalised Makedon. An ἑταῖρος of Alexander, he was almost certainly not coeval with the King, but rather already mature when he settled in Amphipolis in the 350s or early 340s. His birthdate might belong to the late 370s. Laomedon was exiled by Philip in the spring of 336 (along with his brother Erigyios, Harpalos, Nearchos and Ptolemy) for his part in the so-called 'Pixodaros affair' (Arr. 3. 6. 5; cf. Plut. *Alex.* 10. 4, naming only Erigyios), but recalled after Philip's death in October of that year (Arr. 3. 6. 6; for the date see Bosworth, *Conquest and Empire* 23; id., *Arrian* i 45 f.).

He accompanied Alexander to Asia and, because he knew the Persian language (δίγλωσσος ἦν [ἐς τὰ βαρβαρικὰ γράμματα]:[13] Arr. 3. 6. 6), he was given charge of the Persian prisoners taken at Issos. In this respect, it is curious that Alexander chose to send Leonnatos to the captive Persian queens, and not Laomedon (note in Curt. 3. 12. 6-7 the emphasis on language skills), and it is possible that the original source of this information (accidentally or deliberately?) substituted the name of Leonnatos for Laomedon (cf. Heckel, *SIFC* 53 [1981], 272-274). At the Hydaspes he served as one of the trierarchs of Alexander's fleet (Nearchos, *FGrHist* 133 F1 §18. 4 = Arr. *Ind.* 18. 4). Nothing else is known of his career under Alexander.

After the King's death in June 323, Laomedon was awarded the satrapy of Koile-Syria,[14] and it is likely that he aided his old friend

---

[13] Brunt, *Arrian* i 238 (with n.2), following Roos, thinks this is a gloss and proposes deletion. Bosworth, *Arrian* i 283, argues for retention of the words, suggesting that Laomedon could read, but not speak, Persian. Bosworth points out that 'Peucestas is explicitly attested to have been the only Macedonian to speak Persian ...', but it should be noted that Laomedon was, in origin, an Asiatic Greek.

[14] Arr. *Succ.* 1a. 5; 1b. 2; Diod. 18. 3. 1; Curt. 10. 10. 2; Justin 13. 4. 12; Appian, *Syr.* 52 [263]; this was the old Persian satrapy of 'Abar-nahara' (Lehmann-Haupt, 'Satrap' §26; cf. §129 ff.). According to the *Testamentum Alexandri*, this territory

Ptolemy in diverting Alexander's funeral-carriage to Egypt. At Triparadeisos in May 320, his position as satrap was confirmed (Arr. *Succ.* 1. 34; Diod. 18. 39. 6; App. *Syr.* 52 [263]); Ptolemy attempted to 'buy' the territory from him in 319, but Laomedon rejected his offer (App. *Syr.* 52 [264]). Friendship gave way to political expediency and, not long after Antipatros' return to Europe, Ptolemy sent his general Nikanor (otherwise unknown) to capture Laomedon and occupy the satrapy (Diod. 18. 43. 2; cf. Paus. 1. 6. 4; App. *Mithr.* 9 [27], incorrectly saying that Antigonos expelled Laomedon). Laomedon, however, bribed his guards and escaped to Alketas in Karia (App. *Syr.* 52 [265]). What became of him, we do not know. He may have perished along with many of Alketas' supporters at Kretopolis.[15]

was assigned to Meleagros: Jul. Valer. 3. 58; Leo 33; Ps.-Kall. 3. 33. 15; Metz, *LM* 117; cf. Heckel, *LDT* 67.

[15] He may be the father of the Larichos honoured at Priene (*OGIS* i 215, 13); cf. Bosworth, *Arrian* i 283; Habicht, *Gottmenschentum*² 88 f. Judeich's view (*Arch. Jahrb.* 10 [1895], 164 ff.) that Laomedon was the occupant of the Alexander-sarcophagus is incompatible with both the artistic and historical evidence.

2. Harpalos son of Machatas

Literature. Berve ii 75-80, no. 143; Stähelin, *RE* vii.2 (1912), 2397-2401, no. 2. First Flight: E. Badian, 'The First Flight of Harpalus', *Historia* 9 (1960), 245 f.; Green, 222 f.; W. Heckel, 'The Flight of Harpalos and Tauriskos', *CP* 72 (1977), 133-135; Bosworth, *Arrian* i 284 (cf. *Conquest and Empire* 57); Jaschinski, 10-18; E. D. Carney, 'The First Flight of Harpalus Again', *CJ* 77 (1982), 9-11; I. Worthington, 'The First Flight of Harpalus Reconsidered', *G & R* 31 (1984), 161-169; B. Kingsley, 'Harpalos in the Megarid (333-331 B.C.) and the Grain Shipments from Cyrene', *ZPE* 66 (1986), 165-177. Python's *Agen*: B. Snell, *Scenes from Greek Drama* (Berkeley-Los Angeles, 1964), 99-138; D. F. Sutton, 'Harpalus as Pallides', *RhM* 123 (1980), 96; id., *The Greek Satyr Play* (Meisenheim am Glan, 1980), 75-81. Famous Flight: E. Badian, 'Harpalus', *JHS* 81 (1961), 16-43; Jaschinski, 23 ff.; I. Worthington, 'The Chronology of the Harpalus Affair', *SO* 61 (1986), 63-76.

Harpalos son of Machatas (Arr. 3. 6. 4), was in all probability the nephew of Philip's Elimeiot wife Phila (thus Hoffmann 164), whom Satyros (*ap.* Athen. 13. 557c = *FHG* iii, frg. 5) describes as the sister of Derdas and Machatas. This, at least, appears to be the source of Harpalos' importance and the reason for his close association, from the early years, with Alexander. As a nephew of one of Philip's wives, he may well have been brought up at the Court, a *syntrophos* of Alexander — though the evidence for the careers of Alexander's other banished hetairoi suggests otherwise. Machaitas (*sic*), who is found in the circle of notables around Philip, is probably identical with the brother of Phila; an older Harpalos — presumably a brother or a cousin of Machatas and father of Kalas, the later satrap of Hellespontine Phrygia (Stähelin, *RE* vii.2 [1912], 2398, no. 1) — also appears. According to Plutarch (*Apophth. Phil.* 24 = *Mor.* 178f-179a), a certain Macha[i]tas was unjustly fined by Philip II, who had not heard the arguments that had been presented but had fallen asleep during the proceedings. Philip, we are told, would not reverse the decision — although Macha[i]tas launched a vigorous appeal — but made amends by paying the fine he had himself imposed. Plutarch's story (*Apophth. Phil.* 25 = *Mor.* 179a) about the elder Harpalos is somewhat similar, involving the law-courts, and suggests that this man was on intimate terms with Philip.

Two sons of Machatas, Tauron and Philippos, were very likely brothers of Harpalos;[16] Kalas son of Harpalos may have been a cousin,[17]

---

[16]Philippos: Arr. 6. 27. 2; Curt. 10. 1. 20; Plut. *Alex.* 60. 16; cf. Berve ii 384-385, no. 780; Tauron: Curt. 5. 3. 6, 10; Arr. 5. 14. 1; *IG* xii.9 197, 4 identifies Tauron as son of Machatas and proxenos of Eretria; cf. Berve ii 371-372, no. 741.

[17]Arr. 1. 14. 3; Diod. 17. 17. 4 (Kallas); cf. Hoffmann 165. If, however, Harpalos was (like Erigyios) a much older man, it is remotely possible that Kalas was his

as was perhaps Derdas, whom Alexander sent as ambassador to the Skythians beyond the Iaxartes (Curt. 7. 6. 12; 8. 1. 7; Berve ii 131, no. 250). Machatas Sabattara of Europos, voted a proxeny at Delphoi, may also have been a relative (Dittenberger, *Syll.*³ 269J; Hoffmann 164). But we know little about the family, most of whose members vanish without a trace.[18] Even Phila remains an enigma, though she was Philip's (second?) wife. Karanos certainly was not her son, nor a cousin of Harpalos (Heckel, *RFIC* 107 [1979], 386 f.). The royal house of Elimeiotis, which enjoyed considerable prestige during Philip's reign and saw many of its adherents promoted by Alexander, lapses into obscurity after Harpalos' disgrace and Alexander's death.[19]

Alexander's hetairos suffered from a physical ailment. We do not know of what sort, only that it prevented him from pursuing a military career (τὸ σῶμα ἐς τὰ πολέμια ἀχρεῖον ἦν).[20] This was perhaps the origin of his ills. Imposed inactivity drove him to various forms of self-indulgence. But that was yet to come. In 336, he shared in Alexander's misfortunes but soon reaped the rewards of his loyalty. In the turmoil that followed Philip's ill-timed union with Kleopatra, Alexander's hetairoi had, it appears, encouraged and abetted him in his intrigues with Karian Pixodaros; like Alexander, they undoubtedly misconstrued

son. In that event, he would be identical with the Harpalos of Plut. *Mor.* 179a but not a nephew of Phila; Tauron and Philippos might yet be younger brothers.

[18]Kalas vanishes from Hellespontine Phrygia. Cf. Badian, *JHS* 81 (1961), 18: 'there is little support for the orthodox interpretation that Calas was killed on that occasion [sc. in 327].... ...it is more likely that the disappearance of Calas is to be connected with the disgrace of his cousin Harpalus...' (but cf. Billows, *Antigonos* 45, with n.85, for an earlier date). Similarly, Philippos' death in India comes suspiciously soon after Harpalos' flight (Arr. 6. 27. 2; cf. Curt. 10. 1. 20 f.). See also ix 4. 1.

[19]The family may have had connections with the house of Antigonos the One-Eyed. Tauron may have been in the service of Antigonos (*IG* xii.9 197, 4), and in the 2nd century we find a prominent Beroian named Harpalos son of Polemaios (Tataki, *PB*, no. 230); Polemaios was, of course, the name of Monophthalmos' nephew (and, apparently, his brother; cf. Billows, *Antigonos* 16 f.).

[20]Arr. 3. 6. 6. 'Vielleicht hatte er einen hinkenden Gang, worauf die Bezeichnung Παλλίδης (Athen. XIII, 595f) deuten könnte' (Berve ii 76, n.3; cf. Stähelin, *RE* vii.2 [1912], 2397). The nickname Pallides comes from the satyr-play *Agen*, attributed to Python. A. Meineke (*Analecta Critica ad Athenaei Deipnosophistas* [Leipzig, 1867], 280 f.) derives the name from the word 'phallos'. Python perhaps wrote 'Pallides' instead of 'Phallides' to make the word play on Har-palos; for a summary of earlier views see B. Snell, *Scenes from Greek Drama* (Berkeley and Los Angeles, 1964), 104, with n.9. Sutton (*RhM* 123 [1980], 96) derives the name from 'Pallas': 'Harpalos is the "child of Pallas", a gibe at his dealing with the Athenians'. But here we might expect the form Παλλάδης.

Philip's intention to marry the half-witted Arrhidaios to Pixodaros' daughter. For this they were banished for the duration of Philip's reign, Harpalos among them.[21] We do not know where they went. Not far, probably, and they were quick to return once Alexander had come to the throne.

According to Arrian 3. 6. 6 (almost certainly from Ptolemy: Strasburger 34; Kornemann 129-130), Alexander rewarded these companions in various ways (according to their capabilities), once Philip had died and they themselves had returned from exile. But Arrian's report is vague (perhaps deliberately so), and it should not be taken to mean that Harpalos became treasurer immediately, or even, as Berve suggests, 'vielleicht vor Beginn des Perserzuges' (ii 76); Ptolemy's appointment to the office of Somatophylax looks ahead to 330. Harpalos' term of office was, however, a short one, and he soon gave an indication of the course that his life was to follow.

The first flight of Harpalos has in recent years been the subject of much discussion. The evidence is, admittedly, brief and unsatisfactory: Arrian (3. 6. 4-7) alone mentions it, and only in the most cryptic way. Harpalos had been made treasurer by Alexander, as a reward for his loyalty to the Crown Prince in 336 and because he was physically unfit for military service (3. 6. 5-6); his flight occurred shortly before the battle of Issos (ὀλίγον δὲ πρόσθεν τῆς μάχης ἐν Ἰσσῷ γενομένης, 3. 6. 7); and he was persuaded to flee by an ἀνὴρ κακός by the name of Tauriskos. So much for the context and causes.

A 'rational explanation' of Harpalos' flight was attempted by Badian (*Historia* 9 [1960], 246). His conclusion that 'Alexander, *for some reason* [my emphasis], had decided to remove Harpalus from his post and give it to two minor figures', that is, to Philoxenos and Koiranos (Berve, nos. 441, 793), does not convince. Badian further compares the case of Harpalos in 333 with 'what happened to the Hetaeric cavalry after the death of Philotas: the command he had held was divided..., since Alexander...did not want one man to have such power again' (246).[22] But there are three main objections: (i) we have no evidence that the appointment of Philoxenos and Koiranos was the cause and not, in fact, the result of Harpalos' departure; (ii) the political climate at the time of the Philotas affair, which was much later than this, was so different

---

[21]Ptolemy, Erigyios, Nearchos and Harpalos (Plut. *Alex.* 10. 4; cf. Arr. 3. 6. 5, adding Laomedon). For the date see W. Heckel, 'Philip and Olympias (337/6 B.C.)', in *Classical Contributions. Studies in honour of Malcolm Francis McGregor*, edited by G. S. Shrimpton and D. J. McCargar (Locust Valley, N.Y., 1981), 51-57, esp. 55-57; cf. Olmstead, *HPE* 490.

[22]Cf. Badian, *CW* 65 (1971), 79: 'H[arpalus] left because Alexander had reorganized the treasury under two others. He returned when Alexander found this unsatisfactory and asked him to.'

that it cannot be relevant to Harpalos' case; and (iii) the theory omits to account for, as Badian himself later recognised,[23] the role of Tauriskos.

Green (222) argued that Harpalos had gone to Greece on a secret spy-mission 'with defection as his cover-story'. Such a story might have been effective and, indeed, necessary in 333/2, but one wonders why the truth was not made clear after the King's death, or even in the early 3rd century, when Ptolemy wrote his history. Harpalos had been a close friend, and, if his flight was really a 'cover', Ptolemy ought to have said so, in order to save a friend's reputation. In fact, one senses in the existing account a deliberate brevity, a reluctance to divulge all the details of Harpalos' crimes.

Other scholars have concentrated on the context of the flight: soon before the battle of Issos, Alexander's victory over Dareios was far from certain, and Harpalos may have lost heart and fled (so Bosworth, *Arrian* i 284). Perhaps it was the fear that Alexander would not survive the illness that befell him at the Kydnos which drove Harpalos from the Makedonian camp: whoever seized power in Asia might be expected to conduct a purge of the King's friends and relatives (Harpalos was also a nephew of Alexander's step-mother, Phila). Hence, Jaschinski (12-18) believes that Harpalos returned to Europe in order to encourage Alexandros of Epeiros to press his claims to the Makedonian throne; for he was married to Alexander's sister, Kleopatra, and would have had the support of the Queen Mother, Olympias.[24]

The key to Harpalos' first flight must surely be the obscure Tauriskos. Not only does Arrian single him out for attention — and his designation as ἀνὴρ κακός must be significant — but he records the man's fate. Harpalos was, as later events were to show, a man of weak moral fibre. It seems that he and Tauriskos had been up to some sort of mischief. When Arrian 3. 6. 7 says that Harpalos was persuaded by Tauriskos, this must have been persuasion not only to take flight but to commit the crime that necessitated it.[25] Probably the crime involved Harpalos' official position: perhaps, at the suggestion of Tauriskos, who may have befriended him for this very purpose, Harpalos absconded with a

---

[23]*Ibid.*

[24]For a different interpretation of Harpalos' activities in Greece see Kingsley, *ZPE* 66 (1986), 165-177; cf. P. Garnsey, *Famine and Food Supply in the Graeco-Roman World* (Cambridge, 1988), 158 ff.

[25]I was not suggesting in *CP* 72 (1977), 135, as Worthington, *G & R* 31 (1984), 169, n.18 assumes, that this is the meaning of the verb ἀναπείθω (ἀναπεισθεὶς πρὸς Ταυρίσκου ἀνδρὸς κακοῦ Ἅρπαλος φεύγει ξὺν Ταυρίσκῳ). It is merely a logical inference that a man, described as 'bad' or, possibly, 'cowardly', did not induce Harpalos to flee without being in some way involved in his mischief!

sizeable amount of money.[26] Together they fled to Greece. Berve (ii 76), quite rightly, assumes from Tauriskos' intrigues with Alexandros the Epeirot 'daß politische Momente in Spiele waren': Harpalos, as an adherent of the Elimeiot royal house, may have had connections with Alexandros of Epeiros, to whom he sent Tauriskos in the hope of gaining political asylum or, at least, of mitigating his crime. But Tauriskos accomplished little and soon met his end.

Harpalos, however, remained unmolested in the Megarid. Perhaps his lack of fear was prompted, at first, by the failure of Alexander to take action against him and by the hope of safety through the efforts of Tauriskos in Italy. It may also be that Alexander made his first entreaties to Harpalos very shortly after his departure. Tauriskos was a man of no account, intent on enriching himself and clearly expendable. But Harpalos, in view of his noble lineage, and his past friendship to Alexander, could be forgiven his prodigal ways, indeed even reinstated in his former office. He had committed no heinous crime, and there is no reason to suppose that Alexander did not earnestly desire the return of his longtime companion. Little did he suspect that he would be twice burned by the faithless Harpalos.

In 331 Harpalos rejoined Alexander in Phoinikia, where he was promptly reinstated, undoubtedly much to the chagrin of Philoxenos (Arr. 3. 6. 4). The year that followed saw the most decisive blows dealt to the staggering Achaimenid empire: Gaugamela, Babylon, Persepolis. The accumulated spoils were left with Harpalos at Ekbatana, and with them six thousand Makedonian troops, some cavalry and lightly armed infantry, Menidas, Sitalkes, Kleandros and, for a time, Parmenion (Arr. 3. 19. 7; cf. Curt. 10. 1. 1 ff.). Not only did Harpalos control an immense treasure, but he also supplied the needs of Alexander in the east: he regulated the very pulse of the empire. Whatever Alexander required from the west, for war or leisure, Harpalos provided: men, equipment, even books. Perhaps while he wintered in Baktria-Sogdiana (ἐν τοῖς ἄνω τόποις), Alexander received from Harpalos the works of Philistos, tragedies of Euripides, Sophokles, Aischylos, and dithyrambs of Telestos and Philoxenos (Plut. *Alex.* 8. 3; cf. Hamilton, *PA* 21). There were unpleasant duties as well: Parmenion could not have been liquidated without Harpalos' aid (thus Badian, *JHS* 81 [1961], 22 f.). And, after Parmenion's death, Harpalos was, as Berve noted (ii 77), the most important link between east and west.

At an unspecified time, he shifted the seat of his power to Babylon, almost certainly on Alexander's instructions. There he was entrusted

---

[26]It matters little whether the money was stolen in one lump sum or embezzled in smaller amounts over a period of time, as Worthington (*G & R* 31 [1984] 165) argues.

with the royal treasure and the collected revenues (τῶν ἐν Βαβυλῶνι θησαυρῶν καὶ τῶν προσόδων τὴν φυλακὴν πεπιστευμένος, Diod. 17. 108. 4). And he soon won great notoriety. Lavish dinners and splendid gardens, these were harmless extravagances. But they were only the beginning. The King may even have been somewhat amused by the tales of Harpalos' delicacies from the Persian Gulf (Diod. 17. 108. 4), his exotic gardens and fruitless attempts to grow ivy in Media (Plut. *Mor.* 648c-d; *Alex.* 35. 15; Theophrastos, *Hist. Plant.* 4. 4. 1; Pliny, *NH* 16. 144). Yet he will have become less tolerant with each new report and stories that doubtless exaggerated the extent of Harpalos' depravity. In 326, seven thousand infantrymen reached India from Babylon, bearing twenty-five thousand suits of exquisite armour (Curt. 9. 3. 21) and further tales of debauchery. Much of this could be dismissed as malicious gossip, but there was no denying that he had used the imperial treasures to buy and bring to Babylon the Athenian courtesan Pythionike, whom he pampered with gifts while she lived (Diod. 17. 108. 5) and, after she had died, worshipped as Pythionike Aphrodite (Theopompos, *FGrHist* 115 F253 = Athen. 13. 595c, *Letter to Alexander*).[27]

From the resources of the empire, Harpalos erected two great monuments to harlotry: a temple in Babylon and, on the Sacred Way to Eleusis, a tomb, which Dikaiarchos deemed 'worthy of Perikles or Miltiades or Kimon' (Dikaiarchos *ap.* Athen. 13. 594f). The tomb in Attika, impressive still in Pausanias' day (Paus. 1. 37. 4), cost thirty talents, according to Plutarch; Theopompos claimed that both buildings were erected at an expense of 200 talents (cf. Plut. *Phokion* 22. 1-2). And the cause of this extravagance, wrote Theopompos, a woman who was 'thrice a slave and thrice a harlot' (*ap.* Athen. 13. 595a-c = *FGrHist* 115 F253: *Letter to Alexander*). Still Harpalos' passion for courtesans continued unabated: he summoned Glykera from Athens (Theopompos, *FGrHist* 115 F 254; Diod. 17. 108. 6), and ordered her to be revered as a queen in Tarsos; he even erected a statue to her in Syrian Rhossos.

The Alexander who emerged from Gedrosia was not the same man who had forgiven, or even laughed off, Harpalos' earlier indiscretions. Disappointed at the Hyphasis, he had suffered a serious wound in the town of the Mallians, where the lethargy of his troops had left him exposed to enemy fire. The incident fuelled rumours of his death and, with them, defection in the northeastern satrapies. And, even when reports of his demise proved false, few gave much consideration to the possibility, much less the consequences, of his return. Harpalos' crimes, it turned out, could be viewed as part of larger, more sinister, activities, done in concert with Kleandros, Sitalkes, Agathon and others. His

---

[27] For Pythionike see Berve ii 338, no. 676; Diodoros and Plutarch call her 'Pythonike'.

dealings with native women transgressed both law and acceptable morality (Diod. 17. 108. 4: τὸ μὲν πρῶτον εἰς ὕβρεις γυναικῶν καὶ παρανόμους ἔρωτας βαρβάρων ἐξετράπη. Cf. Curt. 10. 1. 1-5, for similar atrocities by the generals who had remained with him), and they brought shame upon the new Great King.

Nevertheless, we are told that, when Kissos and Ephialtes brought the news of Harpalos' first flight, Alexander was so struck with disbelief that he ordered them placed in chains: for he believed that they were surely slandering and falsely accusing him.[28] He did not yet understand the enormity of Harpalos' crime. But patterns of maladministration soon became evident, and nothing short of a purge would restore order and security to the heart of the empire. Harpalos himself had anticipated these measures and fled to Kilikia, whence he would make his way to Attika.[29]

At this juncture, in 324, before Harpalos had made the decision to sail for Athens, the King retained a certain macabre sense of humour and allowed the production in the Makedonian camp of a satyr-play entitled *Agen*.[30] The author was Python, a Byzantine (or possibly Katanian), though it was alleged — quite implausibly — in antiquity that Alexander himself wrote the play. This work, which depicted Harpalos in the character of 'Pallides', mocked his relationships with Pythionike and Glykera, and predicted that Agen (Alexander) would soon punish him for his crimes. For the troops, Harpalos' sex-life served as a useful diversion after the hard campaigning in Baktria and India, and the deprivations of the Gedrosian march. And the view, held by many scholars, that Alexander would not have allowed such political lampooning, fails to take into account the poem of Pranichos or Pierion, which purportedly raised the ire of Kleitos in Marakanda (Plut. *Alex.* 50. 8).[31]

---

[28][ἔδησεν] Ἐφιάλτην καὶ Κίσσον, ὡς καταψευδομένους τοῦ ἀνδρός (Plut. *Alex.* 41. 8). Ephialtes and Kissos are otherwise unknown (see Berve nos. 330, 420, unless the latter can be identified with Kittos the Athenian actor [*IG* ii² 2418]; cf. P. Ghiron-Bistagne, *Recherches sur les Acteurs dans la Grèce antique* [Paris, 1976], 72, 337). For actors as envoys and messengers cf. Thessalos and Aristokritos in the negotiations with Pixodaros (Plut. *Alex.* 10. 1-2; Berve ii 67, no. 125; ii 180, no. 371).

[29]For Harpalos' flight in general see also Arr. *ap.* Phot. *Bibl.* p. 68b;cf. Diod. 17, *argumentum* νγ'.

[30]Cf. Bosworth, *Conquest and Empire* 149; but Worthington, *SO* 61 (1986), 64, follows Beloch iv² 2. 434-436 in dating the production of the play to October 324, at Ekbatana.

[31]Athen. 13. 595e claims that the play was first performed at the Hydaspes; which Snell 109 ff. takes to mean in India, in 326. Droysen i³ 406, n.101, suggests Choaspes instead of Hydaspes; Beloch iv² 2. 434-436 argues that the Medus

While the troops roared at Pallides, a more earnest Harpalos set out for Attika with thirty ships, bringing 6,000 mercenaries and 5,000 talents from the Babylonian treasury.[32] A general uprising, led by Athens, seemed the only way to avoid punishment (Arr. *Succ.* 16 = Anecd. Bekk. p. 145, 18 s.v. ἐκπολεμῶ).[33] But the Athenians were uncertain about how to deal with Harpalos' arrival,[34] and at first rebuffed him. Taking the fleet and his mercenaries to Tainaron in the Peloponnese, Harpalos soon returned to Athens as a suppliant (Plut. *Demosth.* 25. 3), bringing with him 700 talents. Demosthenes who had originally urged that he not be admitted to the city, now accepted a generous bribe,[35] for which he was later indicted by Hypereides, Pytheas, Menesaichmos, Himeraios and Stratrokles (Plut. *Mor.* 846c; 848f),[36] convicted and forced to go into exile (Plut. *Mor.* 846c; Paus. 2. 33. 3 claims that Demosthenes did not take any money; for his exile cf. Diod. 18. 13. 6). Harpalos himself was imprisoned and his money confiscated, but he escaped (Plut. *Mor.* 846b) to Megara (Justin 13. 5. 9); eventually he went to Tainaron and Krete (Plut. *Mor.* 846b).[37] The Athenians, though enticed by Harpalos' bribes, were frightened by the appearance of Alexander's admiral, Philoxenos (Plut.

Hydaspes (Verg. *Georg.* 4. 211, explained by Servius as fluvius Mediae; possibly the Karkheh?) is meant. Goukowsky ii 77 thinks it was the Iranian 'Hydaspes' (Halil-rud), and that the *Agen* was produced at Salmous in Karmania. Cf. Bosworth, *Conquest and Empire* 149 f.

[32] 6,000 mercenaries, 5,000 talents (Diod. 17. 108. 6); 30 ships (Curt. 10. 2. 1).

[33] Harpalos reached Athens before 21 July, 324 (so Badian, *JHS* 81 [1961], 42), and the Athenians were already aware of Nikanor's intention to proclaim the Exiles' Decree at the Olympic Festival. The Athenians were, in fact, on the verge of going to war over this very matter (cf. Ashton, *Antichthon* 17 [1983], 47 ff.); Harpalos' sudden arrival, ironically, delayed rather than prompted the outbreak of this 'Hellenic' War.

[34] Ashton, *Antichthon* 17 (1983), 56 f.: 'The Athenians might well have suspected that he was on a punitive mission from Alexander, who had become aware of their intention to oppose the restoration of the exiles and the consequent surrender of Samos.'

[35] Justin 13. 5. 9. Plut. *Mor.* 846a (1000 darics); *Mor.* 846c (30 talents); *Demosth.* 25 (a golden drinking-cup and 20 talents).

[36] Patrokles or Prokles is probably a corruption of Stratokles (cf. Badian, *JHS* 81 [1961], 32, n.113). Another opponent of Harpalos and those who accepted his money was Deinarchos (*Mor.* 850c-d).

[37] Plutarch details Phokion's involvement with Harpalos. The latter attempted to bribe Phokion with 700 talents; Phokion rejected his bribes, though others accepted (*Phok.* 21. 3-4). Harpalos befriended Phokion's son-in-law, Charikles (21. 5), who was put on trial for his dealings with Harpalos (22. 4). After Harpalos' death, his daughter (by Pythionike?) was raised by Charikles and Phokion (22. 3).

Mor. 531a).³⁸ Ultimately, his money helped finance the Lamian war (Diod. 18. 9. 1); for the Athenians sent some of it to Leosthenes (Diod. 18. 9. 4). But, by this time, it was too late for Harpalos. Disappointed by the Athenians, he sailed away, perhaps intending to go Kyrene, where his forces went after his death. On Krete, he was killed by one of his friends (Diod. 17. 108. 8; Curt. 10. 2. 3), namely Thibron (Diod. 18. 19. 2; Arr. *Succ.* 1. 16; cf. Strabo 17. 3. 21 C837) — though others say he was killed by a servant or by a certain Makedonian named Pausanias (Paus. 2. 33. 4-5).

---

³⁸Hypereides, *Dem.*, col. 8; Paus. 2. 33. 4; Plut. *Mor.* 531a. Olympias and Antipatros had also demanded Harpalos' extradition (Diod. 17. 108. 7). On the chronological problems see, most recently, Worthington, *SO* 61 (1986), 63-76; for the political and legal activities in Athens: W. Will, *Athen und Alexander. Untersuchungen zur Geschichte der Stadt von 338 bis 322 v. Chr.*, Münchener Beiträge zur Papyrusforschung und antiken Rechtsgeschichte, Heft 77 (Munich, 1983), 113 ff. with earlier literature.

3. Ptolemy son of Lagos

Literature. Berve ii 329-335, no. 668; Volkmann, *RE* xxiii (1959), 1603 ff., no. 18; Seibert, *Ptolemaios*; R. M. Errington, 'Bias in Ptolemy's History of Alexander', *CQ* 19 (1969), 233-242; H. Bengtson, 'Ptolemaios I., König von Aegypten', in *Herrschergestalten des Hellenismus* (Munich, 1975), 10-35; Eggermont, 107 ff.; P. Pédech, *Historiens compagnons d' Alexandre* (Paris, 1984), 215-222.

Ptolemy presents an unusual problem: much of what we know about his career in Alexander's lifetime derives from Arrian and, ultimately, from Ptolemy himself. In contrast, the Vulgate tells us little. But, whereas the Vulgate is silent about the minor commands, which Ptolemy may in fact have exaggerated for his own glorification, it does treat him very favourably in the description of three episodes, which Ptolemy himself either omits or disputes.

The son of Lagos[39] and Arsinoë (Porphyry *ap.* Euseb. Arm. *chron.* p. 74, 19 ff. = *FGrHist* 260 F2 §2), purportedly an adherent of a lesser branch of the Makedonian royal house,[40] Ptolemy came from Eordaia (Arr. 6. 28. 4; *Ind.* 18. 5) and may have been brought up at the Court in Pella (cf. A. Bouché-Leclercq, *Histoire des Lagides* i 3). Rumours that he was an illegitimate son of Philip II (Paus. 1. 6. 2; Curt. 9. 8. 22; Aelian, frg. 285; *Suda* s.v. Λάγος) are just that and originated in the early years of the Diadochic age, when blood relationship with the house of Philip had tremendous propaganda value.[41] The only source for Ptolemy's birthdate is of dubious worth: Ps.-Lucian (*Macrob.* 12) places it in 367/6 B.C., a date generally rejected because it conflicts with the popularly accepted view that Ptolemy was coeval with Alexander. The reasons for abandoning this theory have been given above ('Introduction').

In spring 336, Ptolemy and four other hetairoi of Alexander were banished by Philip II for their role in the Pixodaros affair. They had clearly induced the Crown Prince to conduct private negotiations with the Karian dynast through the agency of the actor Thessalos, negotiations which scuttled Philip's own diplomacy. Hence they were exiled, and did not return to Makedonia until after Philip's death.[42]

---

[39]See e.g., Arr. 2. 11. 8; 3. 6. 5. For occurrences of the patronymikon in Arrian, see Seibert, *Ptolemaios* 8 f. On Lagos see also Plut. *de cohib. ira* 9 = *Mor.* 458a-b.

[40]Satyros, frg. 21 = *FHG* iii 165; Theokritos 17. 26, with Gow, *Theocritus* ii 331; Curt. 9. 8. 22; Dittenberger, *OGIS* i 54, line 6; cf. also Wilcken, *RE* ii (1896), 1281, s.v. 'Arsinoë (24)'.

[41]Cf. Errington, in *Entretiens Hardt* 22 (Geneva, 1976), 155 f.

[42]Plut. *Alex.* 10. 4; Arr. 3. 6. 5; that they went to Epeiros, as Bengtson (*Herrschergestalten* 11) suggests, is pure speculation.

Ptolemy almost certainly took part in the Asiatic expedition from the very beginning. He appears to have joined in the pursuit of the Persians who fled from the battlefield of Issos, though he embellished his account with images of the Persians crossing a ravine on the bodies of their own dead (Arr. 2. 11. 8; cf. Bosworth, *ad loc.*, with earlier literature). But we hear of no independent command until late 331, when Alexander reached the Persian Gates. Here Arrian (3. 18. 9) — probably drawing on Ptolemy's own *History* — assigns to him the command of 3,000 troops to guard a route by which Ariobarzanes' men might possibly retreat. Ptolemy's role is (significantly?) omitted by the Vulgate authors, who really had no good reason to diminish his contributions; for there are two later episodes in which the Vulgate clearly invents stories that enhance Ptolemy's reputation (Curt. 9. 5. 21; 9. 8. 22-27; Diod. 17. 103. 6-8). Bosworth (*Arrian* i 328) may be correct in suggesting that 'he cast himself for the role played by Philotas'. Certainly, Ptolemy's lack of achievement up to this point, combined with the conspicuous silence of the Vulgate, raises suspicions about the man's sudden prominence in an account based, most likely, on his own record of events.[43]

In autumn 330, after Demetrios had been deposed (and presumably executed) on allegations of involvement in Dimnos' conspiracy, Alexander appointed Ptolemy Somatophylax (Arr. 3. 27. 5; cf. 6. 28. 4 = Aristoboulos, *FGrHist* 139 F50). Arrian (3. 6. 6), in a passage that anticipates the appointment, regards it as a reward for Ptolemy's loyalty to the King in the past, especially in 337/6 B.C. When Justin (13. 4. 10) writes that he had been 'promoted from the ranks (*ex gregario milite*) on account of his *virtus*', he is merely indicating that Ptolemy, up to this point, had had no unit under his command.[44] It was at about this time that Alexander began to make greater use of his Somatophylakes on an *ad hoc* basis. This is almost certainly because the composition of the unit had changed significantly and its members were all younger men whom the King felt he could trust. Thus, in 329, we find Ptolemy assigned the task of bringing in the regicide Bessos, whom Spitamenes and Dataphernes had arrested

---

[43]Seibert (*Ptolemaios*) makes a valiant attempt to defend Ptolemy, first (4-7) by rejecting C. B. Welles' arguments ('The Reliability of Ptolemy as an historian', in *Miscellanea Rostagni* [1963], 101-116, esp. 107) and then (8-10) by arguing, on the basis of a meticulous study of Arrian's use of Ptolemy's patronymikon, that the officer at the Persian Gates was not, in fact, the son of Lagos. But Bosworth (*Arrian* i 328 f.) is rightly sceptical of Seibert's conclusions; cf. Wirth, *Bibliotheca Orientalis* 30 (1973), 408 f.; see also Heckel, *Athenaeum* 58 (1980), 169, n.7.

[44]In much the same way, Appian (*Syr.* 56 [283]) calls Seleukos στρατιώτης before his appointment as commander of the Royal Hypaspists; noted by Bouché-Leclercq, *Histoire des Lagides* i 2, n.1.

and were prepared to extradite, presumably in exchange for immunity.[45] Here again, Arrian, when he follows Ptolemy (*FGrHist* 138 F14), shows signs of embellishment, and Ptolemy's own role is doubtless exaggerated. But, from his account, we do gain a sense of how delicate the extradition process was and how great the fear of betrayal. Spitamenes and Dataphernes had asked that only a small force be sent to them; Ptolemy's contingent probably exceeded 5,000 men.[46] Alexander had clearly not forgotten Satibarzanes' treachery and the death of Anaxippos (Arr. 3. 25. 2, 5).

That, in 328, Ptolemy commanded one of five columns that swept through Sogdiana is probably true, even though Curtius mentions only three contingents.[47] In late summer or autumn of that year, he attended the banquet in Marakanda where Alexander killed Kleitos. Although it is generally agreed that he made some attempt to restrain Kleitos (Arr. 4. 8. 9 = Aristoboulos, *FGrHist* 139 F29) or Alexander himself (Curt. 8. 1. 45, 48), it could be argued that he had failed to prevent the murder, and it is difficult to determine what, if anything, Ptolemy said about the episode in his *History*.[48] Over the winter, when the Makedonian forces

---

[45] Arr. 3. 29. 6 - 30. 5; long discussion in Seibert, *Ptolemaios* 10-16. Other accounts of Bessos' arrest: Arr. 3. 30. 5 = Aristoboulos, *FGrHist* 139 F24; Diod. 17. 83. 7-9; Curt. 7. 5. 19 ff.; Justin 12. 5. 10-11; *Itiner. Al.* 34.

[46] Three hipparchies of Companions; the brigade of Philotas; one chiliarchy of hypaspists, all the Agrianes and half the archers. Seibert, *Ptolemaios* 11, n.33, following Berve, puts the figure at c. 5000. But the calculation of 300 men per hipparchy (= *ile*) is probably incorrect, since the hipparchies had by this time been reformed (cf. Bosworth, *Arrian* i 375 f.), and the strength of a brigade of *psiloi* (i.e., Philotas' brigade) was not necessarily equal to that of its counterpart in the pezhetairoi.

[47] Arr. 4. 16. 2-3 (they were led by Perdikkas, Hephaistion, Koinos and Artabazos, Ptolemy, and Alexander himself; Curt. 8. 1. 1 assigns the command to Alexander, Hephaistion and Koinos, adding at 8. 1. 10 that Artabazos accompanied Hephaistion). For the campaign see Holt, *Alexander and Bactria* 60-62. Ptolemy's claim to have reported the discovery of oil at the Oxos (Arr. 4. 15. 7-8) is contradicted by Plut. *Alex*. 57. 5 ff. and Curt. 7. 10. 14, and probably untrue (cf. Seibert, *Ptolemaios* 16 f.).

[48] Seibert assumes that he omitted the episode, since it was unflattering to both Alexander and Ptolemy: 'Sehr wahrscheinlich führte Ptolemaios die Kleitoskatastrophe nicht an, da sie auf Alexander ein ungünstiges Licht warf, aber auch auf seine eigene Person wie die der anderen Beteiligten, da sie nach den vorliegenden Quellen die Ermordung des Kleitos hätten verhindern können' (*Ptolemaios* 19). Arrian's citation of Aristoboulos suggests too that the latter's information differed from or supplemented Ptolemy's account. Cf. Errington, *CQ* 19 (1969), 238 f. Whether Curtius was following Kleitarchos or Timagenes, both of whom had reason to flatter Ptolemy, or possibly Ptolemy himself, is unknown.

besieged the fortress of Sisimithres (the Rock of Chorienes), Ptolemy and his fellow Somatophylakes, Perdikkas and Leonnatos, conducted the night operations in shifts (Arr. 4. 21. 4).

In the spring of 327, after Alexander's marriage to Rhoxane and before the departure for India, Ptolemy played a major role in bringing the conspiracy of Hermolaos and the Pages to Alexander's attention. The details of the plot had been divulged to him by Eurylochos, and, in Arrian's version (4. 13. 7), Ptolemy alone informed Alexander. Curtius (8. 6. 22) says that Ptolemy *and Leonnatos* were approached by Eurylochos, and it appears that, in his own *History*, Ptolemy took full credit by suppressing Leonnatos' contribution.[49]

During the Swat campaign, Ptolemy was wounded in a skirmish with the Aspasians near the Choes river (Arr. 4. 23. 3). The wound could not have been serious, for Ptolemy soon afterwards pursued the Indian hyparch up a hill and killed him in single combat, the account of which almost certainly comes from Ptolemy's own pen (Arr. 4. 24. 3-4).[50] Once the Makedonians had advanced beyond Arigaion, Ptolemy was again sent ahead to reconnoitre, and he reported large numbers of enemy campfires (4. 24. 8). In the attack on this concentration of Indian forces, Alexander divided his troops into three contingents, assigning the command of one third to Ptolemy, to whom he assigned the light-armed brigades of Philotas and Philippos, as well as one third of the hypaspists (Arr. 4. 24. 10). While Alexander dealt with the Indians who had rushed down onto the plain, Ptolemy successfully dislodged those who occupied the hills (Arr. 4. 25. 2-3). And Ptolemy himself reported that in the engagement more than 40,000 Indians and 230,000 oxen were captured by the Makedonians (Arr. 4. 25. 4 = *FGrHist* 138 F18).[51] But, despite Ptolemy's tendency to focus in his *History* on his own achievements, there is little to support Curtius' remark that 'Ptolemy took the most cities, but Alexander captured the greatest ones' (8. 10. 21). Not surprisingly, Ptolemy also played a key role in the assault on Aornos in Arrian's version (4. 29. 1-6). The Vulgate knows nothing of it, and Curtius in particular (8. 11. 5) ascribes a similar command to Myllinas

---

Certainly, it could be argued that the attempt to prevent Kleitos' murder, even if unsuccessful, exculpated Ptolemy.

[49]Cf. Errington, *CQ* 19 (1969), 234. Cf. Arr. 4. 25. 3, in which Ptolemy, after reporting in some detail the contributions of his third of the army, and that of Alexander, says only that Leonnatos' troops fared equally well (ὡσαύτως ἔπραξαν).

[50]Jacoby rightly includes Ptolemy's *aristeia* in F18; cf. Brunt, *Arrian* i 421, n.3; and Seibert, *Ptolemaios* 19, with earlier literature in n.54.

[51]Ptolemy has clearly concentrated on his own role in the battle, to the extent of misrepresenting its importance. Leonnatos and Alexander are pushed aside, as Ptolemy emphasizes his own achievement. See Seibert, *Ptolemaios* 21.

(probably the son of Asandros, a Beroian; cf. Tataki, *PB* no. 910; also Berve ii 267 f., no. 542).

The Vulgate preserves a story that Ptolemy was one of many Makedonians wounded at Harmatelia, a town of Brahmins — located by Diodoros and Curtius in the kingdom of Sambus, but placed by Strabo (15. 2. 7 C723, followed by Eggermont 125 ff.) in the land of the Oreitai. These Indians smeared the tips of their weapons with poison extracted from snakes, thus causing the wounded to die in excruciating pain (Diod. 17. 103. 3-6; Curt. 9. 8. 20; Strabo 15. 2. 7 C723). Apart from the implausible tale that Alexander saw in a dream a serpent carrying in its mouth the plant which was the antidote to the poison, it is clear that the whole story is a fiction invented to glorify Ptolemy. Like the false report that Ptolemy saved Alexander's life in the town of the Mallians (Curt. 9. 5. 21; Paus. 1. 6. 2), which is disproved by Ptolemy's own *History* (Arr. 6. 11. 8), this story contains late elements which render it even more suspect. Diodoros (17. 103. 6-7; cf. Curt. 9. 8. 23-24) emphasizes the character and popularity of the later ruler of Egypt; Curtius (9. 8. 22; cf. Paus. 1. 6. 2) adds that Ptolemy was thought to be an illegitimate son of Philip II. The snake itself is thought by some to be connected with the cult of Sarapis (see Eggermont, 112-114, with earlier literature), instituted in Egypt by Ptolemy.[52]

He was responsible for building the funeral-pyre, on which the famed Indian philosopher Kalanos committed suicide amidst the flames shortly before the army reached Sousa (Arr. 7. 3. 2). At Sousa in 324, Ptolemy married Artakama, a daughter of Artabazos (Arr. 7. 4. 6; cf. Phot. *Bibl.* 68b; cf. Plut. *Eum.* 1. 7, who calls her Apame)[53] — hence a sister of Alexander's mistress Barsine — and, along with his fellow Somatophylakes, was awarded a golden crown (Arr. 7. 5. 6).[54]

---

[52]On the problems associated with Sarapis see Fraser, *Opuscula Atheniensia* 7 (1967), 23-45; A. B. Bosworth, *From Arrian to Alexander* (Oxford, 1988), 167 ff.

[53]There is no evidence that Ptolemy had been previously married. The Athenian courtesan Thaïs, who had accompanied the expedition, became Ptolemy's mistress (Plut. *Alex.* 38. 2; Hamilton, *PA* 100) — possibly she joined the expedition in that capacity — and bore him two sons (Lagos and Leontiskos) and a daughter, Eirene, who later married Eunostos, King of Kypriot Soloi (Athen. 13. 576e).

[54]Volkmann (1607) speculates that, at this time, Ptolemy may have been appointed ἐδέατρος (the equivalent of the Roman *praegustator*) or 'King's Taster' (Athen. 4. 171b = Chares, *FGrHist* 125 F1). Apart from the unlikelihood that Alexander would risk the life of a Somatophylax for this purpose, it should be noted that Justin 12. 14. 9 describes the sons of Antipatros (who were Pages of Alexander) as *Philippus et Iollas praegustare ac temperare potum regis soliti....* And it is certainly more likely that Pages or even slaves would have been used as 'Tasters' for the King. Furthermore, Chares speaks of Ptolemy as ἐδέατρος in Book Three of his *History*, much too early for this historical context.

(Berve ii 269).[58] No military activity is attested for Nearchos' stay in Baktria-Sogdiana. But as the Makedonian army approached the Indus, near Dyrta in the land of the Assakenoi, he led a reconnaissance force composed of Agrianes and three chiliarchies of hypaspists under Antiochos (Arr. 4. 30. 5-6);[59] the results of the mission are not spelled out.

In autumn 326, Alexander ordered a fleet to be built at the Hydaspes (Jhelum), and Nearchos was designated its admiral (Arr. 6. 2. 3; Arr. *Ind.* 18. 10). This, at least, is Nearchos' own assertion. His trierarchy (Arr. *Ind.* 18. 4) was, however, a financial responsibility, in the Attic fashion of public service (cf. Plut. *Eum.* 2. 4 ff. for Alexander's shortage of money). The voyage began in the autumn of that year (so Strabo 15. 1. 17 C691), reaching the confluence of the Hydaspes and Akesines (Chenab) on the ninth or tenth day (thus Arr. 6. 4. 1-4; but cf. Brunt, *Arrian* ii 109). Here the fleet suffered considerable damage in the eddies and on the riverbanks where the ships ran aground (Arr. 6. 4. 4 - 5. 4; cf. Curt. 9. 4. 9-14; Diod. 17. 97); Nearchos was entrusted with the repair of the vessels and ordered to sail to the borders of the Mallian territory and meet Alexander, who advanced by land.[60] Of Nearchos' activities from this point, until the fleet reached Patala, nothing is recorded. The descent of the river took, according to Aristoboulos (*FGrHist* 139 F35 = Strabo 15. 1. 17 C692), ten months.[61]

From the Indus delta (perhaps from Xylinepolis, on the island of Killouta: Plut. *Alex.* 66. 1; Pliny, *NH* 6. 96; cf. Arr. 6. 19. 3; thus Capelle 2133; cf. McCrindle 316, n.1), Nearchos and Onesikritos were ordered to sail to the Ocean and in the direction of the Euphrates (Curt. 9. 10. 3; Diod. 17. 104. 3; Plut. *Alex.* 66. 3; Arr. 6. 19. 5; *Ind.* 20 ff.; Strabo 15. 2. 4

---

[58]Badian (*YCS* 24 [1975], 150) assumes that Nearchos was recalled from his satrapy because he 'had not proved up to expectation in his arduous assignment'.

[59]Against the view that Nearchos himself was a hypaspist commander (Berve ii 269; Billows, *Antigonos* 407) see Badian, *YCS* 24 (1975), 150 f.

[60]Arr. 6. 5. 4 places the repair of the ships before Alexander's departure, but Berve ii 270 may be right in seeing the refitting of the fleet as Nearchos' responsibility. Badian, *YCS* 24 (1975), 152 f., sees the damage to the fleet as a sign of Nearchos' incompetence and suggests that Alexander did not allow the fleet to proceed to the junction of the Akesines and Hydraotes 'until his own pilot Onesicritus could take charge of the actual navigation' (153). But Alexander's ship fared no better at the confluence of the Akesines and Hydaspes (Diod. 17. 97; Curt. 9. 4. 9-14), and I see no good reason why Alexander should prefer him to Nearchos.

[61]Calculations based on Aristoboulos' own dates for the departure of the fleet and its arrival at Patala result in a voyage of almost 9 months. Plut. *Alex.* 66. 1 says seven months, Pliny, *NH* 6. 60, only five. But it is not entirely clear what Plutarch and Pliny regard as the starting-point of the voyage; they could be counting from Alexander's departure from the junction of the Akesines and the Indus (cf. Hamilton, *PA* 181 f.). For the chronology in general see Beloch iii^2 2. 305-307, 320 f.

C721). Despite Nearchos' attempts to make it seem otherwise (esp. Arr. *Ind.* 20), the actual naval responsibilities for the expedition were given to Onesikritos, who called himself ἀρχικυβερνήτης (Plut. *Mor.* 331e; Strabo 15. 1. 28 C698; 15. 2. 4 C721; cf. Pliny, *NH* 2. 185: *dux*; 6. 81: *classis praefectus*). Nearchos was commander-in-chief of the expedition (Plut. *Alex.* 66. 3; Badian, *YCS* 24 [1975], 153-160),[62] and his protestations about Onesikritos' mendacity appear to have been aimed at depriving the man of any credit for the undertaking.

The expedition is described in passionate detail by Nearchos (Arr. *Ind.* 20. 1 - 42. 10, contained in *FGrHist* 133 F1) and Onesikritos (*ap.* Pliny, *NH* 6. 96-100 = *FGrHist* 134 F28) themselves.[63] Attacks on the fleet by the natives, who were emboldened by Alexander's departure, forced Nearchos to set out on 21 September (20 Boedromion: Arr. *Ind.* 21. 1; cf. Strabo 15. 2. 5 C721) 325; but the fleet made slow progress, being forced by high winds to put in at a place which Nearchos named 'Alexander's Harbour' (near Gujo; hence east of modern Karachi, if the latter is the Morontobara of *Ind.* 22. 4),[64] where the island of Bibakta, two stades offshore, gave shelter for 35 days (*Ind.* 21. 10-13). When the winds subsided (late October/early November), Nearchos led the expedition westward, establishing a camp at Kokala in Oreitan territory, where he received supplies for ten days from Leonnatos (Arr. *Ind.* 23. 4-7).[65] Malnutrition and poor morale plagued the maritime expedition. Those who had posed disciplinary problems were left with Leonnatos; new sailors were recruited from the army (*Ind.* 23. 8).

With fresh recruits Nearchos advanced to the Tomeros river (Hingol), about three hundred stades east of what Nearchos called the last settlement of the Oreitai at Malana (Arr. *Ind.* 25. 1; mod. Ras Malan). It was at the Tomeros river that Nearchos demonstrated his true talents, which reflect the nature of his training before he came to Makedonia from Krete. He had earlier been used by Alexander as a commander of light infantry (cf. Arr. 4. 30. 5-6), and would be employed in a similar capacity by Antigonos in 317/6 (Diod. 19. 19. 4-5). At this time, he led lightly armed troops, supported by archers on the ships anchored

---

[62]*Suda* s.v. Νέαρχος claims that it was Nearchos who lied about being admiral, when he was in fact a steersman.

[63]For questions of the itinerary and distances see Brunt, *Arrian* ii 518-525, App. xxv: 'Nearchus' Voyages'. For earlier discussions see Tomaschek, *SB Wien* 121 (1890), Abhandlung viii, pp. 1-88; Neubert, *Petermanns Geog. Mitteilungen* 74 (1928), 136-143; J. Seibert, *Alexander der Grosse* (Darmstadt, 1972), 163-165, 292-294, with earlier literature.

[64]So Brunt, *Arrian* ii 371, n.1; Seibert, *Eroberung* 182 (cf. Tomaschek, 12 f.), identifies 'Alexander's Harbour' with Karachi. But see Eggermont, 33 f.

[65]Capelle speaks of 'Rast von zehn Tagen' (2133). We do not know how long Nearchos' men remained at Kokala.

offshore, against the natives, who carried heavy wooden spears (with points hardened by fire), and easily routed them (Arr. *Ind.* 24). Nearchos' force must have included a sizeable contingent of Kretan archers (cf. *Ind.* 28. 3, 5), and, although little is known about him, Archias son of Anaxidotos of Pella appears to have been placed on Nearchos' staff by Alexander for his military expertise.[66]

Particularly difficult was the journey along the Makran coast, skirting the villages of the Ichthyphagoi (or 'Fish-Eaters'), where provisions were scarce — though date-palms grew in places (*Ind.* 27. 2; 29. 1, 5) — and plundering raids yielded little in the way of grain (cf. *Ind.* 27. 6 - 28. 9); whatever animals were carried off, including seven camels (*Ind.* 29. 5), were slaughtered for their flesh. At Mosarna (mod. Pasni? Cf. Brunt, *Arrian* ii 384, n.1; Seibert, *Eroberung* 183), they took on board a Gedrosian guide, Hydrakes (Berve ii 376, no. 760), who led them as far as Karmania (*Ind.* 26. 10 - 27. 1).[67] There, in December 325 (Beloch iii^2 2. 321), Nearchos rejoined Alexander. Diodoros (17. 106. 4) mentions a coastal town named Salmous (Curt. 10. 1. 10 and Strabo 15. 2. 11 C725 are vague, but appear to be following the same source as Diodoros); Plutarch (*Alex.* 67. 7) speaks of the 'capital of Gedrosia' (read 'Karmania'? Thus Badian, *CQ* 8 [1958], 151; cf. Hamilton, *PA* 186), which could be identical with Salmous.[68] Arrian (*Ind.* 33. 2) says they anchored at the mouth of the River Anamis (cf. Arr. 6. 28. 5, on an uninhabited shore of Karmania) in the district of Harmozeia; the King's camp was five days' march inland (*Ind.* 33. 7), and we are treated in Nearchos' own account to the hazards of the journey and Alexander's reluctance to send him back to the coast and subject him to further risks (see Badian, *YCS* 24 [1975], 160-165, rightly sceptical). In fact, it is hard to imagine that Alexander had any other plans for Nearchos than for him to sail on to the mouth of the Euphrates (Curt. 10. 1. 16; Diod. 17. 107. 1; cf. Plut. *Alex.* 68. 6), whereafter he was to sail up the Pasitigris (Eulaios)[69] to Sousa (Arr. 6. 28. 6; *Ind.* 36. 4-9; Pliny, *NH* 6. 99; cf. Arr. *ap.* Phot. *Bibl.* 68a). The last leg of the voyage was considerably easier, and Nearchos' expedition

---

[66]For Archias see Arr. *Ind.* 18. 3; 27. 8 - 28. 7; 34-35; cf. Arr. 7. 20. 7.

[67]Rounding the Ras-al-Kuh headland, the fleet began to sail northwest into the Strait of Hormuz (cf. Arr. *Ind.* 32. 3). Maketa (Ras Musandam, the promontory of Oman) became visible (cf. Strabo 15. 2. 14 C726; Pliny, *NH* 6. 98), and Nearchos rejected Onesikritos' suggestion that they abandon the Karmanian coast and make for it instead (*Ind.* 32. 7, 9-13).

[68]That it was located on the coast is generally doubted: Hamilton, *PA* 187; Bosworth, *Conquest and Empire* 150; Goukowsky ii 54-58; Engels, *Logistics* 117, suggests that the Karmanian capital may have been located at Tepe Yahya; cf. Cook, *PE* 187.

[69]For geographical problems see Bosworth, *Arrian* i 321, and Brunt, *Arrian* ii 525-527.

proceeded to the mouth of the Euphrates and sailed as far as Diridotis, a village of Babylonia (possibly Teredon: Strabo 16. 2. 3 C766, but the identification is not clear).[70] There it was learned that Alexander was not far from Sousa (Arr. *Ind.* 42. 1), and Nearchos sailed back to the Pasitigris, eventually coming to a pontoon bridge, which Alexander's advance force had prepared for the King's crossing to Sousa (*Ind.* 42. 7). The reuniting of the forces occurred in March 324 (Beloch iii^2 2. 321; Capelle, 2133).

Nearchos continued to Sousa, witnessing on the way the self-imolation of Kalanos (Arr. 7. 3. 6 = *FGrHist* 133 F4). At Sousa, he was wedded to the daughter of Barsine and Mentor (Arr. 7. 4. 6; Arr. *ap.* Phot. *Bibl.* 68b) — a fact which explains both Nearchos' support of Barsine's son, Herakles, as Alexander's successor (Curt. 10. 6. 10-12) and his friendship with Eumenes (Plut. *Eum.* 18. 6), who had married Artonis, a sister of Barsine (Plut. *Eum.* 1. 7) — and crowned for his valorous achievements on the Ocean voyage (Arr. 7. 5. 6; *Ind.* 42. 9 gives the impression that Nearchos and Leonnatos were crowned when the fleet and army were reunited; rejected by Badian, *YCS* 24 [1975], 166). From Sousa, Nearchos took Alexander by ship to the mouth of the Eulaios (Arr. 7. 7. 1), but thereafter the King sailed up the Tigris to rejoin Hephaistion at Opis (Arr. 7. 7. 6), while Nearchos conducted the fleet up the Euphrates to Babylon (Arr. 7. 19. 3). Here Nearchos was said to have brought the warnings of the Chaldaian astrologers to the King's attention (Diod. 17. 112. 3-4; Plut. *Alex.* 73. 1, with Hamilton, *PA* 202 f.). Alexander designated him admiral of his planned Arabian fleet (Arr. 7. 25. 4; cf. Plut. *Alex.* 68. 1, with Hamilton, *PA* 187-189), a project cut short by the King's sudden death in Babylon. For it was after a banquet, which he had given in Nearchos' honour (Plut. *Alex.* 75. 4), that Alexander went to the drinking-party in the home of Medios, at which he became fatally ill. Nearchos' part in the plot to poison Alexander is a fabrication of the Polyperchan camp (Metz, *LM* 97-98; Ps.-Kall. 3. 31. 8-9; cf. Heckel, *LDT* 36).

Justin's claim (13. 4. 15) that Nearchos was assigned Lykia and Pamphylia in the division at Babylon appears to be an error, influenced by his earlier administration of the satrapy. But Nearchos clearly returned to Asia Minor and Antigonos' entourage, in whose service he captured Telmissos, where Antipatrides, an old friend of his (Polyainos 5. 35), had been installed, most likely by Attalos and Alketas in 320/19 (cf. Billows, *Antigonos* 408). In 317/6 Antigonos sent him with a lightly armed force into Kossaian territory in order to seize passes of strategic importance to Eumenes (Diod. 19. 19. 4-5). He accompanied Antigonos to Gabiene, and is said to have been one of the officers who begged him,

---

[70]See, however, Tomaschek, 79.

unsuccessfully, to spare the life of the captive Eumenes (Plut. *Eum.* 18). Nearchos is last mentioned as one of four advisors (along with Andronikos, Peithon son of Agenor and Philippos) left by Antigonos with Demetrios Poliorketes in Syria in 313/2 (Diod. 19. 69. 1; chronology: Errington, *Hermes* 105 [1977], 498-500). Soon afterwards, he may have retired into private life, turning his attention to the publication of his historical account, an earlier version of which he had read to Alexander in the last days of his life (Plut. *Alex.* 76. 3).[71]

[71] But see Hamilton, *PA* 211; according to Arr. 7. 25. 4, Alexander was briefing Nearchos on the details of the up-coming naval expedition to Arabia. For Nearchos' literary achievement see Pearson, *LHA* 112-149; Jacoby, *FGrHist* 133, with iiD ('Kommentar') pp. 445-468.

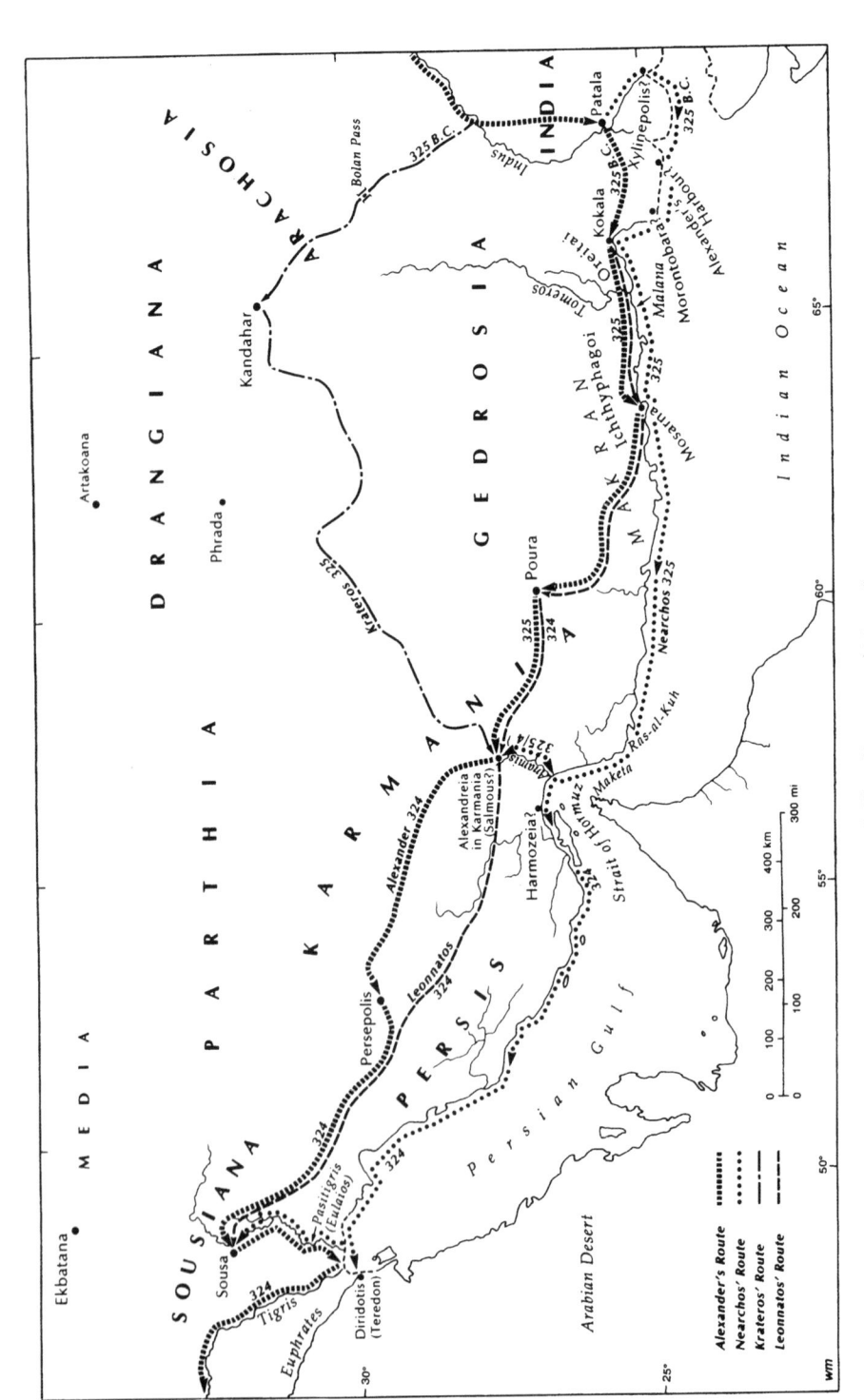

Map II The Voyage of Nearchos

Part II

v. The Somatophylakes

A. CAREER PROGRESS

1. Σωματοφυλακία

The historians of Alexander applied the term σωματοφύλακες not only to the seven-man elite bodyguard (whose title appears to have been οἱ σωματοφύλακες or οἱ σωματοφύλακες οἱ βασιλικοί),[1] but occasionally to members of the Royal Pages (normally the παῖδες βασιλικοί) and the infantry bodyguard (the ἄγημα of the hypaspists) as well. The term is most frequent in Arrian, usually denoting a member of the first group. Not surprisingly, for one of Arrian's sources belonged to the seven-man bodyguard.[2] But Arrian uses the word σωματοφύλακες of the hypaspists on four, perhaps five, occasions,[3] and Diodoros (17. 65. 1) speaks of the institution of the Pages as the σωματοφυλακία. Indeed σωματοφυλακία or *custodia corporis* was the common function of members of these three groups. All were responsible for guarding the Makedonian King, whether in battle, during the hunt or at the Court, and they shared also the adjective βασιλικός ('the King's own'; the Latin *regius* refers, as far as I can see, only to the Pages). Four units were organised specifically for the King's protection: the Pages, hypaspists, the Seven and the cavalry-guard (or ἴλη βασιλική); the term σωματοφύλακες was, however, never applied to the last group.

2. The Education of Aristocratic Youths

Literature. Droysen, *RE* iii (1899), 97, s.v. βασιλικοὶ παῖδες; Fischer, *RE* xviii (1942), 2385-2386, s.v. 'Paides basilikoi'; Griffith, *HMac* ii 401 ff.; E. D. Carney, 'The Conspiracy of Hermolaus', *CJ* 76 (1980-81), 223-231, esp. 227-228; W. Heckel, '*Somatophylakia*: A Macedonian *cursus honorum*', *Phoenix* 40 (1986), 279-294; R. Scholl, 'Alexander der Grosse und die Sklaverei am Hofe', *Klio* 69 (1987), 110-111; Hammond, *Macedonian State* 56-57; id., 'Royal Pages, Personal Pages and Boys Trained in the Macedonian Manner during the Period of the Temenid Monarchy', *Historia* 39 (1990), 261-90.

---

[1] Henceforth the 'Seven', the 'Somatophylakes' or the 'Bodyguard'.
[2] I note twenty-three passages in Arrian where *somatophylakes* are named. Twelve of these name Ptolemy son of Lagos: Arr. 3. 6. 6; 3. 27. 5; 4. 8. 9; 4. 13. 7; 4. 15. 8; 4. 16. 2; 4. 21. 4; 4. 29. 1; 5. 13. 1; 6. 28. 4; 7. 3. 2; 7. 4. 6.
[3] Arr. 1. 6. 5; 1. 24. 1; 3. 17. 2; 4. 3. 2 and 4. 30. 3 (distinguishing between the ἄγημα, i.e., the σωματοφύλακες, and the rest of the hypaspists).

THE MARSHALS OF ALEXANDER'S EMPIRE

(i) Background

The institution of the Pages dates, according to Arrian (4. 13. 1; cf. Aelian, *VH* 14. 48), from the reign of Philip II, apparently inspired by a similar practice at the Persian Court. Curtius (8. 8. 3) and Valerius Maximus (3. 3 ext. 1), however, emphasise its antiquity in Makedonia, and it appears that Dekamnichos and Krateuas ('Krataios', Arist. *Pol.* 1311b; 'Krateros', Diod. 14. 37. 6) may have been Pages of Archelaos.[4] About the Pages of Philip II we are ill informed. Only two are attested by name: Aphthonetos and Archedamos, both punished for disobedience (Aelian, *VH* 14. 48). Diodoros (16. 93. 4-6) gives a sensational account of Pausanias of Orestis, τοῦ δὲ βασιλέως σωματοφύλαξ, who, because of his beauty, had been the lover of Philip II but was supplanted by another Pausanias who perished fighting by the King's side in early 336 B.C. (πρὸ τοῦ βασιλέως στὰς ἁπάσας τὰς φερομένας ἐπ' αὐτὸν πληγὰς ἀνεδέξατο τῷ ἰδίῳ σώματι καὶ μετήλλαξεν: 16. 93. 6). Pausanias of Orestis seems to have been a hypaspist, but his alleged sexual relationship with Philip would have been a product of his younger days, when he served as one of the King's Pages; for it seems that homosexuality was common, if not encouraged, at the Court (cf. Berve i 39). Justin 8. 6. 4-8 provides a similar picture of Olympias' younger brother, Alexandros of Epeiros: raised at Philip's court in the late 350s and early 340s, presumably as a Page, he was reputedly the King's lover. Other young aristocrats were clearly brought up at the Court as *syntrophoi* of Amyntas Perdikka, Arrhidaios and Alexander the Great, just as later Alexander IV was surrounded by young men of the nobility.[5]

(ii) Recruitment

There is general agreement that the παῖδες βασιλικοί were a body of young men, the sons of prominent Makedones (τῶν ἐν τέλει Μακεδόνων

---

[4]Cf. Hammond, *HMac* ii 167; Carney, *PdP* 211 (1983), 271-272.
[5]The *syntrophoi* of Amyntas Perdikka may have included Philotas son of Parmenion (Curt. 6. 10. 24), Hegelochos son of Hippostratos (Curt. 6. 11. 22-29; for his identity see Heckel, *RhM* 125 [1982], 78-87, and i 1. 2), Amyntas son of Antiochos (see Ellis, *JHS* 91 [1971], 15-24), and perhaps the two eldest sons of Andromenes, Amyntas and Simmias (Curt. 7. 1. 11). Amongst Alexander's *syntrophoi* we find Hephaistion (Curt. 3. 12. 16: *is longe omnium amicorum carissimus erat regi, cum ipso pariter eductus, secretorum omnium arbiter...*), Marsyas son of Periandros, historian and half-brother of Antigonos Monophthalmos (*Suda*, s.v. Μαρσύας. Cf. Heckel, *Hermes* 108 [1980], 446-447), and Leonnatos (Arr. *Succ.* 12 = *Suda*, s.v. Λεοννάτος). For Alexander IV's *syntrophoi* see Diod. 19. 52. 4: τοὺς εἰωθότας παῖδας συντρέφεσθαι.

τοὺς παῖδας, Arr. 4. 13. 1; τῶν ἐν Μακεδονίᾳ δοκιμωτάτων τοὺς υἱεῖς, Aelian, *VH* 14. 48; *principum Macedoniae liberos adultos,* Curt. 5. 1. 42, cf. 8. 6. 2; *pueri regii apud Macedonas vocabantur principum liberi,* Livy 45. 6; cf. also Diod. 17. 65. 1; Justin 12. 7. 2), whose function in general was θεραπεία τοῦ βασιλέως. This involved guarding the King while he slept (*custodia corporis,* σωματοφυλακία), bringing his horse to him and accompanying him in the hunt and in battle.[6] Often their tasks were menial (*munia haud multum servilibus ministeriis abhorrentia,* Curt. 8. 6. 2). And it was the King's prerogative to order punishment, which, in the few recorded instances, was severe (Curt. 8. 6. 5; Aelian, *VH* 14. 48); thus a type of Laconic endurance was fostered among these young men (cf. Val. Max. 3. 3 ext. 1).[7] Ultimately they provided the Makedonians with generals and governors (Curt. 5. 1. 42; 8. 6. 6).

Dietmar Kienast has argued that Philip II used Persian models for the organisation of the Court and the army.[8] Whether the Royal Pages were established by Philip himself, or whether the practice dates from the time of Persian rule in Makedonia, cannot be determined. The positions of Dekamnichos and Krateuas at the court of Archelaos suggest the latter — though we cannot identify them with *certainty* as Pages[9] — and Hammond makes a strong case for an early date.[10] That the Makedonians took the Persian court as their model is generally accepted, and we have Xenophon's description of the sons of Persian nobles raised at the court of the Great King: πάντες γὰρ οἱ τῶν ἀρίστων Περσῶν παῖδες ἐπὶ ταῖς βασιλέως θύραις παιδεύονται· ἔνθα πολλὴν μὲν σωφροσύνην καταμάθοι ἄν τις, αἰσχρὸν δ' οὐδὲν οὔτ' ἀκοῦσαι οὔτ' ἰδεῖν ἔστι. θεῶνται δ' οἱ παῖδες καὶ τιμωμένους ὑπὸ βασιλέως καὶ ἀκούουσι, καὶ ἄλλους ἀτιμαζομένους· ὥστε εὐθὺς παῖδες ὄντες μανθάνουσιν ἄρχειν τε καὶ ἄρχεσθαι (*Anab.* 1. 9. 3-4). And whether this institution was intended to unite the aristocratic families of Makedon amicably, or whether these sons served as hostages for the good conduct of their fathers, it is certain that Philip's primary aim

---

[6]Arr. 4. 13. 1: καὶ ὁπότε ἐξελαύνοι βασιλεύς, τοὺς ἵππους παρὰ τῶν ἱπποκόμων δεχόμενοι ἐκεῖνοι προσῆγον καὶ ἀνέβαλλον οὗτοι βασιλέα τὸν Περσικὸν τρόπον καὶ τῆς ἐπὶ θήρᾳ φιλοτιμίας βασιλεῖ κοινωνοὶ ἦσαν.

[7]A Page attending Alexander as he sacrificed endured in silence as a hot coal fell on his arm and burned his skin, fearing to cry out and disrupt the religious ceremony.

[8]*Philipp II. von Makedonien und das Reich der Achaimeniden* (Munich, 1973).

[9]Hammond, *Macedonian State* 56, n.22, argues that Arr. 4. 13. 1 should be taken to mean that the Pages existed already in Philip's time, not that he established the institution.

[10]*Historia* 39 (1990), 261-264.

was stability within the kingdom and at the Court.[11] For, if the practice did not originate with Philip, it was undoubtedly he who extended the membership of the corps to Upper Makedonia.[12]

We are not told how large the corps of the Pages was, or if its number was fixed. In 330 Amyntas son of Andromenes brought fifty young men from Makedonia to serve as Alexander's Pages (Curt. 5. 1. 42; cf. Diod. 17. 65. 1), and Berve (i 37, n.3) estimates that the entire unit numbered in excess of one hundred. N. G. L. Hammond prefers a figure in the range of 200, arguing that the fifty Pages mentioned by Curtius and Diodoros 'probably represented the oldest year'.[13] Other figures are of limited value: sixteen Pages accompanied Perdikkas, son of Orontes, in 323 B.C. (Curt. 10. 8. 3); they were numerous enough to allow the nine conspirators named by Curtius (8. 6. 7-9) to be on guard-duty on the same night in 327; but Berve identifies only thirteen individuals as Pages, Hoffmann fourteen, two of these from Philip's time.[14] The *paides* who appear in Eumenes' army (Diod. 19. 28. 3) and with Alketas in Pisidia (Diod. 18. 45. 3) may have been 'the sons of the native nobility respectively of Cappadocia and Pisidia' (Anson, *AHB* 2 [1988], 132, n.11). More problematical are the two hundred *paides* of Plut. *Eum.* 3. 11 (διακοσίους δὲ τῶν παίδων ὁπλοφόρων), whom A. Spendel (*Untersuchungen zum Heerwesen der Diadochen* [Breslau,

---

[11]Kienast (*ibid.*) 30.

[12]Of the Somatophylakes named by Arr. 6. 28. 4, Leonnatos (Πελλαῖος in this passage and in Arr. *Ind.* 18. 3) came originally from Lynkestis, Perdikkas from Orestis; the *somatophylax* Attalos (Diod. 16. 94. 4), whether Page or hypaspist, was from Tymphaia, as was Alexandros son of Polyperchon, a Somatophylax of Philip III Arrhidaios (Arr. *Succ.* 1. 38). The hypaspist commanders (Curt. 5. 2. 5) include a certain Lyncestes Amyntas, but it is not certain that he belonged to the aristocracy. The Somatophylax Arybbas (Arr. 3. 5. 5) appears to have come from Epeiros, and Neoptolemos, who is called ἀρχιυπασπιστής by Plutarch, *Eumenes* 1. 6, belonged to the Aiakidai and was Epeirot in origin. Cf. also Fox 51; Griffith, *HMac* ii 402-403.

[13]*Macedonian State* 56, n.24. Griffith (*HMac* ii 401), who calculates that about fifty youths may have been added every three years and that 'the Pages at any one time will have numbered about eighty-five.' This strikes me as unnecessarily low.

[14]Berve: Antikles (no. 88), Antipatros (no. 93), Aretis (no. 110), Elaptonius (no. 296), Epimenes (no. 300), Hermolaos (no. 305), Eurylochos (no. 332), Metron (no. 520), Nikostratos (no. 570, probably a corruption of the name Sostratos, though Berve treats them as separate individuals; see Curt. 8. 6. 9, a particularly corrupt passage, and Heckel, *LCM* 6 [1981], 63-64), Sostratos (no. 738), Philippos (no. 777), Philotas (no. 801), and Charikles (no. 824). Hoffmann 179-180: Aphthonetos, Archedamos, Aretis, Hermolaos, Sostratos, Antipatros, Epimenes, Antikles, Philotas, Charikles, Eurylochos, Nikostratos, Elaptonius, Excipinus.

1915], 27) identified as infantrymen. But these examples of individuals, from (apparently) non-Makedonian backgrounds and the Diadochic age, add little to our understanding of Alexander's Pages.

(iii) Terminology

Which raises the question of basic terminology. In the Alexander-historians, the Pages are officially the παῖδες (Plut. *Alex.* 55. 6-7; Diod. 17. 66. 3; 17. 76. 5; 19. 52. 4; Arr. 4. 12. 7; 4. 13. 1-2) or παῖδες βασιλικοί (Diod. 17. 79. 4; Arr. 4. 16. 6; cf. Diod. 17. 36. 5: οἱ δὲ τοῦ βασιλέως παῖδες).[15] In Latin they are *pueri* (Curt. 8. 6. 24; 8. 7. 8; 10. 7. 16; 10. 8. 3-4), *pueri regii* (Curt. 5. 2. 13; Livy 45. 6) or *pueri nobiles* (Curt. 8. 6. 7; 10. 5. 8; cf. Val. Max. 3. 3 ext. 1: *nobilissimi pueri*), though in the last case the 'term' is always further explained; hence it might be unwise to speak of a 'term' at all. As a unit, they are the *regia cohors* or *puerorum regia cohors* (Curt. 8. 6. 7; 9. 10. 26; 10. 8. 3), sometimes merely the *cohors* (Curt. 8. 6. 6; 8. 6. 18; 8. 8. 20). Clearly they were meant to be the King's bodyguards (Diod. 17. 65. 1; Curt. 5. 1. 42; 10. 5. 8), but, while they appear to have been called σωματοφύλακες (though never δορύφοροι) by the Greeks, Roman writers did not apply to them the terms *custodes corporis* or *armigeri*.[16] The rather vague *satellites* is never used, as far as I am aware, to refer to the Pages.[17]

Pages are often described in less precise phrases or in specific terms hitherto disregarded. Some of this terminology will involve descriptions of their functions, age-group, aristocratic affiliations or any combination of the aforementioned. Hence, the *cohors ... quae excubabat ad tabernaculum regis* (Curt. 3. 12. 3; cf. 8. 13. 20; 8. 6. 3: *excubabant, servatis noctium vicibus, proximi foribus eius aedis, in qua*

---

[15]Scholl, *Klio* 69 (1987), 110-111, seeks to distinguish between the *basilikoi paides* and the Pages. Since Diod. 17. 65. 1 calls the Pages υἱοί instead of παῖδες (cf. Curt. 5. 1. 42; 8. 6. 2: *adulti liberi*), Scholl argues: 'Das würde dann ein Anhaltspunkt dafür sein können, dass wir es mit verschiedenen Gruppen bei den Pagen und den königlichen Paides zu tun haben' (111). But Arr. 4. 13. 1 (τῶν ἐν τέλει Μακεδόνων τοὺς παῖδας) leaves little doubt about the origins of the *paides*, and Curt. (5. 1. 42; 8. 6. 2) calls the sons of Makedonian nobles (*principum adulti liberi*) *pueri regii* (= παῖδες βασιλικοί).

[16]All references appear to be to Somatophylakes and hypaspists. *custos corporis*: Curt. 4. 13. 19; 5. 11. 6; 6. 7. 15; 6. 11. 8; 7. 5. 40; 7. 10. 9; 8. 2. 11; 8. 6. 21; 8. 11. 11; 9. 6. 4; 9. 8. 23; 10. 2. 30; 10. 6. 1; Justin 9. 6. 3-4; 12. 12. 3; *ME* 2; cf. Curt. 7. 7. 9. *armiger*: Curt. 3. 12. 7; 4. 7. 21; 4. 15. 29; 5. 4. 21; 6. 1. 5; 6. 8. 17; 6. 8. 19; 6. 8. 24; 7. 1. 14; 7. 1. 18; 7. 2. 13; 7. 2. 28; 8. 1. 45; 8. 2. 11.

[17]Curt. 3. 12. 10; 4. 7. 21; 6. 7. 24; 6. 7. 29; 6. 8. 19; 10. 5. 14; 10. 7. 14; 10. 7. 17; 10. 8. 3; 10. 8. 8; Justin 12. 6. 3; 12. 8. 4; 12. 12. 4.

rex adquiescebat. Cf. also Arr. 4. 13. 1: κοιμώμενον [sc. βασιλέα] φυλάσσειν τούτοις ἐπετέτραπτο) will, by analogy with Curtius 8. 6. 18 (*iam alii ex cohorte in stationem successerant ante cubiculi fores excubituri*), refer to the Pages. To which group one may add an individual *qui ministrare regi solebat* (Justin 12. 14. 6; cf. Curt. 5. 1. 42; 8. 6. 2; Metz *LM* 89: *cum Iolla...praeministro Alexandri.* Cf. Justin 12. 14. 9; Livy 45. 6; Curt. 5. 2. 13; Diod. 17. 36. 5), if he belongs to one of the noble families of Makedonia: that is, not a slave but a boy of aristocratic descent engaged in θεραπεία τοῦ βασιλέως. By contrast, other functions similar to those of the Pages were handled by slaves, and although the Pages were entrusted with the King's horses on occasions, they are not to be identified with the grooms (ἱπποκόμοι); for Curtius makes a clear distinction between Pages and *agasones* (8. 6. 4).[18]

Most important is the terminology that involves age-limits for membership in the unit. Berve (i 37) assumes that a youth entered the ranks of the Pages sometime between the ages of 13 and 15, a 'boy' by ancient and modern standards. But this training must have continued for several years, perhaps until shortly before the age of 20. Hence, the Pages belonged to that group that included *pueri*, μειράκια (Plut. *Alex.* 55. 2; Arr. 4. 13. 1) and presumably νεανίσκοι (Plut. *Alex.* 10. 5). They are *adulti liberi* and *iuvenes* (Curt. 5. 1. 42; 8. 2. 35; 8. 6. 2): for example, Hermolaos, who calls himself a *puer* (Curt. 8. 7. 8), is referred to by Curtius (8. 6. 8) as a *iuvenis*, and the Pages in general are called *iuvenes* at 8. 6. 25. Similarly, the Page Metron (cf. Diod. 17. 79. 4), who received the news of Dimnos' conspiracy against Alexander in 330, is called *iuvenis nobilis* (Curt. 8. 7. 22). But again the difficulty is this: if *iuvenis nobilis* is used regularly as a substitute for *puer regius*, and even if every reference to a Makedonian *iuvenis nobilis* involves an individual who could be a Page, this does not mean that every *iuvenis nobilis* is by definition a Page. We must rule out, however, Berve's claim that Philippos, the brother of Lysimachos, could not have been a Page because Curtius calls him *iuvenis* instead of *puer*.[19]

But if Philippos was not one of the Pages, then we have a group of young men, described in similar terms, who are apparently hypaspists, but not clearly distinguished from the Pages because of the ambiguity of the words that indicate age. Alexandros, Charos and their

---

[18]Cf. Arr. 4. 13. 1. The *hypaspistai basilikoi* found together with the *hippokomoi* at Gaugamela (Arr. 3. 13. 6) are probably an error for *paides basilikoi*.

[19]Curt. 8. 2. 35: *Nobiles iuvenes comitari eum soliti defecerant praeter Philippum. Lysimachi erat frater, tum primum adultus et, quod facile adpareret, indolis rarae.* Berve ii 382: 'Als Page würde er als puer bezeichnet und vermutlich beritten gewesen sein.' Cf. the description of Polemon son of Andromenes: *iuvenis...primo aetatis flore pubescens...* (Curt. 7. 2. 4).

colleagues, *iuvenes promptissimi ex sua cohorte* (Curt. 8. 11. 9-10), belong to this group. Berve originally identified them as Pages (*RE* Supplbd iv [1924], 15, 215), but promoted them to the hypaspists in his prosopography (ii 21, no. 40; ii 408, no. 826). By the same token, we cannot be sure about the status of Pausanias of Orestis, the assassin of Philip II, whom Diodoros calls σωματοφύλαξ and whom Justin describes as *nobilis ex Macedonibus adulescens*.[20] But, whatever we decide about the status of Pausanias, it must apply equally to Leonnatos, Perdikkas and Attalos, who were his fellow *somatophylakes* in 336 B.C. (Diod. 16. 94. 4).[21]

The institution of the Royal Pages marked the beginning of the careers of most, if not all, Makedonian aristocrats (Curt. 5. 1. 42: *magnorumque praefectorum et ducum haec incrementa sunt et rudimenta*). This institution had two restrictions: age and birth. On the latter point, it is important to note that Philip II had opened up the Makedonian aristocracy to highlanders and Greeks (cf. Griffith, *HMac* ii 402 f.). The sons of Philip's newly created non-lowland hetairoi were presumably raised at Pella and enrolled as Pages. Thus we find Leonnatos, who was undoubtedly of Lynkestian origin, referred to as Πελλαῖος in Arrian's only complete list of the Somatophylakes (Arr. 6. 28. 4). Similarly, Lysimachos, whose father appears to have been Thessalian, was raised at Pella along with his brothers.[22] Most notable among Philip's highland hetairoi, whose sons were raised at the Court, were Andromenes and Polyperchon of Tymphaia, Derdas and Machatas of Elimeia,[23] Aëropos of Lynkestis, Orontes, Alexandros

---

[20] Justin 9. 6. 3-4. Pausanias had very recently been sexually abused by Attalos (or his muleteers); at that time his age is given as *primis pubertatis annis* (cf. Polemon, above).

[21] Pausanias could not have been one of the Seven (*pace* Hammond, *GRBS* 19 [1978], 347). Diodoros and Justin emphasise his youth, and it is difficult to imagine that Attalos and his friends could have, with impunity, degraded a man of such high standing. Hammond also identifies the Attalos of Diod. 16. 94. 4 with the uncle of Kleopatra-Eurydike. This Attalos could not have been one of the Seven since he was absent from the Court at the time of Philip's assassination; the identification also implies that Perdikkas and Leonnatos were members of the Seven in 336. See Heckel, *LCM* 4 (1979), 215-216.

[22] Merker, *Chiron* 9 (1979), 31-36, concludes that he was Makedonian (cf. Heckel, *Klio* 64 [1982], 374, written in 1976). Perhaps Lysimachos' appointment indicates that Philip sought regional representation amongst his Somatophylakes (Arybbas was Epeirot). Lysimachos was, however, regarded as Makedonian: Arr. *Ind.* 18. 3; *Anab.* 6. 28. 4; Plut. *Demetr.* 44; Justin 15. 3. 1; Paus. 1. 9. 5.

[23] Derdas (Berve, no. 250; Curt. 7. 6. 12; 8. 1. 7), whom Alexander sent to the Skythians, was probably a member of this family, but we do not know in what

and Antiochos of Orestis. Of the Eordaian nobility we know little, though men like Krateuas (and perhaps Lagos) were especially prominent.[24]

3. The Royal Hypaspists

Literature. Berve i 122-125; Tarn ii 148 ff.; R. D. Milns, 'The Hypaspists of Alexander III — Some Problems', *Historia* 20 (1971), 186 ff., esp. 188-189; id., *CP* 78 (1983), 49; W. Heckel, '*Somatophylakia*: A Macedonian *Cursus Honorum*', *Phoenix* 40 (1986), 285-288; cf. N. G. L. Hammond, 'The Various Guards of Philip II and Alexander III', *Historia* 40 (1991), 396-418.

The greatest difficulty is presented by the hypaspists, or rather by that unit which formed Alexander's personal footguard, Berve's *Hypaspistenleibwache* (i 122 ff.). We know very little indeed about the composition of this group and its relationship to the Pages and the Seven. Yet it is precisely this unit which is vital to our understanding of the organisation of Alexander's *somatophylakes*. The connection between the Pages and the Seven is obvious: (i) Both were exclusive to the Makedonian aristocracy (or, rather, to the sons of Philip's hetairoi), and presumably a man who became a member of the Seven had at one time been a Page. (ii) The Pages and the Seven shared the function of σωματοφυλακία at the Court, guarding the King while he slept; for the Pages guarded the outside of the bed-chamber, the Somatophylakes the inside. Thus we find Eurylochos divulging the details of Hermolaos' conspiracy to Ptolemy and Leonnatos, who were that night on guard within the doors.[25] (iii) At the King's banquets, we

---

capacity he accompanied Alexander. Kalas son of Harpalos became satrap of Hellespontine Phrygia; Tauron son of Machatas commanded the archers, and his brother Philippos was a satrap in India at the time of his death in 324; Harpalos the treasurer may have been their brother as well.

[24]We know very little about Peithon son of Krateuas (Berve ii 311, no. 621) before 323; Ptolemy son of Lagos was rumoured to have been a bastard son of Philip of Makedon by Arsinoë. For Ptolemy's alleged humble origins see Justin 13. 4. 10: *ex gregario milite Alexander virtutis causa provexerat.* Since Ptolemy's birthdate, according to Ps.-Lucian (*Macrob.* 12), was 367/6, it is difficult to determine whether Ptolemy's failure to appear as a Page or hypaspist is due to age or ineligibility for such offices. It is possible that Ptolemy came from a good family, but that suspicions of illegitimacy hindered his promotion. Later in his career, Ptolemy made political hay out of this disadvantage and promulgated the view that he was Philip's bastard son. We know nothing of importance about the early career of his brother Menelaos (perhaps identical with Berve, no. 505).

[25]Curt. 8. 6. 22: *Ptolemaeum ac Leonnatum excubantes ad cubicuili limen....* Cf. A. Giacone, *Storie di Alessandro Magno di Quinto Curzio Rufo*

find in his immediate vicinity, his hetairoi, some Pages (who attended him), the Somatophylakes, who were high in the King's esteem but also protected him, and some of the hypaspists (Curt. 8. 1. 45 ff.; Arr. 4. 8. 8; 4. 8. 9; Plut. *Alex.* 51. 6). The accounts of the Kleitos affair name five of the seven Somatophylakes, and Hephaistion and Leonnatos appear at the banquet that saw the introduction of *proskynesis*.[26]

Now, since the number of the Bodyguard was fixed at seven, it was not possible for more than a very few ever to attain that rank. Apparently, a Somatophylax held office for life (or, at least, until retirement) unless appointment to another post — such as a governorship[27] — or the charge or suspicion of some misconduct led to his replacement (Demetrios: Arr. 3. 27. 5). We are told that the institution of the Pages served as a training-school for future officers and governors (*Haec cohors velut seminarium ducum praefectorumque apud Macedonas fuit*, Curt. 8. 6. 6; cf. 5. 1. 42). Yet, it is inconceivable that every Page, upon 'graduation', advanced directly to a high military or administrative post. Nor is it likely that he fought in the ranks with the common soldiers, amongst the pezhetairoi (or asthetairoi), slingers or archers. There must have been an intermediate stage in what we might call the Makedonian *cursus honorum*. Possibly, the ex-Page was enrolled in the *ile basilike*, though there is not one piece of evidence for this; what evidence we have suggests instead that he joined the *agema* of the hypaspists.

(i) The ἄγημα

To identify and define the *agema* of the hypaspists is, however, no easy task. Berve (i 122-126) argued that the hypaspists were divided into the regular hypaspists — part of which was the *agema*, which corresponded to the *ile basilike* of the cavalry — and the 'Royal Hypaspists', who formed the personal guard of the King (the *Hypaspistenleibwache*). Tarn (ii 148-154) rejected Berve's arguments, claiming that all hypaspists were 'royal' (βασιλικοί) but that the

---

(Turin, 1977), 514, n.14: 'I σωματοφύλακες, generali aiutanti del re, dormivano all'interno dell'appartamento reale, ossia *ad cubiculi limen*; i paggi reali invece vegliavano fuori, *ad cubiculi fores*.'

[26]Kleitos affair: Aristonous (Plut. *Alex.* 51. 6; cf. Ziegler, *RhM* 84 [1935], 379-380); Perdikkas, Ptolemy, Lysimachos and Leonnatos (Curt. 8. 1. 45-46, 48). *Proskynesis*: Hephaistion (Plut. *Alex.* 55. 1; the Lysimachos at 55. 2 is the Akarnanian); Leonnatos (Arr. 4. 12. 2); for the story that substitutes Polyperchon for Leonnatos (Curt. 8. 5. 22), see Heckel, *AJP* 99 (1978), 458-461.

[27]Arr. 2. 12. 2 (Balakros); Arr. 3. 16. 9 (Menes). Peukestas, upon accepting the satrapy of Persis (Arr. 6. 30. 2), ceased to be Somatophylax. His appointment was both honorary and temporary.

original *agema* continued to form the King's personal guard. R. D. Milns has modified that view further, suggesting that one of the three chiliarchies of the hypaspists (formed in late 331; cf. Curt. 5. 2. 5)[28] was the so-called *agema*, and that it was sub-divided into 8 tetrarchies (125 per unit, as in the tetrarchies of Philip V). He proposed 'that each day a "tetrarchia" from the *agema* of the hypaspists was detailed to act as Alexander's personal bodyguards...' (*CP* 78 [1983], 49). Thus, when Arrian (5. 13. 1) says that Alexander embarked Ptolemy, Lysimachos, Perdikkas (roughly half of the Somatophylakes) and Seleukos, with half of the hypaspists, on board a triakonter, Milns takes this to mean about 65 men or half of one tetrarchy of the *agema* (49).

There is an easier solution. The *agema* of the hypaspists was the infantry equivalent of the *ile basilike*, which itself later became known as the *agema* of the cavalry — references to the cavalry *agema* as early as 331/0 are anachronistic (Curt. 4. 13. 26; 5. 4. 21),[29] and we do not know exactly what happened to the *ile basilike* after the division of the Companions between Hephaistion and Kleitos (Arr. 3. 27. 4). Like the Companion Cavalry (ἡ ἵππος ἡ ἑταιρική), which had an ἴλη βασιλική (= ἄγημα in later times), the hypaspists of the Companions (οἱ ὑπασπισταὶ τῶν ἑταίρων)[30] had an ἄγημα βασιλικόν. These *agemata* were both part of and yet distinct from their respective units: the distinction is clearly made between 'the King's own' troops (βασιλικός-ή-όν) and the Companions in general (ἑταῖροι). Thus we find that the Makedonian troops are normally called the King's Companions, whereas only troops specifically organised for the King's protection and under his personal leadership were given the adjective βασιλικός. When Arrian 5. 13. 3 speaks of ὑπασπισταὶ βασιλικοί, the ἄγημα βασιλικόν and οἱ ἄλλοι ὑπασπισταί, he fails to realise that the 'Royal Hypaspists' and the 'royal *agema*' are one and the same.[31]

---

[28] Bosworth, *Arrian* i 148 f., argues for four chiliarchies of hypaspists.

[29] The MSS. of Arr. 1. 8. 3 read τὰ δὲ ἀγήματα καὶ τοὺς ὑπασπιστάς, which Schmieder emended to τὸ δὲ ἄγημά τε καὶ τοὺς ὑπασπιστάς. See Bosworth, *Arrian* i 81-82. Diodoros 19. 27-29 names the *agema* of the cavalry three times, twice speaking of a squadron of 300 men, one each in the armies of Eumenes (19. 28. 3) and Antigonos (19. 29. 5); Eudamos' *agema* numbered only 150 (19. 27. 2).

[30] Arr. 1. 14. 2. Bosworth, *Arrian* i 117 thinks τῶν ἑταίρων is an error which originated as a scribal gloss.

[31] The term 'Royal Hypaspists' comes up only three times in Arrian (1. 8. 4; 3. 13. 6; 5. 13. 4). In the first instance, a distinction is made between 'Royal Hypaspists' and the *agema* (but this *agema* could be the *ile basilike*); in the second (3. 13. 6) we do not know which group of hypaspists Arrian has in mind, and possibly the παῖδες βασιλικοί are meant; and, in the third, Arrian himself

(ii) Royal and Regular Hypaspists

Literature. Berve i 122, 125-129; Tarn ii 148-154; R. D. Milns, 'Philip II and the Hypaspists', *Historia* 16 (1967), 509-513; id., 'The Hypaspists of Alexander III — Some Problems', *Historia* 20 (1971), 186-195; E. M. Anson, 'The Hypaspists: Macedonia's Professional Citizen-Soldiers', *Historia* 34 (1985), 246-248.

That we have in the hypaspists of Alexander two groups — one smaller aristocratic contingent and a larger non-noble unit — is clear from both the origins of the hypaspists and the details about their commanders.³² The regular hypaspists were originally known as pezhetairoi.³³ These are described by Theopompos (*FGrHist* 115 F348) as ἐκ πάντων τῶν Μακεδόνων ἐπίλεκτοι οἱ μέγιστοι καὶ ἰσχυρότατοι ἐδορυφόρουν τὸν βασιλέα καὶ ἐκαλοῦντο πεζέταιροι. I would disagree, however, with Anson's claim that in Philip's time these pezhetairoi were 'only the

has made a mistake, for there we find three separate groups — hypaspists, 'Royal Hypaspists' and 'Royal *agema*'. The adjective βασιλικός is more likely to designate an elite unit than a larger one (3000-4000 men). It is worth noting that the Companion Cavalry never appear as the 'Royal Companion Cavalry' but only the elite squadron receives the adjective 'Royal' (Arr. 3. 11. 8 wrongly separates the ἴλη βασιλική from the 'other Royal Ilai', which is impossible since the adjective βασιλική is the only thing that can distinguish it from the other *ilai*).

³²Unlike the members of the *agema*, the hypaspist officers who were subordinate to Nikanor and later to Neoptolemos (the ἀρχιυπασπισταί) were men of obscure background, of whom only one has an attested patronymikon — Atarrhias son of Deinomenes (Plut. *Mor.* 339b = *de fort. Al.* 2. 7). Antigenes, Atarrhias, Antigonos, two Amyntases, Hellanikos, Philotas and Theodotos were all selected as pentakosiarchs (so Bosworth, *Arrian* i 148 f.) in Sittakene in a contest of valour that would surely have been demeaning for *syntrophoi* of the King (Curt. 5. 2. 5). Two chiliarchs, Adaios and Timandros, who may have been hypaspist-commanders, are also of unknown origin, as is Antiochos, a chiliarch in 327/6; that Nearchos was a chiliarch of the hypaspists (thus Arr. 4. 30. 6) is doubtful (cf. E. Badian, 'Nearchus the Cretan', *YCS* 24 [1975], 150-151, with n.23). The later Argyraspid commander, Teutamos, is equally obscure; he too may have been a pentakosiarch of the regular hypaspists at some point. That the pride of Makedon's aristocratic youth served under such leaders is inconceivable.

³³E. M. Anson, 'The Hypaspists: Macedonia's Professional Citizen-Soldiers', *Historia* 34 (1985), 246-248. But see now A. Erskine, 'The πεζέταιροι of Philip II and Alexander III', *Historia* 38 (1989), 385-394, who argues that the pezhetairoi were Philip's footguard but that these were replaced by the hypaspists in Alexander's reign. The pezhetairoi, however, continued to operate as a 'higher status unit' (394), but Alexander preferred a footguard composed of men of whose loyalty he could be sure.

agema ... one thousand troops as opposed to the later three thousand' (*Historia* 34 [1985], 248). The pezhetairoi of Philip II took the name hypaspists or, more specifically, 'the hypaspists of the Companions' (οἱ ὑπασπισταὶ τῶν ἑταίρων) when the name pezhetairoi came to be applied generally to the Makedonian infantry. The regular hypaspists, who were under the command of Nikanor son of Parmenion until his death in 330 B.C., appear to have developed into the Argyraspids, as is foreshadowed by Diod. 17. 57. 2. The Argyraspids, it may be worth noting, have no attested *agema*.

The *agema*, then, was regarded as separate from the main troop of the hypaspists and it was virtually always with the King (cf. Arr. 1. 1. 11; 1. 5. 10; 1. 6. 9; 3. 1. 4; 3. 17. 2; 3. 18. 5 etc.). The very name ἄγημα points to the fact that it was, in theory, led by the King (τὸ ἡγούμενον or τὸ ἀγούμενον, so Hoffmann 85; or ἤγημα = 'that which leads'). It comprised aristocratic troops (ex-Pages), who were known in Philip's time as *somatophylakes*, a name which was applied to certain hypaspists even in the early years of Alexander's reign. Thus, Ptolemy son of Lagos, who had been a member of this group, sometimes called them by their former name, σωματοφύλακες βασιλικοί. Now, when Alexander led only a portion of the army, he invariably took with him at least some of the hypaspists. In most cases, the terminology is too general to allow us to determine which hypaspists are meant. But there are passages in Arrian which refer to the King leading 'the *agema* and the hypaspists' (1. 1. 11; 1. 8. 3-4), and in the troop-dispositions at Issos and Gaugamela we have 'the *agema* and the hypaspists' or 'the *agema* of the hypaspists and the other hypaspists' (2. 8. 3; 3. 11. 9). Later, we hear of 'the Royal Hypaspists and the hypaspists' in the Ouxian campaign (3. 17. 2) and 'the *somatophylakes* and the hypaspists' in Sogdiana (4. 3. 2); and in India, Alexander leads 'seven hundred of the *somatophylakes* and the hypaspists' (4. 30. 3). Thus it becomes clear that the members of the *agema* were also known as *somatophylakes*. When Diodoros says that Hephaistion was wounded at Gaugamela while leading the *somatophylakes* (τῶν δὲ σωματοφυλάκων ἡγούμενος, 17. 61. 3), he must mean that he was the nominal commander of the *agema*,[34] which differed from the main

---

[34]He appears to have replaced Admetos, who died bravely in the assault on Tyre (Arr. 2. 23. 5; Diod. 17. 45. 6). So Berve i 124. Berve, however, thinks that Hephaistion held this office until around 328/7, when he was appointed to the Seven and replaced by Seleukos. I have argued for 334 as the year of Hephaistion's promotion to the Seven (*Historia* 27 [1978], 227; though I have since changed my mind about the meaning of Diod. 17. 61. 3): that he was both Somatophylax and commander of the *agema* poses no difficulties, but I do not see how Hephaistion could have commanded both his half of the Companion

hypaspist unit in one very significant way — its membership was restricted to the aristocracy. In the following year, Hephaistion was appointed commander of one-half of the Companion Cavalry and replaced as leader of the *agema* by Seleukos son of Antiochos; he in turn may have been succeeded by Kassandros (Justin 13. 4. 18).[35]

(iii) The ἄγημα and the ἑταῖροι

We have already seen that the term ἑταῖροι came to be applied in a flattering way to the Makedonian infantry — but only in the form pezhetairoi ('foot companions'). 'Hetairos' itself was a title reserved for the noble (whether Makedonian by birth or by naturalisation).[36] Arrian refers to members of the 'Royal Bodyguard' or 'Royal Hypaspists' as ἑταῖροι on occasions. In the assault on Tyre (2. 23. 6), '...Alexander took possession of the wall with his Companions (ξὺν τοῖς ἑταίροις).' Here the hetairoi were the hypaspists and not the pezhetairoi of Koinos' brigade, who were, at any rate, on a different ship; for a little earlier we are told that Alexander intended to take the wall 'with his hypaspists' (2. 23. 4). These hypaspists were carried on a single ship, and represented only a fraction of the total number; probably they are the *agema*. At 1. 6. 6 Alexander occupies a hill σὺν τοῖς ἑταίροις, a group made up of *somatophylakes* and hetairoi (1. 6. 5). Seleukos, who leads the 'Royal Hypaspists' (5. 13. 4) is described as Σέλευκος τῶν ἑταίρων to distinguish him from Perdikkas, Lysimachos and Ptolemy who are σωματοφύλακες, that is, members of the Seven (5. 13. 1); and Neoptolemos, who appears to be fighting as a 'Royal Hypaspist' at Gaza (2. 27. 1), is called Νεοπτόλεμος τῶν ἑταίρων τοῦ Αἰακιδῶν γένους (2. 27. 6). Both Seleukos and

Cavalry (Arr. 3. 27. 4) and the hypaspists. Thus, I would place Seleukos' appointment in 330 B.C.

[35]During Alexander's lifetime, the *chiliarchos* was Hephaistion (until 324) and then Perdikkas; Seleukos commanded the *agema*. After Alexander's death, when Perdikkas became *epimeletes* of the Kings, Seleukos became the new *chiliarchos* and the *agema* appears to have passed on to Kassandros. Note that Seleukos did not follow Perdikkas in the order of the hipparchies (as one might wrongly deduce from Diod. 18. 3. 4) during Alexander's lifetime. From Plut. *Eum*. 1. 5 we learn that the order of the hipparchies was (i) Hephaistion, (ii) Perdikkas and (iii) Eumenes. When Perdikkas was advanced to the first hipparchy, he became *chiliarchos*, and Eumenes replaced him in the second hipparchy. By contrast, Seleukos, who was still commander of the *agema* of the hypaspists at Alexander's death, was promoted to command the first hipparchy (which was ἐπιφανεστάτην = Hephaistion's chiliarchy) over the head of Eumenes.

[36]Prominent foreigners could also become hetairoi: for example, Abdalonymos, Bagoas, Demaratos of Korinth, Nithaphon.

Neoptolemos belonged to aristocratic families — one from Orestis, the other Epeiros — and both commanded hypaspists. The term ἑταῖρος is also used of Leonnatos (Arr. 2. 12. 5), just after the battle of Issos, when he was not yet one of the Seven and held no independent command; he was last identified as σωματοφύλαξ in 336, in a context where σωματοφύλαξ undoubtedly means ὑπασπιστὴς βασιλικός.[37]

4. From Royal Page to Royal Hypaspist

The transition from παῖδες βασιλικοί to the ὑπασπισταὶ βασιλικοί required aristocratic youths to fight in an infantry unit for the first — and only — time in their careers. To fight in this way was beneath the dignity of the Makedonian noble, and Amyntas son of Andromenes, quite naturally, objects that he would not give up his horse to the *scriba equitum*, Antiphanes, *nisi pedes militare vellem* (Curt. 7. 1. 34). As Pages the young men of Makedon accompanied their king on horseback, especially in the hunt. In fact, Hermolaos' punishment for striking a boar, instead of yielding the 'kill' to the King, included the removal of his horse (Arr. 4. 13. 2). And, when the Pages were forced to fight, as in the skirmish with the Massagetai at Zariaspa (Baktra) in 328, they did so on horseback (Arr. 4. 16. 6). Thus, it is clear that, as Page and as commander, the Makedonian noble fought on horseback. Why should we expect him to dismount around the age of eighteen and fight as an infantryman instead of joining the Companion Cavalry (ἡ ἵππος ἡ ἑταιρική)?

For the view that the young man joined the Companion Cavalry upon leaving the παῖδες βασιλικοί I can find not one shred of evidence. Aretis ('Ἀρέτις), described by Arrian as ἀναβολεὺς τῶν βασιλικῶν, fought on horseback in the battle at the Graneikos (1. 15. 6). He may have been one of the Pages, whose functions are described as τοὺς ἵππους παρὰ τῶν ἱπποκόμων δεχόμενοι ἐκεῖνοι προσῆγον καὶ ἀνέβαλλον οὗτοι βασιλέα τὸν Περσικὸν τρόπον (Arr. 4. 13. 1; cf. Berve i 38). At Gaugamela, we encounter a certain Aretes ('Ἀρέτης), commander of the Paionians. If Aretis is identical with Aretes, then we see the man at two different stages of his career. But there is nothing to indicate that he was necessarily a cavalryman immediately before his appointment to the command of the Paionians.

On the other hand, we have a number of nobles who are unmistakably infantrymen. The best example is Philippos, the son of

---

[37] σωματοφύλαξ (Diod. 16. 94. 4); *ex purpuratis* (= ἑταῖρος, Curt. 3. 12. 7); Somatophylax (Arr. 3. 5. 5); ἑταῖρος (Arr. 4. 12. 2). Note that Pausanias of Orestis who, like Leonnatos, is σωματοφύλαξ (Diod. 16. 93. 3) in 336, is described by Plut. *Mor.* 170e-f as δορυφόρος, and by Josephus, *AJ* 19. 1. 13 (95), as τῶν ἑταίρων.

Agathokles and brother of Lysimachos. Curtius (8. 2. 35-36) leaves us in no doubt about his status:

> Nobiles iuvenes comitari eum soliti defecerant praeter Philippum: Lysimachi erat frater, tum primum adultus et, quod facile adpareret, indolis rarae. Is pedes, incredibile dictu, per D stadia vectum regem comitatus est, saepe equum suum offerente Lysimacho; nec tamen ut digrederetur a rege effici potuit, cum lorica indutus arma gestaret.[38]

> The young noblemen who formed his usual retinue had given up the chase, all except Philip, the brother of Lysimachus, who was in the early stages of manhood and, as was readily apparent, was a person of rare qualities. Incredibly, Philip kept up with the king on foot although Alexander rode for 500 stades. Lysimachus made him frequent offers of his horse, but Philip could not be induced to leave the king, even though he was wearing a cuirass and carrying weapons.
> (J. C. Yardley, tr.)

Now Berve (ii 382) correctly describes Philippos as 'anscheinend dem Leibhypaspistenkorps Al[exander]s angehörend', adding the note 'als Page würde er als puer bezeichnet und vermutlich beritten gewesen sein' (n.2).

Around the age of eighteen or nineteen, the young noble was ready for more vigorous training; the emphasis now shifted to the military sphere and to fighting on foot. The development of the equestrian arts was appropriate for boys who were not yet full grown, who lacked the size and strength to wield the sarissa, to endure forced marches and to stand up to hardened veterans. For the noble it was a humbling experience, but one that prepared him to lead infantry and, if necessary, to dismount and fight alongside his men (cf. Ptolemy, Arr. 4. 24. 3). In contemporary North American slang, we would call it 'paying one's dues', but in practice it was not radically different from the Spartan system which subjected the children of the *homoioi* to similar and harsher treatment, exempting only the children of the King (as was, apparently, the case in Makedonia as well).

ἐπεὶ δὲ τῆς βασιλείας Ἄγιδι προσηκούσης κατὰ τὸν νόμον, ἰδιώτης ἐδόκει βιοτεύσειν ὁ Ἀγησίλαος, ἤχθη τὴν λεγομένην ἀγωγὴν ἐν Λακεδαίμονι, σκληρὰν μὲν οὖσαν τῇ διαίτῃ καὶ πολύπονον,

---

[38]Justin (15. 3. 11-12) knows the story and attributes similar conduct to Lysimachos himself. *Denique omni ex animo huius facti memoria exturbata post in India insectanti regi quosdam palantes hostes, cum a satellitum turba equi celeritate desertus esset, solus ei per inmensas harenarum moles cursus comes fuit. Quod idem antea Philippus, frater eius, cum facere voluisset, inter manus regis expiraverat.*

παιδεύουσαν δὲ τοὺς νέους ἄρχεσθαι. ... ταύτης ἀφίησιν ὁ νόμος τῆς ἀνάγκης τοὺς ἐπὶ βασιλείᾳ τρεφομένους παῖδας.
(Plut. Ages. 1. 2-4)

Since Agis was the legitimate heir to the throne, it was expected that Agesilaus would spend his life as a private citizen, and he was therefore brought up according to the regular Spartan system of education, which was austere in its way of life, full of hardships, and designed to train young men to obey orders. ... The law exempts the heir-apparent to the throne from the necessity of undergoing this training
(I. Scott-Kilvert, tr.)

The education of aristocratic youths thus led them through stages of both real and mock servitude. As παῖδες/*pueri* (a term that implies both boys and slaves), as hypaspists and as Somatophylakes, they performed duties reserved in other societies for slaves and eunuchs. Like the Persian youths described in Xenophon's *Anabasis*, they learned 'both to rule and to be ruled' (1. 9. 4). The *agema* was the second stage of mock servitude, the King's 'Shield-bearers' or, to use the same medieval analogy from which we adopted the term Pages, 'the King's Squires'. Always at the King's side in battle and under his watchful eye, they were young, vigorous, fast troops. And what better bodyguard for the King than young men eager to exhibit their bravery in the hope of winning a promotion? It was in this capacity, as a member of the *agema* of the hypaspists, that Pausanias died in Philip's defence in the battle with the Illyrians; thus Peukestas protected Alexander in the town of the Mallians.[39] Best explained as members of the *agema* are the *promptissimi iuvenes* of Curtius' account: Charos, Alexandros (8. 11. 9 ff.), Nikanor and Hegesimachos (8. 13. 13-16), Philippos son of Agathokles (8. 2. 35-39; cf. Justin 15. 3. 12) — all men *ex sua cohorte*, but not Pages. If *ex sua cohorte* does not, in fact, refer to the Pages, then we have the words σωματοφύλακες and *cohors* used of young men in different age-classes, i.e., at successive stages of their careers.

Finally, there is an otherwise inexplicable passage in Curtius (7. 1. 18), which attests to the importance of the concept of σωματοφυλακία in the military and political education of the aristocrat. Amyntas son of Andromenes, before speaking in his own defence in 330 B.C., asked that the attire of an *armiger* (= σωματοφύλαξ) be *restored* to him: *ut*

---

[39]Diod. 16. 93. 6 (Pausanias); Arr. 6. 10. 2; Diod. 17. 99. 4; Curt. 9. 5. 14-17 (Peukestas). Curtius adds Timaeus (= Limnaios), also one of the hypaspists (Plut. *Alex.* 63. 5, 8). Diodoros calls Peukestas 'one of the hypaspists'; Arr. 6. 10. 2 says he held the sacred shield from Ilion, which was carried by a member of the hypaspists (Arr. 1. 11. 8).

habitus quoque redderetur armigeri. Now neither Amyntas nor any other son of Andromenes was ever known to have been Somatophylax of the King. But, in all likelihood, Amyntas had served as Page, then as a Royal Hypaspist of Philip II (cf. his brother Attalos, Diod. 16. 94. 4). The lance, which was given to him on the King's orders and which Amyntas held in his left hand (7. 1. 19) — presumably as a gesture that there was no hostile intent — was symbolic: with this weapon, and in his capacity as Royal Hypaspist, Amyntas had 'earned his stripes', proved his loyalty to the Argead house. The testimony of such a man could not be taken lightly.

5. The Commanders of the Royal Hypaspists

5. 1. Admetos

Literature. Berve ii 13, no. 24; Kirchner, *RE* i (1894), 380, no. 5; Tarn ii 151.

A Makedonian officer (perhaps commander of the *agema* of the hypaspists, so Tarn ii 151), and according to Diodoros (17. 45. 6) a man of great bodily strength,[40] Admetos commanded the ship carrying the hypaspists in the naval assault on Tyre (Arr. 2. 23. 2). He displayed great courage, fighting as he did in full view of Alexander, and, being the first to scale the wall, he was killed by a spear (Arr. 2. 23. 5). Diodoros (17. 45. 6) records his death — his skull was split by an axe — in a separate, unsuccessful, engagement and it may be that Arrian conflated the two episodes (Bosworth, *Arrian* i 253).

5. 2. Seleukos son of Antiochos

Literature. Berve ii 351-352, no. 700; Stähelin, *RE* ii.A (1923), 1208, no. 2; Bevan, *House of Seleucus* i 28-73; R. A. Hadley, 'Hieronymus of Cardia and Early Seleucid Mythology', *Historia* 18 (1969), 142-152; Mehl 1-28; Grainger 1-23; cf. Bengtson, *Herrschergestalten* 38-6.

---

[40]The regular hypaspists were recruited, not by region or social class, but for their bodily strength (cf. Theopompos, *FGrHist* 115 F348). This need not, however, mean that Admetos was not aristocratic: both Lysimachos (Justin 15. 3. 3-8) and Seleukos (App. *Syr.* 57 [294]) were noted for their physical strength, and they were undisputedly aristocratic. The name Admetos does occur in the Aiakid house of Epeiros (Thuc. 1. 136. 3; it appears also in 4th century Epeiros: see N. G. L. Hammond, *Epirus* [Oxford, 1967], 796), and Admetos may have been a kinsman of Arybbas and Neoptolemos, both of whom were involved in *somatophylakia*.

Seleukos, the son of Antiochos (Dittenberger, *OGIS* i 413; Justin 13. 4. 17; 15. 4. 3; Arr. *Succ.* 1a. 2)[41] and Laodike (Justin 15. 4. 3; Strabo 16. 2. 4 C750; App. *Syr.* 57; Steph. Byz. s.v. Λαοδίκεια), came, apparently, from Europos[42] in Makedonia. About the father we learn only that he was a prominent officer of Philip II (Justin 15. 4. 3), a claim which we have no reason to doubt. Stories of Laodike's liaisons with Apollo are creations of the Diadochic era and influenced in part by Olympias' alleged affair with Ammon, who visited her in the form of a snake.[43]

Nor is there unanimity about the date of Seleukos' birth. According to Eusebius Arm. (*ap*. Porphyry of Tyre, *FGrHist* 260 F32 §4), he was 75 years old when he died in 281/0. But this dating is suspicious, since it represents the middle ground between the dates of Appian and Justin, and makes Seleukos an exact contemporary of Alexander the Great (cf. Grainger 1). Appian (*Syr.* 63 [331]; 64 [342]) claims that he was 73 years old at the time of his death; Justin (17. 1. 10; cf. Oros. 3. 23. 59) makes him 77 at Korupedion, seven months before he was assassinated by Ptolemaios Keraunos (Justin 17. 2. 4). Appian's evidence would date Seleukos' birth to 354, which helps to explain why we hear nothing of his military career before 326. But both Appian and Justin compare Seleukos' age with that of Lysimachos (Appian: S. 73; L. 70; Justin: S. 77; L. 74), and the matter is confounded by Ps.-Lucian (*Macrob.* 11), who gives Lysimachos' age at his death as 80 and cites Hieronymos of Kardia as his source. Appian and Justin agree on one point: Seleukos was three years older than Lysimachos. Ps.-Lucian may indeed have rounded up Lysimachos' age to include him in a list of octogenarians, but this is more likely to have happened if

---

[41] Also Strabo 16. 2. 4 C749; Appian, *Syr.* 57 [295]; Oros. 3. 23. 10; Libanios 11. 93.

[42] See Steph. Byz. s.v. Ὠρωπός (cf. App. *Syr.* 57 [298]). Oropos is unknown in Makedonia; there are, however, at least two towns named Europos, one in Bottiaia, the other further north in Almopia. The former is preferred by Grainger 4 f.; cf. Hammond, *HMac* i 166 f.; id., *Macedonian State* 93. Connections with Europos make it more difficult to link Antiochos with the royal house of the Orestai and to see Seleukos as a kinsman of Perdikkas son of Orontes, whom he later served and assassinated. A relationship to Ptolemaios son of Seleukos, whose geographic origins are not recorded, is possible (Berve ii 441, Stemma xiii; Grainger 251, Stemma ii), but cannot be proved. Ptolemaios commanded the Tymphaian infantry at Issos, and this suggests that he too may have been Tymphaian, as was his successor Polyperchon son of Simmias. The existence of a sister, named Didymeia, who (according to Malalas 8, p. 198) had two sons, Nikanor and Nikomedes, is accepted by Berve (ii 142, no. 268); Grainger (3-4) is rightly sceptical.

[43] Justin 15. 4. 1-6. For stories of Olympias and Ammon see Plut. *Alex.* 2. 6; 3. 1-2; Justin 11. 11. 3; 12. 16. 2; Gellius, *NA* 13. 4. 1-3. Cf. also Mehl 5-6; Grainger 2-3; Hadley, *Historia* 18 (1969), 144, 152.

his true age approached 75 instead of 70. Furthermore, a birthdate of 352/1 would make Lysimachos' career much more difficult to explain. Hence a birthdate c. 358 for Seleukos appears to be most consistent with all the available evidence.

The early stages of Seleukos' career can be reconstructed with some degree of confidence. Born in Europos, near the Axios river, not long before Alexander himself, he came to Pella in the mid- to late 340s as a Page of Philip II and slightly older *syntrophos* of the Crown Prince. Hence Malalas (p. 203 Bonn) names Pella as Seleukos' birthplace, and Pausanias (1. 16. 1) says that he set out from Pella on the Asiatic expedition.[44] A member of Alexander's hetairoi, his aristocratic standing is virtually proved by his promotion — probably in 330 B.C. — to the command of the Royal Hypaspists. Hephaistion held this office at Gaugamela and must surely have relinquished it when he was appointed hipparch in 330, upon the death of Philotas (Arr. 3. 27. 4). When Seleukos appears as commander of the Royal Hypaspists at the Hydaspes (Arr. 5. 13. 1, 4), he must have held the office for almost four years. Certainly the fact that Seleukos coordinated the infantry (i.e., hypaspists, archers) against Poros (Arr. 5. 16. 3; Curt. 8. 14. 15 incorrectly substitutes Leonnatos for Seleukos in his account of the Hydaspes battle) suggests that by this time he had acquired considerable experience in command — primarily in the campaigns of Baktria and Sogdiana.

For the remainder of Seleukos' career during Alexander's lifetime there is no evidence of military activity, though he must certainly have played a prominent role in the Indus campaign and will most likely have accompanied the King to Gedrosia and the West.[45] At Sousa in 324 he received as his bride Apame, the daughter of Alexander's noble adversary, Spitamenes;[46] she was to become the mother of Antiochos I Soter, and Seleukos later named at least three cities for her.[47] Seleukos is mentioned in connection with perhaps three episodes in Babylonia — a sailing-trip on the marshes near Babylon

---

[44] App. *Syr.* 56 (284) mentions only Makedonia in general.

[45] Thus, too, his troops will have been clearly distinct from those of Antigenes, whom Mehl 15 correctly identifies as 'die kurz zuvor geschaffenen Argyraspiden'.

[46] Arr. 7. 4. 6; cf. Plut. *Demetr.* 31. 5; App. *Syr.* 57 [295-296]; Strabo 12. 8. 15 C578 (the daughter of Artabazos); cf. 16. 2. 4 C750; Pliny, *NH* 6. 132.

[47] App. *Syr.* 57 [295]; Livy 38. 13. 5 (calling Apame the 'sister' of Seleukos); Steph. Byz. s.v. Ἀπάμεια; cf. Strabo 16. 2. 4 C750. If there is any significance in the fact that Apame was the only bride from the Northeast, besides Alexander's wife Rhoxane (as Mehl 18 points out), cannot be determined. At any rate, we do not know the names of all the brides of prominent hetairoi; there may have been others from Baktria and Sogdiana.

(Arr. 7. 22. 5; App. *Syr.* 56 [288-289]); the dinner-party of Medeios the Thessalian (Ps.-Kall. 3. 31. 8?); and the visit to the temple of Sarapis (Arr. 7. 26. 2; Plut. *Alex.* 76. 9) — all associated with the King's death.

In the first of these episodes, Seleukos recovered Alexander's diadem, which had been blown off his head and had settled on some reeds near the tombs of Assyrian kings. In order to keep it dry, Seleukos placed the diadem on his head while he swam back to the King's ship. The actions were regarded as ominous: the diadem, landing near the tombs, foretold the King's death; placed on Seleukos' head, it presaged the kingship of the bearer. But, according to Aristoboulos (*FGrHist* 139 F55 = Arr. 7. 22. 5), it was a Phoinikian sailor and not Seleukos who recovered the diadem, and Justin 15. 3. 13-14 tells a similar story about Lysimachos' future kingship. Such stories circulated in the Diadochic age, almost certainly after 307/6, to support the regal pretensions of one Successor or another. We may place very little faith in their historicity.

That Seleukos attended the dinner-party of Medeios, at which Alexander became fatally ill, may be true. That he was involved in a plot to poison the King is, however, unlikely. To begin with, the sources do not explicitly name him: Ps.-Kallisthenes (3. 31. 8) includes in the list of guests a certain ... ὁ Εὐρώπιος, whom some scholars would identify with Seleukos — that is, Σέλευκος ὁ Εὐρώπιος ('Seleukos the Europian'). But the story of Alexander's final days, which somehow found its way into many manuscripts of the *Alexander Romance*, is at best political propaganda and at worst literary fiction.[48]

The story that Seleukos (accompanied by Peithon, Attalos, Menidas, Demophon, Peukestas and Kleomenes) slept in the temple of Sarapis in Babylon in the hope that Alexander's health might improve (Arr. 7. 26. 2; Plut. *Alex.* 76. 9) has also been challenged by scholars, since the cult of Sarapis is generally thought to have been instituted by Ptolemy I in Egypt.[49] Grainger (218 f.) may be right in assigning this story to the propaganda wars of the Diadochoi as well.

In the factional strife that broke out after Alexander's death in June 323, Seleukos is scarcely mentioned. He is referred to once as a marshal of the second rank: the most powerful leaders in Babylon were Perdikkas, Leonnatos, and Ptolemy; with them, but clearly of lesser importance, were Lysimachos, Aristonous, Peithon, Seleukos and Eumenes (Arr. *Succ.* 1a. 2). Furthermore, some scholars have seen in Seleukos' failure to obtain a satrapy in the Babylonian settlement another indication of the man's inferior status. But Seleukos was clearly a man whom Perdikkas trusted — perhaps wrongly, as events

---

[48]For Seleukos' role see Heckel, *LDT* 40 f., 66.
[49]For a discussion of modern views see Hamilton, *PA* 212 f.

would show. When Perdikkas had eliminated his rival Meleagros and distributed the satrapies, he took steps to secure for himself the 'guardianship' of (first) Philip III Arrhidiaos and (later) Alexander IV. Hence he named Seleukos his second-in-command (at least in the military sphere: *summus castrorum tribunatus*, Justin 13. 4. 17), assigning to him 'the hipparchy of the Companions, which was the most distinguished' (Diod. 18. 3. 4), namely the 'first hipparchy' or 'Hephaistion's chiliarchy' (Arr. 7. 14. 10), which Perdikkas himself had once commanded. As such, he was, in theory, second only to Perdikkas who exercised power 'in the name of the Kings'. But this power depended on Perdikkas' ability to preserve the integrity of Alexander's empire and to impose the 'Royal Will' on the satraps and the *strategos* of Europe. In this endeavour, Perdikkas failed miserably, only to be confronted by a mutiny of his officers — among them Antigenes, Peithon and Seleukos — who murdered him in his tent as the Royal Army was encamped near Memphis (Nepos, *Eum.* 5. 1; cf. Arr. *Succ.* 1. 28, 35; Diod. 18. 33. 2 ff.; Paus. 1. 6. 3; Strabo 17. 1. 8 C794; *Diadochoi Chronicle*, BM 34660, col. 4). For Seleukos, Perdikkas' experiences with the satraps was a valuable lesson. In the future, he too would choose satrapal rank instead of accepting service with the Royal Army in a futile attempt to assert the authority of the Kings.

6. Background and Organisation of the Seven

Literature. W. Heckel, 'The Somatophylakes of Alexander the Great: Some Thoughts', *Historia* 27 (1978), 224-228; id., '*IG* ii^2 562 and the Status of Alexander IV', *ZPE* 40 (1980), 249-250; Billows, *Antigonos* 421-423.

The Somatophylakes, or Seven, create fewer problems and have been much discussed. In the reign of Philip II, their sole purpose may have been to guard the King at the Court, but it must be pointed out that we know so little about the office under Philip that even this is merely an inference drawn from the evidence of the Alexander-historians. Arrian (6. 28. 4) provides the only complete list of Somatophylakes in Alexander's lifetime: εἶναι δὲ αὐτῷ ἑπτὰ εἰς τότε σωματοφύλακας, Λεοννάτον Ἀντέου, Ἡφαιστίωνα τὸν Ἀμύντορος, Λυσίμαχον Ἀγαθοκλέους, Ἀριστόνουν Πεισαίου, τούτους μὲν Πελλαίους, Περδίκκαν δὲ Ὀρόντου ἐκ τῆς Ὀρεστίδος, Πτολεμαῖον δὲ Λάγου καὶ Πείθωνα Κρατεύα Ἐορδαίους· ὄγδοον δὲ προσγενέσθαι αὐτοῖς Πευκέσταν τὸν Ἀλεξάνδρου ὑπερασπίσαντα. Their number was fixed, already in Philip's time, at seven — Peukestas was an exceptional, and temporary, eighth — and may have aimed at some kind of regional representation. Berve (i 27) has collected a list of no fewer than fourteen individuals whom he thought to have held the office during Alexander's lifetime. Nevertheless, although the unit underwent numerous changes in personnel, it may still be possible to reconstruct the list of the seven who held office at the time of Philip's death.

Arybbas, Balakros and Demetrios appear to have been members of the unit in 336, when Alexander came to the throne. Balakros was replaced by Menes, after the battle of Issos (Arr. 2. 12. 2); Menes, in turn, by Perdikkas in late 331 (Arr. 3. 16. 9: Menes became hyparch of Syria, Phoinikia, Kilikia; cf. Curt. 6. 8. 17, calling Perdikkas an *armiger* in 330, which can only mean one of the Seven[50]). Arybbas at his death was replaced by Leonnatos (Arr. 3. 5. 5), one of Alexander's *syntrophoi*. Demetrios, allegedly a member of Dimnos' conspiracy, was removed from office in the land of the Ariaspians and replaced with Ptolemy son of Lagos (Arr. 3. 27. 5), an hetairos of the King. Hephaistion, it seems, replaced Ptolemaios ὁ σωματοφύλαξ ὁ βασιλικός (Arr. 1. 22. 4; cf. 1. 22. 7), who was killed at Halikarnassos and had probably been one of Philip's Bodyguards. Alexander's appointments to the Seven show that he was concerned to replace Philip's men with his own *syntrophoi* or with others whom he felt he could trust: hence we recognise among the newly-appointed Somatophylakes three men who were raised with the Crown Prince — Hephaistion, Leonnatos, Perdikkas — and another, Ptolemy (cf. Arr. 3. 6. 5-6), who, as an ἑταῖρος of Alexander, was banished in 336. If it was, indeed, Alexander's policy to bring his own men into the Seven, then it is not surprising to find Hephaistion as his first appointee. That Ptolemaios, whom Hephaistion replaced, was the first attested member of the Seven to command a division of the army,[51] and we should have no difficulty in seeing Hephaistion as both Somatophylax and commander of the σωματοφύλακες (sc. βασιλικοί), that is, of the ἄγημα τῶν ὑπασπιστῶν (thus Diod. 17. 61. 3). About Menes we know too little to reach any firm conclusions. His appointment in late 333, falling between the promotions of Hephaistion and Leonnatos, may have been political: like Alexander's decision to split the command of the Companion Cavalry between Hephaistion and the more senior Kleitos, Menes' appointment suggests that Alexander could not move too quickly in transforming the hierarchy of command, or, at least, that he did not want to be perceived as doing so.

---

[50]Perdikkas, as a taxiarch from at least 335 onwards, could not have been a hypaspist in 330 B.C. The last reference to the infantry-taxis of Perdikkas comes in the account of the battle at the Persian Gates (Arr. 3. 18. 5), and it may be that Alexander delayed replacing Menes, whom he sent to the coast from Sousa, until he reached Persepolis.

[51]τοῖς δὲ κατὰ τὸ Τρίπυλον ἐκδραμοῦσιν ἀπήντα Πτολεμαῖος ὁ σωματοφύλαξ ὁ βασιλικός, τήν τε Ἀδαίου καὶ Τιμάνδρου ἅμα οἱ τάξιν ἄγων καὶ ἔστιν οὓς τῶν ψιλῶν (Arr. 1. 22. 4).

The appointments of Aristonous, Peithon and Lysimachos are problematical: since we do not know whom they replaced, it may well be that they were appointed originally by Philip II. Lysimachos was born between 362/1 (Ps.-Lucian, *Macrob.* 11) and 356/5 B.C. (Justin 17. 1. 10) and conspicuous for his strength and courage, qualities which may have recommended him to Philip in the first place (cf. Justin 15. 3. 7-8; Theopompos, *FGrHist* 115 F348). The ages of Peithon and Aristonous are not recorded. Certainly we know of no personal connections between any of these three and Alexander, nor did they distinguish themselves in such a way as to warrant promotion during Alexander's reign.

By October 324, the importance of the unit had begun to decline: the position left vacant by Hephaistion's death was not filled; Peukestas' exceptional office was honorary, and he soon departed to the satrapy of Persis; and, of the Somatophylakes who survived Alexander, only Aristonous remained in Babylon with Perdikkas and the Kings. There were no Somatophylakes of the Kings until the settlement at Triparadeisos (320), when Antipatros assigned four of them to Philip III: Autodikos, Amyntas, Alexandros and Ptolemaios (Arr. *Succ.* 1. 38). *IG* ii² 561, a decree of Stratokles (307-301 B.C.) honouring Philippos, Iolaos and (possibly) a third individual, whose name has been lost, suggests that Alexander IV had been assigned three Somatophylakes, bringing the combined total to seven (cf. Heckel, *ZPE* 40 [1980], 249 f., and nos. 5. 1-2 below).

B. THE CAREERS OF THE SOMATOPHYLAKES

1. Somatophylakes appointed in 336 or before

1. 1. Ptolemaios ὁ σωματοφύλαξ ὁ βασιλικός

Literature. Berve ii 337, no. 672.

Ptolemaios, undoubtedly of noble Makedonian descent, may have been the father of Ptolemaios, Somatophylax of Philip III (Arr. *Succ.* 1. 38; Dittenberger, *Syll.* 332, 25, records a gift of land near Spartolos made by Alexander to 'Ptolemaios father of Ptolemaios' [Πτολεμαίωι τῶι πατρὶ τῶι Πτολεμαίου], and confirmed by Kassandros).[52] In 334, Ptolemaios commanded two *taxeis* of hypaspists (those of Addaios and Timandros: see vi 2. 1-2) in the skirmish with those defenders who

---

[52]But see the comments of Billows, *Antigonos* 425-430, nos. 99, 100, and the discussion of Ptolemaios son of Ptolemaios (below).

had made a sortie from the Tripylon at Halikarnassos (Arr. 1. 22. 4 ff.). Ptolemaios himself was killed in the engagement (Arr. 1. 22. 7).

1. 2. Balakros son of Nikanor

Literature. Berve ii 100-101, no. 200; Kaerst, *RE* ii (1896), 2816, no. 1; Baumbach 45, 65, 69; H. von Aulock, 'Die Prägung des Balakros in Kilikien', *JNG* 14 (1964), 79-82; W. Heckel, 'A Grandson of Antipatros at Delos', *ZPE* 70 (1987) 161 f.; id., 'The Granddaughters of Iolaus', *Classicum* 15 (1989), 33; E. Badian, 'Two Postscripts on the Marriage of Phila and Balacrus', *ZPE* 73 (1988), 116 ff.

Balakros[53] son of Nikanor (Arr. 2. 12. 2; Diod. 18. 22. 1) was the father of Nikanor (Harpokration s.v. Νικάνωρ)[54] and possibly of Philippos (Berve ii 383-384, no. 778; Curt. 4. 13. 28; Diod. 17. 57. 3). Born, in all likelihood, in the 380s, he appears to have been politically allied with Antipatros, whose daughter he married (Anton. Diog. *ap.* Phot. *Bibl.* 166, p. 111a-b), perhaps just before the Asiatic campaign. Antipatros son of Balagros, who appears in Delian inscriptions (*IG* xi.2. 287b, 57; 161, 85), was probably their son (Heckel, *ZPE* 70 [1987], 161-162; cf. Badian, *ZPE* 73 [1988], 116-118). Balakros had apparently been a Somatophylax of Philip II, unless he was appointed at the time of Alexander's accession, and served Alexander in that capacity until shortly after the battle of Issos, when he was named satrap of Kilikia (Arr. 2. 12. 2; cf. Diod. 18. 22. 1). He is almost certainly the Balakros of Curt. 4. 5. 13 (not Berve's no. 203), who in 332 joined with Antigonos and Kalas — satraps of Phrygia and Hellespontine Phrygia respectively — in completing the conquest of Asia Minor.[55] As satrap he also controlled finances and minted coins bearing at first his own name, later merely the letter B (von Aulock); perhaps, as Bosworth suggests, he was 'primarily responsible for the payment of the army during the long siege of Tyre' (*Conquest and Empire* 232).[56] Late in Alexander's reign — shortly before Harpalos' arrival at Tarsos — Balakros was killed in an

---

[53]Arrian and Diodoros write 'Balakros'; but the epigraphic form 'Balagros' has the support of Antonios Diogenes (*ap.* Phot. p. 111a-b) and Curt. 4. 13. 28 where 'Phaligrus' appears to be a corruption of Philippus Balagri.

[54]Perhaps Alexander's navarch in 334 (Berve ii 275, no. 555) or the later governor of Alexandreia in Parapamisadai (Arr. 4. 22. 5, 28. 6; Berve ii 275-276, no. 556); though the two may be identical.

[55]Schachermeyr 212: 'Kilikien wurde ... dem Leibwächter Balakros als Satrapie anvertraut. Der mochte auch die Befriedung der Taurosstämme fortsetzen und hierin mit Antigonos zusammenwirken.' Cf. also Briant 70; Bosworth, *Arrian* i 219; id., *CQ* 24 (1974), 58 f; and Billows, *Antigonos* 44-45. I see no reason to assume that Balakros was killed in this campaign.

[56]Hence also the reference to Tyre in Anton. Diog. *ap.* Phot. p.111a-b.

attempt to quell an insurrection by the Isaurians and Larandians (Diod. 18. 22. 1).[57]

1. 3. Arybbas

Literature. Berve ii 85, no. 156; Hoffmann 176-177; Kaerst, *RE* ii (1896), 1497, no. 2.

The name suggests Epeirot origin: Arybbas may even have been a kinsman of Philip's wife Olympias (Berve ii 85).[58] He appears to have been an appointee of Philip II, who may have been aiming at geographical representation amongst the Somatophylakes. Arybbas accompanied Alexander as far as Egypt, where in the winter of 332/1 he died of illness and was replaced by Leonnatos (Arr. 3. 5. 5).

1. 4. Demetrios

Literature. Berve ii 135, no. 260; Kirchner, *RE* iv (1901), 2768, no. 24; Bosworth, *Arrian* i 366 f.

Demetrios' family background is unknown, and the temptation to identify him with the brother of Antigonos Monophthalmos must be resisted: it is highly unlikely that the sources would have been silent about the relationship, considering Demetrios' alleged involvement in Dimnos' conspiracy (Arr. 3. 27. 5; Curt. 6. 7. 15), even more so if Curtius is correct in suggesting that Demetrios played a major role in the organisation of the plot (Curt. 6. 11. 37). Furthermore, Plutarch (*Demetr.* 2. 1) claims that Demetrios Poliorketes (born in 337/6) was named after his uncle. Since he was the elder of Antigonos' sons, this suggests strongly that the honour was bestowed upon the elder Demetrios posthumously, that is, that Antigonos' brother died before 337/6. Plutarch (*ibid.*) adds that there were rumours that Antigonos married Demetrios' mother Stratonike, who had previously been married to his brother, the father of Poliorketes. But here too the sources' failure to mention that Poliorketes' natural father had been executed for conspiring against Alexander creates a deafening silence.

---

[57] For this view, cf. Higgins, *Athenaeum* 58 (1980), 150; Bosworth, *Arrian* i 219 argues for an earlier date, perhaps 'associated with Antigonus' campaigns in Lycaonia during 332 (Curt. iv 5. 13).'

[58] Olympias' brother was brought up at the Court, perhaps as a Page (Justin 8. 6. 4-8), and Alexander's 'royal tutor', Leonidas (Berve ii 235-236, no. 469), was a relative of Olympias as well (Plut. *Alex.* 5. 7). The form of the name in Arrian is Arrybas (on which see Hoffmann 176 f.).

Who Demetrios the Somatophylax was cannot be determined. Arrian (3. 27. 5) claims that Alexander deposed him from office in the land of the Ariaspians, 'suspecting that he had a share in Philotas' conspiracy' (ὑποπτεύσας μετασχεῖν Φιλώτᾳ τῆς ἐπιβουλῆς). Curtius includes his name in the list of conspirators given by Dimnos to his lover Nikomachos (6. 7. 15). Despite his vigorous defence (Curt. 6. 11. 35), he was indicted by a second witness ('Calis': Curt. 6. 11. 37) and executed along with the others (Curt. 6. 11. 38). It is suspicious, however, that Demetrios (the only individual of note to be linked with Dimnos' plot) is given very little attention by Alexander or by the sources. It appears that Demetrios was removed from office, as Arrian says, on a mere suspicion, that his only crime was friendship with Philotas. Curtius' introduction of 'Calis' (not named in 6. 7. 15) as Demetrios' accomplice, suggests contamination from a second source. The original version (of Kleitarchos?) may not have named him at all.[59] Ptolemy son of Lagos replaced him as Somatophylax.

2. Somatophylakes appointed by Alexander III

During the course of his Asiatic campaign, Alexander is known to have appointed at least six Somatophylakes: Hephaistion, Leonnatos, Perdikkas, Ptolemy, Menes, and Peukestas. Only the last two are dealt with here. The others have separate studies devoted to them.[60]

2. 1. Menes son of Dionysios

Literature. Berve ii 257, no. 507; Julien 62, n.2; Lehmann-Haupt, 'Satrap' 157 f.; Brunt, *Arrian* i 278-279, n.11; A. B. Bosworth, 'The Government of Syria under Alexander the Great', *CQ* 24 (1974), 59-60; id., *Arrian* i 319; D. R. Shackleton-Bailey, '*Curtiana*', *CQ* 31 (1981), 176.

Menes son of Dionysios came from Pella (Diod. 17. 64. 5) and was appointed Somatophylax to replace Balakros son of Nikanor, to whom Alexander had entrusted the satrapy of Kilikia in late 333 B.C. (Arr. 2. 12. 2). As Somatophylax he did nothing worthy of record, nor did he hold the office long: towards the end of 331, when the army reached Sousa, he was appointed hyparch of Phoinikia, Syria and Kilikia (Arr. 3. 16. 9; cf. Diod. 17. 64. 5; Curt. 5. 1. 43). Menes' position is not clear and no explanation can be entirely satisfactory. Berve's assumption that he controlled finances, replacing Koiranos of Beroia, is

---

[59]Bosworth (*Arrian* i 366 f.) thinks that Demetrios was executed for his part in Dimnos' conspiracy, and that Ptolemy may have been appointed, in the land of the Ariaspians, to an office which had been vacant for some time.

[60]Hephaistion (**ii 2**); Leonnatos (**ii 3**); Perdikkas (**ii 5**); Ptolemy (**iv 3**).

rejected for want of evidence by Brunt (*Arrian* i 278, n.11). Bosworth thinks Menes replaced Balakros as satrap of Kilikia, assuming control of Syria and Phoinikia as well (*Arrian* i 319; cf. *CQ* 24 [1974], 59-60), but this would place Balakros' death in 332 or 331 (see 1. 2 above).

It is more likely that Alexander employed Menes temporarily as overseer of the area, that the existing satraps and financial officers were responsible to him. Thus the Vulgate refers to Menes and Apollodoros as στρατηγοὺς τῆς τε Βαβυλῶνος καὶ τῶν σατραπειῶν μέχρι Κιλικίας (Diod. 17. 64. 5; cf. Curt. 5. 1. 43, as emended by Shackleton-Bailey, *CQ* 31 [1981], 176). Considering the political situation in Europe and the need to press eastwards against Dareios, Alexander found it necessary to entrust the coastal region to a single individual. Hence he sent Menes to the coast with 3000 talents (Arr. 3. 16. 9; Curt. 5. 1. 43 says 1000), which were to be transported to Antipatros for use in the war with Agis III. It was also his responsibility to see that the discharged Greek veterans found their way back to Europe (Arr. 3. 19. 6).[61] Coins minted in the region bearing the mark M will also belong to the time of Menes' coordination of affairs in this region (see Berve ii 257, following Babelon, *Les Perses Achéménides* LI). Menes' disappearance from the sources, with no indication of his successor, suggests that his position was intended to be temporary.[62]

2. 2. Peukestas son of Alexandros

Literature. Berve ii 318-319, no. 634; id., *RE* xix (1938), s.v., no. 1; A. Momigliano, 'Peucesta', *RFIC* 59 (1931) 245 f.; Hornblower, *Hieronymus,* passim; K. Buraselis, *Das hellenistische Makedonien und die Ägäis* (Munich, 1982), 21, n.70; R. D. Milns, 'A Note on Diodorus and Macedonian Military Terminology in Book XVII', *Historia* 31 (1982), 123 ff.; Billows, *Antigonos* 417-418, no. 90; id., 'Anatolian Dynasts: The Case of the Macedonian Eupolemos in Karia', *CA* 8 (1989), 180, 185.

A resident of Mieza, where Alexander and the Pages were educated by Aristotle, Peukestas son of Alexandros (Arr. *Ind.* 18. 6; cf. *Succ.* 1. 38) was born most likely in the early 350s; Amyntas, a Somatophylax of Philip III Arrhidaios in 320, was his brother (Arr. *Succ.* 1. 38; cf. Berve ii 26, no. 56; see also 4. 2 below). He is first mentioned as a trierarch of the Hydaspes fleet (Arr. *Ind.* 18. 6), an indication of his high standing and financial status. Not much later, in the Mallian campaign, he was

---

[61]These were brought by Epokillos son of Polyeides from Ekbatana (Arr. 3. 19. 5-6).

[62]Somewhat like the position of the Younger Kyros during the last stages of the Peloponnesian war (Xenophon, *Anab.* 1. 1. 2; *HG* 1. 4. 3).

seriously wounded saving the King's life (Curt. 9. 5. 14-18; Arr. 6. 9. 3 - 10. 1-2; 6. 11. 7-8; 6. 28. 4; *Ind.* 19. 8; Diod. 17. 99. 4; Plut. *Alex.* 63. 5; cf. Ps.-Kall. 3. 4. 14-15; *Itiner. Al.* 115). About this most memorable event in Peukestas' career (cf. Diod. 19. 14. 4-5) there is no dispute in the ancient sources, but the question of Peukestas' rank must be addressed.

In his account of the Mallian campaign, Diodoros calls Peukestas εἷς τῶν ὑπασπιστῶν (17. 99. 4), a designation which is undoubtedly correct. Modern misconceptions about the hypaspists have caused unnecessary difficulties. Milns (*Historia* 31 [1982], 123) writes: 'Peucestas, the bearer of the Sacred Shield and soon to be appointed as one of the σωματοφύλακες ... and then satrap of the vital satrapy of Persis ..., was certainly not a junior or middle-ranking hypaspist-officer at the time of the Malli town incident and in all probability was neither the archihypaspist ... nor a chiliarch. It is thus unlikely that he had any association at all with the hypaspists at this time.'

But the evidence points to this very thing. Plutarch (*Alex.* 63. 5, 8) agrees with Diodoros (17. 99. 4) in calling Peukestas a hypaspist; Arrian (6. 9. 3) claims he carried the Sacred Shield from Ilion, having stated earlier (1. 11. 7-8) that the arms taken by the Makedonians from the Temple of Athena at Troy were 'carried before them by the hypaspists'. And Bosworth appears to be on the right track when he writes: 'It seems that there was a small group of ἑταῖροι who acted as shield-bearers for the king, a body distinct from the corps of hypaspists' (*Arrian* i 102). Furthermore, we might ask in what capacity Peukestas accompanied the King into the town of the Mallians. The others who were wounded or killed while defending Alexander were Leonnatos and Aristonous (both members of the Seven), along with Habreas and Limnaios. But Limnaios, who is otherwise unknown, appears only in the Vulgate and in place of Habreas, a 'double pay man' (διμοιρίτης) and, apparently, a regular hypaspist. Now Alexander normally took with him the Agrianes, the *agema* and some of the hypaspists, and in this particular incident, the most vigorous of members of the last two units, climbing different ladders, were the first to enter the city with him. Thus, it seems that Peukestas was the foremost of the Royal Hypaspists; he distinguished himself and won a promotion.

As a reward for his bravery, Alexander made him an exceptional eighth Bodyguard (Arr. 6. 28. 4; cf. 7. 5. 4: he awarded him a golden crown at Sousa in 324) and very soon thereafter assigned him the satrapy of Persis (Arr. 6. 30. 2; cf. Diod. 19. 14. 4-5), which Peukestas administered with such zeal that he adopted Persian dress and became the first Makedonian of record to learn the Persian language (Arr. 6. 30.

3). This conduct, though pleasing to Alexander, earned the disapproval of his countrymen (Arr. 7. 6. 3; cf. 7. 23. 3).[63]

June 323 found Peukestas in Babylon, whither he had brought 20,000 Persian archers and slingers, as well as recruits from the Kossaians and Tapourians (Arr. 7. 23. 1; cf. Diod. 17. 110. 2). He is said to have attended the drinking-party hosted by Medeios of Larisa, at which the King became fatally ill; indeed, it is alleged that he was involved in a conspiracy to poison the King (Ps.-Kall. 3. 31. 8; cf. Heckel, *LDT* 38 f.; 74 f.). Along with Attalos, Peithon, Seleukos and others, Peukestas spent the night in the temple of Sarapis,[64] inquiring about the health of Alexander (Arr. 7. 26. 2). Little is known about Peukestas in the years between Alexander's death and the settlement of Triparadeisos, where in 320 his brother, Amyntas, was appointed Somatophylax of Philip III (Arr. *Succ.* 1. 38). He himself was confirmed as satrap of Persis (at Babylon: Diod. 18. 3. 3; Justin 13. 4. 23; Arr. *Succ.* 1b. 6; cf. *LM* 121; at Triparadeisos: Diod. 18. 39. 6; Arr. *Succ.* 1. 35).

Peukestas' immense popularity in the east and the importance of his satrapy made him a natural leader of the resistance to Peithon, who in 317 tried to revive for himself the position of στρατηγὸς τῶν ἄνω σατραπειῶν, which he had held temporarily under Perdikkas in 323/2 (Diod. 19. 14. 1-3). And he had gathered, in addition to his own forces,[65] contingents led by the satraps Tlepolemos, Stasandros and Sibyrtios; Oxyartes sent troops under the care of Androbazos, and Eudamos came from India (Diod. 19. 14. 6-8). It was this army, assembled to oppose Peithon, that Eumenes sought to bring under his own control in Sousiana (Diod. 19. 15. 1; Plut. *Eum.* 13. 9). But the question of leadership went beyond the rivalry of the respective commanders (Nepos, *Eum.* 7. 1); the division of sentiment appears to have followed racial lines (Diod. 19. 15. 1; cf. Plut. *Eum.* 14. 8 ff.). Peukestas, it appears, did not formally acknowledge Eumenes' leadership, but accepted for the time a joint command in the name of Alexander the Great, a face-saving proposal. Fear of Antigonos, who threatened to remove him from his satrapy and perhaps end his life, induced Peukestas to throw in his lot with Eumenes.[66] But, upon reaching his home province, Peukestas attempted to gain the supreme command through an extravagant show of pomp (Diod. 19. 21. 2 - 23. 1;

---

[63]Diod. 19. 14. 5 says that Peukestas received Alexander's *permission* to adopt Persian dress.

[64]But see Grainger 218 f., and Fraser, *Opuscula Atheniensia* 7 (1967), 23-45.

[65]10,000 Persian archers and slingers; 3000 Makedonian-style infantrymen; 600 Greek and Thrakian cavalry, and 400 Persian horsemen (Diod. 19. 14. 5).

[66]Diod. 19. 17. 5. Reluctantly, Peukestas summoned 10,000 archers from Persia (Diod. 19. 17. 4-6)

cf. Plut. *Eum.* 14. 5), which might have succeeded, had not Eumenes resorted to deception in order to win back the troops. Producing forged letters, purportedly from the Armenian satrap Orontas, Eumenes announced that Olympias had expelled Kassandros from Makedonia and placed Alexander IV on the throne; Polyperchon, the letter alleged, was approaching Kappadokia in order to attack Antigonos from the west (Diod. 19. 23. 2-3; Polyainos 4. 8. 3).

Rivalry between Eumenes and Peukestas was intense (Nepos, *Eum.* 7. 1), despite their friendship in Alexander's lifetime (Plut. *Eum.* 13. 9): Eumenes further undermined Peukestas' authority by bringing charges against the latter's friend Sibyrtios (Diod. 19. 23. 4), and, when he fled, Eumenes led Peukestas on with idle promises (Diod. 19. 24. 1). In the end, however, it was the will of the Makedonian element, almost certainly the Argyraspids, that prevailed and Eumenes, despite an illness contracted in Persia (Diod. 19. 24. 6; Plut. *Eum.* 14. 6), was hailed as the commander-in-chief. In Paraitakene, Peukestas' subordinate position may be seen in the fact that Eumenes had an *agema* of horsemen (300 strong), whereas a corresponding *agema* was shared by Peukestas and Antigenes (Diod. 19. 28. 3).

Perhaps disillusionment affected his performance. Peukestas appears now to have been seeking a pretext for breaking with Eumenes and his ally Antigenes. The dispersal of the troops in winter quarters in Media might have facilitated a withdrawal. But the army of Antigonos had sought to catch the enemy disunited, only to be forced by the weather to make its size and presence known. Native spies on dromedaries (Diod. 19. 37. 6) reported the presence of Antigonos' army, prompting Peukestas to contemplate flight (Plut. *Eum.* 15. 7-8; Diod. 19. 38. 1). Nevertheless, he remained with Eumenes. But the accounts, deriving from Hieronymos (Hornblower, *Hieronymus* 151), are hostile to Peukestas and depict him as overcome by fear (παντάπασιν ἔκφρων ὑπὸ δέους γενόμενος, Plut. *Eum.* 15. 8; cf. Diod. 19. 38. 1); the defeat at Gabiene is attributed to his poor showing in the cavalry engagement (Plut. *Eum.* 16. 9; Diod. 19. 42. 4, 43. 2-3 and esp. 19. 43. 5). After the battle, when it was learned that Antigonos had captured the baggage-camp and was offering to restore their property to those who defected, Peukestas and his Persian force abandoned Eumenes, though only after the desertion of the Argyraspids had sealed his fate (Polyainos 4. 6. 13). That Peukestas betrayed his allies during the battle is almost certainly not the case, for the hostile sources would not have failed to bring this charge against him both through vindictiveness and to exculpate Eumenes.

He himself eluded the fate of the other prominent officers who had surrendered, perhaps through the intervention of Sibyrtios.[67] Antigonos removed him from his satrapy but kept him in his entourage until he returned to Asia Minor, where Peukestas' name resurfaces on an inscription from Karian Theangela.[68] Phylarchos (*ap*. Athen. 14. 614f = *FGrHist* 81 F12) suggests that Peukestas was still active at the Court of Demetrios Poliorketes at some time after the battle of Ipsos. What became of him, we do not know.

3. Problematic Appointments: Lysimachos, Peithon, Aristonous

3. 1. Lysimachos son of Agathokles

Literature. Berve ii 239-241, no. 480; Hoffmann 171-172; Geyer, *RE* xiv.1 (1928), 1, no. 1; Kornemann 255; W. Hünerwadel, 'Forschungen zur Geschichte Königs Lysimachos von Thrakien' (Diss. Zürich, 1910); I. L. Merker, 'Lysimachos — Thessalian or Macedonian?' *Chiron* 9 (1979), 31-36; W. Heckel, 'The Early Career of Lysimachos', *Klio* 64 (1982), 373-381; Sandberger 138 ff., no. 49.

Concerning Lysimachos' career before 323, there are a few undisputed facts: he was the son of a certain Agathokles, and the brother of Philippos (Berve, no. 774) and Autodikos (no. 187), though a third brother, Alkimachos (no. 47), is not positively identified; he was Somatophylax (Arr. 6. 28. 4) and, as such, was wounded near Sangala in India (Arr. 5. 24. 5) and later crowned at Sousa (Arr. 7. 5. 6); he was present at Alexander's death, but in the succession of 323 B.C. he appears to have been inferior to the great generals;[69] he received Thrake as his satrapy. The rest is far from certain.

First there is the matter of Lysimachos' origin: was he Makedonian or Thessalian? Arrian (*Ind*. 18. 3) terms him Pellaian, perhaps merely indicating that he was raised at the court of Philip II;[70] Plutarch (*Demetr*. 44. 6) calls him ὁμόφυλος with Demetrios Poliorketes;[71] hence Justin (15. 3. 1): *inlustri quidem Macedoniae loco*

---

[67] For their fates see Diod. 19. 44. 1. Sibyrtios: Diod. 19. 23. 4 (Πευκέστου μάλιστα φίλος); 19. 47. 3 (on good terms with Antigonos: εὖ διακείμενον τὰ πρὸς αὐτόν); see also Billows, *Antigonos* 432 f., no. 106.

[68] Robert, *Collection Froehner* 1: *Inscriptions Grecques* (1936) no. 52; *Staatsv*. iii 249; Momigliano, *RFIC* 59 (1931), 245 f.; Buraselis 21, n.70; Billows, *CA* 8 (1989), 180.

[69] Arr. *Succ*. 1a. 2: Perdikkas, Leonnatos and Ptolemy are described as οἱ μέγιστοι τῶν ἱππέων καὶ τῶν ἡγεμόνων, whereas Lysimachos, Aristonous, Peithon, Seleukos and Eumenes belong to the group οἱ μετ' ἐκείνους.

[70] Cf. Leonnatos, who was Lynkestian but raised at Pella.

[71] Plutarch refers to the division of Makedonia between the Makedonian Lysimachos and the foreigner Pyrrhos.

natus (cf. Paus. 1. 9. 5). Porphyry of Tyre (*ap.* Euseb. Arm. = *FGrHist* 260 F3 §8), however, claims that Lysimachos was a Thessalian from Krannon, and F. Geyer (*RE* xiv.1 [1928], 1) identifies him with the son of that Agathokles whom Theopompos (*ap.* Athen. 6. 259f - 260a = *FGrHist* 115 F81) describes as Ἀγαθοκλέα δοῦλον γενόμενον καὶ τῶν ἐκ Θεσσαλίας πενεστῶν Φίλιππος μέγα παρ' αὐτῷ δυνάμενον διὰ τὴν κολακείαν. Berve (ii 239) rejects this identification; Hünerwadel (13) observes that, amid the political and military turmoil of the Diadochic age, no charge was ever brought against Lysimachos concerning his alleged Thessalian origin or his father's *kolakeia*. Now Theopompos' scandalous characterisation of Agathokles inspires little confidence: he did not speak highly of Thessalians who supported Philip of Makedon;[72] Agathokles' humble origins can be traced to the historian's malice. We may assume that he was granted Makedonian citizenship, and that his sons, like those of Philip's other hetairoi, were educated at the Court in Pella.[73] Hence, Lysimachos, Philippos and Autodikos all appear to have been involved in σωματοφυλακία.

Alkimachos, however, is not explicitly identified as Lysimachos' brother. But, given the high standing of other members of the family, it appears likely he was the son of the same Agathokles, perhaps even the eldest (Berve ii 23, no. 47). For he attained prominence already during Philip's reign and, after the battle of Chaironeia, went with Antipatros on an embassy to Athens, where he was voted a proxeny (*IG* ii² 239; Hypereides, *Against Demades*, frg. 77 = 19. 2 [Burtt]). In 334 Alkimachos disappears from our sources after being sent to overthrow the oligarchies in the Aiolic and Ionic cities of Asia Minor and to replace them with democracies (Arr. 1. 18. 1-2). Both Alkimachos and his father were men of considerable importance at Philip's Court, and it is likely that the family was firmly entrenched there well before Alexander's accession.

Curtius (8. 1. 14-17) first mentions Lysimachos in the context of the lion-hunt in the forests of Bazeira in Sogdiana (328 B.C.). Lysimachos, presumably in his capacity as Somatophylax,[74] tried to protect the King from a charging lion. Alexander, however, ordered him aside and killed the beast with his own spear, reminding Lysimachos of his

---

[72]Cf. the denigration of Thrasydaios, a Thessalian tetrarch who acted as Philip's ambassador to Thebes in 338: μικρὸν μὲν ὄντα τὴν γνώμην, κόλακα δὲ μέγιστον (*FGrHist* 115 F209). See also Shrimpton, *Theopompus* 168 f. (on Agathokles); cf. 154 (Thrasydaios).

[73]Agathokles himself did not necessarily become 'a citizen of Pella', as Westlake, *Thessaly* 195 contends.

[74]Pausanias (1. 9. 5), who gives a distorted version, does refer to Lysimachos as δορυφόρος, which may be intended to be the equivalent of σωματοφύλαξ. Cf. Berve ii 240, n.2.

misadventure during a lion-hunt in Syria.⁷⁵ Curtius' primary source gave a credible account: *Lysimachus enim quondam, cum venarentur in Syria, occiderat quidem eximiae magnitudinis feram solus, sed laevo humero usque ad ossa lacerato, ad ultimum periculi pervenerat* (8. 1. 15). But three centuries of historiography intervened, and Curtius rejects the story, popular in his own time, that Alexander exposed Lysimachos to a lion (*fabulam, quae obiectum leoni a rege Lysimachum temere vulgavit ab eo casu quem supra diximus ortam esse crediderim*: 8. 1. 17). Pompeius Trogus was the Roman source of that fiction: Seneca, the Elder Pliny and Valerius Maximus seem to have taken it from the *Historiae Philippicae*, but the ultimate source was undoubtedly Hellenistic.⁷⁶ Timagenes of Alexandria may have had a hand in all of this, but one thinks of earlier sources, Douris of Samos and the like.

Plutarch (*Demetr.* 27. 3) gives the lion-story a humorous context, and compares Lysimachos' scars, sustained while he was caged with a lion, with the bites on Demetrios' neck, inflicted by the flute-girl Lamia. Immediately preceding this anecdote is a reference to Lynkeus of Samos, who attended and described in detail a dinner-party given by Lamia in honour of Demetrios (Plut. *Demetrios* 27. 3; cf. Athen. 3. 101e; 4. 128a-b). Douris and Lynkeus were brothers (Athen. 8. 337d; *Suda* s.v. Λυγκεύς), students of Theophrastos of Eresos (Athen. 4. 128a-b), and contemporaries of Lysimachos and Demetrios. Of the content of Douris' historical work we are reasonably well informed;⁷⁷ Lynkeus is more elusive, though it appears that his work was rich in the scandalous gossip of dinner-parties (Körte, *RE* xiii.2 [1927], 2472 f., no. 6). And dinner-parties, such as the one described by Lynkeus, will have been the source of, and the inspiration for, much of the gossip concerning the Diadochoi, and especially the stories about Demetrios, Lamia and Lysimachos (cf. Athen 6. 246e; 6. 261b; 14. 614f - 615a; Plut. *Demetr.* 27. 3). Douris of Samos, on the other hand, is known to have written a somewhat sensational *Makedonian History*.⁷⁸ Of course, neither may

---

⁷⁵Presumably the Sidonian lion-hunt, in which Krateros took part, is meant. The hunt was commemorated by Lysippos' composition (see A. von Salis, *Löwenkampfbilder des Lysipp* [Berlin, 1956], 36-37; Franklin P. Johnson, *Lysippos* [Durham, N. Carolina, 1927], 226-228, with n. 107 on p. 227; Lippold, *RE* xiv.1 [1928], 61) dedicated by Krateros the son at Delphoi (see W. W. Tarn, *Antigonos Gonatas* [Oxford, 1913], 213, n. 145).

⁷⁶For Trogus' account cf. Justin 15. 3. 7-8.

⁷⁷See Jacoby, *FGrHist* iiA 76, for the fragments; iiC (Leiden, 1963), 115-131. J. G. Droysen, *Kleine Schriften zur alten Geschichte* (Leipzig, 1894), ii 207, first suggested Douris as the source of the lion-story.

⁷⁸On Douris in general see R. Kebric, *In the Shadow of Macedon. Duris of Samos*, Historia Einzelschrifen, Heft 29 (Wiesbaden, 1977); for the *Makedonian History*, 36 ff.

have been the source — perhaps Lysimachos, for an unknown reason, circulated the story himself — but there is a strong probability that the author who invented or, at least, promulgated the story that Lysimachos was caged with a lion was a contemporary, or near-contemporary, of the Diadoch; Phylarchos, who belongs to the late 3rd century, is not above suspicion.[79]

Justin provides some clues to how the story may have been elaborated. Lysimachos was reputed for his cultivation of the philosophers — Onesikritos of Astypalaia, a pupil of Diogenes, was present at Lysimachos' court[80] — and already in 324 he had been given the funerary horse of the Indian philosopher Kalanos, whose student he had been (Arr. 7. 3. 4). His devotion to philosophy became proverbial,[81] and the story developed that he pitied the philosopher-historian Kallisthenes, whom Alexander had caged like a wild animal.[82] Lysimachos, who is said to have been a student of Kallisthenes as well,[83] attempted to give him poison in order to end his suffering. For this act, according to Justin, he was caged together with a lion, which he killed by tearing out its tongue (15. 3. 3-8). But Lysimachos was allegedly guilty of similar cruelty (conduct befitting a tyrant), sometime after 300 B.C., when he mutilated and caged Telesphoros the Rhodian for making a tasteless joke about his queen,

---

[79] See esp. *FGrHist* 81 F12, 29, 31.

[80] Plut. *Alex.* 65. 2; on Onesikritos' life and work see T. S. Brown, *Onesicritus: A Study in Hellenistic Historiography* (Berkeley, 1949), esp. 1-23; also Jacoby, *FGrHist* iiB 134; iiD 468-480; Pearson, *LHA* 83-111. According to Plutarch (*Alex.* 46. 4), Onesikritos read Lysimachos the fourth book of his History, which included the tale of Alexander and the Amazons. Lysimachos remarked: 'Where was I when all this happened?'

[81] Against this view, Jacoby iiD 470; according to the *Hypomnemata* of Karystios (*ap.* Athen. 8. 610e) Lysimachos drove the philosophers out of his kingdom.

[82] On the various versions of Kallisthenes' death: Plut. *Alex.* 55. 9; Chares, *FGrHist* 125 F15, says that he died of obesity and a disease of lice; Ptolemy, 138 F17 = Arr. 4. 14. 3, says that he was killed by hanging; Aristoboulos, 139 F33 = Arr. 4. 14. 3, claims that he was imprisoned and thereafter died of illness. See Berve ii 197, n. 408; cf. Brown, *AJP* 70 (1949), 247-248; A. H. Chroust, *Aristotle*, vol. 1 (South Bend, Indiana, 1973), 47 and 304-305. That he was a historian, and not a philosopher at all, is again brought to our attention by E. Badian, *The Deification of Alexander the Great*, Colloquy 21, Center for Hermeneutical Studies in Hellenistic and Modern Culture (Berkeley, 1976), 1; cf. Kroll, *RE* x.2 (1919), 1674-1726; esp. 1676, s.v. 'Kallisthenes (2)'. On his lack of philosophical training see Bosworth, *Historia* 19 (1970), 407-413.

[83] Justin 15. 3. 3-6. Chroust, *op. cit.*, 305, n. 171, assumes that Lysimachos was foiled in his attempt to poison Kallisthenes; he accepts, rather naïvely, the story of Lysimachos' punishment.

Arsinoë.[84] As a result, the lion-story, now removed from its historical context (it takes place neither in Syria nor Bazeira), establishes a precedent for Lysimachos' treatment of Telesphoros and is itself explained in terms of Alexander's cruelty to Kallisthenes. In fact, Alexander's caging of Lysimachos becomes canonised as one of the three great examples of Alexander's cruelty, together with the murder of Kleitos and the punishment of Kallisthenes, in the works of the Roman rhetoricians.[85] But the truth of the whole matter is probably very close to what Curtius tells us: Lysimachos once killed a lion of extraordinary size in Syria, but was severely mauled in the process; on a second occasion, in the Bazeiran woods, Alexander prevented him from making a similar mistake.

Plutarch's comment (*Alex.* 55. 2) about 'men like Lysimachos and Hagnon', who maligned Kallisthenes, should not be taken as a reference to the son of Agathokles (*pace* Pearson, *LHA* 57, n.30), who was clearly well disposed towards the Greek: Berve (ii 241, no. 481; cf. Hamilton, *PA* 14, 153-154) correctly identifies him as Alexander's Akarnanian tutor, the victim of Chares' hostility. It is puzzling, however, that Berve does not credit Lysimachos' participation in the Kleitos episode.[86] There is no good reason to disbelieve Curtius (8. 1. 46). For the political issues that lay behind Kleitos' confrontation with Alexander, Curtius' version demonstrates a sober approach to the affair. Nor does Plutarch's account, which claims that Aristophanes (read 'Aristonous') disarmed the king, vitiate that of Curtius, for the former concerns the removal of Alexander's own sword (which was the first weapon that he might be expected to reach for, if he carried it on

---

[84]Athen. 14. 616c: κακῶν κατάρχεις τήνδ' ἐμοῦσαν εἰσάγων. Whether Arsinoë was in fact prone to vomiting cannot be determined. Seneca, *de Ira* 3. 17. 3-4 describes the cruel punishment of Telesphoros: ...*cum oris detruncati mutilatique deformitas humanam faciem perdidisset; accedebat fames et squalor et inluvies corporis in stercore suo destituti; callosis super haec genibus manibus....* Athenaios was fond of such stories as well: cf. the case of Sotades of Maroneia, the *kinaidologos*, who, according to the account given by his son Apollonios, insulted first Lysimachos and then Ptolemy Philadelphos, and consequently was sunk into the deep in a leaden jar by Ptolemy's admiral, Patroklos (14. 620f-621a).

[85]Seneca, *de Ira* 3. 17. 2, with a veiled reference at 3. 23. 1; also *de Clem.* 1. 25. 1, but details are few; Pliny, *NH* 8. 54, according to whom Lysimachos strangles the lion; Val. Max. 9. 3 ext. 1; Pausanias 1. 9. 5; cf. also Justin 15. 3. 7-8 (Lysimachos tears out the lion's tongue); Lucian, *dial. mort.* 14. 4 (397); Plut. *Demetr.* 27. 3. Dr John Vanderspoel draws my attention to Themistios, *Or.* 7. 94a; 10. 129d-130a; 13. 176a, which mention Kallisthenes, Kleitos and Parmenion, though Lysimachos is absent.

[86]Berve ii 240: '...die Rolle, welche man ihm, freilich mit Unrecht, ... zuschrieb....'.

his person), while the later involves a spear, which Alexander had taken from a bystander (Curt. 8. 1. 45: *Alexander rapta lancea ex manibus armigeri...*). It appears from Plutarch's account (*Alex.* 51. 11) that all the Somatophylakes were present at the banquet, as we should expect. Presumably they did not stand idly by while Aristonous alone attempted to restrain the King. Very likely each one attempted, in his own way, to avert the disaster. Lysimachos, who appears in the company of Leonnatos, Perdikkas, and Ptolemy (all of whom were already Somatophylakes), undoubtedly held the same rank.

Not long after Kleitos' death, Lysimachos' younger brother, Philippos, a Royal Hypaspist, accompanied the King some five hundred stades on foot, refusing to mount the horse of Lysimachos, who rode nearby. Remaining ever by the King's side, both in the pursuit of the supporters of Sisimithres and in the skirmish that followed, Philippos finally collapsed from exhaustion and expired in the King's arms (Curtius 8. 2. 35-39; Justin 15. 3. 12). This story is preceded in Justin (15. 3. 10-11) by a similar one, in which Lysimachos remains at the side of Alexander in India when all others have fallen behind. It is surely a doublet (cf. Berve ii 240, n.4), with an added twist: Appian (*Syr.* 64) and Justin (15. 3. 13-14) relate that Lysimachos (here, one of Alexander's hypaspists!) was wounded when Alexander, leaping from his horse, clipped him with his spear. In an attempt to stop the bleeding, Alexander placed his diadem on Lysimachos' head (*diadema sibi demptum rex adligandi vulneris causa capiti eius inponeret*: Justin 15. 3. 13). That Aristandros (who vanished from the accounts of Alexander, probably with the end of Kallisthenes' historical work) or any other seer prophesied that this act signified that Lysimachos would himself be King defies all credulity.[87] The story is clearly a later invention, as is Aristoboulos' claim (*FGrHist* 139 F54 = Arr. 7. 18. 5) that the seer Peithagoras predicted Lysimachos' victory over Antigonos at Ipsos.

What evidence remains for the early career of Lysimachos is relatively straight-forward. Near Sangala some 1200 of Alexander's troops were wounded, among them Lysimachos the Somatophylax (Arr. 5. 24. 5). He had earlier boarded a thirty-oared vessel at the Hydaspes (with two other Somatophylakes), before the battle with

---

[87] See Berve ii 241, n.2; ii 62-63, no. 117; A. Fränkel, *Die Quellen der Alexanderhistoriker* (Leipzig, 1883), 171 ff. Robinson, *AJP* 50 (1929), 195 ff., argues that Kallisthenes was the source for all references to Aristandros and that he disappears after Kallisthenes' death. Hamilton (*PA* 4) finds this 'hardly conclusive, and as Aristander must have been an old man in 327 it is more reasonable to suppose that he died a natural death soon after.' A similar story regarding Alexander's diadem is told of Seleukos by Arrian 7. 22. 5, a variant on the version given by Aristoboulos (*FGrHist* 139 F55).

Poros, though his role in the actual battle is not described (Arr. 5. 13. 1); presumably he fought in the immediate vicinity of Alexander himself. When Alexander decided to sail down the Indus river system to the Ocean, Lysimachos was one of those from Pella charged with a trierarchy in the Attic fashion (Arr. *Ind*. 18. 3 = Nearchos, *FGrHist* 133 F1). He is named by Arrian in the only complete list of the Somatophylakes (6. 28. 4).

At Sousa (spring 324), Lysimachos and the other Somatophylakes were crowned by Alexander, though unlike Leonnatos, Lysimachos appears to have earned no special distinction (Arr. 7. 5. 6) — unless Alexander rewarded his valour in the Sangala campaign (Arr. 5. 24. 5). Very likely, he took a Persian bride: her name is not recorded, nor her fate. She may have been repudiated after Alexander's death, although it is worthy of note that in 302 B.C. Lysimachos married (albeit only for a brief time) Amastris, whom Krateros had married at Sousa but put aside in favour of Antipatros' daughter, Phila.[88]

According to Pseudo-Kallisthenes (3. 32. 8), Lysimachos, Ptolemy and Perdikkas (*LM* 103 includes the enigmatic Holkias, Berve, no. 580) were summoned to Alexander's death-bed. This may be true, but the claim that Alexander assigned Thrake to Lysimachos (*LM* 111), because he was best qualified to subdue and rule it (Justin 15. 3. 15: *quasi omnium fortissimo*), is a fabrication. Similarly, the charge that Alexander envied him his abilities as a commander (so Aelian, *VH* 12. 16; 14. 47a) must be rejected: rumours circulated in the years that followed Alexander's death that various Successors had, at one time or another, fallen out of favour with Alexander. Such stories reflected, either favourably or unfavourably, upon the individuals in question and were generated by the propaganda mills of this turbulent age.

There remains the thorny problem of Lysimachos' birthdate. His age at Koroupedion is given variously as eighty (Ps.-Lucian, *Macrob*. 11), seventy-four (Justin 17. 1. 10) and seventy (Appian, *Syr*. 64). One is immediately attracted to Ps.-Lucian, who claims the venerable Hieronymos as his source. But Ps.-Lucian does not quote his sources accurately,[89] and the macrobian list, which admits only octogenarians, may have exaggerated Lysimachos' age slightly. If so, then we must abandon the source-critical approach; for we know neither what

---

[88] See Wilcken, *RE* i.2 (1894), 1750, s.v. 'Amastris (7)'; also Berve ii 24, no. 50, s.v. Ἄμαστρις. She was at the time the widow of Dionysios of Herakleia in Pontos.

[89] See the edition of A. M. Harmon, *Lucian*, vol. 1 Loeb Classical Library (Cambridge, Mass., 1913), 229, notes 1 and 2. Berve ii 330 doubts the testimony of Ps.-Lucian, *Macrob*. 11, concerning the age of Ptolemy and (ii 351, n. 5) rejects his authority for the age of Seleukos, though he is less suspicious in the case of Lysimachos (ii 239). See now Mehl 2.

Hieronymos himself wrote nor which sources Justin and Appian followed. We must, therefore, judge Lysimachos' age in the light of the evidence that we have accumulated; and this suggests that he was older. If he was Somatophylax already in Philip's day, then he was probably somewhat older than Alexander, although Justin's date for Lysimachos' birth, 355 B.C., could still stand as the extreme lower limit.

Appian's estimate (seventy years) is disturbingly low. By this reckoning, Lysimachos would have been too young to have been one of Philip's Somatophylakes, and thus must have been appointed during the course of the campaign, probably in the early 320s. But we know of no Somatophylax whom Lysimachos replaced (or could have replaced), nor do we know the time of, or reason for, his appointment. Furthermore, in the early 320s, Alexander had begun to develop the Somatophylakes into his personal military 'Staff'. Four of his trusted friends — Hephaistion, Ptolemy, Leonnatos, Perdikkas — had been promoted to the rank, and Menes' appointment was perhaps the last attempt to placate the 'Old Guard'. How then are we to account for the sudden appointment of the youthful (by Appian's dating) and untried Lysimachos? If there is indeed an explanation of this, then it must be one that applies equally to Peithon and Aristonous, whose careers are remarkably similar. Whom did they replace? When were they appointed? And why? Lysimachos appears to have been appointed Somatophylax before 336 and his relative obscurity during Alexander's reign may be due in part to his family's connections with Philip. Although the family was influential at the Court, Lysimachos and his brothers do not appear to have had any strong personal ties with Alexander.

A study of the evidence for Lysimachos' career under Alexander leads, inevitably, to disappointment. The Alexander-historians have left little record of his activities: few details illuminate his career; the man is all but devoid of characterisation. In fact, there is little in the sources, apart from a handful of references in Arrian, that is not contaminated by the hindsight of historians. The most frequently attested episodes derive from late sources, and these transpose a familiarity with the cruel and miserly Diadoch onto the inconspicuous Somatophylax of Alexander. What little information appears likely to be true is, unfortunately, of very limited interest and value. There is one explanation: Lysimachos attained his rank before Alexander's accession, his fame and power after, and as a result of, Alexander's death.

We may be encouraged by the careers of Philip's other Somatophylakes — Arybbas, Balakros, Demetrios, Ptolemaios, Aristonous and Peithon — who were relatively insignificant under Alexander. The first four — but for the fact that they died (Arybbas, Ptolemaios) or were replaced (Balakros, Demetrios) — are little more than shadows, Peithon and Aristonous virtual mirror-images of Lysimachos, once his history has been stripped of the late and unreliable elements.

3. 2. Aristonous son of Peisaios

Literature. Berve ii 69, no. 133; Kaerst, *RE* ii.1 (1895), 947-948, no. 8; K. Ziegler, 'Plutarchstudien', *RhM* 84 (1935), 379 f.; R. M. Errington, 'Bias in Ptolemy's History of Alexander', *CQ* 19 (1969), 235-236, esp. 240-241.

The son of Peisaios (Arr. 6. 28. 4; *Succ.* 1a. 2; *Ind.* 18. 5), Aristonous is described as both Πελλαῖος (Arr. 6. 28. 4) and of Eordaian origin (Arr. *Ind.* 18. 5), which must mean that he was from Eordaia but raised at the Court in Pella (cf. Leonnatos). Until his name appears in Arrian's list of the Somatophylakes (325 B.C.; Arr. 6. 28. 4, from Aristoboulos, *FGrHist* 139 F50), he is unknown in the *Anabasis*. He may have been appointed to that office before 336, and we have a strong indication that Aristonous was a Somatophylax already in 328. According to Plutarch, a certain Aristophanes, termed σωματοφύλαξ, removed Alexander's sword while the King was quarreling with Kleitos ('Ἀλέξανδρος...τὸ ἐγχειρίδιον ἐζήτει. τῶν δὲ σωματοφυλάκων ἑνὸς Ἀριστοφάνους φθάσαντος ὑφελέσθαι, *Alex.* 51. 5-6). Palmerius emended the text to read 'Aristonous',[90] a simple and sensible correction, which Berve nevertheless regarded as 'nicht nur reine Willkür, sondern auch sachlich falsch' (ii 69, n.2). Aristophanes was retained as an historical figure, a member of the regular hypaspists (ii 74, no. 136). But Ziegler (*RhM* 84 [1935], 379 f.) convincingly rejects Berve's view: for, in the very sentence in which Aristophanes is described as σωματοφύλαξ, the term ὑπασπισταί occurs. The latter were summoned by Alexander, and it is doubtful that Plutarch used two different terms within the same sentence to apply to the same unit.

In 326, Aristonous assumed a trierarchy at the Hydaspes (*Ind.* 18. 5), as did the other Somatophylakes. Arrian (Ptolemy) may have failed to mention his wound in the Mallian town (Curt. 9. 5. 15, 18)[91] because, after Alexander's death, Aristonous supported Perdikkas (Curt. 10. 6. 16); but the golden crown awarded him at Sousa in 324 (Arr. 7. 5. 6) supports Curtius' claim. In 323 B.C., Aristonous espoused the Perdikkan cause (Curt. 10. 6. 16) and in 321/0 served as the commander-in-chief of the expedition against the Kypriot kings who had allied

---

[90]Hamilton, *PA* 143. See Berve ii 69, no. 133.

[91]See Errington, *CQ* 19 (1969), 235 f.; Curt. 9. 5. 21: *Ptolomaeum, qui postea regnavit, huic pugnae adfuisse auctor est Clitarchus et Timagenes; sed ipse, scilicet gloriae suae non refragatus afuisse se, missum in expeditionem, memoriae tradidit.* Cf. Arr. 6. 11. 8.

themselves with Ptolemy (Arr. *Succ.* 24. 6). This undertaking was ill-fated, and Aristonous was apparently forced to surrender to Antigonos. Antipatros, it appears, pardoned him and allowed him to return to Makedonia, possibly on the understanding that he would retire to private life.[92]

But Antipatros' death in late 319 brought political turmoil, and Aristonous joined Polyperchon, now allied with Eumenes and the remnants of the Perdikkan party. Nothing is known of his role in the early stages of Polyperchon's war with Kassandros, but in 316, when Olympias was forced to seek refuge in Pydna, Aristonous, on the Queen Mother's orders, took control of those troops who were still loyal to Alexander's house (Diod. 19. 35. 4). He appears to have accomplished little: once Kassandros had prevailed over Aiakides of Epeiros and Polyperchon, whose armies were weakened by defections, Aristonous thought it prudent to fall back on Amphipolis. This place he defended until early 315 B.C. (Diod. 19. 50. 3), when Olympias ordered him to surrender. Indeed, he had actually defeated Kassandros' general Krateuas at Bedyndia (19. 50. 7-8). Kassandros, at first, guaranteed Aristonous' personal safety (Diod. 19. 50. 8), but he feared him on account of his popularity — which he derived from his high position during Alexander's lifetime — and contrived to have him murdered through the agency of Krateuas' relatives (Diod. 19. 51. 1).[93]

3. 3. Peithon son of Krateuas

Literature. Berve ii 311, no. 621; id., *RE* xix (1938), 220-222; Bengtson, *Strategie* i 178 ff.; Heckel, *LDT* 38-39, 66-67, 74-75.

Peithon son of Krateuas (Arr. *Succ.* 1a. 2) came from Alkomenai in Deuriopos (Strabo 7. 7. 8 C326). He is incorrectly referred to as 'Illyrius' (Justin 13. 4. 13; 13. 8. 10); perhaps the ancients confused his place of origin with Alkomenai in Illyria (so Berve ii 311, n.3). Nothing is known of his career until 326, when he served as a trierarch of the Hydaspes fleet (*Ind.* 18. 6), an honour accorded to all Somatophylakes, to which unit Peithon belonged in 325 (Arr. 6. 28. 4) and presumably already in 336 (see 3. 1 above). Like his fellow Somatophylakes, he received a golden crown at Sousa in 324 (Arr. 7. 5.

---

[92]Cf. the case of Holkias (Polyainos 4. 6. 6).

[93]It is tempting to see in Krateuas a relative (perhaps even the son) of Peithon son of Krateuas, the former Somatophylax. At the time of Aristonous' victory over Krateuas, Peithon's execution at the hands of Antigonos may not yet have occurred; certainly it could not have been known in Makedonia (for the chronology see R. M. Errington, 'Diodorus Siculus and the Chronology of the Early Diadochoi, 320-311 B.C.', *Hermes* 105 [1977], 478 ff.).

6). He appears to have served the King primarily in an advisory capacity — if we assume that the Somatophylakes were automatically included in Alexander's *consilium amicorum*. He is undoubtedly the same Peithon who, along with Seleukos and others,[94] slept in the temple of Sarapis during Alexander's fatal illness.

In the succession struggle that followed the King's death, Peithon appears as an opponent of Arrhidaios' kingship[95] and a supporter of Perdikkas: his proposed joint-guardianship of Rhoxane's child by Perdikkas and Leonnatos, leaving the direction of European affairs to Antipatros and Krateros (Curt. 10. 7. 8-9) was surely a compromise intended to prevent the complete erosion of Perdikkas' authority. In return for his support, Peithon received the satrapy of Media Maior,[96] and also the task of suppressing the Greek rebellion in the Upper Satrapies (Diod. 18. 4. 8; 18. 7. 3-9). For this purpose, he received special powers, perhaps as στρατηγὸς τῶν ἄνω σατραπειῶν (cf. Diod. 19. 14. 1), to levy troops from the neighbouring satrapies and to act as commander-in-chief of the expedition.[97] This command fuelled Peithon's ambitions, and he planned to come to terms with the insurgents and take them into his service; for his intention was clearly ἰδιοπραγεῖν καὶ τῶν ἄνω σατραπειῶν δυναστεύειν (Diod. 18. 7. 4). But Perdikkas, suspecting his designs, gave instructions that the rebels be slaughtered upon their surrender (18. 7. 5). Despite Peithon's intrigues and the cooperation of Letodoros the Ainianian, the troops were moved more by the expectation of plunder than by compassion and carried out Perdikkas' orders (Diod. 18. 7. 6-9).[98]

Rejoining Perdikkas, probably in time to participate in the expedition against Ariarathes of Kappadokia, Peithon eventually

---

[94] Arr. 7. 26. 2 names Attalos (probably the son of Andromenes), Demophon the seer (Berve ii 141, no. 264), Peukestas, Kleomenes (Berve ii 211-212, no. 432), Menidas (Berve ii 257-258, no. 508) and Seleukos. For doubts concerning the historicity of this event see Grainger 218 f.

[95] Curt. 10. 7. 4-5. Curtius' narrative has a contemporary Roman colouring; cf. Martin, *AJAH* 8 (1983) 161-190, who notes that Peithon's role is suspiciously similar to that of Josephus' Chaerea (164, with n.5, and 179). Nevertheless, support for Perdikkas involved, at this time, a rejection of Arrhidaios' claim; Curtius has, in all likelihood, embellished a notice about Peithon in Kleitarchos' original.

[96] Justin 13. 4. 13; Curt. 10. 10. 4; Diod. 18. 3. 1; Arr. *Succ.* 1a. 5; 1b. 2 = Dexippos, *FGrHist* 100 F8 §2. Metz, *LM* 117 (in an unhistorical context); cf. Heckel, *LDT* 66-67, for Peithon's connections with Syria Mesopotamia.

[97] Diod. 18. 7. 3: Peithon was given 3,000 infantry and 800 horse in Babylon, as well as written orders to the satraps to supply a further 10,000 infantry and 8,000 cavalry for the expedition.

[98] See Holt, *Alexander and Bactria* 88-91, who is probably correct in assuming that the massacre 'involved only the 3,000 men with Letodorus' (90).

accompanied him to Egypt, where he was one of the ringleaders of the mutiny near Memphis in 320 (Diod. 18. 36. 5).[99] Thus he gained for a time a measure of the power he desired: with Ptolemy's aid, he and Arrhidaios became *epimeletai* of the Kings (Diod. 18. 36. 6-7), though Ptolemy shrewdly left them with the dregs of the Royal Army and the problems of back-pay. Leading the remnants of the Perdikkan army from Egypt to Triparadeisos in Syria, Peithon and Arrhidaios soon found themselves up-staged by Adea-Eurydike, who spoke on behalf of her husband Philip III and inflamed the troops. Peithon and his colleague thus resigned and the army elected Antipatros in their place (Diod. 18. 39. 1-2); it was enough, for the time, to be reaffirmed as satrap of Media (Diod. 18. 39. 6; Arr. *Succ.* 1. 35).

For the next year, Peithon appears to have remained idle. But Antipatros' death in late 319 left no one to enforce the terms of Triparadeisos: already before the Regent's death, Ptolemy had seized Koile-Syria from Laomedon, and now Antigonos advanced to Hellespontine Phrygia and Lydia to expel Antipatros' appointees there. Monophthalmos used his mandate to crush the remnants of the Perdikkan party as a way of securing Asia for himself. For Peithon, too, it was time to regain lost ground: reviving for himself the title of στρατηγὸς τῶν ἄνω σατραπειῶν, he expelled the Parthian satrap Philippos (Diod. 19. 14. 1, wrongly calling him 'Philotas'), installing in his place his own brother Eudamos. But this move alarmed the neighbouring satraps, who rallied under the leadership of Peukestas and drove Peithon (and presumably Eudamos) out of Parthia (Diod. 19. 14. 2). Hence, when Eumenes contacted Peithon and asked him to support the Kings, Peithon was already trying to win over Seleukos to his own cause (Diod. 19. 14. 3). The two joined in opposing Eumenes (Diod. 19. 12. 1-2, 5; cf. Diod. 19. 17. 2), but Seleukos chose to throw in his lot with Antigonos, perhaps in exchange for the annexation of Sousiana (Diod. 19. 18. 1; cf. Mehl 49 f.).[100]

Stripped of an important ally, Peithon served Antigonos (Diod. 19. 19. 4), even giving him useful advice, which Antigonos rejected at his own peril (Diod. 19. 19. 8). Before the battle of Paraitakene, Peithon was sent by Antigonos to bring reinforcements and pack-animals from Media (Diod. 19. 20. 2), which he supplied in large numbers (Diod. 19. 20. 3; cf. 19. 27. 1). That Antigonos had complete trust in him is doubtful, but he valued his generalship and assigned him control of the less mobile forces while he pursued the enemy with his cavalry (Diod.

---

[99]Justin 13. 8. 10 has Peithon 'the Illyrian' declared an outlaw along with Eumenes and Alketas. Trogus' original almost certainly recorded that Perdikkas was murdered by Peithon.

[100]This was the satrapy of Antigenes (Arr. *Succ.* 1. 35; Diod. 18. 39. 6), who was now serving with Eumenes.

19. 26. 7). In Paraitakene, Peithon commanded the cavalry on the left wing (Diod. 19. 29. 2-3), but his force was routed (Diod. 19. 30. 1-4). Hieronymos may have given him a bad press — just he was to discredit Peukestas in his description of the battle of Gabiene (see 2. 2 above) — since Peithon had failed to cooperate with Eumenes and was plotting to betray Antigonos. As the army moved into Peithon's satrapy (Diod. 19. 32. 3), it was important for Antigonos to keep his goodwill, and we find Peithon closely associated with Antigonos in command right up to the final defeat of Eumenes at Gabiene (Diod. 19. 38. 4; 19. 40. 1; 19. 43. 4). But soon thereafter he was suspected of plotting rebellion. Antigonos, however, deceived him into thinking that he intended to hand over troops to him and to leave him as *strategos* of the Upper Satrapies. Caught off-guard by the dissimulation, Peithon was arrested and executed in 315 (Diod. 19. 46. 1-4; Polyainos 4. 6. 14).[101]

4. The Somatophylakes of Philip III

Arrian (*Succ.* 1. 38) tells us that at Triparadeisos in Syria (320 B.C.), the marshals of the empire redistributed the satrapies and appointed four men as Somatophylakes: σωματοφύλακας δὲ τοῦ βασιλέως Αὐτόδικόν τε τὸν Ἀγαθοκλέους παῖδα καὶ Ἀμύνταν τὸν Ἀλεξάνδρου παῖδα Πευκέστου δὲ ἀδελφὸν καὶ Πτολεμαῖον τὸν Πτολεμαίου καὶ Ἀλέξανδρον τὸν Πολυπέρχοντος.... Three points deserve attention. First, Photios' epitome of Arrian speaks of only one King (τοῦ βασιλέως), despite the fact that he has earlier referred to both Philip III and Alexander IV as 'Kings' (*Succ.* 1. 28, 29; cf. 1a. 1, 1a. 8) and does so again immediately below (τοὺς βασιλέας φρουρεῖν, 1. 38). The four Somatophylakes are nowhere else attested as such. Second, the number four is unusual — Alexander, and apparently his predecessors as well, had seven — and something must account for the change in number. Third, only Amyntas son of Alexandros is further identified: he is the brother of Peukestas. It is assumed, by the author or the epitomator, that the identities of the other three are clear enough. Does this then mean that Ptolemaios son of Ptolemaios was regarded (perhaps even wrongly) by later sources as the son of Ptolemy son of Lagos?

---

[101]In Peithon's place, Antigonos appointed Orontobates, a native of the region, under the watchful eye of Hippostratos and a mercenary force. These defeated the remnants of Peithon's army, which had been augmented by some 800 survivors of Eumenes' force at Gabiene (Diod. 19. 47. 1). Their leaders Meleagros (probably the former ilarch of Alexander, Berve ii 250, no. 495) and Okranes the Mede perished in the engagement; what became of Menoitas (see Berve ii 258-259, no. 510) is unknown. Peithon's own fate was a signal to Seleukos that Antigonos was not to be trusted (Diod. 19. 55. 4) and an example of the latter's ruthless ambition (Diod. 19. 56. 1).

Now the 'King' in question can only be Philip III Arrhidaios. Inscriptions of the Diadochic period sometimes speak of King Philip alone (e.g., *IG* ii² 401), even though the joint-kingship was clearly recognised (see *OGIS* 4; *Ath. Mitt.* 72 [1957], 158, no. 1B, 11; *Hesperia* 37 [1968], 222).[102] And the literary sources, as a rule, spoke not only of the provisions made for the dual kingship (Arr. *Succ.* 1a. 1) but also of its actual existence. Why then does Photios (or Arrian himself?) speak only of Philip III in this instance? It may be that no Somatophylakes were assigned at this time to Alexander IV, who had not yet reached his third birthday. Possibly the provisions for the Somatophylakia of the younger King were omitted by Photios in his abbreviation.

But the restriction of the number of Somatophylakes to four is almost certainly to be explained by the dual kingship, which required that the Seven be shared between Philip III and Alexander.[103] *IG* ii² 561, an Athenian decree of Stratokles, honours certain Somatophylakes of a King Alexander named Philippos and Iolaos; possibly (though there is little room on the stone) a third individual as well. The Alexander of this inscription can scarcely have been Alexander III, since no Somatophylax by either name is attested; nor is it likely that Somatophylakes of Alexander II (r. 369-368 B.C.) were still alive and serving Antigonos and Demetrios, as the decree concerning Iolaos and Philippos indicates. That they were hypaspist officers of Alexander the Great (thus Billows; see below), raises questions about identity and terminology. Most plausibly, these were Somatophylakes of Alexander IV. At Triparadeisos it was presumably decided that the Somatophylakia would be shared by the Kings and that either the number would be increased to eight, with each King receiving four, or that the traditional number of seven would be retained, with Philip III assigned four on account of seniority.[104] Whether Alexander's Somatophylakes were actually appointed at Triparadeisos remains uncertain.

In order to identify Ptolemaios son of Ptolemaios we must consider the criteria for the selection of the Somatophylakes of the Kings. Furthermore, there is the question of whether a Makedonian King, on his accession, normally chose his own Somatophylakes, inherited them from his predecessor, or had them appointed by the Makedonian

---

[102] For a full discussion, see Chr. Habicht, 'Literarische und epigraphische Überlieferung zur Geschichte Alexanders und seiner ersten Nachfolger', in *Akten des VI. Intern. Kongr. für griech. und latein. Epigraphik* (Munich, 1973), 367-377, esp. 369 ff.

[103] Habicht, *ibid.* 374: 'Jeder der beiden Könige hat seine eigenen Somatophylakes, wies dies in der Natur des Amtes liegt...'.

[104] See W. Heckel, '*IG* ii² 561 and the Status of Alexander IV', *ZPE* 40 (1980), 249-250.

nobility. I have spoken above (in the cases of Arybbas, Ptolemaios, Balakros: cf. Peithon, Aristonous, Lysimachos) of Philip II's Somatophylakes, who were inherited by Alexander the Great in 336. Although this is the most reasonable assumption, they may have been appointed for him. One thing is certain: in 336, Alexander could not make changes to the composition of the Seven without serious political fall-out. The case of the dual kingship was somewhat different. Neither King was capable of selecting his own Somatophylakes, the one being mentally deficient, the other an infant. Hence the names of the individuals selected tell us something about the political jockeying that took place at Triparadeisos.

The senior statesman and, undisputedly, the most powerful figure in 320 B.C. was Antipatros: ruler of Makedonia and its European dependencies, commander-in-chief of the Royal Army and guardian of the Kings, he was in a position to dictate the terms of the settlement of Triparadeisos. Of course, his power rested upon the goodwill of many competent governors (Ptolemy, Lysimachos, Peukestas) and on certain Perdikkan commanders who had changed their allegiance (Peithon, Seleukos, Philoxenos, Kleitos). Antigonos Monophthalmos was designated *hegemon* of Asia, responsible for the war against Eumenes and the outlaws of the Makedonian state. But Antipatros knew the man's nature, and the redistribution of the satrapies and the restructuring of command at Triparadeisos reflect a distrust of Monophthalmos' ambitions. Antipatros' son, Kassandros, was appointed Antigonos' χιλιάρχης τῆς ἵππου (Arr. *Succ.* 1. 38; Diod. 18. 39. 7), so that Antigonos could not pursue an independent policy undetected (ὅπως μὴ δύνηται διαλαθεῖν ἰδιοπραγῶν, Diod. 18. 39. 7). Key satrapies, adjacent to Antigonos' own, were occupied by friends of Antipatros: Kleitos (Lydia), Arrhidaios (Hellespontine Phrygia),[105] Philoxenos (Kilikia), Asandros (Karia); Nikanor, perhaps Antipatros' own son (Kappadokia). The deposed satraps, Menandros and Philotas, found employment, and the idle hope of reinstatement, with Antigonos.[106] Philip III's Somatophylakes must also have been selected with a view to keeping Antigonos in check,[107] a policy obscured

---

[105]He had been pressured to resign the guardianship of the Kings, which was then voted upon Antipatros (Diod. 18. 39. 2-3), and the rule of Leonnatos' old satrapy may be regarded as compensation.

[106]Menandros reappears as Antigonos' agent in Kappadokia (Diod. 18. 59. 1; Plut. *Eum.* 9. 8-11). Diod. 18. 50. 5 claims that Antigonos was planning to drive out the satraps of Asia and replace them with his friends (cf. Diod. 18. 62. 7). For Menandros and Philotas see also Billows, *Antigonos* 402 f., no. 71; 423 f., no. 95.

[107]Billows, *Antigonos* 70, view of 'the selections clearly being intended to honour and please great nobles' misses the point.

by the unexpected return of the Kings to Makedonia. For Antipatros had intended, all along, that the Kings remain in Asia (cf. Diod. 18. 18. 7, where Antipatros helps Krateros prepare for his return to Asia: that is, to assume the *prostasia* of Philip III), and he committed them to Antigonos' care (καὶ τούτῳ [sc. 'Αντιγόνῳ] τοὺς βασιλέας φρουρεῖν τε καὶ θεραπεύειν προσταξας, Arr. *Succ.* 1. 38). Hence the following appointees as Philip's Somatophylakes: the brother and son respectively of Lysimachos and Polyperchon (4. 1 and 4. 3 below), staunch allies of Antipatros; the brother of Peukestas (4. 2 below), perhaps because Peukestas was the most reliable of the eastern satraps; Ptolemaios son of Ptolemaios may have been the nephew of Antigonos, as Billows suggests (see 4. 4 below), and thus a conciliatory appointment.

4. 1. Autodikos son of Agathokles

Literature. Berve ii 95, no. 187; id., *RE* Supplbd. iv (1924), 57; Wilcken, *RE* ii (1896), 2602, no. 7.

Autodikos son of Agathokles (Arr. *Succ.* 1. 38) was a younger brother of Lysimachos.[108] He was appointed Somatophylax of Philip III Arrhidaios in 320, but there is no indication of how long he held this office. Autodikos may have remained with the King until his capture by Olympias' forces. He is not named again in the historical accounts, but a statue dedicated at Oropos by King Lysimachos to Autodikos' wife Adeia suggests that he was still alive in the 280s (Dittenberger, *Syll.*³ 373).[109]

4. 2. Amyntas son of Alexandros

Literature. Berve ii 26, no. 56; Kaerst, *RE* i (1894), 2007, no. 20.

The son of Alexandros of Mieza (cf. Arr. *Ind.* 18. 6), Amyntas was the brother of the Royal Hypaspist and Somatophylax, Peukestas, and was himself appointed Somatophylax of Philip III Arrhidaios at Triparadeisos in 320 B.C. (Arr. *Succ.* 1. 38). Otherwise nothing is known about him unless he can identified with the Amyntas who served as

---

[108]His birthdate is difficult to determine. One assumes that he was born at least in the late 340s, unless he was older than Philippos, who died at the end of 328 and could scarcely have been born much later than 348. At any rate, it is conceivable that both Philippos and Autodikos accompanied Alexander III to Asia as Pages.

[109]βασιλεὺς Λυσίμαχος | "Αδειαν τὴν Αὐτοδίκου | τοῦ ἀδελφοῦ γυναῖκα..... Nothing indicates that Adeia was a widow at this time.

hipparch of Perdikkas' expedition against Kypros in 321/0 (Arr. *Succ.* 24. 6, lines 26-27). If this is the case, then the entire force will have gone over to Antigonos and received favourable treatment from Antipatros: Medios of Larisa, the *xenagos* of this expedition, is found in the camp of Antigonos. Antipatros may have found Peukestas a useful ally in the east, to keep both Eumenes and Antigonos in check; for it is perhaps significant that Antipatros did not appoint Peithon's brother Eudamos (or another, if one existed) in place of Amyntas son of Alexandros. The appointment of the latter suggests that Antipatros trusted Peukestas more than he did Peithon.

4. 3. Alexandros son of Polyperchon

Literature. Berve ii 21, no. 39; Kaerst, *RE* i (1894), 1435, no. 13.

Son of the taxiarch and later ἐπιμελετής Polyperchon, Alexandros was thus born before 334 and, in the light of his appointment as Somatophylax of Philip III at Triparadeisos in 320 (Arr. *Succ.* 1. 38), most likely in the 340s. His appointment as Somatophylax was undoubtedly intended to give Polyperchon some input into the management of affairs. Conversely, it may be seen as a way for Antipatros the Regent to keep at his court the relatives of prominent men, who might serve as hostages.

4. 4. Ptolemaios son of Ptolemaios

Literature. Berve ii 335, no. 669; Droysen ii^3 1. 90, n.45; Billows, *Antigonos* 425 f., no. 99, s.v. 'Polemaios I'; 426-430, no. 100, s.v. 'Polemaios II'.

Droysen identified Ptolemaios the father as the son of Seleukos, but this must be ruled out if we accept the view (stated below §6) that Ptolemaios son of Seleukos was coeval with Alexander the Great and a Royal Hypaspist rather than Somatophylax. The Somatophylax Ptolemaios (patronymic unknown; 1. 1 above) deserves consideration (Berve ii 335). This would suggest, however, that Alexander's Somatophylax was closely related to one of the major political figures of 320 B.C., and for this view we have no documented support. That the father was Ptolemy son of Lagos is generally rejected (Berve ii 335: 'der Lagide scheidet selbstverständlich von vornherein aus'!; cf. Droysen, ii^3 1. 90, n.45), though he could conceivably have had a son, born in the late 340s, who died not long after the birth of Keraunos.

Billows (*Antigonos* 425 f., no. 99) has now made a strong case for the identification of Philip III's Somatophylax (Arr. *Succ.* 1. 38) with Polemaios, the nephew of Antigonos Monophthalmos. The confusion of Ptolemaios and Polemaios is common enough in the literary sources. *I.*

Iasos, no. 2 (line 10) shows that this nephew of Antigonos was the son of Polemaios, and it is difficult to resist identifying him with P(t)olemaios son of Philippos (Berve ii 336, no. 671; Arr. 1. 14. 6, 15. 1). The elder P(t)olemaios would thus have been Antigonos' brother; since he died in 313 B.C. (Diod. 19. 68. 5), he cannot be identified with the Somatophylax who died at Halikarnassos (1. 1 above). Polemaios son of Polemaios would therefore have been named Somatophylax as a concession to Antigonos, whose power was restricted by Antipatros' satrapal and military appointments.

5. Somatophylakes of Alexander IV?

5. 1. Philippos son of ?

Literature. Schoch, *RE* xix (1938), 2335, no. 17; Chr. Habicht, 'Literarische und epigraphische Überlieferung zur Geschichte Alexanders und seiner ersten Nachfolger', in *Akten des VI. Intern. Kongr. für griech. und latein. Epigraphik* (Munich, 1973), 367-377, esp. 369 ff., esp. 374, n.35; S. M. Burstein, '*IG* ii^2 561 and the Court of Alexander IV', *ZPE* 24 (1977), 223-225; Heckel, '*IG* ii^2 561 and the Status of Alexander IV', *ZPE* 40 (1980), 249 f.; id., 'Honours for Philip and Iolaos (*IG* ii^2 561)', *ZPE* 44 (1981), 75-77; Billows, *Antigonos* 421-423, no. 93.

IG ii^2 561 names a certain Philippos — his patronymikon cannot be restored with any certainty — who had been a Somatophylax of a Makedonian King; only Alexander can plausibly be restored. Billows suggests identification with Philippos son of Balakros, arguing from the use of the term σωματοφύλαξ that 'Philippos had been ... most probably an officer in the royal squadron of the Hypaspists' (422). But, although σωματοφύλακες is a term that a Makedonian, like Ptolemy son of Lagos, might use of a portion of the hypaspists, because he understood their origins and functions, it is not very likely that an Athenian public document would use the term in such a way; the term ὑπασπιστής does appear, though only once, on an Athenian inscription (*IG* ii^2 329).[110] Even if it were possible that σωματοφύλαξ here means a commander of the hypaspists, it remains highly improbable that Philippos son of Balakros, who had been a taxiarch, or who had, at least temporarily, commanded a brigade of pezhetairoi, would be identified as the holder of a lesser office in an honorary decree, which

---

[110]Cf. A. J. Heisserer, *Alexander the Great and the Greeks. The Epigraphic Evidence* [Norman, Oklahoma, 1980], 3).

included the highlights of his career.[111] Whoever this man was, he was clearly a Somatophylax of Alexander IV and, as such, probably related to one of the influential officers who forged the settlement at Triparadeisos.

5. 2. Iolaos

Literature. Chr. Habicht, 'Literarische und epigraphische Überlieferung zur Geschichte Alexanders und seiner ersten Nachfolger', in *Akten des VI. Intern. Kongr. für griech. und latein. Epigraphik* (Munich, 1973), 367-377, esp. 369 ff., esp. 374, n.35; S. M. Burstein, '*IG* ii² 561 and the Court of Alexander IV', *ZPE* 24 (1977), 223-225; Heckel, '*IG* ii ²561 and the Status of Alexander IV', *ZPE* 40 (1980), 249 f.; id., 'Honours for Philip and Iolaos (*IG* ii² 561)', *ZPE* 44 (1981), 75-77; A. Oikonomides, 'The Decree of the Athenian Orator Hyperides honoring the Macedonians Iolaos and Medios', *ΠΡΑΚΤΙΚΑ Β'* (Athens, 1987), 169-182; Billows, *Antigonos* 394-395, no. 57.

IG ii² 561 identifies a second Somatophylax of King [Alexander] as Iolaos. My reading of lines 6-7 is as follows (*ZPE* 44 [1981], 75): [κα]ὶ Ἰόλαος κ[....9..... γενόμενloι] σωματοφ[ύλακες Ἀλεξάνδρου]. Whether the κ which precedes the lacuna is the beginning of a patronymikon (so Billows 395) or of the word καί is uncertain. Billows identifies Iolaos as a hypaspist officer of Alexander the Great, but this seems unlikely (cf. 5. 1 above).

The temptation to identify Philippos and Iolaos with the sons of Antipatros, who were *somatophylakes* (= Pages; see below Part C, 1. 15, 1. 17) of Alexander the Great, must be resisted. [Plut.] *Vit. X or.* 9 = *Mor.* 849f claims that the Athenian orator Hypereides proposed to honour them as benefactors, since they had poisoned the King. *IG* ii² 561 is a decree of Stratokles (the restoration is virtually certain — despite the efforts of Oikonomides, 169-182), and Iolaos himself was already dead in 317 (Diod. 19. 11. 8). The mention of both Antigonos and Demetrios (lines 11-12) suggests a date later than 317 B.C.: I restore the text of lines 11-14 as: ...στρ[ατευόμενοι μετὰ Ἀντιl]γόνου κα[ὶ Δημητρίου συνηγωνί]|ζοντ[ο ὑπὲρ τῆς ἐλευθερίας καὶ τ]ῆς [δημοκρατίας......12......]. Such language would scarcely be appropriate in the period when Nikanor was holding Athens for Kassandros, who was at that time an ally of Antigonos.

---

[111]Billows (422) may be correct in rejecting my reading Μ[ενελάου Μακεδών], but Β[αλάκρου Μακεδών] fits neither Kirchner's text (which requires 13 letter spaces) or mine (15 letter spaces).

6. The case of Ptolemaios son of Seleukos.

Literature. Berve ii 335 f., no. 670; Hoffmann 174; Beloch iii² 2. 327.

Ptolemaios was probably from Tymphaia (so Berve ii 335) or from Orestis and a relative of Seleukos son of Antiochos (Hoffmann 174). Arrian (1. 24. 1) calls him ἕνα τῶν σωματοφυλάκων τῶν βασιλικῶν, leading some scholars to believe that he was one of the Seven.[112] But this presents problems. In late 334 Ptolemaios led the newly-weds back to Makedonia for the winter (Arr. 1. 24. 1), returning to Gordion in the spring of 333 with these men and substantial reinforcements (Arr. 1. 29. 4; cf. Curt. 3. 1. 24). When we meet him again in 333, he is no longer a Somatophylax but a taxiarch at Issos, where he loses his life. His brigade was now assigned to the Tymphaian Polyperchon (Arr. 2. 12. 2). Berve (ii 336) suggested that Ptolemaios ceased to be a member of the Seven because his mission to Makedonia required him to be away from the King for an extended period, and when he returned Alexander placed him in charge of the Tymphaian infantry. But such a change of command is in fact a demotion. We do not know who replaced him as Somatophylax, and it is hard to imagine that a man would have been willing to give up his high rank for a belated honeymoon. Furthermore, we have the case of Leonnatos, who, although a member of the Seven, was absent from the King's side for short periods without relinquishing the rank of Somatophylax, or of Perdikkas who was taxiarch and then hipparch while he belonged to the Seven. Those who gave up the title of Somatophylax were given other permanent appointments (Menes, Balakros) or had been charged with some crime (Demetrios). It is more likely that Ptolemaios was educated as a Page, served as a member of the *agema* (ἕνα τῶν σωματοφυλάκων τῶν βασιλικῶν), where he distinguished himself, and, on his return from Makedonia, was promoted to taxiarch.

7. Conclusion

Leonnatos' career (see ii 3) best illustrates how a Makedonian noble could progress through the ranks. Unfortunately, his is the only fully-documented example: often an individual is encountered at one stage of his career or mentioned on the occasion of his death. It would have been interesting to follow the career progress of Alexander's Pages, but,

---

[112]Beloch (iii² 2. 327), however, assumes that he was so described through 'Verwechslung mit dem Somatophylax Ptolemaeos, dessen Tod vor Halikarnassos kurz vorher berichtet wird...'.

of those known for certain by name, all except Metron, Aretis, Iolaos and Philippos (and Excipinos?) were executed or fell into disgrace. Metron may be identical with the trierarch at the Hydaspes (Arr. *Ind.* 18. 5; cf. Berve, nos. 519-520), but this would demonstrate only that he was a man of means who continued to prosper under Alexander. Aretis, on the other hand, if Alexander's ἀναβολεύς (Arr. 1. 15. 6; cf. 4. 13. 1: τοὺς ἵππους παρὰ τῶν ἱπποκόμων δεχόμενοι ἐκεῖνοι προσῆγον καὶ ἀνέβαλλον οὗτοι βασιλέα) was in fact one of the Pages, may be identical with the commander of the ἱππεῖς πρόδρομοι at Gaugamela (Arr. 3. 12. 3; cf. Berve, no. 109, s.v. 'Αρέτης), though we know nothing about the intermediate stages of his career. Iolaos was involved in the negotiations between Perdikkas and Antipatros in 323/2 (Arr. *Succ.* 1. 21), but by 317 B.C. he was already dead (Diod. 19. 11. 8); Philippos (probably also a Page of Alexander) served as *strategos* of his brother Kassandros against Aiakides of Epeiros and the Aitolians in 313 (Diod. 19. 74. 3-6). Olympias' brother Alexandros was brought up as a Page at Philip's court, but he soon returned to Epeiros. Nevertheless we do find other Aiakids in higher positions: Neoptolemos as ἀρχιυπασπιστής (Plut. *Eum.* 1. 6) and Arybbas as one of the Seven (Arr. 3. 5. 5).

Amongst the Royal Hypaspists, apart from Perdikkas, Peukestas and Leonnatos, we have Pausanias and his namesake, both of whom were probably Pages of Philip II shortly before 336 B.C. Both died in that year. Philippos son of Agathokles and Limnaios (cf. Charos, Alexandros, Hegesimachos, Nikanor and others) perished during the performance of exceptional deeds and we know nothing of the early stages of their careers. Attalos son of Andromenes appears to have been a member of the *agema* and later a taxiarch.

Perhaps not surprisingly, the best examples of career progress among the Makedonian aristocrats involve the young men who were Alexander's σύντροφοι: Hephaistion, Leonnatos, Marsyas (brother of Antigonos Monophthalmos), Perdikkas, Ptolemaios son of Seleukos, and Seleukos son of Antiochos (perhaps relatives), Attalos son of Andromenes, and others. In 336, when Philip II died, they were still in the very early stages of their careers, and they found that some of the major positions in the Makedonian army were in the hands of slightly older (8-9 years older?) men, many of them the *syntrophoi* of Amyntas Perdikka (born c. 365).[113] Some of this latter group died in battle or were promoted to administrative positions (the final stage of the Makedonian *cursus honorum*), others were eliminated on genuine or trumped-up charges of conspiracy. Alexandros Lynkestes, Philotas,

---

[113] See also W. Heckel, 'Factions and Macedonian Politics in the Reign of Alexander the Great', in *Ancient Macedonia IV* (Thessaloniki, 1986), 293-305, esp. 302 ff.

Demetrios the Bodyguard, all were part of this system, but we know only what rank each man held at the time of his arrest or execution. And it is only an exceptional man, like Leonnatos, who distinguished himself at every stage of his political and military career, who gives us a clear insight into the question of career progress and the concept of σωματοφυλακία.

C. PAGES AND ROYAL HYPASPISTS

1. The Pages

1. 1. Antikles

Literature. Berve ii 44, no. 88; id., *RE* Supplbd iv (1924), 32, no. 8; Hoffmann 180.

The son of Theokritos, Antikles was persuaded by Hermolaos and Sostratos to join the 'conspiracy of the Pages' in 327 (Arr. 4. 13. 4; Curt. 8. 6. 9, slightly different). He was later arrested, tortured and executed (Arr. 4. 13. 7, 14. 3; Curt. 8. 8. 20; cf. Plut. *Alex.* 55. 7; Justin 12. 7. 2).

1. 2. Antipatros

Literature. Berve ii 45-46, no. 93; Kaerst, *RE* i (1894), 2509, no. 15; Hoffmann 179-180.

Antipatros was the son of Asklepiodoros, satrap of Syria (Arr. 4. 13. 4; Curt. 8. 6. 9 has *Antipatrum Asclepiodorumque*. Cf. Hoffmann 180). Convinced by Hermolaos and Sostratos to join their conspiracy, he was later arrested, tortured and executed for his complicity (Curt. 8. 8. 20; Arr. 4. 13. 7, 14. 3; Plut. *Alex.* 55. 7; Justin 12. 7. 2).

1. 3. Aphthonetos

Literature. Hoffmann 179; N. G. L. Hammond, 'Royal Pages, Personal Pages, and Boys Trained in the Macedonian Manner during the Period of the Temenid Monarchy', *Historia* 39 (1990), 261-290, esp. 264 f.

A Page of Philip II, he was scourged for leaving his τάξις (= the *regia cohors*) in order to quench his thirst at an inn (Aelian, *VH* 14. 48: Ἀφθόνητον γοῦν ἐμαστίγωσεν, ὅτι τὴν τάξιν ἐκλιπὼν ἐξετράπετο τῆς ὁδοῦ διψήσας καὶ παρῆλθεν εἰς πανδοκέως). Hammond takes ἀφθόνητον as an adverb rather than a proper name: 'Philip flogged one boy unenviably (ἀφθόνητον) for falling out from an exercise and going into a public house...'. But Ἀφθόνητον must be the object of ἐμαστίγωσεν, and thus the name of the Page in question.

1. 4. Aphthonios (Elaptonius)

Literature. Berve ii 149, no. 296; id., *RE* Supplbd iv (1924), 269; Hoffmann 180.

Named Elaptonius by Curt. 8. 6. 9 (Hedicke emends the name to *Aphtonius*; 'der...Name ist sicher verderbt', Hoffmann 180) as a member of the 'conspiracy of the Pages', he was arrested, tortured and executed (Curt. 8. 8. 20; cf. Arr. 4. 13. 7, 14. 2, who does not name either Elaptonius or Aphthonios; Plut. *Alex.* 55. 7; Justin 12. 7. 2).

1. 5. Archedamos

Literature. Hoffmann 179.

A Page of Philip II, he was put to death for failing to take up arms on Philip's orders: καὶ Ἀρχέδαμον ἀπέκτεινεν [sc. Φίλιππος], ὅτι προστάξαντος αὐτοῦ ἐν τοῖς ὅπλοις συνέχειν ἑαυτόν, ὁ δὲ ἀπεδύσατο (Aelian, *VH* 14. 48).

1. 6. Aretis

Literature. Berve ii 58, no. 110; id., RE Supplbd iv (1924), 46; Hoffmann 179.

Termed by Arr. 1. 15. 6 ἀναβολεὺς τῶν βασιλικῶν (to which Berve ii 58 adds [παίδων]), he fought at the Graneikos river but was unable to hand Alexander a lance since his, like that of the King, had been broken in the engagement. Possibly (*contra* Hoffmann 179) he is to be identified with the commander of the ἱππεῖς πρόδρομοι at Gaugamela (Arr. 3. 12. 3; Curt. 4. 15. 13); Krüger (followed by Roos/Wirth and now P. A. Brunt) reads Ἀρέτην for Ἄρετιν in Arr. 1. 15. 6.

1. 7. Charikles

Literature. Berve ii 407, no. 824; id., RE Supplbd IV (1924), 215, no. 4a; Hoffmann 180.

Charikles son of Menandros (Arr. 4. 13. 7), the satrap of Lydia, was perhaps one of the King's Pages in 327 B.C. Though not party to the Hermolaos conspiracy, he was informed of it by his lover Epimenes (no. 1. 8 below) and brought the matter to the attention of the latter's brother, Eurylochos (thus Arr. 4. 13. 7; Curt. 8. 6. 20 omits Charikles entirely). The matter was revealed to Alexander by Eurylochos, through the agency of Ptolemy and Leonnatos. The conspirators themselves were arrested, tortured and executed, but Charikles and Epimenes were spared (cf. Curt. 8. 6. 26).[114]

---

[114] I have included Charikles in this catalogue with some reluctance; it is not at all certain that he was a Page at this time. He may have been older, with Epimenes as his *eromenos*. There is, however, little doubt that at some earlier point in his career he had been a Page.

1. 8. Epimenes

Literature. Berve ii 150, no. 300; id., *RE* Supplbd iv (1924), 275, no. 3; Hoffmann 180.

The son of Arsaios (Arr. 4. 13. 4, 7; Berve ii 150, following Hoffmann, prints Arseas; Brunt, *Arrian* i 383, 385: 'Arseus') and party to the 'conspiracy of the Pages' (Curt. 8. 6. 9), he appears to have undergone a change of heart (Curt. 8. 6. 20) and revealed the plot either to his lover Charikles (no. 1. 7 above; Arr. 4. 13. 7), who in turn informed Epimenes' brother, Eurylochos, or to Eurylochos himself (Curt. 8. 6. 20), who brought the matter to Alexander's attention (Curt. 8. 6. 22; Arr. 4. 13. 7). Epimenes was spared for his role in alerting Alexander to the danger (Curt. 8. 6. 26).

1. 9. Eurylochos

Literature. Berve ii 159, no. 322; id., *RE* Supplbd iv (1924), 450, no. 5a; Hoffmann 180.

The brother of Epimenes (Arr. 4. 13. 7; Curt. 8. 6. 20), Eurylochos was presumably also the son of Arsaios (Arr. 4. 13. 3). I do not understand why Berve makes him the brother of Charikles and 'nicht, wie Curt. VIII, 6, 20 angibt, des Epimenes' (ii 159, n.1): Arr. 4. 13. 7 says Χαρικλῆς δὲ φράζει Εὐρυλόχῳ τῷ ἀδελφῷ τῷ Ἐπιμένους (cf. Hoffmann 180). Curtius' claim that Epimenes had wished to keep Eurylochos out of the conspiracy (*quem antea expertem esse consilii voluerat*, 8. 6. 20), suggests that Eurylochos was also one of the Pages (if we assume that the plot was restricted to the Pages). Whether Eurylochos learned of the conspiracy directly from Epimenes (Curt.) or through Charikles (Arr.), he brought the matter to Alexander's attention through the agency of Ptolemy (Arr. 4. 13. 7) and Leonnatos (Curt. 8. 6. 22). Eurylochos was handsomely rewarded by the King, who spared Epimenes as well (8. 6. 26).

1. 10. Excipinus (?)

Literature. Hoffmann 180-181; Berve ii 158, no. 318 (Euxenippos).

Hoffmann's (180-181) identification of Excipinus (a *iuvenis* of considerable beauty, so Curt. 7. 9. 19) as a Page is based on no firm evidence.

1. 11. Gorgatas

Literature. Berve ii 113, no. 232; id., *RE* Supplbd iv (1924), 710; Hoffmann 205.

A young man of Makedonian stock, Gorgatas (cf. Gorgias, Hekataios, nos. 1. 12-13) was brought against the wishes of Olympias from her court to Alexander in Asia by Amyntas son of Andromenes (Curt. 7. 1. 38-39). Possibly he was enrolled in the Pages (cf. Curt. 5. 1. 42; Diod. 17. 65. 1).

1. 12. Gorgias

Literature. Berve ii 114, no. 234; id., *RE* Supplbd iv (1924), 710, no. 3a; Hoffmann 205.

A young Makedonian, Gorgias (cf. Gorgatas, Hekataios, nos. 1. 11, 1. 13) was brought against the wishes of Olympias from her court to Alexander in Asia by Amyntas son of Andromenes (Curt. 7. 1. 38-39). Possibly he was enrolled in the Pages (cf. Curt. 5. 1. 42; Diod. 17. 65. 1).

1. 13. Hekataios

Literature. Berve ii 149, no. 293; id., *RE* Supplbd iv (1924), 714, no. 1a; Hoffmann 205.

A young Makedonian, Hekataios (cf. Gorgatas, Gorgias, nos. 1. 11-12) was brought against the wishes of Olympias from her court to Alexander in Asia by Amyntas son of Andromenes (Curt. 7. 1. 38-39). Possibly he was enrolled in the Pages (cf. Curt. 5. 1. 42; Diod. 17. 65. 1).

1. 14. Hermolaos

Literature. Berve ii 152-153, no. 305; Plaumann, *RE* viii (1913), 890-891, no. 1; Hoffmann 179.

Hermolaos was the son of the ilarch Sopolis and was a student of Kallisthenes (Arr. 4. 13. 2; Curt. 8. 7. 2-3), though the latter relationship was unduly emphasised in order to implicate Kallisthenes, who was probably responsible for the education of all the Pages and was most likely innocent (Plut. *Alex.* 55. 6; Curt. 8. 7. 10; 8. 8. 21; Justin 12. 7. 2). After he had been flogged for anticipating the King in the hunt and striking down a wild boar (Arr. 4. 13. 2; Curt. 8. 6. 7), Hermolaos conspired with several other Pages to murder Alexander while he slept (Arr. 4. 13. 4; Curt. 8. 6. 8-10). In Curtius' version (8. 6. 8), it was Hermolaos' lover Sostratos who persuaded him to join a plot against the King. Whether there is any truth to the story of the boar-hunt, we cannot say. But there were clearly political overtones (Arr. 4. 14. 2; Curt. 8. 7. 1 ff.), and the 'conspiracy of the Pages' was symptomatic of the friction between Alexander (and his faithful clique) and the more conservative elements in the Makedonian aristocracy. Betrayed by some of his accomplices and repudiated by his own father (Curt. 8. 7. 2), Hermolaos was arrested and tried (Curt. 8. 7. 1 ff.; Arr. 4. 13. 7-14. 2), and condemned to death by stoning (Arr. 4. 14. 2; Plut. *Alex.* 55. 7; Curt. 8. 8. 20 says that the Pages themselves put to death Hermolaos and his accomplices).

1. 15. Iolaos

Literature. Berve ii 184, no. 386.

Iolaos was the youngest son of Antipatros. That he was a Page is surely implied by Justin (12. 14. 9) who describes him and his brother as *Philippus et Iollas praegustare ac temperare potum regis soliti....* Earlier Justin incorrectly includes another son of Antipatros, Kassandros, who was certainly too old to be a Page in 323 B.C. (*Igitur ad occupandum regem Cassandrum filium dato veneno subornat, qui cum fratribus Philippo et Iolla ministrare regi solebat...*, 12. 14. 6). Iolaos is given the title ἀρχιοινοχόος (Plut. *Alex.* 74. 2; cf. Arr. 7. 27. 2: οἰνοχόος βασιλικός), but I see no difficulty in assuming that he held this position as one of the Pages (cf. Aretis the ἀναβολεύς).

Of his life very little is known. Soon after Alexander's death, he acted as an intermediary for his father and Perdikkas, bringing to Asia in 322/1 his sister Nikaia, the latter's intended bride (Arr. *Succ.* 1. 21). Thereafter, he appears to have returned to Makedonia, to the court of his father. By 317/6, he was already dead: Olympias, as an act of vengeance against her son's 'murderers', overturned his grave (Diod. 19. 11. 8).[115]

1. 16. Metron

Literature. Berve ii 260-261, no. 520.

Makedonian, perhaps the son of Epicharmos from Pydna, a trierarch at the Hydaspes in 326 B.C. (Arr. *Ind.* 18. 5), unless this identification is to be rejected on the grounds of age (so Berve ii 260, no. 519; but we may

---

[115]For his role in the alleged poisoning of the King see Arr. 7. 27. 1-3; Justin 12. 13. 6 ff., esp. 12. 14. 6-9; Curt. 10. 10. 14-19; Plut. *Alex.* 77. 2; [Plut.] *vit. X or.* 849f. See also Heckel, *LDT*.

have a parallel case of rapid promotion if Aretis [1. 6 above] is identical with Aretes). When Kebalinos had no success in bringing the news of Dimnos' plot to the King's attention through Philotas (see Berve, nos. 269, 418, 802), he informed Metron: *nobili iuveni — Metron erat ei nomen — super armamentarium posito, quod scelus pararetur indicat*, Curt. 6. 7. 22; Diod. 17. 79. 4: τῶν βασιλικῶν τινι παίδων (cf. Berve ii 260, who identifies him as a Page). He revealed to Alexander the conspiracy of Dimnos and the role of Philotas (Curt. 6. 7. 23; Diod. 17. 79. 5; cf. Plut. *Alex.* 49. 6; Hamilton, *PA* 136). As a Page, Metron undoubtedly came from a good aristocratic family, and Alexander may have further enriched him for his part in bringing the Dimnos/Philotas affair to his attention. Hence a trierarchy in 326 is not entirely out of the question.[116]

1. 17. Philippos

Literature. Berve ii 383, no. 777; Sandberger 19.

A son of Antipatros, Philippos was the brother of Iolaos (no. 1. 15 above). That he was a Page is surely implied by Justin (12. 14. 9) who describes him and his brother as *Philippus et Iollas praegustare ac temperare potum regis soliti....* Earlier Justin incorrectly includes another son of Antipatros, Kassandros, who was certainly too old to be a Page in 323 B.C. (*Igitur ad occupandum regem Cassandrum filium dato veneno subornat, qui cum fratribus Philippo et Iolla ministrare regi solebat...*, 12. 14. 6). On Philippos Berve comments: 'Es ist möglich, daß er nur Page des Königs war' (ii 383).

It appears that, after the death of Alexander and the settlement of affairs in Babylon, Philippos returned to Makedonia with his brother Iolaos. He later served his brother Kassandros as *strategos* in the campaign against the Aitolians, and won a victory over King Aiakides of Epeiros at Oiniadai in 313 B.C., in which Aiakides himself met his end (Diod. 19. 74. 3-5; Paus. 1. 11. 4; cf. Sandberger 19, no. 5). His successes in Akarnania frightened the Aitolians, who took refuge in the mountains (Diod. 19. 74. 6), but nothing else is recorded about Philippos' generalship or his life. His son Antipatros ruled Makedonia for 45 days in 280 B.C. (Porphyry, *FGrHist* 260 F3 §10),

---

[116]I am tempted to see in the trierarch, Bagoas son of Pharnouches (Arr. *Ind.* 18. 8), the famous eunuch of Dareios III, an identification which Berve (no. 194) rejects. Eunuchs could not have sons, but they certainly did have fathers, and the influence of the eunuch may account for Alexander's ill-advised appointment of Pharnoukes as leader of the force ambushed by Spitamenes at the Polytimetos.

following the death of Ptolemaios Keraunos and the brief reign of the latter's brother, Meleagros (cf. Walbank, *HMac* iii 253).

1. 18. Philotas

Literature. Berve ii 392, no. 801; Hoffmann 180.

Philotas appears to have been the son of a prominent Thrakian Karsis (Arr. 4. 13. 4) and perhaps a Makedonian woman; he would thus have been named for the maternal grandfather (Berve ii 392; Hoffmann 180). In 327, he became involved in the conspiracy of Hermolaos and was tried and executed (Arr. 4. 13. 4, 7; Curt. 8. 8. 20; Plut. *Alex.* 55. 7; Justin 12. 7. 2).

1. 19. Sostratos

Literature. Berve ii 369, no. 738; Hoffmann 179; Heckel, *LCM* 6 (1981), 63-64.

The son of Amyntas (Arr. 4. 13. 3; Berve ii 369, n.2: 'Fälschlich schreibt Itiner. 97 cum Sostrato et Amynta'; cf. Curt. 8. 6. 9, *Antipatrum Asclepiodorumque* and no. 1. 2 above) and lover of Hermolaos (Arr. 4. 13. 3; Curt. 8. 6. 8), Sostratos joined (Arr.) or instigated (Curt.) the 'conspiracy of the Pages' on account of the outrage done to Hermolaos (no. 1. 14 above). For his part he was arrested, tortured and executed (Arr. 4. 13. 3 - 14. 2; Curt. 8. 8. 20; Plut. *Alex.* 55. 7; Justin 12. 7. 2).

Curtius, in a particularly corrupt passage (8. 6. 9), names also Nicostratus (Berve ii 280, no. 570; Hoffmann 180); this is probably a corruption of the name Sostratos (Heckel, *LCM* 6 [1981], 63 f.).

2. Some Royal Hypaspists

2. 1. Alexandros

Literature. Berve ii 21, no. 40; id., *RE* Supplbd iv (1924), 15, no. 34e.

Together with Charos, Alexandros led a band of 30 young men selected from the Royal Hypaspists for the assault on Aornos: *iuvenesque promptissimos ex sua cohorte XXX delegit; duces his dati sunt Charus et Alexander* (Curt. 8. 11. 9-10). Berve in *RE* identified him as 'ein junger Makedone aus dem Pagenkorps Alexanders d. Gr. (dieses ist bei Curt. Ruf. VIII, 11, 9 mit *cohors* gemeint)...'. But in the *Alexanderreich* he assigns Alexandros and Charos to the 'Leibhypaspisten' (cf. Berve ii 382, n.2, for the case of Philippos). Now the 30 *iuvenes ex sua cohorte* appear to be Royal Hypaspists — although the term *iuvenes* is applied by Curtius to the Pages, and Metron in particular, a known

Page, is called *nobilis iuvenis*. Since we are dealing with a continuation of the concept of σωματοφυλακία, the *cohors* appears to be the *agema* of the hypaspists. Alexandros was killed in a valiant assault on Aornos (Curt. 8. 11. 15).

2. 2. Charos

Literature. Berve ii 408, no. 826; id., *RE* Supplbd iv (1924), 215.

A member of Alexander's cohort (Curt. 8. 11. 9-10) but apparently not a Page, he commanded (together with Alexandros) a troop of 30 hypaspists in an assault on Aornos, where he was killed in battle and fell upon the corpse of his friend Alexandros (Curt. 8. 11. 15-16).

2. 3. Hegesimachos (Simachos)

Literature. Berve ii 166, no. 344; cf. Hoffmann 215 'Symmachus'.

A *nobilis iuvenis*, Hegesimachos (along with Nikanor) led a band of young men (*promptissimi iuvenum*, cf. Alexandros and Charos) in an unsuccessful attack on an island in the Hydaspes river (Curt. 8. 13. 13) and perished in the attempt (8. 13. 15-16). Berve (ii 166) identifies him as 'aus dem Korps der Leibhypaspisten'.

2. 4. Limnaios

Literature. Niese i 143 f., n.4; Hoffmann 147; Berve ii 237, no. 474.

Curt. 9. 5. 15-16 : 'Timaeus'. The form Limnaios (Plut. *Alex.* 63; *de fort. Al.* 1. 2 = *Mor.* 327b; 2. 13 = *Mor.* 344d) is certainly correct: a Limnaios son of Harpalos appears in an inscription from Kassandreia (Hatzopoulos, Μελετέματα 5 [1988], 17 f.; cf. A. Henry, 'Bithys son of Kleon of Lysimacheia', in *Owls for Athens* [Oxford, 1990], 179 f.); at Beroia (Tataki 215, nos. 812-814, and p. 423); and at the court of Philip V (cf. Polyb. 18. 34. 4; Schoch, *RE* xiii [1926], no. 3). One of the Royal Hypaspists (Plut. *Alex.* 63. 5), Limnaios accompanied Alexander into the town of the Mallians in India, where he was killed defending the King, who was seriously wounded (Plut. *Alex.* 63. 8; *Mor.* 327b, 344d; Curt. 9. 5. 15-16). Arrian (6. 9. 3; 6. 10. 1-2) does not mention him, and admits that there was disagreement about who defended Alexander on this occasion (6. 11. 7). Arrian names Habreas where the Vulgate sources refer to Limnaios (Berve ii 237 wrongly assumes a confusion of Limnaios and Leonnatos).

2. 5. Nikanor

Literature. Berve ii 277, no. 560; Hoffmann 215.

A *nobilis iuvenis,* Nikanor (along with Hegesimachos) led a band of young men (*promptissimi iuvenum,* cf. Alexandros and Charos) in an unsuccessful attack on an island in the Hydaspes river (Curt. 8. 13. 13) and perished in the attempt (8. 13. 15-16). Berve (ii 277) identifies him as 'vielleicht aus dem Leibhypaspistenkorps'.

2. 6. Pausanias

Literature. W. Heckel, 'Philip and Olympias (337/6 B.C.)', in *Classical Contributions. Studies in honour of Malcolm Francis McGregor,* edited by G. S. Shrimpton and D. J. McCargar (Locust Valley, N.Y., 1981), 51-57, esp. 56.

A young Makedonian of unknown family, identified merely as a lover of Philip II and friend of Attalos (Diod. 16. 93. 4-5), Pausanias was apparently close in age to his namesake from Orestis (2. 7 below), whose rival he had become for Philip's favour. Their homosexual relations with the King had presumably begun during their terms as Pages at the Court. The Orestian is described as τοῦ δὲ βασιλέως σωματοφύλαξ (Diod. 16. 93. 3), and the fact that this Pausanias died fighting on foot in the vicinity of Philip II (πρὸ τοῦ βασιλέως στάς) suggests that he was a Royal Hypaspist, that is, a member of the *agema.* His death occurred in a battle with the Illyrians (Diod. 16. 93. 6), which I would date to early 336 (Heckel, 56).

2. 7. Pausanias of Orestis

Literature. Berve ii 308-309, no. 614; Hoffmann 212; A. B. Bosworth, 'Philip II and Upper Macedonia', *CQ* 21 (1971), 93-105; J. Rufus Fears, 'Pausanias the Assassin of Philip II', *Athenaeum* 53 (1975), 111-135; N. G. L. Hammond, '"Philip's Tomb" in Historical Context', *GRBS* 19 (1978), 331-350, esp. 343.

Pausanias son of Kerastos (Josephus, *AJ* 11. 8. 1 [304]) of Orestis (Diod. 16. 93. 3) is best known as the assassin of Philip II; hence most of what is recorded about him concerns the quarrel with his namesake and rival (2. 6 above; Diod. 16. 93. 3 ff.) and the sordid details of the alleged gang rape instigated by Attalos (Justin 9. 6. 5 ff.; Diod. 16. 93. 7 ff.; Aristotle, *Pol.* 5. 10 1311^b; Plut. *Alex.* 10. 5 includes Attalos' niece Kleopatra as an instigator) and his murder of Philip in an effort to gain some measure of revenge (Diod. 16. 94. 3; Justin 9. 6. 4; Plut. *Alex.* 10. 5-6; Josephus, *AJ* 11. 8. 1 [304]; 19. 1. 13 [95]; Aristotle, *Pol.* 5. 10 1311^b; cf. Aelian, *VH* 3. 45; Val. Max. 1. 8 ext. 9; Cicero, *de Fat.* 3. 5). Pausanias was at the time of Philip's death a σωματοφύλαξ, that is, a Royal Hypaspist (Joh. Antioch. frg. 40; Plut. *de Superst.* 11 = *Mor.* 170e-f calls him δορυφόρος; cf. Justin 9. 6. 4, *nobilis ex Macedonibus adulescens*; Josephus, *AJ* 19. 1. 13 [95], calls him one of Philip's hetairoi). It was alleged that he was incited by Olympias, or even Alexander, to kill Philip (Justin 9. 7. 1 ff.; Plut. *Alex.* 10. 5); Diod. 16. 94. 1-2 claims he was inspired by the sophist Hermokrates. Pausanias was killed by other Royal Hypaspists, as he tried to escape (Diod. 16. 94. 4; cf. Justin 9. 7. 9, where the reference to 'get-away horses' suggests that Justin is compressing a similar story), and his body crucified (Justin 9. 7. 10; 11. 2. 1; cf. *P.Oxy.* 1798; Bosworth, *CQ* 21 [1971], 93 f.; Hammond, *GRBS* 19 [1978], 343 ff.; Welles, *Diodorus* 101, n.2).

2. 8. Philippos

Literature. Berve ii 382-383, no. 774.

Philippos was a brother of Lysimachos (Curt. 8. 2. 35; Justin 15. 3. 12), hence also a son of Agathokles (Arr. 6. 28. 4; *Ind.* 18. 3; *Succ.* 1a. 2). On a campaign in Sogdiana, Philippos accompanied on foot the King (who rode), declining to take Lysimachos' horse (Curt. 8. 2. 35-36). Later, after fighting by Alexander's side, he fainted and died in his arms (8. 2. 37-40). Curt. 8. 2. 35 describes him as follows: *nobiles iuvenes comitari eum soliti defecerant praeter Philippum; Lysimachi frater erat tum primum adultus....* Berve (ii 382, n.2) is certainly correct in assuming that he belonged to the hypaspists: 'als Page würde er als puer bezeichnet und vermutlich beritten gewesen sein.' But the use of the word *iuvenis* does not by itself prove that Philippos was not a Page; cf. the case of Metron (whom Berve himself identified as a Page).

vi. Commanders of Regular Hypaspists

1. The ἀρχιυπασπιστής

The term ἀρχιυπασπιστής appears only in Plutarch (*Eum.* 1. 6), where the Aiakid Neoptolemos is so described. Berve concludes (i 128): 'Der offizielle Titel des Kommandeurs lautete, wenigstens in den letzten Jahren, scheinbar ἀρχιυπασπιστής...'. If this terminology is correct, Neoptolemos was, in all likelihood, the successor of Parmenion's son, Nikanor (whom Arr. 3. 25. 4 calls ὁ τῶν ὑπασπιστῶν ἄρχων), and commander of the hypaspists from 330 until 323.

1. 1. Nikanor son of Parmenion

Literature. Berve ii 275, no. 554; id., *RE* xvii.1 (1936), 266, no. 1.

The second (?) of Parmenion's sons (Arr. 1. 14. 2; 2. 8. 3; 3. 11. 9; Diod. 17. 57. 2; Curt. 3. 9. 7; 4. 13. 27; *Suda*, Harpokration, s.v. Νικάνωρ), Nikanor was the brother of Philotas and Hektor. That he was younger than Philotas is suggested not only by their paternal grandfather's name (Philotas, Arr. 3. 11. 10) but also by the relative importance of their commands: the hipparch of the Companions was unquestionably superior to the ἀρχιυπασπιστής. Philotas was apparently coeval with Amyntas Perdikka and born c. 365; Nikanor can scarcely have been born much later. The prominence of these brothers already in 335/4 must be seen as a reward for Parmenion's help in eliminating Alexander's rival Attalos (Diod. 17. 2. 4-6; 17. 5. 2; Curt. 7. 1. 3), his own son-in-law (Curt. 6. 9. 17). Hence Nikanor, presumably as commander of the hypaspists, was given charge of the phalanx in the Getic campaign of 335 (Arr. 1. 4. 2; cf. Berve ii 275).

At the Graneikos river (334), Nikanor is first named as the hypaspist commander, holding a position just to the right of centre on the Makedonian line, between the Companions and the brigades of the pezhetairoi (Arr. 1. 14. 2). At Issos, Nikanor's hypaspists occupied the far right wing, with the pezhetairoi to their immediate left (Arr. 2. 8. 3; Curt. 3. 9. 7). But in the battle of Gaugamela they were again stationed in the centre between the Companions and pezhetairoi (Arr. 3. 11. 9; cf. Curt. 4. 13. 27). Of Nikanor's actual participation in these battles nothing is known.

Alexander took with him in his pursuit of Dareios, in the final days of that king's life, the most mobile of the infantry, the hypaspists and the Agrianes. But, when it became necessary to proceed only on horseback, he substituted some 500 mounted infantrymen for cavalry and pushed ahead with these *dimachae*, as they were called.[1] Nikanor and Attalos (the commander of the Agrianes) were ordered to follow with the remaining troops (cf. Curt. 5. 13. 19). Although the ἀρχιυπασπιστής would seem to be the superior officer, Arrian (3. 21. 8) treats Nikanor and Attalos as equals — perhaps Attalos was considerably senior, perhaps the special position of the Agrianes in Alexander's army was a factor. Not long afterwards, Nikanor died of illness in Areia (Arr. 3. 25. 4; Curt. 6. 6. 18), where Philotas remained to perform the funeral rites, retaining 2,600 men while Alexander himself continued in pursuit of the rebel Bessos (Curt. 6. 6. 19). Nikanor's successor appears to have been Neoptolemos (1. 2 below).

1. 2. Neoptolemos

Literature. Berve ii 273, no. 548; id., *RE* xvi (1935), 2464, no. 7; Beloch iv² 2. 145-146; Schubert, *Quellen* 162 ff.; G. Wirth, 'Zur grossen Schlacht des Eumenes 322 (PSI 1284)', *Klio* 46 (1965), 283-288; A. B. Bosworth, 'Eumenes, Neoptolemus and *PSI* XII 1284', *GRBS* 19 (1978), 227-237; E. M. Anson, 'Neoptolemus and Armenia', *AHB* 4 (1990), 125-128.

Neoptolemos' patronymikon is unknown, but Arrian (2. 27. 6) introduces him as one of the Aiakidai; hence he was a scion of the Molossian royal house (Beloch iv² 2. 145) and perhaps a relative of Arybbas the Somatophylax (cf. Arr. 3. 5. 5).[2] He probably took part in the Asiatic expedition from the beginning, although he is not mentioned until the campaign of Gaza (late 332), where he was the first to scale the wall (Arr. 2. 27. 6). This act of courage did not go unnoticed by the King, and it is not surprising to find Neoptolemos as the successor of Nikanor son of Parmenion: his designation as ἀρχιυπασπιστής (Plut. *Eum.* 1. 6) must

---

[1] Curt. 5. 13. 8 says they were 300 strong. Cf. Hesychios 1, p.997; Pollux 1. 10. Possibly these included many men from the *agema* who had been trained in horsemanship as Pages of the King.

[2] He may have been related (perhaps distantly) to Perdikkas; for it is highly probable that the Aiakidai intermarried with the royal houses of Upper Makedonia, and the name of Perdikkas' brother, Alketas, was common in the Molossian royal house. We know of at least two marriages between Argeads and Aiakids (Philip and Olympias; Alexandros and Kleopatra); Beroa of Epeiros married the Illyrian Glaukias (Justin 17. 3. 19; Plut. *Pyrrh.* 3. 1-2; cf. Sandberger, no. 22); and Aiakides, the father of Pyrrhos, married Phthia, daughter of Menon of Pharsalos (Plut. *Pyrrh.* 1. 6-7; cf. Sandberger, no. 66).

mean that from 330 until 323 he commanded the regular hypaspists (cf. Berve ii 273).³ Neoptolemos may have been awarded the satrapy of Armenia in the settlement of 323. But the doctored text of Dexippos (*FGrHist* 100 F8 §6 = Arr. *Succ.* 1b. 6, reading Νεοπτολέμου ⟨'Αρμενία, Τληπολέμου⟩ Καρμανία) is suspect since it does violence to the geographical sequence; it is much easier to correct Νεοπτολέμου to Τληπολέμου. Briant (152, n.8) is probably correct to regard him as *strategos* rather than satrap (cf. Plut. *Eum.* 4. 1; 5. 2).⁴ The satrapy was assigned by Alexander to Mithrenes in 331 (Curt. 5. 1. 44); but Orontes, who commanded the Armenians at Gaugamela (Arr. 3. 8. 5), is found ruling it in 317. He may have regained his ancestral territory at Triparadeisos, perhaps through the influence of his friend Peukestas. That Neoptolemos managed only to create havoc in Armenia (Plut. *Eum.* 4. 1), suggests that he was not cooperating with any existing satrap.

When it became clear that war with Krateros and Antipatros was imminent, Perdikkas assigned Kappadokia and Armenia to Eumenes and instructed both his brother Alketas and Neoptolemos to obey the Greek commander (Plut. *Eum.* 5. 2; Diod. 18. 29. 2; Justin 13. 6. 15). Alketas refused to serve, arguing that his Makedonians would be ashamed to fight against Krateros (Plut. *Eum.* 5. 3). Neoptolemos remained with Eumenes but soon intrigued with Antipatros (Arr. *Succ.* 1. 26) and plotted betrayal (Plut. *Eum.* 5. 4), presumably intending to defect with his forces to the enemy once the engagement had begun.⁵ Eumenes, discovering the plot, brought him to battle and defeated him (Plut. *Eum.* 5. 5; Diod. 18. 29. 4-5; Arr. *Succ.* 1. 27; cf. *PSI* xii 1284, with Bosworth, *GRBS* 19 [1978], 227 ff.); Neoptolemos, however, escaped with some 300 horsemen (Diod. 18. 29. 6; cf. Plut. *Eum.* 5. 6; Arr. *Succ.* 1. 27; Justin 13. 8. 5). Taking refuge with Krateros, he persuaded him that the Makedonians in Eumenes' service would receive him favourably (Plut. *Eum.* 6. 1-2); for the mere sight of Krateros would be sufficient to turn the tide of battle. But, when Eumenes learned that Neoptolemos was stationed on the left (Diod. 18. 30. 3; 18. 31. 1), he placed his

---

³Bosworth, *Conquest and Empire* 104, thinks that Neoptolemos' relationship with Alexander (though somewhat distant) may account for his command of the entire hypaspist corps at a time when the King was eliminating larger commands (e.g., the command of the Companion Cavalry was divided between Hephaistion and Black Kleitos after Philotas' death).

⁴Diod. 19. 14. 1, however, calls Philotas (sc. Philippos; cf. Billows, *Antigonos* 90, n.17) *strategos*, although he was clearly satrap of Parthia (Diod. 18. 39. 6; Arr. *Succ.* 1. 35).

⁵Schubert, *Quellen* 163, imagines a more important role for Neoptolemos: that he would keep Eumenes in check in Asia Minor while Krateros and Antipatros proceeded to Egypt.

Makedonian troops opposite him and deployed his barbarians on his own left, facing Krateros (Plut. *Eum.* 6. 7; 7. 3). The stratagem worked, and Krateros, uttering curses against Neoptolemos (Plut. *Eum.* 7. 4), found the enemy stubborn in its resistance. As fate would have it, he perished in the engagement.

The final struggle between Eumenes and Neoptolemos,[6] as reported by Plutarch (*Eum.* 7. 7-12), Diodoros (18. 31) and Nepos (*Eum.* 4. 1-2), derives from a single primary source — Hieronymos (Schubert, *Quellen* 178 f.), who emphasised the long-standing hatred between the two men. That Neoptolemos, who had berated Eumenes as the King's secretary (Plut. *Eum.* 1. 6), found himself overcome in a bitter hand-to-hand struggle (Arr. *Succ.* 1. 27: καὶ πίπτει μὲν Νεοπτόλεμος τῇ αὐτοῦ Εὐμένους τοῦ γραμματέως δεξιᾷ), is perhaps Douris' colouring (cf. Hornblower, *Hieronymus* 196). Felled by his adversary, and prevented by a wound to the knee from rising from the ground, Neoptolemos directed a feeble blow to Eumenes' groin as the Greek was already stripping the armour from his body, a heroic scene which does for Eumenes what Kallisthenes had intended for Alexander in his description of the Graneikos battle. One final thrust to the neck ended Neoptolemos' life (Diod. 18. 31. 5; Justin 13. 8. 8). Since Krateros had already fallen, and with the right wing in disarray, Neoptolemos' death signalled total defeat (Diod. 18. 32. 1; cf. 18. 37. 1). Eumenes' attitude to his defeated adversaries was mixed: he regarded Krateros with honour, Neoptolemos with contempt (Plut. *Eum.* 7. 13). But to have overcome both opponents greatly enhanced his reputation (Diod. 18. 53. 3).

Neoptolemos was a man of great pride and warlike spirit (Arr. *Succ.* 1. 27 calls him ἀνὴρ στρατιωτικὸς καὶ πολέμοις ἠριστευκώς). At some point after 330 he, or perhaps his family, commissioned Apelles to depict him on horseback, fighting the Persians (Pliny, *NH* 35. 96; Pollitt, p. 162). Like many other figures of this period, Neoptolemos did not fare well in the pages of Hieronymos, or even the more sensational Douris. Greek historians depicted him as an arrogant and treacherous knave, humbled by Eumenes of Kardia.

---

[6]It occurred ten days after the initial engagement (Plut. *Eum.* 8. 1).

2. Chiliarchs and Pentakosiarchs

2. 1. Addaios

Literature. Berve ii 12, no. 22; Hoffmann 190-191; Kirchner, *RE* i (1894), 349.

Ἀδδαῖος (Arrian: Ἀδαῖος) is the correct form of the name and is securely attested in inscriptions (see Hoffmann 190-191). A Makedonian of unknown family background, Addaios appears as a brigade (τάξις) commander — presumably of the hypaspists, as the anachronistic use of the title χιλιάρχης suggests (cf. Berve ii 12) — during the siege of Halikarnassos in 334. Here he served under Ptolemaios the Somatophylax, along with Timandros (Arr. 1. 22. 4), and was killed in a skirmish with enemy troops who sallied forth from the Tripylon (Arr. 1. 22. 7).

2. 2. Timandros

Literature. Berve ii 373, no. 746.

Perhaps a chiliarch (cf. Addaios; 2. 1 above; Arr. 1. 22. 7; so Berve ii 373) of the hypaspists, Timandros is named in connection with Addaios as the commander of a τάξις under the general command of the Somatophylax Ptolemaios at Halikarnassos (Arr. 1. 22. 4). Berve's suggestion (ii 373) that he may have been the father of Asklepiodoros (Arr. *Ind.* 18. 3) appears doubtful, since the text seems to be corrupt and Asklepiodoros is probably the son of Eunikos (see Jacoby, *FGrHist* iiB, p. 450). Timandros is not heard of again.

2. 3. Antiochos

Literature. Berve ii 45, no. 90; cf. Kirchner, *RE* i (1894), 2450, no. 13; Badian, *YCS* 24 (1975), 150 f.

A Makedonian of unknown family background, Antiochos first appears in 327 B.C. as a chiliarch of the hypaspists. Alexander sent him, with his chiliarchy and two others, from Dyrta on a reconnaissance mission (Arr. 4. 30. 5-6). Antiochos appears to have been subordinate to Nearchos, who took with him also the Agrianes and the light infantry (ψιλοί). Nothing else is known about him.

2. 4. Atarrhias son of Deinomenes

Literature. Berve ii 90-91, no. 178; Hoffmann 203-204; Kaerst, *RE* ii (1896), 1898.

The only hypaspist commander (excluding the *archihypaspistes* Nikanor) whose patronymikon is attested, Atarrhias son of Deinomenes (Plut. *de fort. Al.* 2. 7 = *Mor.* 339b) is first mentioned as the champion in the military contest in Sittakene which determined the chiliarchs and/or pentakosiarchs of the regular hypaspists (Curt. 5. 2. 5). During his quarrel with Alexander, however, Kleitos alluded to the courage of Atarrhias and the veterans at Halikarnassos (Curt. 8. 1. 36), a claim which seems to be supported by Arrian (1. 21. 5). As the foremost hypaspist officer, after Neoptolemos, Atarrhias appears in charge of the 'police' force that arrested Philotas at Phrada (Curt. 6. 8. 19-22), and he took an active role in demanding the execution of Alexandros Lynkestes (Curt. 7. 1. 5). Nothing further is recorded about Atarrhias, except that he was heavily in debt by the end of the campaign and attempted to defraud the King (Plut. *Mor.* 339b: 'Tarrhias'; cf. Aelian, *VH* 14. 47a: Alexander regarded him as undisciplined). Identification with the homonymous officer of Kassandros, who appears in 317 B.C. (Diod. 19. 36. 2), is possible but cannot be substantiated (rejected by Kaerst, *RE* ii [1896], 1898).

2. 5. Philotas

Literature. Berve ii 398-399, no. 807; id., *RE* xx (1950), 178, no. 5; Bosworth, *Arrian* i 146 f.

Philotas' patronymikon is not given, but Curtius 5. 2. 5 identifies him as Augaeus. Berve ii 398 thinks he may have come from Augaia in Chalkidike; but *Augaeus* might be easily emended to *Aegaeus*. In the contest of valour, held in Sittakene in late 331, Philotas took third place and thus became an officer of the hypaspists (Curt. 5. 2. 5). Bosworth (*Arrian* i 148-149) argues that Curtius has confused matters somewhat and that the victors did not become chiliarchs but rather pentakosiarchs: after the reorganisation of the army, there may have been four chiliarchies (thus Arr. 4. 30. 6; 5. 23. 7), hence eight champions who were appointed pentakosiarchs. Although Curtius does not specify what kinds of troops these men would lead, the names of the first two champions, Atarrhias and Antigenes, make it highly likely that they were, in fact, hypaspists. Philotas may be identical with the man of the same name who, along with Hellanikos, distinguished himself during the siege of Halikarnassos (Arr. 1. 21. 5). This identification, although rejected by Bosworth (*Arrian* i 146 f.), appears to be strengthened by the fact that Atarrhias — like Philotas and Hellanikos, a victor in Sittakene — was also conspicuous at Halikarnassos (Curt. 8. 1. 36). Nothing else is known about about him. Identification with the taxiarch (Berve, no. 803) is impossible.

2. 6. Amyntas

Literature. Heckel, *LCM* 6 (1981), 63.

A Makedonian of unknown origin, Amyntas took fourth place in the contest of valour in Sittakene and received command of a pentakosiarchy, presumably of the hypaspists or of some brigade of light infantry (Curt. 5. 2. 5; cf. Bosworth, *Arrian* i 148 f.). Nothing else is known about this Amyntas, nor is it possible to identify him with any of his namesakes.

2. 7. Antigonos

Literature. Heckel, *LCM* 6 (1981), 63.

Apparently of Makedonian origin, Antigonos is otherwise unknown. In late 331, he finished fifth in the contest of valour in Sittakene and thus became one of the pentakosiarchs of the hypaspists (Curt. 5. 2. 5).

2. 8. Amyntas Lynkestes

Literature. Berve ii 31, no. 63.

An Upper Makedonian, as his ethnic indicates, from Lynkestis, Amyntas placed sixth in the contest in Sittakene (331 B.C.) and was named one of the pentakosiarchs of the hypaspists (Curt. 5. 2. 5). Nothing else is known about him.

2. 9. Theodotos

Literature. Berve ii 176, no. 361.

Theodotos was apparently Makedonian and awarded seventh place in the contest of valour in Sittakene (331 B.C.); hence he became a pentakosiarch of the hypaspists (Curt. 5. 2. 5). He is otherwise unknown. That he was Lysimachos' *thesaurophylax* of the late 280s (Polyainos 4. 9. 4; Geyer, *RE* v.A [1934], 1953, no. 7) is only a very remote possibility; nor can a good case be made for identification with Antigonos Monophthalmos' navarch of 314 (Diod. 19. 64. 5-7); see further Hauben, *Vlootbevelhebberschap* 100, no. 35; Berve ii 176 (undecided) and Billows, *Antigonos* 436, no. 113.

2. 10. Hellanikos

Literature. Berve ii 150, no. 298; Sundwall, *RE* viii (1913), 104, no. 3.

A Makedonian (Hoffmann 195; cf. *IG* x² 2. 421, for the occurrence of the name in Makedonia) of unknown family background — possibly identical with the Hellanikos who distinguished himself at Halikarnassos, along with Philotas (2. 5 above; cf. Bosworth, *Arrian* i 146 f.) — Hellanikos saved some of the Makedonian siege-works from destruction by troops who had sallied forth from the city (Arr. 1. 21. 5; cf. Diod. 17. 24. 5-6; also Curt. 8. 1. 36 and 2. 4 above: 'Atarrhias'). He finished eighth in the contest in Sittakene (Curt. 5. 2. 5), and was thus assigned a pentakosiarchy of the hypaspists.

vii. Commanders of the Argyraspids

Literature. Berve i 128; Tarn ii 151 f.; A. Spendel, *Untersuchungen zum Heerwesen der Diadochen* (Breslau, 1915); R. Lock, 'The Origins of the Argyraspids', *Historia* 26 (1977), 373-378; E. M. Anson, 'Alexander's Hypaspists and the Argyraspids', *Historia* 30 (1981), 117-120; W. Heckel, 'The Career of Antigenes', *SO* 57 (1982), 63.

The Argyraspids, or Silver Shields, are generally believed to have strong connections with the regular hypaspists of Alexander the Great. According to Berve (i 128), they came into being in India 'durch eine Auswahl aus altgedienten Hypaspisten' but were not identical with the entire hypaspists corps; for he draws attention to the existence of hypaspists alongside the Argyraspids at Paraitakene (Diod. 19. 28. 1). But the hypaspists mentioned in the army of Eumenes — they appear also at Gabiene (Diod. 19. 40. 3) — are clearly not the hypaspists of Alexander. Significantly, it is the Argyraspids who pride themselves on their service, and their stainless record, under Alexander, not the hypaspists who are positioned next to them. Spendel (45) regarded the Argyraspids as synonymous with the hypaspists of Alexander (cf. Tarn ii 151 f.; and now Anson, *Historia* 30 [1981], 117-120). But recently, Lock (*Historia* 26 [1977], 373-378) has argued that the Argyraspids were actually three thousand disgruntled veterans from the Royal Army at Triparadeisos who were entrusted with the task of bringing the treasures from Sousa to Kyinda in Kilikia for the satrap Antigenes (Arr. *Succ.* 1. 38).

But four points are immediately apparent: (i) the hypaspists were referred to by at least one primary historian, the common source of Diodoros (17. 57. 2) and Curtius (4. 13. 27), as Argyraspids; (ii) both units are named for their shields; (iii) the hypaspists are generally thought to have numbered 3,000 (i.e., three chiliarchies; and at Paraitakene, Eumenes' hypaspists do number 3,000: Diod. 19. 28. 1), which is the precise figure given for the Argyraspids (Diod. 18. 58. 1; 19. 28. 1); and (iv) Antigenes is associated with both the hypaspists (Curt. 5. 2. 5) in late 331 and the Argyraspids, as early as 320 (Arr. *Succ.* 1. 35). So the links between the two units are very clear. Furthermore, the number of troops assigned to Antigenes to convey the treasures from Sousa to Kyinda was also 3,000.

Now Lock supposes that these 3,000 men became the Argyraspids but were not identical with the hypaspists. This is, I believe, refuted by the points raised above and also by the fact that the Argyraspids are spoken of as a unit which served undefeated under Alexander; Lock's veterans would have been drawn from various battalions and brigades. Furthermore, Curtius (8. 5. 4) says that Alexander's troops adopted splendid new arms on the eve of the Indian invasion; Justin (12. 7. 5) mistakenly calls the entire army the Argyraspids![1] Added to this is the strong likelihood that the hypaspist veterans (now the Argyraspids) were dismissed at Opis in 324, at which time Antigenes accompanied Krateros to Kilikia.[2]

1. Antigenes

Literature. Berve ii 41-42, nos. 83-84; Kaerst, *RE* i (1894), 2399, no. 9; W. Heckel, 'The Career of Antigenes', *SO* 57 (1982), 57-67; id., *LCM* 10 (1985), 109 f.; N. G. L. Hammond, 'Alexander's Veterans after his Death', *GRBS* 25 (1984), 51-61; id., 'Casualties and Reinforcements of citizen soldiers in Greece and Macedonia', *JHS* 109 (1989), 64-65.

A Makedonian officer of uncertain origin (possibly from Pella or Pallene, if Plut. *Alex.* 70. 4-6 conflates Antigenes and Atarrhias[3]),

---

[1] Justin 12. 7. 5: *phaleras equorum et arma militum argento inducit exercitumque suum ab argenteis clipeis Argyraspidas appellavit.* Unless Justin uses *exercitus suus* to mean the hypaspists ('Alexander's own troops'), he has made an error, wrongly calling the whole army the Argyraspids. But this does not make his testimony worthless (*pace* Lock 375; Tarn ii 123 f.). He was aware of the formation of the Argyraspids, but he did not understand exactly who they were.

[2] Hammond (*JHS* 109 [1989], 64) believes that the Argyraspids remained in Babylon in 323, 'to form the Macedonian part of the multiracial phalanx'.

[3] Plutarch claims (*Mor.* 339b = *de fort. Alex.* 2. 7) that a certain Antigenes Πελληναῖος (or possibly Πελλαῖος?) was invincible in war but a slave to pleasure and vice; that he tried to enrol himself amongst the sick in order to return home with Telesippa, the woman he loved (*Mor.* 339c-d; cf. 181a); and that a certain Antigenes, a one-eyed man, tried to defraud Alexander, when he was paying the debts of his veterans (*Alex.* 70. 4-6). In the *Moralia* (339b), Plutarch calls the one-eyed man Tarrhias (almost certainly, Atarrhias son of Deinomenes). And this leads to a virtually insoluble problem: since the man who lost one eye at Perinthos (in 340/39) is described as still young at the time (ἔτι νέος ὤν), and since both Antigenes, the commander of the Silver Shields, and Atarrhias (who distinguished himself at Halikarnassos) were well advanced in years at the time of Alexander's death, we must suppose that there was a younger, one-eyed, man whose name was either Antigenes or

Antigenes was born sometime around 380 B.C.; for he was among the veterans discharged at Opis in 324 (Justin 12. 12. 8; cf. Plut. *Eum.* 16. 7, who claims that none of the Argyraspids, whom Antigenes commanded, was younger than sixty).[4] In all probability, he accompanied Alexander from the start of the expedition, and in late 331 in the military contest held in Sittakene he received second prize and, with it, the rank of chiliarch (or, possibly, pentakosiarch) of the hypaspists (Curt. 5. 2. 5).

He is not mentioned again until the battle with Poros in 326, where he appears along with Tauron and Seleukos in command of a division of infantrymen, though not pezhetairoi (Arr. 5. 16. 3; cf. Curt. 8. 14. 15).[5] Seleukos commanded the σωματοφύλακες (the Royal Hypaspists), Tauron the archers, and Antigenes' force most likely comprised the regular hypaspists. It is, however, unlikely that Antigenes led all the regular hypaspists: his exact functions in the battle at the Hydaspes are not spelled out, but the suggestion that he commanded a brigade of pezhetairoi or that he had authority over the Makedonian infantry in the engagement must be regarded as highly implausible. That Alexander would have entrusted such important units, which were accustomed to be led by the most prominent Makedonian aristocrats, to

Atarrhias. Are we to prefer the evidence of the *Life* to that of the *Moralia*? Or did the error occur in the *Life* because Plutarch confused Antigenes with Antigonos 'the One-Eyed'? We must stop short of identifying this Antigenes with Antigonos the One-Eyed (Tarn ii 314, n.1), since the latter could not have been in Alexander's camp when either of the reported incidents took place (cf. also Hamilton, *PA* 196; but see now Billows, *Antigonos* 27-29). If Plutarch is mistaken in calling him νέος in 340/39, it is still somewhat unusual to find no other source mentioning that the leader of the Silver Shields had lost an eye. Berve's entry (ii 41-42, no. 84) obscures the problem. Nor do I see any reason for identifying the Antigenes of Curt. 5. 2. 5 with the man from Pallene, unless the one-eyed man was, in fact, Atarrhias.

[4] I register here, for the record, Tarn's absurd suggestion (ii 314) that Antigenes was the son and successor of the taxiarch Koinos son of Polemokrates (emending Justin 13. 4. 14, *Susiana gens Coeno* to *Susiana Antigeni Coeni* [sc. *filio*]). Now, even if Tarn's emendation is correct, and Antigenes really was the son of a man named Koinos, the relative ages and the careers of the two famous infantry commanders make it impossible to identify Antigenes as the grandson of Polemokrates.

[5] Of the seven phalanx brigades, two (Polyperchon and Alketas) had remained with Krateros directly opposite Poros' position; three others (Attalos, Meleagros, Gorgias [Krateros]) had been positioned upstream. That leaves two unaccounted for (Peithon [Koinos] and Kleitos). Tarn ii 190 implausibly regards Antigenes as the commander of Koinos' brigade; who replaced Kleitos as taxiarch, we do not know.

a man of Antigenes' relatively low standing, seems unlikely. Nor does it appear that Antigenes had risen to the rank of ἀρχιυπασπιστής, which again appears to have been reserved for men of higher social rank.[6] It may be that only Antigenes' chiliarchy, or possibly his and one other, had crossed the Hydaspes with the King. Antigenes commanded them and perhaps some of the light infantry (the Agrianes and the javelin-men under Balakros). Perhaps on account of his age, and that of his troops, Antigenes is next found in conjunction with Krateros and the ἀπόμαχοι, those no longer fit for active service, patrolling Drangiana and Arachosia before rejoining Alexander in Karmania (Arr. 6. 17. 3).

According to Justin 12. 12. 8, Antigenes was one of the commanders sent back from Opis to Makedonia in 324 in the company of Krateros, Polyperchon, Gorgias, Polydamas, White Kleitos and 10,000 veterans (cf. Arr. 7. 12. 4; Curt. 10. 10. 15). But in late 323 they were still in Kilikia, and only in 322 do we find Krateros in Makedonia (Diod. 18. 16. 4-5) and Kleitos in the Aegean (Diod. 18. 15. 8-9). What became of Polydamas and Gorgias we do not know: neither is heard of again. Antigenes, however, could not have returned to Makedonia, since in 320 he was in Egypt, where he played a leading role in Perdikkas' assassination (Arr. *Succ.* 1. 35; Diod. 18. 39. 6). Has Justin inserted his name in error? Antigenes was certainly old enough and due for retirement. If the Argyraspids are correctly regarded as superannuated hypaspists, we should expect them to be among the 10,000 discharged veterans. And, indeed, Alexander had replaced them with a Persian brigade of Silver Shields (ἀργυρασπίδων τάξις Περσική).[7]

Schachermeyr suggests that Krateros left Antigenes and the 3000 Argyraspids in Kilikia and, after his death, Antipatros picked them up and led them to Syria, whence they were sent in due course to

---

[6]If Antigenes replaced Nikanor as ἀρχιυπασπιστής in 330 — setting aside the question of social status — this raises questions about why Atarrhias, who was awarded the first prize in the contest of valour (Curt. 5. 2. 5; cf. 8. 1. 36, where Kleitos singles him out for praise) and was especially prominent in the Philotas affair (Curt. 6. 8. 19 ff.; 7. 1. 5), was passed over. If Atarrhias did succeed Nikanor, thus explaining his prominence in 330, we cannot account for his replacement by Antigenes at some time before 326. Neoptolemos would thus have succeeded Antigenes in 324 B.C. It appears that we are dealing with three groups of hypaspist commanders: the commanders of the Royal Hypaspists (Hephaistion, Seleukos; possibly Admetos); the ἀρχιυπασπισταί (Nikanor, Neoptolemos); and the chiliarchs of the regular hypaspists (men who rose from the ranks).

[7]Arr. 7. 11. 3; cf. Justin 12. 12. 3-4.

Sousiana (320 B.C.).[8] But this view fails to take into account the fact that Antigenes and the Argyraspids were already in Perdikkas' camp when he invaded Egypt, and that Antigenes and his fellow conspirators murdered him before the news of Krateros' death was known (Diod. 18. 37. 1).[9] And, in fact, Antipatros arrived in Syria *after* Peithon and Arrhidaios led the remnants of the Perdikkan army out of Egypt to Triparadeisos (Diod. 18. 39. 1; cf. Arr. *Succ.* 1. 30). Thus, if Antigenes came from Kilikia to Egypt, it was not in the company of Antipatros.

For this stage of Antigenes' career we must turn to the political situation in Kilikia. When Krateros and the veterans arrived in the satrapy in late 324, it was in turmoil. Harpalos had fled to Greece, ultimately from Tarsos, taking with him the courtesan Glykera and, doubtless, some of the treasures; for it is difficult to imagine that the man who plundered Babylon left Tarsos untouched.[10] Around this time, too, the Pisidians had killed in battle the Kilikian satrap, Balakros (Diod. 18. 22. 1), a former Somatophylax and the son-in-law of Antipatros. Krateros spent the winter and the following spring restoring order to the area, which he was to hand over to the taxiarch Philotas, whom Alexander was preparing to send out from Babylon.[11] When Alexander died suddenly on 10 June 323, Krateros and the veterans remained in Kilikia virtually in a state of limbo; for Perdikkas, with the backing of the army, had cancelled Krateros' orders to replace Antipatros as regent of Makedonia.[12] Late in the year

---

[8]*Babylon* 14, n.10: '...doch hat sie [sc. die Argyraspiden] Krateros, wie mir scheint, nachher nicht nach Makedonien mitgenommen, sondern in Kilikien belassen, worauf sie nach dem Tod des Krateros von Antipater nach Syrien mitgeführt, und von dort nach Susa gesandt wurden.'

[9]But Diod. 18. 33. 1 incorrectly says Περδίκκας δὲ πυθόμενος τὴν κατὰ τὸν Εὐμενῆ νίκην πολλῷ θρασύτερος ἐγένετο πρὸς τὴν εἰς Αἴγυπτον στρατείαν. See Errington, *JHS* 90 (1970), 66, with n. 127; cf. Hornblower, *Hieronymus* 51.

[10]See Berve ii 75-80, no. 143 (Harpalos) and ii 112-113, no. 231 (Glykera). For Glykera in Tarsos: Theopompos *ap.* Athen. 13. 586c; 595d; cf. also B. Snell, *Szenen aus griechischen Dramen* (Berlin, 1971), 104-137. For the date of Harpalos' flight (spring 324): Berve ii 78, n. 1; Badian, *JHS* 81 (1961), 24, 41-43; Worthington, *SO* 61 (1986), 63-76. On Harpalos see also **iv 2**.

[11]For Krateros' departure, Arr. 7. 12. 4; Krateros must have recovered from a serious illness that threatened his life. For Philotas see Berve ii 397-398, no. 804; he is probably identical with the taxiarch, no. 803, and the φίλος of Antigonos (Diod. 18. 62. 4 ff.). He was still in Babylon when Alexander died (see Heckel, *LDT* 36).

[12]Badian, *HSCP* 72 (1967), 183-204. For Krateros' position see **ii 4**.

came Antipatros' appeal for help against the rebellious Greeks (Diod. 18. 12. 1). Krateros left Kilikia in late May or early June 322.[13]

Krateros departed for Makedonia, leaving some of his troops with Kleitos, who took the fleet into the Aegean. The three thousand Argyraspids under Antigenes remained in Kilikia for the time, and Krateros augmented his army with new recruits. Diodoros (18. 16. 4) describes his force in the following words: ἦγε δὲ πεζοὺς μὲν τῶν εἰς Ἀσίαν Ἀλεξάνδρῳ συνδιαβεβηκότων ἑξακισχιλίους, τῶν δ' ἐν παρόδῳ προσειλημμένων τετρακισχιλίους.... At first sight, this seems to say that Krateros' infantryman were composed of two groups: those who had been with Alexander from the start and those who had joined Alexander in the course of his campaigns. But this would be a curious distinction for the historian to make, and it is more likely that those who were picked ἐν παρόδῳ were fresh troops recruited by Krateros on his march to Makedonia, possibly from the satrapies in Asia Minor (Heckel, SO 57 [1982], 61; cf. now Hammond, JHS 109 [1989], 65, n.49, against Brunt, Arrian ii 489).[14] The Argyraspids remained in Kilikia, entrusted with the protection of Philotas' satrapy and the treasury at Tarsos. But in 321 Perdikkas crushed the Pisidians and, in early 320, he moved into Kilikia en route to Egypt. Expelling Philotas, who remained faithful to Krateros, he won over the troops of Antigenes, whom he now led against Ptolemy (Arr. Succ. 24. 2; Justin 13. 6. 16). So it was that Antigenes came to the Nile, where, according to our accounts, he soon turned against Perdikkas, and, in the company of Peithon and Seleukos, murdered him.[15]

If this is indeed how Antigenes came to serve briefly with Perdikkas, then it must be that the Argyraspids were formed before 320: that is, Antigenes joined Perdikkas as the commander of the Silver Shields, which is what the wording of Arrian (Succ. 1. 35: Ἀντιγένει...τῶν ἀργυρασπίδων Μακεδόνων ἡγουμένῳ) implies. It appears that the Argyraspids were formed in India (cf. Curt. 8. 5. 4),

---

[13]Schwahn, Klio 24 (1931), 331 f., thinks Perdikkas' campaign against Ariarathes induced Krateros to leave Kilikia for Makedonia; he is followed by Errington, JHS 90 (1970), 61. We cannot determine the precise chronology, but Diod. 18. 16. 4 synchronises Krateros' arrival in Makedonia with Perdikkas' campaign against Ariarathes: ὑπὸ δὲ τοὺς αὐτοὺς καιροὺς καὶ Κρατερὸς ἐκ Κιλικίας ἀναζεύξας ἧκεν εἰς Μακεδονίαν....

[14]Cf. Schachermeyr, Babylon 169, n.147. Hammond, however, thinks the 4000 veterans left in Kilikia served with Neoptolemos and then Eumenes (GRBS 25 [1984], 56 f.; reiterated in JHS 109 [1989], 65); this is highly improbable (Heckel, LCM 10 [1985], 109 f.); but these were not the Argyraspids.

[15]Arr. Succ. 1. 35; Diod. 18. 39. 6; Nepos, Eum. 5. 1 (adding Seleukos); for Peithon's role see Diod. 18. 36. 5.

took the northern route to Karmania in 325 and set out for Makedonia in 324. If my reconstruction of Antigenes' activities is correct, the Silver Shields could not have been formed any later than 324, and Antigenes was their original commander.

Despite being awarded the satrapy of Sousiana in the settlement of Triparadeisos, Antigenes appears to have seen Sousa on only two occasions between 320 and his death in 315: first in 320, when he conveyed some of the treasure from there to Kyinda (Quinda) in Kilikia, and again in 317, when he accompanied Eumenes to the East. According to Dexippos' epitome of Arrian's *History of the Successors*, in the first division of the satrapies, the marshals of the empire merely confirmed an otherwise obscure Koinos, whom Alexander had installed in the satrapy in 325 (Dexippos, *FGrHist* 100 F8 §6; cf. *LM* 121; Justin 13. 4. 14). What became of him we do not know. Perhaps he was removed by the Perdikkan faction in 320, as was, for example, Archon of Pella, the overseer of Babylon (Arr. *Succ.* 24); perhaps he was pro-Perdikkan and joined Dokimos in flight, condemned *in absentia* by the army in Syria. Nor do we know who administered Sousiana in Antigenes' absence, though Xenophilos is the most likely candidate (Curt. 5. 2. 16; cf. Diod. 19. 17. 3; 19. 18. 1; 19. 48. 6). But Antigenes' satrapal rank may be reflected by the fact that, in the battle of Paraitakene, Antigenes and Peukestas shared an *agema* of 300 horse (Diod. 19. 28. 3).[16]

Antigenes' position in Kilikia must have grown uncertain with the death of Antipatros in late 319 and the actions taken in the following year by Antigonos against Arrhidaios and White Kleitos. Philoxenos, the satrap of Kilikia, had good reason to fear Antigonos, in whose camp the deposed satrap Philotas had found refuge and hope of reinstatement. Letters from Polyperchon and the Kings calling upon the Argyraspids to support their cause and serve with Eumenes had their desired effect (Diod. 18. 58. 1; 18. 59. 3; Plut. *Eum.* 13. 3), and Antigenes welcomed the outlawed Greek, though not without some suspicion and resentment (Nepos, *Eum.* 7. 1). A compromise saw the theoretical command of their forces retained by the spirit of Alexander, in whose tent the commanders met to decide policy (Diod. 18. 60. 1-61. 3; Plut. *Eum.* 13. 7-8; Polyainos 4. 8. 2; Nepos, *Eum.* 7. 1-2). Entreaties and bribes from both Ptolemy (Diod. 18. 62. 1-2) and Antigonos' agents (Philotas and thirty others: Diod. 18. 62. 3-63. 6) were rejected — though Antigenes found his colleague Teutamos wavering in his loyalty, an ominous sign (Diod. 18. 62. 5-6).

---

[16]That is, two *agemata* of 150 horsemen; cf. Diod. 19. 27. 2, where Eudamos has an *agema* of 150 cavalry, which Devine, *AncW* 12 (1985), 76, aptly refers to as 'his satrapal *agema*'.

The royalists soon moved eastward through Antigenes' satrapy (Diod. 19. 15. 5-6), which was now — if it had not earlier been — entrusted to Xenophilos, the commandant of the citadel of Sousa (Diod. 19. 17. 3).[17] Though he resisted Antigonos, the satrapy itself was annexed and assigned to Seleukos (Diod. 19. 18. 1). For Antigenes, hope of recovering Sousiana lay in the defeat of Antigonos and his allies, Peithon and Seleukos; to the Argyraspids, these barred a return to Makedonia which had been pre-empted by the outbreak of the Lamian war. The forces from the Upper Satrapies now joined the cause of Eumenes, led by the orientalising Peukestas (Diod. 19. 14. 2-8), a man of no mean ambition. And their presence, together with Peukestas' rivalry with Eumenes, served rather to bolster the support of the Argyraspids for the latter; Antigenes, who served Eumenes on the written orders of the Kings, was not disposed to support Peukestas, whom he regarded, more or less, as an equal. Instead he asserted the right of the Makedones to select a leader (Diod. 19. 15. 1-2), and Antigenes appears, as the army moved towards the Tigris, to have exercised some kind of joint command with Eumenes (cf. Diod. 19. 17. 4).[18] But, with Antigonos' forces threatening and the oriental element inclining towards Peukestas, the Makedonians opted for Eumenes, calling out for him in the Makedonian tongue (Plut. *Eum.* 14. 8-11).[19]

At Paraitakene, Antigenes' subordinate role is clearly spelled out: together with Teutamos, he leads the Argyraspids and the hypaspists (6,000 men in all; cf. § 2 below), and he shares an *agema* (300 horse) with Peukestas (Diod. 19. 28. 1, 3); Eumenes has a squadron of 300 to himself. But the setback in Paraitakene put Eumenes' supreme command in jeopardy, and Teutamos plotted with other prominent officers to remove the Greek once he served his purpose in the upcoming battle. Plutarch (*Eum.* 16. 2) includes Antigenes in this plot, but this is inconsistent with the other evidence and can be ascribed either to the tendency to lump the commanders of the Argyraspids together or to a source hostile to Antigenes himself. In Gabiene, distressed because their baggage and the camp-followers had fallen into Antigonos' hands, the Silver Shields delivered up Eumenes to the enemy (Diod.

---

[17] He was appointed in late 331 (Curt. 5. 2. 16; Arr. 3. 16. 9 names Mazaros in this context; he may have been the Persian officer whom Xenophilos replaced).

[18] This may simply reflect the fact that their forces were in Antigenes' satrapy (cf. Teutamos' sudden prominence in Paraitakene; see § 2 below). When it was learned that Antigonos was in Media, Antigenes and Eumenes shared the opinion that the army should move back to the coast. But this was rejected by the satraps of central Asia (Diod. 19. 21. 1).

[19] The story is only partially told by Diod. 19. 24. 4 ff. During Eumenes' illness, Antigenes and Peukestas jointly led the army on its march (19. 24. 6).

19. 43. 7-9; Plut. *Eum.* 17; cf. Nepos, *Eum.* 10. 1-2).[20] For this act of treachery they earned the reproach of posterity. Even Antigonos was disgusted with them — or so we are told — and he handed some 1000 of them to Sibyrtios, satrap of Arachosia, ordering him to wear them out and destroy them (Diod. 19. 48. 3; Plut. *Eum.* 19. 3; Polyainos 4. 6. 15).

Antigenes himself was thrown into a pit and burned alive (Diod. 19. 44. 1), on the face of it, a fitting end for a fickle and odious man. Had he not abandoned the cause of Krateros and Philotas in Kilikia, plotted against and murdered Perdikkas in Egypt and then handed over Eumenes to his enemies? Death by fire. But was this justice or a senseless act of barbarity?

Antigenes deserves to be placed in a better light. If he abandoned the faction of Krateros and Philotas, it was because he chose to support Perdikkas, who represented the concept of *Reichseinheit*, spoke for the Kings and commanded the Royal Army. For Antigenes was a traditional Makedonian, a confirmed royalist. If he plotted against Perdikkas, it was because, like the other generals of note, he had become disillusioned with him: Perdikkas was a self-seeking individual with no sense of humanity and little regard for the sufferings of his troops.[21] And as for Eumenes, it is simply not true that he betrayed him. Plutarch (*Eumenes* 17. 1-2) makes it clear that Teutamos and his followers (οἱ περὶ τὸν Τεύταμον) led the betrayal. Polyainos 4. 6. 15 says that Antigonos rewarded Eumenes' captors with gifts, though he punished a large number of the Silver Shields. So it appears that the Argyraspids and their commanders were divided on the matter of Eumenes. Although Antigenes was cruelly executed, there is no mention of Teutamos, who was doubtless among those rewarded by Antigonos (but see further, § 2 below). He had been willing to defect in Kilikia in 318, but had been prevented from doing so by Antigenes (Diod. 18. 62. 4-7). In fact, the record shows that Antigenes was consistently loyal to Eumenes: he willingly obeyed the orders of Polyperchon the regent (Diod. 18. 58. 1), allied himself with Eumenes (18. 59. 3) and resisted the embassies of Ptolemy (18. 62. 1-2), Antigonos (through the agency of Philotas, 18. 62. 4-7), and Seleukos and Peithon (19. 12. 2-3; 19. 13. 1). Hieronymos, in fact, has words of praise for him (ὁ δ' Ἀντιγένης, συνέσει καὶ πίστεως βεβαιότητι διαφέρων, Diod. 18. 62. 6), which he would scarcely have written, had he regarded Antigenes as a traitor.

---

[20]For analyses of the battles of Paraitakene and Gabiene respectively, see Devine, *AncW* 12 (1985), 75-86, 87-96; also Billows, *Antigonos* 94-104.

[21]Justin 13. 8. 2: *sed Perdiccae plus odium adrogantiae quam vires hostium nocebat...*; cf. Diod. 18. 33. 3, 5; 18. 36. 1.

When Antigenes was put to death, it was as one of Eumenes' supporters. Nepos (*Eum.* 12. 4), and perhaps Douris, alleged that Eumenes was strangled without Antigonos' knowledge, an absurd suggestion; Hieronymus, it appears, put the blame on the Makedones, who demanded Eumenes' death, no doubt reviving the charge that he had been responsible for Krateros' fate (cf. Plut. *Eum.* 10. 7-8). And when these sources depict the Silver Shields as arrogant, jealous and seditious, they are unfair to Antigenes, who met his end not, as we are led to believe, for his betrayal of Eumenes, but for his steadfast support of him. Antigonos cannot be exculpated.[22]

2. Teutamos

Literature. Berve ii 372, no. 744; Stähelin, *RE* v.A (1934), 1152-1153, no. 3; Billows, *Antigonos* 85, n.8.

Nothing is known of Teutamos' life before he emerges as co-commander of the Argyraspids. Berve (ii 372) suggests plausibly that he held some office in Alexander's army; he may, however, have been an officer of Antipatros, assigned to the Silver Shields at Triparadeisos — though it is hard to imagine Alexander's veterans accepting such a commander. Nevertheless, Teutamos' political loyalties differed from those of Antigenes, and his role may have been to keep a watchful eye on his colleague. Though inferior to Antigenes, in both his military and administrative offices, Teutamos was nevertheless a man of some importance. Diodoros indicates that both men were satraps:

ἐδίδαξε γὰρ αὐτὸν συμφέρειν ζῆν τὸν Εὐμενῆ μᾶλλον ἢ τὸν Ἀντίγονον· ἐκεῖνον μὲν γὰρ εἰς πλεῖον ἰσχύσαντα παρελεῖσθαι τὰς σατραπείας αὐτῶν καὶ ἀντικαταστήσειν ἐκ τῶν αὐτοῦ φίλων, Εὐμενῆ δὲ ξένον ὄντα μηδέποτ' ἰδιοπραγῆσαι τολμήσειν, ἀλλὰ στρατηγὸν ὄντα φίλοις αὐτοῖς χρήσεσθαι καὶ συμπράξασι φυλάξειν αὐτοῖς τὰς σατραπείας, τάχα δὲ καὶ ἄλλας προσδώσειν.

(18. 62. 6-7)

---

[22]Antigonos had already destroyed Alketas and mutilated his body (Diod. 18. 47), captured and imprisoned Attalos, Polemon and Dokimos (18. 45); though Dokimos appears to have come to terms with Antigonos' wife Stratonike (19. 16); see Simpson, *Historia* 6 (1957), 504 f. Arrhidaios, satrap of Hellespontine Phrygia, was his next victim (18. 51-52); Billows' attempt to identify him with the honorand of *IG* xii.9, 212 is tenuous (*Antigonos* 375, no. 18). And the fall of Eumenes spelled doom for Antigenes, Eudamos, Amphimachos, Peukestas, Peithon, Kephalon and Stasandros (Diod. 19. 44. 1; 19. 46. 1-4; cf. 19. 48. 2-3).

For he (Antigenes) showed him (Teutamos) that it was to his advantage that Eumenes rather than Antigonus should remain alive. The latter, indeed, if he became more powerful, would take away *their satrapies* and set up some of his friends in their places; Eumenes, however, since he was a foreigner, would never dare to advance his own interests, but, remaining a general, would treat them as friends and, if they co-operated with him, *would protect their satrapies* for them and perhaps give them others also.

(R. M. Geer, tr.)

Now, unless Diodoros has made an error, Teutamos' satrapy must have been a minor one; for there is no mention of him or his office in the accounts of the Triparadeisos settlement. Bosworth speculates that the satrapy in question may have been Paraitakene, 'on the borders of Persis and Susiana. Under Alexander it was ruled as a separate entity by the son of the satrap of Susiana, and it may well have been assigned to Teutamus in 321 in return for services rendered.'[23] If Bosworth is right about Teutamos' satrapy — and I suspect that he is —, then the appointment will have been more than a mere reward for past service: it enhances our picture of the political safeguards established at Triparadeisos by Antipatros.

The old Regent had been careful to limit Antigonos' power by assigning, at Triparadeisos, strategically important satrapies to men whom he regarded as loyal to himself. Hence, Kleitos received Lydia, Arrhidaios took Hellespontine Phrygia, and Philoxenos Kilikia. Furthermore, at least three of the Somatophylakes of Philip III (who was intended to remain with Antigonos) — Autodikos, Amyntas, Alexandros — belonged to families which viewed Antigonos' power with suspicion. Antipatros' own son, Kassandros, served as chiliarch of the cavalry so that Antigonos could not pursue his own goals undetected (Diod. 18. 39. 7; Arr. *Succ.* 1. 38). There may have been similar distrust of Antigenes and Peithon, who had betrayed Perdikkas; and Teutamos, as satrap of Paraitakene, would have been well placed to monitor their activities.

Billows (*Antigonos* 85, n.8) makes the interesting suggestion that Teutamos may have commanded Eumenes' hypaspists, also 3,000 strong (Diod. 19. 28. 1; cf. 19. 40. 3, without numbers); for Diodoros (19. 28. 1) says that Antigenes and Teutamos commanded both the Argyraspids and the hypaspists. But Teutamos is regularly described as a commander of the Argyraspids (Diod. 18. 59. 3; 18. 62. 4, 5; cf. 18. 58. 1 and 18. 62. 1, where the 'commanders' of the unit are mentioned; Plut.

---

[23] A. B. Bosworth, 'History and Artifice in Plutarch's *Eumenes*', in P. A. Stadter, ed., *Plutarch and the Historical Tradition* (London, 1992), 66 f.

Eum. 13. 3, 7; 16. 2; Polyainos 4. 8. 2), and Diodoros' references to Antigenes alone constitute a kind of shorthand that can be explained in terms of Antigenes' greater importance as satrap of Sousiana and Teutamos' superior (Diod. 19. 12. 1-2; 19. 13. 2; 19. 15. 2; 19. 21. 1; 19. 41. 1; 19. 44. 1). Eumenes' hypaspists are clearly his own unit, and as such they have no early connection with Teutamos, who in 318 and in 315 is still linked with the Argyraspids. He may have been commander of the hypaspists at Paraitakene and Gabiene, but that was an *ad hoc* arrangement and not his official position.[24]

In 318, Teutamos and Antigenes were instructed by Polyperchon, writing in the name of the Kings, to support Eumenes who had been appointed General of Asia (Diod. 18. 58. 1). These instructions they obeyed and joined forces with Eumenes (Plut. *Eum.* 13. 2-4), whom they congratulated on his escape from Nora (Diod 18. 59. 3). Not entirely at ease with the idea of serving the Greek Eumenes, Teutamos was, nevertheless, willing to accept the theoretical leadership of Alexander (Plut. *Eum.* 13. 7-8; Polyainos 4. 8. 2). He appears to have resisted the appeals of Ptolemy, who had landed at Zephyrion in Kilikia and urged the Argyraspid commanders to abandon Eumenes (Diod 18. 62. 1); but a second embassy, by Antigonos' agent Philotas, would have persuaded Teutamos, had not Antigenes intervened to keep him loyal (Diod 18. 62. 4-6). He commanded the Argyraspids at Paraitakene (Diod. 19. 28. 1); but soon he plotted with some of the other commanders to make use of Eumenes in the coming battle in Media and then to eliminate him (Plut. *Eum.* 16. 2).[25] The conspiracy was, however, reported to Eumenes by Eudamos and Phaidimos. When the Makedonian baggage was captured at Gabiene, Teutamos took the lead in negotiating with Antigonos, who promised to return the property of the Silver Shields in exchange for Eumenes (Plut. *Eum.* 17. 1-2).[26]

---

[24] Hammond, *CQ* 28 (1978), 135 thinks the hypaspists in Eumenes' army were the 'new hypaspists', the successors and 'descendants of the hypaspists'; these had failed at Kamelon Teichos, mutinied against Perdikkas, and were assigned by Antipatros to Antigenes, in addition to the Argyraspids, at Triparadeisos; see, however, Anson, *AHB* 2 (1988), 131-133.

[25] Antigenes is included amongst the conspirators in error, perhaps because it was customary to lump the commanders of the Argyraspids together. For the different attitudes of Plutarch and Diodoros towards the Silver Shields see Hornblower, *Hieronymus* 156.

[26] Justin 14. 3. 11 says the Silver Shields sent a deputation *ignaris ducibus*, which must mean that they did so without the knowledge of Antigenes and other officers in the army, but Teutamos was clearly not ignorant of the proceedings.

What became of Teutamos, we are not told. It appears that he avoided Antigenes' fate by initiating the arrest and betrayal of Eumenes: Plutarch significantly speaks of οἱ περὶ τὸν Τεύταμον (*Eum.* 17. 1). There is no indication that he served under Antigonos — perhaps he was dismissed on account of his age. It is possible that he commanded the remnants of the Silver Shields, whom Antigonos entrusted to Sibyrtios, and thus consigned to difficult service and obscurity.[27]

---

[27]Polyainos 4. 6. 15; Plut. *Eum.* 19. 3; Diod. 19. 48. 3-4 says that the Argyraspids who went with Sibyrtios to Arachosia included 'those who had betrayed Eumenes'. It would be in character for Antigonos to 'double-cross' Teutamos; cf. his treatment of Seleukos (Diod. 19. 55. 2 ff.). I suspect that Xenophilos too was eliminated by Antigonos. Diod. 19. 48. 6 makes it clear that he merely pretended friendship until Sousa was securely in his hands but does not comment on Xenophilos' fate (τοῦτον μὲν οὖν προσδεξάμενος προσεποιεῖτο τιμᾶν ἐν τοῖς μεγίστοις τῶν φίλων, εὐλαβούμενος μὴ μετανοήσας πάλιν αὐτὸν ἀποκλείσῃ). Billows, *Antigonos* 440 (no. 119) is less suspicious: 'Antigonos received him honorably and enrolled him among his *philoi* (i.e., personal staff) .... Xenophilos presumably remained thenceforth in Antigonos's service.' Note that Sousiana was entrusted to neither Seleukos nor Xenophilos, but rather to the native Aspisas (Diod. 19. 55. 1), on whom see Billows, *Antigonos* 376 f., no. 21.

viii. Commanders of Infantry

1. Some Commanders of Pezhetairoi

(i) Terminology: πεζέταιροι and ἀσθέταιροι

A. B. Bosworth ('ΑΣΘΕΤΑΙΡΟΙ', *CQ* 23 [1973], 245-253; cf. *Arrian* i 170 f.) has demonstrated that the term ἀσθέταιροι (or ἀσθέτεροι) is correctly used by Arrian (2. 23. 2; 4. 23. 1; 5. 22. 6; 6. 6. 1; 6. 21. 3) to denote a part of the Makedonian phalanx, and that the reading of the MSS., emended by editors to πεζέταιροι, should be retained; in fact, the validity of the term is virtually proved by Arr. 7. 11. 3 which speaks of the introduction of πεζέταιροι Πέρσαι καὶ ἀσθέτεροι ἄλλοι. There is no longer any doubt that ἀσθέταιροι (or οἱ ἀσθέταιροι καλούμενοι)[1] is the correct way of designating a portion of the Makedonian infantry.

G. T. Griffith has argued that the word is a contraction of ἀριστ-έταῖροι or 'best Companions', just as, for instance, Ἀστόδαμος derives from Ἀριστόδαμος. He sees the term as an honour applied to individual brigades, as it was earned, Koinos' unit being the first to receive this designation. At some time between the battles at the Graneikos river and Issos, Koinos' brigade distinguished itself and became known as the 'best'; hence it occupied the 'first position', adjacent to Nikanor's hypaspists, at Issos, whereas it had held only the second spot (beside Perdikkas) at the Graneikos. In his description of the final assault on Tyre, therefore, Arrian (2. 23. 2) speaks of ἡ Κοίνου τάξις οἱ ἀσθέτεροι καλούμενοι. Hence Griffith (*HMac* ii 712) comments: 'Perhaps it distinguished itself at Granicus or Halicarnassus: perhaps it was always the smartest and the best on the job: perhaps at this time Alexander liked Coenus best.' But we do not know for what reason Alexander changed the order of the brigades: at Issos, Koinos takes up Perdikkas' position, Ptolemaios son of Seleukos replaces Philippos son of Amyntas, and Meleagros has exchanged positions with Amyntas on either side of Polyperchon, who had now replaced Ptolemaios.

---

[1] The participle καλούμενοι accompanies the term on each occasion except 5. 22. 6. πεζέταιροι appears an eighth time, Arr. 7. 2. 1 (without the variant ἀσθέταιροι), unnoticed by Bosworth; but this does not affect the argument in any significant way.

COMMANDERS OF INFANTRY

Meleagros' unit, as far as we know, was never honoured with the title *asthetairoi* — if this is in fact an honour — but moved instead to the third position.

Bosworth's suggestion that ἀσθέταιροι is formed from ἀσιστα-ἑταῖροι, that is, 'closest kinsmen' and that the units of *asthetairoi* hail from Upper Makedonia is more likely to be correct.[2] In all, there appear to have been four brigades so designated, those of Koinos (who commanded the Elimeiot contingent: Diod. 17. 57. 2), Philippos (Tymphaians[3]), Perdikkas (Orestians and Lynkestians: Diod. 17. 57. 2; Curt. 4. 13. 28) and Amyntas.

(ii) The Command Structure (Pezhetairoi)

The commanders of the Makedonian heavy infantry are named by Arrian in his description of the battle-order at the Graneikos: Perdikkas son of Orontes, Koinos son of Polemokrates, Amyntas son of Andromenes, Philippos son of Amyntas, Krateros (son of Alexandros), Meleagros (son of Neoptolemos).[4] Meleagros and Philippos are mentioned together already during the Getic campaign;[5] Koinos and Perdikkas led their own units in the battle with Kleitos and Glaukias (Arr. 1. 6. 9); and the brigades of Perdikkas and Amyntas son of Andromenes are attested at Thebes (Arr. 1. 8. 1-2: Diod. 17. 12. 3 names only Perdikkas). By the time of the battle of Issos, Philippos has dropped out of the list, replaced by Ptolemaios son of Seleukos; but this Ptolemaios died in the battle and was in turn replaced by Polyperchon son of Simmias by the time the army reached Gaugamela. The command structure of the Makedonian heavy infantry undergoes no

---

[2]Cf. Brunt, *Arrian* i lxxix, n.99. But see now Hammond, *Macedonian State* 148-151, for the view that the name derives from 'astoi and hetairoi, meaning "townsmen companions"' (150). For a very different interpretation see Goukowsky, *REG* 100 (1987), 240-255, esp. 243 ff., who sees the *asthetairoi* as elite troops selected from a *taxis* or several *taxeis* of pezhetairoi. Arr. 2. 23. 3 'ne signifie donc pas, comme le croit Bosworth, que la *taxis* de Coenos était formée d'*asthetairoi*, mais plutôt que Coenos a choisi, dans sa *taxis*, des hommes d'élite: "ceux que l'on nomme *asthetairoi*"' (244). I see no good evidence, however, for the view that the *asthetairoi* were portions of, rather than entire, brigades.

[3]This unit was commanded successively by Philippos son of Amyntas, Ptolemaios son of Seleukos, and Polyperchon son of Simmias. For the Tymphaian origin of the troops see Diod. 17. 57. 2: τῶν ὀνομαζομένων Στυμφαίων.

[4]Arrian does not give the patronymika of Krateros and Meleagros in this list.

[5]It is, of course, not certain that these are the taxiarchs. Philippos is a common name; Meleagros could possibly be identical with the ilarch (Berve ii 250, no. 495).

significant changes until the period 328-326, except for the replacement of Amyntas and Perdikkas by their respective brothers, Attalos and Alketas.

In the spring of 328, Alexander left four brigades in Baktria: Polyperchon [Philippos], Attalos [Amyntas], Meleagros, and Gorgias [—]. Arrian does not name the commander-in-chief in this passage (4. 16. 1), but it becomes clear from 4. 17. 1 that he was Krateros. Gorgias' brigade is thus either new or else Krateros' own. Indeed, in the spring of 327, Krateros, Polyperchon [Philippos], Attalos [Amyntas], and Alketas [Perdikkas] are found together in Paraitakene, Krateros still having τὴν αὐτοῦ τάξιν (Arr. 4. 22. 1). Now it is Arrian's practice to refer to the commander-in-chief as having under his authority 'his own brigade' (or 'hipparchy') and those of others.[6] And on this occasion it appears that the actual leadership of the brigade was someone else's responsibility, namely Gorgias'. When the army moved into India (Arr. 4. 22. 7), Perdikkas and Hephaistion (both hipparchs) led Gorgias [—], (White) Kleitos [—] and Meleagros, leaving Alexander with the ἀσθέταιροι (see above): Polyperchon [Philippos], Attalos [Amyntas], Koinos, and presumably Alketas [Perdikkas]. What has happened to Krateros' brigade? Again the obvious explanation is that Gorgias is now in command of it (cf. Bosworth, CQ 23 [1973], 247, n.1; Tarn ii 145). At first glance, it seems odd that Krateros' brigade should be included in the forces of Perdikkas and Hephaistion. But, in the campaigns to come, Krateros leads contingents which include Alketas [Perdikkas] (Arr. 4. 23. 5; 5. 11. 3). So it seems that, in the spring of 326, there were seven brigades named for the following commanders: Gorgias [Krateros], Meleagros, Polyperchon [Philippos], Attalos [Amyntas], Koinos, Alketas [Perdikkas] and Kleitos [new].

Seven phalanx brigades reappear in the battle at the Hydaspes. Krateros remains in the main camp with his own hipparchy and the brigades of Polyperchon [Philippos] and Alketas [Perdikkas].[7] Between this camp and the 'island', Alexander located Meleagros, Attalos [Amyntas] and Gorgias [Krateros],[8] keeping with him Koinos

---

[6]Antiochos commands his own chiliarchy and two others (Arr. 4. 30. 6); at the Hydaspes Koinos leads his own hipparchy as well as Demetrios' (5. 16. 3); in India Peithon commands his own brigade and two hipparchies.

[7]Arr. 5. 11. 3.

[8]Arr. 5. 12. 1. Bosworth, CQ 23 (1973), 247, n.2, argues that Meleagros, Gorgias and Attalos commanded mercenary forces and 'are not attested with battalions and cannot have commanded battalions...'. He points to 'the absurdity of Alexander going into battle with two battalions and leaving five unengaged on the far bank of the Hydaspes...'. But this is exactly what the other evidence for the battle suggests: the leaders of the πεζοί are Seleukos (Royal Hypaspists), Antigenes (regular hypaspists) and Tauron (archers). I find

and Kleitos [new].⁹ But, since Koinos appears subsequently as a hipparch (Arr. 5. 16. 3), we may assume that the leadership of his brigade was assumed by Peithon son of Agenor (cf. 6. 6. 1: τῶν ἀσθεταίρων καλουμένων τὴν Πείθωνος τάξιν).

What became of the heavy infantry brigades after 325 is hard to determine. Attalos and Meleagros returned to Karmania with Krateros (Arr. 6. 17. 3; Antigenes' brigade must have comprised hypaspists). In 324 Polyperchon set out for Makedonia with Krateros (Arr. 7. 12. 4), as did Gorgias and Kleitos (Justin 12. 12. 8); Attalos, Alketas and Meleagros were all still in Babylon when the King died. Many of the 10,000 veterans who accompanied Krateros must have been discharged pezhetairoi, and it appears that there was a reorganisation of the infantry or that only four brigades remained with the King: Attalos, Alketas, Meleagros and Koinos' old unit.

The taxiarchs of the pezhetairoi were amongst Alexander's most influential officers; many went on to become hipparchs or to play major roles in the early wars of the Diadochoi. Most taxiarchs have been dealt with above (Koinos, Krateros and Perdikkas: ii 1, 4-5; Meleagros, Alketas, three sons of Andromenes, White Kleitos and Polyperchon: iii 1-5; Ptolemaios son of Seleukos: vB 6); the remaining three (or four?) are discussed below.

1. 1. Peithon son of Agenor

Literature. Berve ii 310, no. 619; id., *RE* xix (1938), 218-220, no. 2; Billows, *Antigonos* 415-416, no. 88; A. B. Bosworth, 'The Indian Satrapies under Alexander the Great', *Antichthon* 17 (1983), 37-46, esp. 39 ff.; W. Heckel, 'Peithon, Son of Agenor', *Mnemosyne* 43 (1990), 456-459.

Berve (ii 310-312) has five separate entries under the name Πείθων (nos. 619-623).¹⁰ Of these only one appears in the sources without patronymic, a taxiarch mentioned by Arrian (6. 6-7) as participating in the Mallian campaign of 326/5. The temptation to identify him with one of the remaining four is great. But with which one? Peithon son of Sosikles can be ruled out; for he was taken alive by the Skythians in the campaign of 328 and presumably executed (Arr. 4. 16. 6-7). The son of Krateuas, one of the Somatophylakes, is equally unlikely, though

---

it hard to believe that Alexander would place the brigades of three experienced commanders under new and unnamed commanders for this battle only.

⁹Arr. 5. 12. 2. Koinos was by now hipparch, but his brigade kept Koinos' name until his death: cf. 5. 21. 1; only at 6. 6. 1, that is, after Koinos' death [6. 2. 1], does it become known as Peithon's brigade.

¹⁰Cf. Berve's entries in *RE* xix (1938), 218-222, nos. 1-5.

Berve curiously prefers him to the son of Agenor.[11] Berve's own candidate is an otherwise unattested son of Antigenes, who captured a snake of exceptional length during the Indian campaign (Arr. *Ind*. 15. 10): 'Es ist möglich, diesen P[eithon] mit dem gleichnamigen Taxisführer (nr. 623) zu identifizieren, zumal Nearchos einen gemeinen Soldaten bei solcher Gelegenheit kaum mit Namen und Vatersnamen angeführt hätte' (ii 311). This Peithon was undoubtedly a man of higher rank, but it does not follow from the use of the patronymic that he was the taxiarch. I cannot understand why the identification of the taxiarch with Agenor's son, the most obvious one to my mind, is rejected as 'unmöglich' (ii 312).

About this Peithon's background, apart from his father's name, Agenor (Arr. 6. 17. 1; Justin 13. 4. 21), nothing is known.[12] But Arrian introduces a taxiarch of the ἀσθέταιροι,[13] who accompanied Alexander against the Mallians (6. 6. 1) and captured and enslaved those who had fled to a neighbouring fortress (6. 7. 2-3), only shortly before the appointment of Peithon son of Agenor as satrap. Together with Demetrios the hipparch, Peithon the taxiarch conducted further reprisals against the Mallians (Arr. 6. 8. 2-3; perhaps his was one of the two brigades of infantry that accompanied Hephaistion and Demetrios the hipparch into the territory of the 'cowardly Poros' [Arr. 5. 21. 5]). After the appointment of Agenor's son as satrap, Peithon the taxiarch is not heard of again. It appears that, as a reward for his efforts and because of his experience in this region, Alexander appointed the son of Agenor satrap of India from the confluence of the Indus and Akesines rivers to the Indian Ocean (Arr. 6. 15. 4) — that is, the west bank of the Indus, down to the sea and including Patala. That he shared the satrapy with Oxyartes is highly unlikely and editors are right to emend the text of Arrian 6. 15. 4: τῆς δὲ ἀπὸ τῶν ξυμβολῶν τοῦ τε Ἰνδοῦ καὶ Ἀκεσίνου χώρας ἔστε ἐπὶ θάλασσαν σατράπην ἀπέδειξε[ν Ὀξυάρτην καὶ] Πείθωνα ξὺν τῇ παραλίᾳ πάσῃ τῆς Ἰνδῶν γῆς.[14]

As satrap, he campaigned against the rebellious Mousikanos, bringing him captive to Alexander, who crucified him (Curt. 9. 8. 16;

---

[11]Berve ii 312, n.2: 'Nur der Somatophylax käme in Betracht, dieser wäre aber von Arrian als solcher bezeichnet.' Bosworth, *Conquest and Empire* 275, considers it 'highly probable' that Peithon son of Krateuas is the taxiarch.

[12]Speculation about his date of birth is pointless.

[13]Peithon commanded Koinos' former brigade; he had perhaps already done so in the battle at the Hydaspes.

[14]Oxyartes' satrapy is described above (Arr. 6. 15. 3) as Parapamisadai; perhaps this was extended in a south-easterly direction to the confluence of the Indos and Akesines (Chenab) and was thus adjacent to Peithon's.

Arr. 6. 17. 1-2).[15] Although Justin (13. 4. 21) implies that Peithon retained this satrapy after Alexander's death (cf. Curt. 10. 10. 4, without naming him or defining his territory), it appears that, probably after the death of Philippos son of Machatas, he was transferred to the Kophen satrapy (Gandhara), between Parapamisos and the Indus (so Diod. 18. 3. 3; Dexippos, *FGrHist* 100 F8; cf. Bosworth, *Antichthon* 17 [1983], 37-46, esp. 39 ff.). At Triparadeisos (320 B.C.) his position was confirmed (Diod. 18. 39. 6; Arr. *Succ.* 1. 36).[16]

Nothing further is heard of Peithon until 315, when Antigonos appointed him satrap of Babylonia in place of Seleukos, who had fled to Egypt (Diod. 19. 56. 4). Diodoros describes him as Πίθωνα τὸν ἐκ τῆς Ἰνδικῆς καταβεβηκότα, but it is not possible to determine whether he took part in the battle of Gabiene or if he had, perhaps, been recalled from India when Antigonos reformed the administration of the east (Diod. 19. 48. 1-2). His support of Antigonos raises some interesting questions. Did he join Antigonos before the battle of Paraitakene? Thus Berve (*RE* xix [1938], 219): 'er begegnet erst wieder 316 auf Seiten des Antigonos, dem er aus seiner Satrapie Heeresmacht zuführte...'. If so, he could have brought with him only a small force of elephants; for Antigonos had a significant number of the beasts at Kretopolis (18. 45. 1; no specific figure is given, but they were clearly a sizeable force) and deployed 65 of them at Paraitakene and Gabiene, far short of the 120 brought to Eumenes by Eudamos.[17] Furthermore, it will be difficult to explain why Peithon joined Antigonos at this point, when the eastern satraps had uniformly aligned themselves with Eumenes.[18] Of course, he may have been motivated by strong personal friendship towards Antigonos or by fear of Eudamos, who had murdered Poros in the adjacent satrapy (Diod. 19. 14. 8), but neither of these can be documented. Against the view that he fought with Eumenes and surrendered to Antigonos are both the silence of the sources and the fact that Antigonos dealt harshly with the prominent subordinates of Eumenes.[19] Antigonos was certainly not in a position to remove Peithon

---

[15]The capital of Mousikanos' kingdom was probably Alor, which 'is situated at the other end of the ancient caravan route leading from Kandahar on the Iranian plateau by the Khojak and Bolan passes into the Kacchi plain, and then by Shikarpur to Sukkur and Alor on the Indus' (Eggermont 9). For the importance of Mousikanos' rebellion see Eggermont 5-9, 22.

[16]The career of Philippos (Berve ii 384-385, no. 780; cf. 2. 2 below) is in many respects similar to that of Peithon the taxiarch.

[17]Diod. 19. 27. 1 (Paraitakene) and 19. 40. 1 (Gabiene); for Eudamos' elephants see Diod. 19. 14. 8, 15. 5; 27. 2; cf. Plut. *Eum*. 16. 3. See also Devine, *AncW* 12 (1985), 75-86; id., *AncW* 12 (1985), 87-96.

[18]They had, in fact, assembled to oppose Peithon son of Krateuas, who was trying to assert himself as στρατηγὸς τῶν ἄνω σατραπειῶν (Diod. 19. 14. 1; cf. Bengtson, *Strategie* i 176 ff.).

[19]Diod. 19. 44. 1; cf. Heckel, *BNJ* 15 (1980), 43-45; id., *SO* 57 (1982), 57-67.

from India, for he could not even exert his authority over Tlepolemos, Stasanor and Oxyartes (Diod. 19. 48. 1-2). All of which makes it likely that Peithon left India soon after Gabiene, because of the instability there;[20] perhaps he arrived at the same time as, if not together with, Sibyrtios, whom Antigonos reinstated as governor of Arachosia (Diod. 19. 48. 3).

From Babylon he was summoned to Syria in 314/3 — though not necessarily relieved of his satrapy, since no successor is named in the sources[21] — possibly because of his experience in India with elephants, and he became an advisor of Demetrios Poliorketes (Diod. 19. 69. 1), as well as joint commander of his forces (cf. Diod. 19. 82. 1). In 313, Demetrios left Peithon with the elephants and heavily-armed troops to hold Koile-Syria while he tried in vain to deal with the enemy in Kilikia (19. 80. 1). When Demetrios returned and engaged Ptolemy at Gaza, Peithon fought on Demetrios' left wing, sharing the command (Diod. 19. 82. 1); in this engagement, he fell and his body was recovered under truce (Diod. 19. 85. 2).

1. 2. Gorgias

Literature. Berve ii 113, no. 233; Hoffmann 188; Kirchner, *RE* vii (1912), 1597, no. 3.

A Makedonian of unknown origin, Gorgias nevertheless came from a good (Upper Makedonian?) family and belonged to the King's hetairoi.[22] Berve's suggestion that he was born 'spätestens gegen 380' (ii 113) is based solely on Justin (12. 12. 8), who identifies him as a *senex* in 324. Gorgias is first mentioned as taxiarch in 328 — clearly in charge of Krateros' former brigade — in Baktria, together with Polyperchon and Attalos son of Andromenes.[23] These taxiarchs had been left behind to guard Baktria against incursions by the rebel Spitamenes, while Alexander and the greater portion of the army were operating in Sogdiana. When the expedition set out for India, Gorgias' brigade, along with those of White Kleitos and Meleagros, formed part of the advance party led by Hephaistion and Perdikkas (Arr. 4. 22. 7). At the Hydaspes, Gorgias and Meleagros are again found together (this time with Attalos), stationed half-way between the main camp and Alexander's crossing of the river (Arr. 5. 12. 1). To them had been

---

[20]Tarn, *GBI*³ 168; cf. Billows, *Antigonos* 415.
[21]Whether Blitor's authority over Mesopotamia was handed over to Peithon, as Billows (*Antigonos* 415) speculates, cannot be determined.
[22]Justin 12. 12. 8: *ex amicis.*
[23]Arr. 4. 16. 1. Krateros appears to have been the commander-in-chief on this mission (Arr. 4. 17. 1); Gorgias' brigade is undoubtedly Krateros'.

assigned the mercenary forces, but this should not be taken to mean that they no longer kept their own brigades.[24]

Of his later career nothing is known except that in 324 he was sent home from Opis along with Krateros (Justin 12. 12. 8). It is probable, therefore, that he returned to Makedonia in 322 and perhaps fought at Krannon.[25] Plutarch (*Eum.* 7. 6) says that Gorgias, 'one of Eumenes' generals', recognised Krateros' body on the battlefield near the Hellespont in 320. Unless Plutarch or his source has made an error, this could be a different officer with the same name (Berve ii 114 thinks of the young favourite of Olympias, brought to Asia in 331/0 B.C. by Amyntas son of Andromenes [Curt. 7. 1. 38; cf. Berve, nos. 234-235]).[26] On the other hand, not all the generals who left Opis with Krateros in 324 returned to Makedonia, as we know from the case of Antigenes (vii 1). What became of Gorgias, we do not know.

1. 3. Philippos son of Amyntas
and
1. 4. Philippos son of Balakros

Literature. Son of Amyntas: Berve ii 383, no. 775; Treves, *RE* xix (1938), 2547, no. 59. Son of Balakros: Berve ii 383 f., no. 778; Treves, *RE* xix (1938), 2547 f., no. 60; Billows, *Antigonos* 421-423, no. 93.

Arrian (1. 14. 2) names as one of the taxiarchs at the Graneikos Philippos son of Amyntas, an individual otherwise not certainly attested. The Philippos who, together with Meleagros, was responsible for conveying the booty from the Getic campaign back to the Makedonian base (Arr. 1. 4. 5) may have been the same man, but this is not confirmed by a patronymic.[27] It is tempting to see the patronymic Ἀμύντου in Arrian 1. 14. 2 as a scribal error caused by the proximity of the name Amyntas son of Andromenes: ἐπὶ δὲ ἡ Ἀμύντου τοῦ Ἀνδρομένους [sc. τάξις]· ἐπὶ δὲ ὧν Φίλιππος ὁ Ἀμύντου ἦρχε. And, if this is what has happened, Philippos may perhaps be the son of Balakros who intrudes into the Vulgate description of the battle-order at Gaugamela. Arrian 3. 11. 9, in explaining the absence of Amyntas, wrongly calls that man son of Philippos. This leads Bosworth to

---

[24]Cf. Berve ii 113, against Bosworth, *CQ* 23 (1973), 247, n.2.

[25]Plut. *Cam.* 19: 7 Metageitnion = 5 August, 322 (Beloch iv^2 1. 74).

[26]Plut. *Eum.* 7. 6: Γοργίας δὲ τῶν Εὐμένους στρατηγῶν ἔγνω τε καὶ καταβὰς περιέστησε φρουρὰν τῷ σώματι κακῶς ἤδη διακειμένου καὶ δυσθανατοῦντος. An error is not entirely out of the question: cf. the case of Neoptolemos son of Arrhabaios, who died at Halikarnassos fighting for the Persians, according to Arr. 1. 20. 10, but for the Makedonians in Diodoros' version (17. 25. 5; cf. Welles, *Diodorus* 188, n.1).

[27]Cf. Treves, *RE* xix (1938), 2547; Berve ii 383 thinks that the joint command, with Meleagros, suggests strongly that this Philippos is the taxiarch.

assume that one of Arrian's sources (possibly Aristoboulos) recorded the presence of Philippos son of Balakros and that Arrian, although he followed Ptolemy's version, which assigned the command — and, ultimately, the responsibility for the gap in the phalanx — to Simmias, made a mental error and carelessly identified Amyntas as the son of Philippos.[28]

The identification of Philippos son of Amyntas with Balakros' son does, however, make it more difficult to explain why Philippos' brigade was given in (spring?) 333 to Ptolemaios son of Seleukos. The disappearance of Philippos son of Amyntas might be explained by death or misconduct in 334/3, neither recorded by the sources, but Philippos son of Balakros resurfaces, as we have noted, in the Vulgate accounts of Gaugamela (Diod. 17. 57. 3; Curt. 4. 13. 28) as temporary commander of Amyntas' brigade. Beloch (iii² 2. 327 f.) thought that Philippos' brigade was a seventh unit, identical with that named by Arrian (4. 24. 10) in the Indian campaign. But the latter is almost certainly the brigade of light infantry led by Philippos son of Machatas (see 2. 2 below). Either Philippos son of Balakros was a taxiarch in the European campaigns and at the Graneikos, but demoted in favour of Ptolemaios and Polyperchon, or Philippos son of Amyntas must be distinguished from the son of Balakros.[29] In the second event, we must assume that Philippos son of Amyntas died or was removed from office for reasons not recorded by our sources.

2. Commanders of Light Infantry

2. 1. Philotas

Literature. Berve ii 397, no. 803, and ii 397-398, no. 804; id., *RE* xx (1950), 177-178, no. 2, and 179, nos. 7-8; Schoch, *RE* xx (1950), 179-180, no. 10; Julien 20; Milns, *GRBS* 7 (1966), 159 ff.; Bosworth, *CQ* 23 (1973), 252 f.; Heckel, *LDT* 36 f.; Billows, *Antigonos* 423-424, no. 95.

Although Philotas was clearly a Makedonian of high standing, as evinced by his career under Alexander and the Diadochoi, nothing is known of his family or geographical origins. It is tempting to identify him with the officer who, in the company of Lysanias, conveyed the

---

[28] *Arrian* i 300 f.; cf. id., *CQ* 26 (1976), 125, and *Entretiens Hardt* 22 (Geneva, 1976), 9-16.

[29] Against Billows' view (*Antigonos* 421-423, no. 93) that Philippos son of Balakros is the Somatophylax of Alexander named in *IG* ii² 561 and thus a former Royal Hypaspist of Alexander the Great see Heckel, *LDT* 42-43.

Thrakian booty to Amphipolis in 335 (Arr. 1. 2. 1).[30] Otherwise, he is first mentioned as the commander of an infantry brigade sent with Ptolemy son of Lagos to arrest the regicide Bessos. Arrian's wording may be helpful in determining Philotas' true position: Πτολεμαῖον δὲ τὸν Λάγου ἀποστέλλει τῶν τε ἑταίρων ἱππαρχίας τρεῖς ἄγοντα καὶ τοὺς ἱππακοντιστὰς ξύμπαντας, πεζῶν δὲ τήν τε Φιλώτα τάξιν καὶ τῶν ὑπασπιστῶν χιλιαρχίαν μίαν καὶ τοὺς Ἀγριᾶνας πάντας καὶ τῶν τοξοτῶν τοὺς ἡμίσεας (3. 29. 7). Many scholars understand πεζῶν τὴν Φιλώτα τάξιν to mean that Philotas commanded a (seventh) brigade of pezhetairoi. But Arrian uses πεζοί to refer to light and allied infantry as well as to archers (2. 9. 2-3; 3. 5. 6), and τοὺς ἡγεμόνας τῶν πεζῶν are clearly distinguished from ταξιάρχους (Arr. 3. 9. 6). Similarly we read τῶν πεζῶν δὲ τὴν φάλαγγα Σελεύκῳ καὶ Ἀντιγένει καὶ Ταύρωνι προσέταξεν ἄγειν (5. 16. 3) in a context where the brigades of heavy infantry have already been deployed elsewhere and the commanders named led Royal Hypaspists, regular hypaspists and archers respectively. Hence it does not follow from 3. 29. 7 that Philotas commanded heavy infantry; the Philotas named along with Amyntas and Koinos (Arr. 3. 18. 6; cf. Curt. 5. 4. 20, 30, who adds Polyperchon) is almost certainly the son of Parmenion, a cavalry-officer.

When Philotas is next mentioned, in the Aspasian campaign (327/6), his brigade is one of four — Philotas, Attalos, Balakros, Philippos — of which only one, that of Attalos, can have comprised pezhetairoi. Perdikkas and Hephaistion, *en route* to the Indus, had taken Gorgias, Kleitos and Meleagros (Arr. 4. 22. 7); Krateros retained the brigades of Polyperchon and Alketas;[31] hence Alexander was left with only Koinos and Attalos. Balakros' men are undoubtedly light infantry (ψιλοί), and it is highly likely that Philippos (probably the son of Machatas, see 2. 2 below) and Philotas led similar troops.[32]

In 323 Philotas resurfaces as satrap of Kilikia,[33] an appointment which was perhaps made by Alexander himself; for the previous satrap, Balakros son of Nikanor had been killed by the Pisidians during the King's lifetime.[34] He appears to be the Philotas named as

---

[30]This identification is made even more attractive by the possibility that Lysanias is identical with the cavalry commander of Antigonos (Diod. 19. 29. 2; cf. Billows, *Antigonos* 398, no. 64), in which case both found their way eventually into Antigonos' service.

[31]This must be deduced from Arr. 4. 23. 1, 5; 4. 24. 1; 4. 25. 5-6. Gorgias' brigade was formerly Krateros'; Kleitos' was a new (seventh) unit.

[32]Cf. Bosworth, *CQ* 23 (1973), 252 f.

[33]Diod. 18. 3. 1; Justin 13. 4. 12; Arr. *Succ.* 1a. 5 = *FGrHist* 156 F1 §5; Arr. *Succ.* 1b. 2 = Dexippos, *FGrHist* 100 F8 §2; cf. Justin 13. 6. 16. Diod. 18. 12. 1 wrongly calls him the satrap of Hellespontine Phrygia. This is an error for Leonnatos.

[34]Diod. 18. 22. 1: ἔτι ζῶντος Ἀλεξάνδρου.

one of the King's poisoners (Ps.-Kall. 3. 31. 8-9; his name has dropped out of the Metz *Liber de Morte*); the charge was almost certainly fabricated but suggests nevertheless that he was still in Babylon in May/June 323 and did not take up his office until after Alexander's death.[35] Perdikkas removed him from his satrapy in 321/0, perceiving that he was loyal to Krateros (Arr. *Succ.* 24. 2; Justin 13. 6. 16; cf. Boerma 185). Philotas may now have joined the forces of Antipatros, if he did not go directly to Antigonos.

If Philotas had been a φίλος of Antigonos before the settlement at Triparadeisos, Antipatros may have failed to reinstate him as satrap of Kilikia in 320 for this very reason, allowing Philoxenos to remain in office (Arr. *Succ.* 1. 34; Diod. 18. 39. 6).[36] Antipatros may have used the argument that Philotas had been unable to hold Kilikia and, therefore, did not deserve to be restored (cf. Menandros, who abandoned Lydia and was replaced by Kleitos in 320), but his real purpose must have been to offset Antigonos' power in Asia by leaving Kilikia and Lydia in the hands of men more loyal to himself; Diodoros 18. 50. 5 shows that Antigonos wanted to reinstate *his* men in Asia Minor (cf. also 18. 62. 6-7). In 318, Philotas was sent with thirty other Makedonians to seduce the Argyraspids away from their allegiance to Eumenes. For this purpose, he bore a letter from Antigonos himself (Diod. 18. 62. 4). Philotas suborned Teutamos to approach Antigenes in an effort to bring about his defection, but instead the latter succeeded in bringing Teutamos back into Eumenes' camp (Diod. 18. 62. 5-7; cf. Heckel, *SO* 57 [1982], 64-65). Although he read out to the Argyraspids Antigonos' letter, urging them to arrest Eumenes, whom the Makedonians had outlawed at Triparadeisos, he met with no success and returned to Antigonos (Diod. 18. 63. 1-5). Nothing else is known about him.[37]

---

[35]See Heckel, *LDT* 36-37, though I would now withdraw the tentative identification with Philotas Augaeus (Curt. 5. 2. 5).

[36]Philoxenos was Perdikkas' appointee, and we must assume that he remained in office because he had defected to Antipatros after Krateros' defeat at the Hellespont in 320.

[37]Billows, *Antigonos* 103, n.27, suggests that Antigenes may have been killed because 'he had caused the execution of Antigonos's friend Philotas...'. I can see no evidence for this. It is more likely that Antigenes was executed because he supported Eumenes, and because he was regarded as unreliable.

2. 2. Philippos son of Machatas

Literature. Berve ii 384 f., no. 780, and ii 386 f., no. 784; Treves, *RE* xix (1938), 2545, no. 55, and 2545 f., no. 56; Bosworth, *CQ* 23 (1973), 252-253.

Philippos son of Machatas (Arr. 5. 8. 3) was, in all probability, the brother of Harpalos the Treasurer and Tauron, who commanded the archers in the second half of Alexander's campaign. Although Philippos is attested with patronymic only once in the Alexander-historians, his career can be reconstructed with a measure of certainty. He first appears in the Aspasian campaign of 327/6 B.C., leading a brigade of light infantry in that third of the army which Alexander had entrusted to Ptolemy son of Lagos (Arr. 4. 24. 10).[38] At Taxila, Philippos was ordered to govern the newly-formed satrapy east of the Indus (Arr. 5. 8. 3), and on the death of Nikanor (Arr. 5. 20. 7) his province was extended to include Gandhara (Arr. 6. 2. 3), which he restored to order with the help of Tyriespis, the ruler of the Parapamisadai (Berve ii 376, no. 758).[39] As the Makedonian conquests continued, Philippos received additional territory between the rivers Akesines and Indus as far south as their confluence (Arr. 6. 14. 3; 6. 15. 2; cf. Plut. *Alex.* 60. 16), regions which he had himself helped to subdue (Arr. 6. 2. 3; 6. 4. 1; cf. *Ind.* 19. 4).

When Alexander moved south towards Sogdia and the kingdom of Mousikanos (with its capital at Alor; cf. Eggermont 5-9), Philippos remained in the enlarged satrapy, supported by all the Thrakians (presumably under Eudamos' command; see 3. 3 below) and a force of mercenaries, with instructions to found a city at the junction of the rivers and build dockyards (Arr. 6. 15. 2).[40] In 325 Philippos was assassinated by mercenaries, some of whom were killed in the act by the satrap's Bodyguard, others were arrested and executed. Alexander, who learned of Philippos' death as he marched from Gedrosia to

[38] This cannot have been a brigade of pezhetairoi commanded (perhaps) by Philippos son of Balakros (see 1. 3-4 above).

[39] The Philippos who was installed as commandant (phrourarch) of Peukelaotis (= Charsada), under the general supervision of Nikanor, who ruled the Kophen (Gandhara) satrapy (Arr. 4. 28. 6), is unlikely to have been the son of Machatas. But Berve (ii 386, no. 783) equates the commandant of Peukelaotis with the man who campaigned with Tyriespis in Gandhara; the latter Philippos was clearly the son of Machatas.

[40] The city may be the one described by Diod. 17. 102. 4 and Curt. 9. 8. 8 (so Welles, *Diodorus* 413, n.2); Brunt (*Arrian* ii 144, n.3) thinks Curt. 9. 8. 8 could refer to the city founded by Alexander near Sogdia (Arr. 6. 15. 4; cf. Tarn ii 237). I am inclined to believe that both Diodoros (who says the city was founded by Alexander — possibly inaccurate shorthand) and Curtius refer to the latter foundation.

Karmania, appointed Eudamos as his replacement (Arr. 6. 27. 2; Curt. 10. 1. 20). His sudden death, corresponding roughly to the time of Harpalos' misadventures, evokes certain suspicions about Alexander's role in the man's murder.

2. 3. Balakros

Literature. Berve ii 101, no. 201 and ii 101, no. 202; Kaerst, *RE* ii (1896), 2816, nos. 3-4; Bosworth, *CQ* 23 (1973), 252-253.

A Makedonian of unknown family origin, Balakros commanded the javelin-men (ἀκοντισταί), perhaps since the beginning of the expedition. At Gaugamela, these were stationed on the right, where they effectively negated the threat of the Persian scythe-chariots.[41] Balakros is thus also identical with the commander of ψιλοί who campaigned against the Skythians north of the Iaxartes (Syr-Darya) in 329 (Arr. 4. 4. 6: τοὺς ἄλλους ψιλούς, ὧν Βάλακρος ἦρχεν) and in Aspasian territory in 327/6. On the latter occasion, his troops (along with Attalos' brigade of pezhetairoi) belonged to Leonnatos' third of the army (Arr. 4. 24. 10). The same Balakros took some of his men to reconnoitre at Aornos and discovered that the Indians had fled from the rock (Curt. 8. 11. 22). After that he is not heard of again. It is highly doubtful that he is identical with the Balakros who defeated Hydarnes and recaptured Miletos (Curt. 4. 5. 13); that man was probably the son of Balakros, a former Somatophylax and satrap of Kilikia.

3. Commanders of Thrakian Infantry

3. 1. Attalos

Literature. Berve ii 94-95, no. 183; Kaerst, *RE* ii (1896), 2158, no. 6.

A prominent Makedonian, Attalos is first attested as commander of the Agrianes at Issos (Arr. 2. 9. 2); he may have held the position since, at least, the beginning of the Asiatic campaign. At Gaugamela, as at Issos, he is found on the right wing, this time with half the Agrianes and adjacent to Kleitos' *ile basilike* (Arr. 3. 12. 2; cf. Curt. 4. 13. 31). The unit appears to have numbered about 500 from 334 until the reorganisation of the army in the vicinity of Sousa (so Berve i 137 f). Thereafter, the Agrianes formed at least one chiliarchy (Curt. 5. 3. 6 says that Tauron led 1,500 archers and 1,000 Agrianes in the Ouxian

---

[41] Arr. 3. 12. 3; 3. 13. 5. Marsden, *Gaugamela* 66 f., calculates that Balakros' javelin-men numbered about 1,000; they were presumably of Thrakian origin.

campaign). When Alexander rushed ahead in pursuit of Bessos, who had by this time arrested Dareios III, he ordered Attalos and the Agrianes, as well as the hypaspists under Nikanor, to follow as lightly equipped as possible; the rest of the infantry were to continue at their normal pace (Arr. 3. 21. 8). This is our last reference to Attalos. He may have retained his command until at least the end of the expedition. Certainly there is no record of his replacement by another officer.

3. 2. Ptolemaios

Literature. Berve ii 337, no. 673; Volkmann, *RE* xxiii.2 (1959), 1594 f., no. 8.

The commander of the Thrakians, Ptolemaios was apparently the Makedonian officer in charge of all Thrakian infantry, except the Agrianes, during the first half of the expedition. Of the native commanders, only Sitalkes is known to us. Ptolemaios is first mentioned when he returned from the coast of Phoinikia and Kilikia to Alexander in 329 at Zariaspa (Arr. 4. 7. 2; cf. Curt. 7. 10. 11: he returned with 5000 mercenaries), having been sent there in the winter of 331/0 to accompany Menes the hyparch and the discharged Thessalian cavalrymen (cf. Arr. 3. 16. 9). On his departure for the coast, he was replaced by Eudamos (3. 3 below). What became of Ptolemaios after his return to Baktria is unknown.

3. 3. Eudamos

Literature. Berve ii 154, no. 311 (Εὔδημος); Willrich, *RE* vi (1909), 893, no. 5.

The form of the name is variously given: Curtius writes 'Eudaemon'; Arrian and Plutarch have Εὔδαμος, Εὔδημος appears in Diodoros. A man of unknown origin, though probably Makedonian, Eudamos was apparently ὁ τῶν Θρᾳκῶν στρατηγός (Curt. 10. 1. 21 calls him *dux Thracum*). Thus he may have replaced Ptolemaios (3. 2 above) in 331 (as is hesitantly suggested by Berve ii 154); possibly, however, he led the newly-recruited Thrakians who accompanied Amyntas son of Andromenes to Sousa (Arr. 3. 16. 10; Curt. 5. 1. 41 says Babylon), whence Alexander had sent those Thrakians currently serving with Ptolemaios to Phoinikia and Kilikia (Arr. 3. 16. 9, with 4. 7. 2). He was entrusted with the Indian satrapy once administered by Philippos (son of Machatas), who had been assassinated in 325 (Curt. 10. 1. 20), and he may have been installed originally as *strategos* in the kingdom of Poros, whom he later killed (Diod. 19. 14. 8); Arrian says that the temporary control of Philippos' satrapy should be shared by Eudamos and Taxiles (6. 27. 2), but this need not imply that Eudamos was

Taxiles' *strategos*.⁴² After Alexander's death, he murdered Poros and moved westward to join Eumenes and the rulers of the eastern satrapies in their war with Antigonos (Diod. 19. 14. 8, 15. 5; 19. 30). He was taken prisoner by Antigonos in the battle of Gabiene and executed, ostensibly, for his crime against Poros (Diod. 19. 44. 1).

3. 4. Sitalkes

Literature. Berve ii 357, no. 712; Schoch, *RE* iiiA (1929), 381 f., no. 2; cf. Hoffmann 182.

Apparently a prince of the Odrysian royal house (cf. Kaerst i³ 332 f., n.1; Hoffmann 182; Bosworth, *Arrian* i 171), possibly even the son of Kersobleptes, Sitalkes commanded the Thrakian javelin-men (ἀκοντισταί) since at least the beginning of the Asiatic campaign, and in this capacity served also as a hostage for the good conduct of his father; according to Frontinus (*Strat.* 2. 11. 3; cf. Justin 11. 5. 3), Alexander took the sons of Thrakian kings with him in order to ensure the loyalty of their fathers at home (cf. Ariston: ix 3. 4). Sitalkes first appears in the Pisidian campaign, in the attack on Sagalassos (334/3). Here the natives had occupied a hill-fort near the city and could only be dislodged by an attack of the lightly armed troops — the archers and Agrianes on the right, Sitalkes' javelin-men on the left (Arr. 1. 28. 4). Doubtless, the latter played an important role in defeating the enemy, though Arrian's account concentrates on the activities of the right wing, where Alexander himself was present (1. 28. 5-8).

In late 333, Sitalkes accompanied Parmenion, when he occupied the 'other' Gates that led from Kilikia to Syria (Arr. 2. 5. 1; for their location see Bosworth, *Arrian* i 192 f.). And, at Issos (Arr. 2. 9. 3), as at Gaugamela (Arr. 3. 12. 4), he was stationed on the left wing. In 330, he remained with Parmenion at Ekbatana and later received, through the agency of Polydamas, orders to kill the old general (Arr. 3. 26. 3-4). But, when Alexander returned from India, Sitalkes like his colleagues, Kleandros, Herakon and Agathon, who had participated in the murder of Parmenion, was found guilty of maladministration and executed (Arr. 6. 27. 4; cf. Curt. 10. 1. 1).

---

⁴²Alexander clearly trusted Taxiles, but not Poros.

COMMANDERS OF INFANTRY

4. Commanders of Other Allied Troops

4. 1. Balakros son of Amyntas

Literature. Berve ii 100, no. 199; Kaerst, *RE* ii (1896), 2816, no. 2; Hoffmann 176, n.82.

A prominent Makedonian, Balakros assumed the command of the allied infantry upon Antigonos' appointment as satrap of Phrygia (Arr. 1. 29. 3). As their commander he fought at Issos, Tyre and Gaza, but he was left behind with Peukestas son of Makartatos as *strategos* of the troops in Egypt in 331 (Arr. 3. 5. 5; Curt. 4. 8. 4 names only Peukestas). His command was given to Karanos (Arr. 3. 5. 6, Κάλανος).

4. 2. Karanos (Kalanos)

Literature. Berve ii 186-187, no. 395; id., *RE* Supplbd iv (1924), 854, 'Kalas (2)'; Schoch, *RE* Supplbd iv (1924), 854, 'Kalanos (2)'; W. Heckel, 'Some Speculations on the Prosopography of the Alexanderreich', *LCM* 6 (1981), 64, 69-70.

The commander of the allied infantry from 331 to 330, Karanos took office when his predecessor, Balakros son of Amyntas, was appointed *strategos* in Egypt (Arr. 3. 5. 5-6) and retained it until the allied infantry were dismissed in 330 at Ekbatana. Although Arrian calls him 'Kalanos', this form (as a proper name or nickname) is simply not Makedonian. In fact, it was unusual enough to prompt Plutarch to explain how it came to be applied to the Indian philosopher Sphines: ἐπεὶ δὲ κατ' Ἰνδικὴν γλῶτταν τῷ Καλὲ προσαγορεύων ἀντὶ τοῦ χαίρειν τοὺς ἐντυγχάνοντας ἠσπάζετο, Καλανὸς ὑπὸ τῶν Ἑλλήνων ὠνομάσθη (*Alex*. 65. 5). Understanding the infantry commander's fate depends, in part, on what we make of his name. Berve, following Hoffmann, sees Καλανός as a corruption of Κάλας. I suspect, however, that Καλανός is a simple error for Κάρανος inspired perhaps by the proximity of the name Βάλα-κρος. He may be identical with Berve's Karanos (no. 412) and also with Arrian's Koiranos (Arr. 3. 12. 4; Berve ii 219, no. 442), both of whom commanded ξύμμαχοι ἱππεῖς (cf. Brunt, *Arrian* i 262, n.1). Thus he would have been promoted from infantry to cavalry commander (for the remainder of his career see ix 5. 3).

5. Commanders of the Archers

The organisation and command structure of Alexander's archers is virtually impossible to determine. Arrian mentions both Makedonian (Arr. 3. 12. 2; cf. 2. 9. 2) and Kretan (Arr. 2. 9. 3) units, and the few attested commanders have names that are recognisably Makedonian

(Antiochos, Kleandros, Klearchos) or Kretan (Eurybotas, Ombrion). But the division of command becomes blurred: Arrian's terminology, here as elsewhere, is vague and the man identified specifically as commander of the Makedonian archers, Brison (Arr. 3. 12. 2), may be identical with the Kretan Ombrion (5. 5-6 below). Berve's attempt (i 131 f.) to distinguish between the ranks of στρατηγὸς τῶν τοξοτῶν and τοξάρχης is misguided and fruitless (see 5. 2-3 below).

Diodoros (17. 17. 4) gives the combined number of archers and Agrianes as 1,000 at the time of Alexander's crossing into Asia. Thus the archers by themselves can scarcely have numbered more than 500 (cf. Berve i 132). But the reform of the army at Sousa in late 331 saw them increase to at least 3,000: Tauron commanded 1,500 in the land of the Ouxians (Curt. 5. 3. 6), and these constituted only a portion of the force; in 327 not fewer than three chiliarchies are attested (Arr. 4. 24. 10). Berve (i 133) may be correct in assigning the command of the reformed archers to Tauron son of Machatas.

5. 1. Eurybotas

Literature. Berve ii 158, no. 320; Kirchner, *RE* vi (1909), 1321.

A Kretan by birth, Eurybotas perished in the attack on Thebes (335 B.C.) while commanding the archers (Arr. 1. 8. 4). His successor is not named.

5. 2-3. Klearchos and Kleandros

Literature. Kleandros: Berve ii 205, no. 423; Kroll, *RE* xi (1922), 558, no. 5. Klearchos: Berve ii 205, no. 424; id., *RE* Supplbd iv (1924), 908 no. 6a; Heckel, *LCM* 6 (1981), 64-65.

Arrian 1. 22. 7 discusses the casualties at Halikarnassos, saying that forty of Alexander's men died, among them Ptolemaios the Somatophylax and Klearchos the commander of the archers (ἐν τούτοις Πτολεμαῖός τε ὁ σωματοφύλαξ καὶ Κλέαρχος ὁ τοξάρχης). But later (1. 28. 8) he lists amongst the dead in a skirmish with the Pisidians a certain Kleandros 'general of the archers' (Κλέανδρός τε ὁ στρατηγὸς τῶν τοξοτῶν). Now possibly there were two commanders of archers who perished in successive campaigns. It was clearly dangerous work: Eurybotas the τοξάρχης had been killed in the attack on Thebes in the preceding year (Arr. 1. 8. 4; see 5. 1 above). But Kleandros and Klearchos are easily confused. When Arrian speaks of the leader of the ξένοι (3. 6. 8) he writes: ἐπὶ δὲ τοῖς ξένοις, ὧν ἡγεῖτο Μένανδρος, Κλέαρχος αὐτῷ ἐτάχθη. But at Gaugamela (Arr. 3. 12. 2) these men are found under the command of Kleandros son of Polemokrates. In this case as well Berve (ii 204 f.) distinguishes between the two commanders (nos. 422 and 425); Brunt, *Arrian* i 240, n.8, identifies them.

Kleandros and Klearchos are probably one and the same, their appearance in two separate passages of Arrian attributable to confusion. One of Arrian's sources reported the death of the commander of the archers in the context of the battle at Halikarnassos, the other in the Pisidian campaign; the former called him Klearchos and the latter Kleandros. Arrian copied both versions, failing to notice that the same commander was involved. Berve (i 132), however, obscures the issue when he distinguishes between the ranks of στρατηγὸς τῶν τοξοτῶν and τοξάρχης. But Berve's own scheme breaks down: Kleandros, who in his opinion (ii 205) succeeded Klearchos, was στρατηγός, replacing a man who was τοξάρχης. Similarly, Antiochos, who is described by Arrian as ὁ ἄρχων τῶν τοξοτῶν (3. 5. 6; cf. 2. 9. 2), succeeds Kleandros and is himself replaced by Ombrion, another ἄρχων. There is clearly no distinction to be made between the στρατηγὸς τῶν τοξοτῶν and the ἄρχων τῶν τοξοτῶν (= τοξάρχης). Hence one cannot preclude identification of Kleandros and Klearchos on the ground that one outranked the other.

5. 4. Antiochos

Literature. Berve ii 45, no. 91; Kirchner, *RE* i (1894), 2450, no. 13.

Although his name suggests a Makedonian origin, nothing is known about Antiochos' background. He commanded the archers at Issos (Arrian 3. 5. 6: ἄρχων τῶν τοξοτῶν), stationed with the Makedonian archers on the right side next to the Paionians.[43] He appears to have succeeded Kleandros or possibly Klearchos in 334/3 (see 5. 2-3 above). In 332/1, Antiochos died of unknown causes — perhaps in Egypt, possibly in earlier campaigning. Alexander replaced him with the Kretan Ombrion (below).

5. 5-6. Brison or Ombrion?

Literature. Brison: Berve ii 110-111, no. 223; Hoffmann 195; Kaerst, *RE* iii (1899), 858, no. 1; Krause, *Hermes* 25 (1890), 77; Ombrion: Berve ii 288, no. 582; Bosworth, *Arrian* i 302.

Arrian (3. 5. 6) says that in Egypt (332/1 B.C.) a Kretan named Ombrion replaced the dead Antiochos as commander of the archers (ἄρχων τῶν τοξοτῶν). But, at Gaugamela, Arrian names as commander of the Makedonian archers a certain Brison, whom Alexander had stationed

---

[43] Arr. 2. 9. 2. The Kretan archers were on the left (2. 9. 3); cf. Curt. 3. 9. 9.

on the right wing between the Agrianes and the so-called 'old mercenaries' (οἱ ἀρχαῖοι καλούμενοι ξένοι) under Kleandros (3. 12. 2). Brison's origins are unknown, nor is he heard of again. The case for identifying him as Makedonian is not strong.[44] Bosworth may be right in suspecting that 'Arrian's text has been corrupted by contraction: i.e. for ὧν Βρίσων read ὧν ⟨'Ομ⟩βρίων' (*Arrian* i 302). Ombrion, too, vanishes from history: the next attested commander of the archers is Tauron son of Machatas.

5. 7. Tauron son of Machatas

Literature. Berve ii 371-372, no. 741; Hoffmann 201; cf. Billows, *Antigonos* 450, no. 139.

The son of Machatas (*IG* ix.9, 197), hence a brother of Philippos and Harpalos and an adherent of the royal house of Elimeia, Tauron first appears in late 331. Alexander, intending to attack a town of the Ouxians, sent him with a force of 1,500 mercenary archers and 1,000 Agrianes to occupy the heights above that town (Curt. 5. 3. 6; cf. Diod. 17. 67. 4-5). Arrian (3. 17. 4) assigns to Krateros the command of this force, which in his version was intended to cut down the Ouxians who fled to the heights. Now it may be that Tauron commanded only the archers, with the supreme command belonging to Krateros. But Bosworth (*Arrian* i 321 ff.) argues persuasively for two different engagements fought on the journey from Sousa to the Persian Gates. Tauron's manoeuvre was carried out successfully and the appearance of the archers and Agrianes disheartened the Ouxians who were now under attack by Alexander (Curt. 5. 3. 10).

Tauron is not mentioned again until 326, this time with the title τοξάρχης, in the battle with Poros (Arr. 5. 14. 1). Along with Seleukos and Antigenes, he commanded infantrymen who were clearly not pezhetairoi (Arr. 5. 16. 3; cf. Curt. 8. 14. 15, wrongly substituting Leonnatos for Seleukos). According to Diodoros (17. 88. 5) the archers were used to make a direct attack on Poros himself.

The next stages of his life are difficult to reconstruct. His career undoubtedly suffered because of his relationship to Harpalos, whose flight to Greece in 324 was an overt act of rebellion. He reappears in the late 4th century, honoured at Eretria together with Myllenas son of Asandros (*IG* xii.9, 197), a γραμματεύς of Alexander. Since most of the honorific decrees of Eretria in this period concern men in the service of Antigonos and his son, it appears that Tauron too became an Antigonid supporter (Billows, *Antigonos* 450, 'Taurion').[45]

---

[44]Hoffmann 195 includes him among the Makedones.

[45]It is tempting to postulate a family connection between the Antigonids and the royal house of Elimeia: a certain Harpalos appears, perhaps as

6. Commanders of Greek Mercenaries

6. 1. Menandros

Literature. Berve ii 255, no. 501; Geyer, *RE* xv (1932), 706 f., no. 5; Heckel, *LDT* 39 f.; Billows, *Antigonos* 402 f., no. 71.

A Makedonian hetairos of Alexander (Arr. 3. 6. 7) and father of the Page Charikles (Arr. 4. 13. 7), Menandros commanded mercenary infantry from perhaps 334 until the spring of 331 B.C. We are told only that, in the spring of 331, Menandros relinquished the command of the ξένοι to Kleandros in order to become satrap of Lydia.[46] Of his activities as satrap during Alexander's lifetime we know very little: he appears to have been responsible for sending some 2,600 Lydian infantry and 300 cavalrymen, who reached Alexander near Artakoana in 330.[47] In 323, Menandros brought fresh troops to Alexander in Babylon (7. 23. 1) and attended the dinner-party given by Medius, at which the King became fatally ill. It is alleged in the pamphlet on 'The Last Days and Testament of Alexander the Great' that Menandros was guilty of complicity in the plot to poison the King (Ps.-Kall. 3. 31. 8; *LM* 97-98), but this appears to be hostile propaganda spread by the Polyperchon faction.[48]

Menandros was confirmed as satrap of Lydia in the settlement at Babylon (Arr. *Succ.* 1a. 6; 1b. 2; cf. 1. 26; Curt. 10. 10. 2; Diod. 18. 3. 1; Justin 13. 4. 15), but he was soon humiliated by Perdikkas, who assigned control of the satrapy to Kleopatra, the sister of Alexander the Great, leaving Menandros in charge of the army (Arr. *Succ.* 25. 2). He soon defected to Antigonos, who had returned from Europe, having incited Antipatros and Krateros to war with Perdikkas. In the settlement of

---

governor of Beroia, in the mid-third century (Tataki, *PB* 116, no. 228) in the service of Antigonos Gonatas; a later Harpalos son of Polemaios (Tataki, *PB* 116-117, no. 230) was Perseus' ambassador to Rome in 172. Polemaios was, of course, the name of Antigonos Monophthalmos' nephew (cf. Tataki, *PB* 255, no. 1082). Furthermore, Tauron is honoured along with Myllenas son of Asandros (possibly another Beroian; cf. Tataki, *PB* 231-232, no. 910); Asandros son of Agathon, satrap of Karia, is described by Arr. *Succ.* 25. 1 as welcoming Antigonos κατὰ γένος ἐπιτήδειος ὤν.

[46] Arr. 3. 6. 7-8. The MSS. have Κλέαρχος, which appears to be a mistake for Κλέανδρος (so Brunt, *Arrian* i 240, n.8; cf. Bosworth, *Arrian* i 285). Cf Arr. 3. 12. 2; 3. 26. 3; 6. 27. 4. For Menandros' satrapy see also Dittenberger, *Syll.*³ 302, 4-5; Arr. 7. 23. 1.

[47] Curt. 6. 6. 35. It had perhaps been one of Menandros' first tasks, upon taking charge of the satrapy, to secure these reinforcements for the King.

[48] See Heckel, *LDT*.

Triparadeisos, Menandros was relieved of his satrapy, which was assigned instead to White Kleitos. Menandros, for his part, took refuge with Antigonos, who appears to have promised to restore Lydia to him. Though Menandros served Antigonos faithfully, especially in the events following the battle of Orkynii (Plut. *Eum.* 9. 8-12; cf. Diod. 18. 59. 1-2), there is no clear indication that Antigonos kept his word. Nor can we say what became of Menandros.[49] Menandros commissioned a painting of himself by Apelles, apparently during Alexander's lifetime (Pliny, *NH* 35. 93, wrongly 'King of the Karians'; cf. Pollitt, p. 162).[50]

6. 2. Kleandros son of Polemokrates

Literature. Berve ii 204, no. 422, s.v. Κλέανδρος; Kroll, *RE* xi 558, no. 6; Badian, 'Harpalus', *JHS* 81 (1961), 21-23; Berve ii 205, no. 425, s.v. Κλέαρχος; Schoch, *RE* Supplbd iv (1924), 908, no. 7a.

The son of Polemokrates (Arr. 1. 24. 2) and, in all probability, the brother of Koinos (cf. 1. 24. 1), Kleandros served Alexander since at least the beginning of the Asiatic campaign. In late 334, before Alexander invaded Lykia and Pamphylia, he was sent to recruit mercenaries from the Peloponnese (Arr. 1. 24. 2; Curt. 3. 1. 1: on the date see Heckel, *Hermes* 119 [1991], 124 f.). He rejoined Alexander at Sidon in early 332, bringing with him 4,000 mercenaries (Arr. 2. 20. 5; cf. Curt. 4. 3. 11). Arrian (3. 6. 8) says that Alexander, when he assigned the satrapy of Lydia to Menandros (replacing Asandros), appointed 'Klearchos' commander of the ἀρχαῖοι ξένοι, but this is clearly an error for 'Kleandros' (Brunt, *Arrian* i 240, n.8; Bosworth, *Arrian* i 285; Heckel, *LCM* 6 [1981], 65), who led this unit soon afterwards at Gaugamela (Arr. 3. 12. 2).

In the following year, Kleandros remained with Parmenion in Ekbatana and, on orders brought by Polydamas, orchestrated the old general's murder (Arr. 3. 26. 3-4; cf. Curt. 7. 2. 19 ff.). In 324, he was summoned to Karmania, along with Herakon, Sitalkes and Agathon, and executed on charges of maladministration and crimes against the native population (Arr. 6. 27. 4; Curt. 10. 1. 1-7, who does not mention Kleandros' own death but adds [10. 1. 8] that 600 common soldiers, who carried out the orders of Kleandros and his fellow officers, were executed *en masse*).[51]

---

[49]I cannot understand why Berve ii 255 says that Menandros died in 321. Billows, *Antigonos* 403, thinks that Antigonos left Menandros behind as *strategos* of Kappadokia, where he may have died c. 317/6.

[50]Unless Pliny has confused him with Asandros, the later satrap of Karia.

[51]Curtius' allegation that Kleandros raped a virgin of the native aristocracy and gave her to his slave as a concubine (10. 1. 5) may go back to Kleitarchos

6. 3. Herakon

Literature. Berve ii 168-169, no. 354; Sundwall, *RE* viii (1913), 528, no. 1.

An officer, presumably of Makedonian origin, Herakon remained in Ekbatana with Parmenion and, together with Kleandros, Agathon and Sitalkes, was involved in the old man's murder (Curt. 10. 1. 1). He may have commanded mercenary troops, though nothing specific is recorded about his unit. Little else is known about his career except that he had apparently been shifted to an administrative post in Sousa — perhaps at the same time as Harpalos moved from Ekbatana to Babylon.[52] He was summoned to Karmania in 324 with his colleagues (named above) and there charged with maladministration and temple-robbery (Curt. 10. 1. 1 ff.; Arr. 6. 27. 3-4). Though Kleandros and Sitalkes were found guilty and executed, Herakon was acquitted, only to be indicted by the natives in Sousa on similar charges and this time required to pay the penalty (Arr. 6. 27. 5).

6. 4. Andronikos son of Agerros

Literature. Berve ii 39, no. 78; Kaerst, *RE* i (1894), 2162, no. 10; E. D. Carney, 'The Death of Clitus', *GRBS* 22 (1981), 153 ff.

A noble Makedonian, Andronikos was the father of Proteas (and perhaps also Theodoros: Berve ii 176, no. 362; cf. Carney, *GRBS* 22 [1981], 152, with n.10) and in all likelihood the husband of Lanike, daughter of Dropidas and sister of Black Kleitos.[53] Andronikos first appears in 330 as the officer sent by Alexander (in accordance with their request) to the 1500 Greek mercenaries who had served with Dareios III but, upon his death, were prepared to surrender to the Makedonians (Arr. 3. 23. 9; Artabazos went with him, presumably as a guide). Andronikos returned with these men and interceded on their behalf with the King, who spared their lives and appointed

---

(for similar charges against Harpalos, cf. Diod. 17. 108. 4: εἰς ὕβρεις γυναικῶν καὶ παρανόμους ἔρωτας βαρβάρων ἐξετράπη).

[52]Somewhat different is Berve's view (ii 168): 'Da H. von Arr. III, 26, 3 bei Parmenions Ermordung unter den in Ekbatana anwesenden Strategen nicht genannt wird und später (324) wegen Beraubung eines Heiligtumes in Susa bestraft wurde (Arr. VI, 27, 5), darf man annehmen, dass er Ende 330 mit seinem Kontingent von Parmenion nach Susa beordert ward.'

[53]If this identification is correct, then Andronikos will have also have been the father of the two *anonymi* who died at Miletos in 334 (Curt. 8. 2. 8; cf. Arr. 4. 9. 4; Heckel, *L'Antiquité Classique* 56 [1987], 136, nos. 40-41).

Andronikos their commander (Arr. 3. 24. 5: καὶ ἐπέταξεν αὐτοῖς Ἀνδρόνικον, ὅσπερ ἤγαγέ τε αὐτοὺς καὶ ἔνδηλος γεγόνει οὐ φαῦλον ποιούμενος σῶσαι τοὺς ἄνδρας). Not long afterwards, Alexander sent him, along with Karanos, Erigyios and Artabazos against the rebel Satibarzanes.[54] There is no record of Andronikos' death in the campaign, in which Erigyios is said to have slain Satibarzanes with his own hand (Arr. 3. 28. 3; cf. Curt. 7. 4. 32-38), and it appears that he retained his command.

Carney (*GRBS* 22 [1981], 157) suggests that he may have led the 1500 mercenaries whom Alexander sent against Spitamenes in 329, but their commander was clearly Menedemos (see 6. 5 below). In this campaign, Andromachos commanded 60 Companions, Karanos the 800 mercenary cavalry; and Pharnouches (a Lykian) led the expedition (Arr. 4. 3. 7). That leaves Menedemos in charge of the infantry, a point which may explain his prominence in the Vulgate (Curt. 7. 6. 24; 7. 7. 31 ff.; 7. 7. 39; 7. 9. 21; cf. *ME* 13). I do not see how Menedemos could be an error for Andronikos; but Curtius (7. 6. 24) does give Menedemos 3,000 infantry, in addition to 800 cavalry, and it is remotely possible that Andronikos served under him. Carney (*GRBS* 22 [1981], 157 f.), however, takes matters one step further and argues that the poem (composed by Pranichos or Pierion) which angered Kleitos and provoked the quarrel with Alexander (Plut. *Alex.* 50. 8) dealt with the Polytimetos campaign and thus made light of the death of his brother-in-law. Certainly the identification of Proteas as 'son of Lanike' creates the impression that his father was already dead in the final years of Alexander's life (Athen. 4. 129a; Aelian 12. 26).[55] That Proteas forgave Alexander for his murder of Kleitos is not unreasonable; despite the apologetic tone of most sources, there is no reason to suppose that Alexander faked his grief. But, it is less likely that Proteas would have remained on intimate terms with a king who condoned the ridiculing of his father; and, indeed, it was not Kleitos but other older Makedonians who first found the poem objectionable. If Andronikos son of Agerros did perish in the Polytimetos (Zeravshan) fiasco, this episode will not have been the subject of Pranichos' (Pierion's) composition.[56]

---

[54]Curt. 7. 3. 2; Arrian's failure to mention him (3. 28. 2-3) is not serious; Andronikos will have been subordinate to Erigyios and Karanos.

[55]Berve is correct to distinguish him from Andronikos of Olynthos (ii 39-40, no. 79).

[56]Holt, *Alexander and Bactria* 78 f., n.118, argues that the poem mocked the battle at Baktra in which the harpist Aristonikos fell (Arr. 4. 16. 6) — he was honoured at Delphoi with a bronze statue, depicting him holding the lyre in one hand, a spear in the other. The suggestion is tantalising, and ἔναγχος ('recent') does suit this episode better than the more remote Polytimetos battle,

6. 5. Menedemos

Literature. Berve ii 256, no. 504; Stähelin, *RE* xv (1932), 787, no. 2.

Nothing is recorded about Menedemos' family or geographical origins; the name is attested in Makedonia (*IG* ii² 1335, 35), and we may be dealing with a Makedonian officer rather than a Greek mercenary leader. Menedemos appears only in connection with the campaign in which he was killed, that at the Polytimetos (Zeravshan) against Spitamenes (329 B.C.). Here he commanded 1500 mercenary infantry, as we may deduce from Arrian's description (4. 3. 7): Andromachos led 60 Companions, Karanos 800 mercenary cavalry; the Lykian Pharnouches was (allegedly) in charge of the entire expedition. Hence Menedemos must have been the commander of the mercenary infantry. But Curtius, who names only Menedemos in his account (7. 6. 24; 7. 7. 31 ff.; 7. 7. 39; 7. 9. 21; cf. *ME* 13), gives him 3000 foot soldiers in addition to 800 horse (7. 6. 24), a figure rejected by Berve (ii 256) without good reason. Whether Andronikos son of Agerros served under Menedemos (see 6. 4 above) cannot be determined.

The mercenaries, largely through the incompetence of their Makedonian commanders, were lured into an ambush and virtually annihilated by Spitamenes.[57] Menedemos himself perished in the engagement and was duly buried by Alexander when he returned from the Iaxartes (Curt. 7. 9. 21; *ME* 13).

---

but Plutarch (*Alex.* 50. 8) clearly refers to τοὺς στρατηγοὺς ... τοὺς ἔναγχος ἡττημένους, and Aristonikos could scarcely belong to that number.

[57] According to Arr. 4. 6. 2, forty cavalry and 300 infantrymen escaped.

ix. Commanders of Cavalry

1. Hipparchs of the Companion Cavalry

The title given to Philotas son of Parmenion, the most famous commander of the Companions, is not recorded by any ancient source, but it is very likely that he was hipparch; for his successors in 330 are certainly so designated (καταστήσας ἐπὶ τοὺς ἑταίρους ἱππάρχας δύο, Ἡφαιστίωνά τε τὸν Ἀμύντορος καὶ Κλεῖτον τὸν Δρωπίδου [Arr. 3. 27. 4]). As hipparch he commanded the eight squadrons of the Companions, including the ἴλη βασιλική, which was led by Kleitos. These appear to have numbered 1800 in all and to have excluded the πρόδρομοι ἱππεῖς — who were led successively by Amyntas son of Arrhabaios (Arr. 1. 14. 1: Graneikos),[1] Protomachos (Arr. 2. 9. 2: Issos), and Aretes (Arr. 3. 12. 3: Gaugamela) — and the Paionian scouts, commanded by Ariston. The common source of Diodoros and Curtius wrongly thought that Philotas' command did not include the ἴλη βασιλική, and that the other seven squadrons of the Companions were separate from Philotas' squadrons, though attached to Philotas' command at Gaugamela. Hence Diodoros 17. 57. 1 writes: ἐπὶ μὲν οὖν τὸ δεξιὸν κέρας ἔταξε τὴν βασιλικὴν εἴλην, ἧς εἶχε τὴν ἡγεμονίαν Κλεῖτος ὁ μέλας ὀνομαζόμενος, ἐχομένους δὲ ταύτης τοὺς ἄλλους φίλους, ὧν ἡγεῖτο Φιλώτας ὁ Παρμενίωνος, ἑξῆς δὲ τὰς ἄλλας ἱππαρχίας ἑπτὰ τεταγμένας ὑπὸ τὸν αὐτὸν ἡγεμόνα. This is echoed by Curtius 4. 13. 26-27: *In dextro cornu locati sunt equites, quos agema appellabant; praeerat his Clitus, cui iunxit Philotae turmas, ceterosque praefectos equitum lateri eius adplicuit. Ultima Meleagri ala stabat, quam phalanx sequebatur.* But Arrian 3. 11. 8 makes it clear that Philotas led all the Companions (ξυμπάσης τῆς ἵππου τῶν ἑταίρων), and that these comprised eight squadrons, including that of Kleitos.

Philotas clearly did not command the four squadrons of πρόδρομοι (cf. Arr. 1. 14. 1; 2. 9. 2; 3. 12. 3), and this suggests, when one considers also Diodoros 17. 17. 4, that the eight squadrons of Companions comprised 1800 men and the πρόδρομοι and the Paionians — five squadrons

---

[1]Diodoros' claim (17. 17. 4) that the prodromoi were commanded by Kassandros (or possibly Asandros) appears to be an error (cf. Berve ii 201, no. 414, s.v. Κάσσανδρος); but see Adams, *AncW* 2 (1979), 111-115.

altogether — another 900. The most important hipparchs of the Companions in the period following the death of Philotas (i 2. 2) have received thorough study in earlier chapters: Black Kleitos (i 3); Koinos (ii 1); Hephaistion (ii 2); Krateros (ii 4); Perdikkas (ii 5); White Kleitos (iii 4). Two others are discussed below, Demetrios son of Althaimenes (1. 1) and Eumenes of Kardia (1. 2).

1. 1. Demetrios son of Althaimenes

Literature. Berve ii 134, no. 256; Kirchner, *RE* iv (1901), 2768, no. 25; Hoffmann 183; cf. also Osborne, *Naturalization* i 69-71, D21; C. Schwenk, *Athens in the Age of Alexander* (Chicago, 1985), 132-134, no. 24; Heckel, *ZPE* 87 (1991), 40 f.

Demetrios son of Althaimenes is the only one of the eight ilarchs named at Gaugamela who attained prominence in the latter half of Alexander's Asiatic campaign. Although he is first mentioned in the battle-order at Gaugamela, where he was stationed between Herakleides and Meleagros (Arr. 3. 11. 8), he may have held the rank of ilarch since 334, if not earlier. He is not heard of again until the Swat campaign of 327/6, when he is sent — this time designated as 'hipparch' — with Attalos son of Andromenes and Alketas son of Orontes (perhaps under the leadership of Polyperchon: Curt. 8. 11. 1) against the town of Ora (Arr. 4. 27. 5), which was captured after Alexander's arrival (4. 27. 9). In the battle at the Hydaspes, Demetrios' hipparchy crossed the river with Alexander and was detailed on the right with that of Koinos (Arr. 5. 16. 3). His last recorded command was in the Mallian campaign (326/5 B.C.): he and Peithon the taxiarch, along with some lightly armed troops, were sent to subdue those Mallians who had taken refuge in the woods near the river (Arr. 6. 8. 2-3).[2]

Demetrios vanishes from our records. That he was the only one of Alexander's original ilarchs to attain prominence may be due to his family connections. But at these we can only guess. If Hephaistion was indeed the son of Amyntor son of Demetrios (Kirchner, *PA* 750), who was honoured by the Athenians in 334/3 B.C. (*IG* ii^2 405 = Osborne, *Naturalization* i 69-71, D21; cf. Schwenk, no. 24),[3] then we could, at least tentatively, postulate a relationship between Hephaistion and Demetrios. The stemma that follows is, of course, purely hypothetical.

---

[2] The river is presumably the Hydraotes (Arr. 6. 7. 1).
[3] On Hephaistion see **ii 2**.

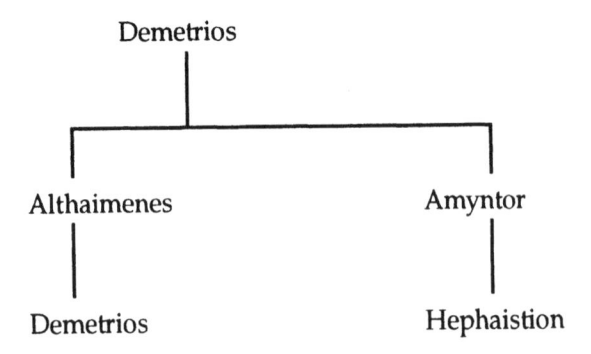

```
            Demetrios
               |
   ┌───────────┴───────────┐
Althaimenes              Amyntor
   |                        |
Demetrios              Hephaistion
```

1. 2. Eumenes son of Hieronymos

Literature. Berve ii 156-158, no. 317; A. Vezin, *Eumenes von Kardia* (Tübingen, 1907); Kaerst, *RE* vi (1909), 1083 f., no. 4.

Eumenes son of Hieronymos (Arr. *Ind.* 18. 7) of Kardia (Plut. *Eum.* 1. 1; Nepos, *Eum.* 1. 1) was unique among the hipparchs of the Companion Cavalry in being of non-Makedonian origin. Born in the Thrakian Chersonese in 361/0,[4] Eumenes came to Philip's court in his twentieth year (Nepos, *Eum.* 13. 1), apparently the son of a politically prominent Kardian. Stories found in Douris (Plut. *Eum.* 1. 1) and other Hellenistic sources (cf. Aelian, *VH* 12. 43) that depict Hieronymos as a poor waggoner or funeral musician, are inventions of the gossip-mongers and virtually disproved by the threat posed to Eumenes by the ruling tyrant of Kardia, Hekataios. This man's enmity may have had its origins in political upheavals as early as the 340s, in which Hieronymos played a significant role, and it continued into the reign of Alexander and beyond.[5]

We are not told in what capacity Eumenes served Philip, only that he did so for seven years (Nepos, *Eum.* 1. 4-6, cf. 13. 1; Plut. *Eum.* 1. 1-3). It seems likely, however, that he was secretary (γραμματεύς) of Philip and Alexander successively (Arr. 5. 24. 6-7; cf. Plut. *Eum.* 1. 6; at 1. 4 he is called ἀρχιγραμματεύς; cf. Metz, *LM* 116: *hypomnematographus*). In the Indian campaign he was given his first recorded military command

---

[4]He was forty-five when he died in 316/5 (Nepos, *Eum.* 13. 1).

[5]Plut. *Eum.* 3. 7: ἦν γὰρ αὐτοῖς πατρική τις ἐκ πολιτικῶν διαφορῶν ὑποψία πρὸς ἀλλήλους· καὶ πολλάκις ὁ Εὐμένης ἐγεγόνει φανερὸς κατηγορῶν τοῦ Ἑκαταίου τυραννοῦντος καὶ παρακαλῶν Ἀλέξανδρον ἀποδοῦναι τοῖς Καρδιανοῖς τὴν ἐλευθερίαν. For Hekataios' tyranny see Berve, *Tyrannis* 314; Hornblower, *Hieronymus* 8 f., dates the establishment of the tyranny to the period after Philip II's death.

(cf. Plut. *Eum*. 1. 5): after the capture of Sangala, Eumenes was instructed to take 300 horsemen to two neighbouring Kathaian towns in order to induce their surrender (Arr. 5. 24. 6). The mission accomplished little, for the Indians, on hearing of Sangala's fall, deserted their towns. No further military activity is attested for Eumenes. In late 324, after the death of Hephaistion, he assumed command of Perdikkas' hipparchy when the latter advanced to Hephaistion's position (Plut. *Eum*. 1. 5; cf. Nepos, *Eum*. 1. 6). As it turned out, the position was, for the most part, honorary: Alexander died soon afterwards, and the realignment of commands at Babylon soon saw Eumenes as satrap of Paphlagonia and the unconquered region of Kappadokia (Diod. 18. 3. 1; Curt. 10. 10. 3; Plut. *Eum*. 3. 3-4; Nepos, *Eum*. 2. 2; Arr. *Succ*. 1b. 2 = Dexippos, *FGrHist* 100 F8 §2; App. *Syr*. 53; cf. Metz, *LM* 116); he was to become Perdikkas' most reliable lieutenant.[6]

Eumenes' wealth and importance at the Court are evident on two occasions. At the Hydaspes, he was assigned a trierarchy, and in 324 at Sousa he was honoured by a marriage to Artonis, the daughter of Artabazos and sister of Barsine (Arr. 7. 4. 6; cf. Arr. *ap*. Phot. *Bibl*. 68b; Plut. *Eum*. 1. 7). She is probably the wife to whom Antigonos returned Eumenes' remains in 315 (Plut. *Eum*. 19. 2; hence also the mother of the children mentioned in the same passage). About Eumenes' career under Alexander little else is known, though a few anecdotes illuminate his character. Although he, like several others, had found Hephaistion difficult to deal with (Plut. *Eum*. 2. 1-3), he took the precaution of being amongst the first to praise Alexander's friend when he died at Ekbatana (Plut. *Eum*. 2. 9-10), thereby not only deflecting the King's ill will but possibly procuring for himself a significant cavalry command. Stories of his avarice may be exaggerated (Plut. *Eum*. 2. 4-6), but Eumenes appears to have had his share of 'cash-flow' problems (Plut. *Eum*. 16. 3). Despite his later prominence in the wars of the Diadochoi, Eumenes was hindered throughout his career by his Greek origins.[7]

---

[6]Arr. *Succ*. 1a. 2 lists him as one of the officers of second rank in Babylon in 323. For his alleged presence at the dinner-party of Medios see Ps.-Kall. 3. 31. 9; Metz, *LM* 98.

[7]See Anson, *AncW* 3 (1980), 55-59, and Hornblower, *Hieronymus* 156 ff.; cf. also H. D. Westlake, 'Eumenes of Cardia', *Bulletin of the John Rylands Library* 37 (1954), 309-327; reprinted in *Essays on the Greek Historians and Greek History* (New York, 1969), 313-330.

2. Ilarchs of the Companion Cavalry

2. 1. Ariston

Literature. Berve ii 74, no. 137; Hoffmann 182; Kirchner, *RE* ii (1896), 951, no. 28.

Nothing is known about the family and background of Ariston, who was undoubtedly a Makedonian of high standing. He is first attested at Gaugamela, where his squadron of Companions was stationed between those of Glaukias and Sopolis on the right wing (Arr. 3. 11. 8); he may have been an ilarch since at least the beginning of Alexander's reign. Otherwise, nothing is known about the man. Berve (ii 74) identifies him tentatively with the man who brought the remains of Krateros to his widow, Phila (Diod. 19. 59. 3).[8]

2. 2. Glaukias

Literature. Berve ii 111, no. 226; Kirchner, *RE* vii (1912), 1398, no. 3; Hoffmann 182.

Glaukias' place and date of birth are unknown, as are other details concerning his family.[9] Undoubtedly an adherent of the Makedonian nobility, he is attested but once in the Alexander historians — as an ilarch at Gaugamela, where his squadron was positioned between those of Kleitos (ἴλη βασιλική) and Ariston (Arr. 3. 11. 8). How long he served in this capacity, and what became of him, we do not know. Glaukias the ilarch may be identical with Kassandros' henchman, who murdered Alexander IV and Rhoxane at Amphipolis in 310 (Diod. 19. 52. 4; 19. 105. 2-3; cf. Berve ii 111).

2. 3. Herakleides son of Antiochos

Literature. Berve ii 167, no. 347; Sundwall, *RE* viii (1913), 459, no. 17.

Herakleides son of Antiochos (Arr. 3. 11. 8) was clearly of Makedonian origin. He commanded the Bottiaian squadron of Companion cavalry in the Triballian campaign (Arr. 1. 2. 5) and retained his office until at

---

[8] I am inclined to identify this man with Ariston of Pharsalos (Berve ii 75, no. 139); see Heckel, *LDT* 43.

[9] He may have had connections with Illyria, where two men of that name are attested in this period, but the name is too widespread in the Greek world to permit any firm conclusions.

least the battle of Gaugamela (Arr. 3. 11. 8). Thereafter he disappears from our sources.

2. 4. Meleagros

Literature. Berve ii 250, no. 495; Geyer, *RE* xv.1 (1932), 480, no. 5 (= no. 6); Hoffmann 183; Heckel, *LDT* 40.

Meleagros' background is unknown, but it is clear from his position that he belonged to a prominent Makedonian family. He commanded a squadron of the Companion Cavalry at Gaugamela (Arr. 3. 11. 8; Curt. 4. 13. 27) and may have served as ilarch since at least the beginning of the Asiatic expedition. His connections with the Somatophylax, Peithon son of Krateuas, in whose service we find him in 317/6 (Diod. 19. 47. 1), may go back into Alexander's reign and beyond.

2. 5. Pantordanos son of Kleandros

Literature. Berve ii 298, no. 605; Hoffmann 183-184.

Apart from the father's name, Kleandros,[10] nothing is known about Pantordanos or his family. He commanded the so-called 'Leugaian' squadron[11] in the battle of Issos, occupying at first the left wing but then being transferred (along with the squadron of Peroidas: 2. 6 below) to the right, just as the battle began (Arr. 2. 9. 3). Pantordanos is not heard of again, and the battle-order at Gaugamela (Arr. 3. 11. 8) shows that he had been replaced.[12] Arrian (2. 10. 7) says that some 120 Makedonians of note (τῶν οὐκ ἠμελημένων Μακεδόνων) died at Issos, but names only Ptolemaios son of Seleukos. It is not impossible that Pantordanos fell on the battlefield, but, since Arrian drew attention to

---

[10] Arr. 2. 9. 3. That he was the son of Kleandros son of Polemokrates is not impossible but highly unlikely: this would push Kleandros' birthdate back to c. 390, which might suit Kleandros' connections with Parmenion but would not be consistent with the date of Koinos' (his brother's) birth (c. 370). Whether Kleandros the τοξάρχης (Berve ii 205, no. 423) was a relative cannot be determined. The name is far too common in Makedonia to permit identification on this basis alone.

[11] Leugaia appears not to be a Makedonian toponym, and attempts have been made to emend the text (cf. Beloch iii² 2. 326; Berve i 105, n.3). Bosworth, *Arrian* i 211, may be right in seeing the name not as 'a regional adjective but a native Macedonian title for the squadron'.

[12] By Ariston, Demetrios, Glaukias, Hegelochos or Meleagros (cf. Berve i 107, with table).

his manoeuvre at the beginning of the battle, it would be unusual for him to omit his death, had it occurred.

2. 6. Peroidas son of Menestheus

Literature. Berve ii 317, no. 631; Hoffmann 184-185.

The commander of the squadron from Anthemos, Peroidas appears to have accompanied Alexander from the beginning of the campaign. At Issos, his *ile* was transferred, along with that of Pantordanos (2. 5 above), from the left to the right wing before the battle began (Arr. 2. 9. 3). His role in the engagement is not further attested. Like Pantordanos, he was no longer an ilarch at Gaugamela, and it seems unlikely that either (or both!) perished at Issos.[13] Who his replacement was is unclear: Ariston, Demetrios, Glaukias, Hegelochos and Meleagros all appear for the first time at Gaugamela, though two of them may well have been ilarchs at Issos.

2. 7. Sokrates son of Sathon

Literature. Berve ii 367, no. 732; Hoffmann 186; Bosworth, *Arrian* i 120.

The son of Sathon (Arr. 1. 12. 7), Sokrates commanded the squadron from Apollonia since at least the beginning of the Asiatic expedition. In 334, he joined Amyntas son of Arrhabaios and the four squadrons of prodromoi in a scouting mission from Hermotos in the direction of the river Graneikos (Arr. 1. 12. 7). At the river, he was again stationed next to Amyntas on the right wing (Arr. 1. 14. 1), and their units, along with an infantry brigade led by Ptolemaios son of Philippos, initiated the fighting by being the first to cross to the opposite bank (Arr. 1. 14. 6-15. 1).[14]

Arrian does not name Sokrates again. No full list is provided for the battle of Issos (late 333), but Sokrates is no longer amongst the ilarchs at Gaugamela (Arr. 3. 11. 8). If Curtius (4. 5. 9) is not mistaken,

---

[13] Arrian does not, however, record the deaths of all prominent officers: but for a chance reference in Curt. 6. 11. 22, we would not know of Hegelochos' death (apparently at Gaugamela).

[14] Ptolemaios son of Philippos (Berve ii 336, no. 671) is almost certainly the Somatophylax who died at Halikarnassos (Arr. 1. 22. 4, 7; cf. Berve ii 337, no. 672) and, as Billows (*Antigonos* 425, no. 99, s.v. 'Polemaios I') suggests, the brother of Antigonos Monophthalmos. For the problem of Ptolemaios' command see Bosworth, *Arrian* i 120.

Sokrates took over, temporarily, the governorship of Kilikia; for Balakros, whom Alexander had appointed after the battle of Issos (Arr. 2. 12. 2), is soon found campaigning at, and capturing, Miletos (Curt. 4. 5. 13). Berve assumes that the Platon, who brought reinforcements from Kilikia to Alexander in 331/0 (Curt. 5. 7. 12), is actually Sokrates — with the Vulgate or Curtius himself confused by the names of two prominent philosophers (ii 367; cf. ii 429, Abschn. II, no. 67, s.v. Πλάτων; rejected by Bosworth, CQ 24 [1974], 59, n.1). Curtius, however, calls Platon 'an Athenian' and, if Berve's theory is correct, we have a confusion of both the man's name and his nationality. What became of Sokrates the ilarch we do not know.

2. 8. Sopolis son of Hermodoros

Literature. Berve ii 368-369, no. 736; Hoffmann 186.

Sopolis son of Hermodoros[15] commanded the Amphipolitan squadron of Companion cavalry since at least the Triballian campaign of 335 (Arr. 1. 2. 5), in which he appears together with Herakleides son of Antiochos, who led the Bottiaians. He is attested again at Gaugamela, where his squadron was stationed between those of Ariston and Herakleides (Arr. 3. 11. 8). That he belonged to the Makedonian aristocracy is indicated not only by his important cavalry command but also by the fact that his son, Hermolaos, served as one of Alexander's Pages in 327. In the winter of 328/7 Sopolis was sent from Nautaka, in the company of Menidas and Epokillos, to bring new recruits from Makedonia (Arr. 4. 18. 3). There is no record of his return to Alexander's camp, and we may assume that, after the disgrace of his son in 327, he did not think it wise to do so. Alexander may have sent orders that he be arrested and, perhaps, executed.[16]

3. The πρόδρομοι ἱππεῖς and the Paionians

The Prodromoi or Sarissophoroi ('Lancers'; for the equation see Arr. 3. 12. 3 and Curt. 4. 15. 13) comprised four squadrons of the Companion Cavalry (Arr. 1. 12. 7; 4. 4. 6), distinguished from the eight regular *ilai* by their name and equipment — they carried a *sarissa*, longer than the

---

[15] Arr. 3. 11. 8. Nothing is known about Hermodoros.

[16] But this is far from certain. It appears that Asklepiodoros, father of Hermolaos' fellow-conspirator, Antipatros, was a trierarch of the Hydaspes-fleet (Arr. *Ind.* 18. 3, with Jacoby's emendation); cf. Heckel, *Ancient Macedonia* iv 300.

cavalryman's spear but shorter than the *sarissa* of the pezhetairoi[17] — and led collectively by a single hipparch; the names of their individual ilarchs are unknown. The Prodromoi are last heard of in 329,[18] whereafter, it appears, they were incorporated into the reformed hipparchies of the Companions. Tarn (ii 157 f.) argued that they were of Thrakian origin, but the consensus of modern scholarly opinion now regards them as Makedonian (Berve i 129; cf. Brunt, *JHS* 83 [1963], 27 f.; Milns, *JHS* 86 [1966], 167; Griffith, *HMac* ii 411; Bosworth, *Conquest and Empire* 262 f.; id., *Arrian* i 110). Their commanders were unquestionably Makedonian.

3. 1. Amyntas son of Arrhabaios

Literature. Berve ii 29-30, no. 59; Kirchner, *RE* i (1894), 2006, no. 5; Bosworth, *Arrian* i 109.

The son of Arrhabaios (Arr. 1. 12. 7; 1. 14. 1, 6; 1. 28. 4) and brother of the defector Neoptolemos (Arr. 1. 20. 10; but Diod. 17. 25. 5 puts him on the Makedonian side; cf. Welles, *Diodorus* 188, n.1). He was presumably the grandson of Aëropos and the nephew of Alexandros the Lynkestian. Berve ii 29 identifies him tentatively with the Amyntas who, along with Klearchos, was sent by Philip as an envoy to Thebes in 338 B.C. (Marsyas, *FGrHist* 135/6 F20 = Plut. *Demosth.* 18. 1-2). Given the frequency of the name in Makedonia, this is far from certain; Berve's no. 62 comes to mind, though even he must be ruled out if the correct form of the man's name is actually Anemoitas (Demosth. 18. 295). More likely is Berve's identification of the son of Arrhabaios with that Amyntas who, along with Attalos and Parmenion, led the advance force in Asia Minor in 336-334 (Justin 9. 5. 8).

In 334, he led the scouting party (4 *ilai* of prodromoi, and the squadron of Sokrates son of Sathon; see 2. 7 above) from Hermotos in the direction of the Graneikos (Arr. 1. 12. 7), and in the battle at that river, his squadrons (sarissophoroi and Paionians: Arr. 1. 14. 1) were stationed on the right wing and initiated the assault on those Persian forces who occupied the opposite riverbank (Arr. 1. 14. 6 - 15. 1; cf. 1. 16. 1). Later in that year, Amyntas reappears in the battle at Sagalassos, commanding the entire left, a task normally assigned to Parmenion but given to Amyntas in the latter's absence (Arr. 1. 28. 4). All three attested commands show that the son of Arrhabaios was an officer of high standing, militarily competent and trusted by the King. This

---

[17]See Markle, *AJA* 81 (1977), 323-339, esp. 333 ff.; Manti, *AncW* 8 (1983), 73-80.

[18]Arr. 4. 4. 6.

makes his disappearance from history all the more intriguing, as Berve ii 29 f. rightly notes. Had he died — in battle or from illness — in the first year of the campaign, the sources would almost certainly have recorded the fact. More than likely, his disappearance is to be explained by the arrest of his uncle Alexandros.

The battle of Sagalassos was, of course, chronologically later than the arrest of Alexandros Lynkestes (cf. Arr. 1. 25), unless there is some truth to Diodoros' claim that Alexandros was arrested shortly before the battle of Issos (Diod. 17. 32. 1-2; cf. Curt. 7. 1. 6). But the arrest was conducted in secret, by Amphoteros, the brother of Krateros (Arr. 1. 25. 9-10), and was probably not revealed to Alexander's army until all forces had reunited at Gordion. Bosworth rejects the identification of Amyntas' father with the suspected regicide Arrhabaios, and wonders why Amyntas would have been removed after the arrest of his uncle, if 'he had successfully survived the treason of his father and his brother' (*Arrian* i 109). For Alexander in Makedonia — where he was doubtless influenced by Antipatros, Alexandros' father-in-law — it may have seemed possible to give Amyntas another chance. But with the apparent treason of Alexandros, Amyntas' presence became dangerous and his removal a necessity (cf. Heckel, *Ancient Macedonia* iv [Thessaloniki, 1986], 299, with n.22). His successor was apparently Protomachos (below).

3. 2. Protomachos

Literature. Berve ii 329, no. 667; Ziegler, *RE* xxiii.1 (1957), 985, no. 4.

A Makedonian of unknown family background, Protomachos is once attested: at Issos, he commanded the Prodromoi (τῶν ἱππέων τοὺς προδρόμους, Arr. 2. 9. 2).[19] He replaced Amyntas son of Arrhabaios (3. 1 above) in this office, perhaps, as Berve ii 329 suggests,[20] at Gordion in spring 333. But by the time of the Gaugamela campaign (summer 331) he had himself been replaced by Aretes (3. 3 below). What became of him is unknown.

---

[19] Hoffmann 200 incorrectly says he held this command at the Graneikos river.

[20] But not 'als Nachfolger des Hegelochos'. Hegelochos may have held a special command over the prodromoi and 500 lightly armed troops (Arr. 1. 13. 1), but this office, reported between Amyntas' scouting mission (Arr. 1. 12. 7) and the latter's command of the prodromoi at the Graneikos (1. 14. 1, 6) looks suspiciously like an error on Arrian's part, ascribable perhaps to the conflicting reports of Ptolemy and Aristoboulos (cf. Bosworth, *Arrian* i 114). That Hegelochos ever commanded the four squadrons of prodromoi, only to be demoted at Gaugamela (Arr. 3. 11. 8), is highly unlikely.

3. 3. Aretes

Literature. Berve ii 58, no. 109; Kaerst, *RE* ii (1896), 678, no. 1; Bosworth, *Arrian* i 303, 305 f.; cf. i 122.

Aretes is named only in the accounts of the battle of Gaugamela, where he commanded the sarissophoroi (Curt. 4. 15. 13), having replaced, at some point between late 333 and mid-331, Protomachos (3. 2 above). At Gaugamela, he was stationed on the right wing (Arr. 3. 12. 3; cf. Bosworth, *Arrian* i 303), next to the ilarch Ariston, who commanded the Paionians (cf. Curt. 4. 9. 24). During the engagement, Aretes was sent to relieve the cavalry of Menidas, who were under heavy attack from the Skythian horse (Arr. 3. 13. 3; 3. 14. 1, 3; Curt. 4. 15. 13, 18). Nothing else is known about Aretes, who may, however, be identical with Ἀρέτις (Berve ii 58, no. 110), Alexander's ἀναβολεύς at the Graneikos (Arr. 1. 15. 6: most editors, following Krüger, read Ἀρέτης, but Bosworth, *Arrian* i 122, rejects this reading and, by implication, the identification; cf. Hoffmann 179; *SEG* xvii 141).

3. 4. Ariston: Commander of the Paionians

Literature. Berve ii 74 f., no. 138; Kirchner, *RE* ii (1896), 951 f., no. 32; Marsden, *Gaugamela* 31, 48, 50; I. L. Merker, 'The Ancient Kingdom of Paionia', *Balkan Studies* vi (Thessaloniki, 1965), 35-46, esp. 44-46; Atkinson, *Curtius* i 384 f.

Ariston appears to have been a member of the Paionian royal house, possibly even the brother of Patraos and father of the later king Audoleon (cf. Kaerst, *RE* ii [1896] 2279, s.v. 'Audoleon'; for the apparent grandson, Ariston son of Audoleon, see Polyainos 4. 12. 3; cf. Merker, *Balkan Studies* vi 45). His service with Alexander, like that of Sitalkes and others, helped to ensure the loyalty of his nation to Makedon in the King's absence (Frontinus, *Strat.* 2. 11. 3; cf. Justin 11. 5. 3; see also Sitalkes: viii 3. 4). From the beginning of the expedition, he commanded the single *ile* of Paionians, who occupied a position on the right at the Graneikos (Arr. 1. 14. 1) and at Issos (Arr. 2. 9. 2). In 331 the Paionians fell in with some 1,000 cavalrymen left by Mazaios in the vicinity of the Tigris (Curt. 4. 9. 24-25) and routed them; Ariston for his part slew in single-combat their leader Satropates (Atropates?) and brought his head to Alexander (Curt. 4. 9. 25; Plut. *Alex.* 39. 2; Merker, *Balkan Studies* vi 44 f. argues persuasively that the incident is commemorated on the coinage of Patraos).[21]

---

[21]See also Atkinson, *Curtius* i 384 (cf. Marsden, *Gaugamela* 31, n.4), who suggests that Curtius may have misplaced the episode. Unless there really was an earlier engagement at the Tigris, Ariston's *aristeia* may have occurred about

At Gaugamela, Ariston and his Paionians were again stationed on the right wing, together with the prodromoi, immediately behind Menidas' mercenary horse (Arr. 3. 12. 3; cf. Bosworth, *Arrian* i 303; Marsden, *Gaugamela* 48) and concealing from enemy view the Agrianes, archers and ἀρχαῖοι ξένοι. In the initial engagement, Ariston brought the Paionians up to aid Menidas, who was hard-pressed by the Skythian and Baktrian cavalry and, supported by the prodromoi and Kleandros' mercenaries, succeeded in breaking the enemy formation (Arr. 3. 13. 3-4). Nothing else is known about him.

4. Commanders of the Thessalian Cavalry

4. 1. Kalas son of Harpalos

Literature. Berve ii 188, no. 397; id., *RE* Supplbd. iv (1924), 854, no. 1; Baumbach 29, 43, 56; E. Badian, 'Harpalus', *JHS* 81 (1961), 18; Billows, *Antigonos* 38-40, 44-45.

Kalas son of Harpalos (Arr. 1. 14. 3; Diod. 17. 17. 4, where the form Κάλλας occurs; cf. Hoffmann 196) was, in all probability, a kinsman — probably a cousin[22] — of Harpalos the Treasurer (iv 2), hence an adherent of the Elimeiot royal house. In the spring of 336, he crossed into Asia Minor with Parmenion, Attalos and (presumably) Amyntas son of Arrhabaios (Justin 9. 5. 8-9; cf. Diod. 16. 91. 2). Berve ii 188 regards Kalas as Attalos' successor, and it may be that he was sent to Asia later, with Hekataios, in order to secure Attalos' elimination; for Harpalos was at that time one of Alexander's most trusted hetairoi.[23] Kalas' conduct of the war in the Troad was far from successful: he nearly lost Kyzikos to Memnon (Diod. 17. 7. 3-8; Polyainos 5. 44. 5) and

---

3 days later, when the Makedonian army encountered some 1,000 stragglers (Curt. 4. 10. 9-11; cf. Arr. 3. 7. 7 - 8. 2). Certainly, it is more likely that Alexander should send a single *ile* of Paionians against them than against a cavalry force of 1,000. It does, however, make Ariston's victory somewhat less heroic. Marsden, *Gaugamela* 31, goes further and suggests that 'he was hauled over the coals by Alexander afterwards' for killing Satropates, who might have given the Makedonians valuable information about enemy numbers and deployments.

[22]It is remotely possible, though unlikely, that he was the Treasurer's son. We have no proof that the infamous Harpalos was coeval with Alexander (see iv 2).

[23]The fact that Parmenion shared the command with one Elimeiot and secured a second (Koinos) as a son-in-law may represent a political realignment for the old general; ironically, their relatives contributed in no small way in his demise.

was driven back into Rhoiteion (Diod. 17. 7. 10).²⁴ Memnon's successes in 335/4 may be attributed only in part to his generalship; Alexander, preoccupied with the turmoil in Greece had been forced to leave Parmenion and Kalas to their own devices.

When the Asiatic campaign began in 334, Kalas was appointed hipparch of the Thessalian cavalry (Diod. 17. 17. 4), which he commanded at the Graneikos (Arr. 1. 14. 3), though he and the other officers on the left were subordinated to Parmenion (Arr. 1. 14. 1). But he was soon assigned the satrapy of Hellespontine Phrygia and took up residence in Dakyleion, which Parmenion occupied (Arr. 1. 17. 1-2).²⁵ The Thessalian horse were turned over to Alexandros Lynkestes (4. 2 below), with whom Kalas secured that portion of the Troad known as 'Memnon's Land' (Arr. 1. 17. 8; cf. Polyainos 4. 3. 15).²⁶

Of Kalas' administration of the satrapy little is known. In 333, Paphlagonia was annexed to his territory (Arr. 2. 4. 2, where 'Phrygia' stands for 'Hellespontine Phrygia'; Curt. 3. 1. 24), and Kalas cooperated with Antigonos Monophthalmos (Phrygia) and Balakros son of Nikanor (Kilikia) in stamping out Persian resistance to Makedonian authority in Asia Minor (Curt. 4. 5. 13; cf. Billows, *Antigonos* 43-45; for more detailed discussion see i 5). Memnon of Herakleia (*FGrHist* 434 F12 §4) records a defeat at the hands of a Bithynian dynast named Bas no later than 328/7 B.C. (cf. Bosworth, *Arrian* i 127, with further literature). This need not have been the occasion of Kalas' death, nor is it likely, as Billows suggests (*Antigonos* 45, with n.85), that the campaign against Bas, and Kalas' death, occurred in the late 330s. Alexander appointed Demarchos satrap of Hellespontine Phrygia, probably late in the campaign (Arr. *Succ.* 1a. 6). Badian's suggestion (*JHS* 81 [1961], 18) that Kalas was removed

---

²⁴Cf. McCoy, *AJP* 110 (1989), 423 f.; Judeich 305 f.

²⁵Bosworth, *Arrian* i 127, points out that the appointment was a logical one, given Kalas' experience in the area. Similarly, Alexander later appointed Peithon son of Agenor and Philippos son of Machatas as satraps of areas in which they had actively campaigned. For Dakyleion see Ruge, *RE* iv (1901), 2220.

²⁶For this campaign see Bosworth, *Arrian* i 131; Memnon and his brother Mentor undoubtedly had estates there, but 'Memnon's Land' clearly refers to the realm of the mythical Memnon and not the estates of the Rhodian general, as Berve ii 188 maintains (see Strabo 13. 1. 11 C587). Alexandros and Kalas took with them the Peloponnesians and other allies except the Argives (Arr. 1. 17. 8). Bosworth, *ibid.*, assumes that these are the allied infantry, normally commanded by Antigonos, though the latter was in Priene at the time (Tod ii 186). Certainly, if Alexandros and Kalas took with them the Thessalian horse, it is less likely that the allied force comprised the cavalry squadrons of Philip son of Menelaos (4. 3 below).

from office in the aftermath of Harpalos' misconduct is attractive but lacks proof.

4. 2. Alexandros son of Aëropos

Literature. Berve ii 17-19, no. 37; Kaerst, *RE* i (1894), 1435, no. 12; A. B. Bosworth, 'Philip II and Upper Macedonia', *CQ* 21 (1971), 93 ff.; E. D. Carney, 'Alexander the Lyncestian: The Disloyal Opposition', *GRBS* 21 (1980), 23-33.

A son of Aëropos (Arr. 1. 7. 6; 1. 17. 8) of Lynkestis (Diod. 17. 32. 1; 17. 80. 2; Curt. 7. 1. 5; 8. 8. 6; Justin 11. 2. 2; 11. 7. 1), Alexandros was probably an adherent of that canton's royal house. His brothers, Heromenes and Arrhabaios (Arr. 1. 25. 1), were both executed for their alleged complicity in the 'plot' to assassinate Philip II (cf. Justin 11. 2. 2); Alexandros himself had married a daughter of Antipatros (Curt. 7. 1. 7; Justin 11. 7. 1; 12. 14. 1; Diod. 17. 80. 2 wrongly calls his father-in-law 'Antigonos'; for the marriage of Alexandros Lynkestes and his descendants see Habicht, 'Zwei Angehörige des lynkestischen Königshauses', in *Ancient Macedonia* ii [Thessaloniki, 1977] 511-516; cf. Heckel, *Classicum* 15 [1989], 32 f., 37).

Although his brothers were executed for their alleged roles in the murder of Philip (Arr. 1. 25. 1; Justin 11. 2. 1-2; cf. Diod. 17. 2. 1; Plut. *Alex.* 10. 7), Alexandros was spared on account of his connections with Antipatros (thus Badian, *Phoenix* 17 [1963], 248) and because he was the first to hail his namesake as 'King' (Arr. 1. 25. 2; Justin 11. 2. 2). He was promptly appointed *strategos* of Thrake (Arr. 1. 25. 2). Indeed, at Thebes it was rumoured in 335 that the approaching Makedonian army was led by Alexandros Lynkestes, coming from Thrake; for certain politicians had encouraged a false report that Alexander the Great was dead (Arr. 1. 7. 6). When the Asiatic expedition began in 334, Alexandros accompanied the King, who clearly did not trust him with the *strategia* of Thrake in his absence. For the Lynkestian it was undoubtedly a demotion that was offset by his succession to Kalas' hipparchy, when the son of Harpalos received the satrapy of Hellespontine Phrygia (Arr. 1. 25. 2); the King's *consilium* may have voiced suspicions about Alexandros' reliability (Arr. 1. 25. 5).[27]

Alexandros was hipparch for only a few months, in which time he helped Kalas establish himself in the Troad (Arr. 1. 17. 8; cf. Polyainos 4. 3. 15). But soon incriminating evidence came to the attention of Parmenion. A Persian by the name of Sisenes was intercepted as he bore a letter from Dareios III to Alexandros Lynkestes, offering him 1,000

---

[27] It is not clear whether the hetairoi, who in 334/3 expressed the view that Alexander had been unwise in giving the hipparchy to the Lynkestian, had actually voiced this opinion several months earlier.

talents of gold if he assassinated his king.²⁸ Alexandros was arrested, through the agency of Amphoteros, whom Alexander sent to Parmenion's camp from Phaselis over the winter of 334/3.²⁹ Deposed from office and kept under guard until 330, he was eliminated in the aftermath of the Philotas affair (Curt. 7. 1. 5-9; Diod. 17. 80. 2; Justin 12. 14. 1). The Thessalian horse were entrusted to Philippos son of Menelaos (below).

4. 3. Philippos son of Menelaos

Literature. Berve ii 384, no. 779, and ii 387, no. 785; Treves, *RE* xix (1938), 2548, no. 61.

Philippos son of Menelaos was clearly a Makedonian, though his precise origin is unknown. He is first attested as hipparch of the allied cavalry (from the Peloponnesos) at the Graneikos (Arr. 1. 14. 3), a unit which he appears to have led from the very beginning of the Asiatic expedition. Philippos' name does not reappear until the accounts of Gaugamela, where he leads the Thessalian cavalry (Arr. 3. 11. 10; Diod. 17. 57. 4; Curt. 4. 13. 29); his former hipparchy is now commanded by Erigyios son of Larichos (**iv 1. 1**). It appears that Philippos was promoted to hipparch of the Thessalians in the winter of 334/3, after the arrest of Alexandros Lynkestes (Arr. 1. 25; see 4. 2 above), or at the latest in the spring of 333 at Gordion; at that time Erigyios was assigned the allied cavalry, though neither is mentioned by name until the battle of Gaugamela.

---

[28] Arr. 1. 25. 3, according to whom the Great King was responding to a letter from Alexandros carried by the deserter Amyntas son of Antiochos (Berve ii 28 f., no. 58). The message may have come from Dareios' Chiliarch, Nabarzanes (Curt. 3. 7. 12).

[29] Amphoteros son of Alexandros was the brother of Krateros (see **ii 4**). His role is mentioned only by Arrian (1. 25. 9-10). Diodoros (17. 32. 1-2), however, places the arrest of Alexandros shortly before the battle of Issos and says that the King was warned against the Lynkestian by Olympias; Curtius 7. 1. 6 speaks of two informants against Alexandros, gives a radically different version of the arrest of Sisines (3. 7. 11-15; cf. Atkinson, *Curtius* i 183 ff.), and appears to have discussed Alexandros Lynkestes in the lost second book of his *History* (cf. Heckel, *Hermes* 119 [1991], 125). But Curt. 7. 1. 6 (*tertium iam annum custodiebatur in vinculis*) follows a primary source (Kleitarchos?) dating the arrest of Alexandros to autumn 333 (i.e., not long before Issos); in this context, most sources describe Parmenion's suspicions that Philippos of Akarnania had been bribed by Dareios to poison Alexander (Curt. 3. 6. 1-17; Plut. *Alex.* 19. 4-10; Val. Max. 3. 8 ext. 6; Ps.-Kall. 2. 8. 4-11; Jul. Valer. 2. 24; Seneca, *de Ira* 2. 23. 2; also Arr. 2. 4. 8-11).

After the battle of Issos,[30] Philippos and the Thessalians were taken by Parmenion to Damaskos, where they captured the Persian treasures and many relatives of Persian notables (Plut. *Alex.* 24. 1-3). Probably, like Erigyios, Philippos remained with Menon son of Kerdimmas in Koile-Syria between early 332 and spring 331 (Arr. 2. 13. 7). At Ekbatana, however, Alexander dismissed the Thessalian cavalry, and Philippos was reassigned to the command of the mercenary horse (Arr. 3. 25. 4; cf. Berve ii 384), replacing Menidas, who remained in Media with Parmenion. Philippos remained for some time in Ekbatana and rejoined the King in Areia ('on the way to Baktra', Arr. 3. 25. 4), bringing the mercenary cavalry, the *xenoi* of Andromachos, and those of the Thessalians who had volunteered to continue serving Alexander (Arr. 3. 25. 4; Curt. 6. 6. 35 says the Thessalians numbered 130). The son of Menelaos is not heard of again. He may, however, have been identical with the later satrap of Baktria and Sogdiana (Berve ii 387, no. 785), whom Alexander appointed after the death of Amyntas son of Nikolaos (Berve ii 30, no. 60).[31] This Philippos retained his satrapy in the settlement of 323 (Diod. 18. 3. 3; Dexippos, *FGrHist* 100 F8 §6; Metz, *LM* 121; Ps.-Kall. 3. 33. 22; cf. Justin 13. 4. 23, confused) but was shuffled to Parthyaia in the reorganisation at Triparadeisos in 320 (Diod. 18. 39. 6; Arr. *Succ.* 1. 35). Some three years later, he was deposed and killed by Peithon son of Krateuas, who installed his own brother Eudamos as satrap of Parthyaia (cf. Diod. 19. 14. 1, who calls him 'Philotas, *strategos* of Parthyaia').[32]

4. 4. Polydamas

Literature. Berve ii 322-323, no. 648; Hoffmann 200; Scherling, *RE* xxi.2 (1952), 1602, no. 7; Atkinson, *Curtius* i 439.

At Gaugamela, the Thessalian cavalry with Parmenion on the left wing came under extreme pressure from the Persians led by Mazaios. In

---

[30]For the Thessalian cavalry at Issos see Arr. 2. 8. 9; 2. 9. 1; 2. 11. 2-3; Curt. 3. 9. 8; 3. 11. 3, 13-15; Diod. 17. 33. 2.

[31]If this identification is correct, Philippos cannot have been the son of Menelaos honoured in *IG* ii^2 568 + 559, who was still alive in the late 300s. I am grateful to Dr Richard Billows for sending me an unpublished paper on the Philippoi in Alexander's time.

[32]Cf. Billows, *Antigonos* 90, n.17, who, at least in the index, equates the satrap of Parthyaia with the son of Menelaos. Such errors in names are not infrequent in Diodoros' text: cf. 18. 12. 1: 'Philotas' for 'Leonnatos'; 19. 44. 1: 'Kelbanos' for 'Kephalon' (cf. Heckel, *BNf* 15 (1980), 43-45); see also Rubincam, *AHB* 2 (1988), 35.

consequence Parmenion was forced to call upon Alexander for help (Plut. *Alex*. 33. 9-10; Diod. 17. 60. 7); in Curtius' version (4. 15. 6-7) the message was carried by a certain Polydamas, identified by Hoffmann (200; followed by Berve ii 322) as Makedonian. Atkinson (*Curtius* i 439) comments: 'Polydamas...was a friend, and perhaps contemporary of Parmenion, in whose liquidation he played a despicable part.... Arrian's silence on Parmenion's message to Alexander ... casts doubt on the historicity of the episode, and it is therefore natural to ask whether Polydamas was introduced into this story because of the role he later played in Alexander's attack on Parmenion (cf. Kaerst 395).' It may be that Curtius drew attention to Polydamas in this context for dramatic effect, but this should not lead us automatically to conclude that Curtius fabricated Polydamas' role: the other extant vulgate authors, all give abbreviated accounts; their common source (Kleitarchos?) may, however, have named Polydamas. Berve ii 322 tentatively identifies him with the son of Antaios from Arethusa (Dittenberger, *Syll.*³ 269K), the only securely attested Makedonian of that name.

But Polydamas' role becomes more plausible if we assume that he was not Makedonian at all but Pharsalian. Arrian (3. 11. 10) describes Parmenion leading the left, accompanied by the Pharsalian horse (καὶ ἀμφ' αὐτὸν οἱ τῶν Φαρσαλίων ἱππεῖς). Our Polydamas may have been one of the King's Thessalian hetairoi — like Ariston (Berve, no. 139), also of Pharsalos, and Medios of Larisa (no. 521) — and may have been included in, or perhaps commanded, Parmenion's guard (cf. Curt. 7. 2. 11). Whether he was related to the great Polydamas of the second quarter of the fourth century, or indeed one of that man's children, whom Jason of Pherai held hostage (Xen. *Hell.* 6. 1. 18), is impossible to say. That he had young brothers (*fratres*) who were left behind as hostages, when he rode to Ekbatana to secure Parmenion's execution (Curt. 7. 2. 12), seems unlikely.[33] There is, at any rate, no compelling reason for identifying Polydamas as Makedonian; the assumption that he was Pharsalian makes it less likely that Curtius invented his role at Gaugamela.

In late 330, Polydamas was sent to Ekbatana to secure Parmenion's execution (Arr. 3. 26. 3; Curt. 7. 2. 11 ff.; Strabo 15. 2. 10 C724; cf. Diod. 17. 80. 3)[34] and was nearly lynched by Parmenion's troops after the order was carried out (Curt. 7. 2. 29). Nothing else is known of his

---

[33] Berve suggested *filii* for *fratres*; perhaps they were nephews (ἀδελφιδοῦς for ἀδελφός is an easy slip)?

[34] According to Strabo, Polydamas and his Arab guides made the thirty-day trip in only eleven days.

career, except that he was dismissed with the veterans at Opis and returned to Makedonia with Krateros (Justin 12. 12. 8).

5. Commanders of Other Allied Horse

5. 1. Agathon son of Tyrimmas

Literature. Berve ii 6-7, no. 8; Hoffmann 191; Kaerst, *RE* i (1894), 760, no. 7.

The son of Tyrimmas (Arr. 3. 12. 4), Agathon was apparently of Makedonian origin (so Hoffmann 191) and commander of the Thrakian cavalry between 334 and 330. He is attested at the Graneikos river (Arr. 1. 14. 3) and at Gaugamela (Arr. 3. 12. 4; he was stationed on the left wing with Sitalkes and Koiranos[35]). Although in the latter case Agathon's troops are described as 'Odrysians', he will have been the commander of the entire Thrakian cavalry (so Berve ii 6; cf. Brunt, *Arrian* i 263, n.7). In mid-330, he remained behind at Ekbatana, with his cavalry unit and in the company of Parmenion, Kleandros, Herakon and Sitalkes. He soon played a role in the elimination of Parmenion (Curt. 10. 1. 1). But in 325/4, Agathon was charged with maladministration when Alexander returned from India. Together with Herakon, Kleandros and Sitalkes, he met the King in Karmania, where he was arrested and presumably executed (Curt. 10. 1. 1 ff.; cf. Arr. 6. 27. 3 ff.).

5. 2. Anaxippos

Literature. Berve ii 37, no. 72; Kirchner, *RE* i (1894), 2098, no. 2.

A Makedonian of unknown family background, Anaxippos is described as one of Alexander's hetairoi (Arr. 3. 25. 2). In 330, he was sent with 40 *hippakontistai* (Berve ii 37, incorrectly 60) to prevent the plundering of Areia (Arr. 3. 25. 2). But he was betrayed by the rebellious satrap Satibarzanes, who slaughtered the horsemen and Anaxippos himself (Arr. 3. 25. 5).

---

[35] Possibly Karanos? But Roos' emendation to this effect is rejected by Bosworth, *Arrian* i 303.

5. 3. Koiranos (Karanos?)

Literature. Berve ii 219, no. 442; (Koiranos); Berve ii 200 f., no. 412 (Karanos); Brunt, *Arrian* i 262, n.1; Heckel, *LCM* 6 (1981), 70; Bosworth, *Arrian* i 303; N. G. L. Hammond, 'The Macedonian Defeat near Samarcand', *AncW* 22 (1991), 41-47.

Arrian (3. 12. 4) calls the commander of the allied horse (ξύμμαχοι ἱππεῖς) in 331 Koiranos. Possibly this is an error for Karanos (thus Roos emends the text; cf. Brunt, *Arrian* i 262, n.1; Heckel, *LCM* 6 [1981], 70) but Bosworth, *Arrian* i 303, argues for retaining Κοίρανος. Koiranos is not heard of again; Karanos, on the other hand, is found commanding similar troops later in the the campaign. Together with Erigyios, and with Artabazos as a guide, Karanos was sent against the rebellious satrap of Areia, Satibarzanes (Arr. 3. 28. 2); his role in the campaign is overshadowed by Erigyios, who is said to have killed Satibarzanes in hand-to-hand combat (Arr. 3. 28. 3; cf. Curt. 7. 4. 33-40). In 329, at the Polytimetos (Zeravshan) river, where he was ambushed and killed by Spitamenes (Arr. 4. 3. 7; 4. 5. 7; 4. 6. 2), Karanos' troops were 800 μισθοφόροι ἱππεῖς, but it may be that the allied horse continued to serve Alexander as mercenaries. For his earlier career see viii 4. 2.

6. The Mercenary Cavalry (μισθοφόροι ἱππεῖς)

6. 1. Menidas

Literature. Berve ii 257 f., no. 508; J. R. Hamilton, 'Three Passages in Arrian', *CQ* 5 (1955), 217 f.; Kroll, *RE* xv (1932), 851 (Menidas).

A prominent Makedonian officer, Menidas appears in all extant texts without patronymikon. Arrian (3. 5. 1) records that, in the winter of 332/1, Menoitas son of Hegesandros brought 400 mercenaries[36] to Alexander in Memphis. 'Menoitas' may, however, be an error for 'Menidas' (so Hamilton, *CQ* 5 [1955], 217 f.; *contra* Bosworth, *Arrian* i 275) and, if so, Menidas will have been the son of Hegesandros and commander of 400 mercenary cavalry from 332/1 onwards. At Gaugamela, Alexander positioned the mercenary horse on the right tip of his angled line, followed by the prodromoi and Paionians, with the Agrianes, archers and Kleandros' mercenary infantry in reserve (Arr. 3.

---

[36] It is not specified whether these are cavalry or infantry, but Hamilton, *CQ* 5 (1955), 217 f. comments: 'Four hundred seems to me too small a number [i.e., for infantry] and certainly in no other case is so small a number of infantry reinforcements recorded'.

12. 2-3). Menidas had been instructed to attack the enemy cavalry, should they attempt to outflank the Makedonians (Arr. 3. 12. 4). This is precisely what happened, but Menidas' force proved inadequate (Arr. 3. 13. 3), owing to their small numbers, and had to be supported by the prodromoi, Paionians and the mercenary infantrymen, which managed to break the Persian formation (Arr. 3. 13. 3-4). Very different is Curtius' account, which depicts Menidas' skirmish with the enemy as an, apparently unauthorised, attempt to save the baggage. But his efforts were half-hearted, and he abandoned the position 'less a champion of the baggage than a witness to its loss'.[37] In the end, Alexander, reluctantly, sent the prodromoi under Aretes to repulse the Skythians who were plundering the camp (Curt. 4. 15. 13-18). Curtius appears to have based his narrative on an account that sought to vindicate Parmenion and, in the process, depicted Menidas — arguably one of the heroes of Gaugamela who was wounded in action (Arr. 3. 15. 2; Diod. 17. 61. 3; Curt. 4. 16. 32) — as cowardly and inept;[38] he was, of course, destined to become one of Parmenion's assassins (Arr. 3. 26. 3-4).

In 330, Menidas was left behind at Ekbatana with Parmenion's forces (Arr. 3. 26. 3), and he must have played some part in the execution of the old general (3. 26. 4; cf. Berve ii 258). The command of the mercenary cavalry was turned over to Philippos son of Menelaos (4. 3 above), who brought them to Alexander in Areia (Arr. 3. 25. 4; cf. Curt. 6. 6. 35). Menidas rejoined Alexander at Zariaspa (Baktra) over the winter of 329/8, in the company of Ptolemaios (the commander of the Thrakians) and Epokillos (Arr. 4. 7. 2: Μελαμνίδας should be emended to read Μενίδας, so Hamilton CQ 5 [1955], 217; Curt. 7. 10. 11 says he and Ptolemaios brought 5,000 mercenaries: 4,000 infantry and 1,000 cavalry). In the following year, Menidas was sent out from Nautaka, together with Epokillos and the ilarch Sopolis to recruit new forces in Makedonia (Arr. 4. 18. 3). It appears that these reinforcements did not reach Alexander until his return to Babylon (Arr. 7. 23. 1: the cavalry which Menidas led were probably new recruits).[39] Menidas is last attested sleeping in the temple of Sarapis in Babylon when the King had become fatally ill (Arr. 7. 26. 2: but cf. the comments of Grainger 218 f.).[40]

---

[37]Curt. 4. 15. 12. J. C. Yardley, tr.

[38]Thus Atkinson, Curtius i 440 f., followed by Devine, AncW 13 (1986), 91. Bosworth, Arrian i 304 f., glosses over the problem of Menidas' treatment.

[39]See, however, Badian, JHS 81 (1961), 22, with n.39, who believes that Menidas did, in fact, return to Alexander with reinforcements, presumably during the Indian campaign. We must assume that Sopolis did not return to Alexander, considering his son's role in organising the conspiracy of the Pages.

[40]I do not see why Berve ii 258, with n.4, following Ausfeld, thinks that Dardanos in Ps.-Kall. 3. 31 (Arm.) is Menidas.

6. 2. Andromachos son of Hieron

Literature. Berve ii 38, no.75; Kaerst, *RE* i (1894), 2152, no. 6.; Hammond, *AncW* 22 (1991), 41-47.

The son of Hieron, Andromachos is first attested commanding mercenary cavalry at Gaugamela (Arr. 3. 12. 5), though nothing is known of his actual conduct in the battle. In 330 he remained briefly in Ekbatana, but soon rejoined the King in Areia in the company of Philippos son of Menelaos (Arr. 3. 25. 4). In the following year, Andromachos is found leading 60 Companions — in the company of Karanos (who commanded 800 mercenary horse; Arr. 4. 3. 7), Pharnouches and Menedemos (viii 6. 5) — at the Polytimetos river (mod. Zeravshan). The campaign ended in disaster for the Makedonian forces who were ambushed in the river by Spitamenes (Arr. 4. 3. 7; 4. 5. 5 - 6. 2). Though some troops did escape from the river, it appears that all their officers, including Andromachos, perished.[41]

6. 3. Epokillos son of Polyeides

Literature. Berve ii 150 f., no. 301; Kirchner, *RE* vi (1909), 228; Hoffmann 195 f.

Epokillos son of Polyeides (Arr. 3. 19. 6; on the father's name see Hoffmann 195 f.) is known to us only as an officer in charge of transporting troops to and from Alexander's camp. In 330, Epokillos escorted the discharged allied cavalry to the coast, leading his own squadron of cavalrymen, presumably mercenaries (Arr. 3. 19. 6).[42] He returned to the King at Zariaspa (Baktra) at the end of winter 329/8, accompanied by Ptolemaios, the commander of the Thrakians, and Menidas (Arr. 4. 7. 2, reading Μελαμνίδας; Curt. 7. 10. 11, 'Maenidas', emended by Hedicke to 'Melanidas'; but cf. Hamilton, *CQ* 5 [1955], 217). With the latter and the ilarch Sopolis, Epokillos left Baktria in the winter of 328/7 to bring reinforcements from Makedonia (Arr. 4. 18. 3).

---

[41]Arr. 4. 6. 2 says that forty cavalrymen and 300 infantry escaped. If Andromachos had been among them we should expect Arrian to have mentioned the fact. Curt. 7. 6. 24; 7. 7. 31 ff. gives an account of the Polytimetos disaster in which Andromachos is not mentioned. Identification of the son of Hieron with the navarch who served at Tyre (Arr. 2. 20. 10) is remotely possible, but incapable of proof (Berve ii 39, no. 77).

[42]Alexander had dismissed the Thessalians, and the Thrakian cavalry remained in Ekbatana with Agathon (5. 1 above); it is doubtful that the King would have spared his Makedonian cavalry for this escort duty. Hence it is likely that Epokillos' horsemen were mercenaries.

What became of him, we are not told. Only Menidas is known to have rejoined Alexander (Arr. 7. 23. 1; 7. 26. 2).

Appendices

APPENDIX I: HEPHAISTION'S CHILIARCHY

Except for Antipatros' role as *strategos autokrator* of Europe, no part of the 'compromise' at Babylon has given modern scholars less trouble than Perdikkas' designation as Chiliarch. Typical is R. M. Errington's assessment:

> The remainder of the compromise is now comparatively straightforward. Perdiccas' position was fully understood by Arrian and it creates no difficulty: he was to be 'chiliarch of the chiliarchy which Hephaestion had commanded'; and Arrian further defines this as 'supervisor of the whole kingdom'. The command of Hephaestion's chiliarchy implied the Grand Viziership, and this has generally been recognised. The Persian Grand Vizier was effectively the second-in-command of the whole Persian empire after the King: Perdiccas as Macedonian chiliarch was second-in-command of the whole Macedonian empire, clearly including Europe. With an idiot king Perdiccas was effectively in the position which Alexander had indicated for him, recognised as the most powerful single individual in the empire.[1]

The view that the Chiliarchy of Hephaistion was the equivalent of the Persian office of hazarapati- (Ktesias, *FGrHist* 688 F15 §46; Aelian, *VH* 1. 21; Hesychios s.v. ἀζαραπατεῖς), the officer who was second to the King in authority (Nepos, *Conon* 3. 2), has found almost universal acceptance.[2] But Arrian (*Succ.* 1a. 3) explains that 'to

---

[1] Errington, *JHS* 90 (1970) 56; but, for a different approach see Griffith, *JHS* 83 (1963), 74, n.17, and Bosworth, *CQ* 21 (1971), 131-133.

[2] Thus we have the following comments: 'Die Chiliarchie, die Perdikkas in Babylon bestätigt wurde, bedeutet zwar an sich nur das Kommando über die erste Hipparchie der Hetairenkavallerie, also an sich einen militärischen Rang; mit ihm hatte jedoch Alexander das persische Amt des Großwesirs, des Ersten nach dem Großkönig im Reich..., verschmolzen' (Bengtson, *Strategie* i 66). 'Wenn also Alexander einen Hipparchen seiner Hetaerenreiterei, den

chiliarch the Chiliarchy of Hephaistion' implied the 'guardianship of the entire kingdom' (τὸ δὲ ἦν ἐπιτροπὴ τῆς ξυμπάσης βασιλείας). And Diodoros (18. 48. 5) says that in 319 B.C. Antipatros revived the Chiliarchy for his son, Kassandros, and thus made him 'second in authority'.

ἡ δὲ τοῦ χιλιάρχου τάξις καὶ προαγωγὴ τὸ μὲν πρῶτον ὑπὸ τῶν Περσικῶν βασιλέων εἰς ὄνομα καὶ δόξαν προήχθη, μετὰ δὲ ταῦτα πάλιν ὑπ' Ἀλεξάνδρου μεγάλης ἔτυχεν ἐξουσίας καὶ τιμῆς, ὅτε καὶ τῶν ἄλλων Περσικῶν νομίμων ζηλωτὴς ἐγένετο. διὸ καὶ Ἀντίπατρος κατὰ τὴν αὐτὴν ἀγωγὴν τὸν υἱὸν Κάσανδρον ὄντα νέον ἀπέδειξε χιλίαρχον.

The position and rank of chiliarch had first been brought to fame and honour by the Persian kings, and afterwards under Alexander it gained great power and glory at the time when he became an admirer of this and all other Persian customs. For this reason Antipater, following the same course, appointed his son Cassander, since he was young, to the office of chiliarch.

(R. M. Geer, tr.)

Now chiliarchies and chiliarchs of a purely military nature existed within both Persian and Makedonian armies (Aesch. *Pers.* 302-305; Hdt. 7. 81; Xenophon, *Cyr.* 2. 1. 23; 3. 3. 11; 4. 1. 4; 7. 5. 17; 8. 6. 1; *Oecon.* 4. 7; Arr. *Tact.* 10. 5 ff.; Hesychios s.v. χιλίαρχος; Arr. 1. 22. 7; 3. 29. 7; 4. 24. 10; 4. 30. 5-6; 7. 14. 10; 7. 25. 6; *Succ.* 1a. 3; 1b. 4; Curt. 5. 2. 3; Athen. 12. 539e = Phylarchos, *FGrHist* 81 F41); these, furthermore, were natural developments from existing Makedonian units (Arr. *Tact.* 10; cf. also Curt. 5. 2. 3). And it seems logical that the commander of the

---

Hephaistion, zum Chiliarchen ernannte, so lag darin sicher eine Nachahmung persischer Hofsitte' (Brandis, *RE* iii [1899], 2276). 'Hier spätestens ward er [sc. Hephaistion] zum Chiliarchen und damit zum ersten Würdenträger des Reiches ernannt' (Berve ii 173). 'Die beherrschende Figur der frühesten Diadochenzeit ist kraft seiner amtlichen Stellung und seiner machtvollen Persönlichkeit Perdikkas, der Erste unter den Leibwächtern, seit Hephaistions Tode mit der Wahrnehmung der Geschäfte des Chiliarchen betraut.... Das war nach den einleuchtenden Darlegungen von Brandis, Plaumann und Berve nichts anderes als ein Grosswesirat, das Alexander in Anlehnung an persische Regierungstradition für seinen Seelenfreund Hephaistion geschaffen hatte' (Schur, *RhM* 83 [1934], 130). For the *hazarapati*- see P. J. Junge, 'Hazarapatis', *Klio* 33 (1940), 13-38; E. Benveniste, *Titres et noms propres en iranien ancien* (Paris, 1966), 67-71; also Schachermeyr, *Babylon* 31-37.

Great King's cavalry should be regarded as the most prestigious officer in the army, hence also his chief executive officer. The rank of *magister equitum* comes to mind. In Makedonia before Alexander's reign no such position existed. Neither Kleitos, as commander of the Royal Squadron (*ile basilike*), nor Philotas the hipparch of the 'Companions', served as the King's second-in-command — but rather this function was carried out by Parmenion in Asia (or by Antipatros or Parmenion in Europe). It was only with Alexander's attempt to give greater military authority to his best friend, Hephaistion, that the foremost cavalry officer became the King's military chief-of-staff.

Upon the death of Philotas, the command of the 'Companions' was shared by Hephaistion and Black Kleitos (Arr. 3. 27. 4; cf. Bosworth, *Arrian* i 364 f.), but we have no record of Hephaistion ever commanding even the half assigned to him. In Sogdiana he leads one-fifth of the army (Arr. 4. 16. 2) or, if Curtius (8. 1. 1) is correct, one-third of the forces north of the Oxos river, in conjunction with the satrap, Artabazos (cf. Curt. 8. 1. 10). It was at about this time, when Kleitos had been designated Artabazos' successor, or immediately after Kleitos' murder in autumn 328, that the command structure of the Makedonian cavalry, augmented by reinforcements, was changed. The enlarged unit was divided into hipparchies — in place of the previous *ilai*, to which the term hipparchies was sometimes (anachronistically) applied — which were likewise 'chiliarchies'.

Political pressure, as well as military considerations, had prevented Alexander from assigning the entire cavalry to Hephaistion in 330. Now, in late 328, he was faced with a similar problem. But whereas in 330 it had been necessary to placate the 'Old Guard', the failure to increase the number of troops under Hephaistion's command in 328 was predicated by a need to promote several 'New Men', formerly taxiarchs, to the rank of hipparch: Koinos, Perdikkas, Krateros. In order to offset this apparent 'demotion' of Hephaistion, Alexander assigned to him the honorific, 'first hipparchy (or Chiliarchy)'. Hence Griffith remarks that the unit was called 'Hephaistion's Chiliarchy' in order to 'distinguish it from other chiliarchies'.[3] And this suits both Arrian's description of Hephaistion's Chiliarchy (7. 14. 10) and the promotion of officers from one hipparchy to the next, as related by Diodoros (18. 3. 4), Appian (*Syr.* 57 [292]) and Plutarch (*Eum.* 1. 5). Hephaistion was probably designated χιλιάρχης τῆς ἵππου (cf. Arr. *Succ.* 1. 38), in imitation of the Persian practice, in spite of commanding only one hipparchy. Arrian's remark (7. 14. 10) that

---

[3] *JHS* 83 (1963), 74, n.17.

Hephaistion's Chiliarchy was left vacant after his death has generally been regarded as incorrect and attributed to Ptolemy's bias. Perdikkas succeeded him as commander of the 'First Hipparchy' (which Diod. 18. 3. 4 describes as ἡ ἐπιφανεστάτη) and thus, *de facto*, as the 'chiliarch of the cavalry'.

The so-called 'Compromise' settlement at Babylon — which saw the recognition of Arrhidaios as King (with Rhoxane's child as *symbasileus*, should it turn out to be male), Krateros as *prostates*, Perdikkas Chiliarch of Hephaistion's Chiliarchy and Meleagros hyparch (Arr. *Succ.* 1a. 3; cf. 1b. 4, an arrangement echoed by Justin 13. 4. 5: *castrorum et exercitus et rerum*[4] *cura Meleagro et Perdiccas adsignatur*) — represented a defeat for Perdikkas' political ambitions; for he managed only to retain the authority he had exercised at the time of Alexander's death. And now Krateros was technically his superior, Meleagros his watchdog. But Krateros' absence made it easier to eliminate Meleagros and exercise the *prostasia* of Arrhidaios' kingship, to which he soon added the guardianship of Alexander IV (thus Diod. 18. 23. 2). Hence Perdikkas distributed the satrapies 'in the name of King Philip' and assigned to Seleukos the 'First Hipparchy', that is, Hephaistion's Chiliarchy (Diod. 18. 3. 4; cf. Justin 13. 4. 17: *summus castrorum tribunatus Seleuco, Antiochi filio, cessit*).

In this capacity, Seleukos accompanied Perdikkas and eventually helped to murder him near Memphis (Nepos, *Eum.* 5. 1). Guardianship of the Kings passed in turn from Peithon and Arrhidaios to Antipatros (Diod. 18. 36. 6-7; 18. 39. 1-2), who left them in the charge of Antigonos, the *hegemon* of Asia. He was instructed τοὺς βασιλέας φρουρεῖν τε καὶ θεραπεύειν, and Kassandros was designated his χιλιάρχης τῆς ἵππου (Arr. *Succ.* 1. 38; cf. Diod. 18. 39. 7). The *Heidelberg Epitome* places the assignment of Babylonia to Seleukos and the appointment of Kassandros as Chiliarch side by side. Seleukos had clearly relinquished Hephaistion's Chiliarchy to Kassandros, whose relationship to Antigonos was similar to that of Seleukos to Perdikkas.[5] By now the title 'Hephaistion's Chiliarchy' may have become defunct. At the time of his death, Hephaistion was Alexander's dearest friend, his foremost commander (by virtue of his command of the first hipparchy; see Plut. *Eum.* 1. 5; Diod. 18. 3. 4; App. *Syr.* 57 [292]), and husband of Alexander's sister-in-law, Drypetis. But

---

[4]Thus the MSS. Seel wrongly adopts Madvig's emendation 'regum'. There was only one 'King' at this time.

[5]Except that Perdikkas exercised the offices of Antipatros and Antigonos as *epimeletes* and *hegemon*.

Alexander's own death precipitated many changes in the army, which accompanied the gradual disintegration of the empire. Also, it is likely that the distinction that Hephaistion's name had given to the Chiliarchy had now become meaningless.

Kassandros and Antigonos soon fell out and, on the former's advice, Antipatros took the Kings to Makedonia (Arr. *Succ.* 1. 42; Diod. 18. 39. 7 abbreviates events and obscures the process). Whether Antipatros appointed a Chiliarch we do not know. Polyperchon was undoubtedly the obvious candidate. On his death-bed in autumn 319, Antipatros recognised Polyperchon as guardian of the Kings and *strategos* of Europe, again appointing Kassandros as Chiliarch (Diod. 18. 48. 4-5). But Kassandros rebelled against Polyperchon's authority. The office of Chiliarch was unquestionably one of second rank, desired by none of Hephaistion's successors — Perdikkas, Seleukos, or Kassandros. In the almost three years that Perdikkas exercised power in Asia he did so as *prostates* or *epimeletes,* not as Chiliarch.

APPENDICES

APPENDIX II: THE FATHER OF LEONNATOS

Arrian gives Leonnatos four different patronymika, each apparently derived from an independent primary historian. Arr. *Anab*. 3. 5. 5 (Ptolemy?) has Ὀνάσου, 6. 28. 4 (Aristoboulos) Ἀντέου. Arr. *Succ*. 1a. 2 (Hieronymos or Douris) is closer to the latter with Ἄνθους, but *Indike* 18. 3 (Nearchos) gives Εὔνου. How could there have been so much uncertainty about the name of Leonnatos' father? The problem is not one of knowledge but of transmission. The troublesome passages are *Indike* 18. 3 and *Anab*. 3. 5. 5. The former reads: τριήραρχοι δὲ αὐτῷ ἐπεστάθησαν ἐκ Μακεδόνων μὲν Ἡφαιστίων τε Ἀμύντορος καὶ Λεόννατος ὁ Εὔνου καὶ Λυσίμαχος ὁ Ἀγαθοκλέους καὶ Ἀσκληπιόδωρος ὁ Τιμάνδρου.... Jacoby (*FGrHist* iiB, p. 681; cf. iiD, p. 450) argues plausibly that Εὔνου is an error for Εὐν⟨ίκ⟩ου, the patronymikon of Asklepiodoros and emends the text to read: τριήραρχοι δὲ αὐτῷ ἐπεστάθησαν ἐκ Μακεδόνων μὲν Ἡφαιστίων τε Ἀμύντορος καὶ Λεόννατος ὁ ⟨* καὶ Ἀσκληπιόδωρος ὁ⟩ Εὐν⟨ίκ⟩ου καὶ Λυσίμαχος ὁ Ἀγαθοκλέους καὶ Ἀσκληπιόδωρος ὁ Τιμάνδρου.... Here the mention of two men named Asklepiodoros caused the first to drop out of the list and the patronymikon of the first to be corrupted into Εὔνου and wrongly given to Leonnatos.[6] It is more difficult, perhaps impossible, to explain the corruption of the name in *Anab*. 3. 5. 5: σωματοφύλακα δὲ ἀντὶ Ἀρρύβα [τὸν] Λεοννάτον τὸν Ὀνάσου ἔταξεν· Ἀρρύβας γὰρ νόσῳ ἀπέθανεν. The scribe may have been influenced by the similarity of ἀντί (which occurs also in the following sentence) and Ἀντέου, and there could be some connection between νόσῳ and the corrupt Ὀνάσου. But it is idle to speculate.[7] Ἀντέου is, at least, corroborated by the form Ἄνθους, and the consensus of scholarly opinion favours this form (cf. Hoffmann 170; Berve ii 232).

The *Suda* claims that Leonnatos was related to Philip's mother, the Lynkestian Eurydike,[8] and this has the support of Curtius (10. 7. 8).

---

[6]Hammond's attempt to distinguish the son of Eunos from the son of Anteas (*ZPE* 82 [1990], 172, n.8) should be rejected: Leonnatos son of Anteas would thus be the only Somatophylax not assigned a trierarchy at the Hydaspes.

[7]Onasos is a Greek name (cf. Pape-Benseler 1061, s.v.), but it is otherwise unknown in Makedonia.

[8]See also A. N. Oikonomides, 'A New Inscription from Vergina and Eurydice the Mother of Philip II', *AncW* 7 (1983), 62-64

I propose the following stemma, based on Hammond's genealogy of the Lynkestian royal house (*HMac* ii 16):

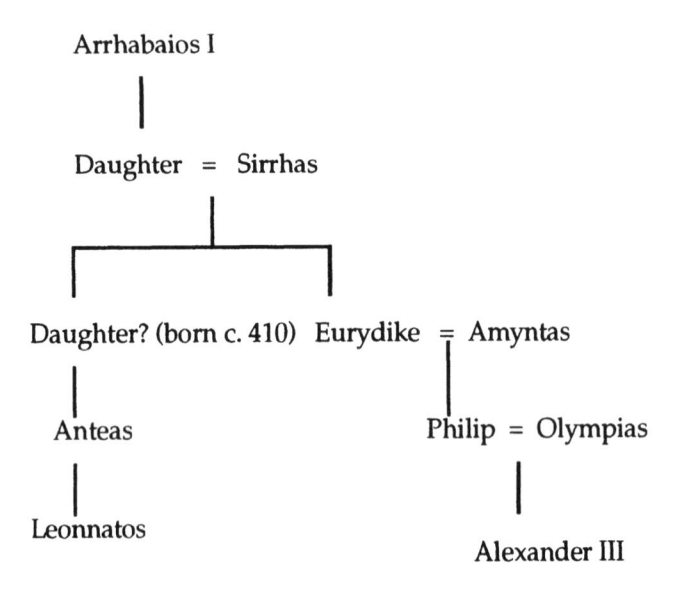

```
                    Arrhabaios I
                         |
              Daughter = Sirrhas
         ┌───────────────┴───────────┐
   Daughter? (born c. 410)    Eurydike = Amyntas
         |                              |
       Anteas                    Philip = Olympias
         |                              |
      Leonnatos                   Alexander III
```

APPENDICES

APPENDIX III: THE BATTLE OF AMORGOS

It has generally been recognised that the decisive battles of the Lamian War were those fought at sea by the Makedonian admiral Kleitos (surnamed 'the White') in 322 B.C. Yet this is anything but obvious from Diodoros 18. 15. 8-9:

τῶν δὲ Μακεδόνων θαλασσοκρατούντων οἱ Ἀθηναῖοι πρὸς ταῖς ὑπαρχούσαις ναυσὶν ἄλλας κατεσκεύασαν, ὥστε γενέσθαι τὰς πάσας ἑκατὸν ἑβδομήκοντα. τῶν δὲ Μακεδονικῶν νεῶν οὐσῶν διακοσίων καὶ τεσσαράκοντα τὴν ναυαρχίαν εἶχε Κλεῖτος. οὗτος δὲ ναυμαχήσας πρὸς Εὐετίωνα τὸν Ἀθηναίων ναύαρχον ἐνίκησε δυσὶν ναυμαχίαις καὶ συχνὰς τῶν πολεμίων νεῶν διέφθειρε περὶ τὰς καλουμένας Ἐχινάδας νήσους.

> Since the Macedonians had command of the sea, the Athenians made ready other ships in addition to those which they already had, so that there were in all one hundred and seventy. Cleitus was in command of the Macedonian fleet, which numbered two hundred and forty. Engaging with the Athenian admiral Evetion he defeated him in two naval battles and destroyed a large number of the ships of the enemy near the islands that are called the Echinades.
>
> (R. M. Geer, tr.)

The passage does, however, provide a good starting-point for an examination of several points relating to the naval operations in the Lamian War.

The wording of Diodoros is ambiguous: either Kleitos fought two sea-battles and then destroyed numerous Athenian ships near the so-called 'Echinades' islands or the battle of the 'Echinades' was the second of Kleitos' two naval victories. The latter is clearly the more likely interpretation. The Athenians ships must surely have been destroyed by Kleitos in a *naumachia*, and that *naumachia* will have been the second of the two mentioned by Diodoros, who perhaps used καὶ...διέφθειρε... rather than a subordinating participle to avoid the false impression that both battles were fought near the 'Echinades'. Otherwise we must follow Goukowsky in assuming that Kleitos fought three sea-battles against Euetion — at Abydos, Amorgos and the 'Echinades'.[9] But this creates a number of difficulties.

---

[9]P. Goukowsky, ed., *Diodore de Sicile. Bibliothèque Historique: Livre xviii* (Paris, 1978), *ad loc*.

373

Diodoros (18. 10. 2) gives the Athenian naval strength at the outset of the war as 240 ships (cf. Justin 13. 5. 8: 200 ships), which appears to be the paper strength of the fleet, unless he has confused the numbers of the respective fleets. But Diodoros (18. 15. 8: τῶν δὲ Μακεδόνων θαλασσοκρατούντων οἱ Ἀθηναῖοι πρὸς ταῖς ὑπαρχούσαις ναυσὶν ἄλλας κατεσκεύασαν, ὥστε γενέσθαι τὰς πάσας ἑκατὸν ἑβδομήκοντα) appears to indicate that the Athenians had already suffered one reverse in the Lamian War and were now preparing supplementary forces. This setback, according to the structure of Diodoros' narrative, occurred before the arrival of Kleitos and must be equated with the battle at the Hellespont. The victorious Makedonian fleet was thus the one sent by Alexander before his death, and this numbered 110 ships. The Athenians, under Euetion, must have sailed originally to the Malian gulf, where they gave support to Leosthenes' forces, which soon besieged Antipatros at Lamia. When news reached them that Antipatros had summoned Leonnatos from Hellespontine Phrygia, a portion of the fleet — thought to be sufficient to deal with the 110 Makedonian ships — was deployed to the Hellespont only to be defeated near Abydos.

That there was a sea-battle at the Hellespont is clear from two Athenian inscriptions, IG ii[2] 398 and 493, the former dated convincingly to 322/1-320/19.[10] The relevant passages read: τῆς δὲ ναυμαχί[α]ς τῆς ἐν Ἑλλη[σπόντωι γενομένης | π]ολλοὺς διέσ[ωισεν καὶ ἐφόδια δοὺ]ς ἀπέστειλε[ν καὶ αἴτιος ἐγένετ|ο τ]οῦ σωθῆναι... (ii[2] 398a, following M. B. Walbank's text); καὶ ἐπὶ πολέμου τοῦ προτέρου τῶν ἐκ τῆς ναυμαχίας πολλοὺς τῶν πολιτῶν συνδιέσωισεν καὶ ἐφόδια δοὺς ἀπέστειλεν εἰς τὴν πόλιν (ii[2] 493, honouring Nikon of Abydos). The battle, as the decree in honour of Nikon suggests, was fought in the vicinity of Abydos, and its purpose, from the Athenian standpoint, was clearly to gain control of the Hellespont and prevent Makedonian reinforcements (brought by Leonnatos from Hellespontine Phrygia) from entering Europe and coming to the aid of Antipatros in Thessaly. But it should be noted that neither the inscriptional nor the literary sources mention Kleitos in connection with the battle near Abydos. Thus, if Kleitos fought only two sea-battles against Euetion, the second was at the so-called 'Echinades' islands and the first must have been somewhere other than the Hellespont.

If the battle at the Hellespont was preliminary to Leonnatos' crossing, as is generally supposed, it must have taken place as T. Walek

---

[10]See M. B. Walbank, 'Athens grants Citizenship to a Benefactor: IG II[2] 398a + 438', AHB 1 (1987), 10-12, with earlier literature.

suggests in March 322.¹¹ But Cary (383) points out that Kleitos could not have left the Levant before April and would not have reached Abydos until about the end of that month, by which time he would have been too late to aid Leonnatos' crossing. Thus, if the battle of Abydos preceded Leonnatos' entry into Europe, it must have been fought by Antipatros' fleet, as Ferguson noted,¹² the only logical consequence of our reconstruction.

Antipatros summoned reinforcements from Asia before moving south into Thessaly (autumn 323), appealing to both Krateros and Leonnatos for aid (Diod. 18. 12. 1). But Antipatros must have pinned his hopes primarily on Leonnatos, who was the closest of the satraps in Asia. Kleitos, who had accompanied Krateros from Opis to Kilikia, will scarcely have begun assembling his fleet before Antipatros' appeal, and his purpose in assembling it must have been to secure the crossing of the Hellespont for Krateros and not for Leonnatos. But Krateros' position was very different from that of Leonnatos. His legal position was in doubt: Alexander had sent him to replace Antipatros as regent of Makedonia, but Perdikkas had cancelled these orders;¹³ the army in Babylon had entrusted to him the προστασία of Philip Arrhidaios' kingdom, but Perdikkas clearly controlled the Royal Army and the King himself. Thus, Krateros' late arrival in Europe must be explained, in part, by the outcome of Leonnatos' battle with Antiphilos (May? 322).

The battle of Krannon occurred on 7 Metageitnion, which Beloch (iv² 1. 74) equates with 5 August, 322. Unlike Leonnatos, Krateros did not recruit troops in Makedonia but came directly to the Peneus, where he joined forces with Antipatros and relinquished the supreme command to him. Since the engagement was fought very soon after his arrival, it appears that Krateros did not cross the Hellespont much before the beginning of July. And this begins to make Ashton's date of 26 or 27 June, 322, for the battle of Amorgos look very attractive.¹⁴

The *Marmor Parium* (*FGrHist* 239 B9) informs us that in the archonship of Kephisodoros (323/2 B.C.) the Athenians were defeated

---

¹¹T. Walek, 'Les opérations navales pendant la guerre lamiaque', *RPh* 48 (1924), 28, dating Leonnatos' death to May 322.

¹²W. S. Ferguson, *Hellenistic Athens* (London, 1911), 17, but n.1 on that page shows that Ferguson too thought that the battle of Abydos was one of the two mentioned at Diod. 18. 15. 8.

¹³Arr. 7. 12. 4-5; Diod. 18. 4. 1-6; cf. Badian, *HSCP* 72 (1967), 183 ff.

¹⁴N. G. Ashton, 'The *Naumachia* near Amorgos in 322 B.C.', *ABSA* 72 (1977), 10-11.

by the Makedonians near the island of Amorgos: ἀπὸ τοῦ πολέμου τοῦ γενομένου περὶ Λαμίαν Ἀθηναίοις πρὸς Ἀντίπατρον καὶ τῆς ναυμαχίας τῆς γενομένης Μακεδόσιν πρὸς Ἀθηναίους περὶ Ἀμοργόν, ἣν ἐνίκων Μακεδόνες, ἔτη πεντήκοντα ἐννέα, ἄρχοντος Ἀθήνησιν Κηφισοδώρου. The battle is alluded to in Plutarch's *Demetrios* 11. 4, in a discussion of the character of Stratokles of Diomeia, but the *de fort Al.* 2. 5 (= *Mor.* 338a), shows that the Makedonian navarch in this battle was Kleitos. Hence, unless the so-called 'Echinades' can in some way be located near Abydos or Amorgos (thus Cary's map, p. 1 opp.), Kleitos' two sea-battles did not include the one at the Hellespont.

Now it is generally assumed that the battle of Amorgos alone is mentioned by the Parian Marble 'because for the Athenians it was the most decisive battle of the campaign'[15] and that it was 'the antithetic parallel to the Athenian-inspired victory at Salamis in 480 B.C.'[16] As a result it is also considered Kleitos' last major sea-battle in 322. But the Parian Marble may have singled out the battle near Amorgos because it was the last naval engagement in the year of Kephisodoros.[17] The engagement of the 'Echinades' islands belonged to the next archon-year. Furthermore, Morrison has argued that, since the Athenians towed their wrecks back to Peiraieus, they did not suffer serious losses, because 'a heavily defeated fleet usually had to surrender its wrecks to the enemy, for whom they were a mark of victory' (*JHS* 107 [1987], 94). Plutarch deliberately underestimates the Makedonian victory, when he says that Kleitos acted the part of Poseidon after sinking a mere 'three or four Greek ships', in order to mock the admiral for his hybris. But the clear implication of the two passages in Plutarch is that Amorgos did not symbolise the end of Athenian sea-power. And this is further supported by Diodoros' emphasis on the heavy Athenian losses at the 'Echinades' (συχνὰς τῶν πολεμίων νεῶν διέφθειρε περὶ τὰς καλουμένας Ἐχινάδας νήσους).

Thus the Athenians, having failed to prevent Leonnatos' crossing in March as a result of their defeat at Abydos, strengthened their existing fleet and determined to prevent Kleitos from entering the Aegean. A fleet sailing from the Levant would enter the Aegean, passing Rhodes, and proceed north, keeping Kos on its right and Astypalaia and Amorgos on the left. A sea-battle off Amorgos is thus very easy to

---

[15]Thus J. S. Morrison, 'Athenian Sea-Power in 323/2 B.C.: Dream and Reality', *JHS* 107 (1987), 93.

[16]Ashton, *ABSA* 72 (1977), 1, summarising earlier opinions.

[17]Ashton, *ABSA* 72 (1977), 10-11, argues plausibly that the battle took place at the very end of June 322.

explain, strategically, and its timing — late in the year of Kephisodoros — can also be understood in terms of Krateros' late departure from Kilikia.

Cary, however, thinks that Kleitos commanded the fleet at Abydos, and that the Athenians were contesting not the crossing of Leonnatos but Krateros. But, if the battle of Amorgos followed the one at the Hellespont, the question arises: Why was the second engagement fought there? I can see no good reason why Kleitos, having secured Krateros' crossing into Europe, should sail south towards Amorgos. The engagement there can best be explained as an attempt to intercept the new Makedonian fleet, which ought have been arriving from the Levant some time in June. Furthermore, it will not have been clear to the Athenians whether Kleitos' ultimate destination was the Hellespont, the Malian gulf or Peiraieus. Hence the vicinity of Amorgos was the obvious point at which to make the interception. The decisive sea-battle of the Lamian war was yet to come. This was fought before the summer ended in the Malian Gulf, near Cape Echinos and the Lichades Islands (see Map III).

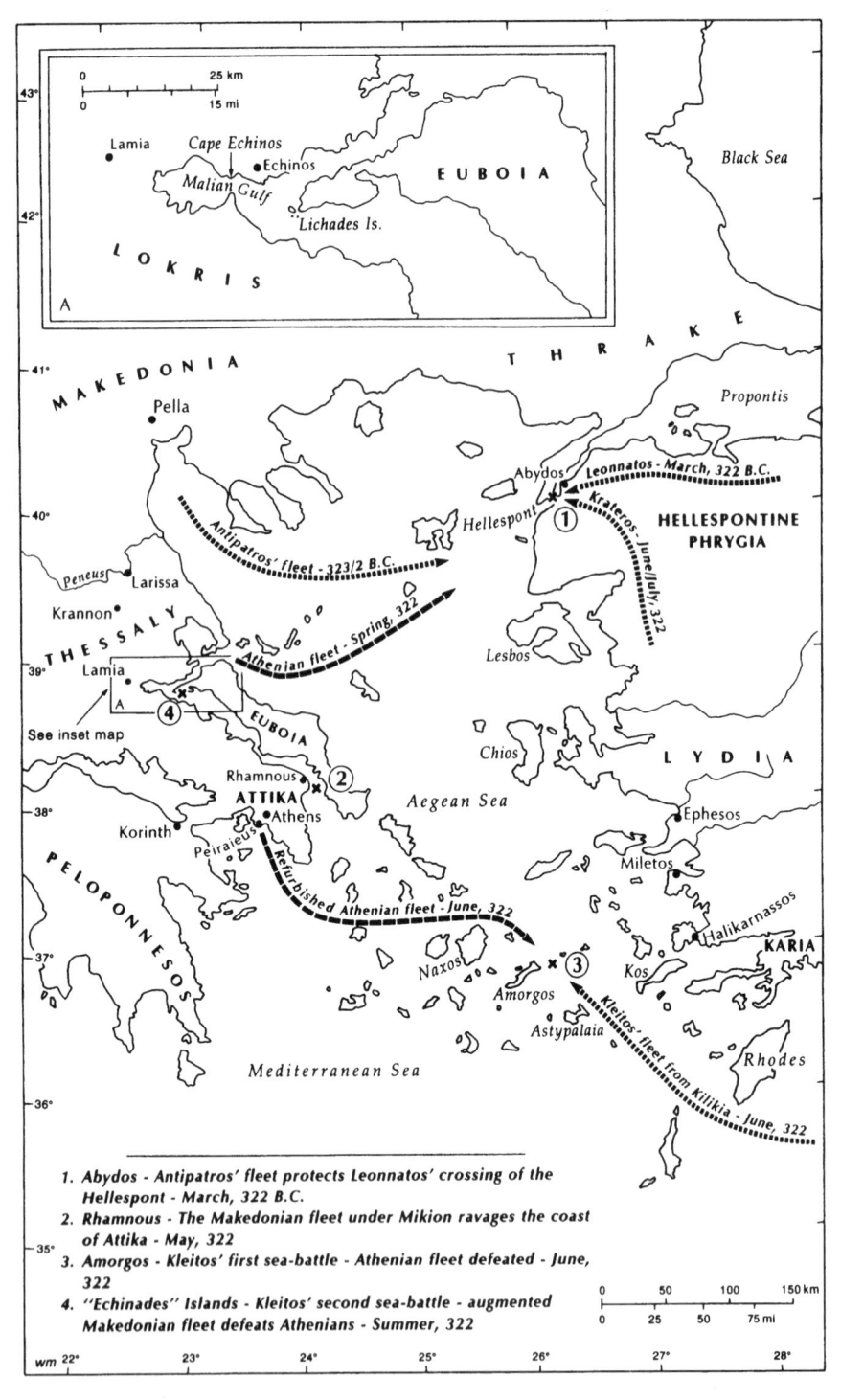

Map III The Naval Battles of the Lamian War (322 B.C.)

APPENDIX IV: ARTAKOANA

Artakoana (Chortakana: Diod. 17. 78. 1) and Alexandreia in Areia appear to have been separate settlements (so Bosworth, *Arrian* i 356 f., locating Artakoana 'somewhere along the Hari Rud in the vicinity of Herat'); but Engels (*Logistics* 91) believes Artakoana may have been 70 miles northeast of Kalat-i-Nadiri, and thus possibly in the modern Soviet Union. In 330, Alexander accepted the surrender of Satibarzanes at Sousia (Tus: Engels, *Logistics* 85; cf. Seibert, *Eroberung* 118 f.), reinstating him as satrap of the Areians (Arr. 3. 25. 1). Learning that Bessos had fled to Baktria and was now styling himself 'King of Asia', Alexander set out for Baktra by the shortest route.[18] But it was soon reported to him that Satibarzanes had rebelled and massacred Anaxippos and the mounted javelin-men with him (Arr. 3. 25. 5). Thus, he turned back, leaving the bulk of the army with Krateros, and arrived two days later at Artakoana — some 600 stades (about 66 miles) — where Satibarzanes had taken refuge (Arr. 3. 25. 6). Krateros, it appears from Arrian, did not join him until after the capture of Artakoana and the appointment of a new satrap, Arsakes, in Areia (Arr. 3. 25. 7-8). But, if we trust the evidence of the Vulgate, Arrian (or his sources) omitted entirely Krateros' important contribution to the suppression of the revolt in Areia.

Curtius (6. 6. 20 ff.) tells us that, when Alexander had turned back to deal with Satibarzanes, the rebel fled with his cavalry in the direction of Baktria; cf. Arr. 3. 25. 7, showing that they abandoned Artakoana (Σατιβαρζάνης ... ξὺν ὀλίγοις ἱππεῦσι τῶν Ἀρείων ἔφυγε. Curt. 6. 6. 22 says there were 2,000 cavalrymen with Satibarzanes). Some 13,000 Areians took refuge at a rocky outcrop, which can only have been Kalat-i-Nadiri (Engels, *Logistics* 87-89; cf. Green 337). These were blockaded by Krateros (Curt. 6. 6. 25) and finally 'smoked out' by Alexander (Curt. 6. 6. 25-32). But Curtius then goes on to say:

> hinc ad Craterum, qui Artacana obsidebat, redit. Ille omnibus praeparatis regis expectabat adventum, captae urbis titulo, sicut par erat, cedens.
>
> (6. 6. 33)

---

[18]Via the Merv Oasis, according to Engels, *Logistics* 89, and Bosworth, *JHS* 101 (1981), 20; but Seibert, *Eroberung* 119, opts for the easterly route over the Zulfikar pass and Bala Murghab to Baktra (Balkh).

> From here Alexander returned to Craterus, who was engaged in the siege of Artacana and who, after making the necessary preparations, was awaiting the king's arrival in order to cede to him the honour of taking the city, as was right and proper.
>
> (J. C. Yardley, tr.)

Engels (*Logistics* 90) appears to be suggesting that Kalat was where Alexander left Krateros when he turned to deal with Satibarzanes at Artakoana, which was 600 stades distant. It seems unlikely, however, that Satibarzanes' people would have flown in the direction of the main Makedonian force in order to find refuge there. Schachermeyr (313) correctly noted that Alexander instructed Krateros' troops to follow in the direction of Artakoana. Furthermore, to seek Artakoana in 'the region 70 miles north to east of Kalat' (Engels, *Logistics* 91) makes little sense, if Alexander was moving northeast, in the direction of Baktria. Satibarzanes had been left behind in Areia and it was apparently on the road to his capital, Artakoana, that he slaughtered Anaxippos and his men. That this satrapal capital was located to the north and east of Kalat-i-Nadiri is highly unlikely. It is better located in the vicinity of Herat, if not at Herat itself (thus Olmstead, *HPE* 46, n.55; cf. Seibert, *Eroberung* 120, with n.74 on the location of Alexandreia in Areia; the rock to which Satibarzanes fled was probably Naratu). And it is clear that Alexander had to turn back from his initial attempt to invade Baktria. When he did move on to Baktria the second time it was through Drangiana, Arachosia and Parapamisos, that is, along the Helmand valley.

APPENDICES

APPENDIX V: THE MARRIAGE OF ATTALOS AND ATALANTE[19]

Shortly after Alexander's death, dissension arose between the leaders of the cavalry and the phalanx over the matter of the succession: the cavalry-officers, notably Perdikkas, favoured the, as yet unborn, son of Rhoxane — he would, of course, require a regent; the phalanx opted for the mentally deficient Arrhidaios, whom they were already hailing as King, under the title Philip III.[20] Meleagros son of Neoptolemos, a taxiarch throughout Alexander's reign and the most distinguished of the infantry commanders who remained in Babylon, espoused Arrhidaios' cause most vehemently.[21] Justin, however, adds an interesting detail: he says (13. 3. 2) that the Perdikkan party sent Meleagros *and Attalos* to the infantry in order to win them over, but that these men neglected their duties and took up the cause of the phalanx instead (*legatos ad mitigandos eorum animos duos ex proceribus, Attalum et Meleagrum mittunt, qui potentiam ex vulgi adulatione quaerentes omissa legatione militibus consentiunt*). Justin goes on to say that this Attalos sent men to murder Perdikkas (*Attalus ad interficiendum Perdiccam, ducem partis alterius, mittit ... percussores*), but that the assassins lacked the resolve to carry out their mission (13. 3. 7-8).

Justin's Attalos (apparently unknown to Berve)[22] is clearly the son of Andromenes, as the phrase *ex proceribus* implies; also, as a taxiarch like Meleagros himself, he would have been a suitable candidate for such an embassy. But his role in the events of 323 has, unfortunately, been coloured by the preconception that Attalos was already Perdikkas' relative and staunch supporter. Thus G. Wirth supposes that Attalos' name was included in this passage for dramatic effect.[23] Schachermeyr believes that Attalos, son of Andromenes, was in fact sent to the phalanx, but that Justin suffered a *lapsus memoriae* and ascribed to him actions taken by Meleagros alone.[24] Attalos, he argues, would not have instigated the murder of his own brother-in-law; Justin

---

[19] For an earlier discussion see W. Heckel, 'On Attalos and Atalante', *CQ* 28 (1978), 377-382.

[20] Berve ii 385-386, no. 781, s.v. Φίλιππος 'Αρριδαῖος; the fullest account is given by Curt. 10. 7. 1 ff.; cf. Justin 13. 2. 6 ff.; Diod. 18. 2. 2-4; Arr. *Succ.* 1a. 1.

[21] Berve ii 249-250, no. 494, s.v. Μελέαγρος. See also **iii 1**.

[22] Berve ii 92-93 does not go beyond Alexander's death in his discussion of Attalos, although he normally includes important details from the period of the succession.

[23] *Helikon* 7 (1967), 291, n.37.

[24] *Babylon* 125.

must be in error. Schachermeyr concludes that Justin made the mistake 'da [er] bei Trogus wohl kaum vermerkt fand, dass Attalos ein Schwager des Perdikkas gewesen sei...'.[25] Meleagros is singled out by all the sources because he was the most important of these legates sent to the infantry (Justin names only two, but Diod. 18. 2. 2 implies that there were more), and because he was liquidated by Perdikkas on account of his intrigues and his 'treason'. Attalos was thus overshadowed by Meleagros, and his role can only be understood if his relationship with Perdikkas is placed in the proper historical context.

Now, as it happens, it makes little difference whether Attalos or Meleagros instigated the attempted murder, though, if it was the former, we should have virtual proof that he was not yet married to Perdikkas' sister. What does matter is that both Attalos and Meleagros were actively supporting the cause of the conservative phalanx, which is exactly what we should expect. And it is totally wrong to argue that relationship by marriage prevented Attalos from opposing Perdikkas. We know only as much as Diodoros tells us: that, at the time of her death in 320 B.C., Perdikkas' sister, Atalante, was Attalos' wife (18. 37. 2). Knowledge of this union has, however, prejudiced our interpretation of Attalos' role in the events of 323.

Atalante's presence in her brother's camp in Egypt demands an explanation. Unlike the Persian aristocracy, the Makedonians did not customarily bring their womenfolk along on campaigns. We have the unequivocal example of the 'newly-weds' — including Meleagros, Ptolemaios son of Seleukos, and Koinos — who returned to their wives over the winter of 334/3; Koinos' wife, the daughter of Parmenion, remained in Makedonia raising their son.[26] And it would be difficult to imagine that Attalos summoned her from Makedonia to the main theatre of the war in order that he might see the wife from whom he had been separated for some ten to fourteen years. There is only one plausible reason for Atalante's presence: she had only recently been summoned to Asia by Perdikkas in order that she might marry Attalos. It was a political union, much like (though on a smaller scale) the marriage-alliances that Perdikkas himself sought by bringing to Asia

[25]*Ibid.*

[26]For Koinos' marriage to Parmenion's daughter see Curt. 6. 9. 30, supported by Arr. 1. 24. 1; 1. 29. 4. See also Dittenberger, *Syll.*³ 332, where the son, Perdikkas, is named, and Berve ii 215-218, no. 439, s.v. Κοῖνος, and 312-313, no. 626, s.v. Περδίκκας. Those women who did come to Asia, such as Stratonike and Phila, joined their husbands after they had been appointed satraps and had taken up permanent residence in Kelainai and Tarsos.

Minor Nikaia and Kleopatra (Diod. 18. 23; Justin 13. 6. 4-7; Arr. *Succ.* 1. 21, 26). Atalante's marriage to Attalos concluded an earlier agreement between Perdikkas and the son of Andromenes.

When Alexander died, the most prominent leaders of the phalanx (Krateros and Polyperchon, along with Gorgias, White Kleitos, and the hypaspist/argyraspid commander, Antigenes) were absent in Kilikia; Koinos had died shortly after espousing the cause of the common soldiery at the Hyphasis. The remaining taxiarchs included Meleagros, Attalos and Alketas, as well as a commander of light infantry, Philotas. To judge from the hostility of the phalanx towards Perdikkas, Alketas' influence cannot be regarded as significant, and, when Perdikkas and his supporters were forced to withdraw from Babylon, Alketas could scarcely have remained behind. There is no reason to suppose that the other three supported Perdikkas. Meleagros certainly did not, while Philotas remained loyal to Krateros, and Perdikkas later deposed him from the satrapy of Kilikia for this very reason.[27] Attalos too belonged to this conservative faction: he had been a friend of the other Philotas, Parmenion's son, and was, in the late stages of the campaign, associated with those taxiarchs who opposed Alexander's orientalism.[28] These men put up a united front against Perdikkas, who attempted to preserve the unity of the empire and Alexander's oriental policies. Attalos, by virtue of his family-connections and his leadership of the conservative pezhetairoi, very likely shared the sentiments of the common soldiery, whom Meleagros had incited. Only in 321/0 B.C. does he appear as a supporter of Perdikkas, together with his brother Polemon.[29]

We are told that, not long after the rift occurred between the cavalry and the infantry, Perdikkas effected a reconciliation. The cavalry had cut off the grain-supply to the city, and the infantry was

[27]Justin 13. 6. 16: *Cilicia Philotae adempta Philoxeno datur;* cf. Arr. *Succ.* 24. 2: Φιλώταν μὲν τὸν ξατράπην τῆς χώρας ἐπιτήδειον τοῖς ἀμφὶ Κρατερὸν γιγνώσκων παρέλυσεν τῆς ἀρχῆς, Φιλόξενον δὲ ἀντ' αὐτοῦ ἄρχειν κατέστησεν. See also Berve ii 397-398, no. 804, s.v. Φιλώτας. He must be identical with Berve's no. 803, although he commanded light infantry and not pezhetairoi.

[28]For their opposition to Alexander's policies see Plut. *Alex.* 47. 9-10 (Krateros); Curt. 8. 5. 22 ff. (Polyperchon); Curt. 8. 12. 17-18 (Meleagros); and Curt. 9. 3. 3-16, 20; Arr. 5. 27. 2-28. 1 (Koinos). Cf. Niese i 194, n.1: 'da Attalos mit Meleagros eng verbunden war und sicherlich neben ihm ein hohes Amt bekleidete.'

[29]Arr. *Succ.* 24. 1; cf. 1. 25, where Polemon alone is mentioned. See Badian, *HSCP* 72 (1967), 189, n.34.

uncertain about which course of action to take: should the matter be decided by arms or diplomacy? Suspicion prevailed, and the ill will of the troops soon turned against Meleagros, whom they held chiefly responsible for their predicament.[30] We are told that the negotiations were carried out by Pasas the Thessalian, Amissos of Megalopolis and Perilaos (Perillos),[31] but we are not told who the peacemakers among the infantry were. Meleagros was given, for the moment, the rank of hyparch — in essence, he was Perdikkas' lieutenant — but he was soon liquidated without much opposition.[32] The key to Perdikkas' success in achieving this reconciliation, and in eliminating the troublesome Meleagros, was his ability to win the support of Attalos, who doubtless had a considerable following in the phalanx.

To seal this alliance, Perdikkas offered his sister, Atalante, to Attalos as wife. She was summoned some time later and arrived in Asia Minor in order to complete the arrangement and consummate the marriage. When Attalos was sent out with the fleet, she remained with her brother and, ultimately, shared his fate.[33] For Attalos, the alliance was a costly miscalculation. Atalante bound him to a losing cause.

---

[30]Curt. 10. 8. 5 says that the soldiers were angry with Meleagros because he instigated the attempted murder of Perdikkas. This would argue against Justin's (13. 3. 7) claim that Attalos was responsible, but it does not alter the fundamental fact that Attalos was nevertheless a supporter of the phalanx against the leaders of the cavalry. Niese (i 194, n.1) is probably wrong in believing that Attalos instigated the murder, though he correctly draws attention to Attalos' close connections with Meleagros. Attalos may well have read the changing mood of the army and exploited the bad feeling towards Meleagros. For the mood of the army see Curt. 10. 8. 9; for their deliberation on a course of action 10. 8. 12, which surely exaggerates the conditions in Babylon (*itaque inopia primum, deinde fames esse coepit*), after only one week's siege (Curt. 10. 10. 9).

[31]Curt. 10. 8. 15. Berve ii 25, 306-307, 317, nos. 53, 608, 630, s.vv. Amissos, Πάσας, Πέριλλος.

[32]For Meleagros' death see Diod. 18. 4. 7; Arr. *Succ.* 1a. 4; Justin 13. 4. 7-8; Curt. 10. 9. 7-21, esp. 20-21.

[33]Diod. 18. 37. 2. The 'daughters of Attalos' who accompanied Olympias to Pydna in the winter of 317/6 and were captured along with Rhoxane and Alexander IV (Diod. 19. 35. 5), may have been the children of Attalos and Atalante. Like Rhoxane and her son, they will have returned to Makedonia with Antipatros after the settlement of Triparadeisos. See W. Heckel, 'Fifty-two *Anonymae* in the History of Alexander', *Historia* 36 (1987), 118 (A38-39).

APPENDICES

APPENDIX VI: ASANDROS SON OF PHILOTAS

Berve ii 87, no. 165, identifies Asandros son of Philotas as 'anscheinend Bruder Parmenions und demnach vermutlich um 380 geboren' (cf. Kaerst, *RE* ii. 2 [1896] 1515, no. 2); Welles (*AHW* 39), calling him Parmenion's cousin, could possibly be closer to the truth. There are four references to Asandros[34] (though Curt. 7. 10. 12 reads *aelexander* or *alexander* in the MSS., Schmieder restores *Asander*), but only one identifies him: Ἄσανδρος ὁ Φιλώτα (Arr. 1. 17. 7). Though Philotas is a common name, Berve casts aside his usual caution (ii 397-399: 'Gleichsetzung mit einem der anderen Träger des Namens ist bei dessen Häufigkeit zu unsicher') and describes Asandros as 'anscheinend Bruder Parmenions' (ii 87; followed by Badian, *TAPA* 91 [1960], 329). The case for identification is, in fact, very weak. Moreover, if Asandros were Parmenion's brother, Alexander's act of recalling him from Sardeis to the main camp (Curt. 7. 10. 12) in order to have him executed cannot have been politically astute. This could only have revived unpleasant memories and accentuated the sufferings of the house of Parmenion. It is remarkable that his arrival created no recorded sensation in Alexander's camp, although there was a dissident faction in the army, which disapproved of Parmenion's murder (Diod. 17. 80. 4; Justin 12. 5. 4 ff.; Curt. 7. 2. 35 ff.). Even in Hegelochos' case, which bears only a superficial similarity, there is evidence of discontent. If we make Asandros Parmenion's brother, we create a historical situation that the sources must have suppressed, i.e., the reaction of Alexander's camp to Asandros' arrival. See W. Heckel 'Asandros', *AJP* 98 (1977), 410-412; also Bosworth, *Arrian* i 130.

---

[34] He is appointed satrap of Lydia (Arr. 1. 17. 7) and, later, together with Ptolemaios (identified as a brother of Antigonos Monophthlamos by Billows, *Antigonos* 425 f., no. 99, s.v. 'Polemaios I'), defeats Orontobates (Arr. 2. 5. 7, with Bosworth, *Arrian* i 195 f.). In 331, he is replaced as satrap by Menandros (Arr. 3. 6. 7).

General Bibliography

Adams, C. D., 'The Harpalos Case', *TAPA* 32 (1901), 121-153.
Adams, W. L., 'Cassander and the Crossing of the Hellespont: Diodorus 17. 17. 4', *AncW* 2 (1979), 111-115.
—, 'The Royal Macedonian Tomb at Vergina: An Historical Interpretation', *AncW* 3 (1980), 67-72.
—, 'Antipater and Cassander: Generalship on Restricted Resources in the Fourth Century', *AncW* 10 (1985), 79-88.
Adcock, F. E., *The Greek and Macedonian Art of War* (Berkeley, 1957).
Altheim, F., 'Proskynesis', *Paideia* 5 (1950), 307.
Anderson, A. R., 'Heracles and his Successors: A Study of a Heroic Ideal and the Recurrence of a Heroic Type', *HSCP* 39 (1928), 7-58.
Anson, E. M., 'Eumenes of Cardia' (Diss. Univ. of Virginia, 1975).
—, 'The Siege of Nora: A Source Conflict', *GRBS* 18 (1977), 251-256.
—, 'Discrimination and Eumenes of Cardia', *AncW* 3 (1980), 55-59.
—, 'Alexander's Hypaspists and the Argyraspids', *Historia* 30 (1981), 117-120.
—, 'The Meaning of the Term Macedones', *AncW* 10 (1984), 67-68.
—, 'The Hypaspists: Macedonia's Professional Citizen-Soldiers', *Historia* 34 (1985), 246-248.
—, 'Macedonia's Alleged Constitutionalism', *CJ* 80 (1985), 303-316.
—, 'Diodorus and the Date of Triparadeisus', *AJP* 107 (1986), 208-217.
—, 'Hypaspists and Argyraspids after 323', *AHB* 2 (1988), 131-133.
—, 'Antigonus, the Satrap of Phrygia', *Historia* 37 (1988), 471-477.
—, 'The Persian Fleet in 334', *CP* 84 (1989), 44-49.
—, 'Neoptolemus and Armenia', *AHB* 4 (1990), 125-128.
—, 'The Evolution of the Macedonian Army Assembly (330-315 B.C.)', *Historia* 40 (1991), 230-247.
Anspach, A. E., *De Alexandri Magni expeditione Indica* (Leipzig, 1903).
Ashton, N.G., 'The *Naumachia* near Amorgos in 322 B.C.', *ABSA* 72 (1977), 1-11.
—, 'The Lamian War: a false start?' *Antichthon* 17 (1983), 47-63.
—, 'The Lamian War — *stat magni nominis umbra*', *JHS* 104 (1984), 152-157.

Atkinson, J. E., 'Primary Sources and the Alexanderreich', *Acta Classica* 6 (1963), 125-137.
—, *A Commentary on Q. Curtius Rufus' Historiae Alexandri Magni. Books 3 and 4* (Amsterdam, 1980).
Aulock, H. von, 'Die Prägung des Balakros in Kilikien', *JNG* 14 (1964), 79-82.
Austin, M. M., *The Hellenistic World from Alexander to the Roman Conquest* (Cambridge, 1981).
Aymard, A., 'Sur l'Assemblée Macédonienne', *REA* 52 (1950), 115-137.
Badian, E., 'The Eunuch Bagoas: A Study in Method', *CQ* 8 (1958), 144-157.
—, 'The Death of Parmenio', *TAPA* 91 (1960), 324-338.
—, 'The First Flight of Harpalus', *Historia* 9 (1960), 245-246.
—, 'Harpalus', *JHS* 81 (1961), 16-43.
—, 'Alexander the Great and the Loneliness of Power', *AUMLA* 17 (1962), 80-91.
—, 'The Death of Philip II', *Phoenix* 17 (1963), 244-250.
—, *Studies in Greek and Roman History* (Oxford, 1964).
—, 'Orientals in Alexander's Army', *JHS* 85 (1965), 160-161.
—, 'The Administration of the Empire', *G & R* 12 (1965), 166-182.
—, 'The Date of Clitarchus', *PACA* 8 (1965), 5-11.
—, 'Agis III', *Hermes* 95 (1967), 170-192.
—, 'A King's Notebooks', *HSCP* 72 (1967), 183-204.
—, 'Alexander the Great, 1948-67', *CW* 65 (1971), 37-83.
—, 'Nearchus the Cretan', *YCS* 24 (1975), 147-170.
—, *The Deification of Alexander the Great*, Colloquy 21: *Center for Hermeneutical Studies in Hellenistic and Modern Culture* (Berkeley, 1976).
—, 'A Comma in the History of Samos', *ZPE* 23 (1976), 289-294.
—, 'The Battle of the Granicus: a new look', in *Ancient Macedonia* ii (Thessaloniki, 1977), 271-293.
—, 'The Deification of Alexander the Great', in *Ancient Macedonian Studies in Honor of Charles F. Edson*, H. J. Dell ed. (Thessaloniki, 1981), 27-71.
—, 'Eurydice', in *Philip II, Alexander the Great, and the Macedonian Heritage*, edited by W. L. Adams and E. N. Borza (Washington, D.C., 1982), 99-110.
—, 'Greeks and Macedonians', in *Macedonia and Greece in Late Classical and Early Hellenistic Times. Studies in the History of Art*, no. 10 (Washington, D.C., 1982), 33-51.
—, 'Alexander in Iran', in *Cambridge History of Iran* ii, I. L. Gershevitch ed. (Cambridge, 1985), 420-501.

—, 'Alexander at Peucelaotis', *CQ* 37 (1987), 117-128.
—, 'Two Postscripts on the Marriage of Phila and Balacrus', *ZPE* 73 (1988), 116-118.
—, 'History from "Square Brackets"', *ZPE* 79 (1989), 59-70.
Balcer, J. M., 'Alexander's Burning of Persepolis', *Iranica Antiqua* 13 (1978), 119-133.
Bauer, Georg, *Die Hiedelberger Epitome. Eine Quelle zur Diadochengeschichte* (Greifswald, 1914).
Baumbach, A., *Kleinasien unter Alexander dem Grossen* (Diss. Jena, publ. Weida i. Th., 1911).
Bellen, H., 'Der Rachegedanke in der griechisch-persischen Auseinandersetzung', *Chiron* 4 (1974), 43-67.
Beloch, K. J., *Griechische Geschichte*, 2nd ed., vols. 3-4 (Berlin and Leipzig, 1922-1927).
Bengtson, H., *Die Strategie in der hellenistischen Zeit: Ein Beitrag zum antiken Staatsrecht.* Münchener Beiträge zur Papyrusforschung und antiken Rechtsgeschichte, Heft 26 (Munich, 1937-1952).
—, 'Φιλόξενος ὁ Μακεδών', *Philologus* 92 (1937), 126-155.
—, *Herrschergestalten des Hellenismus* (Munich, 1975).
—, *Philipp und Alexander der Grosse* (Munich, 1985).
—, *Die Diadochen. Die Nachfolger Alexanders des Grossen* (Munich, 1987).
Benoist-Méchin, J., *Alexander the Great: The Meeting of East and West*, Mary Ilford, tr. (New York, 1966).
Benveniste, E., 'La ville de Cyreschata', *Journal Asiatique* 234 (1943-45), 163-166.
—, *Titres et noms propres in iranien ancien* (Paris, 1966).
Bernhardt, R., 'Zu den Verhandlungen zwischen Dareios und Alexander nach der Schlacht bei Issos', *Chiron* 18 (1988), 181-198.
Berthold, R. M., *Rhodes in the Hellenistic Age* (Ithaca and London, 1984).
Berve, Helmut, *Das Alexanderreich auf prosopographischer Grundlage*, 2 vols (Munich, 1925-1926).
—, 'Die angebliche Begründung des Königskultes durch Alexander', *Klio* 20 (1926), 179-186.
—, 'Die Verschmelzungspolitik Alexanders des Grossen', *Klio* 31 (1938), 135-168.
—, *Die Tyrannis bei den Griechen* (Munich, 1967).
Bevan, E. R., *The House of Seleucus*, vol. 1 (London, 1902).
Bickerman, E., 'La lettre d'Alexandre le Grand aux bannis grecs', *REA* 42 (1940), 25-35.

—, 'Sur un passage d'Hypéride (Epitaphios, col. VIII)', *Athenaeum* 41 (1963), 70-85.
Bieber, M., *Alexander in Greek and Roman Art* (Chicago, 1964).
Billows, R., 'Anatolian Dynasts: The Case of the Macedonian Eupolemos in Karia', *CA* 8 (1989), 173-205.
—, *Antigonos the One-Eyed and the Creation of the Hellenistic State* (Berkeley and Los Angeles, 1990).
Blänsdorf, J., 'Herodot bei Curtius Rufus', *Hermes* 99 (1971), 11-24.
Bödefeld, H., 'Untersuchungen zur Datierung der Alexandergeschichte des Q. Curtius Rufus' (Diss. Düsseldorf, 1982).
Boerma, R. N. H., *Justinus' Boeken over de Diadochen, een historisch Commentaar. Boek 13-15 cap. 2* (Amsterdam, 1979).
Borza, E. N., 'Alexander and the Return from Siwah', *Historia* 16 (1967), 369.
—, 'The End of Agis' Revolt', *CP* 66 (1971), 230-235.
—, 'Fire from Heaven: Alexander at Persepolis', *CP* 67 (1972), 233-245.
—, 'Alexander's Communications', *Ancient Macedonia* ii (Thessaloniki, 1977), 295-303.
—, 'The Royal Macedonian Tombs and the Paraphernalia of Alexander the Great', *Phoenix* 41 (1987), 105-121.
—, *In the Shadow of Olympus. The Emergence of Macedon* (Princeton, 1990).
Bosworth, A. B., 'Aristotle and Callisthenes', *Historia* 19 (1970), 407-413.
—, 'Philip II and Upper Macedonia', *CQ* 21 (1971), 93-105.
—, 'The Death of Alexander the Great: Rumour and Propaganda', *CQ* 21 (1971), 112-136.
—, 'ΑΣΘΕΤΑΙΡΟΙ', *CQ* 23 (1973), 245-253.
—, 'The Government of Syria under Alexander the Great', *CQ* 24 (1974), 46-64.
—, 'The Mission of Amphoterus and the Outbreak of Agis' War', *Phoenix* 29 (1975), 27-43.
—, 'Arrian and the Alexander Vulgate', in *Fondation Hardt, Entretiens* 22 (Geneva, 1976), 1-46.
—, 'Errors in Arrian', *CQ* 26 (1976), 117-139.
—, 'Alexander and Ammon', in *Greece and the Ancient Mediterranean in History and Prehistory. Studies presented to Fritz Schachermeyr*, K. Kinzl ed. (Berlin, 1977), 51-75.
—, 'Eumenes, Neoptolemus and *PSI* XII 1284', *GRBS* 19 (1978), 227-237.
—, 'Alexander and the Iranians', *JHS* 100 (1980), 1-21.
—, *A Historical Commentary on Arrian's History of Alexander, Books i-iii* (Oxford, 1980).

—, 'A Missing Year in the History of Alexander the Great', *JHS* 101 (1981), 17-39.
—, 'The Indian Satrapies under Alexander the Great', *Antichthon* 17 (1983), 37-46.
—, 'Alexander the Great and the Decline of Macedon', *JHS* 106 (1986), 1-12.
—, *Conquest and Empire. The Reign of Alexander the Great* (Cambridge, 1988).
—, *From Arrian to Alexander: Studies in Historical Interpretation* (Oxford, 1988).
—, 'History and Artifice in Plutarch's *Eumenes*', in *Plutarch and the Historical Tradition*, ed. by P. A. Stadter (London, 1992), 56-89.
Bouché-Leclercq, A., *Histoire des Lagides*, vol. 1 (Paris, 1903).
Breloer, B., *Alexanders Kampf gegen Poros* (Stuttgart, 1933).
—, *Alexanders Bund mit Poros: Indien von Dareios zu Sandrokottos*, Sammlung orientalistischen Arbeiten 9 (Leipzig, 1941).
Briant, Pierre, *Antigone le Borgne* (Paris, 1973).
—, 'D'Alexandre le Grand aux diadoques: le cas d'Eumène de Kardia', *REA* 74 (1972), 32-73; 75 (1973), 43-81.
—, *Rois, Tributs et Paysans* (Paris, 1982).
Brown, T. S., *Onesicritus: A Study in Hellenistic Historiography* (Berkeley, 1949).
—, 'Callisthenes and Alexander', *AJP* 70 (1949), 225-248.
—, 'Clitarchus', *AJR* 71 (1950), 134-155.
—, 'Alexander's Book Order (Plut. *Alex.* 8)', *Historia* 16 (1967), 359-368.
—, 'Hieronymus of Cardia', *AHR* 53 (1947), 684-696.
Brunt, P. A., 'Persian Accounts of Alexander's Campaigns', *CQ* 12 (1962), 141-155.
—, 'Alexander's Macedonian Cavalry', *JHS* 83 (1963), 27-46.
—, 'The Aims of Alexander', *G & R* 12 (1965), 205-216.
—, 'Alexander, Barsine and Heracles', *RFIC* 103 (1975), 22-34.
—, ed., *Arrian*, Loeb Classical Library, 2 vols. (Cambridge, Mass., 1976, 1983).
Buckler, J., *Philip II and the Sacred War*, Supplements to Mnemosyne 109 (Leiden, 1989).
Buraselis, K., *Das hellenistische Makedonien und die Ägäis*, Münchener Beiträge zur Papyrusforschung und antiken Rechtsgeschichte, Heft 73 (Munich, 1982).
Burn, A. R., 'Notes on Alexander's Campaigns', *JHS* 72 (1952), 81-91.
—, 'The Generalship of Alexander', *G & R* 12 (1965), 140-154.
—, *Alexander the Great and the Middle East* (London, 1973).

Burstein, S. M., *Outpost of Hellenism: The Emergence of Heraclea on the Black Sea* (Berkeley and Los Angeles, 1976).
—, 'IG ii² 561 and the Court of Alexander IV', *ZPE* 24 (1977), 223-225.
—, 'The Tomb of Philip II and the Succession of Alexander the Great', *EMC* 26 (1982), 141-163.
Carney, E. D., 'Alexander the Great and the Macedonian Aristocracy' (Diss. Duke University, 1975).
—, 'Alexander the Lyncestian: The Disloyal Opposition', *GRBS* 21 (1980), 23-33.
—, 'The Conspiracy of Hermolaus', *CJ* 76 (1980/81), 223-231.
—, 'The Death of Clitus', *GRBS* 22 (1981), 149-160.
—, 'The First Flight of Harpalus Again', *CJ* 77 (1982), 9-11.
—, 'Regicide in Macedonia', *PdP* 211 (1983), 260-272.
—, 'Olympias', *Anc. Soc.* 18 (1987), 35-62.
—, 'The Career of Adea-Eurydike', *Historia* 36 (1987), 496-502.
—, 'The Sisters of Alexander the Great: Royal Relicts', *Historia* 37 (1988), 385-404.
Caroe, O., *The Pathans* (London, 1962).
Cary, M., *A History of the Greek World from 323 to 146 B.C.*, 2nd edition (London, 1951).
Casson, S., *Macedonia, Thrace and Illyria* (Oxford, 1926).
Cauer, F., 'Philotas, Kleitos, Kallisthenes: Beiträge zur Alexander-geschichte', *Neue Jahrbücher für classische Philologie*, Supplbd 20, 1894.
Cawkwell, G. L., 'The Crowning of Demosthenes', *CQ* 19 (1969), 161-180.
—, 'Agesilaus and Sparta', *CQ* 26 (1976), 62-84.
—, *Philip of Macedon* (London, 1978).
Charbonneaux, J., 'Antigone le Borgne et Démétrios Poliorcète sont-ils figurés sur le sarcophage d'Alexandre?' *Rev. des Arts* 2 (1952), 219-223.
Chroust, A. H., *Aristotle*, vol. 1 (South Bend, Indiana, 1973).
Cloché, P., *Alexandre le Grand et les essais de fusion entre l'Occident gréco-macédonien et l'Orient* (Neuchatel, 1953).
—, *La Dislocation d'un Empire*, Paris, 1959.
Cohen, G. M., 'The Marriage of Lysimachus and Nicaea', *Historia* 22 (1973), 354-356.
—, 'The Diadochoi and the New Monarchies', *Athenaeum* 52 (1974), 177-179.
Cook, J. M., *The Persian Empire* (New York, 1983).
Cross, G. N., *Epirus: A Study in Greek Constitutional Development* (Cambridge, 1932).

Cust, R. H. Hobart, *Giovanni Antonio Bassi, The Man and the Painter, 1477-1549* (London, 1906).
Davies, J. K., *Athenian Propertied Families: 600-300 B.C.* (Oxford, 1971).
De Sanctis, G., 'Perdicca', *SIFC* 9 (1931), 9-24.
Develin, R., 'The Murder of Philip II', *Antichthon* 15 (1981), 86-99.
—, 'Anaximenes (*FGrHist* 72) F4', *Historia* 34 (1985), 493-496.
—, *Athenian Officials: 684-321 B.C.* (Cambridge, 1989).
Devine, A. M., 'Grand Tactics at Gaugamela', *Phoenix* 29 (1975), 374-385.
—, 'The *Parthi*, the Tyranny of Tiberius and the Date of Q. Curtius Rufus', *Phoenix* 33 (1979), 142-159.
—, 'The Location of Castabulum and Alexander's Route from Mallus to Myriandrus', *Acta Classica* 27 (1984), 127-129.
—, 'The Strategies of Alexander the Great and Darius III in the Issus Campaign (333 B.C.)', *AncW* 12 (1985), 25-38.
—, 'Grand Tactics at the Battle of Issus', *AncW* 12 (1985), 39-59.
—, 'Diodorus' Account of the Battle of Paraitacene', *AncW* 12 (1985), 75-86.
—, 'Diodorus' Account of the Battle of Gabiene', *AncW* 12 (1985), 87-96.
—, 'Demythologizing the Battle of the Granicus', *Phoenix* 40 (1986), 265-278.
—, 'The Battle of Gaugamela: A Tactical and Source-Critical Study', *AncW* 13 (1986), 87-116.
—, 'The Battle of the Hydaspes: A Tactical and Source-Critical Study', *AncW* 16 (1987), 91-113.
—, 'The Macedonian Army at Gaugamela: Its Strength and the Length of Its Battle-Line', *AncW* 19 (1989), 77-80
Diels, H., and Schubart, W., *Didymos: Kommentar zu Demosthenes (Papyrus 9780)*, Berliner Klassikertexte 1 (Berlin, 1904).
Dittberner, W., *Issos: Ein Beitrag zur Geschichte Alexanders des Grossen* (Diss. Berlin, 1908).
Dittenberger, W., *Sylloge Inscriptionum Graecarum*, 3rd edition, vol. 1 (Leipzig, 1915).
Dixon, Patricia, see French, Valerie.
Dobesch, G., 'Alexander der Grosse und der korinthische Bund', *GB* 3 (1975), 73-149.
Droysen, Hans, *Heerwesen und Kriegführung der Griechen* (Freiburg i. Br., 1889).
Droysen, J. G., 'Zur Geschichte der Nachfolger Alexanders', *RhM* 2 (1843), 387-414; 511-530.
—, 'Zu Duris und Hieronymos', *Hermes* 11 (1876), 458-465.

—, 'Alexanders des Grossen Armee', *Hermes* 12 (1877), 226-252.
—, *Geschichte des Hellenismus*, 3rd edition, vols 1-2 (Basel, 1952).
Edmunds, Lowell, 'The Religiosity of Alexander', *GRBS* 12 (1971), 363-391.
Edson, C. P., 'The Antigonids, Heracles and Beroea', *HSCP* 45 (1934), 213-246.
—, 'Early Macedonia', in *Ancient Macedonia*, vol. 1 (Thessaloniki, 1970), 17- 44.
Egge, R., *Untersuchungen zur Primärtradition bein Q. Curtius Rufus* (Freiburg i. Br., 1978).
Eggermont, P. H. L., 'Alexander's Campaign in Gandhara and Ptolemy's List of Indo-Scythian Towns', *Orientalia Lovaniensia Periodica* 1 (1970), 63-123.
—, *Alexander's Campaigns in Sind and Baluchistan and the Siege of the Brahmin Town of Harmatelia* (Leuven, 1975).
Ehrenberg, V., *Alexander and the Greeks*, Ruth Fraenkel von Velsen tr. (Oxford, 1938).
Ehrhardt, C., 'Two Notes on Philip of Macedon's First Interventions in Thessaly', *CQ* 17 (1967), 296-301.
Ellis, J. R., 'Amyntas Perdikka, Philip II and Alexander the Great: A Study in Conspiracy', *JHS* 91 (1971), 15-24.
—, 'The Step-Brothers of Philip II', *Historia* 22 (1973), 350-354.
—, 'Alexander's Hypaspists Again', *Historia* 24 (1975), 617-618.
—, *Philip II and Macedonian Imperialism* (London, 1976; repr. Princeton, 1986).
—, 'The Assassination of Philip II', in *Ancient Macedonian Studies in honor of Charles F. Edson*, H.J. Dell ed. (Thessaloniki, 1981), 99-137.
Endres, H., 'Krateros, Perdikkas und die letzten Pläne Alexanders des Grossen', *RhM* 72 (1917-1918), 437-445.
Engel, R., 'Anmerkungen zur Schlacht bei Orkynia', *MusHelv.* 28 (1971), 227-231.
—, Zur Chronologie von Perdikkas' Massnahmen am Vorabend des ersten Koalitionskrieges 321 v. Chr.', *RhM* 115 (1972), 215-219.
—, 'Die Überlieferung der Schlacht bei Kretopolis', *Historia* 21 (1972), 501-507.
—, 'Polyäns Stratagem IV 6, 8 zur "Seeschlacht am Hellespont"', *Klio* 55 (1973), 141-145.
—, 'Zwei Heeresversammlungen in Memphis', *Hermes* 102 (1974), 122-124.

—, *Untersuchungen zum Machtaufstieg des Antigonos I. Monophthalmos. Ein Beitrag zur Geschichte der frühen Diadochenzeit* (Kallmünz, 1976).

Engels, D. W., *Alexander the Great and the Logistics of the Macedonian Army* (Berkeley and Los Angeles, 1978).

—, 'A note on Alexander's Death', *CP* 73 (1978), 224-228.

—, 'Alexander's Intelligence System', *CQ* 30 (1980), 327-340.

Ensslin, W., 'Die Gewaltenteilungen im Reichsregiment nach Alexanders Tod', *RhM* 74 (1925), 297-308.

Errington, R. M., 'Bias in Ptolemy's History of Alexander', *CQ* 19 (1969), 233-242.

—, 'From Babylon to Triparadeisos: 323-320 B.C.', *JHS* 90 (1970), 49-77.

—, 'Macedonian "Royal Style" and its Historical Significance', *JHS* 94 (1974), 20-37.

—, 'Arybbas the Molossian', *GRBS* 16 (1975), 41-50.

—, 'Samos and the Lamian War', *Chiron* 5 (1975), 51-57.

—, 'Alexander in the Hellenistic World', in *Fondation Hardt, Entretiens* 22 (Geneva, 1976), 137-179.

—, 'Diodorus Siculus and the Chronology of the Early Diadochoi, 320-311 B.C.', *Hermes* 105 (1977), 478-504.

—, 'The Nature of the Macedonian State under the Monarchy', *Chiron* 8 (1978), 77-133.

—, *A History of Macedonia*, trans. by C. Errington (Berkeley and Los Angeles, 1990).

Erskine, A., 'The πεζέταιροι of Philip II and Alexander III', *Historia* 38 (1989), 385-394.

Fears, J. Rufus, 'Parthi in Q. Curtius Rufus', *Hermes* 102 (1974), 623-625.

—, 'Pausanias, The Assassin of Philip II', *Athenaeum* 53 (1975), 111-135.

—, 'Silius Italicus, *Cataphracti*, and the Date of Q. Curtius Rufus', *CP* 71 (1976), 214-223.

Ferguson, W. S., *Hellenistic Athens* (London, 1911).

Fontana, M. J., *Le Lotte per la Successione di Alessandro Magno dal 323 al 315* (Palermo, 1960).

Fortina, Marcello, *Cassandro, Re di Macedonia* (Turin, 1965).

Foss, C., 'The Battle of the Granicus: A New Look', in *Ancient Macedonia* ii (Thessaloniki, 1977), 495-502.

Foucart, P., 'Étude sur Didymos', *Mem. de l'acad. des Inscript. et Belles-Lettres* 38 (1909), 138-145.

Foucher, M., *Sur la Frontière Indo-Afghane* (Paris, 1901).

Fox, Robin Lane, *Alexander the Great* (London, 1973).

—, *The Search for Alexander* (Boston and Toronto, 1980).

Fraenkel, Arthur, *Die Quellen der Alexanderhistoriker* (Breslau, 1883, repr. Aalen, 1969).
Fraser, P. M., 'Current Problems concerning the early History of the Cult of Sarapis', *Opuscula Atheniensia* 7 (1967), 23-45
Fredricksmeyer, E. A., 'Alexander the Great and the Macedonian Kausia', *TAPA* 116 (1986), 215-227.
French, Valerie, and Dixon, Patricia, 'The Pixodaros Affair: Another View', *AncW* 13 (1986), 73-86.
—, 'The Source Traditions for the Pixodaros Affair', *AncW* 14 (1986), 25-40.
Fuller, J. F. C., *The Generalship of Alexander the Great* (London, 1958).
Garnsey, P., *Famine and Food Supply in the Graeco-Roman World* (Cambridge, 1988).
Gebauer, Kurt, 'Alexanderbildnis und Alexandertypus (D19)', *MDAI (A)* 63-64 (1938-1939), 1-106.
Geer, R. M., *Diodorus of Sicily*, Loeb Classical Library, vols. 9-10 (Cambridge, Mass., 1947-1954).
Gehrke, Hans-Joachim, *Phokion: Studien zur Erfassung seiner historischen Gestalt*, Zetemata, Heft 64 (Munich, 1976).
Geiger, Wm., *Alexanders Feldzüge in Sogdiana*, Programm der K. Studienanstalt zu Neustadt, Schuljahr 1883-1884.
Geyer, Fritz, *Makedonien bis zur Thronbesteigung Philipps II.* Historische Zeitschrift, Beiheft 19 (Munich and Berlin, 1930).
Ghiron-Bistagne, P., *Recherches sur les Acteurs dans la Grèce antique* (Paris, 1976).
Giacone, A., *Storie di Alessandro Magno di Quinto Curzio Rufo* (Turin, 1977).
Golan, D., 'The Fate of a Court Historian: Callisthenes', *Athenaeum* 66 (1988), 99-120.
Goldstein, J. A., *The Letters of Demosthenes* (New York, 1968).
Gomme, A. W., *A Historical Commentary on Thucydides*, vol. 1 (Oxford, 1945).
Goukowsky, P., *Essai sur les origines du mythe d'Alexandre*. 2 vols. (Nancy, 1978-81).
—, 'Makedonika', *REG* 100 (1987), 240-255.
Gow, A. S. F., *Theocritus*, 2 vols. (Cambridge, 1965).
Grainger, J., *Seleukos Nikator. Constituting a Hellenistic Kingdom* (London, 1989).
Granier, F., *Die makedonische Heeresversammlung. Ein Beitrag zum antiken Staatsrecht* (Munich, 1931).
Green, Peter, *Alexander of Macedon* (London, 1974).

—, *Alexander to Actium: The Historical Evolution of the Hellenistic Age* (Berkeley, 1990).
Greenwalt, W. S., 'The Search for Arrhidaeus', *AncW* 10 (1984), 69-77.
—, 'Amyntas III and the Political Stability of Argead Macedonia', *AncW* 18 (1988), 35-44.
—, 'Polygamy and Succession in Argead Macedonia', *Arethusa* 22 (1989), 19-43.
Griffin, A., *Sikyon* (Oxford, 1982).
Griffith, G. T., *The Mercenaries of the Hellenistic World* (Cambridge, 1935).
—, 'Alexander's Generalship at Gaugamela', *JHS* 67 (1947), 77-89.
—, 'Μακεδονικά. Notes on the Macedonians of Philip and Alexander', *Proceedings of the Cambridge Philological Association* 4 (1956-1957), 3-10.
—, 'A Note on the Hipparchies of Alexander', *JHS* 83 (1963), 68-74.
—, 'The Macedonian Background', *G & R* 12 (1965), 125-139.
—, 'Alexander and Antipater in 323 B.C.', *PACA* 8 (1965), 12-17.
—, *Alexander the Great: The Main Problems* (Cambridge, 1966).
—, 'The Letter of Darius at Arrian 2. 14', *PCPS* 14 (1968), 33-48.
—, 'Philip of Macedon's Early Interventions in Thessaly (358-352 B.C.)', *CQ* 20 (1970), 67-80.
Grilli, A., 'Il 'Saeculum' di Curzio Rufo', *PdP* 168 (1976), 215-223.
Grimmig, F., 'Arrians Diadochengeschichte' (Diss. Halle, 1914).
Grote, Karl, *Das griechische Söldnerwesen der hellenistischen Zeit* (Diss. Jena, publ. Weida, 1913).
Gruen, E. S., 'The Coronation of the Diadochoi', in *The Craft of the Ancient Historian: Essays in Honor of Chester G. Starr*, edited by J. Eadie and J. Ober (Lanham, Md., 1985), 253-271.
Grzybek, E., 'Zu Philipp II. und Alexander dem Grossen', in *Ancient Macedonia* iv (Thessaloniki, 1986), 223-229.
Gunderson, L., 'Quintus Curtius Rufus', in *Philip II, Alexander the Great and the Macedonian Heritage*, edited by W. L. Adams and E. N. Borza (Washington, D.C., 1982), 177-196.
Guthrie, W. K. C., *A History of Greek Philosophy*, vol. 6 (Cambridge, 1981).
Habicht, Christian, *Gottmenschentum und griechische Städte*, Zetemata, Heft 14, 2nd edition (Munich, 1970).
—, 'Samische Volksbeschlüsse der hellenistischer Zeit', *MDAI(A)* 72 (1957), 152 ff.
—, 'Der Beitrag Spartas zur Restitution von Samos während des Lamischen Krieges', *Chiron* 5 (1975), 45-50.
Hackmann, F., *Die Schlacht bei Gaugamela* (Halle, 1902).

Hadley, R.A., 'Hieronymus of Cardia and early Seleucid Mythology', *Historia* 18 (1969), 142-152.
—, 'Royal Propaganda of Seleucus I and Lysimachus', *JHS* 94 (1974), 50-65.
—, 'The Foundation Date of Seleucia-on-the-Tigris', *Historia* 27 (1978), 228-230.
Hamilton, J. R., 'Alexander and his so-called Father', *CQ* 3 (1953), 151-157.
—, 'Three Passages in Arrian', *CQ* 5 (1955), 217-221.
—, 'The Cavalry Battle at the Hydaspes', *JHS* 76 (1956), 26-31.
—, 'Alexander's Early Life', *G & R* 12 (1965), 116-125.
—, *Plutarch, Alexander: A Commentary* (Oxford, 1969).
—, 'Alexander among the Oreitae', *Historia* 21 (1972), 603-608.
—, *Alexander the Great* (London, 1973).
—, 'The Origins of Ruler-Cult', *Prudentia* 16 (1984), 3-16.
—, 'The Date of Quintus Curtius Rufus', *Historia* 37 (1988), 445-456.
Hammond, N. G. L., *Epirus* ((Oxford, 1967).
—, 'Alexander's Campaign in Illyria', *JHS* 94 (1974), 66ff.
—, 'A Cavalry Unit in the army of Antigonus Monophthalmus: Asthippoi', *CQ* 28 (1978), 128-135.
—, 'A Note on "Pursuit" in Arrian', *CQ* 28 (1978), 136-140.
—, '"Philip's Tomb" in Historical Context', *GRBS* 19 (1978), 331-350.
—, 'The Battle of the Granicus River', *JHS* 100 (1980), 73-88.
—, 'Some Passages in Arrian concerning Alexander', *CQ* 30 (1980), 455-476.
—, 'Training in the Use of the Sarissa and its Effect in Battle 359-333', *Antichthon* 14 (1980), 53-63.
—, *Alexander the Great. King, Commander and Statesman* (London, 1981).
—, *Three Historians of Alexander the Great* (Cambridge, 1983).
—, 'Alexander's Veterans after his Death', *GRBS* 25 (1984), 51-61.
—, 'Some Macedonian Offices: c. 336-309 B.C.', *JHS* 105 (1985), 156-160.
—, 'A Papyrus Commentary on Alexander's Balkan Campaign', *GRBS* 28 (1987), 331-347.
—, 'The King and the Land in the Macedonian kingdom', *CQ* 38 (1988), 382-391.
—, 'The Royal Journal of Alexander', *Historia* 37 (1988), 129-150.
—, 'Casualties and Reinforcements of Citizen Soldiers in Greece and Macedonia', *JHS* 109 (1989), 56-68.
—, *The Macedonian State. Origins, Institutions and History* (Oxford, 1989).

—, 'Royal Pages, Personal Pages and Boys Trained in the Macedonian Manner during the Period of the Temenid Monarchy', *Historia* 39 (1990), 261-290.
—, 'Inscriptions concerning Philippi and Calindoea in the Reign of Alexander the Great', *ZPE* 82 (1990), 167-175.
—, 'The Macedonian Defeat near Samarcand', *AncW* 22 (1991), 41-47.
—, 'The Various Guards of Philip II and Alexander III', *Historia* 40 (1991), 396-418.
Hammond, N. G. L., and Griffith, G. T., *A History of Macedonia II: 550-336 B.C.* (Oxford, 1979).
Hammond, N. G. L., and Walbank, F. W., *A History of Macedonia III: 336-167 B.C.* (Oxford, 1988).
Hampl, F., *Alexander der Grosse* (Göttingen, 1958).
—, 'Alexanders des Grossen *Hypomnemata* und letzte Pläne', *Studies Presented to D. M. Robinson*, Washington University Publications, vol. 2 (St Louis, Mo., 1953), 816-829.
Harris, Ramon I., 'The Dilemma of Alexander the Great', *PACA* 11 (1968), 46-54.
Hatzopoulos, M. B., 'Dates of Philip II's reign', in *Philip, Alexander the Great and the Macedonian Heritage*, edited by W. L. Adams and E. N. Borza (Washington, 1982).
—, 'A reconsideration of the Pixodarus Affair', in *Macedonia and Greece in Late Classical and Early Hellenistic Times*. Studies in the History of Art, vol. 10 (Washington, 1982), 59-66.
—, 'Succession and Regency in Classical Macedonia', in *Ancient Macedonia*, vol. 4 (Thessaloniki, 1986), 279-292.
Hauben, Hans, 'The Command Structure in Alexander's Mediterranean Fleets', *Anc. Soc.* 3 (1972), 55-65.
—, 'An Athenian Naval Victory in 321 B.C.', *ZPE* 13 (1974), 56-67.
—, 'A Royal Toast in 302 B.C.', *Anc. Soc.* 5 (1974), 105-119.
—, *Het Vlootbevelhebberschap in de vroege Diadochen tijd (323-301 v. C.): Een prosopographisch en institutioneel onderzoek* (Brussels, 1975).
—, 'The Expansion of Macedonian Sea-Power under Alexander the Great', *Anc. Soc.* 7 (1976), 79-105.
—, 'Rhodes, Alexander and the Diadochi from 333/332 to 304 B.C.', *Historia* 26 (1977), 307-339.
—, 'The First War of the Successors (321 B.C.): Chronological and Historical Problems', *Anc. Soc.* 9 (1977), 85-120.
Hayum, A., *Giovanni Antonio Bazzi - 'Il Sodoma'* (Diss. Harvard, 1968, publ. New York, 1976).
Heckel, W., 'Amyntas, Son of Andromenes', *GRBS* 16 (1975), 393-398.

—, 'The Flight of Harpalos and Tauriskos', *CP* 72 (1977), 133-135.
—, 'The Conspiracy *against* Philotas', *Phoenix* 31 (1977), 9-21.
—, 'Asandros', *AJP* 98 (1977), 410-412.
—, 'The *Somatophylakes* of Alexander the Great: Some Thoughts', *Historia* 27 (1978), 224-228.
—, 'Kleopatra or Eurydike?' *Phoenix* 32 (1978), 155-158.
—, 'On Attalos and Atalante', *CQ* 28 (1978), 377-382.
—, 'Leonnatos, Polyperchon and the Introduction of *Proskynesis*', *AJP* 99 (1978), 459-461.
—, 'The *Somatophylax* Attalos: Diodoros 16. 94. 4', *LCM* 4 (1979), 215-216.
—, 'Philip II, Kleopatra and Karanos', *RFIC* 107 (1979), 385-393.
—, 'Alexander at the Persian Gates', *Athenaeum* 58 (1980), 168-174.
—, 'Kelbanos, Kebalos or Kephalon?' *Beiträge zur Namenforschung* 15 (1980), 43-45.
—, 'Marsyas of Pella, Historian of Macedon', *Hermes* 108 (1980), 444-462.
—, 'IG ii^2 561 and the Status of Alexander IV', *ZPE* 40 (1980), 249-250.
—, 'Honours for Philip and Iolaos: IG ii^2 561', *ZPE* 44 (1981), 75-77.
—, 'Some Speculations on the Prosopography of the Alexanderreich', *LCM* 6 (1981), 63-70.
—, 'Polyxena, the Mother of Alexander the Great', *Chiron* 11 (1981), 79-86.
—, 'Two Doctors from Kos?' *Mnemosyne* 34 (1981), 396-398.
—, 'Leonnatus and the Captive Persian Queens: A Case of Mistaken Identity', *SIFC* 53 (1981), 272-274.
—, 'Philip and Olympias (337/6 B.C.)', *Classical Contributions. Studies in Honour of Malcolm Francis McGregor*, edited by G. S. Shrimpton and D. J. McCargar (Locust Valley, N.Y., 1981), 51-57.
—, 'The Career of Antigenes', *SO* 57 (1982), 57-67.
—, 'Who Was Hegelochos?' *RhM* 125 (1982), 78-87.
—, 'The Early Career of Lysimachos', *Klio* 64 (1982), 373-381.
—, 'Adea-Eurydike', *Glotta* 61 (1983), 40-42.
—, 'Kynnane the Illyrian', *RSA* 13-14 (1983-84), 193-200.
—, 'The Boyhood Friends of Alexander the Great', *Emerita* 53 (1985), 285-289.
—, 'The Macedonian Veterans in Kilikia', *LCM* 10 (1985), 109-110.
—, 'Chorienes and Sisimithres', *Athenaeum* 64 (1986), 223-226.
—, 'Factions and Macedonian Politics in the Reign of Alexander the Great', in *Ancient Macedonia* iv (Thessaloniki, 1986), 293-305.
—, '*Somatophylakia*, a Macedonian *cursus honorum*', *Phoenix* 40 (1986), 279-294.

—, 'A Grandson of Antipatros at Delos', *ZPE* 70 (1987), 161-162.
—, '*Anonymi* in the History of Alexander the Great', *L'Antiquité Classique* 56 (1987), 130-147.
—, 'Fifty-two Anonymae in the History of Alexander', *Historia* 36 (1987), 114-119.
—, *The Last Days and Testament of Alexander the Great: a Prosopographic Study*, Historia Einzelschriften, Heft 56 (Stuttgart, 1988).
—, 'The Granddaughters of Iolaus', *Classicum* 15 (1989), 32-39.
—, 'Peithon, Son of Agenor', *Mnemosyne* 43 (1990), 456-459.
—, 'Q. Curtius Rufus and the Date of Cleander's Mission to the Peloponnese', *Hermes* 119 (1991), 124-125.
—, 'Hephaistion "the Athenian"', *ZPE* 87 (1991), 39-41.
Hecker, A., 'Epistola Critica', *Philologus* 5 (1850), 414-512.
Heisserer, A. J., *Alexander the Great and the Greeks. The Epigraphic Evidence* (Norman, Oklahoma, 1980).
Helmreich, F., *Die Reden bei Curtius*, Rhetorische Studien 14 (Paderborn, 1927).
Herzfeld, E., *The Persian Empire* (Wiesbaden, 1968).
Heskel, Julia, 'The Political Background of the Arybbas Decree', *GRBS* 29 (1988), 185-196.
Higgins, W. E., 'Aspects of Alexander's Imperial Administration: some modern methods and views reviewed', *Athenaeum* 58 (1980), 129-152.
Hoffmann, Otto, *Die Makedonen: ihre Sprache und ihr Volkstum* (Göttingen, 1906).
Hofstetter, J., *Die Griechen in Persien. Prosopographie der Griechen im persischen Reich vor Alexander*, Archaeologische Mitteilungen aus Iran, Ergänzungsband 5 (Berlin, 1978).
Holt, F. L., 'The Hyphasis "Mutiny": A Source Study', *AncW* 5 (1982), 33-59.
—, *Alexander the Great and Bactria. The Formation of a Greek Frontier in Central Asia*, Supplements to Mnemosyne 104 (Leiden-New York, 1988).
Hornblower, J., *Hieronymus of Cardia* (Oxford, 1981).
Hornblower, S., *Mausolus* (Oxford, 1982).
—, *The Greek World 479-323 B.C.* (London, 1983).
Hünerwadel, W., 'Forschungen zur Geschichte des Königs Lysimachos von Thrakien' (Diss. Zürich, 1910).
Instinsky, H. U., *Alexander der Grosse am Hellespont* (Godesberg, 1949).

Janke, A., *Auf Alexanders des Grossen Pfaden. Eine Reise durch Kleinasien* (Berlin, 1904).
Jaschinski, S., *Alexander und Griechenland unter dem Eindruck der Flucht des Harpalos* (Bonn, 1981).
Johnson, Franklin P., *Lysippos* (Durham, North Carolina, 1927).
Judeich, W., *Kleinasiatische Studien. Untersuchungen zur griechisch-persischen Geschichte des IV. Jahrhunderts v. Chr.* (Marburg, 1892).
Julien, Paul, *Zur Verwaltung der Satrapien unter Alexander dem Grossen* (Weida, 1914).
Junge, P. J., 'Hazarapatis', *Klio* 33 (1940), 13-38.
Kaerst, Julius, 'Zum Briefwechsel Alexanders des Grossen', *Philologus* 56 (1897), 406-412.
—, *Geschichte des Hellenismus*, 2nd edition (Berlin-Leipzig, vol. 1, 1927, vol. 2, 1926).
Kaiser, W. B., 'Der Brief Alexanders des Grossen an Dareios nach der Schlacht bei Issos' (Diss. Mainz, 1956)
Kampe, Fr., 'Jahresberichte über griechische Historiker', *Philologus* 4 (1849), 111-146.
Kanatsulis, D., *Antipatros. Ein Beitrag zur Geschichte Makedoniens in der Zeit Philipps, Alexanders und der Diadochen* (Thessaloniki, 1942).
—, 'Antipatros als Feldherr und Staatsmann in der Zeit Philipps und Alexanders des Grossen', *Hellenika* 16 (1958/59), 14-64.
—, 'Antipatros als Feldherr und Staatsmann nach dem Tode Alexanders des Grossen', *Makedonika* 8 (1968), 121-184.
Karttunen, K., 'Taxila: Indian City and a Stronghold of Hellenism', *Arctos* 24 (1990), 85-96.
Kebric, R. B., *In the Shadow of Macedon: Duris of Samos*, Historia Einzelschriften, Heft 29 (Wiesbaden, 1977).
Keil, J., 'Ephesische Bürgerrechts- und Proxeniedekrete aus dem vierten und dritten Jahrhundert v. Chr.', *JÖAI* 16 (1913), 231-248.
Keller, Erich, 'Alexander der Grosse nach der Schlacht bei Issos bis zu seiner Rückkehr aus Aegypten', *Historische Studien*, Heft 48, 1904.
Khlopin, I. N., 'Die Chronologie und Dynamik des Feldzuges Alexanders des Grossen nach Mittelasien', *Anc. Soc.* 11/12 (1980/81), 151-172.
Kienast, Dietmar, *Philipp II. von Makedonien und das Reich der Achamieniden*, Abhandlungen der Marburger Gelehrten Gesellschaft, Jahrgang 1971, no. 6 (Munich, 1973).
—, 'Alexander und der Ganges', *Historia* 14 (1965), 180-188.
Kingsley, B., 'The Cap that Survived Alexander', *AJA* 85 (1981), 39-46.

—, 'The Kausia Diadematophoros', *AJA* 88 (1984), 66-68.
—, 'Harpalos in the Megarid (333-331 B.C.) and the Grain Shipments from Cyrene', *ZPE* 66 (1986), 165-177.
Kleiner, G., *Diadochen-Gräber* (Wiesbaden, 1963).
Klotzsch, Carl, *Epirotische Geschichte bis zum Jahre 280 v. Chr.* (Berlin, 1911).
Köhler, Ulrich, 'Über die Diadochengeschichte Arrians', *SB Berlin* (1890), 557-588.
—, 'Über das Verhältniss Alexanders des Grossen zu seinem Vater Philipp', *SB Berlin* (1892), 497-514.
Kornemann, Ernst, 'Zur Geschichte der antiken Herrscherkulte', *Klio* 1 (1901), 51-146.
—, 'Die letzten Ziele der Politik Alexanders des Grossen', *Klio* 16 (1920), 209-238.
—, *Die Alexandergeschichte des Königs Ptolemaios I. von Aegypten* (Leipzig, 1935).
Kraft, K., *Die 'rationale' Alexander*, Frankfurter Althistorische Studien, Heft 5 (Frankfurt, 1971).
Krause, A., 'Beiträge zur Alexander-Geschichte', *Hermes* 25 (1890), 62-81.
Krumbholz, P. *De Asiae Minoris Satrapis Persicis* (Leipzig, 1883).
Laqueur, R., 'Zur Geschichte des Krateros', *Hermes* 54 (1919), 295-300.
Lepore, E., 'Leostene e le origini della guerra lamiaca', *PdP* 10 (1955), 161 ff.
Lévêque, P., *Pyrrhos* (Paris, 1957).
Lobel, E., ed., *Oxyrhynchus Papyri XXX*, Egyptian Exploration Society, Graeco-Roman Memoirs, no. 44 (London, 1964).
Lock, Robert, 'The Date of Agis III's War in Greece', *Antichthon* 6 (1972), 10-27.
—, 'The Origins of the Argyraspids', *Historia* 26 (1977), 373-378.
—, 'The Macedonian Army Assembly in the Time of Alexander the Great', *CP* 72 (1977), 91-107.
Luschey, Heinz, 'Der Löwe von Ekbatana', *Archaeologische Mitteilungen aus Iran* 1 (1968), 115-122.
McCoy, W. J., 'Memnon of Rhodes at the Granicus', *AJP* 110 (1989), 413-433.
McCrindle, J. W., *The Invasion of India by Alexander the Great* (London, 1896; repr. 1969).
McQueen, E. I., 'Quintus Curtius Rufus', in *Latin Biography*, ed. T.A. Dorey (London, 1967), 17 ff.
—, 'Some Notes on the Anti-Macedonian Movement in the Peloponnese in 331 B.C.', *Historia* 27 (1978), 40-64.

Macurdy, Grace, 'Queen Eurydice and the Evidence for Woman Power in Early Macedonia', *AJP* 48 (1927), 201-214.
—, 'The Political Activities and the Name of Cratesipolis', *AJP* 50 (1929), 273-278,
—, 'The Refusal of Callisthenes to Drink to the Health of Alexander', *JHS* 50 (1930), 294-297.
—, 'Roxane and Alexander IV in Epirus', *JHS* 52 (1932), 256-261.
—, *Hellenistic Queens: A Study of Woman-Power in Macedonia, Seleucid Syria and Ptolemaic Egypt*, Johns Hopkins University Studies in Archaeology, no. 14 (Baltimore, 1932).
Manti, R. A., 'The Cavalry Sarissa', *AncW* 8 (1983), 73-80.
Markle, M. M., 'The Macedonian Sarissa, Spear and Related Armor', *AJA* 81 (1977), 323-329.
—, 'Use of the Sarissa by Philip and Alexander of Macedon', *AJA* 82 (1978), 483-497.
Marsden, E. W., *The Campaign of Gaugamela* (Liverpool, 1964).
Martin, Thomas R., 'Quintus Curtius' Presentation of Philip Arrhidaeus and Josephus' Accounts of the Accession of Claudius', *AJAH* 8 (1983), 161-190.
Mehl, A., *Seleukos Nikator und sein Reich. 1. Teil: Seleukos' Leben und die Entwicklung seiner Machtposition* (Leuven, 1986).
—, 'ΔΟΡΙΚΤΗΤΟΣ ΧΩΡΑ', *Anc. Soc.* 10/11 (1980/81), 173-212.
Meineke, A., *Analecta Critica ad Athenaei Deipnosophistas* (Leipzig, 1867).
Melber, J., 'Über die Quellen und den Wert der Strategemensammlung Polyäns. Ein Beitrag zur griechischen Historiographie', *Jahrbücher für classische Philologie*, Supplbd 14 (1885).
Mendels, D., 'Aetolia 331-301: Frustration, Political Power and Survival', *Historia* 33 (1984), 129-180.
Merkelbach, R., *Die Quellen des griechischen Alexanderromans*, Zetemata, Heft 9 (Munich 1954; 2nd edition, 1977).
Merker, I. L., 'The Ancient Kingdom of Paionia', in *Balkan Studies* (Thessaloniki, 1965), 35-46.
—, 'Lysimachus — Thessalian or Macedonian?' *Chiron* 9 (1979), 31-36.
Merlan, P., 'Isocrates, Aristotle and Alexander the Great', *Historia* 3 (1954), 60-81.
Mikrojannakis, E., 'The Diplomatic Contacts between Alexander III and Darius III', in *Ancient Macedonia* i (Thessaloniki, 1970), 103-108.
Milns, R. D., 'Alexander's Macedonian Cavalry and Diodorus xvii. 17. 4', *JHS* 86 (1966), 167-168.
—, 'Alexander's Pursuit of Darius through Iran', *Historia* 15 (1966), 256.
—, 'Alexander's Seventh Phalanx Battalion', *GRBS* 7 (1966), 159-166.

—, 'Philip II and the Hypaspists', *Historia* 16 (1967), 509-512.
—, *Alexander the Great* (London, 1968).
—, 'The Hypaspists of Alexander III — Some Problems', *Historia* 20 (1971), 186-195.
—, 'A Note on Diodorus and Macedonian Military Terminology in Book XVII', *Historia* 31 (1982), 123-126.
—, 'A Note on Arrian's *Anabasis* 5. 13. 1', *CP* 78 (1983), 47-50.
Miltner, F., 'Die staatsrechtliche Entwicklung des Alexanderreiches', *Klio* 26 (1933), 39-55.
—, 'Alexanders Strategie bei Issos', *JÖAI* 28 (1933), 69-78.
Missitzis, L., 'A Royal Decree of Alexander the Great on the Lands of Philippi', *AncW* 12 (1985), 3-14.
Momigliano, A., 'Peucesta', *RFIC* 59 (1931), 245-246.
—, 'La Cronaca Babilonese sui Diadochi', *RFIC* 60 (1932), 462-484.
Morrison, J. S., 'Athenian Sea-Power in 323/2 B.C.: Dream and Reality', *JHS* 107 (1987), 88-97.
Müller, O., *Antigonos Monophthalmos und 'Das Jahr der Könige'* (Bonn, 1973).
Murison, C. L., 'Darius III and the Battle of Issus', *Historia* 21 (1972), 399-423.
Neubert, M., 'Die Fahrt Nearchs nach dem konstanten Stadion', *Petermanns Geog. Mitteilungen* 74 (1928), 136-143.
Neuhaus, O., 'Der Vater der Sisygambis (und das Verwandtschaftsverhältniss des Dareios III Kodomannos zu Artaxerxes II und III)', *RhM* 57 (1902), 610-623.
Neumann, C., 'A Note on Alexander's March-Rates', *Historia* 20 (1971), 196-198.
Niese, B., *Geschichte der griechischen und makedonischen Staaten seit der Schlacht bei Chaeronea* (Gotha, 1893, repr. Darmstadt, 1963).
Noret, J., 'Un fragment du dixième livre de *La succession d'Alexandre* par Arrien retrouvé dans un palimpseste de Gothenbourg', *L'Antiquité Classique* 52 (1983), 235-242.
Oertel, F., 'Zur Ammonssohnschaft Alexanders', *RhM* 89 (1940), 66-74.
Oikonomides, A., 'A New Greek Inscription from Vergina and Eurydice the Mother of Philip II', *AncW* 7 (1983), 62-64.
—, 'The Decree of the Athenian Orator Hyperides Honoring the Macedonians Iolaos and Medios', *ΠΡΑΚΤΙΚΑ Β'* (Athens, 1987), 169-182.
—, 'The Elusive Portrait of Antigonos I, the "One-Eyed" King of Macedonia', *AncW* 20 (1989), 17-20.
Olmstead, A. T., *History of the Persian Empire* (Chicago, 1948).
Osborne, M. J., *Naturalization in Athens*, 3 vols. (Brussels, 1981-1983).

Papastavru, J., *Amphipolis: Geschichte und Prosopographie*, Klio, Beiheft 37 (Leipzig, 1936).
Pearson, Lionel, *The Lost Histories of Alexander the Great* (New York, 1960).
Pédech, P., *Historiens compagnons d'Alexandre* (Paris, 1984).
Pedrizet, Paul, 'Venatio Alexandri', *JHS* 19 (1899), 273-279.
Perrin, B., 'Genesis and Growth of an Alexander-Myth', *TAPA* 26 (1895), 56-68.
Picard, C., 'Sépultures des compagnons de guerre ou successeurs macédoniens d'Alexandre le Grand', *Journal des Savants* (1964), 215-228.
Pollitt, J. J., *The Art of Ancient Greece: Sources and Documents* (Cambridge, 1990).
Pomeroy, S. B., *Women in Hellenistic Egypt from Alexander to Cleopatra* (New York, 1984).
Pope, H., *Foreigners in Attic Inscriptions* (Philadelphia, 1947).
Prentice, W. K., 'Callisthenes, the Original Historian of Alexander', *TAPA* 54 (1923), 74-85.
Prestianni-Giallombardo, A. M., 'Eurydike-Kleopatra. Nota ad Arr. *Anab.* 3, 6, 5', *ASNP* S. III, 11 (1981), 295-306.
Rackham, H., *Pliny: Natural History*, Loeb Classical Library, vol. 9 (Cambridge, Mass., 1968).
Ramsay, W. M., 'Military Operations on the North Front of Mount Taurus, III: The Imprisonment and Escape of Dokimos (Diod. XIX 16)', *JHS* 40 (1920), 107-112.
—, 'Military Operations on the North Front of Mount Taurus, IV: The Campaigns of 320 and 319 B.C.', *JHS* 43 (1923), 1-10.
Rawlinson, H. G., *Bactria* (London, 1912).
Rehork, J., 'Homer, Herodot und Alexander', in *Beiträge zur Alten Geschichte und deren Nachleben. Festschrift für F. Altheim* (Berlin, 1969), 251-260.
Renard, M., and Servais, J., 'A propos du mariage d'Alexandre et de Roxane', *L'Antiquité Classique* 24 (1955), 29-50.
Reuss, F., *Hieronymos von Kardia* (Berlin, 1876).
—, 'König Arybbas von Epeiros', *RhM* 36 (1881), 161-174.
Richter, G. M. A., *The Portraits of the Greeks* (London, 1965).
Ritschl, F., 'De Marsyis rerum scriptoribus', *Opuscula Philologica*, vol. 1 (Leipzig, 1866), 449-470.
Ritter, Hans-Werner, *Diadem und Königsherrschaft. Untersuchungen zu Zeremonien und Rechtsgrundlagen des Herrschaftsantritts bei den Persern, bei Alexander dem Grossen und im Hellenismus* (Berlin-Munich, 1965).

Robinson, C. A., Jr., 'The Seer Aristander', *AJP* 50 (1929), 195-197.
— 'Two Notes on the History of Alexander the Great', *AJP* 53 (1932), 353-359.
—, *The Ephemerides of Alexander's Expedition* (Providence, R. I., 1932).
—, 'Alexander the Great and Parmenio', *AJA* 49 (1945), 422 ff.
—, 'Alexander's Brutality', *AJA* 56 (1952), 169-170.
—, ed., *The History of Alexander the Great*, Brown University Studies XVI, vol. 1 (Providence, R.I., 1953).
Roebuck, C., 'The Settlements of Philip II with the Greek States in 338 B.C.', *CP* 43 (1948), 73-92.
Roisman, J., 'Ptolemy and his rivals in his history of Alexander', *CQ* 34 (1984), 373-385.
Romane, J. Patrick, 'Alexander's Siege of Tyre', *AncW* 16 (1987), 79-90.
Rosen, K., 'Die Reichsordnung von Babylon (323 v. Chr.)', *Acta Classica* 10 (1967), 95-110.
—, 'Die Bündnisformen der Diadochen und der Zerfall des Alexanderreiches', *Acta Classica* 11 (1968), 182 ff.
Rubincam, C. R., 'The Historiographical Tradition on the Death of Evagoras', *AHB* 2 (1988), 34-38.
Rubinsohn, Z., 'The 'Philotas Affair' — A Reconsideration', *Ancient Macedonia* ii (Thessaloniki, 1977), 409-420.
Rutz, W., 'Zur Erzählungskunst des Q. Curtius Rufus. Die Belagerung von Tyros', *Hermes* 93 (1965), 370 ff.
—, 'Zur Erzählungskunst des Q. Curtius Rufus', in *ANRW* 32.4 (Berlin, 1986), 2329-2357.
Ruzicka, S., 'Curtius 4. 1. 34-37 and the "Magnitudo Belli"', *CJ* 79 (1983), 30-34.
—, 'War in the Aegean, 333-331: A Reconsideration', *Phoenix* 42 (1988), 131-151.
Ryder, T. T. B., *Koine Eirene: General Peace and Local Independence in Ancient Greece* (Oxford, 1965).
Salis, A. v., *Löwenkampfbilder des Lysipp* (Berlin, 1956).
Sandberger, F., *Prosopographie zur Geschichte des Pyrrhos* (Stuttgart, 1970).
Sauppe, H., 'Die neuen Bruchstücke des Hyperides', *Philol.* 3 (1848), 610-658.
Schachermeyr, F., 'Das Ende des makedonischen Königshauses', *Klio* 16 (1920), 332-337.
—, 'Zu Geschichte und Staatsrecht der frühen Diadochenzeit', *Klio* 19 (1925), 435-461.
—, *Alexander der Grosse: Ingenium und Macht* (Graz, 1949).

—, 'Die letzten Pläne Alexanders', *JÖAI* 41 (1954), 118-140.
—, *Alexander in Babylon und die Reichsordnung nach seinem Tode* (Vienna, 1970).
—, *Alexander der Grosse: Das Problem seiner Persönlichkeit und seines Wirkens* (Vienna, 1973).
Schaefer, Arnold, *Demosthenes und seine Zeit*, vol. 3 (Leipzig, 1887).
Schmitt, H. H., *Die Staatsverträge des Altertums*, vol. 3 (Munich, 1969).
Schneider, R., *Olympias, die Mutter Alexanders des Grossen* (Zwiekau, 1886).
Schober, L., *Untersuchungen zur Geschichte Babyloniens und der Oberen Satrapien von 323-303 v. Chr.* (Frankfurt, 1981).
Scholl, R., 'Alexander der Grosse und die Sklaverei am Hofe', *Klio* 69 (1987), 108-121.
Schubart, W., See Diels, H.
Schubert, R., 'Der Tod des Kleitos', *RhM* 53 (1898), 98-117.
—, 'Die Porusschlacht', *RhM* 56 (1901), 543-562.
—, *Die Quellen zur Geschichte der Diadochenzeit* (Leipzig, 1914).
Schur, W., 'Das Alexanderreich nach Alexanders Tode', *RhM* 83 (1934), 129-156.
Schwahn, W., 'Die Nachfolge Alexanders des Grossen', *Klio* 23 (1930), 211-238; 24 (1931), 306-332.
Schwarz, F. v., *Alexanders des Grossen Feldzüge in Turkestan* (Munich, 1893; 2nd edition, Stuttgart, 1906).
Schwenk, Cynthia J., *Athens in the Age of Alexander. The Dated Laws and Decrees of 'The Lykourgan Era' 338-322 B.C.* (Chicago, 1985).
Seibert, J., *Historische Beiträge zu den dynastischen Verbindungen in hellenistischer Zeit*, Historia Einzelschriften, Heft 10 (Wiesbaden, 1967).
—, *Untersuchungen zur Geschichte Ptolemaios' I.*, Münchener Beiträge zur Papyrusforschung und antiken Rechtsgeschichte, Heft 56 (Munich, 1969).
—, *Alexander der Grosse*, Erträge der Forschung, no. 10 (Darmstadt, 1972).
—, *Die politischen Flüchtlinge und Verbannten in der griechischen Geschichte* (Darmstadt, 1979).
—, *Das Zeitalter der Diadochen*, Erträge der Forschung, no. 185 (Darmstadt, 1983).
—, *Die Eroberung des Perserreiches durch Alexander den Großen auf kartographischer Grundlage* (Wiesbaden, 1985), TAVO Beiheft, Reihe B, no. 68.
Servais, J., See Renard, M.

Shackleton-Bailey, 'Curtiana', *CQ* 31 (1981), 175-180.
Shrimpton, G. S., *Theopompus the Historian* (Montreal and Kingston, 1991).
Simpson, R. H., 'Antigonus, Polyperchon and the Macedonian Regency', *Historia* 6 (1957), 371-373.
—, 'A Possible Case of Misrepresentation in Diodorus XIX', *Historia* 6 (1957), 504-505.
—, 'Antigonus the One-Eyed and the Greeks', *Historia* 8 (1959), 385-409.
Smith, R. R. R., *Hellenistic Royal Portraits* (Oxford, 1988).
Smith, Vincent, *The Early History of India. From 600 B.C. to the Muhammadan Conquest, including the Invasion of Alexander the Great*, 4th edition, revised by S. M. Edwardes (Oxford, 1924).
Snell, B., *Scenes from Greek Drama* (Berkeley and Los Angeles, 1964).
Sofman, A. S., and Tsibukidis, D. I., 'Nearchus and Alexander', *AncW* 16 (1987), 71-77.
Sohlberg, D., 'Zu Kleitarch', *Historia* 21 (1972), 758-759.
Spendel, A., *Untersuchungen zum Heerwesen der Diadochen* (Breslau, 1915).
Stadter, P. A., 'Flavius Arrianus: The New Xenophon', *GRBS* 8 (1967), 155-161.
Stähelin, Felix, 'Die griechischen Historikerfragmente bei Didymos', *Klio* 5 (1905), 55-71; 141-154.
Stark, F., *Alexander's Path from Caria to Cilicia* (New York, 1958).
Stein, Sir Aurel, 'Alexander's Campaign in the Indian North-west Frontier', *Geog. Journal* 70 (1927), 417-540.
—, *On Alexander's Track to the Indus* (London, 1929).
—, 'The Site of Alexander's Passage of the Hydaspes and the Battle with Porus', *Geog. Journal* 80 (1932), 31-46.
—, 'An Archaeological Journey in Western Iran', *Geog. Journal* 92 (1938), 313-342.
Stewart, A., 'Diodorus, Curtius, and Arrian on Alexander's Mole at Tyre', *Berytus* 35 (1987), 97-99.
Stiehle, R., 'Zu den Fragmenten der griechischen Historiker', *Philol.* 9 (1854), 462-514.
Strasburger, Hermann, *Ptolemaios und Alexander* (Leipzig, 1934).
—, 'Alexanders Zug durch die gedrosische Wüste', *Hermes* 80 (1952), 456-493.
—, 'Zur Route Alexanders durch Gedrosien', *Hermes* 82 (1954), 251.
Sumner, G. V., 'Curtius Rufus and the "Historia Alexandri"', *AUMLA* 15 (1961), 30-39.
Sutton, D. F., 'Harpalus as Pallides', *RhM* 123 (1980), 96.

—, *The Greek Satyr Play* (Meisenheim am Glan, 1980).
Tarn, W. W., *Antigonos Gonatas* (Oxford, 1913).
—, 'Heracles, Son of Barsine', *JHS* 41 (1921), 18-28.
—, *Alexander the Great*, 2 vols. (Cambridge, 1948).
—, *The Greeks in Bactria and India*, 3rd edition (Cambridge, 1951).
Tataki, A. B., *Ancient Beroea: Prosopography and Society* (Athens, 1988).
Teodorsson, Sven-Tage, 'Theocritus the Sophist, Antigonus the One-Eyed, and the Limits of Clemency', *Hermes* 118 (1990), 380-382.
Thomas, C. G., 'Alexander's Garrisons: A Clue to his Administrative Plans?' *Antichthon* 8 (1974), 11-20.
Tomaschek, W., 'Topographische Erläuterung der Küstenfahrt Nearchs vom Indus bis zum Euphrat', *SB Wien* 121 (1890), Abhandlung viii, 1-88.
Treves, P., 'La reggenza di Cratero', *RFIC* 10 (1932), 372-374.
—, 'Hyperides and the Cult of Hephaestion', *CR* 53 (1939), 56-57.
Tritle, L., *Phocion the Good* (London, 1988).
Tritsch, W., *Olympias. Die Mutter Alexanders des Grossen* (Frankfurt, 1936).
Tronson, A., 'Satyrus the Peripatetic and the Marriages of Philip II', *JHS* 104 (1984), 116-126.
—, 'The Relevance of *IG* ii^2 329 to the Hellenic League of Alexander the Great', *AncW* 12 (1985), 15-19.
Tsibukidis, D. I., see s.v. Sofman, A. S.
Unz, R., 'Alexander's Brothers', *JHS* 105 (1985), 171-174.
Vatin, C., 'Lettre adressée à la cité de Philippes par les ambassadeurs auprès d'Alexandre', in Πρακτικα Β΄ (Athens, 1984), 259-270.
Veith, G., 'Der Kavalleriekampf in der Schlacht am Hydaspes', *Klio* 8 (1908), 131-153.
Vezin, A., *Eumenes von Kardia* (Diss. Tübingen, 1907).
Vitucci, G., 'Il compromesso di Babilonia e la προστασία di Cratero', *Miscellanea A. Rostagni* (Turin, 1963), 63-67.
Vogelsang, W., 'Early Historical Arachosia in South-East Afghanistan', *Iranica Antiqua* 20 (1985), 55-99.
—, 'Some Observations on Achaemenid Hyrcania: A Combination of Sources', in *Achaemenid History* iii, edited by A. Kuhrt and H. Sancisi-Weerdenburg (Leiden, 1988), 121-135.
Wachsmuth, C., 'Zur Metzer Alexander-Epitome', *RhM* 56 (1901), 150-154.
—, 'Bemerkungen zu griechischen Historikern', *RhM* 56 (1901), 215-226.
Walbank, F. W., *A Historical Commentary on Polybius*, vol. 1 (Oxford, 1957).

Walbank, M. B., 'Athens grants Citizenship to Benefactor: *IG* ii² 398a + 438', *AHB* 1 (1987), 10-12.
Walek, T., 'Les opérations navales pendant la guerre lamiaque', *RPh* 48 (1924), 23-30.
Wardman, A. E., 'Plutarch and Alexander', *CQ* 5 (1955), 96-107.
Wehrli, C., 'Phila, fille d'Antipater et épouse de Démétrius, roi des Macédoniens', *Historia* 13 (1964), 140-146.
—, *Antigone et Démétrios* (Geneva, 1969).
Welles, C. Bradford, *Royal Correspondence in the Hellenistic Period* (New Haven, 1934).
—, 'The Discovery of Sarapis and the Foundation of Alexandria', *Historia* 11 (1962), 271-298.
—, ed., *Diodorus of Sicily*, Loeb Classical Library, vol. 8 (Cambridge, Mass., 1963).
—, 'The Reliability of Ptolemy as an Historian', in *Miscellanea A. Rostagni* (Turin, 1963), 101 ff.
—, *Alexander and the Hellenistic World* (Toronto, 1970).
Welwei, K. W., 'Der Kampf um das makedonische Lager bei Gaugamela', *RhM* 122 (1979), 222-228.
Westlake, H. D., *Thessaly in the Fourth Century B.C.* (London, 1935).
—, 'Eumenes of Cardia', *Bulletin of the John Rylands Library* 37 (1954), 309-327 = *Essays on the Greek Historians and Greek History* (London, 1969), 313-330.
Wilcken, Ulrich, *Alexander the Great*, G. C. Richards, tr., with introduction and notes by E. N. Borza (New York, 1967).
Will, Ed., *Histoire politique du monde hellenistique (323-30 av. J.C.)*, vol. 1 (Nancy, 1966).
—, 'The Succession to Alexander', in *CAH* vii.1 (Cambridge, 1985), 23-61.
—, 'The Formation of the Hellenistic Kingdoms', in *CAH* vii.1 (Cambridge, 1985), 101-117.
Will, W., *Athen und Alexander. Untersuchungen zur Geschichte der Stadt von 338 bis 322 v. Chr.*, Münchener Beiträge zur Papyrusforschung und antiken Rechtsgeschichte, Heft 77 (Munich, 1983).
Williams, J. M., 'A Note on Athenian Chronology, 319/8-318/7 B.C.', *Hermes* 112 (1984), 300-305.
—, 'Demades' Last Years, 323/2-319/8 B.C.: A "Revisionist" Interpretation', *AncW* 19 (1989), 19-30.
Willrich, H., 'Wer liess König Philipp von Makedonien ermorden?' *Hermes* 34 (1899), 174-182.

—, 'Krateros und der Grabherr des Alexandersarkophags von Sidon', *Hermes* 34 (1899), 231-250.

Wirth, Gerhard, *Studien zur Alexandergeschichte* (Darmstadt, 1985) = *Studien*.

—, 'Zur grossen Schlacht des Eumenes 322 (PSI 1284)', *Klio* 46 (1965), 283-288 = *Studien* 204 ff.

—, 'Zur Politik des Perdikkas 323', *Helikon* 7 (1967), 281-322.

—, 'Nearchos, der Flottenchef', *Acta Conventus XI, 'Eirene'*, (Warsaw, 1972), 615-639 = *Studien* 51 ff.

—, 'Alexander zwischen Gaugamela und Persepolis', *Historia* 20 (1971), 617-632 = *Studien* 76 ff.

—, 'Dareios und Alexander', *Chiron* 1 (1971), 133-152 = *Studien* 92 ff.

—, 'Nearch, Alexander und die Diadochen. Spekulationen über einen Zusammenhang', *Tyche* 3 (1988), 241-259.

Woodcock, G., *The Greeks in India* (London, 1966).

Worthington, I., 'The First Flight of Harpalus Reconsidered', *G & R* 31 (1984), 161-169.

—, 'Plutarch, *Demosthenes* 25 and Demosthenes' Cup', *CP* 80 (1985), 229-233.

—, 'The Chronology of the Harpalus Affair', *SO* 61 (1986), 63-76.

—, '*IG* ii^2 1631, 1632 and Harpalus' Ships', *ZPE* 65 (1986), 222-224.

Wüst, F., *Philipp II. von Makedonien und Griechenland in den Jahren von 346 bis 338*, Münchener historische Abhandlungen, Heft 14 (Munich, 1938).

—, 'Zu den Hypomnemata Alexanders des Grossen: das Grabmal Hephaistions', *JÖAI* 44 (1959), 147-157.

Ziegler, K., 'Plutarchstudien', *RhM* 84 (1935), 369-390.

CONCORDANCE

The following list of individuals treated in *The Marshals of Alexander's Empire* is arranged in English alphabetical order. It provides the numbers assigned to these individuals by H. Berve in the second volume of his *Das Alexanderreich auf prosopographischer Grundlage* (Munich, 1926), together with the Chapter-Section (i 2; or sometimes with sub-section: i 2. 3) and page references in *The Marshals*.

BERVE	NAME	MARSHALS	PAGE
22	Addaios (Adaios)	vi. 2. 1	303
24	Admetos	vA 5. 1	253
8	Agathon	ix 5. 1	361
37	Alexandros s. of Aëropos	ix 4. 2	357
39	Alexandros s. of Polyperchon	vB 4. 3	283
40	Alexandros	vC 2. 1	295
45	Alketas	iii 2	171
56	Amyntas s. of Alexandros	vB 4. 2	282
57	Amyntas s. of Andromenes	iii 3. 1	176
59	Amyntas s. of Arrhabaios	ix 3. 1	352
63	Amyntas Lynkestes	vi 2. 8	305
65	Amyntas (= 57)	iii 3. 1	176
—	Amyntas	vi 2. 6	305
72	Anaxippos	ix 5. 2	361
75	Andromachos	ix 6. 2	364
78	Andronikos	viii 6. 4	341
83	Antigenes	vii 1	308
84	Antigenes (= 83)	vii 1	308
87	Antigonos	i 5	50
—	Antigonos	vi 2. 7	305
88	Antikles	vC 1. 1	289
90	Antiochos	vi 2. 3	303
91	Antiochos	viii 5. 4	337
93	Antipatros s. of Asklepiodoros	vC 1. 2	289
94	Antipatros s. of Iolaos	i 4	38
—	Aphthonetos	vC 1. 3	289
—	Aphthonios (= Elaptonius)	vC 1. 4	289
—	Archedamos	vC 1. 5	290
109	Aretes	ix 3. 3	354

110	Aretis	vC 1. 6	290
137	Ariston	ix 2. 1	348
138	Ariston	ix 3. 4	354
133	Aristonous	vB 3. 2	275
136	Aristophanes (= 133)	vB 3. 2	275
156	Arybbas	vB 1. 3	261
165	Asandros	App. VI	385
178	Atarrhias	vi 2. 4	304
181	Attalos s. of Andromenes	iii 3. 3	180
182	Attalos	i 1. 1	4
183	Attalos	viii 3. 1	332
184	Attalos (= 181)	iii 3. 3	180
187	Autodikos	vB 4. 1	282
199	Balakros s. of Amyntas	viii 4. 1	335
200	Balakros s. of Nikanor	vB 1. 2	260
201	Balakros	viii 2. 3	332
202	Balakros (= 201)	viii 2. 3	332
203	Balakros (= 200)	vB 1. 2	260
223	Brison (= 582?)	viii 5. 5-6	337
824	Charikles	vC 1. 7	290
826	Charus (Charos)	vC 2. 2	296
256	Demetrios s. of Althaimenes	ix 1. 1	345
260	Demetrios	vB 1. 4	261
294	Elaptonius (= Aphthonios)	vC 1. 4	289
300	Epimenes	vC 1. 8	291
301	Epokillos	ix 6. 3	364
302	Erigyios	iv 1. 1	209
311	Eudemos (= Eudamos)	viii 3. 3	333
317	Eumenes	ix 1. 2	346
320	Eurybotas	viii 5. 1	336
322	Eurylochos	vC 1. 9	291
318	Euxenippos (= Excipinus)	vC 1. 10	291
226	Glaukias	ix 2. 2	348
232	Gorgatas	vC 1. 11	292
233	Gorgias	viii 1. 2	326
234	Gorgias	vC 1. 12	292
235	Gorgias (= 233?)	viii 1. 2	326
143	Harpalos	iv 2	213
341	Hegelochos	i 1. 2	6
344	Hegesimachos (Simachos)	vC 2. 3	296
293	Hekataios	vC 1. 13	292
298	Hellanikos	vi 2. 10	306

CONCORDANCE

357	Hephaistion	ii 2	65
347	Herakleides	ix 2. 3	348
354	Herakon	viii 6. 3	341
305	Hermolaos	vC 1. 14	292
—	Iolaos	vB 5. 2	285
386	Iolaos	vC 1. 15	293
395	Kalanos (= 412: Karanos)	viii 4. 2	335
397	Kalas	ix 4. 1	355
412	Karanos (= 395: Kalanos)	viii 4. 2	335
422	Kleandros s. of Polemokrates	viii 6. 2	340
423	Kleandros (= 424: Klearchos)	viii 5. 2-3	336
424	Klearchos (= 423: Kleandros)	viii 5. 2-3	336
425	Klearchos (= 422: Klearchos)	viii 6. 2	340
427	Kleitos s. of Dropidas	i 3	34
428	Kleitos	iii 4	185
439	Koinos	ii 1	58
442	Koiranos (= Karanos?)	ix 5. 3	362
446	Krateros	ii 4	107
464	Laomedon	iv 1. 2	211
466	Leonnatos	ii 3	91
474	Limnaios (= Timaeus)	vC 2. 4	296
480	Lysimachos	vB 3. 1	267
493	Melamnidas (= Menidas)	ix 6. 1	362
494	Meleagros s. of Neoptolemos	iii 1	165
495	Meleagros	ix 2. 4	349
501	Menandros	viii 6. 1	339
504	Menedemos	viii 6. 5	343
507	Menes	vB 2. 1	262
508	Menidas	ix 6. 1	362
510	Menoitas (= Menidas)	ix 6. 1	362
519	Metron	vC 1. 16	293
520	Metron (= 519)	vC 1. 16	293
544	Nearchos	iv 4	228
548	Neoptolemos	vi 1. 2	300
554	Nikanor s. of Parmenion	vi 1. 1	299
560	Nikanor	vC 2. 5	297
570	Nikostratos (= 738: Sostratos)	vC 1. 19	295
582	Ombrion	viii 5. 5-6	337
605	Pantordanos	ix 2. 5	349
606	Parmenion	i 2. 1	13
—	Pausanias	vC 2. 6	297
614	Pausanias	vC 2. 7	297

619	Peithon s. of Agenor	viii 1. 1	323
621	Peithon s. of Krateuas	vB 3. 3	276
623	Peithon (= 619)	viii 1. 1	323
627	Perdikkas	ii 5	134
631	Peroidas	ix 2. 6	350
634	Peukestas	vB 2. 2	263
774	Philippos s. of Agathokles	vC 2. 8	298
775	Philippos s. of Amyntas	viii 1. 3	327
777	Philippos s. of Antipatros	vC 1. 17	294
778	Philippos s. of Balakros	viii 1. 4	327
779	Philippos s. of Menelaos	ix 4. 3	358
780	Philippos s. of Machatas	viii 2. 2	331
783	Philippos (see no. 780)	viii 2. 2	331
784	Philippos (= 780?)	viii 2. 2 (n.39)	331
—	Philippos	vB 5. 1	284
801	Philotas s. of Karsis	vC 1. 18	295
802	Philotas s. of Parmenion	i 2. 2	23
803	Philotas	viii 2. 1	328
804	Philotas (= 803)	viii 2. 1	328
805	Philotas (= 802)	i 2. 2	23
807	Philotas	vi 2. 5	304
644	Polemon	iii 3. 4	183
648	Polydamas	ix 4. 4	359
654	Polyperchon	iii 5	188
667	Protomachos	ix 3. 2	353
668	Ptolemaios (Ptolemy)	iv 3	222
669	Ptolemaios s. of Ptolemaios	vB 4. 4	283
670	Ptolemaios s. of Seleukos	vB 6	286
671	Ptolemaios s. of Philippos (= 672)	vB 1. 1	259
672	Ptolemaios	vB 1. 1	259
673	Ptolemaios	viii 3. 2	333
700	Seleukos	vA 5. 2	253
704	Simmias	iii 3. 2	179
712	Sitalkes	viii 3. 4	334
732	Sokrates	ix 2. 7	350
736	Sopolis	ix 2. 8	351
738	Sostratos	vC 1. 19	295
741	Tauron	viii 5. 7	338
744	Teutamos	vii 2	316
361	Theodotos	vi 2. 9	305
746	Timandros	vi 2. 2	303